984.046 K74b

Knudson, Jerry W.

JUN   01

Bolivia, press and
 revolution, 1932-1964

MAR 1 1 1987			
APR 1 8 1989			
MAY 1 2 2007			

GAYLORD 72   PRINTED IN U.S.A.

BOLIVIA

Press and Revolution 1932-1964

Jerry W. Knudson

UNIVERSITY
PRESS OF
AMERICA

LANHAM • NEW YORK • LONDON

Copyright © 1986 by

University Press of America,® Inc.

4720 Boston Way
Lanham, MD 20706

3 Henrietta Street
London WC2E 8LU England

Library of Congress Cataloging in Publication Data

Knudson, Jerry W.
   Bolivia, press and revolution, 1932-1964.

   Bibliography: p.
   Includes index.
   1. Bolivia—Politics and government—1879-1938.
   2. Bolivia—Politics and government—1938-1952.
   3. Bolivia—Politics and government—1952-1982.
   4. Press and politics—Bolivia—History—20th century.
   5. Bolivian newspapers—History—20th century.
   I. Title.
   F3326.K68   1986   984.046   85-26391
   ISBN 0-8191-5137-8 (alk. paper)
   ISBN 0-8191-5138-6 (pbk. : alk. paper)

For my mother

Mabelle Cousins Knudson

and in memory of my father

Jay Curtis Byron Knudson

ACKNOWLEDGEMENTS

When research first began on this book in Bolivia in 1968, I was working in the Biblioteca del Congreso in the congressional building fronting on the Plaza Murillo in La Paz. For months an elderly gentleman in charge there helped me wrestle large bound volumes of newspapers from the topmost shelves of a room adjoining the reading room with the aid of a stepladder. It was an arduous task. Finally, one morning in early July I said to encourage him, "I will be leaving in August." He looked at me and asked, "What year?"

As it turned out his humor was prophetic of my relationship with Bolivia. Summers engendered more summers of research. Thus, field research for this book was carried out in Bolivia during the North American summers of 1968, 1971, 1973, 1976, 1982 and 1985. It would be impossible to thank all of those Bolivians who helped me in my quest; many are acknowledged in the oral history interviews in this book, but to all I extend my deepest gratitude for allowing me to poke around in their national attic.

Particular thanks should go, however, to the staffs of the Biblioteca Nacional in Sucre, and the Biblioteca del Congreso, Biblioteca de la Universidad Mayor de San Andrés, and Biblioteca Municipal, all in La Paz. In the United States, assistance came from the Library of Congress and the New York Public Library. One special bibliographical reference should be noted. The only file of Los Tiempos of Cochabamba available for this period anywhere in the world is at the Library of Congress in Washington, D.C. During the newspaper's first period of existence (1943-1953) libraries in La Paz were not collecting provincial newspapers, and the files of Los Tiempos itself were destroyed when mobs of campesinos attacked and burned the newspaper plant on November 9, 1953.

Special thanks go to Lola Januskis, Latin American bibliographer of Samuel Paley Library at Temple University. I also gratefully acknowledge financial assistance from Temple University, which awarded me a Study Leave and Grant-in-Aid to further the research and writing of this book.

Through the years, portions of my Bolivian research have been published elsewhere. For example, I collected the Chaco

War dispatches of Augusto Céspedes which appeared in Bolivia as Augusto Céspedes, Crónicas heroicas de una guerra estúpida (La Paz: Librería Editorial Juventud, 1975).

More important for purposes of this book, however, has been "The Press and the Bolivian National Revolution," a 48-page pamphlet published by Journalism Monographs, No. 31 (November 1973). A pilot study for this book, it was sent to various Bolivian specialists for comment and criticism, as work on the book progressed, and I am indebted to the following individuals for replying in detail: Robert J. Alexander, Robert D. Barton, Philip W. Bonsal, William E. Carter, James W. Carty, Jr., Rowland Egger, Dwight B. Heath, Douglas Henderson, Jacobo Liberman Z., Christopher Mitchell, Eduardo Ocampo Moscoso, Edward J. Sparks and James W. Wilkie.

Moreover, portions of three chapters of this work have appeared separately:

- "U.S. Coverage since 1952 of Bolivia: The Unknown Soldier of the Cold War," Gazette, International Journal for Mass Communication Studies, Vol. 23, No. 3 (1977), pp. 185-197.

- "'La Calle,' un precursor de la Revolución Nacional Boliviana," Historia Boliviana, Vol. II, No. 2 (1982), pp. 111-119.

- "Shock of Recognition: The Bolivian Press Views the Mexican and Cuban Revolutions," Proceedings of the Pacific Coast Council on Latin American Studies. Vol. 9 (1982), pp. 83-89.

Readers may wish to see the following related articles, also by the author:

- "México y Bolivia, dos revoluciones," Revista de IBEAS [Instituto Boliviano de Estudios y Acción Social] (October 1968), pp. 18-22.

- "The Impact of the Catavi Mine Massacre of 1942 on Bolivian Politics and Public Opinion," The Americas, A Quarterly Review of Inter-American Cultural History, Vol. 26, No. 3 (January 1970), pp. 254-276.

- "The Bolivian Immigration Bill of 1942: A Case Study in Latin American Anti-Semitism," American Jewish Archives, Vol. 22, No. 2 (November 1970), pp. 138-158.

- "Anti-Semitism in Latin America: Barometer of Social

Change," <u>Patterns of Prejudice</u>, Vol. 6, No. 5 (September-October 1972), pp. 1-11.

- "Press Women of Bolivia," <u>Matrix, Women in Communications</u> (Winter 1973-74), pp. 8-9 and 21.

- "Bolivia--Where Critics Need Courage," <u>IPI [International Press Institute] Report</u>, Vol. 23, No. 1 (January 1974), pp. 1 and 18.

- "Bolivia's Popular Assembly of 1971 and the Overthrow of General Juan José Torres," <u>Special Studies No. 52</u>, Council on International Studies, State University of New York of Buffalo (April 1974). 70 pp.

- "Licensing Newsmen: The Bolivian Experience," <u>Gazette, International Journal for Mass Communication Studies</u>, Vol. 25, No. 3 (1979), pp. 163-175.

- "Treatment of the Indian in the Bolivian Press: The Majority as Minority," <u>Studies in Third World Societies</u>, No. 10 (December 1979), pp. 25-39.

- "Bolivia Struggles Towards Freedom," <u>IPI Report</u>, (November 1982), p. 5.

I also thank the Juvenal Aparicio family of Bolivia, whose sons studied in my Latin American history classes at the University of Kentucky and who shared their home in La Paz with me one summer. Finally, all of our teachers are important to us, but I acknowledge especially Calder M. Pickett of the University of Kansas who taught me the responsibilities of journalism, and the late C. Alan Hutchinson of the University of Virginia who taught me the richness and texture of Latin American history.

Philadelphia   Jerry W. Knudson
September 1985

CONTENTS

Introduction

THE BOLIVIAN NATIONAL REVOLUTION

It has become increasingly clear that the press is not tangential to the political process of any society--merely reporting or commenting on the events of the day--but rather an integral part of that process. The gathering, writing, editing, and display of the news in either the print or electronic media gradate its importance, setting the agenda for the audience. In other words, this process tells readers or listeners or viewers what the press considers is significant in the world around them. But, whether in a free or closed society, there may be distortions of reality, whether caused by economic considerations (reader interest) or ideological persuasion (reader guidance). Also, there is the ever-growing problem of the reporter gaining access to information and the intense pressures of getting the news out as quickly as possible. In other words, there are sins of commission and omission. And there is deliberate propaganda--ideas, facts, or allegations spread intentionally to further one's cause or to damage an opposing cause. Such was the case in the role of the opposition press in fomenting and carrying out the Bolivian National Revolution (1952-1964), the second social and economic revolution in Latin American history. It is this function of the opposition Bolivian press in helping to bring about social change which this study will examine. The account stretches from the formation of the Chaco War generation of dissident writers beginning in 1932 to the overthrow of the National Revolution by the Bolivian military in 1964.

The historical method has been used in the belief that history is concerned--or should be concerned--not only with what actually happened in any given time and place, but also with what people thought was happening, as revealed to them through the means of public information. Thus, in the historical sense since the advent of newspapers, it does not matter whether the news was accurate or inaccurate--or later if editorial comment was reasoned or polemical--if readers believed either and acted on that belief. To this extent, the press takes on a reality of its own as a catalyst in the political process. Thus, in my view, newspapers--especially once they reached mass audiences--should be regarded by historians as primary rather than secondary sources in studying the

1

formation of public opinion rather than as sources of historical fact.

We in the United States, bombarded with print and electronic news, have perhaps become more media sophisticated, setting our own agendas through a wide--though shrinking--variety of sources or questioning what we are told. But this was not true of the simpler society in Bolivia during the first half of the Twentieth Century. The press had credibility. As Carlos Montenegro, intellectual mentor of the Movimiento Nacionalista Revolucionario (MNR, National Revolutionary Movement) which launched radical social changes in Bolivia after gaining power in 1952, phrased it:

> The public did not have, throughout half a century, any other source of cultural nutrition than journalism, and it learned to attend to and judge things in consultation with the printed [newspaper] page. This was little less than an oracle for current opinion. [1]

But the exact impact of the press in any given historical situation is extremely difficult to determine. Unlike analysis of current events when scientifically formulated and distributed questionnaires can measure how the public perceives the news, the historian must rely on references to the press and public opinion from other sources. We may not always know with certitude the effect certain propaganda devices had--except through oral history interviews with surviving participants and observers of the Bolivian National Revolution, which the author has been conducting since 1968.

And we can always examine the historical record--the newspapers themselves--to determine at least what was offered to the public. In the case of Bolivia, these events occurred before the advent of television there, and the historical record for radio has been lost because tapes were reused or never made. A few radio speeches by MNR propagandist Roberto Hinojosa were reprinted in the opposition press. But most pre-revolutionary Bolivians, as Montenegro said, got their news and views from the printed page. Therefore, the author has examined, issue by issue, the oligarchical and revolutionary press of the period in the capital of La Paz, center of political, social, and economic power, and Los Tiempos of Cochabamba, which had the second largest circulation in the country.

It might be objected that the press was of little importance in Bolivia because newspaper circulations were low, and the vast majority of Bolivians could not read or even speak Spanish. What significance, then, did the urban newspapers have for the Indians of the countryside--about 60 percent of

the population--or for the country as a whole? Concerning the
first objection, it must be remembered that before 1952 Bolivia
was an elite society. Thus, the 50,000 readers of La Razón,
owned by tin magnate Carlos Víctor Aramayo and the newspaper
which had the highest circulation in Bolivia, constituted one-
fourth of the approximately 200,000 adult, literate, property-
owning males who were allowed to vote in a country of about
three million people. Although 50,000 is considered small
circulation in Western industrialized societies, it was large in
Bolivia and, more importantly, it reached the opinion-makers.
It was this middle and upper class audience who held the reins
of social, economic, and political power--or aspired to it.
Therefore, it was a group well worth cultivating, whether by
the right represented by La Razón or by the left represented
by La Calle, founded in 1936 and the spokesman for the MNR
after its formation in 1941. Moreover, there is considerable
secondary circulation in Latin America; one study showed that
four persons read the same copy of a newspaper in Colombia,
for example. Most telling, if the Big Three mining interests
did not believe in the power of the press to sway public opinion
in Bolivia, why did each of them maintain a newspaper in La
Paz? They were certainly not very lucrative investments. In
addition to Aramayo's La Razón, the other "tin barons," Simón
I. Patiño--reputed to be the sixth wealthiest man in the world--
owned a third interest in El Diario, and Mauricio Hochschild
controlled Ultima Hora. These were class newspapers which, it
will be demonstrated, wielded political power, looking out for
the social and economic interests of their owners.

As for the second objection concerning illiteracy of the
masses, one should not overlook the communication of ideas by
word of mouth. Newspapers are still posted on the walls of
buildings in downtown La Paz where one can see literate
campesinos--moving into the cholo or mixed culture--reading
aloud to their less fortunate fellows. When the MNR embarked
on land reform in 1953, Demetrio Canelas, owner of Los Tiempos
of Cochabamba and also president of the Land Owners Association, opposed the land reform vehemently in the pages of his
newspaper. On November 9, 1953, the Indian peasants of the
area converged on Cochabamba and sacked and burned the
printing plant of Los Tiempos, which did not reappear until
1967. Likewise, mobs--many of whom were probably illiterate--
prevented the reopening of La Razón in La Paz immediately
after the MNR gained power in April 1952. The newspaper
never reappeared. This revenge upon these two newspapers
suggests that even illiterate lower class Bolivians know what the
oligarchical press had been saying about them--or, more accurately, not saying about them and their needs.

Given the striking social inequalities of Latin America and

other areas of the Third World, it seems significant to study the role of the MNR press in Bolivia in helping to bring to power a democratic leftist movement. What were the accomplishments of the Bolivian National Revolution? Briefly, after a propaganda drive dating back to the Chaco War (1932-1935), the MNR after gaining power in 1952 first moved swiftly to nationalize Bolivia's major resource, the largest tin mines, owned by Patiño, Hochschild, and Aramayo. Each had annual incomes, for the most part untaxed, far exceeding the Bolivian national budget. And, as noted, each had newspaper spokesmen in La Paz. With their economic power and journalistic support they could and did control Bolivian political life as well. The MNR writers called them "the mining super-state," and nationalization of their properties had as much symbolic as economic significance.

Secondly, the MNR granted universal suffrage to incorporate the Quechua and Aymará Indian masses, about 60 percent of the population, into national life. Along with the agrarian reform, which brought the Indian into the money economy, the universal vote also broadened the MNR's political base in the countryside. On the road to revolution, the MNR had tapped the support of the middle class and workers of the cities--and to a lesser extent the tin miners. But after 1952 everyone, male or female (over the age of eighteen if married or twenty-one if single), without property or literacy restrictions, could cast his or her colored ballot in all elections, including that for the presidency every four years.

Thirdly, although this reform was more or less forced upon the MNR, the party embarked on massive land redistribution after 1953. It was the last of the major reforms and came about only after the campesinos or Indian peasants began seizing land and terrorizing landowners in the rich agricultural district near Cochabamba and elsewhere. In the final tally, Bolivia redistributed one-third of her agricultural lands to formerly landless peasants. Before 1952 these were pongos or serfs who had to give free labor to the landowner in return for the use of small subsistence plots. As late as 1952, before the MNR came to power, advertisements in La Paz newspapers for the sale of large properties indicated how many Indians went with the land. Víctor Paz Estenssoro, major architect of the MNR and three-time revolutionary president, considers the land reform to have been the greatest achievement of the Revolution. [2]

How was it possible that the MNR carried out these three major reforms within only twelve years in power? Part of the answer is that public opinion in Bolivia had been prepared for these changes. It is my thesis that the Bolivian National

Revolution would not have succeeded to the extent it did if the MNR had not aroused and sustained the social conscience of the middle class through newspapers and literature. It was the triumph of a propaganda campaign waged for twenty years before the MNR came to power in 1952 and so successful that the revolutionary changes were not dismantled by the military after 1964.

It is, of course, possible to exaggerate the influence of the press. Thus, it is not suggested here that MNR propaganda was the only catalyst in the Bolivian revolutionary process--which would be a gross distortion of history--but it was a major one. Almost all of the early leaders of the MNR were journalists--with the exception of Víctor Paz Estenssoro--and those who survive insist on the importance of propaganda to their cause. As La Nación, the official MNR newspaper after 1952, once declared:

> Traditionally, the MNR is a party of journalists. The founding staff was [in 1941] almost totally composed of newspapermen who marked the awakening of the conscience of the Bolivian majorities from that memorable nucleus of revolutionary thought that was La Calle. [3]

Even a competitor of the MNR, Guillermo Lora, leader of the Trotskyite Partido Obrero Revolucionario (POR, Revolutionary Worker Party) concedes this. He has entitled a still unpublished manuscript about the MNR, "From a propaganda group, to a party of masses." [4]

And Paz Estenssoro himself said before the National Press Club in Washington, D.C., in 1963:

> Our purpose was simple. It was to facilitate, through the press, the attainment of the objectives for which we were fighting. In other words, it was an attempt to enlist the help of the press for our revolution. [5]

Finally, this study is not intended to be a history of Bolivian journalism of the period, although that is included for essential background. Nor is it intended to be a political history, but since newspapers do not exist in a vacuum, their reporting of and reactions to major political events are examined in detail. This, then, is intended to be a social history of the interaction between the press and Bolivian society which culminated in the Bolivian National Revolution.

5

Chapter 1

DISSENT AND THE CHACO WAR

> The skirmishes triumph in this hypocritical
> and treacherous war that the land of the
> Chaco has declared with its dust and mud.

> --Augusto Céspedes,
> El Universal, March 22,
> 1933

Just as the disastrous Chaco War with Paraguay (1932-1935) marked a watershed in Bolivian history, it also ushered in the modern era of Bolivian journalism. Before the senseless conflict that cost Bolivia much suffering and a big chunk of her national territory, newspapers had been limited in circulation and had served the political interests of specific persons or parties. Personalism was the keynote of the period as individual owners or editors left their unmistakable marks on the journalistic products they conveyed to the public. There was no mass-based press which addressed itself to the interests of the nation as a whole. Indeed, if there had been such a press, Bolivia might have been spared the excruciating experience of losing 50,000 young men, 70,000 square kilometers of land, and 50 million dollars--the origins of an inflation that was to cripple the country.

As it turned out, a small segment of the Bolivian press matured during the Chaco War. Two newspapers in particular, La República and El Universal, developed a social consciousness and came to oppose the war which they regarded as immoral and foolhardy. They were the only voices in the public arena that had the courage to speak out against the prevailing opinion of reckless jingoism. They came to be the dissenting spokesmen of the popular majorities, but they paid dearly for the privilege. El Universal, which claimed an unprecedented 34,000 readers at the height of the Chaco War, was closed five times by President Daniel Salamanca during the conflict. [1] La República was closed permanently in October 1933, the victim of a war mentality that would brook no opposition. [2]

At the same time, the established press of Bolivia was discredited for supporting the war with enthusiasm. Gustavo

7

A. Navarro, who wrote under the Bulgarian pseudonym of "Tristán Marof," called the leading newspapers of La Paz "houses of journalistic prostitution." Navarro, an independent socialist, continued: "Defamation is the order of the day, like applause. There is not a line which is not controlled. The applause is not for the better or more worthy, but for the mediocre, the vile, or the castrated." [3]

This sycophant press bayed for war and puffed up the military leaders who ineptly conducted it. Roots of the conflict went back to the colonial period when the boundaries between Bolivia and Paraguay were never firmly established in the Chaco Boreal, a no man's land of desert and savanna covering an area slightly smaller than Texas. Beginning in the early Twentieth Century, both countries began building lines of fortines or crude wood-and-mud fortifications to occupy effectively the disputed territory. Standard Oil discovered petroleum in the western section of the Chaco after 1922, and that exacerbated the situation, but the coming conflict was essentially one of empty nationalism. Bolivia had lost her outlet to the sea in the War of the Pacific (1879-1883) in which Chile roundly defeated Peru and Bolivia, and she was interested in a river outlet to the Atlantic through the Chaco. Paraguay, on the other hand, had met ignominious defeat at the hands of Argentina, Uruguay, and Brazil in the War of the Triple Alliance (1864-1870), which cost Paraguay almost two-thirds of her population. Thus, both countries, defeated humiliatingly on their perimeters, turned inward and began inching farther and farther into the disputed Chaco. National pride in both cases required vindication, and skirmishes began to accelerate after Paraguay attacked Fort Vanguardia near the Pilcomayo River in 1928. All-out hostilities commenced in June 1932, but war was not declared until May 10, 1933, with two more years of ugly trench warfare before a truce of exhaustion in 1935. Bolivia had the superior army, trained by German General Hans Kundt, and a larger population, but Paraguay had shorter supply lines and was fighting for what was deemed her homeland. She steadily pushed Bolivian soldiers back to the foothills of the Andes, as the League of Nations in its first great test--before the Italian invasion of Abyssinia--was unable to stop the slaughter. Chile supported Bolivia with aid and supplies, and Argentina backed Paraguay, but charges that the international oil companies had fanned the conflict were never sustained. The confrontation was the bloodiest struggle in the western hemisphere since the United States Civil War. [4]

The tragedy of the Chaco War underscored the many dislocations in Bolivian life. Indians ignorant of Spanish or even the meaning of the word "Bolivia" were hauled to the faraway front in the desolate Chaco Boreal to fight for an incomprehensible cause. Moreover, the tropical lowland pained their lungs, expanded through centuries by the thin air of the altiplano. Corruption gripped their superiors, who profited from fat war contracts or shirked their duties. As one newspaper writer said back in the capital, Bolivian military officers showed up only for the cocktail hour. The country also suffered a primitive technology. "Against the modern installation of the mines," the same writer observed, "there remained in the countryside the plow of the Egyptians." Bolivian diplomats were incompetent or venal, he added, which "placed the country in the backrooms of all the chanceries." [5]

First to recognize the inadequacies of Bolivia for the war being ballyhooed by the old guard political leaders and the oligarchical press was La República, a morning daily founded in 1921 by President Bautista Saavedra (1921-1925) to advance his political fortunes in a schism within the Republican party. The newspaper's opposition to the Chaco conflict--although it ultimately urged vigorous prosecution of the war--would cause it to be closed permanently by the Salamanca government in 1933. But La República was accustomed to its role within the opposition; it had been closed frequently by the old-line Republican government that fell in 1930 when Hernando Siles (1926-1930), last of the party's presidents, was overthrown by General Carlos Blanco Galindo. [6] La República survived as spokesman for the Socialist Republican Party, and former President Saavedra wrote frequently for its pages. [7]

In 1932, as war clouds loomed over the Chaco, the editor of La República was Pedro Zilveti Arce, who urged a course of moderation for Bolivia amidst the outcries of jingoism. The newspaper then sold for ten centavos a copy, which can be compared to the 500 bolivianos that the second MNR newspaper La Tarde commanded in 1962 after the inflation brought on by the Chaco struggle and ten years of revolutionary changes. This represented an increase of 5,000 percent and underscores one of the most difficult problems that the post-Chaco generation had to face.

At the time, La República adopted a patriotic stance on the Chaco but gradually moved to a position opposing the war. In discussing "The question of the Chaco" in February 1932, an editorial proclaimed, "As to the Chaco, the national opinion is united: not to cede eight inches [un palmo] of lands to the adversary who argues hypothetical rights with us." [8] Still, the newspaper was cautious. It reminded its readers in March 1932 that Salamanca had declared when Fortín Vanguardia was attacked in 1928: "War should not be an adventure for Bolivia. Let's go to the Chaco not to conquer or die, but to conquer." La República stated that such histrionics might have their place, but Bolivia needed "a vast labor of preparation in the diverse aspects that surround a modern war"--such as arms and munitions, rapid means of communication, economic backing, and provisions of forces. Also, the newspaper warned, Bolivian leaders should not forget matters on the international scene, where the country needed "an organization of foreign propaganda in order to bring the necessary elements of judgement to world consciousness, so that it might form its own criterion and free itself from contrary and fallacious arguments." [9]

In April 1932, less than two months before the outbreak of full-scale fighting in the Chaco, La República pointed out the dangers inherent in the nation's drift toward war in an editorial headlined "Warlike atmosphere." The newspaper called for "serenity, tact, and fortitude. Precipitate steps can only bring calamities that will compromise the prestige and solidarity of our cause." Paraguay must be contained, La República conceded, but Bolivian reacquisition of the Chaco must wait "until our resources and prestige as a nation permit us to face [the problem] in all its consequences." [10] On other occasions, the newspaper was conciliatory, as when it noted "Paraguayan alarmism" and declared, "The Bolivian position defends our territory and such an attitude cannot alarm anyone..." [11]

La República believed that it was speaking to the common man if not the masses in Bolivian national life, and in May 1932 it warned this audience that they would be "The propitiatory victims" of all-out fighting in the Chaco. This column concluded, "What is evident and certain is that the victim of this pugilism has to be the country [itself]. It will be all of us inhabitants and residents of Bolivia who will have to pay the piper." [12] Meanwhile, La República kept up its continuous, scathing attacks on President Salamanca, such as an article headlined "The salamanquista dictatorship." [13]

Far from letting up in its criticism after undeclared war broke out in June 1932, La República stepped up its attacks, looking behind the scenes to see who had dragged Bolivia into what might turn out to be a hopeless military involvement. The newspaper's writers did not have to dig very deep to discover that la Rosca, Bolivia's small traditional elite, had instigated the war and were profiting from it. For the first time in Bolivian journalism this coterie--which had a very real psychological presence--was lambasted in the press. In July 1932, La República headlined its analysis, "The two great entities into which Bolivia is divided are WITH THE ROSCA or AGAINST THE ROSCA." [14] The newspaper also scored the diplomatic failures which had led to the Chaco impasse, and urged "the widest and absolute amnesty" for Bolivians everywhere as the formal declaration of war neared. [15]

10

El Universal, which pioneered in the discussion of social issues in the Bolivian press and opposed the Chaco War, announces on May 10, 1933, the formal declaration of war by Paraguay.

Nevertheless, the country was at war and Bolivian sensibilities reached deeper than opposing a government from behind an editorial desk. La República declared on July 20, 1932, "All of us Bolivians will lend our decided aid to the Government, in defense of the sovereignty and honor of our country. But we want the certainty that there is a definite plan; we want to know that in peace or war we are not marching from tomb to tomb." [16]   Two days later La República called for a declaration of war against Paraguay, noting that Bolivia could count on Argentine neutrality. [17]   In the first burst of militaristic enthusiasm, the newspaper began printing such articles as "War is of divine essence," but it soon returned to its former position of demanding accountability at home and prosecution of the war with dispatch. [18]

As Bolivia lost battle after battle and morale declined in both the military and at home, La República had the courage to ask for the resignation of Salamanca on October 27, 1932.   In the months ahead, the embattled president exiled journalists associated with La República and El Diario, along with opposition political party leaders. [19]   More editorial attacks against Salamanca followed.   On November 20, 1932, La República printed its most stinging rebuke of the president under the headline UNTIL WHEN?   The newspaper asserted, "The game of Salamanca has been discovered.   The country knows that his egolatría, his animosity, and his egoism are placed above national honor and integrity, that he has permitted that they be trampled upon by the last country on earth, Paraguay.   It is enough then to ask: Until when [will we allow] Salamanca to abuse our patience?"   Two days later, La República followed up its rhetorical question by blazoning in a headline and subhead: THE NECESSITY OF VICTORY DEMANDS THE RESIGNATION OF SALAMANCA.   "It is the corpses of those who have remained planted in the Chaco, the prisoners who have been hanged from the gallows, who demand it.   It is the supreme necessity for victory that imposes it." [20]

Such frontal assaults on the authority of the president did not go unchallenged.   Salamanca believed that the dissident press was impeding the war effort, and he dealt with La República and El Universal in a heavy-handed fashion--closing the papers frequently, exiling journalists, accusing the press of being unpatriotic.   This harassment was sporadic, however, and the newspapers always bounced back with sharper barbs for the war leadership.   In the case of La República, however, Salamanca deemed the newspaper too noxious to be tolerable. On October 7, 1933, the council of ministers ordered permanent closing of La República within three months, and the newspaper which had pioneered in criticism of the Chaco War was never to appear again. [21]

If the Chaco War broadened the base of a few newspapers which criticized such conditions, it also tempered a generation of young writers for the propaganda struggle ahead. A handful of war correspondents, foremost among them Augusto Céspedes and Carlos Montenegro, brought home to readers in La Paz the reality--and futility--of the war. Most Bolivians of the altiplano had never even been to the Chaco; for them, their men might just as well have been fighting on the far side of the moon. But writers such as Céspedes painted vivid and poignant pictures of the harsh conditions on the battle front, adding to the rising tide of antiwar sentiment at home.

The ministry of war in February 1933 invited four La Paz journalists to travel to the zone of war operations. They were Céspedes for El Universal, Guillermo Céspedes Rivera for La Razón, Francisco Villarejos for Semana Gráfica, and Rodolfo Costas for Radio Nacional. El Diario and Ultima Hora did not send correspondents. Later, when the latter proclaimed that the journalistic mission to the Chaco had been a failure, Céspedes maintained it was mere sour grapes because the newspaper itself had failed to send a correspondent to the Chaco. Even when its "fearful directors" were drafted, Céspedes teased in 1975, they remained safely in La Paz. "The most epic reporter of Ultima Hora," he added, "got as far as Villa Montes, then 600 kilometers from the line of fire, as an employee of the agency of the Banco Central, where he was seized by an attack of war panic and was evacuated to La Paz." [22]

Céspedes, today Bolivia's most gifted living writer and only one of three Latin American authors invited to the Soviet Union for a conference in 1971, was only twenty-nine when he made the arduous journey to the Chaco front. The events of the Chaco War were to make him an international literary figure after the publication in 1936 of his Sangre de mestizos (Blood of Half-Breeds), acidic vignettes of the Chaco fighting. One of these short stories, "El Pozo" ("The Well") has been translated and anthologized in many languages and has come to symbolize the inexorable senselessness of the Chaco conflict. The genesis of Sangre de mestizos can be found in Céspedes' forty-five dispatches written for El Universal between February 13, 1933, and November 18, 1934. The writer was in the Chaco for fourteen months, ten of which he served as a soldier, fighting at the battle of Candado. Even as a combatant, Céspedes continued to write for El Universal, although his dispatches were frequently censored. [23]

What kind of picture of the Chaco did Céspedes convey to

the readers of El Universal, accustomed to the quiet calm of the Prado and the beer gardens and nightclubs of Obrajes in La Paz? Many times he referred to the Chaco as a landscape conjured up by Dante. Years later, flying over the region in an airplane, he described it as "that geological remnants sale of a disappeared planet..." [24] After the war, in an article he wrote for La Nación of Santiago de Chile, Céspedes cited the heat as the single most overpowering presence of the Chaco. No soldier could forget "the sun of the Chaco, incendiary and brutal, [which] bakes the sand and boils your brains." [25]

During the course of the war itself, Céspedes described the heat at Villa Montes on his way to the front in February 1933:

> Heat by day and heat by night invades every hour and every place, magnificent as a hog, somnolent, inescapable; the people of Villa Montes are condemned to perpetual heat. They live submerged in a Turkish bath. It is one of the points on this planet which has fever, like Senegal, the Gold Coast, or Sumatra. One sweats without a timetable. With the smallest effort one feels it run down the skin, down the spine, and down the chest--vipers of sweat, with a head that feels like a pearl tiepin. [26]

Semi-arid and covered with scrub brush and cactus, the Chaco was parched and dusty in the winter and drenched and muddy during the summer. Céspedes called Villa Montes a "green oven" with temperatures of 40 degrees centigrade. He described the enervating heat as "inappropriate to write as to do Swedish gymnastics." [27] Water was an extreme problem during the dry period; there was not a single river in the Chaco between the 19th meridian and the Pilcomayo. Soldiers were forced to rely upon sporadic waterholes or cañadas, but since much of the Chaco was an almost perfectly flat plain, there were hundreds of square kilometers in which not a single cañada could be found. Trucks brought water to the troops for as far as 100 to 150 kilometers over primitive roads; meanwhile, Bolivian soldiers would urinate on their sizzling machineguns to cool them down. [28]

Transportation was an extremely severe problem for the Bolivians because they were fighting across the breadth of their country where no roads had ever been developed. Céspedes described his journey from Villa Montes to Fortín Ballivián in February 1933 with the sardonic humor for which he became famous. Only traffic in convoys were allowed beyond Villa Montes so that vehicles could aid each other. Céspedes could not decide which was worse: the roads or the trucks. The former were "rough trails upon which the passage of even pack horses would be problematic." As for the latter, "the trucks of the Chaco are more... long-suffering than mules of the Yungas." At one time on the journey beyond Villa Montes, thirteen trucks--the entire convoy--were stuck in the sea of mud. When a caterpillar hauled the last one out, the first ones would be stuck again. The convoy made only four kilometers within seven hours. [29]

After the mud came dust. Céspedes sent a dispatch from Fort Ballivián which noted that "the dust which covers [the road] is atomized so finely that when the wheels of the trucks run through it, they leave an undulant and tremulous wake, as if they were cutting water." Indeed, the dust was so deep that the differential of the truck left a third track in the road. [30] Yet Céspedes was so impressed with the opening up of the Chaco to mechanized travel that he wrote:

> Whoever writes the history of the Chaco will have to write first the history of its roads, not simply as a geographical premise, but as the foundation of this arduous war. Because a true history will not be done with outlines nor the cartographic drawing of lines, but the lively, painful, fatiguing and shaking history of the distances through which they opened the roads. [31]

Throughout his dispatches, Céspedes drove home again and again the theme that the worst enemy for the Bolivian soldiers--greater even than the barefoot pilitas as their Paraguayan adversaries were called--was the natural environment. Not only was there the dissolving and enervating heat, but also the intimidating psychological factor of the Chaco's sheer presence. After Céspedes made a 21-day journey across 500 kilometers of the region's width, from Entre Ríos to Muñoz, he wrote that "the Chaco plain extends with irritating uniformity." [32] On another occasion he described the area as "the scrubland of the indifferent Chaco, without relief, imperturable as a sleeping vampire." [33] Only the war, Céspedes added as a postscript, gave the Chaco destiny. [34] After the armistice of June 14, 1935, Céspedes in Santiago de Chile published his valedictory statement on the Chaco War in two articles in La Nación. He summed up the scope and tenor of all of his dispatches when he declared:

> There was in them [the soldiers] something visible, but in the Chaco War, sordid war of insects lost in the inexorable landscape and a treacherous universe of thickets and sand, there were no panoramas nor poses. Everything was invisible, especially

heroism... [35]

Also filing stories for El Universal on the unvarnished
truth about what was happening at the front was Carlos
Montenegro. His later book published in 1943, Nacionalismo y
coloniaje (Nationalism and Colonialism) was to be a watershed
between the pessimism and defeatism of Alcides Argüedas and
the affirmative call for greater national self-awareness by a
generation of revolutionary writers. Although Montenegro's
book was published during the administration of Gualberto
Villarroel, the conditions described applied also to the Bolivian
press at the time of the Chaco War. That is why the work of
such war correspondents as Céspedes and Montenegro was so
important in bringing home to the man in the streets of La Paz
the reality of a war glossed over by the traditional capital
press. El Universal performed a great public service in publishing their dispatches despite the harassment of military
censorship and the ever-present threat of closure by the government.

Possessing a theoretical and analytical mind, Montenegro
was not as gifted a descriptive writer as Céspedes. He lacked
the humor and punch of the latter, but he was sensitive to the
tragedy unfolding in the Chaco. Bookish and somewhat shy,
with somber eyes that stared from behind horn-rimmed glasses,
Montenegro did not seem to be the ideal type for a war correspondent, but his thirty-five dispatches to El Universal printed
throughout 1934 chronicled a generation on trial. His column
was first headlined, "Those of Us Who Go to War," and later,
"With the Combatants." [36] Soon after arriving at the front in
March 1934, Montenegro wrote:

This war has nothing spectacular nor transcendent
for the soldier. It is a war such as the younger
generations comprehend it: an event without ante-
cedent nor posterity, in which one fulfills his duty
without exaggerated fear, and in which are frightful
not the machine-guns nor the grenades, not death,
but the trenches, the mud, the heat, the thirst--that
is to say, life itself. [37]

There was also an emotional and romantic reaction to the
Chaco War. In one early dispatch Montenegro discussed the
writers and artists who had come to the front. It was the
biggest happening of their lifetime, and they were not going to
miss the opportunity to strike creative paydirt. As Alberto de
Villegas, author of Sombras de mujeres (Women's Shadows), put
it, "No one should say as a writer what he has not experienced
as a soldier." Montenegro put it more strongly: "The campaign
has brought [to the front] all of the men. I have the

16

impression that no one remains in the cities except those who renounce the future." The journalist continued:

> The men of arts and letters acquire here a new sense: the sense of maximum emotional profundity that only a war like this can give--a war in the desert that chokes with heat and blinds with wind.. [producing] the image of a mountainous desert, silent, deserted, dense, asphyxiating, tragic. [38]

But the ideas and impressions which these writers formed in the Chaco would take months and in some cases years to gestate. Perhaps the most telling effect of their experiences at the war front was the sense of camaraderie they developed which later was to weld together much of the younger generation that was to lead Bolivia into her revolutionary experience after the war.

Another effect which must not be minimized was the profound realization that journalism and propaganda were as necessary to win the war as rifles and bullets. In Germany, Joseph Goebbels was making propaganda a high art, and his concepts trickled down to Bolivian writers, but it was the Chaco War itself which convinced young intellectuals that they had been living in a vacuum of information, a vacuum which had led the country into this deadly struggle. Moreover, Bolivia itself was scarcely known in the exterior; it was thought of as a small, self-contained feudal state perched astride the Andes at the top of the world, peopled with quaint Indian women in bowler hats and aristocratic-looking llamas.

In early 1933, looking toward the future, El Universal declared that one windfall on the Chaco War would be that Bolivia would become known in the outside world and no longer be just a colored patch on a map. The editorial stated, "Above everything else, it is necessary to launch an intensive propaganda, no longer for what refers only to the rights that we defend with our arms, but also as to the industrial, commercial and agricultural possibilities of the country." [39] The word "propaganda" did not have an invidious meaning at that time, and El Universal realized that the best propaganda was the unembellished truth. Thus, the factual dispatches of its correspondents Céspedes and Montenegro were recognized as beneficial to the Bolivian cause: "The interesting reports from their pens reach not only the Bolivian public but also outside the Republic. And one cannot deny this is valuable for the propaganda that the country needs to combat the lying and cynical [accounts] of the enemy." [40]

El Universal, the most sophisticated La Paz newspaper at

that time, printed in late 1934--as Bolivian reverses on the battlefield continued to mount--a letter dispatch from a correspondent in Berlin on the propaganda techniques of Joseph Goebbels, minister of propaganda in the Third Reich. The writer noted, "The German people are reminded not only every day, but every hour, of the program and purpose of Hitler's government. The press, radio, oratory, spectacles, gathering and ceremonies are the means which are utilized." As an example, the correspondent cited the thousands of athletes who ran to the Saar to welcome it back to the Fatherland. Goebbels was quoted as saying that all the accomplishments of the Third Reich would have been impossible without his work, "converted into a model for the entire world." The banner headline over this article proclaimed, PROPAGANDA IS THE VOICE OF ORDER. [41]

In Bolivia, on the other hand, official propaganda efforts were scattered and ineffective. The Centro Nacional de Defensa y Propaganda--raised to ministry level in 1938 by a hero of the Chaco War, President Germán Busch--had been created early in the struggle as a mixed government and private enterprise. Radio Illimani also was established at that time as the governmental station, but it reached only the national territory. [42] The Centro was attached after a year to the ministry of war, but it was mainly defensive, existing to censor cables sent out by press services. Paraguay, by contrast, had launched a propaganda offensive, bringing foreign--especially Argentine--correspondents to observe the action at the front, producing film of the fighting for worldwide distribution and sending Paraguayan cultural missions to Latin American capitals. "That kind of effort, with correspondents in the theatre of operations--genuine journalists--and agents outside the republic is what Bolivian propaganda requires," observed El Diario in early 1935. The newspaper made the point, belatedly, "Now it is an axiomatic truth that wars are won not only with cannon or machine-guns; the artillery of the presses and tribunes is as decisive for the triumph of a cause" as the fortunes of war. [43]

The ineptness of the Bolivian foreign propaganda campaign--as riddled with graft and corruption as other areas of leadership--was exposed in one instance by El Universal. The Bolivian writer Luis Azurduy, returning home after five years abroad, reported that 70,000 Argentine pesos had been sent to the Bolivian legation in Buenos Aires for propaganda but soon disappeared. One Lt. Col. Moreira, the military attaché, had been told he had 10,000 pesos for expenses, but when he presented a bill for 350 pesos, there was no money available. The Círculo Intelectual Argentino Boliviano wanted to rent the Cervantes theater for 200 pesos to show Bolivian art, but they too were turned down. The only work of propaganda that Azurduy had noticed during his long stay in Buenos Aires was two or three "rectifications" published in La Nación and La Prensa, and a note or official communication printed in a neighborhood newspaper, even though the information was available in any of the major newspapers. And who would buy it? "Hardly twenty conservatives of Florida Street," Azurduy concluded. [44]

Toward the end of the war, after President Daniel Salamanca had been overthrown by the military and was replaced with Vice-President Jose Luis Tejada Sorzano on November 27, 1934, things improved on the propaganda front. The new president had the good sense to send two excellent writers on peace propaganda missions: Jorge Canedo Reyes to Peru and Augusto Céspedes to Chile. This was one month before the end of the campaign in 1935. In Chile, Céspedes wrote his Sangre de mestizos, contributed to the principal newspapers and reviews of Santiago and Valparaíso, conducted conferences, and transmitted messages from Chilean intellectuals for the repatriation of prisoners. [45]

Thus, the lesson was driven home to the men who later were to form the MNR that the value of effective propaganda could not be minimized. One of the surprising turns of the Chaco War was that even the oligarchial press became aware of this as Bolivian troops were pushed steadily westward. In early 1935, El Diario reprinted an editorial from the newspaper Alas of Potosí:

> Many times we have expressed the necessity of putting the country in the state of general war, in such a manner that all of its elements will fulfill the specific functions in which they can serve better the interests of the nation: the military man in the trenches, the chemist in his laboratories, the teacher in the lecture hall, the intellectual--or better yet the studious one as Unamuno said--armed with his pen and illustrating to the foreign element the things of our country and its peculiarities.

El Diario itself, in introducing the reprint, called for "the intellectual mobilization of the press" in the nation's darkest hour. [46]

But the propaganda that most helped to end the war was not the official efforts launched at home and abroad nor the spirited reportage of such correspondents as Céspedes and Montenegro. The most telling blow against those who were misconducting the war--and by indirection against the old order itself in Bolivia--was delivered in the editorial opposition to the fighting in the pages of El Universal and La República. Recent studies have shown that editorial comment is less effective than once supposed--that persons tend to read only those newspapers or magazines with whose points of view they already agree. Their own views may be reinforced by what they read but rarely changed. Nevertheless, in the La Paz journalistic arena it was so unusual for two newspapers to go against a great national crusade that their pronouncements carried disproportionate weight. Opposition to the national government--except in the intramural sparring of political cliques who rotated in power--was unheard of in Bolivia. This was the beginning of a mass press in the country, and in a sense a reader of El Universal voted in a street referendum on the Chaco War every time he plunked down his ten centavos to buy a copy. Circulation rose to 34,000 during the height of the Chaco fighting, augmented by the brilliant dispatches of Céspedes and Montenegro, but stimulated even more by the editorial voice of the opposition. [47]

Whether a direct response to the stimulus or not, El Universal came into being in early December 1932 when the fighting in the Chaco had been underway for six months. Under its masthead was the slogan: "Its ear attentive to all the world vibrations. Its heart placed in the Fatherland. And its intelligence at the service of the culture." [48] El Universal was like a breath of fresh air in the rather stultifying journalistic circles of La Paz. The new newspaper bared itself to the winds of change elsewhere in the world by starting a daily column on "Foreign opinion through the editorial column" and a front-page feature, "What the cable doesn't say." Biographical vignettes were printed from time to time on "Men of the Chaco." [49] El Universal printed some of the photographs of Bazoberry, the Mathew Brady of the Chaco War, and experienced its own war losses. Author of the popular column, "Man of the Street," Lisimaco ("Maco") Gutiérrez Granier, was killed in the fighting. [50]

The newspaper also pioneered in the use of humorous, bright or catchy headlines--a practice that was to become the hallmark of La Calle (1936-1946), spokesman for the MNR. Faced with ever more heavy-handed censorship, El Universal proclaimed in a headline in late 1934: "There are no serious motifs to write about--It is indispensable to deal with themes apart from the grandeur of the state. Some reflections upon frivolities and foolishness." [51] Nor were the copy editors of the upstart newspaper averse to editorializing blatantly in their headlines. When the press of Asunción reported that Bolivian prisoners of war returned home had been treated well in their captivity, El Universal headlined the account in a two-line

20

banner on the front page, PARAGUAYAN CYNICISM IS WITH-
OUT PARALLEL IN THE WORLD. [52]   On another occasion,
when Bolivian troops captured 50 Paraguayan officers and 1,000
soldiers, El Universal recalled that Archbishop Bogarín of
Asunción had told a captive Bolivian priest, Luis A. Tapia, that
Bolivians would never capture more than 100 Paraguayans at a
time.   The newspaper headlined its story, "The Paraguayan
Archbishop Bogarín has turned out to be a liar.--His predictions do not have an atom of inspiration from Providence."
[53]   Puncturing pretensions at home as well as abroad, El
Universal noted ironically in a 1935 headline, "There are many
ways of sacrificing oneself for his country, his God and his
woman.--But the most painful is being national representative;
therefore [only] the most patriotic fancy it." [54]

The man responsible for this new brand of journalism was
Armando Arce, who became editor of El Universal on March 18,
1933.   La Calle was founded by Arce and Céspedes after El
Universal was closed by the government in 1935.   The latter
newspaper thus became a training ground for the La Calle
experiment, which was to be the longest and most sustained
propaganda effort in Latin American history.   For example, El
Universal crusaded against the high cost of drugs and medi-
cine--as a 25 percent inflation swept the country.   The newspaper noted that what did cost 2.5 bolivianos now ran as high as
12 bolivianos. [55]   Again, El Universal found that families of
soldiers were left destitute, "condemned to misery," while their
breadwinners were fighting at the front. [56]   The newspaper,
which was rapidly becoming the popular conscience of Bolivia,
also urged that the riches accumulated by war speculators be
investigated and turned over to war orphans. [57]

In a forthright way, El Universal widened the range of its
editorial sights to take in the big tin magnates and great landowners.   Decrying war profiteering as GOLD AND BLOOD in
early 1935, the newspaper in its columns attacked those who
were not contributing to the national defense.   Evasion of even
the minimal taxes prescribed by law had been notorious in
Bolivian life, but for the first time a newspaper was saying
something about it:

El Universal believes that the moment has arrived in
which the potentates of Bolivia should contribute
spontaneously to the defense, but not with the
derisive 50 or 100 bolivianos that any ragamuffin
gives, but rather [the contribution] should be at the
level of the great luxury and prosperity that the rich
lead in this war and at the level of their earnings.
[58]

Statements such as these opened up a new era in Bolivian journalism because the rich and the powerful--who owned most of the other newspapers--were no longer out of bounds for criticism or social accountability. It is scarcely any wonder that El Universal was closed five times during its brief existence (1932-1935). The newspaper thrived on controversy, however, and its editor Armando Arce found the formula that was to make it popular as well as hard-hitting. If there were heavy articles of social import, these were brightened with titillating headlines. One daily feature, "In Jail," would have done justice to the police drama and humor first exploited by the Fleet Street press and later by James Gordon Bennett of the New York Herald in the 1840s. [59] With his combination of popular features and serious articles, Arce was following in the footsteps, whether he knew it or not, of Joseph Pulitzer, who believed that sensationalism was all right if it lured the barely literate reader onto the editorial page or into the other more serious departments of the newspaper. Like a good teacher who knows when to crack a joke, El Universal kept its readers entertained while giving them also the first renegade thought in Bolivian political history.

Early in the Chaco War, El Universal was torn between its independent judgement and the patriotic hysteria which gripped everyone. Thus, after the formal declaration of war on May 12, 1933, the newspaper reprinted part of General Hans Kundt's message to the troops:

Soldiers of Bolivia, you must economize, above all your munition. Let each cartridge used be one enemy less. The merit is in the valor of your bayonets and in the firm will to conquer. Forward, Bolivians. Subordination and steadiness. Your general, Hans Kundt. [60]

The Prussian call to arms by a man who had revamped and trained Bolivia's military establishment seemed incongrous for Indian conscripts, but Carlos Montenegro found that they fought well. [61] The Guaraní soldiers of Paraguay, derisively called pilas or barefoot men by their adversaries, were even more tenacious, however. Although the Indians had been more closely integrated into national Paraguayan life--with a Guaraní newspaper, El Enanito founded at Ayala as early as 1935--the authorities were loathe to admit that their culture rested upon an Indian base. Thus, El Universal quoted an Asunción newspaper in 1933 as saying, "The cross between the white and Guaraní Indian originated in Paraguay a product superior to [both] the white and Indian." Commented El Universal, "That is due undoubtedly to providential intervention, since the whites who intervened in that cross were all Bishops..." [62]

Whenever possible, the humor of El Universal was brought into play as in 1934 when the newspaper cited an Argentine journalist of Radio Universal of Buenos Aires who was surprised to find on a visit to Asusción that the pilas were not an invention of Bolivian propaganda. He reported that even the Paraguayan journalists of the capital city "walk very felinely sporting some stockings of green and blue cotton, and nothing more as pedestrian footwear.... They walk with their socks hitched up but without shoes and they say they know the cobblestones of their streets as well as I know the history of Imperial Rome." [63]

Part of the job of El Universal--as with the other dailies in La Paz--was to combat untrue or misleading propaganda by Paraguayan or Argentine sources. This the newspaper was willing to do; although it came to oppose the war vehemently, its Bolivian nationalism came first, at least in the early stages of the conflict. Thus, El Universal exposed to the light of public scrutiny in La Paz such stories as one originating in El Pueblo of Argentina in 1933. The Argentine newspaper published a letter from La Paz denouncing the shanghaiing of Peruvians who wandered across the Bolivian border looking for work or to sell their products and then found themselves fighting on the Chaco front. Even Peruvian servants and waiters working in La Paz were stripped of their ID's and dragooned to the front, the letter maintained. It estimated that some 1,000 Peruvians were forced to serve illegally in Bolivian trenches. [64] Charges can flow both ways, however. Later in the war, an article in El Universal charged that the Paraguayans were shooting Bolivian villagers on the border who refused to enlist in the Paraguayan army. [65]

Again, in 1934, El Universal pointed out that three "fantastic" allies of the Paraguayan army were these rumors fanned by the press of Asunción: that Bolivia was in an anarchic and revolutionary condition, there was "uncontainable desertion" of the altiplano troops from the Chaco front, and epidemics raged in Bolivian towns. [66] The second point was probably not far from the truth, for La Calle reported after the war that around 16,000 Bolivian deserters were living in Argentina alone, where they had formed the Unión Nacional de Exilados (National Union of Exiles). [67]

El Universal during the Chaco War had to fight defeatism and negative propaganda on the home front as well. For example, the newspaper hooted in early 1934 when Archbishop Peirini, leader of the Bolivian church, said in a sermon at the Chapel of Lourdes in Sucre that Bolivian military disasters were due to the lack of people's faith and, above all, to the recent laws of civil marriage and absolute divorce. [68]

A break in the political stalemate and the seemingly unending series of military reverses came on November 27, 1934, when the aging and inept President Daniel Salamanca was imprisoned by the military during a tour of the Chaco front. To appease international opinion, civilian Vice-President José Luis Tejada Sorzano was installed in the presidency after Salamanca's forced resignation, but it was clear that it was the army which was in the driver's seat from that moment on, including General Enrique Peñaranda, chief of staff, Colonel David Toro, and Major Germán Busch, all of whom had participated in the coup.

The news of the dismissal of Salamanca hit the newspapers of La Paz the following day. El Universal, trying to smooth over the abrupt change of leaders, put a false light on things by saying that the decree signed by Tejada Sorzano in assuming the presidency of the republic was necessary because Salamanca "has established himself in the field of operations in the Southeast, and there exist grave matters of state that demand urgent solution." Tejada Sorzano offered two paragraphs to the press stating that the country's most imperious duty was to maintain order and to back the army. El Universal which had been closed five times by the Salamanca government, was jubilant. The newspaper declared, "The last twenty-four hours have been the best that we have had in these last four years. It is unnecessary to explain why." [69]

Details of the overthrow of Salamanca were sketchy. A plane was bringing the text of his renunciation from Villa Montes but El Universal printed a radio-telegraph version of five lines: "To the Nation: In view of sufficient reasons that weigh on my spirit, I hereby renounce and definitely relinquish the office of Constitutional President of the Republic." It was reported that Salamanca resigned at 3 a.m. But people in the streets of La Paz were wondering if it were a golpe or coup d'etat. El Universal reported that the political situation had been resolved "pacifically" and "voluntarily." Peñaranda was to continue to head the army and "absolute tranquility reigns." [70]

In January 1935 El Universal was able to offer its readers a Paraguayan version of Salamanca's ouster, given to the United Press in Asunción by Lt. Nesto Cárdenas, a prisoner-of-war who had witnessed the events at Villa Montes. He said that Salamanca was going to replace Peñaranda with Brigadier General José L. Lanza. Peñaranda and his fellow officers surrounded Salamanca's house in Villa Montes with 240 men on the night of November 27, 1934. Peñaranda gave Salamanca a resignation to copy in his own hand; when he handed it over to his chief of staff, the ex-president said, "Señor Peñaranda, this is the only maneuver that you have done well." Lanza entered

24

the room, tore off his insignias and threw them in Salamanca's face, shouting, "There you have these insignias that I have won with honor and sacrifice." [71] Rafael Salamanca, son of the former president, later recounted from his exile in Buenos Aires how he had shoved his pistol against Peñaranda's chest to defend his father. The general was allegedly intoxicated during his confrontation with Salamanca. [72]

On November 30, 1934, three days after the transition of power in the Chaco, El Universal drew a historical parallel between Salamanca and the president who led the country to defeat in the War of the Pacific, Hilarión Daza, who deserted his troops in 1880 and fled to Europe. The newspaper editorialized that as in the case of Daza fifty-four years earlier, "history will applaud the gesture of the army command which... has eliminated at Villa Montes the most regrettable and harmful of the presidents of Bolivia." [73] At the same time that El Universal attacked the deposed president, it lauded the new regime because for the first time it saw the possibility to bring reform to Bolivia through the socially conscious younger military officers. Thus, a headline, proclaimed, "We are under a well educated and kind government. Courtesy in police measures, improvement in treatment of the guilty." [74] Again, a headline in El Universal proclaimed that the new government was different "not only in appearances, faces and language. There is a total transformation--within the government, also in gestures. A parallel that has no other parallel." [75] It was clear that El Universal was experiencing the heady honeymoon period that follows the overthrow of one ruler and lasts until entrancement with the new becomes sour.

At the same time, the newspaper continued its investigations of war profiteering under the former regime and also pushed for a general mobilization. In late 1934 El Universal attacked frauds in the management and investment of war funds under the Genuine Republican party that had supported Salamanca. [76] Also coming under the editorial gun was corruption in the allocation of divisas or international exchange rates. [77] Believing that the war had not been prosecuted with dispatch, El Universal predicted in late 1934 that general mobilization was "very probable" and supported this step editorially. [78]

Nevertheless, opposition to the Chaco War grew steadily in the pages of El Universal as the newspaper struggled desperately to extricate the nation from the morass into which it had fallen. As the year 1935 opened, Augusto Céspedes posed the question in print which was causing most Bolivians frustration and anguish: WHAT TO DO? [79] As the League of Nations proved impotent to stop the bloodletting, El Universal headlined its editorial "The slaughter continues." [80] When La Noche of Lima published an article demonstrating there was no petroleum in the disputed area of the Chaco, El Universal gave it prominent display with the headline, "The petroleum myth of the Chaco War.--Irrefutable demonstration of 'La Noche.'" [81] When mutilated prisoners-of-war were exchanged, various Bolivian ex-prisoners related the experiences of their captivity in Paraguay through the columns of El Universal. [82] This was an effective device because the war was brought home in human terms unequalled since the dispatches of Céspedes and Montenegro early in the conflict. Readers in La Paz learned perhaps for the first time how enlisted men were treated in the Chaco, in contrast to the arrogance and disdain of many of their officers.

As truce negotiations finally got underway in Buenos Aires in May 1935, El Universal printed glaring headlines and accounts of the progress--or lack of it--between May 27 and the final headline, THE TRUCE IS SIGNED, of June 12. Hostilities ceased in the Chaco at noon on Friday, June 14, 1935, but the biggest headline of the war appeared on June 11, THERE WILL BE PEACE, with the news that Tejada Sorzano had announced he would sign the agreement. As both Bolivian and Paraguayan trenches were razed in the Chaco, the final peace conference opened on July 1, 1935, in Buenos Aires. [83]

As negotiations in the Argentine capital dragged on for three more years, echos of the Chaco war reverberated bitterly in the pages of El Universal, which maintained a standing column on "Things about the War." In one installment Julio Zauzo Cuenca recalled with distaste those "national tourists [who had gone to] the trenches of the Chaco Boreal." Visiting "firemen" and groups such as the Feminine Patriotic Leagues had used badly needed transportation to go to the front where, according to Zauzo Cuenca, they did nothing except "visit some position... where they were able to make themselves present for posterity through an artistic photograph..." [84]

On the cultural side, El Universal discussed the stinging effects of the Chaco War on Bolivian art and reproduced some of the savage paintings of that conflict by Cecilio Guzmán de Rojas; when these works were exhibited in Buenos Aires, a critic of La Prensa of that city called them "a requisition against the war." [85] The impact of the war upon the world of letters would be felt later. Meantime, El Universal discussed the problems of returning veterans and prisoners-of-war under the headline, "Those who fought in the Chaco want peace and tranquility." The newspaper also printed the long list of Bolivian prisoners who had died in Paraguayan POW camps. [86] Nor did it let up in its investigations into war profiteering;

thus, on June 26, 1935, El Universal referred in a headline to RICH MEN IN THE SHADOW OF THE CROSSES of the Chaco dead. The newspaper exhorted its readers, "you must aid us to discover the scandals [affaires] of the war...." [87]

Nevertheless, there was still some romanticization of the Chaco conflict, a kind of instant replay of glory as when the retrospective articles and memoirs began to appear. In one such excursion into nostalgia, El Universal printed an article in August 1935 headlined, "In a single day, Paraguay had 500 casualties opposite Fort Boquerón." [88] And earlier, when General Peñaranda met in the war zone immediately after the truce with Lt. Col. José Félix Estigarribia, the Paraguayan army commander whose own casualties ran as high as 40,000, El Universal duly reported that he gave Peñaranda the pistol he had carried during the three-year Chaco campaign. At the same time, the newspaper began using its back pages to report sports once more. [89]

El Universal made its valedictory statement on the Chaco War in an editorial, "It is necessary to break with the past," published on July 4, 1935, a few weeks before the newspaper was to close its doors. It had not commented on the Chaco truce of June 14 before this time, and the gestation period produced the most insightful and prophetic view of the effect of the Chaco conflict on Bolivian politics and society that appeared in the Bolivian press in that era. The editorial noted, "It is certain that the war and its consequences have revealed the failure of the old men [who were] responsible for the armed conflict that they did not foresee nor try to evade..." The Chaco generation, on the other hand, those who fought in the desert or suffered in the prisoner-of-war camps, "have earned their doctorates in sacrifice..." They were the ones who should now lead the country rather that the old guard which was still making pretensions of hanging on. The editorial continued:

> The war is an abyss that divided the future from the past.... This is the epoch of radical solutions, not of bargaining terms. It should be defined whether the government is going to continue being the source of enrichment for incompetent persons, or if it is going to be the instrument of recuperation for the country, in the hands of the younger classes, prepared to direct the public with honesty, renovating passion and the patriotic love they acquired in the trenches during the three years of the tragedy brought on by the ineptitude and lack of scruples of the men of the past. [90]

With the return of peace, it was almost as if El Universal's mission had ended. Perhaps with no more reports from the fighting front, the newspaper could not survive its loss of street sales, but it seems more likely that it simply bowed out at a graceful time: it had witnessed the overthrow of Salamanca and the final hush on the battlefields--two causes for which it had struggled for three years. And in a sense El Universal was not to die, for it had been a fertile training ground for the men--especially Armando Arce--who would found La Calle a year later to hammer out on the anvil of public opinion the issues which the Chaco War had brought to the forefront. A new newspaper was needed for a new time and a new political party, the National Revolutionary Movement, but it was sad for many to see El Universal disappear. It had spoken out with more courage than any previous newspaper in the history of Bolivian journalism. In its last issue, the headline on the front page was that Estigarribia had rendered homage to the dead soldiers of both countries in the Chaco campaign when he spoke to all the Paraguayan nation by radio. Also on that front page was a local story that a 21-year-old Bolivian youth had admitted killing twenty-seven persons in his short life. Emperor Hirohito's wife was expecting her sixth child, and il Duce's forces were rampaging into Ethiopia. With these news items lumbering at its back, El Universal closed quietly on August 23, 1935, without editorial comment or explanation. [91]

The newspaper was dead, but it had set a precedent of independent opposition that was to be fruitful in the turbulent post-Chaco years. El Universal differed from La República in that the latter, however outspoken its dissent, was still the voice in the traditional manner of the political party of Saavedra. But El Universal was the cooperative effort of a group of young men, headed by editor Armando Arce, dedicated to examining the moral chasms in Bolivian life revealed by the Chaco War. This examination did not come to a halt when the fighting stopped; if anything, the analytical process was accelerated by the shame and disgust of the Chaco defeat. The country faced internal problems all the more serious because the traditional political parties had been discredited. A rampant inflation sapped the pockets of the middle sector from which the leadership for the Bolivian National Revolution was to come. Two-thirds of the population, composed of Quechua and Aymará-speaking Indians, were almost completely outside national life, living in miserable hovels, dying prematurely from poor diets and lack of medical care, having no chance at an education, alone, forgotten, despised. Very few of the Indian communities had survived with their own land while the great landowners or terratenientes farmed just enough of their enormous acreages to maintain their lifestyles in La Paz or the capitals of Europe. Meanwhile, the Big Three tin companies

28

brooded over national life with what was perceived as malevolent power, making and breaking Bolivian presidents, monopolizing the press of La Paz, shooting striking miners at Catavi.

So much unfinished business--all made painfully clear by the debacle of the Chaco War--prompted Armando Arce and Augusto Céspedes to launch another independent daily in 1936, one year after the demise of El Universal. With the experience of the first newspaper under their belts, the two men--along with Carlos Montenegro and José Cuadros Quiroga--made the new newspaper, La Calle, into one of the most effective opposition newspapers in Latin American history. After the Movimiento Nacionalista Revolucionario (MNR) was formed in 1941 by the economist Víctor Paz Estenssoro and a group of deputies and young journalists who included the founders of La Calle, the newspaper became the new party's spokesman. The MNR, however, disclaimed any official connection with La Calle, which became the gutter scrapper of La Paz journalism partly because the party did not want to seem to be imitating the traditional forms of Bolivian journalism with newspapers placed at the disposal of individual politicians or parties.

At any rate, La Calle in 1936 was clearly the successor to El Universal, dedicated to continuing the struggle against the power of the great mine owners and large landholders. The very name of La Calle (The Street) signaled its editorial policy. In Spanish American culture, houses are places of safety and retreat, built solidly and flush against the street, which is a trafficway of persons and ideas, a place of potential danger. Thus, those who were to help form the MNR announced that they would carry their fight to the street against the entrenched enclaves of la Rosca.

The significance of La Calle demands that it be given extensive treatment in two chapters. Nevertheless, it was a direct outgrowth of the Chaco War and the earlier experience with El Universal and therefore should be mentioned here. Oscar Delgado has written a biographical sketch of Armando Arce which asserts that as editor of both El Universal and La Calle throughout its turbulent ten-year existence (1936 1946) the journalist was in "elbow-to-elbow" contact with Paz Estenssoro, the major architect of the MNR who served Bolivia three times as revolutionary president, and with a group of independent deputies who formed the MNR in 1941 and made Paz Estenssoro their leader. [92] The latter group included Hernán Siles Zuazo, second-in-command of the MNR and president from 1956 to 1960 while Paz Estenssoro was ambassador to England.

The most impressive thing about the formative years of the MNR on the long march to power from the aftermath of the

29

Chaco War to 1952 was that so many of its key personnel were newspapermen. This is not surprising in Latin America where journalistic activity is considered a legitimate intellectual pursuit, but it is astonishing when one considers the large number of MNR leaders who cut their teeth on newspaper work as fulltime journalists and not simply as collaborating dilettantes. To name only the most important, there were Armando Arce, Augusto Céspedes, José Cuadros Quiroga (who drafted the platform for the MNR in 1941), Carlos Montenegro, and Hernán Siles Zuazo. As La Nación, official newspaper spokesman of the Revolution for twelve years, once declared:

> Traditionally, the MNR is a party of journalists. The founding staff was almost totally composed of newspapermen who marked the awakening of the conscience of the Bolivian majorities from that memorable nucleus of revolutionary thought that was La Calle. As the years passed, those men occupied high functions in the government and in diplomacy, but almost always as a consequence of their activity displayed in the press. [93]

It is not generally known that Hernán Siles Zuazo, MNR president from 1956 to 1960, also was a newspaper editor in the tense days following the Chaco War. The traditional political parties were morally bankrupt, and social issues were boiling to the surface. The socialist military governments of two Chaco heros, Lt. Col. David Toro (1936-1937) and Lt. Col. Germán Busch (1937-1939), sought to wrestle with labor unrest and the malaise of dissatisfaction. Toro nationalized in 1937 the Standard Oil concessions given out in 1922, a spectacular move that provided grist for the nationalistic propaganda mills, but one which did not save his regime. Busch promulgated a labor code and constituted himself dictator to push through other social and economic reforms; in 1939 he ordered tin mine owners to turn all of their foreign earnings over to the state, and in return they would receive bolivianos. But the pressures exerted upon Busch were so great from la Rosca that the distraught president apparently shot himself to death on August 23, 1939, ending the first attempted reform movement in Bolivian history. A junta of old-guard army officers handed power over to rightwing General Enrique Peñaranda (1940-1943) after elections were held, dashing the hopes for reform held by young liberals.

The death of the youthful and attractive Busch and the return of military conservatives to power stimulated the appearance of a new newspaper in La Paz to complement the work of La Calle. Hitting the streets on June 24, 1940, it bore as its name the acronym INTI which stood for independence, nationalism, work, and equality. Although its editor was future MNR president Hernán Siles Zuazo, the newspaper has been overlooked in the few sketchy accounts of Bolivian journalism that have been published. Rodolfo Salamanca Lafuente, for example, does not even mention INTI in his recent overview of the Bolivian press, [94] but it was a significant newspaper that carried forward the tradition of El Universal, including its use of humor to shock or persuade. A satirical column on the front page of INTI, entitled "But When the Rooster Crows..." was one of the newspaper's most popular features. It was necessary for street sales, just as was La Calle's similar column, "Dark Alley," because neither newspaper had the backing of a wealthy patron or political party. Each day INTI attacked a different member of Congress in another column, "The Horrors of Loreto." The newspaper also printed incisive political cartoons, something relatively new to Bolivian journalism, including some by Alandia Pantoja, the muralist. [95]

What else was INTI publishing? One of its major themes was revealing the plight of Bolivia's Indians and pleading for its improvement. This was something practically unheard of in the history of Bolivian journalism for the topic was taboo in the established press and deemed of no interest to urban readers in the more popular newspapers. An editorial, for example, came to the "Defense of the Indians," and a woman writer, Martha Mendoza, analyzed "The tragedy of the Indians." She quoted Franz Tamayo, the great cholo educator, who said, "What does the Indian do for the State? Everything! What does the State do for the Indian? Nothing!" [96]

In other areas, INTI opened its columns to José Antonio Arze, leader of the Marxist Partido de la Izquierda Revolucionaria (PIR, Revolutionary Left Party) founded in 1940, who had no other outlet for his political thought. [97] Looking backward, INTI reported that Busch had wanted to nationalize the railroads, and reviewed editorially Toro's book, Mi actuación en la guerra del Chaco (My Action in the Chaco War). [98] Dealing with the present, the newspaper attacked Peñaranda frontally, declaring in a headline shortly before its closure in 1941, "The men who serve General Peñaranda today [Joaquín Espada and Demetrio Canelas] accused him of being the perpetrator of the Chaco disaster." [99]

Early in its career, INTI called for a "Moral revolution" in Bolivian life and stated its journalistic philosophy in these terms:

INTI, following the norm that its founders fixed at the time of launching it, as an eminently nationalist and investigative organ, from its very initiation began

the arduous and misunderstood task of pointing out
with the accusing finger a series of scandals and
irregularities unlawful for the State. Thus we
denounced the flour affair, the activities of Jews [see
Chapter 4], speculation with articles of prime necessity, the petroleum maneuvers, the matter of official
cars... the expenses of ex-President Quintanilla, etc.
[100]

This statement of principles, which was borne out in the
practices in INTI, placed the newspaper clearly in the main-
stream of modern journalism. It was not a spokesman for a
political hack, nor did it represent the special interests of any
one political party; it attempted to speak for all the people and
to create a steady audience of middle-class readers in La Paz.
This was not easy, however provocative or entertaining the
newspaper might be, because INTI was competing with La Calle
for the same audience, and large segments of Bolivian society
did not read newspapers at all. Thus, having financial troubles, INTI was sold to Carlos Salinas Aramayo on April 2, 1941,
and the new editor for the publication became Gover Zarate M.
[101]

Nevertheless, the tone and editorial crusading of INTI did
not change with the new owner. An editorial on April 6, 1941,
entitled "The tradition of 'INTI'" explained that the sale was
necessary "in order to incorporate important capital into the
enterprise to enlarge the installations and modernize them to the
point of making this spokesman, which has essentially popular
roots, into a great modern daily that otherwise would lose its
strict and pure orientation [which is] independent and populist." [102] A front-page editorial a few days later by the new
owner, Carlos Salinas Aramayo, entitled "Something that is
necessary to say," declared: "...INTI will continue being, as
up to today, the newspaper of the people and for the people."
A new masthead proclaimed "INTI, the newspaper of the people," and the editor began printing front-page editorials. [103]
The new proprietor apparently meant what he said for soon the
newspaper was crusading against the ministries of education,
economy, and the treasury. When the government protested,
INTI denied that its attacks were partisan. The newspaper had
changed ownership, it said, but "not with the intent of serving
the interest of any party or political group." [104]

Celebrating its first anniversary and looking forward to its
"Second year of labor," the newspaper editorialized on June 24,
1941, "INTI came forth through the enthusiasm of a nucleus of
youths who endeavored to give birth to an organ of the press
that would interpret, with the greatest fidelity possible, the
desires of the popular mass, making itself into a defender of

the majority classes of the nation." The editorial expressed satisfaction at the continued editorial campaigns after the change in ownership. [105]

The nationalism of INTI extended to a topic everyone was talking about after the Chaco War--the official propaganda effort. The concept of this function was born from the bitter defeat that Bolivia suffered at the hands of her smaller and supposedly weaker neighbor. By 1941, the newspaper reported, offices of propaganda flourished at every level of government, national, departmental, and local. Every branch, even the police, had its sección prensa (press section), but in the outside world Bolivia remained unknown. This, INTI maintained, was the fault of the chancellery, noting "our country, as far as the exterior is concerned, is something like the territory of the moon." The newspaper concluded that the offices of propaganda did not justify their existence, [106] but the problem lay deeper than that. Bolivia was far from being a nation in the modern sense of the word; it was deeply divided between the men of the countryside and the men of the cities, between Indian and cholo and white, between the capital and outlying provinces, between wealth and poverty, between human dignity and human degradation. The patchwork quality of the official propaganda effort after the Chaco War simply reflected the fragmentation of Bolivian life itself.

In another vein, reflecting its admiration for Germany as World War II progressed in Europe, INTI attacked the "False Panamericanism" of the Franklin Delano Roosevelt administration. The newspaper recalled that Bolivia had always supported the inter-American idea strongly. Even the Nineteenth Century despot Mariano Melgarejo had made, in one grand flourish, all people of the Americas "Bolivian citizens." But what had Bolivia derived from her dedication to the Panamerican idea? One need only look at the Chaco War, the newspaper concluded, when no one came to the aid of Bolivia, leaving the country exposed to a hostile world opinion. [107]

Frustration such as this led INTI to attack Peñaranda directly as a do-nothing president who was simply marking time for the status quo. The newspaper implied that the older military man who had commanded Bolivian armies as chief of staff during the Chaco War was nothing more than a front for the tin interests, as would become painfully clear during the Catavi mine massacre in December 1942. In other words, Peñaranda was a caretaker president bridging the gap between the reforms of Toro and Busch--and what? At considerable risk--because Peñaranda was heavy-handed in closing opposition newspapers--INTI editorialized in July 1941: "We should not hide the truth because [the truth] is the obligation of the independent press. General Peñaranda, through the action of his immediate collaborators, has lost 80 percent of the sympathy with which the people conveyed him to the first magistracy of the Nation." [108]

A few days later, an article by José Manuel Pando appeared under the headline, "Who governs, Peñaranda or the Rosca?" The essay appeared on July 16, 1941, which is the last issue on INTI in the newspaper's files in the Biblioteca del Congreso. Since such collections in Bolivia are notoriously incomplete, it is difficult to determine if this was indeed the last issue of INTI. But if the article by Pando did not seal the newspaper's fate, it was indicative of the kind of journalism which the authorities could not stomach. Since it discusses most of the problems brought to light by the Chaco War, problems which had never been examined in the pages of most Bolivian newspapers before, it is well to present the article in its entirety, since it was emblematic of the new wave of Bolivian journalism:

Bolivia, upon attaining independence [1825], had about three million square kilometers. Its territorial patrimony at the present time comprises no more than one million square kilometers. Its initial population was little less than a million inhabitants. Today it counts some three million, two million of which are Indians. A million are mestizos who endure miserable economic conditions. And there are scarcely some few thousand "aristocratic mestizos" and whites who can enjoy the relative comforts which civilization offers.

THE MINING ASPECT

The mines produce huge profits for their owners, especially in the tin market. [But] these profits are not even translated into decent salaries for the laborers who work [the mines], who leave their lungs in pieces in the centers of Catavi, Siglo XX, Llallagua, Potosí, etc. There are thousands of tubercular men and those who have aged prematurely. The national treasury continues receiving pitiful taxes that hardly are enough to sustain a bureaucracy recruited from the increasingly pauperized sectors of the middle classes. And there is no money in the treasury coffers for all of the poor employees, except for the magnates of Masonry and the secret roscas. Meanwhile there are no schools, we lack roads, the people continue hungry, some privileged live comfortably, go to Europe and lead a life of luxury and pleasure. A good Government protects the small mining industry.

34

It constructs sanitary mining towns through both the Enterprises and the State. It watches out for the health of the workers. But there is nothing like that in force today. All because the government is subjected to la Rosca!

OUR AGRICULTURE

Let's go on to the agricultural question. The lands are found in the hands of some few latifundistas [large landowners] who limit themselves to the extent necessary for their personal gain. The campesinos [Indian farmers] receive salaries of hunger. Pongueaje [serfdom] subsists. The community Indians contemplate with sadness that their small properties are diminished. Meanwhile the power and greed of the hacendados grow. The small farmers suffer from bank mortgages. In order to take home a loaf of bread they have to serve as slaves for the exploiting firms. These have all the products in abundance and, when they are scarce in the country, ah!... then we have the paradoxical case of having to import potatoes from Holland in order to fill the pantries of the potentates.

THE RAILROAD NETWORK

There is financial confusion. A lack of political orientation. Educational anarchy. Sterilization of the productive forces and, above all, a suicidal and criminal indifference of the Government to the problems of the Nation. We live beneath the tyranny of imports, surrendered to the uncontrolled voracity of some few but "powerful" commercial enterprises. The railroad network serves only for facilitating the exportation of minerals and for yielding another excessive margin of earnings to Mr. Pickwoad and a handful of gringos...

ECONOMIC BANKRUPTCY

The inhabitants of the interior of the Republic live in provincial isolation, cultivating petty regional rancors which frequently bring the danger of civil wars. The authorities ignore what happens in Oruro, Sucre, Tarija, Cochabamba, the Beni and other Departments. Banking capital, in close alliance with the mining interests, sucks whatever it can from the country through usurious loans. The [national] finances-- especially now in the hands of one of those guilty of the debacle of the Chaco--are in a singularly disastrous state. The taxes oppress people without resources. There is a public debt truly astronomical. Money is sky-high. Before the material conflict with Paraguay the Bolivian peso was quoted at 18 peñiques. Today it is one of the most depreciated currencies of the Continent, for it is quoted at scarcely little more than one peñique. The country is asphyxiating in an inflation that they are trying to remedy uselessly with artificial measures. [109]

This article by José Manuel Pando, which was to be continued but apparently never was, reveals the flavor of Bolivian journalism in the post-Chaco generation. There was no effort toward objectivity in supposedly news columns; rampant editorial comment appeared in such columns whether the articles were signed or not. These writers were in effect practicing an early version of advocacy journalism which swept aside the "cult of objectivity" to arrive at a deeper truth. Other distinguished writers for INTI, Nazario Pardo Valle and Carlos Montenegro, wrote in a similar vein, but the newspaper folded in July 1941 after the trumped-up Nazi putsch (see Chapter 4) brought reprisals against German firms in La Paz who then had to stop the little aid they had been giving INTI. [110] The work of these writers can accurately be described as propaganda, and by winning over the social consciences of the thin middle sector of Bolivian life, they prodded one of the hemisphere's most backward countries into launching the second social and economic revolution in Latin American history.

This small group of writers would not have been driven to this task, however, had it not been for the wrenching effect upon them of the Chaco War. The roots of social abuse which their propaganda exploited lay deeply embedded in Bolivian history, but the savage Chaco conflict bared them for all to see. Stunned and disillusioned by that senseless struggle, the revolutionary generation produced books and articles to exorcise the national past. They recalled their own bitter experiences in the Chaco, both as war correspondents and common soldiers. They founded newspapers such as La Calle and INTI. Their typewriters poured forth a torrent of words, establishing an entirely new genre in Bolivian letters--the newspaper of protest, divorced from any traditional political party and resting shakily on popular support. Through constant and dramatic repetition they stressed the glaring inequities in Bolivian life and advocated a true nationalism.

In a sense, the MNR writers were spokesmen for the less articulate military men who had sworn in Paraguayan prisoner-of-war camps to rediscover the razón de patria. It was they

36

who formed the secret lodge RADEPA in pursuit of a lost nationhood. It was they who helped bring Toro and Busch to power and toppled Peñaranda in 1943, inaugurating the period of co-rule between the MNR and Major Gualberto Villarroel (1943-1946) which convinced the party to go it alone without military collaboration after 1952. But the significance of the work of social protest writers should not be minimized in this formative early period. The almost single-handed opposition of La República to the Chaco War, ultimately costing the newspaper its very existence, was an object lesson in courage not lost upon the generation of younger writers. The war correspondence of Augusto Céspedes and Carlos Montenegro in the columns of El Universal demonstrated that literary devices could be used to bring the horror--and humor--of the war home to La Paz readers. This was nothing new in Bolivian letters, since journalism and literature are more frequently intertwined in Latin America than elsewhere in the world, but the dazzling performance of these two men marked the emergence of new giants on the Bolivian literary scene. If journalism is literature under pressure, they used it to wage their own war of protest. INTI was founded in 1940 as another independent daily, one which carried on briefly in the tradition of El Universal, but the fusion of all these intellectual forces and journalistic developments occurred in the newspaper La Calle, which more than any other single entity paved the way for the Bolivian National Revolution.

Chapter 2

LA CALLE: THE EARLY YEARS

Bolivia has two resources: tin and some writers.

--Augusto Céspedes

La Calle is the outcry of a national desperation.

--El Tiempo of Mexico, 1944

No newspaper in Latin American history fought a longer or more uphill battle against entrenched economic privilege than La Calle (1936-1946) of Bolivia. Although its quest for social justice in Bolivian life was marred by early anti-Semitic campaigns (see Chapter 4), La Calle confronted and ultimately defeated the large landowners--whose semi-feudal rule dated from colonial times--and the tin consortiums of the Twentieth Century. It had no competitor in the hemisphere for courage and staying power except perhaps the militantly socialist Regeneración which in the early years of this century helped to undermine the dictatorial rule in Mexico of Porfirio Díaz (1876-1911). Regeneración was driven underground and forced to publish clandestinely in the United States until its principal editor Ricardo Flores Magón was captured by United States agents and imprisoned in the federal penitentiary at Leavenworth, Kansas, until his death in 1922. The editors and writers of La Calle, on the other hand, lived to witness the fruits of the successful Bolivian National Revolution launched in 1952. Founders and activists in the MNR, they managed to keep publishing La Calle above-ground, although it faced almost constant police harassment and was closed temporarily by every Bolivian regime from its founding in 1936 until Villarroel gained power in 1943. Unlike Regeneración, however, La Calle did not advocate violent and immediate overthrow of the government. It supported, with reservations, the "military socialist" regimes of Colonel David Toro (1936-1937) and Major Germán Busch (1937-1939). [1]

With concerted effort and driven by a strong sense of

39

nationalism, the men who put out La Calle launched a propaganda campaign that was to last for ten years. It exposed the many injustices and dislocations in Bolivian life, which shall be described in detail in succeeding chapters. La Calle in its first five years of existence also helped to coalesce the Movimiento Nacionalista Revolucionario (MNR), founded on January 21, 1941, into a viable political grouping. Guillermo Lora, leader of the Trotskyite Partido Obrero Revolucionario (POR, Revolutionary Worker Party), founded in exile in Argentina in 1934 and which competed with the MNR for support in the mining districts, has entitled a still unpublished study about the MNR, "From a propaganda group, to a party of masses." [2] Indeed, La Calle was the handbook of militancy for the MNR until the appearance of Carlos Montenegro's Nacionalismo y coloniaje (Nationalism and Colonialism) in 1943, which gave the party its theoretical moorings. Thereafter, La Calle continued to serve as the MNR's standard bearer in the harsh day-to-day struggles when the party shared power with Major Gualberto Villarroel (1943-1946). In short, the newspaper aroused and sustained a social conscience in the middle sector and lower classes which made possible the social revolution which began in 1952.

La Calle was founded at that crucial watershed in Bolivian history when reform military elements wrested control of the country from the corrupt and inept civilian and higher military leadership during the closing phase of the Chaco War. When it became inescapably clear that Bolivia was losing that conflict, Major Germán Busch, chief of the army general staff, seized President Daniel Salamanca on November 27, 1934 while he was making a tour of the front. After an interim rule by the civilian vice-president, José Luis Tejada Sorzano, the younger Busch handed the government over to the older and supposedly more experienced Toro, who served as president of the Junta Militar de Gobierno. Recognizing the need to have their own journalistic spokesman in La Paz, the Revolutionary Committee, which included Augusto Céspedes and Armando Arce, decided to launch La Calle. [3] The first editor of the "Morning Daily of the Socialist Party" was Nazario Pardo Valle, who performed this function until Arce could return to La Paz from the Chaco.

Joining a field of five other newspapers in La Paz, then a city of about 200,000 population, La Calle was unique in the history of Bolivian journalism. Many other periodicals had been formed as personal vehicles to further the presidential aspirations of individuals but never before had a newspaper taken upon itself the task of speaking for a whole class of people--the underdogs of Bolivia's lopsided social structure. La República and El Universal had opposed the Chaco War and INTI had broken barriers in discussing domestic social problems, but it

40

remained for La Calle to prepare public opinion for social revolution in Bolivia.

The first edition of La Calle appeared on June 23, 1936, on the same day that the Democratic convention opened in Philadelphia to decide upon a second term for Franklin Delano Roosevelt. The price of the six-column, eight-page edition was only ten centavos; only eight advertisements in the first edition led to widespread speculation that the newspaper was subsidized by the Toro government. [4] La Calle vehemently denied this, declaring that it received not a single centavo in subvention:

> Our daily costs ten centavos simply because we do not edit it to make money, to enrich ourselves, to make a business with this newspaper. We decided from choice only to cover its costs--which happily are covered at ten centavos--and that's enough for us. [5]

Actually, as La Calle noted in early 1937, the new newspaper sold for 50 percent less than the other dailies of La Paz in an obvious effort to gain the widest possible audience. In effect, La Calle launched a journalistic revolution in Bolivia as profound as Benjamin Day had started in 1833 by selling his New York Sun for a penny in street sales, divorcing the United States press from its traditional political support. Still, it was an uphill battle. In the inflation which wracked Bolivia in the wake of the Chaco War, a working man with two children needed 17.10 bolivianos each day for necessities, and one could almost buy a loaf of bread at fifteen centavos as a copy of La Calle for ten centavos. [6] In the first letter to the editor of La Calle, which appeared on its second day of publication, Enrique Araníbar Claure, a veteran of the Chaco War, applauded the ten-centavo price of La Calle, especially since food prices had risen four times from what they were before the war. In these times of "galloping inflation," he declared, "one must preach...by example, esteemed comrade, for only in that way can the newspapers have moral authority." His letter closed, "The watchword of all the socialists and exploited ought to be: EVERYONE BUY 'LA CALLE,' THE ONLY DAILY THAT DOES NOT EXPLOIT THE PEOPLE." [7]

The low newsstand price for La Calle began to pinch, however, when the cost of newsprint rose seven times since the newspaper began publishing. La Calle warned editorially:

> The increase in the price of newsprint gives rise to a danger that is urgent to resolve: the absorption of the press by the capitalist enterprises which in no way serve the national interests but rather those of

41

rosquismo and of a certain political sector avid of predominance and permanent exploitation. [8]

La Calle urged the Socialist State to modify exchange rates for newsprint, but this was not done. On one hand, the newspapers of La Paz had to fight off censorship, and on the other they clamored to get the official printing. At the same time, censorship under the "military socialist" regimes was light but omnipresent. In July 1936 the Junta of Government issued a communique prohibiting public debate on the economy and advising the press to document carefully its accusations. [9] In the same month, a letter from Colonel Germán Busch, chief of the general staff, complained of divulgation of Bolivia's military structure in the La Paz daily press. Although Bolivia was under a state of siege, censorship had not been invoked but rather self-censorship. [10]

As for an official press, La Calle had to deny its own status as such while also driving off the pretensions of others. Thus, an editorial in La Calle on November 12, 1936, noted for some time a rumor had been circulating that La Calle was an official organ, receiving a state subsidy. The newspaper denied this strongly and challenged anyone with proof of the accusation to submit it to the professional Association of Journalists. [11] At the same time, La Calle tried to scare off others who might get the official printing, as it mocked in the column, "The Lamp of Diógenes," started by "George Bernard Chopp:"

'La Razón,' daily sustained by the dinosaur mining interests, asks in an extensive article that an official gazette be published. It wants, as in the time of Salamanca, to be offered a strong subvention to publish decrees, report debates and [print] official announcements. [12]

On the first anniversary of its publication, La Calle admitted that it was "an essential vehicle of opinion" or "a spokesman" for military socialism, but not "an official organ of the regime." The newspaper explained its origins:

La Calle was born shortly after the socialist revolution, with the design of fulfilling an elevated social and historic mission: that of pointing out vigorously and with profound conviction the principles that gave origin to the revolutionary movement, placing itself at the front of the reactionary press that even now misses no motive nor occasion to undermine the socialist structure of the present regime. [13]

42

With limited resources, La Calle fell back on its own wits to win a wider readership among the middle and lower classes of La Paz. No other newspaper quite like it had ever appeared in the capital's journalistic arena, and residents there still talk and laugh about its saucy stories and pungent headlines. Even the upper classes could not resist reading it occasionally to be properly outraged. La Calle adopted the format of a serious newspaper, with pages dedicated to national and international news--the latter edited by Augusto Céspedes from the AP and Havas wires--to compete with the deans of the La Paz press: El Diario founded in 1904 and La Razón founded in 1917. But La Calle went further and whetted reader interest by its wit and humor. The front-page column, "Dark Alley," became the talk of the town with its short humorous paragraphs ground out day after day mainly by Céspedes.

In a sense, La Calle reverted to the personal journalism of an earlier era to puncture the pretensions of the wealthy and haughty--and to reveal with sarcasm and invective the gaping wounds in Bolivian society. Much like an underground newspaper in the United States in the 1960s, La Calle eschewed the "cult of objectivity" and presented its side with vigor and raucous humor, mixing opinion and fact throughout all the columns of the paper. Each issue had one editorial plainly labeled as such, but the lead article over the masthead on the front page and other "articles" elsewhere in the newspaper were compounded of rumor, personal jibes, and liberal doses of opinion.

La Calle resorted to these and other devices to pull readers away from the established and more staid newspapers of La Paz. La Razón, owned by the tin-mining Aramayo family, was regarded as one of the best-edited newspapers in Latin America, but as much bias was present in its pages, although more carefully disguised, as in La Calle. The same was true of El Diario, dean of the capital press in which Simon I. Patiño held 36 percent ownership. La Calle did not try to compete with these two major newspapers directly by imitating modern Western news practices, but rather through the use of sensational headlines, slashing personal attacks and humor. In a semi-literate society these devices were successful in drawing readers into the raison d'etre for the newspaper: its hard-hitting articles on the social conditions of Bolivia and the editorials based on those articles.

La Calle forged its own path on a trial-and-error basis. For the first year of the newspaper's existence, sports news-- such an important staple in Latin American newspapers-- was used only as an occasional filler, but a sports page, "The Sporting World," became a regular feature in 1937 in an apparent effort to attract more readers. The first editorial cartoon appeared on June 28, 1936, but this device appeared only rarely thereafter. Perhaps there was not enough money to hire a cartoonist, or perhaps La Calle simply preferred to wage its war of propaganda with words--much more in keeping with Spanish American culture--rather than with images. Cultural news was not given so much space as in La Razón and El Diario, with their Sunday literary supplements, but La Calle gave its reduced coverage of such matters a sharper social focus. Book reviews began to appear on July 1, 1936, under the heading, "Bibliographical Production, Publications Received," a heading changed three days later to "Bibliographical Spectator." Socially conscious books and articles, which were beginning to appear with increasing frequency in Bolivia, were give the greatest attention. The same was true for art criticism after a "Popular Culture" page edited by A. Ramírez was begun on September 13, 1936. For example, articles appearing on this page dealt with the revolutionary sculpture of Marina Núñez del Prado, what the National Museum was and could become, and socialist art in general. [14]

A sampling of some of the general articles in the early years of La Calle reveals that it went further than any Bolivian newspaper before it in dealing with serious national problems--some brought up and discussed in newsprint for the first time in the history of the country. El Universal and INTI had pointed the way, but La Calle took up with gusto where they left off. Never before had any publication dared to deal in such forceful terms with the need for educating the Indians, governmental blindness in dealing with the vast Indian majority of Bolivia's people, and the problem of maldistribution of land. [15] La Calle led in a campaign against venereal disease--a topic that would have shocked the sedate and insulated readers of the traditional newspapers--and called for socialized medicine in a country where most people went without any medical attention whatsoever. [16] Although the relationship between church and state had never aroused much controversy in Bolivia because the clergy was so weak and compliant, La Calle also entered this forbidden area of discussion. The newspaper urged the "nationalization" of Bolivian priests, forcing foreigners who would not become citizens to leave since the physical head of the Roman Catholic Church was charged to be no longer the Pope but Mussolini. [17] La Calle discussed the role of the church in the socialist state and finally urged editorially the separation of church and state in Bolivia. [18] Although the newspaper took civic pride in the history and beautification of La Paz, [19] then a city of 200,000 persons, it argued for inexpensive housing rather than more spacious and beautiful avenues. [20] "Children live in Bolivia in absolute abandonment by the state," proclaimed the headline of one article,

44

followed by another which offered a plan to protect stray children. [21] Education was of paramount importance for La Calle, but it urged a system of schools that would reflect the social reality of Bolivia rather than rote learning and the traditional humanities training which led to an over-abundance of lawyers. The newspaper called for special vocational schools for the working class, just wages for school teachers, and integral reform of the entire educational system. [22] One of the newspaper's most difficult areas of commentary was the plight of Bolivian labor. La Calle demanded adequate wages and protection for the incipient class and endorsed the Labor Code adopted during the Busch period. Later in the Villarroel regime, however, the newspaper had to call for labor discipline in the common struggle of what was already called "the National Revolution." [23]

These may have seemed heavy topics for a newspaper addressed to a street audience, but they were dressed up in outrageous headlines and interspersed with lighter material throughout the newspaper. Armando Arce wrote most of the salty headlines for La Calle, headlines that would become topics of conversation on street corners by amused readers. To give only a few examples, the newspaper delighted in poking fun at itself, its competitors and Bolivian life in general. An article blasting the road service was headlined, "Not even Tarzan can travel the road to Coro-Coro." Slaps at political opponents were commonplace; referring to the PIR leader, La Calle declared "R.[icardo] Anaya fears assassination of the PIR deputies, but not even dogs would bark at them." [24] Concerning the political aspirations of a former president, the newspaper proclaimed, "Tejada Sorzano needs a promoter of the style of Phineas Taylor Barnum." [25] Plays on words were also used to advantage in headlines. Arce delighted in calling the Frente Democrática Anti-Fascista (FDA, Anti-Fascist Democratic Front) the Frente de Atrás (Backward Front). [26] And when all else failed, the editors of La Calle coined their own words for special taunts, such as using the pidgin English word YANQUILANDIA in a headline to refer to the United States. [27] La Calle printed an article by Jose M. Gutiérrez in order to refute that socialism had failed in the world or had degenerated into democratic individualism. The headline read HANDS UP: CHRIST, MARX, AND LENIN! and the refutation noted that the Bolivian author was "professor for life of constitutional law in a country that is not constituted or is constituted by pongos [serfs]." [90]

This comment was mild when compared with invective hurled at political figures in headlines and the stories themselves. Verbal violence led to physical violence, much as in the era of the frontier press in the United States. Within five

45

months after La Calle began publication, a mob broke into its office at noon, pummeling everyone in sight and seeking to prevent further publication. A banner headline on the front page the next day proclaimed with characteristic immodesty, ALL THE PEOPLE ARE WITH 'LA CALLE.' [29] The tables were turned when militant MNR members invaded the plant of El Diario and beat up its editor, J. S. Canelas. Not content to let the fisticuffs suffice, La Calle noted in a subhead the following day, referring to Canelas' editorial about the incident: "It seems that the blows [to the head] have caused cerebral commotion for Don J. S. Canelas." [30] The verbal attack continued the next day: "The encephalitis of the director of 'El Diario' has become more grave, but he continues writing..." [31]

On another occasion, an attack was made upon the writer of another La Paz newspaper who used the pen-name Julius Brutus. La Calle headlined its reply, JULIUS BRUTUS EDITORIALIZES LIKE THE MISSING LINK OF HOMO STUPIDUS. At issue was the writer's insistence that Villarroel's cabinet members should resign because of the famous Blue Book issued by Spruile Braden to combat Juan Domingo Perón's election in 1946 and which also revived concocted attacks upon the MNR. The reply, signed by "Carlos Darwin," gives much of the flavor of the personal quality of Bolivian journalism during the social readjustments which wracked the country in the wake of the Chaco War:

It was believed that Julius Caesar Brutus was suffering from retarded muyumuyu or galloping meningitis, but reading his editorial of yesterday has convinced the public that he is not sick in the head, but rather that he is constitutionally a cretin. [32]

The virulence of such attacks offended some and delighted others. Even some members of the upper classes which found unthinkable the reforms demanded by La Calle derived pleasure from the sheer exuberance of its personal attacks. On the other hand, La Calle was considered so scandalous that the University of San Andrés in La Paz refused to keep a file of it. When the writer asked for it there, the librarian replied, "Oh, we don't have that. That was a very dirty newspaper." [33] On another occasion, Alcides Molina, comptroller for the Peñaranda government, said he refused to read La Calle to safeguard his "spiritual hygiene." [34]

Another source of amusement and pleasure for the readers of La Calle--and perhaps the most popular department of the entire newspaper--was the daily series of short humorous paragraphs boxed on the front page under the heading,

Callejón oscuro ("Dark Alley.") Many of these items were darts shot at the opposition press in a rivalry that was not altogether unfriendly. On the day of the first issue of La Calle, three of the nine paragraphs in the column dealt with the opposition press in what appeared to be camaraderie but was actually backhanded insults from an upstart newspaper:

- A bourgeois salutes our powerful colleagues 'El Diario' [founded in 1904] and 'La Razón' [established in 1917]. Perhaps it will not be superfluous for us to wish them a 'long life.'

- We greet also 'Ultima Hora,' declaring that we are sorry not to accompany her in her afternoon sallies. And we lament not being able to hail 'La República' and 'Antorcha,' dailies for which we have reserved abundant and savory material. But 'we do not kick the down and out.'

- It is sufficient to give notice that this number is edited within the greatest confusion possible. It is the disorder of 'THE STREET' itself. [35]

The heart of La Calle, however, lay in its editorial comments, which were taken quite seriously indeed. There was usually one editorial clearly labeled as such and appearing in the same place on the fourth page of each issue, although the lead "news story" atop the masthead on the front page was usually editorial in reality. The first issue of June 23, 1936, contained two editorials explaining the new daily's political position. In the first, "The socialist voice," La Calle noted that the "counter-revolutionary" Republican elements had been purged from the government three days earlier, while the Partido Socialista pledged "the cooperation of its maximum energy" to work with the government of Colonel David Toro. Promising to use "its honest and sincere eloquence" in "a convulsive hour," La Calle clearly identified itself as a spokesman for the military socialism of the Toro government:

It is an hour of sharp profiles when the journalistic voice of socialism [La Calle] makes itself heard with the people... we consider it indispensable to leave to the socialist army all the room for maneuver it requires to fulfill loyally its pledge, to make itself worthy of the continental expectation which the revolution of May 17, 1936, aroused in America... [36]

In its second editorial, headlined "We are going to take the Revolution in tow," La Calle served notice that it was not going to be merely a passive observer but rather an active participant in the experiment of military socialism unfolding in Bolivia.

47

The editorial said however optimistic reports might be, no one could say that the revolution was running on the tracks. There was, in fact, infiltration of the government by elements of "new pigmentation" as socialists to sabotage the Toro regime. "As soon as possible," the editorial concluded, "We are going to make a campaign so that once and for all the government will take on an unmistakable socialist appearance, without suicidal vacillations or temporizing with the reaction." [37]

At the same time that La Calle made its editorial position clear, it also announced in its first issue that its columns would be open to all the people. While letters to the editor are rare in Latin American journalism, it is a long-standing practice that those with grievances can come to the newspaper's offices, where they will be presented in a small news story if not settled on the spot. La Calle, however, billing itself as champion of the people, made its invitation in this regard much stronger than usual:

> LA CALLE, socialist daily that has as its primal end
> to serve the people, asks the public to come to our
> house to formulate whatever denunciation against the
> bosses, owners of factories, arbitrary authorities,
> and complaints in general, so that from these columns
> we can make a campaign of social purification, now
> that it is no longer possible to continue with the same
> method and procedure as before, cause of the collec-
> tive malaise. The pages of LA CALLE, as we have
> said, are at the disposition of all the exploited in
> general, the only manner of demonstrating our faith
> and sympathy with the proletarian people. Comrade
> worker: come to formulate, through this daily, which
> is yours, all the complaints and reclamations that you
> consider urgent and just. [38]

The imagery of the street--its hustle and bustle, its thievery and good works, its contradictions as a place to stroll or flee--continued to dominate La Calle during the ten years (1936-1946) of its existence. This imagery suggested many of the titles of La Calle's columns: "From the Window" begun on June 25, 1936; "Street Lamp" initiated on June 27, 1936; "Corner of the Unemployed" started on January 18, 1942, and "A Loiterer's Comments" launched in March 1945. The terminology struck a responsive chord among the inhabitants of La Paz as the city became larger, more impersonal and more unmanage-able. Bolivia's political parties, first formed in the 1880s, never mediated in the struggle for survival of the lower classes, and these parties thus were anathema to the middle sector after the Chaco War. Newspapers such as La Calle and INTI filled the void, as unemployment and the cost of living skyrocketed. Part of the appeal of La Calle was its tough insistence to call things what they were, as the simple metaphor of the newspaper's title itself was explained in the column, "Man of the Street," which first appeared on June 24, 1936:

...let's go immediately to the street because there is the best permanent lecture hall of learning. Whether on the expensive pavement of Comanche stone or upon the twisted cobblestones of the suburban lanes, we the poor passengers have the best book to learn about life and also the most rapid and painful means to leave it... From the central street, noisy and vibrating with traffic, to the silent and dirty passageway, we see things every day if the time and work necessary to win our daily bread permit. [39]

By far the most popular column of La Calle, however, was "Dark Alley" which published short paragraphs on the front page reminiscent of the humor of Mark Twain. Some were designed only to entertain readers, while others dealt satirical or ironic punches to the midriffs of serious social problems. Usually, there was a mixture of both in the same front-page column, so the reader invariably got his social conscience whetted while a smile flickered on his lips. Consider, for example:

• The government has created a burial allotment for school teachers and their families so that these can now die of hunger with complete confidence. [40]

• Paraguay is not keeping its promise in the matter of the return of prisoners. She promised to return free men and is returning instead married men. [41]

• "La Razón" condemns the bad custom of urinating from doors on the street. Candido Gil does it from his window so as not to go against the newspaper. [42]

• We hear that certain proprietors are raising the rents for their tenants and in order to oblige them to pay, they are cutting off the water to make them surrender through thirst. Not for nothing were we in the Chaco, caray! [43]

• Today the national picture, 'The Campaign of the Chaco,' is being shown. Many of the deserters who did not concur in the campaign can rehabilitate themselves by attending the [Cine] Paris. [44]

• The Center of Propaganda and Defense has conceded citations of the same category to an agricultural review and to

LA CALLE. This is because frequently we occupy ourselves with certain domestic animals. [45]

• The body of a working girl has been found in a vat of chicha [a popular alcoholic drink] after fermenting twelve days. The political cadaver of Tejada [Sorzano] has fermented for twelve years and still gives no chicha. [46]

• Colonel Toro has indicated that he will govern with the most capaces [capable]. The rosqueros heard bad and rejoice, believing that he will govern with the most rapaces [rapacious]. [47]

• The lightening bolt that God sent to the Pope proves one of two things: either a lightening ray got away from God, or else the divine marksmanship is failing. [48]

• The 'Friends of the City' are proposing to organize for the fair of Alacitas an exposition and raffle of miniatures, which without doubt will be under the auspices of the minister of education. [49]

Such humor, punctuated with biting social commentary, soon became the most popular feature of La Calle, according to those Bolivians who remember the newspaper with affection and nostalgia. After the demise of La Calle in 1946, nothing similar to "Dark Alley" has since been seen in the Bolivian press. Thereafter, humor has been limited to signed columns usually dealing with one topic and lacking the vaudeville-like staccato punches of the eight or nine items which appeared in "Dark Alley" daily. It required considerable stamina and ingenuity to grind out these items day after day; the brunt of the task fell to the fertile mind of Augusto Céspedes, who concocted many of the jokes from items gleaned in the international news he edited, but "Dark Alley" was really a group effort, as most of the other departments on the newspaper. Items for the following day would be hatched in the banter of staff members over lunch or enjoying a mid-afternoon beer. [50]

The importance of this column should not be under-estimated, however. It served as a major circulation builder for La Calle, especially among the middle and upper classes who abhorred the newspaper's social stands but could not resist the funny jibes and insults of "Dark Alley," much as some persons will buy a certain newspaper for a favorite sports column or comic strip. The placement of "Dark Alley" on the front page of La Calle departed from Bolivian journalistic tradition and emphasized the significance the editors attached to the humorous column. The purpose of the column was taken so seriously by the editors, in fact, that the column appeared blank on the day that the news of the suicide of Germán Busch broke, with a note explaining that the jocose comments of "Dark Alley" would be inappropriate at such a tragic moment in Bolivian history. The blank column was bordered with inverted rules producing black margins, revealing that in three years "Dark Alley" had achieved institutional status.

Another favorite pastime of "Dark Alley" was to poke fun at and discredit the opposition newspapers owned by La Rosca. The vehemence of the repeated attacks on other newspapers was something new in Bolivian journalism because never before had there been a popular opposition newspaper with the circulation and subsequent power of La Calle, under which Céspedes raised the craft of the insult to a high art. Journalists tend to be touchy about their craft, disliking criticism intensely even though they themselves deal constantly in public criticism, but "Dark Alley" spared no one nor anything:

- 'Ultima Hora' greeted yesterday the appearance of LA CALLE. Thank you, colleague, and may you never find yourself in the street, especially in the ultima hora [final hour]... of your existence. [51]

- Our afternoon colleague [Ultima Hora] has published on its editorial page a picture of don Enrique Finot so touched up that it should have been on the page of movie ads. [52]

- Logically, 'La Razón' should be issued today without an editorial because the masons have declared themselves on strike and with them the manufacturers of bricks. [53]

- 'El Diario' expresses editorially that 'one cannot give an ignorant and illiterate worker the right to take part in public affairs.' In its concept, only the gentlemen who possess these conditions should take part. [54]

- After two days of boycott by those who stuff the sections of the newspaper, our colleague 'Ultima Hora' has returned to sell itself again, as usual. [55]

- An inoffensive information that we gave five days ago about a colleague selling itself has been copied to the letter by the same colleague, after five days of looking for jokes in LA CALLE. [56]

- Trotsky was exiled from Oslo for making Communist propaganda. The Bolivian Trotskyites [in Masas], in place of defaming LA CALLE, should protest that exile with the courage to which they are accustomed, that is, by radio. [57]

51

- The early appearance is announced of 'La Reforma,' a penal review that don José Carrasco [publisher of El Diario] will direct. Until now it has been the readers of 'El Diario' who have suffered all the penalties. [58]

- For every ox that is butchered there will be imported a cow. In such a way there will be rotation in the direction of 'La Razón.' [59]

While such tidbits may appear inane--and in fact reminiscent of the jolly joustings of country weekly editors in the United States until not so very long ago--the cumulative effect of this continuous attack upon the established press was to change the face of Bolivian journalism. Before La Calle, newspapers were taken in dead seriousness by upperclass readers in the political battles of the Nineteenth and early Twentieth centuries. The prestige of the press, in their view, was not to be tampered with. As an upstart contender in the La Paz journalistic arena, La Calle had little to fear in belittling its own profession but everything to gain by puncturing the pretensions of the older newspapers either established or owned by the mining interests. It mocked those "oracle[s] of current opinion" with a murderous glee that was to undermine the very concept of authority in Bolivia.

Attacks upon the opposition press also occurred in the news columns and editorials of La Calle. Singled out for particular abuse were Ultima Hora, owned by tin-mining magnate Mauricio Hochschild, and La Razón, owned by the Aramayo family which had also made its fortune in tin. Assaults on El Diario, dean of the capital press, having been founded in 1904, were less frequent, perhaps because the exact extent of the shares of the newspaper owned by Simón I. Patiño, Bolivia's tin king, was unknown. At one time it was said that he owned 36 percent of the newspaper. [60] But the two other major newspapers of La Paz, clearly spokesmen for the Aramayo and Hochschild interests, made irresistible targets for La Calle.

In 1937 La Calle had a particularly satisfying occasion for pinning back the ears of Ultima Hora. The Hochschild newspaper had attacked the ministry of commerce and industry for deciding a case in favor of the owner of the building which housed Ultima Hora's press--a fact not reported to the public in the newspaper's attack upon the ministry. Denouncing its opponent for judging a cause in which the newspaper itself was an interested party, La Calle seized the occasion to launch into the time-honored merits of unselfish journalism:

A newspaper is a tribune; it exercises its mastery of the press obeying a body of doctrine; therefore, when the doctrine fails, practically there has ceased to exist the character and essence of what our fathers understood and certainly our sons will understand by journalism. [61]

When Ultima Hora admitted its vested interest in the case, La Calle proclaimed, WE HAVE OBLIGED 'ULTIMA HORA' TO EXHIBIT ITS PUSTULES IN PUBLIC. [62]

La Calle was levelling its guns not only at the three major newspapers of La Paz, which could be understood in any competitive journalistic situation, but also at the kind of elite and insensitive society which those newspapers represented. As La Calle phrased it in a headline, 'ULTIMA HORA' IS NOT ONLY A DISGRACE: IT IS A MORBID SYMPTOM. In the body of the story itself, the La Calle writer charged, "'Ultima Hora' has not represented any national ideal other than the patriotic ideal of enriching its proprietor." [63]

When La Calle asked several times that an investigating commission be set up to look into the manner in which "enormous" fortunes were made during the Chaco War, [64] the newspapers of la Rosca were not exempt from the charges. A letter from "Juan Pueblo" (John Q. Public) charged that Ultima Hora itself was one of the most fortunate "neuveau riches of the war" because it had received highly favorable exchange rates to buy newsprint, ink, and other materials. [65] Using the terminology of Montenegro's Nacionalismo y coloniaje, La Calle in a headline branded Ultima Hora as colonialist since the overthrow of Peñaranda on December 20, 1943 for opposing the reforms of the Villarroel period, but conceded that the newspaper had posed as nationalist before the first genuine reforms in Bolivian history. [66]

Ultima Hora was not alone in suffering the wrath of La Calle. Many scathing attacks were launched against the prensa rosquera as a tightly-knit group determined to preserve the privileges of the mining "super-state." It was obvious to everyone that the three newspapers representing Bolivia's mining interests acted more or less in concert when questions of social justice or private profits were concerned. Changing their tactics to a more conciliatory attitude toward Villarroel when it became apparent he would be around for awhile, the mining press began to toady toward the new president, causing La Calle to charge this was "a fraudulent dissimulation to disorient the people." [67]

La Razón was an especially favorite whipping boy because of the pretensions of its owner Carlos Víctor Aramayo. The Aramayo consortium was the smallest of the Big Three, but resistance to social change was stronger in La Razón (see Chapter 6) than in any of the other newspapers representing the mining interests. Bolivians resented the fact that Carlos Víctor Aramayo was educated at Oxford, where he affected an English accent, and continued to live in England after graduation. Hochschild at least lived in Bolivia, and he was thus not the butt of so many personal thrusts as Aramayo, ridiculed for his choice to live as a London dandy, or the other wealthy expatriate, Patiño, whose ostentatious display of wealth and negation of his mestizo background also were subjects for lampoon.

Aramayo rankled La Calle most because his newspaper La Razón was highly effective, literate, well-edited--generally conceded to be one of the best in Latin America (by those not bothered by the retrograde editorial positions adopted by the newspaper). It knew its audience well--the thin upper crust of those who profited by mining and landowning in Bolivia--and catered to them. La Calle, irritated by the Western journalistic practices introduced by La Razón, once called it the DAILY MAIL ALTOPERUANO. [68] La Calle knew that Aramayo took a personal interest in the newspaper's editorial policy, and once ran an editorial entitled, "The grammar of Aramayo's editorials is as poor as their contents." [69] When La Razón criticized the MNR as "The group [that comes] before the country," La Calle responded with a blistering editorial, "The Aramayo company [comes] before the country." [70] La Calle also charged that La Razón workers forged MNR communications and sent them to other newspapers, making the party appear to be in hopeless disarray. One such forgery stated that W. Hugo Patiño had been named provisional chief of the MNR departmental command. On the same day, February 17, 1946, other erroneous information was released to the press that 200 MNR militants of the Avanzada Busch had resigned in protest from the party. [71]

The kind of journalism which La Calle introduced into Bolivia, however, was more than intramural sniping to undermine the opposition press--or to present serious ideas in humorous form in "Dark Alley" to be more easily grasped by the man in the street. La Calle followed traditional form in having an editorial page, although it limited itself to one editorial each day--filling the rest of the page with personal columns--while the other La Paz newspapers usually had three or four editorials in each issue. Actually, the lead "news story" atop the masthead on the front page of La Calle was usually editorial in reality, also. See, for example, RESORTING TO BEGGING of March 18, 1937. The front page story declared that an appeal for 10 million bolivianos by the minister of education and indigenous affairs from private capital was not resorting to begging for alms, but rather "demands something to which the State has a plain right because the individual fortune is formed on the base of the badly paid effort of the worker, in this case the Indian..." [72]

Fact and opinion were inextricably mixed throughout the columns of the newspaper, reverting to the personal journalism of an earlier era. And, as we have seen, La Calle made no attempt to disguise opinion in supposedly news columns with accurate headlines; the headlines blatantly proclaimed that here was a partisan newspaper fighting a partisan fight.

Armando Arce wrote most of the editorials for La Calle, signing some of them, and they can be considered the weakest part of the newspaper. Editorials are usually the least read part of any newspaper, and editorials in Latin American newspapers tend to be even more pompous than their English counterparts. While the other staff members were spreading ideas through humorous paragraphs, ostensible news stories and outrageous headlines, Arce was sanctimonious in proclaiming the purity of the editorial campaigns of La Calle:

> One does not see in the campaigns of LA CALLE passion, personal hatreds, acrimony inspired in malevolence or the sickly desire of damaging through simple scandal or scandalous passion; when this newspaper claims for the rights of the State and the people, it assumes a transcendental personality, it makes history, it embodies the sentiment of the Nation. [73]

Such lofty words had little meaning for those who bought La Calle, however, because scandal was precisely what the newspaper was dealing in and what the public was paying for. The most telling blows against entrenched economic privilege that La Calle dealt came in a series of exposé articles, sometimes buttressed with formal editorial comment. The first such campaign by La Calle was directed at the past government of José Luis Tejada Sorzano who succeeded Daniel Salamanca when he was deposed on November 27, 1934, during the course of the Chaco War; Tejada Sorzano stayed in power until May 17, 1936, a few days before Colonel David Toro launched Bolivia's experiment in "military socialism." As apparently the last of the old guard of civilian Bolivian politicians, Tejada Sorzano was a perfect target for the barbed shafts of La Calle. Blame was placed on his brief tenure as president to explain the severe problems which Toro inherited. In its very second issue of June 24, 1936, La Calle opened fire on Tejada Sorzano and Ormachea Zalles, minister of the treasury, for allowing tin production to decline in February and March 1936 in "a notorious way," doing nothing to correct the situation in the hope of sabotaging the next administration. La Calle charged Tejada Sorzano and his officials with fanning the country's crisis as it tottered on the point of collapse following the Chaco War, pilfering public funds, distributing trips abroad to favorites, setting up bogus industries to take advantage of preferential exchange rates, and remaining silent in respect to "the monstrous business deals carried out in the name of the war." Commented La Calle:

> This is the quality of the great men of the Liberal bourgeoisie who, caught between the interest of their privileged caste on one side and the existence of the country on the other, did not hesitate to sacrifice the country and to place in danger its economic existence if that would mean for them a means of pressuring the nation through hunger. [74]

La Calle called for a public trial of Tejada Sorzano and Ormachea Zalles and promised a series of articles revealing the facts of the case. The series lasted throughout June and July of 1936 and totaled eleven installments which savagely attacked the former president. It was charged specifically that Tejada Sorzano had cancelled a tax of 8,500 pounds sterling (one million bolivianos) against the English firm, Fabulosa Mines Consolidated. [75] This was later corrected to indicate the considerable tax had been settled for a mere 6,000 bolivianos. The company's defense was simply that it had been taxed for "nominal" entries in its records, which La Calle considered fraudulent bookkeeping. [76] The persistent editorial campaign by the newspaper paid off on July 5 when President Toro sent a note to Pablo Guillén, attorney general, ordering him to investigate the Fabulosa circumstances as reported in La Calle. [77] Meanwhile, the newspaper discovered that the original tax of 8,500 pounds was cancelled despite a judicial decree from the Supreme Court of Justice ordering that it be paid. Thus, thanks to the investigative reporting of La Calle, the entire matter was thrown back into the courts where public scrutiny could watch the outcome more carefully. [78]

What became known as el affaire Fabulosa was illustrative of the types of campaigns that La Calle would wage throughout its ten stormy years of existence. The Fabulosa scandal was made to order for the newspaper because it contained all the ingredients which would anger the nationalistic senses of Bolivian readers: a foreign company extracting Bolivia's irreplaceable mineral riches without returning anything to the country, taking advantage of the graft and corruption of Bolivia's highest officials, and even ignoring the orders of the country's highest court. It was this kind of story--and there were unfortunately many such skeletons in Bolivia's national closet--that La Calle learned to tell with perfection, turning a complacent generation into a generation of disgust.

Still, it was "Dark Alley" which had the last word on the Fabulosa affaire, whose every possibility had been exhausted to discredit the Liberal party. Two items commented:

> The government has ordered that the charge made by 'La Calle' against 'La Fabulosa' be investigated. Considering that many 'distinguished' gentlemen will have to be prosecuted, Pablo Guillén, attorney general, has decided not to wear a coat and tie as long as the proceedings last. [79]

> Colonel Toro says that certain jobs such as elevator operators in public buildings will be given exclusively to invalids, which will benefit the Liberal party, which is an invalid anxious to come up again in the world... [80]

Not nearly as effective as the classic combination of exposé articles and editorial comment which characterized the presentation of the Fabulosa affaire was a series of columns on the editorial page under the standing heading of "Monkeys of Wall Street." Bolivian readers had been familiar with the ogre of Wall Street--the CIA scapegoat of an earlier period--since the publication of Tristán Marof's novel Wall Street y hambre (Wall Street and Hunger) in 1931, but the title of La Calle's series was unfortunate in that those who extracted Bolivia's raw materials on exceedingly favorable terms or forced loans difficult to repay were more rapacious than "monkeys." Moreover, the individual financial or business leaders attacked in the column, such as Charles Calvino of Standard Oil, meant little to the Bolivians. The attacks which were to come later upon Patiño, Hochschild, and Aramayo were to be much more successful because the targets were as familiar as household words. In the "Monkeys of Wall Street" column, dropped after twelve installments in June and July of 1936, English names were misspelled and facts garbled. The series probably had few readers and little impact. [81]

La Calle obtained much greater propaganda effect when it could play the role of David and slay the giant of Standard Oil. The newspaper, founded on June 23, 1936, could not claim sole credit for the nationalization of the New Jersey corporation's holdings in Bolivia on March 27, 1937, because the issue had been boiling almost since the original concession to Standard on March 3, 1921. Nevertheless, the articles by Carlos Montenegro in La Calle against Standard Oil, expanded into a 137-page pamphlet in 1938, [82] did much to establish the climate of opinion which finally convinced President Toro to make the drastic move. When Standard Oil was evicted from Bolivia, La Calle declared in one of its more vigorous editorials:

> Standard Oil of Bolivia came, through the influence of its economic power, to build itself into a kind of super-state within the country. And, not withstanding the proved immorality and countless decrepit motives made evident [by] Standard, [the company] counted always on the sinful cooperation of [Bolivian] rulers, politicians, authorities, and--it causes disgust to say it--also on journalists who were for sale. [83]

La Calle also took advantage of the occasion to warn Bolivia's own mining interests that they were not invulnerable to action by the State. The newspaper charged that despite rising world tin prices, Bolivian producers were restricting production or did not export all they produced to force the government to reduce the percentage of the exchange rate (divisas) they must pay to the State. The case of Standard Oil, La Calle declared, should be "a warning to the mining magnates who propose to strangle the State." Their arrogant attitude might exceed government tolerance, La Calle threatened, "and give opportunity to the immediate application of one of the most important postulates of socialism, which is the reversion of the mines to the State." [84]

The nationalization of Standard Oil by Bolivia--preceding by a year similar action by Mexico against United States oil firms--was the first such action by a Latin American country, and La Calle realized that the mere expulsion of Standard Oil from Bolivia would not be the end of the matter; both repercussions in the world press and demands by the United States company for indemnification would have to be met head- on. Until the claims of Standard Oil were finally settled in 1942, the issue was almost constantly in the columns of La Calle. Headlines and comments tell the story of the newspaper's longest and most bitter campaign.

Immediately after nationalization, La Calle claimed that the people of Bolivia supported the action, and also printed favorable comments from the foreign press. [85] To the giants of the world press who considered the move unfair or ill-advised, La Calle responded that Standard Oil was maliciously moving to sabotage Bolivia. The newspaper charged that "the gold of Standard is using its marvelous resources to provoke the institutional bankruptcy of the country" by allegedly bribing the judges of the Bolivian Supreme Court who were deciding the case. "It is clear that Standard has declared war on Bolivia!" the newspaper exclaimed in a lead "news" story. [86] To win over domestic public opinion to its side, La Calle claimed in another lead news story that Standard's reserves were being exhausted elsewhere in the world, and hence such a tenacious fight to retain its holdings in Bolivia. [87] An editorial linked Bolivia's entrance into the Chaco War with Standard's supposition of vast oil reserves there, and the matter was brought up again in La Calle when the peace treaty with Paraguay was finally signed in Buenos Aires in July 1938. [88]

More than anything else, however, La Calle resented with enormous bitterness the payment to Standard Oil for its confiscated property made by the Peñaranda government to elicit loans from the United States, anxious to settle the matter in the early years of World War II. La Calle was even more incensed that the Bolivian government would accept the settlement claims as a proceeding in the national Supreme Court at Sucre. As the litigation there dragged on and on, La Calle denounced this affront to Bolivian nationhood throughout 1938 and 1939. The newspaper found suspicious the technical delay which followed delay in the long-drawn-out legal maneuverings, implying in a series of editorials that Peñaranda had instructed the Supreme Court to find in favor of Standard Oil once public sentiment had cooled down. [89] When the first major decision came in March 1939 that the directors of Standard Oil in Bolivia had no judicial personality before the Supreme Court, La Calle railed at the decision as "unrighteous and inadmissible" and "insubstantial" because it did not clearly throw out Standard's claims. Even more objectionably, it meant that the matter would be settled diplomatically outside the revealing spotlight of public opinion. [90]

The newspaper's fears were realized when Bolivia signed an agreement with Standard Oil in Rio de Janeiro on January 27, 1942, agreeing to pay the United States firm $1,500,000 within 90 days, plus 3 percent interest per year since nationalization in 1937. [91] La Calle printed the full text of the agreement, and soon thereafter the Unión Boliviana Defensora del Petróleo (Bolivian Union for the Defense of Petroleum) was formed with MNR leader Víctor Paz Estenssoro elected president. The settlement with Standard Oil outraged a broad segment of Bolivian public opinion; even the conservative Demetrio Canelas published a letter critical of the government's decision in El Imparcial of Cochabamba, which was reprinted in La Noche of La Paz. Canelas wrote that the government had made "an arrangement dishonorable for the name of Bolivia." But La Calle, always selective in choosing its allies, pointed out that Canelas, chief of the Genuine Republican Party, discussed the petroleum issue only after a questionnaire was submitted to him by El Imparcial. "In other words," stated La Calle, "Dr. Canelas only defends the petroleum when his tongue is pulled." [92] La Calle denounced the arrangement with Standard Oil as indemnization, although the agreement was made to appear to be a simple contract of sale of the company's equipment to Bolivia. [93] Later, the MNR newspaper pointed out that Bolivia would have to borrow money to pay the settlement, doubly ironic because she was receiving such low prices for her tin so badly needed in wartime. [94] When Congress began an inquiry into the terms of the settlement on November 11, 1942, La Calle gave extensive coverage and prominent display to the debate until the matter was over-shadowed by the Catavi massacre of December 21, 1942. [95]

In the field of international news, the biggest story of La Calle's early years was the Spanish Civil War and the newspaper gave the most complete coverage of the conflict of any of the newspapers in La Paz. Six full pages were devoted to the Spanish Civil War in the issue of La Calle of October 12, 1936, alone. La Calle was openly sympathetic to the Republican cause, which partially refutes those who charged later that the early MNR was oriented toward the Axis powers in World War II. Perhaps the MNR, formed in 1941, was impressed by those who were the victors in the agony of Spain, but at the time those who were to form the party passionately defended the cause of democracy in Spain. Soon after the outbreak of the conflict, La Calle presented a series on "A Synthetical History of the Spanish Revolution" which ran for 16 installments in September 1936. [96] To background the news, entire pages were devoted to "The Page of Spain--Spanish Citizenship" edited by Professor V. Burgaleta. [97] Even more innovative was La Calle's practice of inviting prominent domestic and foreign writers to offer their comments and opinions on the Spanish holocaust. Peruvian writer Gamaliel Churate, for example, wrote a chilling prophecy, "What is happening to Spain will happen in Bolivia." [98] The most interesting in this series, however, was an interview with Carlos Montenegro, who was to become the intellectual and philosophical mentor of the MNR. Montenegro clearly saw the collision of ideologies in Spain as the opening episode of a Europe on the point of an "epileptic" convulsion. With deeper insight, he described Spain as the "mummy of Europe" suffering "a barbaric awakening of its energies." Sadly, Montenegro observed that "the great majorities of opinion can be subdued by armed minorities" and he warned his fellow countrymen:

> Every people which delays its ideological and social development, suffers these revolutionary fevers that consume with the high temperature of hatred, voraciously and dizzily, the...spirit of the people.

Spain, feverish now, is rising from its pregnant torpor of centuries of humiliations and silence.

Montenegro incorrectly predicted that the Republicans would win the struggle in Spain, but he fervently hoped that both sides would unite in nationalistic unity and turn their common hatred toward the foreign enemy. [99]

On October 12, 1938, after Spain had become the battleground of Europe, La Calle received this message from the Spanish Republican charge d'affaires in La Paz, José María Lucas Parra:

LA CALLE is the only newspaper in La Paz which does honor to its name, gathering together in its columns the popular desires and the defense of the true Spanish people. [I am] personally gratified and [thank you] in the name of those titans who defend inch by inch the soil of the Mother Country from the foreign invasion. [100]

And when the end finally came in 1939 to the conflict which wracked Spain, decimated half her people, and served as a dress rehearsal for the tragedy which was to engulf Europe and much of the world, La Calle concluded its brief but sad editorial comment, "The defeat of Spain is the defeat of the highest and most sacred principles of humanity and nationality." [101]

La Calle's concern with the fate of Spain revealed that it was more than a parochial newspaper, but most of its energies were still concerned with the political struggles unfolding at home. Brought into being as the journalistic vehicle to support "military socialism" in Bolivia, La Calle became disenchanted with David Toro, a victim mainly of mounting inflation and the renewal of diplomatic relations with Paraguay on May 25, 1937. When Toro finally renounced on the night of July 13, 1937, and was replaced as president of the Junta de Gobierno by the younger Lt. Col. Germán Busch, La Calle rejoiced.

What others considered disintegration of reform elements within the military, La Calle saw as a fresh opportunity. Headlining its editorial commenting on the overthrow of Toro "New revolutionary stage," La Calle commended the army for "an intelligent control over its own elements whom it eliminates when it understands that their transitory labor is concluded in order to give way to more active and clearer forms in the conduct of the affairs of the State." Drawing sustenance from the Mexican Revolution, La Calle reminded its readers that "men pass but the revolution remains..." [102] The newspaper also sided with the Busch regime in denouncing its predecessor in the revolutionary manifesto of July 15, 1937. In an editorial, La Calle charged that the "oligarchial class..., during the government of Colonel Toro, gained total power through economic control of the country." [103] Toro from his exile in the Chilean port city of Arica replied that he was dismissed from office simply because he had declared his intention of calling elections. La Calle duly reported the denial of this made by the national department of propaganda, [104] and supported the new Busch regime with such lead articles as "Saving the principles of 1936." [105]

Toro had outlawed all political parties, and La Calle applauded the formation of the Socialist Party by Tristán Marof in 1938, who presaged much of the program of the MNR and later was to come into deadly conflict with it:

The background of its promoter Tristán Maroff [sic] who in another period alarmed, perhaps justifiably, the tranquil and moderate classes, on this occasion has served rather to awaken confidence around a man who has sacrificed himself during long years for his ideals and who, presently, has presented himself with sincere declarations of nationalism, balance, and justice, adapting his principles to the Bolivian reality. [106]

Relations between Marof and those who wrote and published La Calle were soon to sour, however, as the independent socialist leader ridiculed the superficial and uncoordinated reforms of "military socialism." As he declared in the Chamber of Deputies in 1940:

Never was there socialism in the government; never has there been socialism in Bolivia. Socialist fraud one would have to say. A chuquisaqueño [resident of Sucre] without intelligence but ingenious as a good chuquisaqueño [Colonel Toro] introduced this political farce in the government in order to grab power more easily. Therefore I say that it is a lie that socialism has arrived in this government. [107]

Denied access to the columns of La Calle, which was booming Busch as the savior of Bolivia, Marof announced that he would explain his political position in the pages of La Razón, spokesman for the tin-mining Aramayo family. Although Marof's political party had never caught on, this infuriated La Calle which implied in "Dark Alley" that Marof had sold out to the industrialists. In an incident that reveals much of the flavor of the personal journalism of the period, Marof sued La Calle for "defamatory libel." [108] Actually, although a special court for libel actions exists under Bolivian law, it has never been called into session, which explains the excesses of the earlier period and the greater propensity for the government itself to impose censorship or to urge self-regulation by the newspapers themselves. [109] At the time, La Calle found Marof's action surprising, coming from "a professional defamer and daily slanderer." After all, La Calle pressed on, "he is a unique pearl, a traitor to the country and a clean-shaved Communist, who writes in a daily of the right whose proprietor he insulted vilely when he wore a beard." [110] Marof responded by publishing a manifesto attacking the MNR in which he declared he had spent "more than fifteen years in the service of the workers." La Calle's rejoinder exacerbated the dispute, calling Marof's statement "a confession of his ineptitude and mediocrity, for in fifteen years he has not succeeded in collecting more than four cats for his 'workers' party." The newspaper contended that the Partido de la Izquierda Revolucionaria (PIR, Revolutionary Left Party), a Marxist party formed in 1940, had outstripped Marof's party in two years, and the MNR itself, founded in 1941, in one year. [111]

The verbal duel between Marof and Carlos Montenegro, who wrote the attacks in La Calle, ended in physical violence. On the afternoon of June 18, 1943, according to La Calle's version of the incident, Montenegro and his wife were chatting with another woman in the street Genaro Sanjinés when Marof approached them and insulted Montenegro, who then knocked Marof down. When the socialist leader got up, he allegedly pulled out a pistol and aimed it at Montenegro, but his wife struck Marof's arm in time to deflect the bullet, which struck a nearby jewelry shop. Marof fled, later successfully claiming immunity from prosecution as a deputy. Commented La Calle, "the cur Tristán Marof walks the streets armed, provoking and insulting people like a drunken prostitute." [112]

The matter did not end there. After the attack on Montenegro, MNR thugs wrecked the printing press of Marof in Ingavi street and scattered his type. The socialist leader obtained the arrest of MNR members Gastón Vclasco and Juan Valverde Figueroa. Marof then rented the printing press of Fernando Loayza Beltrán and dashed off another broadside against the MNR, released on Sunday, June 20, 1943. The MNR got its two men released from jail but charged that Marof was then "persecuting" two MNR youth leaders, Alfonso Gumucia and Alfonso Finot. [113] By this time, the breach between Marof and the MNR was complete and irreparable; the MNR not only lost the support of a distinguished and potentially valuable ally but also gained a life-long enemy whose later personal attacks on Paz Estenssoro cannot be dismissed lightly. [114]

Before the split, Marof and La Calle could agree on the merits of the administration of Germán Busch (1937-1939). Child of the elite and member of the Bolivian military establishment he seemed as unlikely a candidate as Toro to lead the country's first genuine reform effort. But Busch was younger and more idealistic, sensitive to the point of neurasthenia, and to this day older Bolivians remember him with affection. The backlash of the Chaco War which propelled him into the presidency at the age of thirty-three, alarmed la Rosca, the Bolivian elite, who reacted swiftly to the danger which Busch presented to them. Carlos Víctor Aramayo, owner of La Razón, was charged with financing an abortive rebellion at Palmar on March 26, 1938, led by the ousted President Toro. [115] But Busch would not be intimated. His far-reaching reform decree of June 7, 1939--a symbolic date used by the MNR to announce its program in 1942--struck at the heart of the mining interests by requiring that all expatriate profits be deposited first in the Banco Central de Bolivia to be returned to the owners at the government's discount. [116] With that decree, which was never enforced, Busch signed his own death warrant. He died August 23, 1939, and the pressure exerted upon him by the tin companies was blamed for his death, an apparent suicide. Controversy would swirl around the circumstances of his death later, but at the time La Calle proclaimed in a two-line banner headline: THE MOST ILLUSTRIOUS AND VALIANT OF THE BOLIVIANS COMMITTED SUICIDE YESTERDAY. Subheads read, "Germán Busch, man of America. Deceit by the government and fatigue precipitated his end." Editorially, La Calle commented, "Busch [who had assumed dictatorial control on April 24, 1939] possessed the unanimous confidence of the country which concentrated in his person all the evolutionary possibilities of an epoch of resurrection." [117] Newspapers were forbidden to publish between August 24 and 29, 1939, because of the tense atmosphere surrounding Busch's sudden death, but when publication was allowed to resume, Tristán Marof made the most accurate estimation of Busch's career in the pages of La Calle:

> Busch, an honest military man, is the compelling transition in the historic process of the middle class, sentimental and nationalist, toward another [more] mature socialism with theory and with exact knowledge of our problem. [118]

In the transition period following the suicide of Busch, the writers of La Calle and others who were to form the MNR on January 25, 1941 coalesced more and more as a coherent

La Calle, later the chief spokesman for the MNR, laments on August 24, 1939, the suicide of President Germán Busch, one of the leaders of "military socialism." "Dark Alley" (lower right) appeared blank on this day.

grouping. Any chance of reform by the military seemed foregone as rightwing General Carlos Quintanilla served as provisional president between August 24, 1939 and the installation of
duly elected Enrique Peñaranda on April 15, 1940. In the
printshop of La Calle, in coffee-houses and cafes, and in the
homes on interested individuals, the groundwork of the MNR
was carefully laid. Although the new political grouping did not
announce its official program until June 7, 1942, it elected ten
deputies in 1941, mainly through the support of La Calle and
because of the unrest which continued to grip Bolivia. At
first, the new party treaded softly, cautiously. When it elected
eight deputies and one senator on May 17, 1942--still before its
official program was even announced--the new party had
offended no one for it received these kind words from the
conservative El Diario:

> ...all of them [the elected MNR deputies] are fer-
> vently carrying out the patriotic norms which the
> party has imposed upon them, and they have a man-
> date for correction, honesty, and civic virtues which
> no one can doubt. In the last Congress their rep-
> resentatives took part in an outstanding, efficacious,
> and valiant manner...[119]

This type of conciliatory attitude was to mark the end of
the honeymoon, however, between the MNR and the established
press for years of struggle and mutual conflict were to lie
ahead. The upstart newspaper La Calle boosted the nascent
MNR to national prominence. Since the political party was such
a small group of like-minded persons, La Calle in its early
years was essential in acting as a national sounding board for
the party. The MNR found the arrangement mutually convenient for the party never shrank from controversy--or even
violence--in getting its message across. For its part, La Calle
had a sure attention getter in the crusades of the MNR and the
oratory of Víctor Paz Estenssoro or the anti-Semitic harangues
of José Cuadros Quiroga. The MNR itself was raucous and
brash and fitted in well with the type of shock journalism which
La Calle had been practicing for five years before the appearance of the MNR. In a sense, the party and the newspaper
cannot be separated for the men who edited and wrote for La
Calle were among the prominent ones who formed the MNR in
1941. They started out being propagandists and ended up in
the political arena themselves. In fact, their political and
journalistic functions were so entwined that it is almost impossible to say where one began and the other stopped. La Calle, a
radically different element in Bolivian journalism, nurtured and
propelled into national prominence the radically different political party of the MNR.

Chapter 3

LA CALLE: THE STREET FIGHTERS

Bolivia is a kind of laboratory, a microcosm of the continent.

--Augusto Céspedes

Who were the newspapermen who were to become the first true revolutionaries--in the sense of effecting profound social change--in Bolivia's history? As La Nación, official spokesman for the MNR during its twelve years in power (1952-1964), once declared:

Traditionally, the MNR is a party of journalists. The founding staff [in 1941] was composed almost totally of newspapermen who awakened the conscience of the Bolivian majorities from that memorable nucleus of revolutionary thought that was La Calle. [1]

Four men guided the destiny of the newspaper--Augusto Céspedes, Armando Arce, and José Cuadros Quiroga did the most work in getting La Calle out each day, and Carlos Montenegro contributed columns and articles. Paz Estenssoro never wrote directly for La Calle, but he did contribute pieces to Semanario Busch, a weekly edited by Montenegro which appeared in 1941, and to Revista de Economía Boliviana which also put out a few issues under the editorship of Luis Peñaloza, [2] who later was the first writer to chronicle the origins of the Bolivian National Revolution with his Historia del Movimiento Nacionalista Revolucionario, 1941-1952 (La Paz, 1963). In one sense, however, Paz Estenssoro was a mainstay of La Calle for as MNR deputy emerging as leader of the party, his impassioned oratory and economic discourses filled many columns of La Calle.

Journalism and literature are more closely identified in Latin America than elsewhere in the world, and the younger Bolivian men of letters used both after the Chaco War to wage their own war of protest. There is no hostility between intellectuals and the press, no condescension toward the press by the former nor defensive attitude toward scholars and literary figures by the latter. Latin American newspapers frequently

67

print substantial literary sections which present original fiction and poetry by national writers, along with commentaries on the work of the world's creative community.

In Bolivia, however, before the appearance of La Calle these sections in the oligarchial press were elitist, fawning upon European writers and deprecating Bolivian authors. The most striking example of this was the frosty silence on the part of the established press toward Augusto Céspedes' Metal del diablo (The Devil's Metal), a work of social realism that was a thinly disguised biography excoriating the cruelty and indifference of Simón I. Patiño, the tin king of Bolivia. Appearing shortly before the overthrow of Villarroel in 1946, the book eventually sold more copies than any other in Bolivian history. Yet the three newspapers representing the vested tin interests ignored it completely. La Noche, a newspaper with a small circulation in La Paz, reviewed Metal del diablo and spoke out on the injustice done to Céspedes by the practically monopolistic press of La Paz. The review closed with a pointed question: Why was Céspedes ostracized by the press of his own country?

> Political reprisal? In part, perhaps. But more than that, cowardice. And not exactly before the prospect of criticizing adversely Metal del diablo but rather before the perspective of having to praise it. [3]

The "Tin Curtain," as one MNR writer called it, descended also upon Montenegro's Nacionalismo y coloniaje when it appeared in 1943. Published in a press run of only 1,000 copies, it was the bellweather of the Bolivian National Revolution, but scarcely known elsewhere because the established La Paz press barred reviews or comments upon the work. La Nación noted later, "It was said in the United States about the MNR that its was a revolution without books, as it was said of certain other countries that theirs were books without revolution." [4] This referred to neighboring Peru, where the Marxist-oriented José Carlos Mariátegui had issued a call for revolution in 1928 with his famous Siete ensayos de interpretación de la realidad peruana (Seven Interpretive Essays on Peruvian Reality). Yet Peru experienced no profound social change until the populist, technocratic revolution started by General Juan Velasco Alvarado in 1968.

Bolivia, on the contrary, had both books and a revolution, and foremost among the writers of La Calle who brought it about was Montenegro. His book Nacionalismo y coloniaje (Nationalism and Colonialism) was an affirmative call for a better informed people and greater national self-awareness. It would be tempting to call Montenegro the Mariátegui of Bolivia, but perhaps the comparison should be reversed if one wishes to juggle time. Although historical realities were quite different between Bolivia and Peru, social conditions were much the same. It required forty years for the filtered ideas of Mariátegui to have any effect in Peru, whereas Montenegro pumped enough nationalistic fervor into the MNR with Nacionalismo y coloniaje that the revolution was effected within nine years.

Before Montenegro, Bolivian leaders had been dominated by the pessimism and defeatism of Alcides Argüedas' classic Pueblo enfermo (Sick People) of 1909, with its notorious dictum, "Wherever you place your finger in Bolivian life, you will produce pus." Disdain and deprecation were considered stylish after Argüedas. As late as the Chaco War, for example, a Bolivian president was quoted as saying, "You can plant turnips on the shoulders of the Bolivian people." [5] Between 1920 and 1929 Argüedas wrote a six-volume history of Bolivia, which carried the story of the country from independence to 1921, with the dominant theme that of a grotesque and tragic history. He also contributed articles to El Diario, owned mainly by Patiño. [6] In 1944, during the Villarroel reform interlude, Argüedas published an article in La Razón, owned by Aramayo, on "How and why nations crumble." In it he stated, "Every revolt in our [Latin American] countries is a backward leap in their history and political, spiritual and material development." Considering this challenge to the 1943 coup which brought Villarroel to power, La Calle replied sardonically that with 191 leaps backward Bolivia should be arriving "at the lower paleolithic period!" In his article, Argüedas had compared Bolivia with Byzantium, and La Calle firmly answered, "Bolivia is a convulsive and turbulent country because it wants to rid itself of the dominating caste which, as with Argüedas, always remains enjoying the fruits of the country despite the change in rulers." [7] La Calle also charged in 1944 that Patiño had paid for the writing of Argüedas' Historia de Bolivia and that now Aramayo was paying for its serialized re-publication in La Razón to denigrate the Villarroel coup d'etat and to pave the way for the overthrow of that regime. La Calle claimed it was a well known fact in Bolivia that day after day during the Chaco War the Paraguayan national radio broadcast portions of Argüedas' work to depict the Bolivian foe as weak and vulnerable. The MNR newspaper described Argüedas as "the only author of [Bolivian] books about whom it can be said that he gave [intellectual] weapons to our international enemies." [8] On an earlier occasion, La Calle called Argüedas a "ventriloquist" speaking for the powerful tin-mining companies. In a passage that could only have come from the trenchant pen of Augusto Céspedes, La Calle stated:

In Argüedas there has operated--since his boyhood--a

69

physiological inversion: his stomach performs the function of his brain, and what was the brain is now scarcely the chyme of his digestion. And, when this inversion faces a crisis, the auxiliary organs of digestion come to his aid: then Argüedas thinks with his heart, and the heart descends to exercise the stomach's duty. And [this all happens] when Argüedas eulogizes the millionaires...passing his tongue like the buffing rag of a shoeshine boy over the shoes of Patiño. [9]

Montenegro evaluated the work of Argüedas in a more serious manner, finding his work destructive, with Bolivia doomed to morbid introspection unless the underlying causes of its semi-colonial economic subordination were revealed and righted. Montenegro found much of Bolivian literature slavishly imitative of Argüedas, casting up only the reprehensible in national life. But Montenegro criticized more severely the oligarchial press which he felt held the country in the throes of a chronic inferiority complex. It was no secret to anyone that the Big Three tin magnates held sway in the La Paz daily press until the appearance of La Calle. Simón I. Patiño, the discoverer of tin at Llallagua at the close of the Nineteenth Century, held a major interest in El Diario; Mauricio Hochschild dominated Ultima Hora, which was frequently called "the tin elephant of the afternoon" by La Calle; and Carlos Víctor Aramayo owned La Razón outright. [10]

These newspapers, in Montenegro's view, were servile to interests alien to the achievement of Bolivian nationhood. Hochschild, a German Jew naturalized in Argentina, was the only one of the Big Three who resided in Bolivia. In 1924 Patiño was counted among the five richest men in the world, but both he and his son Antenor seldom visited the source of their wealth, and Aramayo, educated at Oxford, also spent most of his time in Europe. Montenegro argued that these three La Paz daily newspapers supported the kind of elite government that would allow the Big Three to continue to take out of Bolivia untaxed tin earnings that made up 78 percent of the country's foreign exchange.

Moreover, Montenegro argued, the daily journalism of La Paz, depending as it did on United States and European wire services, was alien to the Indian and cholo (mixed) culture of Bolivia. Montenegro continued:

But the greatest wound which capitalist journalism inflicted on our people was creating a cunning and artificial way of thinking in the Bolivian literate classes... The public did not have, throughout half a

70

century, any other source of cultural nutrition than journalism, and it learned to attend to and to judge things in consultation with the printed [newspaper] page. This was little less than an oracle for current opinion. [11]

In summary, Montenegro's Nacionalismo y coloniaje, influenced by Marx and Spengler, was the first major interpretation of Bolivian history since Gabriel René-Moreno published his Ultimos días coloniales en el Alto Perú (Final Colonial Days in Upper Peru) in 1896. Montenegro's thesis was that three anti-national groups had dominated the history of Bolivia: (1) classes that in the early years of independence wanted to perpetuate the colony; (2) cultural and political European forms inappropriate for Bolivia; and (3) international capitalism which was stripping the country of its irreplaceable natural wealth. [12]

Born in Cochabamba in 1903, Montenegro was active in journalism before his premature death from cancer in 1953 in New York. He married the sister of a close friend and fellow Chaco War correspondent, Augusto Céspedes. Montenegro contributed occasionally to La Calle, [13] but most of his creative and scholarly energy went into the writing of Nacionalismo y coloniaje. But when José Antonio Arze, who founded in 1940 the Marxist-Leninist Partido de la Izquierda Revolucionaria (PIR, Revolutionary Left Party), attacked La Calle in 1936 in his weekly Acción Socialista, Carlos Montenegro was the man selected to answer the charges that La Calle was supporting a mere reformist regime. [14] Once a secondary school teacher and lawyer who defended the poor, Montenegro was designated secretary of the short-lived Partido Socialista in 1936. He was also sometimes out of La Paz on government missions and therefore not able to write extensively for La Calle, as when he served as secretary for the Bolivian delegation to the Chaco peace conference held in Buenos Aires in 1936-1937. Upon his return he gave his views of the conference in the pages of La Calle. [15] In 1938 Montenegro justified, ex post facto, the seizure a year earlier of the Standard Oil property in Bolivia and cancellation of its concessions with a polemical booklet, Frente al derecho del estado el oro de la Standard Oil (El petróleo, sangre de Bolivia) (Standard Oil's Gold versus the Law of the State [Petroleum, Bolivia's Blood]) in which he also characterized oil companies as "the new Attila, scourge of weak nations." [16]

For their journalistic opposition to the Peñaranda government which gained power after the suicide of Busch in 1939, Montenegro and other MNR writers were kept under guard in villages of the interior tropical provinces of Bolivia under the pretext that they had participated in the trumped-up putsch

71

Nazi of July 1941. (See Chapter 4.) But he continued to write under the pseudonym of "Kisiabó," the name of the region to which he had been sent along with Céspedes and Hernán Siles. When released Montenegro started the Semanario Busch in 1941, an MNR weekly named for the martyred president Germán Busch. [17] After the overthrow of Peñaranda in December 1943, Montenegro served briefly as minister of agriculture in the cabinet of Villarroel and later was sent as ambassador to Mexico in 1944. During the sexenio, the six-year period from the overthrow of Villarroel in 1946 to the successful MNR revolution of 1952, Montenegro founded and edited the review SEA or Síntesis Económica Americana while in exile in Buenos Aires where he supported himself by writing editorials for La Prensa, the prestigious Argentine newspaper confiscated by Juan Domingo Perón in 1951. Dissatisfied with what he regarded as the biased and frequently erroneous reports from Latin America by the existing wire services, Montenegro attempted to form the Servicio Intercontinental de Periodistas (Journalists' Intercontinental Service), presenting the work of Latin American newsmen free of capitalist restraints, but the project floundered. After Bolivia's successful revolt of 1952, he was named ambassador to neighboring Chile. [18] He continued to work on a projected Historia de Cochabamba, [19] but was dead within a year. There seems to have been a falling-out between Montenegro and Paz Estenssoro after 1952, [20] but from his deathbed in New York, his last words for the Bolivian National Revolution reportedly were, "Tell Paz never to isolate himself from the working masses." [21]

The MNR always held Montenegro foremost among its intellectual precursors. When La Calle reviewed Nacionalismo y coloniaje, which won first prize in a national contest sponsored by the Association of Journalists in 1943, the newspaper declared that Montenegro had achieved a "national re-discovery." [22] His influence was increasingly recognized as the Revolution progressed. As La Nación noted in 1955, "The debt which our people owes him is that he gave back the panoramic vision of our history, demonstrating that a scientific comprehension of our past and our present was possible, in order to establish the bases for a future." Before Montenegro, the official MNR newspaper continued, Bolivia had always been at the margin of history, existing only as "a small self-contained world of castes and feudal struggles." But Montenegro's scalpel had cut through Bolivian life to expose a sharp national duality, and he urged the solidarity of workers of the cities with the exploited of the mines and countryside. In short, La Nación concluded, Montenegro had "formed the revolutionary generation that fights today for our country." [23]

As the years passed, the praise became more extravagant.

René Zavaleta Mercado, writing on the seventh anniversary of Montenegro's death, described him as the "dead brother and live father of the Bolivian revolutionaries," adding that "almost all Bolivian intellectuals are his disciples." Zavaleta, who published three booklets analyzing the political course of the MNR, [24] complained bitterly that Fernando Díez de Medina in his Literatura boliviana, published in 1959, had given only a few minor paragraphs to Montenegro, dismissing him as a "pamphleteer" while at the same time devoting lengthy analysis to an economic essay on nationalization of the tin mines by Ricardo Anaya, leader of the defunct PIR which had collaborated in the overthrow of the MNR and Villarroel in 1946. [25] On the contrary, Zavaleta declared that Montenegro's "interpretation of the independent movement and the unmasking of constitutional rule [were] the first to appear in Bolivia." Montenegro's only possible Bolivian intellectual precursor was Franz Tamayo, he added, who was born in 1879 and had stressed cultural indigenismo. [26] Gabriel René-Moreno ultimately had fled Bolivia, and Alcides Argüedas had exported nothing but vile judgements on his own culture, Zavaleta concluded. In 1960, José Fellmann Valarde, then minister of education and fine arts, observed that Montenegro "gave us consciousness of being Bolivians against the old pessimistic history and taught us that we have all the elements to make a great homeland." [27] Interestingly enough, when a portrait of Montenegro was unveiled in the offices of La Nación on the occasion when Fellmann spoke, present was a representative of the Popular American Revolutionary Alliance (APRA) of neighboring Peru, the Indian journalist Manuel Cenzano who had known Montenegro when both were exiles in Argentina. [28]

Montenegro may have been the brightest star in the firmament of MNR theoreticians and planners, but he was not the guiding light of La Calle itself. Too aloof to engage in verbal brawls himself, he left that task to the three men who got the paper out day after day: Augusto Céspedes, a socially realistic writer; Armando Arce, the self-effacing editor; and José Cuadros Quiroga, who did much through his clever headlines and writing to add to the popular appeal of the newspaper.

By far the most colorful of these three men was Augusto Céspedes, called "Chueco" by his friends because of his bow-legged gait. Born in Cochabamba in 1940, this man--short, with a well-groomed mustache--came to be the most famous Bolivian writer of his generation. If he had not given up his works of fiction to concentrate on historical books supporting the MNR cause, he might well have been a serious contender for the Nobel Prize for Literature. As things turned out, Latin American literature was not fashionable in the world literary community when Céspedes was writing his works of social

73

realism although they were appreciated in the Soviet Union. Céspedes was one of only three Latin American authors invited to the USSR for a writers' congress in 1971. As many intellectuals who had made the pilgrimage before him, Céspedes said in an interview in 1973, "I had not imagined anything about the USSR, but for me it is the society of the future." [29]

The journey from the provincial town of Cochabamba to Moscow was filled with adventure of many kinds for Céspedes. When Hernando Siles was president in 1927 during the first crisis with Paraguay, Céspedes was already writing for newspapers, and in 1926-1927 he edited the newspaper El Comercio in Cochabamba. He recalled that he always felt a "natural inclination" to write, and added, "I believe the writer obeys a kind of internal mandate, a social mandate that compels him to write." [30] As a young correspondent for El Universal, he covered the Chaco fighting both as a reporter and later as a soldier; he was in the Chaco 14 months and fought in the battle of Candado. (See Chapter 1). His dispatches have been collected under the title Crónicas heroicas de una guerra estúpida (Heroic Stories of a Stupid War) (1975), [31] which revealed the genesis of his later collection of vitriolic vignettes of the senseless struggle, Sangre de Mestizos (Blood of Half-Breeds, 1936). Although fictional, these stories--written in Santiago de Chile after the war--were based on actual Chaco experiences with the exception of the best known, "El Pozo," anthologized in many languages around the world. Céspedes recalled in 1973 that "El Pozo" was entirely imagination. The story centers on a well being dug in the harsh and dry lands of the Chaco, going deeper and deeper--on and on endlessly--as the Chaco War itself, until the men had even forgotten the purpose of what they were doing.

When it appeared in 1936, Sangre de mestizos created an immediate sensation and launched Céspedes to literary fame. A sample of the contemporary reviews of the book will demonstrate this. The noted Chilean critic Pedro Olerón wrote, "There is no way of calumniating [this book] with criticism....the principal character, the war, buzzes constantly above the story, like a hot and tragic wind." [32] José Luis Saravia wrote in La Calle that Sangre de mestizos "is the magnificent epic of the aching florescence of mestizaje....There is no analysis in the book of Céspedes; there is vibrating reality. Each image is the synthesis of an aspect of the war in all of its brutal realism, and in this resides much of [the book's] valor, because the suggestion flows from its pages in a vigorous form and opens an unlimited field to the analytical capacity of the reader." [33] Luis de Iturralde, secretary of the Bolivian legation in Lima, also wrote a review of Sangre de mestizos which appeared in El Comercio on March 14, 1937, and was reprinted in La Calle. He

Augusto Céspedes spearheaded a generation of dissident writers after the Chaco War. Active in the MNR, he gave up writing novels of social realism and his journalistic efforts to reinterpret Bolivia's past.

75

stated, "With 'Sangre de Mestizos' the short story in Bolivian literature has come of age, individualizing and emancipating itself." Referring to Céspedes' early journalistic work in La Paz before the Chaco War, Iturralde wrote, "He did not wound with his pen as so many others by the ruinous insult. Céspedes, a skillful and fine humorist, used only irony--suave venom in small doses that produced frightful consequences--in order to examine minutely and patiently the elected idols or scribblers of paper." [34]

From that moment on, Céspedes became a force to be reckoned with on the literary and political landscape of Bolivia. He was so outspoken in his opposition to the United States in the early years of World War II (See Chapter 4), that the New York Herald Tribune called him Bolivia's leading Nazi. Actually, however, Céspedes--who served as a deputy for a total of eight years--advised David Toro to call elections in 1937 and Germán Busch to call them in 1938. Both pleas went unheeded, and Céspedes was the only deputy who protested the closing of Parliament in 1938. [35] Céspedes maintained later that he was the only writer in Bolivia to protest the Busch dictatorship. When he criticized the "totalitarian" declarations of Chancellor Eduardo Díez de Medina, La Calle was closed. When the pro-government La Nación published a list of public figures whom Céspedes had attacked, the writer replied in La Calle: "[The list] is false with reference to some of them, but it is incomplete because there are many, many more. They are innumerable. Thus as some adulate, I combat. A revolutionary writer, I do not expect a post from any of them, something that will astonish the avid ones." [36] Céspedes had been vice president of the commission of foreign affairs of the National Convention in 1938. With this experience he was selected to direct the international section of La Calle; later, he was identified as sub-editor. [37]

Céspedes had his own political ambitions because he was a restless man anxious to effect social change as quickly as possible. His early political career suffered serious setbacks, however, as voters seemed somewhat put off by his literary fame. When he ran for deputy from Cochabamba in 1940, for example, Céspedes received the endorsement of the Peruvian Aprista leader Luis Alberto Sánchez, who wrote, "One can no longer say that America copies Europe and that there are no original writers, from the moment in which there was an Augusto Céspedes." [38] Céspedes also ran for deputy from Bustillo in 1942, but was defeated both times. In 1944, however, his third try, he received 1,627 votes in the mining district of Bustillo, more than any other candidate for deputy except Franz Tamayo in La Paz. [39]

Céspedes became secretary general of the Junta de Gobierno that ruled Bolivia during the Villarroel period and moved closer to the sides of the democracies as the Axis powers were losing in Europe. In a speech over Radio Illimani in early 1944, for example, he declared: "At this moment the world disputes raw materials and liberty. Within this dynamic, we are not far from either of these two motives of the conflict." Bolivia was "an element of international consideration" for her raw materials, Céspedes said, adding "For our desire of liberty, we are united with the nations that fight under that banner." [40] Even earlier, the weekly Tiempo of Mexico recalled that Céspedes had stressed in 1941 that the MNR was a friendly partisan of the United Nations fighting fascism around the world. [41] In 1945-1946, as a reward for his faithful party services, Céspedes served as Bolivian ambassador in neighboring Paraguay where he came to know and respect the pilas or barefooted Paraguayan soldiers whom he had faced across the trenches of the Chaco War. [42]

Céspedes' second literary work created more of a political furor than had Sangre de mestizos (1936). Appearing exactly ten years later, Metal del diablo (The Devil's Metal) was a thinly disguised exposé of the luxurious living and questionable business practices of Bolivia's tin king, Simón I. Patiño. The book, polemical in a socially realistic fashion, did much to speed nationalization of the tin mines (See Chapter 8). When the Buenos Aires edition of 1946 was reviewed in Tiempo of Mexico City, Simón I. Patiño was more than 83 years old. In 1924 he had been counted among the five richest men in the world. He returned to Bolivia and built three fabulous mansions--one in Cochabamba and two in Oruro--but he seldom lived there, preferring the holiday spots of Europe. The Tiempo review charged that Wall Street friends of Patiño had imposed the policy of non-recognition of Villarroel upon the United States government. Although Patiño was not mentioned by name in the book, it apparently missed out on an important hemisphere literary prize because of its controversial nature. According to the rules of the Office of Intellectual Cooperation in Washington, D.C., a jury in each country would select its best book for the final contest. The still unpublished Metal del diablo won in Bolivia in 1941 but not in the North American capital-- contrary to all expectations. According to the Tiempo writer, it seemed that one of the secretaries of Patiño had read the manuscript and threatened a libel suit if it were honored with the prize. Thereupon, wrote the Tiempo author, the novel was dropped from the competition. [43]

Before Céspedes announced his candidacy as deputy from the province of Bustillo de Potosí in 1942, his second try for elected public office, he had spent time in the province at the

mines of Uncîa, Catavi, and Llallagua gathering material for
Metal del diablo. Céspedes announced his candidacy in a letter
to the minister of government, General Felipe M. Rivera, on
April 7, 1942. Thus, his fledgling political steps occurred
almost exactly ten years to the day before the MNR revolution
of 1952. At the time, Céspedes was assistant editor of La Calle
and a member of the directing committee of the MNR. Like
Montenegro, he was disgusted by the charade of the Chaco War
(in which both fought) and combined his literary and journalistic talents with direct political action. In 1942, Céspedes noted
that a state of siege continued despite the approaching elections
of May, whereas the law provided that a siege must be lifted
twenty days before elections. Céspedes also objected to legal
processes against two MNR candidates--Monroy Block for having
"pronounced a discourse against the army" and Mendoza López
"for having acclaimed communism." These were false charges,
Céspedes maintained, and even if they were true, they would
not be against Bolivian laws. Both candidates were being held
under "preventive detention." Céspedes said he had supported
the candidacy of Peñaranda in 1940 because he felt the man
would give "a popular feeling" to the government, but now
Céspedes opposed him. If elected deputy, Céspedes declared
that he would take up the problems of wages, worker and living
conditions, and the Código del Trabajo (Labor Code of the
Busch period). He conducted his campaign in the densest
worker district of Bolivia. [44]

Running as a deputy against the entrenched military
government of General Enrique Peñaranda in 1942 was not an
easy task. La Calle was closed on occasion, broadsides were
confiscated, newsboys harassed. In his letter announcing his
candidacy, Céspedes said simply, "From the government we only
ask an effective tolerance for our propaganda...We have always
fought the extraordinary measures of the Army; we opposed the
laws of social repression and muzzling the press; we legalized
the government of Busch and when he closed the Convention,
we protested, separating ourselves from the government for we
considered that Parliament is a prosecuting institution, indispensable so that Bolivia will not be converted into an ayllu
[communal village] subjected to the autocracy of a patrón." In
other aspects, Céspedes was saying things which had seldom
been heard in Bolivia, such as, "I believe that our mining
industry is the only objective value that includes us a State
and as a people in the international capitalist world." This did
not mean, however, that Céspedes agreed with the state of
things. Far from it, for he added, "We believe that Bolivia is
a nation and not a mere deposit of continental riches." [45]

El Diario summarized Céspedes' letter announcing his
candidacy, and the afternoon newspaper Tierra commented in an

78

editorial titled, "Neither Nazi sabotage nor Communist boycott in Bolivian politics," Augusto Céspedes " has assumed a valiant and definitive position upon declaring his role as opposition candidate to the government of General Peñaranda. In recent times there is an absolute lack of civil spirit, which resembles an exotic flower [rather than an] attitude of true civil government and manhood." [46]

Nevertheless, Céspedes lost the race, stating that his campaign of 14 days, shortened for lack of funds, had been impossibly brief. Céspedes did obtain insights into the workers' mentality, however, which was to serve him well on both La Calle and later as editor of La Nación. For example, he recalled after the campaign that a "poor ignorant man" named Augado was haranguing the mine-workers with the slogan, "Workers of the world, unite!" Commented Céspedes:

> In my numerous speeches, I have emphasized before the workers that that classic manifestation is malicious propaganda for the enemies of the country, who try to make the Bolivian worker lose his patriotic spirit. My theme has been: "Bolivia for the Bolivians.' The only thing which interests us is the welfare of the Bolivian worker. The workers of Chile, Germany, Russia, or the United States mean nothing to us [for] they earn minimum salaries of ten dollars and when they come here they are patrones. [47]

Céspedes was not always the serious politician or political writer. In 1942, when the world was caught up in the throes of war, Céspedes commented on a dispatch from New York about the morals trial of Errol Flynn who allegedly had been involved with 17-year-old Betty Hansen. The dispatch, something typical for La Calle to use, contained many succulent details from the verbatim testimony in the court trial, such as the question put to Ms. Hansen, "Did they [your panties] button or did they zip?" Concluded Augusto Céspedes: "Right now is being exhibited in the cinemas of New York the latest picture of Errol Flynn, called 'Desperate Journey' in which the hero of the screen, after a series of fabulous adventures, flees miraculously from the power of the Nazis. All this in order to fall into the Court of Justice of Los Angeles!" [48] This bit of floss is worthy of mention because it reveals the technique of La Calle: to seize on the most innocuous or blatantly prurient themes both to attract readers to its pages and to expose the foibles of the rich and powerful.

Céspedes himself loved films, however, and was always impressed by film stars. On a cultural exchange trip to the United States in 1943, Céspedes wrote a series of "Letters from

Hollywood" for La Calle, always wearing the same pin-striped suit when posing with various stars. Among others, he interviewed Rita Hayworth, Edward G. Robinson, Jinx Faulkenberg, Joan Crawford, Bette Davis, Gail Russell, and Arturo de Cordova. [49] His most lasting impression of the film capital, however, which was then considering making a picture of Metal del diablo, was that one could not drink after midnight. [50]

Back home, Céspedes found the political scene in turmoil. One of his major opponents in the pages of La Calle at this stage of his career was Javier Paz Campero, a leading lawyer for the Hochschild company and organizer of the short-lived Partido Socialista de Estado. It was a classic confrontation because both men despised what the other believed in. Recounting the past as if it were a litany of shame, La Calle pointed out in 1943 "Facts [which] prove that the Unified Socialists are fascist fellow travelers and antidemocratic." In 1937, the newspaper recalled, the party had dissolved all political parties except the Partido Socialista de Estado headed by Paz Campero. In a sharp counterattack to charges that Céspedes and the MNR were Nazis of fascist sympathizers, the article continued that in 1937 and 1939 the Unified Socialists had exiled persons, confined others, and used government funds indiscreetly. In 1939 they decreed a dictatorship in Bolivia, dissolved Parliament by force and arrogated its powers, including the death penalty by simple vote of the Consejo de Gabinete (cabinet advisory board) made up of the PSE. Moreover, its foreign policy was sympathetic to Germany, Italy, and Spain, and without agreement of the other American republics it recognized the Empire of Ethiopia established by Mussolini, "placing the seal of approval thus on invasion and conquest." Bolivia under the Unified Socialists also was the first government in America to recognize Franco--when he was still fighting at Burgos. [51]

Attacking the Partido Socialista Unificado (PSU), organized in 1940 and which did well in the congressional elections under Peñaranda, La Calle ran an article headlined "Imperialists and anti-imperialists act unified for the 'cause.'" This was another attack on Paz Campero who preferred the concept of Panamericanism of the United States to that of indoamericanismo (Indian-Americanism) of the Andean countries. Wrote Céspedes: "A socialist party which rejects Indoamericanism is negating, after all, its own theoretical substance. Indoamericanism, with geographic, historic, economic, and ethnic content is opposed to Imperialism. It [Indoamericanism] is a South American creation because it intends to organize itself as an expression of the semicolonial countries, and it is the typically socialist creation because it was born with a sense of liberation of the exploited masses--Indians and mestizos--in

80

order to protect their rights before the great potency of the North, not in antagonism but in the spirit of genuine cooperation and fraternity." [52]

The Socialist parties, which frequently were such in name only, faded from the scene, however, as the more broadly based nationalism of the MNR and similar parties came to hold sway. The steady stream of propaganda in the pages of La Calle was boosting the MNR to national prominence, especially after the springboard of the Catavi interpellation. La Calle came to assume the conscience of the nation, inheriting the mantle partly from INTI and El Universal, but adding its own strong and vibrant voice to the journalism arena of La Paz. In the ideological pulls and struggles of the early years of World War II, La Calle, after being awed by the early German and Italian successes, pleaded for a third course between the two opposing camps of the democracies and dictatorships, stressing Bolivia's own national identity. A headline in September 1943 read, "Really, nationalism is incapable of doing what entreguismo [giving away national resources] did--The work of the traditional statesmen." [53]

La Calle also fought for civilian liberties after Bolivia went on a war footing in April 1942. In 1943, for example, the newspaper proclaimed, "The decree of security of the state is dictated only to strangle the legal opposition." The decree was set for December 13, but Céspedes said it was a reproduction of a law decree of interior security of the state considered when Bolivia declared was on the Axis powers in April 1942, which La Calle then denounced as unconstitutional. In 1943 the newspaper pointed out that Bolivia had been in a state of war since April 1942 but civil liberties had not been touched. Céspedes quoted Wendell Wilkie as saying that the success of the United Nations "will be in direct proportion with the exactitude with which those who find themselves in power are able to express the will of their peoples." [54]

Nevertheless, the suppressive decree was issued and went into effect on December 13, 1943. In the afternoon, the government seized copies of the leftist weekly Pregón and closed the paper. Two days later Enrique Baldivieso, president of the Chamber of Deputies, sent a letter to Peñaranda saying, "With the Law-Decree of security, the Government of Bolivia declares an inoffensive war against the potencies of the Axis and an effective [war] against the Bolivian citizens." [55]

After the overthrow of Villarroel in 1946, the journalists who had formed the MNR, along with others, fell upon hard times. Many fled to Argentina, including Céspedes and Carlos Montenegro, who both worked on the distinguished Buenos

Aires newspaper La Prensa after it was confiscated by Juan Domingo Perón in 1951 and handed over to the powerful national trade union, the Confederación General de Trabajo (General Confederation of Labor, CGT). When asked in 1973 if he had not found it embarrassing to work on a confiscated newspaper, Céspedes replied, "Not a bit. Carrying out a revolution is like marrying a woman--you cannot marry only part of her." In other words, some civil liberties had to be foregone until Perón was able to place his social revolution on firmer footing. Céspedes believed that the press of the right (See Chapters 6 and 7) crushed the revolutionary process in his own country; the government was too lenient in allowing freedom of the press to operate in a highly volatile situation. The powerful newspapers--La Razón, El Diario, and Ultima Hora--did not have a proportion commensurate with the standards or needs of the people, Céspedes pointed out; on the contrary they were periódicos millonarios o de lujo (millionaire or luxury newspapers) far removed from the situation of the vast number of Bolivians. During the period of the sexenio, from the overthrow of Villarroel until the successful MNR revolt (1946-1952), the party had only one brief voice in La Paz when La Noche, edited by Mario Torres, presented the views of the MNR in an unostentatious way for several months in 1948-1949. Otherwise it was a bleak and hostile environment for the MNR until En Marcha began appearing in 1951 (See Chapter 5). [56]

After the MNR revolution of 1952, Céspedes became the fifth editor of the official newspaper, La Nación, serving between 1956 and 1959 during the presidency of Hernán Siles Zuazo. It was Víctor Paz Estenssoro, however, the economist who was the major architect of the MNR and revolutionary president in 1952-1956 and 1960-1964, who appointed Céspedes to the post. It was a brilliant selection for no one could come close to Céspedes' sparkling wit, and he served longer than any of the other eleven editors, lending credence which an official journal ordinarily would not have.

As director of La Nación, Céspedes eschewed objectivity and embraced the cause of the socially committed writer. In his first editorial of April 17, 1959, he noted that "each man sees things in accordance with what he is...his origin, his race, his class, his ideas--a thing that occurs in a particularly clear way in the realm of social events that...do not admit of that independence which the spokesman of the ex-ruling class proclaim." Céspedes reiterated that La Nación, founded on October 12, 1952, was affiliated with the MNR and was thus accountable for the outcome of the Revolution. It was, he maintained, a newspaper "that is movimientista because together with the MNR it had made that Revolution and is rendered accountable because no Bolivian can feel himself divorced from the great vital acts of this people." Céspedes added, "Revolutionary journalism wants to be another of the instruments of the revolution, not only the observer but also the expression of it." Therefore, he concluded, "La Nación does not have to subscribe to a similar idol of 'objectivity'..." [57]

Céspedes' credo for the socially committed writer was stated even more emphatically in his acceptance speech when he received the national prize for literature in 1957 for El dictador suicida (The Dictator Self-Destroyed), an historical account of the rule and fate of Germán Busch. In that speech, Céspedes defined the duty of writers in "semi-colonial" countries. Literary men in advanced countries did not need to feel a debt to further nationalism, he asserted, "but on the contrary, in the under-developed countries there is almost no more than raw materials and some writers." Céspedes declared it was far from his intention to affirm that the function of the writer should be that of the guerrilla fighter. (After 1961 he refused to accept any more national prizes for literature, hoping thereby to encourage younger writers and sway them from the course of direct action.) But, noting his own career, he said, "I who left abandoned in my juvenile years, the artist who could have been, in order to dedicate the greater part of my time to politics, [hoped] to find a conciliating solution between this politician and that novelist." In this reconcilation, he was to produce El presidente colgado (The Hanged President, 1966), an examination of events leading up to the death of Villarroel, and Salamanca o el metafísico del fracaso (Salamanca or the Metaphysics of Failure, 1973), an analysis of the man who served as president during most of the Chaco War. In his 1957 speech, Céspedes presaged these accomplishments by declaring, "I essayed then an interpretative medium that permitted me to shelter simultaneously the literary man and the politician; that is I wrote a history." For that effort, he won the national literary prize for El dictator suicida, published in Chile in 1956. It was a watershed in the creative life of Augusto Céspedes, one imposed upon him by the Revolution itself. As he concluded his acceptance speech, he emphasized that "the mission of the writer in the oppressed countries consists in forming the national conscience; he should be miner, peasant, and explorer of the national conscience, the only durable possibility which the contours of our small world and our cultural dependence allow us." [58]

The third member of the literary and journalistic faction of the early MNR was Armando Arce, a less well known figure of Bolivian journalism. Arce was born into a comfortable family but was defrauded of his patrimony by his guardian after the death of his father. With only a high school diploma, Armando Arce became a journalist and worked for eleven years on El

Diario, for which Montenegro and Céspedes also once reported, becoming editor-in-chief. He left that position voluntarily to found El Universal in 1932, an independent daily which under his leadership was the first to launch vigorous campaigns for social and economic reforms in Bolivia (see Chapter 1). Both Montenegro and Céspedes contributed to this newspaper during its three years of life (1932-1935) against enormous odds. Finally, it was closed permanently by the government. Then, after a year's interval, Arce and Céspedes founded La Calle, dedicated to continuing the struggle against the power of the great mine owners and large landholders. [59]

Arce, who was somewhat awkward in the political arena, took journalism very seriously indeed. He was a rarity among the reporters and editors of his day because he devoted full time to his profession, eking out a meager living. And he was a man of immense personal courage. Speaking to the Association of Journalists on May 22, 1943, in an address that was broadcast only seven months before Peñaranda was overthrown, Arce talked on "the history of Bolivian journalism tied to the national life," the theme that was to dominate Carlos Montenegro's Nacionalismo y coloniaje published the same year. The study of national journalism, Arce said in his speech, should be the first step for an "analytical and truthful" history "of a nation whose vigorous qualities have been criminally disdained and caricatured by its pseudo-historians." (This was obviously a reference to Alcides Argüedas and his followers who seemed to export nothing but deprecation for their native land.) Those who have "the inescapable duty of reconstructing the country should begin by reconstructing its history," and in the process those who worked in the popular press were indispensable. "The journalist is, in reality, the engineer who raises the spiritual structure of a nation and through extension, he can construct the future of the world." [60]

Like Céspedes and other intellectuals, Arce succumbed to the temptation of running for public office. His candidacy for deputy from the department of La Paz in 1944 climaxed ten years of journalistic labor. As La Calle said, "The candidacy of Armando Arce implicitly means the candidacy of the daily." Continuing in this vein, the newspaper added, "Armando Arce has no necessity of exhibiting any program because his program is printed in a thousand and more numbers of this newspaper which every morning strikes the conscience of Bolivia like an alarm bell." [61] An election-day statement by Arce himself declared, "I am not an ambitious nor unscrupulous person nor a parvenu to civismo; I am not an imposter of the political holiday, but rather a proven servant of the people." If he were not elected, he continued, it would be more than a mere personal defeat "but a defeat for the people by the people

84

themselves." [62] But Arce, who was somewhat shy and withdrawn and therefore not an effective campaigner, finished last in a field of six candidates with only 920 votes. [63]

The most effective service which Arce could offer the party, however, was not in the political field but as an accomplished propagandist. In early 1946, for example, in a speech over Radio America, Arce declared that only the people could judge the MNR. He denounced "the mountains of dirty propaganda thrown to the wind by the servants of La Rosca." He added, "facing the people of Bolivia is a powerful mechanism, whose major material argument constitutes the millions set aside with interested generosity by those who have made of Bolivia the richest and most extensive field of exploitation and whose surrenders in the course of half a century add up to astronomical sums in dollars and pounds sterling; a field of business that its users do not resign and will not resign themselves to lose." [64]

As the Villarroel government was caught ever more tightly in the squeeze between support by the MNR and opposition by the PIR, the verbal battle in the capital's newspapers heated up as well. When La Calle did not appear between March 3 and 8, 1946, because of the Carnival festival, La Razón took advantage of the occasion to attack Arce's speech upon accepting leadership of the Comando Departmental of the MNR in La Paz (the country was divided into 45 such commands in a monolithic organization.) La Razón deemed "fantastic" Arce's claim that a volante or broadside had been profusely distributed in opposition to the Villarroel regime, naming names of military and civilian leaders whose heads should literally roll "for the tranquility and the free and unrestricted empire of the mining super-state within the country." Arce immediately went on local radio stations in La Paz to give a reply to La Razón's attack. The major thrust of his argument was a question: What about the appeal to Nuremberg trials for army and MNR leaders of the Villarroel revolution suggested by José Antonio Arze in the Communist newspaper El Siglo of Santiago earlier in the year and reprinted "with much complacency" in El Diario? [65]

A serious scandal besmirched the Villarroel government when twelve prominent opponents of the regime, including senators and generals, were found killed alongside a road in an isolated part of the Yungas, or sub-tropical valleys to the east. These "murders of November 1944," as they came to be called, did not come to light until much later. In 1946 La Calle kept intimating that the man responsible for the killings was Gustavo Chacón, ex-minister of foreign relations, who had engineered the massacre to make it appear that the Villarroel government was responsible. Pedro Zilveti Arce (no relation to Armando Arce) wrote a letter to El Diario which stated: "As for the attacks that Señor Chacón has suffered from the official daily, it seems the most natural thing for Señor Armando Arce to try to avoid all clearing up of the mystery that continues causing anguish to Bolivia because, according to all the versions, it was in his [Arce's] house where the crimes [the murders of November 1944] had their beginning of execution, as will be proved in good time." Arce replied briskly that La Calle had tried repeatedly to clear up the matter, such as in an article headlined, CHACON SHOULD SPEAK. Arce stated further that "I am disposed to appeal before whatever court, however inquisitorial it may be, to sustain the integrity of my public and private conduct." In fact, he launched a judicial action to clear his name, but nothing seems to have come of this. [66] After the MNR gained power in 1952, Arce felt constrained to write a brief book about the incident, entitled, Los fusilamientos del 20 de Noviembre de 1944 y el Movimiento Nacionalista Revolucionario (The Executions of November 20, 1944, and the National Revolutionary Movement.)

The charges against Arce were almost certainly unfounded; at least, they did not hurt him within the MNR ranks. Oscar Delgado has written a biography of Arce, who frequently used the penname "Reporter Juanito," which asserted that as an editor of both El Universal and La Calle the journalist was in "elbow-to-elbow" contact with Paz Estenssoro, who served Bolivia three times as president, and with the group of independent deputies who later formed the MNR and made Paz its leader. An editor of the MNR's official newspaper after gaining power, La Nación, Hugo González Rioja also noted that Arce "perhaps did not foresee that what happened almost fatally to every Bolivian intellectual would happen to him: he would wind up in the political jousting field." [67] In 1958 he became interventor of the departmental command of the MNR in the strategic and key point of La Paz and later chief of the same organization. [68] In addition to his journalistic skills, he was a dedicated and hard-headed revolutionary. In his capacity as chief party figure in La Paz, for example, he addressed the youth of the MNR, stressing that "The ABC's of revolutionary technique, or what we might call the 'sociology of the Revolution' [is that] no Revolution is possible without a revolutionary party." Arce, whose services to the Revolution have not been fully recognized outside a close circle of his surviving friends, went on to say:

> The revolutionaries who have grown up in the revolutionary epic are habitually doctrinaires, rigid and hostile to every compromise. The myth of the revolution does not admit on the other hand deception and

slyness; for the people, the revolution is always a moral action, generous, even religious, and they want nothing else except that the revolutionary chiefs radiate a pure, simple, severe force that corresponds to that ideal. [69]

Because he was a master propagandist, one who could paint a favorable picture of the Revolution abroad, Arce was dispatched to serve successfully as ambassador in Peru, Colombia, and Mexico. One scholar has suggested, however, that the reason Arce and others of the early MNR were rewarded with ambassadorial plums was simply the traditional stratagem to keep them from interfering in politics at home. [70]

Given the backgrounds of these three men who, along with José Cuadros Quiroga (see Chapter 4), guided the destinies of La Calle, what did the newspaper find to talk about in its later years? We shall examine its reportage and comment on events from the overthrow of Peñaranda in 1943 to the overthrow of his successor Villarroel and the final closing of La Calle in 1946. If La Calle established itself as a street fighter in its first years of existence, it met its greatest test in its later years as an opponent of a repressive government and then unofficial spokesman for a controversial government.

Enrique Peñaranda was inaugurated as the duly elected president of Bolivia on April 15, 1940. Three years later, La Calle analyzed his performance in office: "Those of the right have gained power over the Peñaranda government, coming to consolidate an influence which they rarely had, with consequences prejudicial for the country in these three years, perhaps those of the most decisive importance for the national destinies." [71]

By the time this editorial note was published, the handwriting was already on the wall for the Peñaranda government. One of his mistakes was exerting a heavy hand when conciliation would have been more appropriate. The law-decree of security of 1943 was the best example of this. La Calle quoted an editorial from La Razón, the Aramayo organ, declaring that the law-decree "If it affects the determination of the Constitution, it will not do so more than in theory. [Opponents] do not take into account the benevolent attitude of the first magistrate...which, in other hands, would be dangerous..." To emphasize its dismay and disgust with this attitude of the rule of men over law, La Calle liberally sprinkled this excerpt with exclamation points. [72]

Repression rarely works, however, and La Calle saw its propaganda pay off when Peñaranda, who had ordered troops into the Catavi dispute, was overthrown exactly one year after the Catavi massacre. Dr. José Francisco Socarrás, visiting professor of psychology and anthropology from the Universidad Nacional of Colombia, witnessed the events of December 20, 1943, when Peñaranda was overthrown, and gave a disinterested outsider's view when interviewed by Harold Zuñiga for Acción Política of Bogotá. Socarrás said, "In reality, it was a revolution made by telephone. The capture of the central station of communications in La Paz was its fundamental episode." There was no participation by the masses in the revolt, but traffic workers under Major Taborga defected to the rebels. A regiment of friendly artillery camped outside La Paz fired continually into the air to keep government officials and the military inside their houses. Simply the noise dispersed Peñaranda's presidential guard. Rebels called the chief of the general staff by telephone and told him to go to the presidential palace to prevent a revolt that was about to break out. He fell into the trap, carrying a light machine-gun, when his car collided with another carrying prisoners of the director of police and other important officials. The revolt was the work of 96 individuals, Socarrás said. Mobs then took to the streets, gutting the houses of Peñaranda and his officials. The ease of the revolt, the Colombian educator said, "gives an idea of the prestige, the organization, and the force of the defeated government." As for the matter of recognition of the new Villarroel government, "The people associate the United States with Patiño, Aramayo, and Hochschild," Socarrás said. Secretary of State Cordell Hull's decision of non-recognition "has provoked a profound resentment reopening ancient wounds, awakening old disappointments, and placing in operation the anti-imperialist literature of some years ago." Socarrás added. [73]

La Calle exulted in the overthrow of Peñaranda because the law-decree of security had been used to lock the newspaper for three months. The newspaper reappeared with a banner headline on December 21, 1943, THE REVOLUTION TRIUMPHS! A smaller banner headline read, "Most popular in the political history of Bolivia." A cutline over a picture of a mob read, "The people gave a response to the massacre." [74] December 21 had been the first anniversary of the Catavi mine violence. Commented La Calle, "Catavi is the symbol, it is the sign, it is the patrón of what those [la Rosca] would do in Bolivia if the people did not maintain themselves vigilant and upright, ready to crush definitively and energetically the reaction that [already] has begun to move in the shadows.... We mention Catavi...because Catavi constitutes the bloody experience of what the inhuman, dark, and traitorous mechanism is capable of, which had garroted until yesterday three million human beings in Bolivia." In a statement of editorial policy, La Calle declared in a signed editorial by Armando Arce that its position today was the same as yesterday. Two groups, he declared, made the revolution--the young military men and the MNR. La Calle workers therefore had decided-- Arce and his companions--to place La Calle openly at the service of the MNR. The "most difficult, dangerous, and greatest responsible" stage of the struggle had only begun, Arce wrote, adding:

> This work [of effective liberation and sovereignty] is not concluded. One must follow the most rugged and difficult of roads because when the Revolution recently began, on the same day that the audacity, the valor, and the faith of a handful of men overpowered the oligarchial hydra, they left it with life making gigantic rancor and aggrandizing ambitions. [75]

Events were to prove these predictions accurate. Foreign embassies did not believe, for example, that the defeat of Peñaranda and the installation of Villarroel represented the wishes of the majority of the Bolivian people, so La Calle suggested "a gigantic demonstration" to convince them. [76] The new government also was attacked by left-over diplomats who were said to be "sabotaging" it. These included Alberto Ostría Gutiérrez in Chile, David Alvéstegui, former editor of La Razón, in Brazil, and Alfonso Finot in Mexico. La Calle declared that these men--and others of a small clique--had parceled out among themselves the diplomatic plums under the ancién regime for twenty years. [77]

In the propaganda counterattack, La Calle hauled all of the skeletons out of Peñaranda's closet which it could find--or pretended to find. The corruption and improvidence of the former chief executive were vigorously attacked. In a fraction of the last fiscal year, La Calle noted, Peñaranda imported 99 cases of table wine, 94 cases of whiskey, 51 cases of other wine, and five cases of aguardiente. [78] Even more spectacular than the revelation of the former president's drinking habits were allegations of padding official accounts. Thus, the investigative commission for crimes against the state, established by the Villarroel government, revealed in its first report that the state had charged one million bolivianos for a Diesel motor worth 12,000 bolivianos. [79] Other private debts of Peñaranda also were billed to the state, La Calle maintained, while the controller apparently looked the other way. The newspaper listed 34 separate items which Peñaranda had purchased for his private house and finca, totaling 25,809 bolivianos and all paid for by the state. [80] Even more serious was the charge that Jorge Peñaranda, brother of the ex-president, had contracted a debt of three million bolivianos, all paid with money from the budget. [81] Later, 33 more personal debts of the house and estate charged against the state by Peñaranda were listed. These allegedly occurred in April 1943 and totaled 36,114 bolivianos. [82] Again, it was alleged that four peñarandista candidates received a total of 136,938 bolivianos, along with other "loans" during the elections of 1942. [83] Finally, as a capstone to its post-mortem of the Peñaranda regime, La Calle gleefully reported that the cost of the Peñaranda trip to the United States, where he had been warmly welcomed by President Franklin Delano Roosevelt and received an honorary doctor of laws degree from Columbia University, was 5,121,331 bolivianos, including costs for the entire retinue. [84] Altogether, La Calle maintained, Peñaranda had misspent almost three billion bolivianos in his three and a half years in office. [85]

On April 14, 1944, La Calle noted, "Today concludes the legal period of General Peñaranda['s rule].--Pillage, drunken orgies, falsifications, and killings define that period." The newspaper charged that Peñaranda had frozen German and Japanese funds ostensibly to demonstrate cooperation with the United Nations, but actually only to unfreeze them clandestinely later for distribution among his sycophants. [86] In a manifesto from Arequipa, Peñaranda declared he would continue governing legally--along with his cabinet. An afternoon daily in La Paz, unnamed, also informed capital readers that Peñaranda had asked Villarroel for permission to return to Bolivia. Would the doctor honoris causa of Columbia University become a member of the constituent convention? asked La Calle. [87]

In the midst of this sniping, the Villarroel government closed La Razón, the newspaper of tin magnate Carlos Víctor Aramayo, in March 1944. To counter criticism of the move, La Calle reprinted two editorials from La Razón when the MNR newspaper itself had been closed in December 1943. At that time, the Aramayo newspaper declared, "The situation of national journalism is passing through a period of crisis.... The conflict has been inevitable. It has resulted in the advisory group of ministers to take violent determinations [the closure of La Calle]. It is lamentable that knowingly it has given occasion for this." In the second editorial, also of December 18, 1943, La Razón stated that professional solidarity had its limits, and the Aramayo newspaper would not support La Calle in this crisis. [88] When it was closed in 1944, the director of La Razón sent a note to the governing junta saying, "fortunately, our history does not register a single case of such extreme rigor that La Razón must continue paying idle workers." "Bravooooo!" hooted La Calle, printing the order by Peñaranda and his cabinet that La Calle, INTI, and Busch would have to continue paying workers during the four months La Calle was closed after the so-called "Nazi putsch" of 1941. [89]

The last word that was heard from General Enrique Peñaranda came in 1946, a few months before the overthrow of Villarroel, when an Associated Press story from Lima quoted him as attacking the "Nazis" then in the Bolivian government. For his documentation, he cited the notorious Department of State Blue Book and asserted that documents of the German legation, then in the hands of the Bolivian chancery, would prove that German subsidies were being paid to members of the present Bolivian government. Peñaranda declared it was "a false democratic gesture" for Villarroel to join the United Nations one day after the revolution and "comical" for Villarroel to break relations with Franco. This "democratic farce," Peñaranda was quoted as saying, was completely destroyed when Villarroel "appealed to genuinely Nazi methods in order to terrify public opinion and remain in power, when he martyred cruelly more than twelve outstanding citizens [allegedly in November 1944] among whom figured ex-members of my cabinet, senators, and high chiefs of the army." The proof of this? Peñaranda cited the continued state of siege and "the incessant violations of constitutional guarantees." Commented La Calle acidly, "By the declarations transcribed, one may suppose that for the first time in his life General Peñaranda has read a book, the Blue Book..." [90]

Actually, La Calle had an easier time pursuing its propaganda course under Villarroel because the government was active in social reforms--frequently mild and symbolic, but reforms nonetheless. On the other hand, it was difficult for La Calle to assume the role of supporter rather than challenger because it had been created to oppose oligarchial governments, and it had done this for seven years. But the reforms issued from the presidential palace in La Paz gave La Calle the opportunity to lead rather than to follow. Early in his presidency, Villarroel organized a commission of minimum salaries; when it was later revealed that some workers in the Colquiri mine got only 6.5 bolivianos a day, Villarroel issued a decree raising salaries 20 percent for the lowest paid and 10 percent for the highest. [91] Also, when a railroad strike wracked the country in 1946, the Villarroel government granted a 30 percent increase--up to 1,000 bolivianos for the lowest levels to 10 percent for the highest--above 4,000 bolivianos. Also, the rather elaborate social laws in existence but seldom enforced were applied, in many cases for the first time, in conformance with the Magruder Commission recommendations. [92]

Most importantly, a decree of April 3, 1945, effected the Busch law of June 17, 1937 by ordering that the state control 100 percent of the divisas or exchange earnings on tin. [93]

In the social sphere, the Convention established by Villarroel voted 58 to 16 to give women suffrage in municipal elections if they were 21 and had completed elementary school. [94] Labor and Indian groups were not neglected. On June 10, 1944, the Sindical Congress of Mining Workers opened in Huanuni with 25 unions present representing 45,000 workers. [95] More significantly, Bolivia's First Congress of Indians opened in La Paz on May 10, 1945, with thousands of campesinos coming from throughout the country to attend. On this occasion, Villarroel said, "Today begins the work of the government that will watch over you as a father over his sons." At the close of the congress, José Gómez Esparza, the Mexican ambassador to Bolivia, declared, "This indigenous congress will have a vibrant echo throughout all of the continent." [96] On the last day of the meeting, some 1,500 Indians assembled spontaneously at Jesús de Machaca to salute the congress, unheard of previously in Bolivian history. [97]

Political difficulties plagued the new government, however. First came the thorny problem of recognition, which was not solved until the three MNR members of Villarroel's cabinet resigned on February 11, 1944. They were Carlos Montenegro, minister of agriculture; Major Alberto Taborga, minister of government; and Augusto Céspedes, secretary general of the Junta de Gobierno. [98] Previously only Argentina had recognized the new regime. La Razón, after decrying lack of recognition for five months, then declared that recognition was worthless. [99] At home, political opposition continued to mount, despite the granting of a general amnesty by Villarroel on July 22, 1944, and 21 months of monetary stability under the national revolutionary government. [100] Apparently the first student demonstration against the new regime erupted on October 5, 1945, when students demonstrating in the streets of La Paz against Perón also shouted "Down with Villarroel!" and "Down with the military government!" [101]

As charges of authoritarian rule mounted against Villarroel, La Calle pointed out, "There is no precedent in the days following a revolution in which there has been conceded in Bolivia such wide liberty of the press." For example, one newspaper had published a cable of resignation by an employee in the commercial section of the Washington, D.C. embassy, saying that "it is proved" that the revolution of December 20, 1943, has a Nazi character, and Nazi elements existed in the Junta. Another daily printed comments by Sumner Welles, "The recent change of government in Bolivia should be watched carefully." But, and La Calle applauded this further statement by Welles, "Even the semblance of all exterior pressure should be avoided. Such pressure undoubtedly would provoke a nationalist reaction." This, commented La Calle, was exactly what was happening. [102] When the Department of State announced on January 24, 1944, that it would not recognize the Villarroel regime, La Calle commented, "Foreign pressure will be welcomed if it serves, as now, to unite all of the Bolivians..." [103] To legitimize his government, in addition to dismissing the three MNR members from his cabinet, Villarroel held elections in July 1944. The elections, which served to give the head of state a constitutional mandate also vindicated the December 20 revolution. Parties supporting Villarroel were the MNR, Socialists, and Independents. Four old-guard parties, including the Marxist PIR, formed the Democratic Union in opposition. [104]

At the same time, the government tended to become as oppressive as its predecessor. In November 1944 Villarroel confiscated Radio Oruro in the mining city south of La Paz and renamed it Radio Rosendo Bullaín. [105] To better relations with the press, Villarroel began weekly Thursday press conferences on June 7, 1945. He was the first Bolivian head of state--and the last--to do so, and the questions were far-ranging. Yet Villarroel used this device to keep the recalcitrant press in line, declaring in his fourth press conference "that the liberty of thought does not mean the liberty of imagination." [106]

On the other hand, there was a movement for greater cultural self-awareness and self-esteem during the Villarroel period. Otero Reiche introduced a motion into the Convention asking that a commission be created to revise textbooks to eliminate deprecations on the national past and to edit an anthology of the best Bolivian literature. Reiche said Bolivian libraries were empty and the people were ignorant of the work of such towering figures as Gabriel René-Moreno. He also said, the newspaper summarized, "that the writer and artist in Bolivia have not received any stimulus on the part of the State." [107]

Politically, the biggest task facing the Villarroel government, and one in which La Calle played its part, was attempting to convince the world that the Bolivian government was not fascist. On December 18, 1945, the Anti-fascist Democratic Front was formed by the traditional parties, joined by the PIR. This alliance of the parties of the right was similar to the Unión Nacional of the Toro period; the Concordancia of the Quintanilla presidency, and the Democratic Alliance of Peñaranda. What, La Calle asked, did the four traditional parties--the Liberals, the anti-Saavedra Republicans, the Genuines, and the Unified Socialists--do during fifty years of rule? Toro congratulated Mussolini on his invasion of Ethiopia, Quintanilla was a friend of Hitler, and the traditional parties distributed free copies of Mi lucha (Mein Kampf). [108]

A propaganda ploy of the opposition occurred when it was announced that copies of a broadside had been circulated in Sucre urging the organization of "Popular tribunals to judge and shoot at once not only the directors responsible for all the calamity the country has suffered since December 20, 1943, but also the collaborators of the present regime." [109] Villarroel said he wanted all public officials to know the risk they ran, but at the same time pressure was brought to bear on reporter Federico Joffre Salinas, who supplied the story to the national news agency Inforvianas. When he was suspended and a suit instituted against him, Joffre wrote a three-column letter to La Calle documenting that he got the information from the Sucre Tribuna Universitaria, a student newspaper. [110]

As the heat was intensified against the Villarroel government, La Calle began a daily column on February 20, 1946--five months before the overthrow of that regime--entitled, "Why the National Revolution is being attacked." After the elections of early May 1946, in which the opposition abstained, an editorial in La Calle was headlined, "There lacks little for an assault upon the Government." The editorial noted that the opposition press, by exaggerating electoral violence, was paving the way for a takeover of the Villarroel government. [111] The first attempt at this occurred on June 13, 1946. Blaming "the plutocratic press" [112] for supplying "Money for the civil war," La Calle scored the deceit of the mining press, quoting La Razón of May 24, only a few days before the attempted takeover: "We seek for the country only the rule of the Constitution, which is the judicial norm, and we are enemies of revolutions, disorder, and subversion." [113]

Putting down the attempted revolt brought forth ecstatic headlines in La Calle. Five banner headlines on the front page, along with pictures of Villarroel and Paz Estenssoro, read VIVA THE NATIONAL REVOLUTION; VIVA THE POPULAR GOVERNMENT; VIVA THE GREAT M.N.R.; VIVA THE REVOLUTIONARY ARMY and THE ROSQUERA SUBVERSION. Firing broke out early in the morning of June 13, 1946, in scattered barracks around La Paz, but the majority of the army proved loyal to Villarroel. The rebels seized arms at the El Alto airport and planned to bombard the city, but the guardian of the armory, an MNR militant, fixed the bombs so they would not explode. Two rebel lieutenants seized two planes to fly over and bomb the city. The bombs did not explode but one pierced the roof of the Congress building and lodged one meter from the national seal, while another ripped through the roof of a building near the La Calle offices.

94

At high noon Villarroel went on the radio to deliver an address to the Bolivian people, reprinted in full later on the front page of La Calle, along with a brief boxed commentary. The president declared that the revolution had passed another test. The counter-revolt had been launched by those whose economic interests were hurt, but it was just that those who had money should contribute more to the collective necessities. The Revolution had been slow to date, Villarroel asserted, because the old institutions had to be destroyed first. The government alone, he stressed, would act against the insurgents because Bolivia needed all of her precious blood. "The permanent tolerance of the Government was interpreted as weakness," he concluded, "and the counter-revolutionaries tried to ignore that the faith of generous hearts is worth more than money which corrupts and stains."

The incident was important also because it revealed how distorted and unobjective the reporting in La Calle was in a pressure situation. The newspaper reported that 1,000 MNR members heeded the call to fight, were armed, and demanded orders. "What patriotic anxiety, what spirit of sacrifice, what love for the Popular Revolution!" La Calle gushed. "That youth who asked for orders and nothing more than orders to leave for the front of the fighting, that is the youth which offers to the people the work of Social Justice that the National Liberating Revolution is carrying out." La Calle advised its readers:

Go to the neighborhoods of the poorer classes and see what is happening. In each home there is a trench; in each family of the people a bulwark of the Popular Government; in the chest of each man there is a burst of holy indignation; on the lips of each woman there are words of encouragement for the men who sustain the Popular Government, which the sons of the country aid and which resists--today also triumphally--those avaricious and miserable powerful ones who have caused the ruin of the nation and the misery of the Bolivian majority, fattening themselves in fifty years of unmerciful exploitation. But those will never return to govern again.

It should be emphasized that this type of exhortation occurred in ostensibly objective news columns and not on the editorial page. There an editorial, "The people," congratulated the citizens of La Paz on their swift action to put down the counter-revolt: "It was certainly a beautiful and admirable spectacle." [114] This editorial was reprinted on the following day, when the banner headline on the front page read ORDER RE-ESTABLISHED. Instigators of the revolt, La Calle claimed, were "Cowardly millionaires;" the conspiracy had begun in the regal mansions, continued in the offices of the "venal press" and ended with the suborning of soldiers. This front-page editorial concluded, "Look now at what you have done. There are the corpses, still not cold, of your victims. Criminals!" Another editorial praised "The military honor" for most army elements remaining loyal to the government. [115]

The attempted revolt of June 13, 1946 brought reprisals in the form of expropriation of La Razón and Ultima Hora, two of the largest dailies of La Paz and owned by Aramayo and Hochschild, respectively. The decree effecting the expropriation was signed on the very day of the unsuccessful coup d'etat. La Calle on June 14 printed the text of the decree, which pointed out that Article 17 of the constitution stated that "private property is guaranteed always as long as it is not prejudicial to the collective interest..." Article 109 gave the state authority "for imperious reasons of necessity or public security" to confiscate private property "when it does not fulfill a social function." The decree noted that some daily editorial industrial enterprises "have converted themselves into organs of sedition, occasioning the alteration of the constituted order." Therefore, the expropriation, to be paid for with bonds, of La Razón and Ultima Hora would be carried out by the prefect of the department of La Paz "to the end that they serve the national interests." Until the indemnification could be agreed upon, the supreme government would be in charge of the indicated enterprises. [116] On June 17, the prefect of the department issued a decree (auto prefectural) stating owners of the newspapers or their representatives had ten days to designate their appraisers, [117] but the appraisal never came about because Villarroel was overthrown on July 21, 1946. The actions of La Razón under state ownership will be examined later (see Chapter 6) but here it is important to point out that with the expropriation of La Razón and Ultima Hora for the first time in Bolivian history newspapers of the right felt the wrath of the central government. Always before it had been little fly-by-night leftist publications which had been closed, or La Calle which had been harassed and ultimately closed. This is not to justify the silencing of two opposition voices in Bolivia, but it does indicate that the shoe could be worn on either foot.

Whatever the provocation, it seems to have been a mistake of the first magnitude for the Villarroel government to clamp down on the opposition press. Repression is like pruning a plant: the leaves and branches may be cut back for awhile but the roots simply grow deeper. The silencing of La Razón and Ultima Hora was not unique in the Villarroel government. According to a hostile critic, Julio Díaz Argüedas, the Villarroel regime tried to "muzzle" the Bolivian press and to impose

96

self-censorship on the other dailies through "threats and strong fines." The official press such as Pregón, Cumbre, and La Calle simply could not compete with Julio César Canelas of El Diario (brother of the editor of Los Tiempos of Cochabamba); David Alvéstegui of La Razón, and Jorge Canedo Reyes of Ultima Hora. The latter was allegedly brutally beaten in police headquarters for having criticized the police for frequenting gambling casinos. Also during the Villarroel period, a national radio chain was established. According to Díaz Argüedas, if independent stations would not broadcast the official notices of Radio Illimani, they would be suspended, fined, or subjected to the arrest of their directors. [118]

At the close of Villarroel's reign, however, events were closing in on him--events which the official press such as La Calle could not dominate and events which the confiscated newspapers were impotent to ameliorate because they had lost their credibility. With inexorable timing, the opposition forces, which included the strange bedfellows of the parties of the right along with the Stalinist PIR, closed in on the hapless resident of the presidential palace who was becoming increasingly isolated from public opinion. With the opposition press expropriated on June 13, 1946, the same day as the unsuccessful revolt against the government, La Calle inexplicable became as dull as dishwater in the days preceding the successful July 21 revolution, carrying such stirring editorials as "The agency of the Agricultural Bank in Cobija." La Calle never commented on the closure of La Razón and Ultima Hora, merely printing the decree as a news story and later as the required legal advertisement. [119] Perhaps La Calle tried to soothe mounting resentment against Villarroel by a low-key approach, but it seems more likely that even at this early date the newspaper and its MNR mentors saw the handwriting on the wall and were putting distance between themselves and Villarroel.

The teachers' strike, whipped up by the PIR and supported by students, was the beginning of the end for the Villarroel regime. On July 9, 1946, La Calle ran an editorial calling the strike "counter-productive." The teachers had never had higher pay, the paper claimed, although it was still insufficient. The government was considering a "prudent readjustment," La Calle reported, and the strike therefore was "precipitous." [120] On July 10 in the evening, 120 students and political leaders fired pistols and revolvers at the national palace, the prefecture, and Radio Illimani, wounding several Carabineros and bystanders. The police used only tear-gas to disperse the mob which revealed one of the weaknesses of Villarroel's position. As July progressed, there were almost daily confrontations between the students, who had recruited numerous partisans by this time, and the police. Villarroel refused to the very end to order the army to fire into crowds of civilians, and with this desire to avoid civil bloodshed he paid with his life.

On July 12, La Calle came out with an editorial entitled "Problems which cannot be ignored." It stated that the difficulty with teachers' pay was not solved during the month of winter vacation because of oligarchial obstruction. The editorial implied that the PIR and extreme right were milking the situation for all it was worth. Paz Estenssoro as minister of the treasury had created a special tax for public education—nevertheless, after two months, the problem had not been settled. The editorial alluded to "the problems of political order that are everywhere, whether they be questions of salaries or property." [121] In a front-page two-line banner headline, La Calle proclaimed, LA ROSCA CANNOT NOW, AS IN 1930, OVERTURN GOVERNMENTS USING UNWARY STUDENTS. A subhead read, "Although these hiss, the people benefitted by the revolution know more than the university students." [122]

In the same issue, the title of an article on an inside page declared, "The revolution voted the biggest education budget in South America." The subhead added, "But there are petty teachers who are ignorant of the work of the Popular Government." In a historical retrospective, the article noted that Hernando Siles (1926-1930) had tried to increase support for public education, but the mining oligarchy—fearful of an enlightened citizenry claiming its rights—had thwarted him. During subsequent rightist governments, teachers had been paid only every three or four months. Under Villarroel, on the other hand, the education budget had increased from 14.03 percent in 1944 to 18.16 in 1946, claimed to be the highest in South America. It was also claimed to be three time that of the Quintanilla government and twice that of Peñaranda—a total of 201,381,537 bolivianos despite falling government income. [123]

Other labor sectors supported the teachers. A general strike was called for July 18 by the Federación Obrero Sindical (Worker Union Federation) but at noon on that day the inspector general of work said on the radio that posters announcing the strike had been forged and all outstanding differences had been referred to conciliation or arbitration. Yet ominously in the same issue of La Calle it was announced that the salaries of other public employees and workers would have to be cut in order to raise the pay of the teachers. [124]

In the final days of La Calle, which after ten years of life would not survive the overthrow of Villarroel on July 21, 1946, the newspaper returned to its cause of fighting vigorously for greater social justice in Bolivia. An editorial calling for

"Greater seriousness in the revolution" warned that--after four attempted golpes or coups d'etat--La Rosca was once again gathering its forces to defeat the government. Its final and most potent weapon, La Calle maintained, was the prensa millonaria (millionaire's press) where the oligarchy taught "whatever was convenient for the goals of subversive reaction." [125]

The final push against Villarroel came on July 21 when sparse groups of fighters, whipped up by the death of a student on the previous day, surrounded the national palace. All of the military except the president's colorados honor guard refused to support the government, so the fighting was soon over. Mobs then took to the streets and hanged the corpse of Villarroel and several of his aides from lampposts in the Plaza Murillo. The propaganda by the opposition that Villarroel had conducted an oppressive, dictatorial, and Nazi-fascist government had been successful. The MNR, which withdrew from the government a few days before the overthrow, lost prestige and would require six years to regroup. Its newspaper La Calle was wrecked by student mobs, and the newspaper which had enlightened the conscience of Bolivia never appeared again. This was its last editorial on July 18, 1946, entitled "The revolution is overcoming obstacles." Opposition, La Calle noted, was natural to every true revolution: if the oligarchy did not obstruct, it would mean that they had lost nothing and the people had gained nothing. "Many years will have to elapse in this struggle at whose initiation we participated," La Calle said, adding, "In these days of provocative agitation from la Rosca, if there is anything interesting for its consequence in the near future, it is the delimitation of positions." The editorial ended on a note of criticism of Villarroel: "...if the experience acquired in more than two years was not taken advantage of, that would accuse incapacity in its conduction. Far from that, what the revolutionary people wait for is the success of a sure political [system] purified of errors and vacillations." [126]

Thus, the newspaper conducted by "street fighters" would meet its fate in actual street conflict, as students wrecked La Calle's plant in 1946. This did not mean that the newspaper had been unsuccessful, however. Through 10 years of constant effort it had softened up public opinion which would make possible the enunciation of these goals by Paz Estenssoro in the election of 1951 and the subsequent justification of the armed rebellion itself. Why was La Calle not revived as the official MNR newspaper in 1952? As Augusto Céspedes recalled, Paz Estenssoro realized after the success of the 1952 revolt that La Calle was too closely identified in the public mind as a newspaper of opposition and therefore "not for this government."

[127]   Carlos Montenegro was to die of cancer in New York in 1953, and Armando Arce and José Cuadros Quiroga were to pass into relative obscurity.   Only Augusto Céspedes survived as editor later of La Nación and through his own literary and historical work.

Nevertheless, La Calle had made its mark on Bolivian life. As Tristán Marof (Gustavo A. Navarro), a bitter enemy of the MNR because he had not been included in its ranks, put it, "Bolivian politics have never been the same since the appearance of La Calle." Marof insisted that La Calle had been subvented by the German embassy at a time when Roberto Prudencio was announcing openly in Parliament, "I am a Nazi," and José Cuadros Quiroga was pro-Nazi.   In fact, Marof continued, La Calle had in miniature the same techniques as Goebbels: brutal irony and satire. [128]

The charge of Nazi tendencies was the most handy club which the opposition could wield against La Calle, and the charge has stuck through the years, especially in view of the anti-Semitic articles.   Leaving these aside for a moment, the best epitaph for La Calle came from Jacobo Libermann, a young man who later was to serve as propaganda director for the Paz Estenssoro government.   In 1973 Libermann recalled:

> La Calle made history in this country.   It was a small newspaper, very modest, of eight pages, somewhat disorganized, technically primitive, but it had a great impact on public opinion because it was delineating the major lines of a new kind of politics, national interests and projections, and it denounced the things that were strangling this country.   [In short], it...expressed the point of view of insurgent nationalism. [129]

Nevertheless, the path to that expression of nationalism was marred with the blatant anti-Semitism and on occasion pro-Nazi sentiment that marred the MNR press before and during the rule of Major Gualberto Villarroel (1943-1946). This, the greatest single controversy surrounding the MNR, demands closer attention as the democracies tried to stamp out totalitarianism in the world while the MNR marched to a different drummer in Bolivia.

Chapter 4

THE MNR AND VILLARROEL: NAZIS OR NATIONALISTS?

> ...the press, the institutes, the great men
> of Bolivia dream of Mussolini and Hitler,
> explaining in the streets and plazas and
> even in [parliamentary] discourses that the
> only way of governing this backward coun-
> try is with a dictatorship in which all
> initiative would be projected from above,
> while those below could offer only a passive
> submission...   It is useless to deny that
> Nazism has penetrated Bolivia.

--Tristán Marof,
The Nazi Danger in Bolivia
(1941) [1]

> What kind of putsch was it which tried to
> overthrow democracy in Bolivia and defy
> the United States with only three unarmed
> journalists?

--La Calle, July 19, 1942

The MNR always had to fight off labels easily applied by
opponents at home and throughout the hemisphere, but difficult
to remove once they were stuck on.   Those who formed the
MNR in 1941 were first called fascists by some in the passions
of World War II and then Communists by others in the strained
atmosphere of the Cold War.   In the earlier period, the United
States Department of State considered the MNR to be Nazi-
Fascist.   Although the MNR and younger military officers
toppled General Enrique Peñaranda on December 20, 1943, the
Villarroel regime which they formed was not recognized by the
United States--nor by any Latin American republic except
Argentina--until June 23, 1944, after the demand was met that
three MNR leaders be removed from the cabinet. [2]

With the world at war, the vision of United States Department of State officials was colored by temporary emotion.   Their
doubts were fed by anti-Semitic propaganda published in La

101

Calle and other MNR periodicals; Bolivian admiration of Adolf Hitler and authoritarian rule in the 1930s and early years of World War II; MNR efforts to cut off Jewish immigration to Bolivia, especially in the restrictive immigration bill of September 1942; and alleged early ties between the MNR and the regime of Juan Domingo Perón in neighboring Argentina. All of these factors caused the United States Department of State to participate in the trumped-up "Nazi putsch" charge of July 1941, in which the MNR was unjustly incriminated.

Anti-Semitism appeared relatively late in Bolivia but had always been just below the surface of the nation's life waiting to be exploited. With very few Jewish residents, the country was among the first in Latin America to open its doors in June 1938 to European Jews displaced by the Nazi holocaust. Under the young military leader Germán Busch, Bolivia welcomed Jewish agricultural settlers. Yet friction was bound to develop, as the Jews abandoned the few bleak agricultural colonies that were actually established to migrate to the cities, [3] where they competed with small entrepreneurs.

When Nazi-inspired agitation developed, Busch banned in May 1939 the wearing of insignias and "the propaganda of international political doctrines." [4] Admiration for the Third Reich permeated the ranks of Bolivian Army officers, however, who had been trained by German General Hans Kundt before the Chaco War, and the postwar military regimes highly esteemed authoritarian rule. Bolivia was the first country in the Americas to recognize the fascist rule of Francisco Franco in Spain and later to applaud the conquest of Abyssinia by Italy. [5] In Bolivia itself, Busch abolished the elected Convention and established a dictatorship on April 24, 1939.

One of the most fervent admirers of the German and Italian totalitarian systems was the young journalist Roberto Hinojosa. Although he was exiled in Mexico during the Toro and Busch regimes (1936-39), his books and polemical tracts were read and discussed in Bolivia. As his enchantment with the Mexican Revolution faded, Hinojosa embraced more and more ardently the National Socialism unfolding in Germany. He despised the self-styled "military socialism" implanted in Bolivia after the Chaco War, calling the proposed reforms "flowers of painted paper, nothing more." The call to patriotism by the Bolivian army disgusted him because "our nationhood consists of nothing more than the flag, the national hymn and an illiteracy rate of 90 percent." [6]

More than anything else, the attraction of Nazism for Hinojosa lay in its possible power to oppose the United States, for whom he blamed all the ills of Latin America. In 1935, for example, he wrote, "The revolutions, the barracks revolts, the tyrannies, the wars--the Chaco War--all our history of blood and shame points to Yankee imperialism as responsible, which became the owner of our lands and the conscience of our political traitors." [7] By 1936 Hinojosa was denouncing the "hypocritical Hebrews" and the "absurd Jews" who he believed controlled international capitalism. He saw as his mission "to enunciate in journalistic form the decadence of capitalist civilization..." [8] Finally, before spewing his anti-Semitic hatred from Radio Illimani during the Villarroel regime, Hinojosa published two pamphlets on The Myth of the Rhine (The Life, Passion and Glory of Adolf Hitler) and Ecce Homo (The Life, Passion and Miracles of Adolf Hitler). [9]

A figure of Bolivian life largely unknown outside his native country--despite the fact that many United States libraries contain some of his books--Hinojosa deserves closer attention. Born in Cochabamba, he studied in Buenos Aires where he formed a group to attack the town of Villazón on the Bolivian-Argentine border in June 1930 where they seized the customs house and $40,000 before being repulsed. This was Hinojosa's grand gesture as a revolutionist because for the rest of his life he was a wandering pariah, publishing articles and books and seeking a fame which eluded him. To Augusto Céspedes, the young Bolivian was "a leftist adventurer...who did not have any very solid method." [10] To Tristán Marof, Hinojosa was also "an adventurer who had no real ideas." He was an elemental individual who produced no serious works, in Marof's view, or any that had profound content. On the contrary, Hinojosa's works of propaganda were not intended to be serious; they were written for the people; they were the inconsistent works of a street orator. Nevertheless Hinojosa, who was related to Villarroel and thus became a member of the MNR, did have a great facility with words and became a demagogue for the MNR cause. [11] Victor Paz Estenssoro was more charitable toward Hinojosa, describing him as "one of the first of the absolute left in Bolivia" although he was a "non-systematic" Communist. [12]

Hinojosa first burst upon the Bolivian consciousness with the foolhardy raid upon Villazón in 1930. Recounting the event five years later, El Diario denounced the "Communist Roberto Hinojosa" who had launched the attack on Villazón during the last days of President Hernando Siles. Since that time, the Tribunal of Military Justice had been investigating the "Vandalic sacking" of the town before Hinojosa and others fled to Argentina--the beginning of a fourteen-year exile for the young adventurer that would take him to revolutionary Mexico. The military court designated Hinojosa as "the instigator and intellectual author, the same who deceived his comrades, making them believe he would distribute riches to them and other advantages which he came to avail himself..." The labor union of Villazón involved in the escapade was absolved of guilt, and its director Domingo Ampuero was placed in liberty. [13]

Later, La Nación published a short biographical sketch of Hinojosa, describing him as an "international fighter" who arrived back in Bolivia in February 1944 where his propaganda harangues over Radio Illimani were to result in his death when Villarroel was overthrown two years later. Always somewhat embarrassing to the MNR in later years because of his adamant anti-Semitic position and flirtation with Nazism, Hinojosa was commended upon his return to Bolivia in 1944 for his "peregrinations through the jails of America as a consequence of his intransigent revolutionary position." [14]

Although La Calle, the gutter scrapper of MNR journalism, was the most vociferous champion of anti-Semitism in Bolivia, anti-Semitic material also appeared in other newspapers in La Paz. Thus, El Diario, spokesman for the Patiño mining interests, printed a sub-headline to a story on the personality of Hitler in 1935, "Thanks to the clear-sightedness and energy of its leader, Germany is on her way toward a better and greater future to which she has unquestionable rights..." [15] Earlier, El Universal, the newspaper which served as the nation's conscience by opposing the Chaco War, expressed hatred toward the Jews quite early. In 1933, for example, three years before La Calle was founded, El Universal was declaring: "the German Jews have been treated as they treated Our Lord Jesus Christ..." But, the newspaper continued, if the German anti-Semites forced all Jews to leave, "they will obtain no other end except to lose the little gold which that country still has, since it is absolutely impossible for a Jew to move even a meter without carrying with him all the gold that he keeps." [16] El Universal also printed editorials titled "Undesirable elements" and stories with such headlines as, "Russian and Polish Jews are becoming the owners of La Paz." [17]

It was La Calle, however, that launched the most virulent anti-Semitic campaign which Bolivia had ever known. Anti-Jewish jokes were appearing in "Dark Alley" only ten days after La Calle began publication in June 1936. [18] On the other hand, in its beginning months of publication La Calle supported Busch strongly enough to endorse his open-door policy on Jewish immigration. An editorial supported Minister of Immigration Julio Salmón's statement that there should be no racial or religious barriers to immigration in the underpopulated Latin America countries, with this disclaimer: "Semitism constituted into an international capitalistic organization is dangerous for any people, whether they be young or old, but the mass of

Jewish workers who, fleeing from racist persecution seek in Bolivia a field for their activities, will not be anything other than a factor of indispensable progress." The editorial concluded, "In some political entities...they boast of anti-Semitism. This is an affair exclusively of Europe, whose pernicious influences should not reach us, who have more important things of our own to occupy us." [19]

Despite this opening note of good will, La Calle soon became extremely critical of the Jewish immigrants and insensitive to their fate in Europe. In 1938, for example, a headline on the front page stated, FIFTY THOUSAND JEWS ARRESTED IN GERMANY, while an inside editorial merely criticized Mussolini for closing the Rotary Clubs in Italy. [20] By 1939 La Calle was clamoring for an end to Jewish immigration to Bolivia. In one article, the newspaper asked, "Where are the rich Jews who came to our country? In Bolivia there remain only the Semites stripped of their fortunes." [21]

La Calle's editorial campaign against further Jewish immigration was successful: on April 30, 1940, Busch's open door was slammed shut by his successor Peñaranda, but the matter did not stop there. An editorial later that month deplored the arrivals of Jews by train in La Paz, and another in March 1940 commented on "the popular alarm" that swept Bolivia as Jews continued to enter the country. [22] In August 1940 an article with the screaming headline MORE JEWS...MORE JEWS... denounced the "uncontainable" immigration of Semites and concluded, "It is urgent that the representatives of all localities promote a parliamentary action to save the country from this pestilence." [23]

Time and time again, however, the MNR deputies were outvoted in Congress on immigration policy. They failed to block a supreme resolution allowing the entry of 4,000 Jewish families. [24] They dissented again when a colonization project was proposed for the northern tropical department of the Beni which would allow the admission of technical and professional Jews under forty who would agree to stay there for five years. [25] And when a bill in the Chamber of Deputies would have authorized Jewish immigrants already in Bolivia to bring their families from abroad, La Calle demurred:

The humanitarianism of the honorable deputies could be employed better...[such as] preoccupying themselves as yesterday with the situation of the Bolivian worker and with the fate of the Indian of whose miseries certain Jew-favoring representatives speak with contempt, while they are moved to tears when they remember the Semites. [26]

The trickle of Jews to landlocked Bolivia on the roof of the world brought in its chain a government scandal which provided a heyday for the opposition press. In May 1939, some 3,000 persons were reported to have entered the country with illegal documents; permits allegedly had been sold in Europe for 200 to 1,500 dollars each. Thus, a sum of four million dollars had been mulcted from the Jews. When the scandal broke, it created a furor in the press which promptly dubbed it THE JEWISH AFFAIRE, the front-page banner headline of INTI when the matter was first reported on December 3, 1940. La Calle charged that it was the venality of the Jews who had corrupted Bolivian consuls Eduardo Díez de Medina and Carlos Virriera Pacieri, both dismissed after a congressional interpellation. [27] Díez de Medina, former minister of foreign affairs, signed 1,200 blank visas in advance, with the names of the applicants to be filled in later upon payment of the fees. When he read his defense before the Chamber of Deputies on December 5, 1940, he quoted a La Paz reporter who had written, "There are each day [as results of Jewish immigration] new cafés, clean bars, beauty parlors, establishments where the desires of the client are anticipated." But he was interrupted by shouts from public spectators in the galleries, "We want potatoes! We don't want cafés or beauty parlors!" [28] Thereafter, verification of passports was put under charge of the Hicem Association in Paris, a permanent central agency for Jewish migration. [29]

In this charged atmosphere of fear and denunciation, it was not difficult to go one step further and claim that the anti-Semitism of the MNR revealed that it was affiliated with or influenced by the German Nazi movement. Leading the attack on this front was the independent socialist Gustavo A. Navarro who had adopted the Bulgarian pen-name Tristán Marof in honor of the Soviet Revolution. Marof had first awakened the Bolivian conscience with his works Renacimiento del Alto Perú (1918), La justicia del Inca (1926) and La tragedia del altiplano (1934), which first called for agrarian reform and nationalization of the tin mines. Always a loner, Marof refused to serve in the administration of Busch, although he was invited to do so by Carlos Montenegro; later, Marof was confined to Fortín Campero for four months during Busch's presidency. From the very beginning, Marof opposed the MNR, which he denounced as opportunistic and reformist, and which he claimed had stolen all his ideas. [30]

Marof was founder of the Partido Socialista Obrero de Bolivia (Socialist Worker Party of Bolivia), which elected four deputies in 1940, and from that base he denounced what he called "creole Nazism" in a broadside of 1941. Leveling his considerable rhetorical powers against the MNR, Marof charged that the MNR deputies had formed a bloque nazificanate in the

106

Chamber of Deputies since 1940, parading under the name of Nationalists, but actually receiving instructions from the German legation and forming a fifth column. Marof also charged that Paz Estenssoro was plotting revolution with the German Ambassador Ernst Wendler, and he attacked Walker Guevara Arze who supposedly declared, "In order to free ourselves from the Anglo-Yankee imperialism, it is necessary to ally ourselves with the 'German imperialism.'" In the 1941 broadside, Marof denounced the personal attacks upon him in "the Nazi daily," La Calle, which he referred to as "that newspaper without talent, written by frustrated and adventurous literary small fry without scruples..." He also declared, "It is an old and known system of Nazi propaganda to discredit by every means the socialist leaders who oppose their designs." [31]

The most sensational attack upon the MNR, however, for its alleged Nazi sympathies centered on the so-called "putsch Nazi" of July 20, 1941. The Peñaranda government cashiered Major Elías Belmonte, the Bolivian military attaché in Berlin, for allegedly conspiring with Ernst Wendler, the German ambassador in La Paz, to stage a Nazi-style coup in Bolivia. Peñaranda officials produced a photostatic copy of a letter from Belmonte to Wendler, stating that the time had come for the coup. Recent research has shown that the copy of the letter, given to the Bolivian government by the United States Department of State, was actually faked by British Intelligence in an effort to solidify opposition in South America to the Axis powers in World War II. [32] The forged letter did not mention the MNR, but the party's leaders were rounded up and imprisoned for four months, and its three opposition publications--La Calle, Semanario Busch and INTI--were closed, along with La Prensa and Radio America in Cochabamba. Augusto Céspedes has debunked the "putsch Nazi" in four separate writings spanning thirty years, and it is from this combined denial by an MNR insider that the present account is drawn. [33]

Significantly, the alleged "putsch Nazi" occurred within forty days of the founding of the MNR, indicating that it probably was used to quell this new opposition. [34] Expecting a crackdown, La Calle denounced the upcoming plot against the MNR on May 11 and June 29, 1941. General Demetrio Ramos, minister of government, resigned rather than be a party to the plot. In the meantime, the Peñaranda government denied the existence of a Nazi complot to defeat the government and impose a totalitarian regime. [35] On the other hand, the Argentine newspapers La Prensa and Crítica jumped the gun and claimed the "putsch" was put down a month before it happened. John Lehar of the Associated Press reported that Peñaranda had dismissed all German military training missions, and that the German colony in La Paz was stirring up agitation against

Standard Oil, whose property had been confiscated in 1937. In a later dispatch, he reported, "It is said that the opposition leftists are aided by the German community." Actually, however, according to Céspedes, the Germans did not control more than 3 percent of Bolivian commerce, and the last German mission had left Bolivia in 1927. [36]

The question of Nazi infiltration in Bolivia through the MNR triggered a virulent journalistic duel in La Paz. Ultima Hora, owned by Jewish tin magnate Mauricio Hochschild, called the MNR organ La Calle "the Nazi morning paper," which responded by labeling Ultima Hora "the Jewish afternoon daily." In answer to a specific taunt from the latter, La Calle replied, "We are not anti-Semites, but neither are we circumcised." [37] La Razón in June 1941 declared that 90 percent of Bolivian Army officers were Nazis. And on July 20, 1941, the day of the alleged "putsch," the Aramayo organ declared that it had been warning the public about Nazi infiltration for two years, and all of its dire predictions had come true. La Razón, which had not opposed the closing of the three MNR organs in La Paz on July 20, stated on July 25 that under the state of siege "there will be no press censorship... This measure, which proves the principles of respect for liberty of the press by the government, will bring greater truthfulness to the news that will be published." [38]

Even more serious for the free flow of information was the imprisonment of three editors and writers of La Calle--Armando Arce, Augusto Céspedes and Carlos Montenegro--which was designed to have a chilling effect on future propaganda efforts. Moreover, the government decreed that salaries of all workers on the closed publications must continue to be paid, and the three journalists were hustled off to internment in the interior for four months. [39]

The "putsch Nazi" also caused an international furor. At the time, news reports from Bolivia conjectured that if the complot had succeeded, World War II would have been brought to America because neighboring states would have invaded Bolivia. [40] This is precisely the effect which British Intelligence had wanted, for the forged Belmonte letter concluded that a coup in Bolivia would eventually engulf all of South America "and we shall commence an era of purification, order and work." [41] The authors of the letter had gauged the tenor of their time correctly, for most of the hemisphere's press did not question the authenticity of the charges made by the Peñaranda government. Critica of Buenos Aires, for example, called Belmonte "the Aymará traitor to the American cause." [42]

Since the "putsch Nazi" momentarily silenced the MNR propaganda effort and was to affect the later combativeness of the movement, it is useful to examine it in greater detail--and from an MNR perspective. On July 19, 1942, La Calle printed an anniversary retrospective which for the first time presented the MNR's account of the encounter. On July 20, 1941, the account stated, El Diario broke the news by printing that the Peñaranda government had documents proving that German Ambassador Wendler was paying for propaganda in La Calle and Radio Nacional, and was suborning Army officials to stage a Nazi putsch and install Major Elías Belmonte, military attaché of the Bolivian embassy in Berlin, in the presidency. Until he could arrive from Germany, "a general" would hold power. El Diario declared that the totalitarian methods of this government would have been "concentration camps, torture, cancellation of [freedom of the] press and of parliament...[and] obligatory work." [43]

With the declaration of a state of siege, Carabineros occupied the streets of La Paz, closing all entertainment places and preventing crowds from gathering. Radios later announced that Céspedes, Arce and Ondarza had been imprisoned in La Paz, and Montenegro and Schrott in Cochabamba. General Candia, minister of defense, flew to Cochabamba on July 20 and returned to La Paz two days later, declaring to La Razón that an indictment (sumario) would determine which officers were in contact with the German legation. Ultima Hora, however, published a later interview with Candia in which he denied that any military elements were involved in the alleged putsch. [44]

When news of the putsch broke, there began what Céspedes later referred to as a drama by Pirandello, [45] with all of the newspapers of La Paz joining in the act. Minister Murillo told the press that the government had "abundant documentation" of the putsch. To La Razón he said, "For the government to have taken a measure of this magnitude, it must be backed with irrefutable documents." La Razón considered the unmasking of the putsch "a journalistic triumph." The newspaper declared that the plot had been intended to provoke armed conflict between Peru and Ecuador, and to cancel contracts for tin and wolfram and send them to Germany. ("Surely by submarines from Lake Titicaca," Paz Estenssoro commented during the later congressional interpellation.) The remainder of the La Paz press followed the lead of La Razón. Ultima Hora, which asserted the putsch originally was set for July 28, said the plan had been prepared by the Gestapo, and added, "All of the anti-democratic campaign [by the MNR press] was merely a means of dissimulating the true intention of submitting [national control to Germany] by the Army official Belmonte and his Bolivian civil and military friends, together with those who [already] had surrendered their body and soul to German Nazism." [46]

To counter such stringent attacks, the MNR issued a broadside on July 22, two days after the arrest of its three leading journalists, which was the first piece of propaganda to bear the party's initials. Headlined WE AGAINST THE TRAITORS, the document denounced the "coarse and ridiculous intrigue plotted by the orphans of popular support [the Peñaranda government] who betrayed the country in war and betray it in peace." The broadside, which bore the names of eight of the founders of the MNR, [47] concluded with what amounted to the MNR's declaration of independence:

> The impostors who domineer the country cannot conceive that a political group can act without a foreign master. The MNR recognizes neither bosses nor masters. Its leaders are not marked by the sign of ignominy or servility or treason. Neither robbery nor business, nor the opulence of the great rosquera lifestyle, based on the salaries distributed by foreign capitalism, stains its conduct. [48]

It required courage in the Bolivia of Peñaranda to sign one's name to such a document, and for their impassioned declaration the eight men were arrested and detained incomunicado by the police. The new arrests did not convince the public that a complot had existed, however, and so the government decided to make public the photostatic copy of the Belmonte "letter," which was published as an engraving in El Diario. A year later, La Calle called the effect counterproductive, for some hyphenations and Spanish usages in the concocted letter were clearly not authentic. By July 23, even El Diario began to have its doubts. The only physical evidence the government could produce was a radio receiver found hidden in the Transocean news agency. Also, the claim that the MNR members had planned to attack the government on bicycles was met with laughter in the streets of La Paz. Hugo Salmón, chief clerk of the ministry of government, had resigned in protest on July 21. El Diario commented that although some believed the Nazis were involved with national elements, "others think [the incident] dealt only with a stratagem to displace the opposition..." [49]

When Congress reconvened on August 6, 1941, the MNR deputies who had escaped the wrath of the police launched an inquiry directed to the ministers of government, foreign relations, treasury and economy. Parliamentary immunity had not saved MNR deputy Rafael Otazo from the arrests following the appearance of the broadside, but he was released in time to return for the opening of Congress. During the round-up of the MNR leaders, Paz Estenssoro was in his hometown of Tarija, but he quickly returned to La Paz to lead the interpellation.

In the course of the heated debate on the alleged putsch, the four MNR deputies gained support from other elements of the political spectrum. On the right, Enrique Hertzog, senator from La Paz and leader of the Genuine Republicans, wrote a letter to Espada, minister of the treasury, on July 22, in which he declared, "All of the persons with whom I have talked, or at least nine out of every ten, do not believe in the fiction that the dailies are telling and many are inclined to think that the Government, in order to free itself of certain enemies, has found no better means than inventing this tale of Nazism." On the left, PIR deputy Alfredo Arratia said in the debate, "I am also with those deputies who do not believe in the Nazi putsch...I believe rather that this has been invented in order to exclude from the political arena a part of the opposition that was characterizing itself by the violence of its attacks." [50]

The four ministers questioned all assured Congress that abundant documentation would back up the government's action, but none was ever forthcoming. On August 11, the Chamber of Deputies, composed almost entirely of representatives of the traditional parties, voted to ask the executive to turn over its proof of the alleged putsch to the recently formed congressional committee named to investigate "anti-Bolivian" activities. In a five-page response, Peñaranda refused to do so.

Blocked on that front, the MNR pressed for executive justification of the state of siege imposed on July 19 but not legalized by Peñaranda until July 31. In the congressional interpellation, Paz Estenssoro derided "the invention of the Nazi putsch [which] demonstrates a Machiavellian intelligence." He argued that the MNR, which was not even mentioned in the Belmonte letter, was dragged into the Nazi witch hunt simply because the party had been denouncing further tax concessions to the Big Three mining interests:

With faith in the campaigns of the independent press removed, [the government] could fix new rebates to the mining industry; it could fix 'with equity' the tax for the heirs of the first millionaire of South America, Simón I. Patiño... Moreover, the government found an excellent occasion to castigate certain journalists, who had exceeded in their festive attacks on some ministers, with a double sanction: confinement and a financial penalty that obliges the closed dailies to continue paying salaries to their workers as long as the closure lasts.

111

Paz Estenssoro also turned the charges back upon the accusers, declaring, "The methods which the Executive is [now] employing are 100 percent Nazi and he uses them in the name of Democracy." [51]

When the other MNR leaders were released four months later from confinement in tropical villages of the East, where Montenegro had continued to write under the pseudonym of Kisiabó, [52] they waged a campaign for exoneration. In the pages of La Calle, which was allowed to resume publication, they pointed out that they had never been indicted for anything, and they would welcome the chance to clear their names in court. They also issued the second bulletin or broadside of the MNR, this one addressed to Alberto Ostria Gutiérrez, the minister of government who had recently been reassigned as ambassador to Chile. Headlined LISTEN, SR. OSTRIA, the handbill implored the chancellor to present his proof against the MNR before leaving for Santiago. "You slander us and go away," it stated, concluding that if Ostria did not present the "abundant and irrefutable documents" the government claimed it had in its possession to back up the Belmonte letter, Ostria would convert himself from "a prestigious personage of the conservative parties into a irresponsible and obscure intriguer." [53] But no documents were released by Ostria, who later attacked the MNR in two books that were more polemical than objective. [54]

When the Chamber of Deputies debated a new immigration bill in September 1942, the anti-Semitism of the early MNR again boiled to the surface. Introduced by MNR deputy Hernán Siles Zuazo, who was to become revolutionary president between 1956-60, the measure would have excluded all Jews, Asians and Negroes from the racially mixed country of Bolivia. For weeks, while acrimonious debate swirled around the proposal, La Calle conducted a vicious anti-Semitic campaign. [55] For example, it proclaimed that if colonization amendments to the bill were to be enacted, "Soon we will have to lament the demolishing effects of new inundations of 'farmers' with very beaked noses, so hooked that thousands of kilometers away they seem to have snagged certain 'fathers of the country' to prepare the new assault on the promised land." [56] This was a reference to the Jewish passport affaire of 1939 which again became ammunition for the MNR propagandists. La Calle commented, "With the cold sophistry of Nazism [the opposition] is trying to defend the Israelites. This is a cunning desire to blind the eyes of the people so the business of selling passports to Jews may continue." [57] La Calle also declared, "Only totalitarian means will permit new Jewish immigration to Bolivia. The immense national majority, the foundation of democracy, opposes and repudiates the ominous big-nosed immigrants." [58] A

112

headline blared, DELIVERY OF THE COUNTRY TO THE JEWS IS
PLOTTED BEHIND THE PEOPLE'S BACKS. In the story itself,
La Calle warned that 40,000 Jews were waiting "to fall like a
ravenous invading horde upon the cities of Bolivia." [59]
Although articles such as this bore no bylines, José Caudros
Quiroga wrote many of them. [60]

Among the capital's newspapers, only Ultima Hora, the
afternoon daily owned by Jewish tin Magnate Mauricio Hochschild, sought to stem the tide of abuse. [61] The newspaper
countered, for instance, that it was unfortunate there were no
mirrors in the Chamber of Deputies so the nation's lawmakers
could see how ridiculous it was for Bolivia to seek only white or
Christian immigrants. Satirical thrusts such as this appeared
in the column, El gorro de dormir ("Nightcap"), which also
observed that if only racial purity were to prevail in Bolivia,
"Parliament will have to remain without a quorum." [62]   On
another day, the column published mock telegrams from Hitler,
Goebbels and the Gestapo congratulating the Chamber of Deputies on the immigration bill under consideration. The one
supposedly from Goebbels concluded, "Bolivia is preparing this
noble land to offer selected Aryan examples. It is necessary
now [once Jews are excluded] to clean out the Indians." A
"telegram" from the Holy Father to Catholic deputy priests
Tumiri Javier and Tomás Chávez Lobatón, who supported the
excluding immigration bill, stated, "Permit me to remind you
that Christ was a Jew and the Catholic Church does not permit
persecution of races. You had better exchange your clerical
collars for Black Shirts." [63] Editorially, Ultima Hora commented:

> There is in Bolivia no political or religious or econ-
> omic or social reason for the furious anti-Semitism
> that some elements are developing. What is the
> source of this? Follow the string and you will arrive
> at the ball of yarn of Nazi action and propaganda,
> which exist despite all the prohibitions. [64]

The Hochschild organ sought to prove this. When a
deputy cited the spurious Protocols of the Elders of Zion to
document what he considered to be the Jewish menace, Ultima
Hora claimed he had obtained reference to the book from the
pamphlet Illustrative and Informative Material for Orators published by the German Office of Propaganda. Ultima Hora also
pointed out that the Protocols had been declared "immoral and
pornographic literature" by the pre-Nazi Nuremberg Court of
Justice in 1931 and by a Swiss court in 1935. When Henry
Ford's The International Jew also was cited as an authoritative
source, Ultima Hora published in Spanish the full retraction and
apology made by Ford in the Dearborn, Michigan, Independent

113

when he withdrew the four-volume work from circulation in 1929. [65] When Deputy Chacón affirmed in the session of October 1, 1942, that there were 25,000 Jews already in Bolivia, Ultima Hora reported that according to the Ministry of Immigration, there were only 3,955. "We have here," commented the newspaper acidly, "a deputy who has been defrauded by his professor of arithmetic." [66]

La Calle won the opening skirmish, however, as the restrictive immigration bill was passed by the Chamber of Deputies in a vote of 41 to 24 on September 21, 1942. This perhaps attests in part to the increased influence of La Calle, for a similar measure had been defeated 34 to 17 on November 12, 1941. [67] The 1942 bill later died in the Senate, but the entire episode was important as it indicated that the MNR was willing to seize upon any issue to boost itself to power. By selecting Jews as the scapegoat of Bolivia's profound social and economic problems, the MNR revealed its anti-Semitic bias, but that did not necessarily mean that the political party was controlled by the Germans. Nevertheless, Paz Estenssoro has expressed regret over these early tactics which he later considered unnecessary and counter-productive. [68]

Memories of the alleged Nazi putsch were revived again when the United States Department of State published its famous Blue Book on the eve of the Argentine election in 1946, charging pro-Nazi activities in Argentina and linking these to the MNR in Bolivia. Designed to hinder the presidential aspirations of Juan Domingo Perón, it actually enhanced the dictator's popularity as the Blue Book, released through the office of the United State Ambassador Spruille Braden, aroused much anti-American feeling and cinched Perón's success at the polls. On May 25, 1946, Augusto Céspedes demolished the myth of the so-called putsch and the reliability of the Blue Book in an article which covered four pages in La Calle. Interim chancellor Pinto had given Céspedes a copy of the Blue Book, which was circulated among the chanceries of the hemisphere, and asked him to comment upon it. In his reply of May 15, 1946, published ten days later in La Calle, Céspedes made these points:

• Among general criticisms of the Blue Book was the fact that phrases criticizing "pseudo-democracy" and "false and surrendering" regimes were used but "in no part of the document appears an invitation to establish a democracy pure of these opprobrious qualifiers." To criticize the kind of democracy Bolivia has known, as Céspedes had been doing in editorials in La Calle, does not deny adhesion to true democracy. Does the MNR platform use "fascist language" as the Blue Book charged? If so, Harold Lasky used it in his book Crisis of

114

Democracy; Scott Nearing used it in Democracy is Enough, and Josef Stalin, "the world-famous leader of anti-fascism," used it in his book, Fundamentals of Leninism. Céspedes also quoted Sumner Welles' speech of February 10, 1946 pledging non-intervention in the internal affairs of other countries.

• As for the concrete charges that Paz Estenssoro and the MNR were involved in the pro-Nazi activities of Major Belmonte that led to his dismissal from office and the expulsion of German Ambassador Wendler, Céspedes--after recounting all of the facts once again--concluded, "All of the foregoing demonstrates that the 'Nazi putsch' lacked reality and that only propaganda gave it an artificial life that the memorandum of the Department of State [included in the Blue Book] took seriously." The eleven MNR leaders ultimately accused of being involved in the plot were accused of being Nazis for allegedly having participated in the Nazi putsch, Céspedes pointed out, and they were accused of having participated in the putsch because they were Nazis.

• The position of La Calle also came under attack in the Blue Book, which stated that the newspaper, directed by Céspedes, had backed the MNR and in the course of 1941 came to be that party's official spokesman, receiving German subventions. It is known, the Blue Book asserted, that Paz Estenssoro received money from Nazi agents Elsner and Flosbach to carry out pro-German propaganda. Céspedes, Montenegro and José Cuadros Quiroga were said to have accompanied the MNR chief in these transactions. In his reply, Céspedes bore down heavily on the "proof" of this assertion, which said merely "It is known..." The MNR writer denounced this allegation as "a lie and a calumny."

• According to the Blue Book, La Calle during 1943 had printed MNR discourses delivered in Congress "expressing anti-Semitism, hostility to the democracies and other doctrines of Nazi origin." Céspedes, who was a careful grammarian, noted that according to the structure of this sentence, "it appears that the democracies are included among the doctrines of Nazi origin." As for the charge of anti-Semitism, Céspedes pointed out that the immigration bill was approved by the majority of the Chamber of Deputies where the MNR had only four deputies.

• The proof of the allegation that the MNR was hostile to the United States was an appendix reprinting an editorial which Céspedes had written for the July 4, 1941, issue of La Calle and which was reprinted on July 4, 1942. Céspedes had given a copy of the editorial to Allan Dawson of the United States Embassy staff in La Paz. Entitled "Bolivia and the great nation of the North," it noted the vast differences in historical rhythm, racial composition and economic force of the United States and Bolivia. The editorial continued, "that almost religious conception of democracy would result somewhat artificial as long as its benefits are not demonstrated with optimum evidence as in the model country." Therefore, the United States should recognize the autonomy of small countries and not tie political systems to mutual aid. The Bolivian people "hope that the United States before imposing a manufactured democracy which will exhaust our riches, offers rather a restorative impulse that will mobilize our productive capabilities and raise the Bolivians from the colonial condition in which they now find themselves so that they can form themselves effectively in the files of continental Democracy as a free State and not as mere vassals exploited by foreign companies." Dawson, the United States Embassy official to whom Céspedes gave his editorial, later was twice hospitalized in mental wards after his mission to Bolivia, according to Céspedes, where he offered the editorial as proof of the statements in the Blue Book, "along with other 'experts' in Bolivian questions..."

• Céspedes also pointed out that Armando Arce and not himself had always been editor of La Calle, adding that the newspaper thrived on opposing existing governments in Bolivia, having been closed by the Toro, Busch and Peñaranda regimes.

• Finally, the Blue Book said that both Céspedes and Montenegro were the principal civil adherents of Major Belmonte, calling him "the hope of Bolivia." Commented Céspedes: "It is one of the few truths that the memorandum contains. I declared that in respect to Belmonte through both public and private words."

In conclusion, Céspedes believed that the memorandum, included later in the Argentine Blue Book on the eve of Perón's election, was written by "some imaginative and sensational reporter" or it was the product of "bureaucratic routine" to justify the policy of non-recognition of the Villarroel government. Céspedes concluded, "It is not in the search for and commentaries on documents in chanceries, although they can come to amount to an enormous tonnage in brute weight, where one can find the causes and resolve the destiny of the popular revolutions of America, but in a more cordial comprehension of the characteristics of the history, the people and the economy of the semi-colonial countries." [69]

Despite the forged Belmonte letter and the exaggerated fears of the Blue Book, however, there is ample evidence that the MNR--and particularly La Calle--was considerably anti-Semitic in its formative years. Even this can be misleading, however. As Céspedes explained in a recent interview, the Germany Embassy distributed free information from the German news service, and almost all newspapers used it. "Really," Céspedes commented, "there was a sympathy in Bolivia for the cause of Germany, not for the Nazi-Fascists, but as an enemy of our oppressor, the United States. Germany was not our oppressor." [70]

Whether inspired by German propaganda or not, anti-Semitism was long a staple in the pages of La Calle and other newspapers. In 1941, for example, INTI printed a rare editorial cartoon under the heading, "The Bolivians 'Made in Judea' are moving." The caption under the cartoon stated: "Abraham, Isaac, Solomon, Jacob and [illegible] are all 'farmers,' recently arrived in the country. In order to do honor to their condition as such, they have begun 'to plant' distrust concerning 'Nazism' in order 'to harvest' later the magnificent business for which their insatiable voracity has such an appetite. They defend the 'DIMOKRACIAS" against the bad 'boilivianos.' They are very good." [71] The caption, including slurs on the manner in which the Jewish immigrants pronounced Spanish, was based mainly on the provision, believed to be widely violated, that Jews coming to Bolivia since Busch's open-door policy must become farmers in the rural areas of the country.

Again, in 1942, an editorial in La Calle lambasted the Hochschild-Aramayo consortium for objecting to the continuation of the German high school in La Paz because of alleged Nazi influence there. Commented La Calle: "What the disciples of Hochschild want is, simply, that there not be in Bolivia pedagogy nor philosophy of any kind that is not Jewish; that is to say, that which deceives systematically the youth in order to present to them the only ideal of business, usury and the utility of [precious] metal as an exclusive objective in life." [72]

The temporary union of the Hochschild and Aramayo interest also brought fears that the Jewish entrepreneur would dominate the policy of La Razón, founded in 1917, long an organ of the Republican party, and more recently the property of Aramayo. On the anniversary of its founding, La Calle printed an article headlined, "Born Bolivian and now internationalized, the organ of the Jewish consortium [La Razón] completes 25 years." The opening paragraph asserted, "According to the Jewish technique of universal domination, the press is the instrument that should act in their hands in order to manipulate national opinion. The Jew prefers not to found a newspaper, but rather to exercise his influence through the means of one which already has a national reputation." Thus, since the creation of the Hochschild-Aramayo consortium, La

Razón had been converted into "a defensive spokesman of the commercial interests, into a mercantile agency, into an office of blacklists and, finally, into a propagandistic enterprise for the transactions of the H-A corporation..." [73]   On another occasion, a subhead in La Calle declared, "The 'Nazis,' the Communists and even the democrats conspire, but not us, says the Jewish afternoon newspaper." [74]

Meanwhile, La Calle kept up a steady barrage of attacks on the continued favorable policy on Jewish immigration. A headline in early 1942 blared, 10,000 JEWS WILL ENTER THE COUNTRY UNDER THE NAME OF 'CHRISTIAN POLES!' Shortly thereafter, another headline declaimed, STOP THE PERNICIOUS IMMIGRATION! Subheads declared, "On the proximate elections depends whether the Bolivian citizens can fight against the invasion of the Hebrews...! The people should know the deputies that defended the Bolivians and those who voted to bring in more Jews." [75]

While José Cuadros Quiroga wrote most of these attacks in the pages of La Calle, the anti-Semitic virus affected others as well. Even Carlos Montenegro, the most intellectual member of the early MNR coterie, was not immune. Commenting in 1942 on two recent books, Stefan Zweig's Brazil, Land of the Future and Emil Ludwig's biography of Bolívar, Montenegro wrote, "These two Jewish writers have very much to write about concerning their race, their religion, and even Germany, the country from which they have been thrown out as undesirables." Zweig in his book saw Brazil as a haven for the displaced Jews of the world. Montenegro rejoined, "To call it [Brazil], 'land of the future' is inevitable for a Hebrew." Most of Montenegro's attack was leveled upon Ludwig, however, who in an earlier book on Abraham Lincoln had said that the Emancipator was "assassinated on Good Friday, like a prophet." Montenegro asked, "Who was the prophet assassinated on Good Friday? Jesus Christ! His assassins were the Jews who crucified him for religious reasons." Montenegro could easily have demolished Ludwig's condescending and ethnocentric account of Bolívar on its own demerits, but instead he descended to attack the author's religion, even dragging up the superficial and historically unsound belief that the Jews were responsible for the death of Jesus. As for the emancipator of South America, Montenegro wrote, "The Jews have always felt a profound aversion for Bolívar. Karl Marx denigrates him with passion, accusing him of being a traitor, a coward, an ambitious man, enemy of the people... The fact is that Bolívar is the triumph of the mestizo man, the American, and as such he didn't need to be 'the elect of God' to sack and enslave free men, as the Jews do as the [so-called] superior race." In conclusion, the MNR writer declared, "Ludwig and Zweig come to prepare the

118

soil for the poppies of their Jewish drug, mortal for the liberty of the spirit." [76]

On every possible occasion, La Calle seized upon racial, religious or ethnic identifications in its vehement anti-Semitic crusade. In 1942, for example, headlines proclaimed, JEWISH COMMUNISTS MIXED UP IN POLITICS ARE SWEPT FROM THE ARGENTINE TERRITORY; and SEMITIC INCRUSTATION IN THE PUBLIC OFFICES. [77] On another occasion, the newspaper headlined an editorial "National sovereignty against the Jewish enterprise," referring to the vote in the Chamber of Deputies of 40-37 to annul elections in Sud Lopez where a Hochschild candidate apparently had won. [78] Another headline, written with the irony with which La Calle was famous, declared BOLIVIA CELEBRATES THE JEWISH NEW YEAR PLEASED AND EXHILARATED, while the subhead read, "The sons of Israel redeemed us from nudity and barbarism." [79] Humorous jibes also were taken against Jews, as in the column, Callejón Oscuro ("Dark Alley") which printed such items as: "If the Honorable [Demetrio] Canelas does not eject the galleries full of Hebrew girls, these will descend to the floor to sell cigarets or other articles necessary to the masculine sex." [80]

Remaining as a backdrop to these sallies was the question of what was going to be done about Jewish immigration. When Peñaranda slammed shut Busch's "open-door" to Jewish immigrants on April 30, 1940, he added that the government should formulate a new immigration law. Defeated in 1942, with the aid of the MNR, the project surfaced again during the administration of Gualberto Villarroel. The problem of identification with anti-Semitic elements delayed recognition of the Villarroel regime for six months and continued to plague the new president. In 1944 after a dispatch by Agencia Overseas stated that Villarroel's government indeed was anti-Semitic, the president issued a stout denial. He said that such a thing would be "absurd" in mestizo Bolivia and that criticism of the Jews had been directed only against the sale of passports and the fact that not even half a percent of the Jewish immigrants had actually become farmers. [81] In October 1945 the project of Jewish immigration was resurrected when Villarroel sent a proposed law with a special message to the Convention.

But an article accompanying the publication of these items in La Calle expressed fear that the new project would open up the passport and other official frauds again in the name of "humanitarianism." Jews were an undesirable element, La Calle stressed again, citing terrorist Jews in Palestine and anti-Nazis sacking Jewish shops in Cairo. [82] In 1946, shortly before the overthrow of Villarroel, Ultima Hora wrote, "It should not cause surprise that between the MNR, which ridicules and persecutes the Jews according to the ideas of Hitler, and the PIR which repudiates the struggle of races, democracy has made a pact with the PIR." La Calle countered by printing the text of the PIR project of September 21, 1942, which would have moved all "agricultural" Jews from the cities to permanent concentration camps in the countryside, or would have expelled them from Bolivia. [83]

In the popular mind, the question of anti-Semitism and pro-Nazi sympathies seemed closely linked. The propaganda could flow either way. In 1943, for example, Javier Paz Campero, leader of the Unified Socialists, declared in the Chamber of Deputies that it was his party's "honorable mission also to defend the Jews or Semites, that noble persecuted race that is the pride of humanity." Augusto Céspedes, answering Paz Campero in the columns of La Calle, pointed out that nine members of the Unified Socialists had voted for complete expulsion of the Jews from Bolivia a year before. Did that make them Nazis? Céspedes continued, "The destroyed ones of Judaism, thrown out of Europe by Hitler, who have arrived in Bolivia do not constitute for this country anything but a parasitic group that begins by contending for the necessities of life with the middle and working classes [and ends up] consolidating itself in a new exploitative class that will weigh, along with the others, upon the Bolivian people." In all fairness, it should be noted that in this article Céspedes denounced both the Allies and Germany as war progressed around the globe. He derided those Bolivians who repeated "the formulas of foreign imperialism that, some with the name of 'Democracy' and other with the name of 'New Order,' fight for the raw materials and the enslavement of the peoples with emerging economies, without hitting the nail on the head concerning their national necessities, in fact rejecting the identification of our own problems." [84]

Not all the resentment stemming from a backward and stagnant economy and a highly stratified social structure was directed against the Jews during the Villarroel period, however. There were other scapegoats, notably the Masonic Lodge. Although this secret fraternal order had played an important part in the Bolivian movement for independence from Spain, by the mid-Twentieth Century it had lost its charm. The wealth and social position of members of the order created suspicion in the eyes of the MNR leaders and their followers. After a concerted editorial campaign in 1944 by La Calle, the Convention voted to bar Masons from serving on the Supreme Court. [85] Even after that success, the campaign continued. Once again, distrust and hatred were spewed forth from the columns of the MNR newspaper. On one occasion, for example, a headline proclaimed, THE MASONIC LODGES HAVE CONTROL OF THE

COUNTRY'S ECONOMY. "--But 'La Razón' compares them to the Christianity of Rome...!" [86] Again, a headline read, SMOKE SCREEN OF MASONRY. "--All of the powerful men [are said to have been] Masons, but Masonry [is said to be] harmless. But in the present time the Masonic organization has gained control of the mechanism of the Bolivian state in service of the international plutocracy." [87] Critics of the MNR noted that Masons were being purged in Germany, too, where Hitler claimed them to be a secret homosexual organization, but in Bolivia the conflict seems to have been class in nature: the well-born or well-to-do gravitated toward the Masonic lodge, which was also outside the traditional Catholic culture of Bolivia.

Noting the pungent duels with scapegoats in the MNR press does not answer the central question, however, as to how the incipient party felt about the Axis themselves. After all, anti-Semitism existed in the world long before the rise of the Third Reich, and many people in the United States and elsewhere were anti-Semitic without being pro-Nazi. From the beginning, however, it can be noted that there was a decided sympathy in La Calle for the Axis powers, especially Germany. In some respects this propaganda was an effort to see the complexities of the world rather than to reduce everything to simplistic terms. In 1940, for example, the year before the MNR was formed, La Calle was saying:

> It is becoming a little false [for] the propaganda made by certain news agencies to assure that in the present war is being decided the destiny of liberty and right on one side and that of violence and barbarism on the other. The epoch of 1914 has already passed in which such formulas were used. The present war is not precisely against the democracy that certain empires would defend, but rather a readjustment that Germany should unavoidably seek in order to exist. [88]

INTI, the independent newspaper edited by Hernán Siles Zuazo, was rapturous in its praise for National Socialism in Germany; on the eighth anniversary of Hitler's assumption of power, the newspaper declared in 1941 that Bolivia, with its great territorial losses throughout its history, had much to learn from liebensraum. The editorial, entitled "The lesson of Hitler," compared the Third Reich to the French Revolution and continued:

> The lesson of Hitler and of the New Germany is a lesson of optimism, of saving energy and of a blind necessity in triumph, because only the force that

engenders this and only the triumph [itself] form the propitious atmosphere for the development of an ample possibility of life... The victory of this war is unquestionable because that victory has been created in the total and complete sacrifice of a people, great for their discipline, their learning and their will. [89]

INTI also pointed out that the concept of neutrality for the Americas raised at the conferences of Panama and Havana had been broken by lend-lease and concession of air and naval bases in the western hemisphere by the United States to "democratic" European states. [90] In 1941 INTI, replying to an editorial in El Diario denouncing fascist influence in Bolivia, declared, "The Nazi danger in the form in which that propaganda presents it does not exist [in Bolivia]." The reply added, "Those are off base who pretend that democracy is absolute and intolerant..." [91] Also in 1941, INTI charged that its criticism of the minister of the treasury lowering taxes for the great mine-owners and increasing taxes on consumer goods, borne by the middle class and poor families, had been met by the government with charges of "Nazi influence" as during the Chaco War when the newspaper had been denounced for its "Communist influence." [92] It must be added, however, that on several occasions INTI argued editorially for Bolivia's continued neutrality in World War II--perhaps the most that pro-Nazi sympathizers could hope for. [93]

For such assertions the opposition press in Bolivia wound up on the infamous blacklist of the United States Department of State. This was especially damaging to newspapers because the blacklist brought lack of newsprint as a consequence. Thus, in 1942 La Calle was constrained to render homage to the national holiday of July 16, 1809, in only its regular number of pages, although lavish editions on the date of Murillo's independence cry had been customary in Bolivia. Fighting back, La Calle editorialized, "It is certain that, even to celebrate Murillo, a newspaper of the people of La Paz must possess the benevolence of the Department of State... And the fact is, however much one speaks of Democracy, we are presently living that exile in the very womb of our country [as Murillo said about the Spanish] in which, in order to render homage to our heroes, we must count previously on the authorization of foreigners." [94] La Calle also reported that leaders of the opposition were getting anonymous telephone calls saying, "Take care because we are going to place you on the BLACK LIST." [95]

What irked the MNR leaders most was that any opposition to the Peñaranda government was considered Nazi-inspired. Thus, in June 1943, La Calle discussed this point in an article under the headline, "Everything that is rebellion is attributed to the Nazi system." The accompanying article stated, "Moreover, the people can no longer be deceived with the mystification of 'Nazi-fascism' which the democratic dissemblers use to shelter peculations and treasons. There is no Nazi-fascism against the servants of Patiño, Hochschild and Aramayo, but rather uncontainable Bolivianism in the march of a people who have placed themselves on their feet." [96]

On the other side of this political controversy were men such as Tristán Marof (Gustavo A. Navarro), who led the fight as an independent deputy and long-standing social critic against what was deemed to be Nazi infiltration into Bolivia. In 1943 he distributed a broadside headlined, "Tristán Marof denounces the vile creole Nazi calumniators." in which he declared that the MNR was Nazi. He added, "It is an old and well known technique of Nazi propaganda to discredit through every means the socialist leaders who oppose their designs." [97] Marof first made the charge that the MNR was Nazi in La Razón, which brought blistering reprisals from La Calle. The MNR newspaper condemned the independent socialist leader as ignorant and opportunistic. He had recently shaved off his beard, a well-known trademark on the Bolivian political scene, which led La Calle to attack the "bearded Trotskyite who shaved in the belief that thus he would go down better with the millionaires." [98] A few days later, Marof was again singled out for demolition as a "spy of the minister of government." He was attacked for not serving in the Chaco War, when actually he was in enforced exile, and once again for shaving his beard: "Thus as the patrón makes his pongo bathe to serve in the house, the Rosca made Marof shave his beard since his aspect was not suitable to enter and ask money at the buffets of the Rosca." In a more substantive vein, La Calle charged that Marof had received 30,000 bolivianos from the Swiss consulate for his anti-Nazi crusade. The newspaper reminded its readers that in 1941 he had voted with the Peñaranda government to mobilize the railroads and miners so their salaries could not be increased. La Calle also claimed that the government had printed and distributed 5,000 copies of Marof's pamphlet, "Nazi infiltration in Bolivia." [99]

And so the battle seesawed back and forth in the early 1940s. There were gains and setbacks for the MNR: the New York Herald Tribune called Augusto Céspedes, the gifted writer and frequent contributor to the pages of La Calle, the "No. 1 Nazi of the Bolivian government" while the magazine Tiempo of Mexico City came forth with the belief that neither Paz Estenssoro, featured on the cover, nor Céspedes was Nazi. [100] Opposition to the alleged Nazi connections of the MNR came from other international sources. In January 1944, for example, the Associated Press announced that the Free World Association was awaiting State Department approval to send a delegation of prominent Americans to Bolivia to stimulate pro-democratic elements, get them to eliminate Nazi influence, and include in the government the PIR of José Antonio Arze "and other decidedly democratic elements, partisans of the United Nations." This news story enraged La Calle, which called the contemplated trip "an open and officious intervention, denigrating and offensive for any free and sovereign nation." [101]

At home, shifting political alignments took advantage of the Nazi hysteria, which caused La Calle to comment, "Instead of liquidating Nazism, they pass the time indicating they will form 'fronts.'" [102] In 1944, La Calle ridiculed the idea that Tristán Marof's Socialist Worker Party and the Peñaranda exiles were going to form "an anti-Nazi bloc." [103] But at the same time, displaced Supreme Court members issued a manifesto charging that the National Convention was dominated by fascists. [104]

It was, however, in the international arena where charges of anti-Semitism and pro-Nazi sympathies hurt the MNR most. A prime example of this was when the renowned Mexican labor leader Vicente Lombardo Toledano came to Bolivia in late 1942 and urged his fellow workers not to fight the Jews, as had been done during the attempted excluding immigration bill. La Calle, which previously had expressed admiration for the Mexican Revolution, was furious. In a two-page, unsigned open letter headed LISTEN, LOMBARDO TOLEDANO and subheaded "And listen also all men of the left," La Calle admitted that Lombardo Toledano "has been one of the pilots of socialist thought in America" but affirmed that he knew nothing of conditions in Bolivia. "Judiasm has found in Bolivia its promised land," the newspaper stated. "Upon the tired shoulders of the Bolivian worker has fallen a new exploiter, more voracious and unmerciful than those we were enduring." La Calle added, "We cannot deny that Nazism has sent its agents to Bolivia as to all parts," but Lombardo Toledano should give details so Bolivia could "destroy those enemies." The open letter concluded, "Lombardo Toledano has not arrived here. Here has come only the expected enemy of fascism: more than that, Yankee imperialism has sent us one of its own." [105]

There were some friendly foreign voices for the Villarroel government, however. In early 1944, for example, the Chilean journalist García Hernández interviewed José Tamayo, minister of foreign relations, who denied any Nazi influence in the government. The interview was published in El Mercurio of Santiago de Chile on January 15, 1944, and concluded with a reference to "this struggle of pure Bolivianism opposite the regressive forces of an industry [tin] surrendered to the most

absurd of the capitalisms..." [106]   One foreign political group
which split on the question of Nazi influence in the MNR and
the Villarroel government was the progressive Alianza Popular
Revolucionaria Americana (APRA, Popular Revolutionary American Alliance) in nearby Peru.   While APRA writer Manuel
Seoane had been deprecating the Villarroel revolution from exile
in Chile, APRA member Luis Alberto Sánchez wrote that the
Bolivian MNR leaders had lost their Nazi fondness in 1940 when
the United States began aiding England, a development confirmed by Pearl Harbor.   Neither, Sánchez wrote, was the
Bolivian revolution "a mere echo of the Argentine revolution."
Perhaps it was in part, he added, but not completely.   But the
Argentine revolution was clerical, had strengthened neutrality,
and had not denied the political system itself.   In Bolivia, on
the other hand, "The regime [of Peñaranda] as constituted in
its final days could not subsist.   It has not lasted despite the
financial bonanza which tin [in World War II] produced." [107]

Taking sharp issue with this was the APRA indianista
novelist Ciro Alegría, whom La Calle charged with confusing the
PIR platform with that of the MNR in an article, "Facing the
Bolivian problem the PIR gives a clear reply."   In a caption to
a photograph, the original article had described "The army
organized by Germans, imbued with Nazi ideas, some of whose
chiefs do not want democracy but rather the despotic fascist
order."   Actually, the PIR had signed a pact with the "feudal
oligarchy" on May 30, 1944, La Calle pointed out, concluding
with a parting shot, "So things go, Cirito..." [108]

In the early years, the MNR played a competitive role with
the PIR (Party of the Revolutionary Left), a Marxist political
grouping formed in 1940 which played a significant part in the
radicalization of the labor movement.   The party's leader, José
Antonio Arze, exploited the so-called Nazi connections of the
MNR without offering any proof.   In 1944, La Calle pointed out
that the PIR leader had received more than 10,000 bolivianos
for attending two sessions of the National Convention--for a
total of fifteen minutes--and 50,000 bolivianos for a trip to the
United States where he told the Associated Press that the
Villarroel government was Nazi-fascist.   The director general of
propaganda in Bolivia issued a communique branding Arze as a
disloyal traitor and a liar. [109]   But Arze continued his
charges, as in February 1946 when he declared in Santiago de
Chile that the Bolivian authorities "should prepare judgments
similar to those of Nuremberg for the members of the MNR and
the army in Bolivia."   Alfonso Gumucio Reyes, the Bolivian
consul in Buenos Aires, responded that every Bolivian had the
right to express his opinion about his country but that Arze
was no Bolivian, having evaded service in the Chaco War after
he tried to blow up munition supplies in La Paz and then fled

to Peru. [110]   As things turned out, a troublesome propagandist against the MNR cause was eliminated for the time being when Arze and other PIR leaders were expelled from the party on March 20, 1946, as "servile elements, traitors to the proletarian cause and enemies of the country." [111]

In June 1946, only a month before the overthrow of Villarroel, the Mexican writer Juan Miguel de Mora published an article in Asi of Mexico City that was favorable to the MNR-Villarroel coalition. The defect of the MNR in the eyes of some observers, de Mora stated, "consisted in its furiously Bolivian character and enemy of concessions to foreign capital." In reality, the prestigious Mexican publication continued, the MNR leaders "are dangerous for the huge interest of imperialism in Latin America, not through being Nazis, but through being patriots." The attempted revolts against Villarroel on December 20, 1944, and April 29 and May 27 of 1945 bore this out, the Asi writer maintained. [112]

Despite such occasional bouquets, however, the overwhelming preponderance of press opinion in the hemisphere was against the Villarroel government. It was very difficult during the passions of World War II to shake off a "Nazi" label, and there was in fact some substance to the charges. Jacobo Libermann, later to be propaganda director for the MNR in power, recalled that the party's admiration of Hitler ended when the German forces were stopped at Stalingrad in the winter of 1942-1943. [113]   This stimulated a sharp counterattack upon the accusers of the MNR. In June 1943, La Calle declared, "Bolivia is the ayllu [communal village] where the right of the colono [serf] to present reservations to the high politics of entreguismo [surrendering natural resources] is disregarded. If he opposes [such a policy] it is because the Nazis have taught him to do so." The editorial continued, "As for the Axis, we are strangers to it through race, geography, economy and ideology. It is with the United States that Bolivia should collaborate..." [114]

The Russian victory at Stalingrad and the Allied victory in Europe produced other startling changes in Bolivian policy. In November 1945, for the first time in Bolivian history the parliament (National Convention) rendered homage to the USSR--under MNR leadership--on the twenty-eighth anniversary of the Soviet revolution. La Calle commented, "As with our National Revolution [under Villarroel], the Russian revolutionaries also were calumniated. And also the plutocratic alliances tried to destroy, in vain, the popular government of the USSR. But the formidable example of energy and sacrifice has lasted now for twenty-eight years. It is the definitive triumph of the Great Revolution of October." [115]

In similar vein, an article by Juan Pérez in La Calle in February 1946 criticized an article by Fabián Vaca Chávez in La Razón which had expressed hatred of the USSR. Turning charges of Nazi-fascist influence back upon their opponents, La Calle claimed that the "democrats" of 1946 were those who had supported Hitler as the best antidote to Stalin. The MNR newspaper continued:

It pleases us very much to see that today we are all democrats, including those who some years ago dedicated whole pages of their newspapers to deify the beautiful Adolf. The beautiful Adolf no longer exists. He is hardly a nebulous shadow in which some cretins still believe through hatred of the people, of the social glebe, and who in the darkest corner of their conscience maintain alive a little flame of adoration for whom they judged to be the Demigod of this epoch. [116]

Pressing this line of attack, La Calle in April 1946 noted that David Alvéstegui, editor of La Razón, had taken advantage of the theft of Mussolini's remains to write an editorial denouncing "fascist experiments" in Bolivia, a clear slap to the authoritarian Villarroel regime. Under the headline, THE STOLEN REMAINS OF MUSSOLINI SHOULD BE HIDDEN IN [THE OFFICES OF] 'LA RAZÓN,' La Calle quoted a letter which Alvéstegui purportedly had written to the Bolivian Chancery when he was ambassador to Italy. The letter dated May 7, 1936, stated in part:

I have had the opportunity to attend the two most GRAND manifestations that Rome has seen in its history: GRAND because of the imposing aspect of the congregated masses; GRAND because of the enormous political and historical significance which they have had; GRAND because of the special consequences which have been derived from them (the conquest of Abyssinia and the defeat of pacifism). [These have been] an unforgettable spectacle because of its greatness and magnitude, which will last in the memory of those of us who have experienced it... [117]

Events closer to home brought the onus of fascist connections more closely to bear upon the MNR. The Grupo de Oficiales Unidos (GOU, Group of United Officers) seized power in neighboring Argentina in June 1940 and witnessed the election of Juan Domingo Perón as president despite--or perhaps because of--the strictures of United States Ambassador Spruille Braden and the Blue Book. When the authoritarian Perón was installed in office on June 4, 1946, a delegation of MNR deputies went to Buenos Aires--less than two months before the overthrow of Villarroel--to be present at the inauguration. As one of them, Augusto Céspedes, recalled in a magazine article when Perón gained power the second time in 1973, "It was then a question of North American propaganda to point out that both forces [the Bolivian and Argentine revolutions] were identified in a common Nazi-fascist root." [118]

Then began a witch hunt directed as a spin-off to the nascent MNR in Bolivia. The United States experts claimed that the GOU, a group of military officers to which Perón belonged, had instigated and formed the secret lodge RADEPA in Bolivia, the group of progressively minded officers to which Villarroel belonged. But RADEPA was formed immediately after the Chaco War, Céspedes pointed out, and therefore was very anterior to the GOU. It later caused suspicion when after the fall of Villarroel on July 21, 1946, many of the MNR leaders sought refuge in Perón's Argentina. But after an abortive attack on the border town of Villazón, forty or fifty of these exiles were imprisoned and others, including Paz Estenssoro, expelled temporarily from Argentine territory.

Did Perón have any influence in the early years on the Bolivian National Revolution? Céspedes reasoned in 1973, "[This] was the tragic falsehood of the supposed connection of the Bolivian nationalism with that of Perón, for if it had existed, the presidency of Perón would have been an invincible reinforcement to the government of Villarroel." On the contrary, the Perón government considered it more prudent to demonstrate a complete rupture with the fallen MNR government in 1946 and open, rather, friendly relations with the reactionary government of Enrique Hertzog. As proof of his pudding, Céspedes cited the fact that Perón had supported the opposition candidate Gabriel Gozálvez in the 1951 Bolivian elections in which Paz Estenssoro gained a plurality but apparently not a majority. [119]

Nevertheless, the ghost of collusion with Perón was to haunt the MNR during the sexenio, its six years out of power between 1946 and 1952, and to create a bad international image for the fledgling political group. This stemmed from the Villarroel period itself; thus, in 1944 an American newsman reported that Paz Estenssoro had not only interviewed the German ex-ambassador but had received millions of Argentine pesos to overthrow Peñaranda in 1943. A reporter for El Tiempo of Mexico City denied this, stating that when Paz Estenssoro was teaching at the University of Buenos Aires he had no contact with anyone outside university circles. The United States reporter's story had been filed from Montevideo,

El Tiempo pointed out, "with the irresponsibility that characterizes the yellow press of certain news agencies of the United States. But the accusation is unjust and dangerous." [120]

Repercussions of these allegations were felt in the parliamentary halls of Bolivia. In September 1944, Augusto Céspedes declared in the National Convention, speaking on international matters, "Whether the Argentine government is or is not Nazi is nobody's business except that of the Argentine people themselves." Bolivia should not align herself with any one foreign nation in the postwar period, Céspedes reasoned, for how could one choose between the United States and the USSR? Céspedes told the anecdote of a donkey whose owners beat him every day until he died and then made drums with his skin. An onlooker reflected, "Poor donkey, you were beaten in life and you continue being beaten after death." That, Céspedes concluded, was the condition of Bolivia, torn between masters. [121]

When the inter-American conference was held at Chapultepec in 1945, MNR sources supported the reincorporation of Argentina into the group of western hemisphere nations. An editorial, "Maturity of the Argentine case," asked for good treatment of Argentina at the upcoming chancellors' meeting in Mexico City. [122] When the gathering rejected Argentina's demand to the Panamerican Union to be reincorporated into "the continental agreement," La Calle commented, "It does not correspond to the Conference of Chancellors to constitute themselves into an inquisitorial tribunal for the political classification of the Argentine government" because it is a de facto government. On the contrary, the MNR newspaper stated, the Conference should take favorable action toward Argentina "because the economic and spiritual gravitation of that country is unquestionably strong." [123] Finally, acting upon urging by the Chapultepec Conference, Argentina declared war on the Axis on March 27, 1945, clearing her way for participation in the United Nations and dispelling some of the rumors about fascist influence in Bolivia. [124] These charges were revived by Ambassador Spruille Braden in the Argentine elections of 1946, circulated in the Blue Book which also damaged Bolivia. The charges prompted groups such as the Frente Democrática Antifascista (Anti-Fascist Democratic Front) to send a telegram supporting José P. Tamborini of the Unión Democratica (Democratic Union) for the presidency, but Perón won by more votes than even the populist Hipólito Irigoyen early in the century. [125]

When Perón was inaugurated on June 4, 1946, the jubilation of the Argentine people in the streets of Buenos Aires could be heard over the radio in Bolivia. La Calle commented editorially, "A revolutionary combatted with fury by the international press of the oligarchies, coaligned against the liberty of the peoples, that colonel who was soon identified as the encarnation of the democratic desires of social justice, faced all reactionary assaults until his energy, always revitalized by the abundance of popular forces, dominated the tremendous storm of the plutocratic hatred." [126]

In one respect, the pages of La Calle during these early years of the MNR should not be taken to reflect the views of the party as a whole. Whether to excuse themselves or not, the surviving members of the MNR maintain that it was José Cuadros Quiroga who wrote most of the anti-Semitic articles in the early years of La Calle. Therefore, a brief examination of his career in in order. Cuadros Quiroga belonged to the left before the Chaco War and for that reason did not go to partici- pate in the fighting; rather, he fled to Peru with José Antonio Arze of the PIR. As Augusto Céspedes recalls, Cuadros Quir- oga became "almost fascist" when he returned after the war. He joined the MNR and became known as a violent enemy of communism. After working on newspapers in Cochabamba and also on El Diario, he worked as an editor on La Calle for the ten years of its existence, becoming well known for his pungent headlines, biting humor in the column Callejón Oscuro ("Dark Alley") and anti-Semitic diatribes. He never wrote books or pamphlets, but during the Hernán Siles Zuazo government (1956-1960) he served as minister of government, from which position he fought mine labor leader Juan Lechín vigorously and then abandoned politics until his death in 1973. Céspedes considers him to have been "one of the best journalists that Bolivia has produced," but he recognized Cuadros Quiroga's essential instability, noting that he "swung from one extreme to the other, finally finding his equilibrum in nationalism." [127]

Nevertheless, the anti-Semitic articles of Cuadros Quiroga would not have been printed in La Calle if they did not meet the general approval of the MNR. After all, Hernán Siles was publishing exuberantly pro-Nazi material in INTI where Cuadros Quiroga had no influence. On balance, it must be remembered that National Socialism was attractive to many persons of diverse political views for its apparent ability to lift Germany out of the economic and political chaos of the Great Depression; the success of the German-American Bund in the United States attests to that. Also, as Céspedes has pointed out, Germany offered an alternative to the type of domination which Bolivia had been receiving at the hands of the United States. Was the MNR in the early 1940s therefore fascist? It is true that La Calle, almost the only voice we have for measuring the party's will during this period, attacked the United States and England vehemently and defended Germany strongly up until the defeat of the German forces at Stalingrad in 1943, but the newspaper also conducted a long campaign in favor of the Spanish Republic and against Franco and the Spanish Falange. In this respect, the MNR was as democratic--or more so--as any of its contemporaries, but the party believed that Bolivia should have the right to choose its own allies, even if that meant selecting a country that was at war with the United States. [128]

As for its anti-Semitic stance, which caused the MNR much embarrassment in later years, one must understand the party's rationale. It was not a matter of hatred used to exploit class divisions, but something quite different in a poor and undeveloped country, compared to an industrialized nation. In the pages of La Calle and in the parliamentary debate on the immigration bill of 1942, the MNR was trying to point out that the attention paid to the Jews on the part of the oligarchy and its representatives drew attention away from the real, immediate and more pressing problems of the workers and campesinos in Bolivia. In this sense, the MNR's position on immigration, where previous Jews had failed to become the farmers they had promised to be, was nationalist rather than bigoted. As Paz Estenssoro declared in parliament:

> Moreover, as before, we see another of the arguments which they have wielded in order to prove us to be Nazis: anti-Semitism. And [they do] that because we would have implanted the necessity of a policy of economic defense before the dangers of an invasion of Jewish peddlers, trying therefore to identify us with the Third Reich in regard to racial superiorities and, in sum, to the ravaging of the Jews. We do not pretend to stop this Jewish avalanche because they are Jews; no, we oppose it because it constitutes an unproductive immigration.

The Jews were used to a higher standard of living than Bolivians, Paz Estenssoro continued; rather than dedicate themselves to agriculture, as agreed, they became competitors of small entrepreneurs in the cities. The Jew would become "the lender, the smuggler, in sum the eroder of the vitality of the people; he, son of that unfortunate country that gave us Prophets and gives, even today, great minds which are the pride of humanity." [129]

In conclusion, an unfortunate series of related incidents came to brand the MNR as fascist in its early years. The so-called Nazi putsch of 1941 was such a transparent attempt to silence a few MNR journalists that not even the opposition believed it. Nevertheless, the charge of Nazi influence was made and it stuck despite all efforts to dispel it, cropping up again in the Blue Book of 1946 and in Alberto Ostria Gutiérrez'

A People Crucified of 1956. The Nazi label came mainly from the pages of La Calle itself, however. Stemming perhaps partly from German influence in the Bolivian military, there was much admiration for German and also Italian solutions in a disintegrating world. And finally, there was much rabid anti-Semitism, stemming in part perhaps from the presence of Hochschild and the fear of further economic and social dislocations if large numbers of Jews were allowed to immigrate to Bolivia. These may have been justifiable motives on the part of a young, inexperienced and vehemently nationalistic party such as the MNR, but the propaganda campaign in La Calle which accompanied the parliamentary debates far exceeded the bounds of propriety and human decency. As a result of the tragic confluence of all of these elements, the MNR went under with Villarroel, whose overthrow and murder in 1946 was a backlash to anti-authoritarian rule throughout the world upon the close of World War II and the defeat of the Axis powers.

Chapter 5

EN MARCHA: TRIUMPH AND TRANSITION

A good newspaper is a nation talking to
itself.

--Arthur Miller

The overthrow of Gualberto Villarroel on July 21, 1946, did not solve the acute problems of Bolivian life; at most, the ruling class bought six years of uneasy truce while those problems continued to fester.   MNR historians call the period from the murder of Villarroel to their own ascension to power in 1952 the sexenio: it was six years of persecution for the out-lawed MNR but also a time of maturing.   During that period of repression, the MNR struck deeper roots in the social discontent in Bolivia.   Its newspaper La Calle had been destroyed and many of its top leaders were in exile in Argentina and else-where, but Hernán Siles Zuazo was leading the resistance in the streets of La Paz.   Raúl Murillo y Aliaga started up En Marcha before the 1951 elections to give the party a more militant voice, although it was forced to publish clandestinely most of the time.   Victor Paz Estenssoro has called En Marcha "a very important factor" in the ultimate success of the MNR; through a period of suspicion and reprisals, it kept alive the hopes of a growing number of the disenchanted middle class that reform eventually would come to Bolivia. [1]

In 1960, as the party looked back on the history of its own press, La Tarde--the second MNR daily founded in 1959--stated that the three main sources of the party's intellectual strength and propaganda had been the economic studies of Paz Estenssoro, parliamentary debates such as those following the Catavi massacre and the press itself.   The official newspaper of the Villarroel interlude was El Nacional, a title resurrected by General Juan José Torres during his brief ten months in power in 1970-1971.   At the time of Villarroel, José Manuel Pando brought out the weekly Pregón to cultivate non-governmental support and complement the MNR organ La Calle.   During the sexenio Paz Estenssoro published two significant pamphlets from Buenos   Aires,   "Revolution   and   Counter-Revolution"   and

133

"Judgement and Sentence against the Bolivian Oligarchy." Probably more important, however, was the clandestine journalism of the sexenio, which included printed broadsides, mimeographed flyers and even carbon copies. There was also an active propaganda effort in the exterior, led by Carlor Montenegro in Buenos Aires and Germán Quiroga Galdo in Lima. [2]

The immediate transition period after the toppling of Villarroel posed propaganda problems for the underground MNR that at the time seemed insurmountable. For one thing, the press of the "mining super-state" had triumphed. There is no doubt that the elite opposition press, incited mainly by La Razón, the organ of tin-mining tycoon Carlos Victor Aramayo, was instrumental in overthrowing the Villarroel regime. In the early days of the sexenio, the reactionary press gloated over the role it had played in that upheaval. La Razón proclaimed, "The newspapermen who from the tribune of 'La Razón' were the promoters of the uprising, were defending liberty of thought and pointing out the road of rebellion to the people." [3] Ultima Hora, backed by miner Mauricio Hochschild, added, "Whoever believes that the movement of July 21 was unexpected... is in error. That movement was prepared by the press." [4] La Razón asserted later, in words that were to be forgotten by its owner when that newspaper was not allowed to reopen by the MNR after 1952, "The government of Villarroel committed an error that eventually was to become fatal: it gave temporary liberty to the press." [5]

There is other evidence that the mining company press played a direct role in the downfall of Villarroel only thirty-eight days after the confiscation of La Razón and Ultima Hora. In the attempted coup d'etat on June 13, 1946, La Razón printed broadsides urging La Paz mobs to seize Villarroel and his supporters with the injunction, "Leave no one alive!" [6] When the teachers' strike and student demonstrations reached their peak on July 21, La Razón workers rushed to the newspaper building and seized it from the pro-government forces. In a self-incriminating feat of journalistic prowess, these workers had an extra on the streets--distributed free--on the very afternoon of the revolt. Seven lines of banner headlines proclaimed: UNIVERSITY STUDENTS ONCE MORE RECONQUER THE WIDEST LIBERTY FOR THE BOLIVIAN PEOPLE: THE COWARDLY TYRANNY THAT MASSACRED WOMEN AND CHILDREN HAS BEEN CRUSHED BY ALL THE HEROIC PEOPLE. Lesser headlines read, "Torrents of blood were shed by the regime in its desire to continue its domination." [7]

Moreover, La Razón became a handmaiden to the new government just as it had served the oligarchial regimes before the reform interlude of Villarroel. Immediately after his over-throw, the newspaper sent bundles of its latest editions to various parts of Bolivia by airplane to help consolidate the new regime, a junta headed by Supreme Court Justice Néstor Guillén until Tomás Monje Gutiérrez, who was to call elections in 1947, took over on August 15, 1946. La Razón's editorial position concerning the post-Villarroel government was emphatic: the Aramayo newspaper declared that the army would return to its traditional mission of maintaining public order and defending Bolivia's frontiers "rather than placing its sword at the disposal of bastard interests." [8]

One strain upon the memory of the MNR as it strived to recuperate from its failure of co-governing with the reform military elements was the charge that it had deliberately sacrificed Villarroel to the angry mobs outside the Palacio Quemado on July 21, 1946. This accusation was to plague the party throughout the sexenio and even into its own period in power after 1952. Specifically, Alfonso Finot, MNR member who was director of press and information under Villarroel, made the sensational charge in 1948 that Paz Estenssoro, feeling betrayed by the military after the three MNR members had been dismissed from the Villarroel cabinet, ordered the telephone lines cut from the presidential palace to all elements of the army on the night of July 20, 1946, leaving the president isolated and subject to the fury of the mob the next day. In an article first published in La Razón on March 11, 1948, Finot wrote that he had been present in the alcaldía municipal (mayor's office) when Paz Estenssoro, also infuriated because the military had not provided the MNR members with any transportation to seek refuge on the eve of the impending storm, ordered two MNR politicians to go to the telephone central to cut the lines, giving them a list of key numbers to sever. [9]

After the tragic denouement of that alleged decision, Finot began an odyssey that was to take a decade and a half of his life. First he sought refuge in the Paraguayan embassy and later was exiled to Paraguay and Argentina. In his penniless days in Buenos Aires, Finot felt so compelled to bring the matter to public attention that he typed, numbered and signed 20 copies for circulation among his friends and anyone else interested. [10] He returned to Bolivia in March 1952, but after the successful MNR insurrection of April 1952, he was imprisoned by the MNR which allegedly tried to force him to recant his statements about the final hours of the Villarroel regime. Refusing, he was exiled once again and could not return to Bolivia until 1961; thus, his slender 32-page tract cost him fifteen years of exile and the animosity of both parties contending for the future of Bolivia.

After Finot's account appeared in print, it received much wider circulation in the book by Alberto Ostría Gutiérrez, Un pueblo en la cruz, El drama de Bolivia (A People Crucified, The Drama of Bolivia, 1956), translated into English in 1958. [11] Ostría Gutiérrez, a conservative diplomat and constitutional lawyer opposed to the MNR, also revived the stories (see Chapter 4) of the alleged early connections between the party and the German Nazis in Bolivia.

The MNR has always vehemently denied the allegations by Finot concerning the fall of Villarroel. When these charges were again brought into play in the months preceding the crucial elections of May 1951, in which Paz Estenssoro was the MNR presidential candidate although he was still in exile, the party leader swung into action. From Buenos Aires he wrote an open letter published in Ultima Hora citing the testimony of Captain Milton López that the Palacio de Gobierno had telephone communications until 5:30 a.m. on July 21, 1946. Finot, defending his account, retaliated with a letter published in El Diario repeating the declarations of the commander-in-chief of the army, General Damaso Arenas, who had remained in the government palace until the last minute, that "the telephone connections were interrupted." Finot also obtained the affirmations, published in the press of La Paz, by Colonel José Pinto, minister of national defense in the Villarroel government, and Colonel Antonio Ponce, minister of public works, that the narrative of Finot was accurate. [12] The Bolivian writer also had the satisfaction of noting in later years that the Chilean journalist, Arturo Matte Alessandri, editor of Las Noticias de Ultima Hora of Santiago, had questioned Paz Estenssoro during a visit to La Paz in 1960 about the veracity of the story that the telephone lines were ordered cut. The MNR chieftan reportedly replied, "We took that measure because treachery was coming from the general staff and the ministry of defense." [13]

The position of the MNR in confronting and refuting such stories was awkward at best. How could the militantly nationalistic party claim Villarroel as a precursor and martyr--a dramatic symbol of resistance during the sexenio--if people believed that the MNR had left the beleaguered president to his fate? Did the party in a coldly calculated way, which opponents would later brand as opportunism, deliberately seek to manufacture a martyr? Or, assuming that Finot's version was correct, was it simple vengeance? Paz Estenssoro, questioned about these matters in 1973, said that he never replied to the charge by Ostría Gutiérrez that Villarroel had been sacrificed because it was as "absurd" as the earlier allegations of a Nazi putsch (see Chapter 4), wild-eyed propaganda by those seeking to discredit the MNR at any price. Paz Estenssoro in retrospect did not feel that either Finot or Ostría Gutiérrez was worthy of reply. The latter had started writing Un pueblo en la cruz (A People Crucified) as ammunition against the MNR in the 1951 elections; selections were published in La Razón a week before the voting, but Paz Estenssoro maintained it had no impact because the Bolivian people did not believe it. As for Finot, he was expelled from the MNR and was bitter, Paz Estenssoro believed. The former MNR president denied the statement by a United States bibliographer that the MNR, once in power, had tried to destroy all the copies of Finot's work, Así cayó Villarroel (How Villarroel Fell). Paz Estenssoro also pointed out that he had maintained a cordial relationship with the widow of Villarroel when the MNR leader was exiled in Argentina. [14]

At the time, the MNR made a bid for power during the twenty-day civil war which began on August 27, 1949. A general strike of railroad and factory workers had been underway since June 1, and the arrest of Senator Juan Lechín, the magnetic labor leader, touched off open violence in the mining centers. This mushroomed into the civil war of August, according to the MNR plan to capitalize on scattered labor strikes, but the effort failed, primarily because of lack of communication and coordination. Under the leadership of General Froilán Calleja, MNR elements occupied the cities of Potosí, Sucre, Cochabamba and Santa Cruz, along with smaller towns in the interior. The call to arms was not heeded in La Paz, however, and any revolutionary movement in Bolivia needs the capital city--the center of political and economic power--if it is to succeed. For the first time in Bolivian history cities were bombed from the air, as the MNR won over some pilots of Lloyd Aereo Boliviano who made bombing runs on La Paz and Cochabamba. The civil war was quelled, with the rebels arrested or forced into exile, but the country lay prostrate, bleeding from internal wounds. President Enrique Hertzog Garaizabal, who had been in poor health, turned the government over to Vice-President Mamerto Urriolagoitia on October 16, 1949. In an effort to reconcile national differences, presidential elections were called for May 1951, with all parties allowed to participate. [15]

Unable to gain power through armed struggle, the MNR prepared for the elections of 1951, which the party did not expect to win. As the MNR presidential candidate Paz Estenssoro commented later, "We never believed that we could attain power through elections. Nevertheless, we considered it necessary and opportune for the Party to join in the elections because... that would permit a formal triumph as a step toward a revolutionary seizure of power." [16] To justify the image of the popular will thwarted at the polls, it was imperative to rack

137

up the biggest turnout possible, and so party planners turned their attention more keenly to the devices of propaganda.

Actually, that effort had never been lost sight of during the sexenio. According to Paz Estenssoro, four or five folletos or pamphlets were published in Buenos Aires and Montevideo for clandestine distribution in Bolivia. At Tartagal on the Argentine border, Humberto Salas Linares bought a small mimeograph machine and ran off a broadside every day for two years, similar to the pasquines (lampoons or satirical writings) of the independence days. The ingenuity of these early propagandists, imposed by the challenge of infiltrating a closed society, seemingly knew no bounds. For example, in an international auto race between Buenos Aires and Caracas, a Bolivian contender was an MNR member who smuggled pamphlets into Bolivia in his car. Perhaps the secret delight of reading and possessing forbidden material also added to its effectiveness. When Paz Estenssoro was on his way to the first meeting of campesinos at Pucara in 1952, an Indian stopped his car and asked the driver, "Is comrade Paz Estenssoro there?" The MNR president got out of the car and greeted the campesino, who then proudly showed him one of the pamphlets from the sexenio period which he took from his back pouch. [17]

The MNR needed something more sustained than these spasmodic and at times homespun efforts, however. As the elections of May 1951 approached, party leaders in La Paz decided to launch a newspaper to fill the void left by the destruction of La Calle in 1946. The Comité Político (political committee) of the MNR in La Paz designated two of its members, Raúl Murillo y Aliaga and Mario Sanjinés Uriarte, to organize a newspaper since the MNR was frozen out of the established press. Los Tiempos of Cochabamba did give the MNR an occasional page to report its doings (see Chapter 7) but there was no outlet in La Paz. The first difficulty in starting a new publication was getting the government's authorization, certain to be denied to the MNR. Murillo already had an authorization for a non-political newspaper he had planned to call En Marcha, and it was agreed that this would become the first official periodical of the MNR. Even the title was appropriate as a symbol of the struggle and persecutions which the MNR had endured during the extended march of the sexenio. When the first issue appeared on March 13, 1951, the government was flabbergasted; the minister of government and chief of police accused the MNR of not having an authorization for publishing a newspaper, and they were astonished when they saw Murillo's permit. [18]

Murillo, who had been a member of the rightwing Falange Socialista Boliviana (FSB, Bolivian Socialist Falange) founded in

1937, was only twenty-eight years old when he took over the demanding task of editing En Marcha. Still, he had edited the review Continental and the weekly Acción, among other publications. At first two other editors listed under the masthead were Mario Sanjinés Uriarte and José Fellmann Velarde, but shortly Murillo came to be cited alone. [19] In an interview in 1973, Murillo recalled that he had written articles and editorials--"at times the whole newspaper." Because of police harassment, it was not issued regularly, getting out nine issues before May 1951 elections and a few thereafter. En Marcha was established specifically to influence those elections or, in Murillo's words, "to orient the electoral process and channel popular consciousness." [20] En Marcha bought its press from the ministry of labor, and the price of the newspaper went from 20 centavos to 150 bolivianos, a nightmarish example of the inflation which wracked Bolivia at that time. [21]

Murillo, who guided the propaganda effort (although he called it "the process of diffusion") of the MNR during the sexenio, had this concept of the role of En Marcha: "It was the only means of expression that the people had--through the MNR--to vent their general, national and popular anxieties against the government at that time, to state their necessities, their complaints and above all to orient the thought of the militancy of the party toward the objectives that we had to pursue." There was a press run of between 10-15,000 copies for each issue; actually, there was a greater demand for En Marcha but it could not be satisfied due to lack of paper and limited printing facilities. It should be borne in mind, however, that the newspaper had considerable secondary circulation. Copies were passed surreptitiously from hand to hand as popular opinion against the repressive governmental rule continued to mount.

En Marcha served two functions: not only did it disseminate the undiluted political thought of the MNR, together with militant calls to action, but it also financed the elections of 1951. Sales of the newspaper maintained the departmental commands of the MNR in the interior of the republic. Bundles of En Marcha would be shipped to them and be sold for 50 centavos each when other newspapers were going for 5 bolivianos. This would insure the widest distribution of the MNR's message, but contributions were also welcomed from those who wanted to give more. In Potosí, for example, one man bought a copy of En Marcha for 500 bolivianos. It must be remembered that the newspaper was not sold normally, however; it was sold as forbidden merchandise. The newsboys of La Paz, who favored the MNR, sold En Marcha clandestinely, slipping it between the pages of El Diario or La Razón and charging for both.

Buyers might face getting beat up by the police, as did everyone else connected with En Marcha. As soon as a new number appeared, Murillo recalled, there would immediately be "a wave of persecutions." Members of the editorial staff and street vendors of the newspaper had to fight violently--with clubs--on many occasions when the government tried to impede the distribution of En Marcha. Time and again the police assaulted the editorial offices and printing plant of the newspaper, closing the press, scattering the type, destroying machinery. As Murillo recalled, "Every time the newspaper came out it was a field battle." The editor, who had been a member of the MNR since the early stages of the party's formation, was jailed many times and once was confined to the Isla de Coati, an island prison camp in Lake Titicaca, but he always managed to escape and return to La Paz where he got out another number of En Marcha.

The audience sought by this robust renegade of Bolivian journalism was the middle class, the opinion makers whose support the MNR desperately needed, and the workers, who were beginning to be class conscious and were the only organized part of the lower classes. En Marcha was distributed at the mining centers around the country, which were bastions for the MNR, and the party also tried to reach the seemingly inert mass of campesinos, some of whom were trying to organize MNR comandos (commands) in the countryside. The MNR was organized in a hierarchy of forty-five departmental or provincial commands throughout the country to insure discipline. Thus, En Marcha served both to reinforce the militancy of the MNR and to win converts, or at least to gain the electoral support of those who were not party members. As Murillo described the effect of his newspaper on the 1951 elections, "It was the instrument of orientation of the rank and file of the party and, something more, it raised the fighting morale of the people... toward the objectives that the MNR was seeking." To achieve this, En Marcha printed some messages from Paz Estenssoro in his Buenos Aires exile, but this was extremely difficult. Communication was haphazard and dangerous; those who got out the newspaper did it essentially on their own, exercising their own judgement. After En Marcha appealed so spectacularly to popular emotions, the MNR organizers in La Paz decided to launch a series of publications for the party, which would come out more or less two times a month throughout the country. These publications were designed to appeal to specific interest groups. Among them were Frente Sindical (Union Front) for workers; Democracia (Democracy) for the middle class; Rebelión (Rebellion) for women, and Resistencia (Resistance) for the youth. [22]

The significance of En Marcha in boosting the MNR on its road to power demands that its trajectory be examined in greater detail. No copies of the newspaper can be found in any of the public libraries of Bolivia; rather, it must be consulted in the private collection of its editor Raúl Murillo y Aliaga in his printing shop in La Paz. When the first issue appeared on March 13, 1951, about two months before the scheduled elections, it was an historic moment. A two-line banner headline proclaimed, THEY ARE BLOCKING THE ENTRY [LNTO BOLIVIA] OF THE CHIEF OF THE M.N.R. DOCTOR VICTOR PAZ ESTENSSORO. The accompanying story explained that the party leader had gone into exile in Paraguay and Argentina in 1946 with only a salvoconducto or safe-conduct pass. His passport should still be good, but the government had refused to issue him one since 1947. Nevertheless, the story indicated that Paz Estenssoro "would shortly be in La Paz to preside over his candidacy," which was announced in this issue of En Marcha. The selection of the vice-presidential candidate would be made by a special commission with only one member elected by each of the departmental commands and one by the national political committee.

The symbolism which the MNR wished to convey to the Bolivian people became apparent in this first issue of En Marcha. Prominently displayed on the front page were pictures of Paz Estenssoro, "The chief of the National Revolution," and Villarroel, "The martyr of the National Revolution." A sense of history or tradition is extremely important in Hispanic culture, and by appropriating Villarroel as their precursor--even though he had dismissed the three MNR members from his cabinet--the party was signaling its ties to the past. This symbolic search for moorings was repeated many times as En Marcha sought to drum up support for the MNR candidates in the elections of May 1951. On one occasion, the newspaper discussed "The social and economic work carried out by the Villarroel-Paz Estenssoro Government." On another, the entire back page was given over to a picture of Villarroel with the headline, THE MARTYR OF THE NATIONAL REVOLUTION. At still another time, a front-page article analyzed "The armed forces facing the supreme historical obligation, Busch and Villarroel." [23]

In similar vein, the newspaper reported the speech that Federico Alvarez Plata gave upon opening the fifth convention of the MNR in which he declared, "Because we are the national majority, we are the most appropriate to carry out the pacification of the country." An article by Paz Estenssoro, I ACCUSE... was a summary of his pamphlet printed in Buenos Aires in 1948, "Judgement and Sentence against the Bolivian Oligarchy." It consisted of 100 points of indictment against the ruthlessness of wealth and power in Bolivia, ending with the

Catavi massacre. This summary was reprinted in the second issue of En Marcha "at the request of numerous persons who have not been able to acquire our first number..." [24] In the first issue, a series of "Letters to the People" was started, with the first directed to the miners, who were demanding freedom for imprisoned Juan Lechín, executive secretary of the Federación Sindical de Trabajadores Mineros de Bolivia (FSTMB, Bolivian Mine Workers Federation), the first miners' federation in Bolivia, formed in 1944. It is not surprising that the editors of En Marcha would direct their first special appeal to the miners because the MNR from the beginning had sought to tap this source of organized strength which could also be counted on to come to the party's assistance in the event of a violent showdown. Other "Letters to the People" printed before and immediately after the elections of May 1951 were addressed to the public and private employees and to the military. [25]

Police harassment against the MNR also was reported in this first issue of the party's official newspaper. En Marcha recounted how the police had stopped a broadcast of Paz Estenssoro, apparently taped in Buenos Aires, at Radio Amauta in La Paz on March 11, 1951, and had seized other material at Radio Bolivia, where one employee was arrested. Undaunted, En Marcha published the text of the entire speech, covering an entire page of its second issue. The editors were well aware that they could gain the sympathy of their readers if it were demonstrated, as in the above case, that the government was treating their candidate harshly and unfairly.

In other ways, En Marcha employed relatively sophisticated propaganda devices. One was the CARTEL DE COMBATE (Placard of Combat), a saying or slogan presented as a front-page boxed feature in every number of the newspaper. In the first issue, for example, En Marcha quoted perhaps the best-known statement of Gualberto Villarroel, "I am more a friend of the poor than enemy of the rich." In the second issue, the words of wisdom came from Franz Tamayo, the great cholo educator and writer who commanded respect from most segments of Bolivian society. He was quoted as saying, "The only servitude that does not defile is that to the law." En Marcha also put new words to huaynos, popular songs of Bolivia, to instill a patriotic or fighting spirit among its readers. [26] Occasionally, editorial cartoons would be used, as one which proclaimed, "ENOUGH! Fewer bullets and more bread!" The editors also realized that they could not go against the grain of Bolivian habits and customs if they wanted to get their message across. Thus, in the second issue which came out shortly before Easter, there was a prominent picture of Christ and a prayer for Holy Week, although the MNR could hardly be described as religious in outlook. [27]

The big news of the second issue, however, was the announcement of the candidacy for vice-president of Hernán Siles Zuazo, who accepted the designation from his exile in Santiago de Chile. Siles, born in La Paz in 1913, was the son of former President Hernando Siles (1926-1930) and had been active in the MNR since its founding in 1941. The younger Siles had contributed articles both to La Calle and the weekly Semanario Busch, but he first gained the attention of those who were to form the MNR as founder and editor of the daily newspaper INTI (see Chapter 1). Franz Tamayo issued a personal salute to Hernán Siles Zuazo in a later issue of En Marcha. [28] Meanwhile, a groundswell of public opinion was beginning to surge for the MNR ticket: the Federación de Ex-Combatientes, the powerful organization of Chaco War veterans, came out for Paz Estenssoro, and En Marcha claimed, ALL OF THE CAMPESINOS SUPPORT THE M.N.R. [29]

While some of its articles were hortatory, En Marcha also was a newspaper of substance. There were serious analyses of national economic realities by Paz Estenssoro from its very inception. For example, in the second issue of En Marcha an editorial discussed "The small miners and Washington." Declining tin prices were wrecking the country's economy, but the Bolivian representatives at the foreign ministers' meeting in Washington, D.C., really represented Chilean interests, En Marcha charged, and foreign consortiums such as Patiño Mines and Aramayo Mines. The newspaper concluded, "The delegates of Bolivia will not defend the interests of this producer nation because they have been and they are simple subalterns of anti-Bolivian capital." [30] In headlines, emotionally charged words sought to convey a simple but strong message to the readers; shibboleths cropped up time after time that were becoming established in the revolutionary rhetoric, such as this headline from the third issue of En Marcha: BOLIVIA AGAINST THE SUPER-STATE.--ECONOMIC POWER AND POLITICAL POWER.--THE SUPER STATE.--ITS TREASON TO BOLIVIA. [31]

As the hour of the May 6, 1951 elections approached, En Marcha found more concrete matters to occupy its attention. The most serious candidate the MNR had to confront was Gabriel Gosálves, heading the ticket of the Partido Alianza Social Demócrata (Social Democratic Alliance Party), a last-ditch combination of old guard parties determined to block the election of Paz Estenssoro. The MNR chief appeared to have clear sailing if the elections were honest because the only other leftist candidate in the field was José Antonio Arze of the Partido de la Izquierda Revolucionario (Party of the Revolutionary Left) which had miniscule support, whereas the opposition was fractured four ways. [32] The fact that six political parties had put candidates in the running revealed that Bolivia was facing a crisis in her old order that might not be solved at the polls. The MNR resented the fact that its candidate, Paz Estenssoro, was not even allowed to be in the country to campaign on his own behalf. In a public relations move, Gosálvez, the main conservative opposition candidate, petitioned Urriolagoitia to let Paz Estenssoro re-enter the country, and the president replied that it was perfectly all right with him, but the MNR leader was under judicial action for stirring up the civil war of 1949. One Bolivian observer, Alfredo Ayala, believed that the forced absence of Paz Estenssoro was beneficial to the MNR cause "because the psychology of our people is emotive and of a general tendency to be the adversary of he who holds power in his hands." [33] Straws in the wind indicated also that the elections might not be fair; En Marcha reported at the end of March that the government had given the Carabineros (national police) five sets of identification papers each to vote five times for Gosálvez and his vice-presidential running mate, Roberto Arce. [34]

The government clearly was running scared, violating the general amnesty proclaimed in the months before the elections by exiling more top political leaders. En Marcha headlined this development, MORE POLICE OUTRAGES, when the authorities exiled Deputy Guillermo Lora to Chile. Lora, leader of the Trotskyite Partido Obrero Revolucionario (POR, Revolutionary Workers' Party) founded in 1920, had come back to the country clandestinely to answer charges that he and the POR were the "intellectual instigators" of the Catavi massacre of 1949. Police accused him of "subversive travels" but they obviously simply wanted to get rid of one more political opponent. Juan Lechín, the powerful mine workers' union leader, also was exiled to Chile; police said he was involved with Lora and other elements in plotting revolution. Yet, En Marcha pointed out, police maintained there was "complete tranquility in all of the territory of the Republic." The newspaper also advised its readers that police had tried to close it since its last issue had appeared in the streets. [35]

The major task of En Marcha, however, was to build up the image of Paz Estenssoro in the few weeks remaining before the elections. The leader of the MNR was an outstanding orator who had proved his mettle in the heated debates during the Catavi inquiry of 1943, but some party members feared that he was too mild and soft-spoken--too much of the economics professor--to fare well in the rough and tumble of the national political arena. Others pointed out that the public had dubbed him el mono (the monkey) because of his spectacles and sagging jowls and that this nickname showed he could win the people's affection. In an editorial En Marcha called Paz Estenssoro a

144

"caudillo" [commander]... complete man... a piece of the people's heart." But the newspaper hastened to explain what it meant: "One is not dealing with the old type of caudillo whose force rested on awakening primitive emotions in the mass. One is dealing with a modern guide who translates and places himself at the front of the banners of a people to carry them to triumph. All of a generation is represented in men like Victor Paz, and there you have the spirit of his fight." [36]

In early April, as the pace of the campaign stepped up, it seemed that the MNR chief would return to Bolivia after all. In its fourth issue En Marcha went all out to exhort the party faithful to be at El Alto, the airport on the altiplano above La Paz, to greet him. A banner headline on April 5 proclaimed PAZ ESTENSSORO ARRIVES TODAY. A subhead added, "All of the people to receive him!" and for the first time En Marcha began printing the V-signal made by two extended fingers and standing for Venceremos! (We Will Conquer!) The caption under a picture of Paz Estenssoro read, "The people of Bolivia salute the chief of the National Revolution." Fearing perhaps that their candidate might be barred at the last moment, the editors of En Marcha printed a statement by Froilán Calderón, head of the MNR judicial commission, to Federico Alvarez Plata, executive secretary of the party, indicating that Paz Estenssoro had met all government requirements to run in the May 6 elections. Also in this fourth issue, the MNR was putting some distance between itself and the Partido de la Izquierda Revolucianario (PIR, Party of the Revolutionary Left) whose leader Jose Antonio Arze had come out as a presidential candidate. The Marxist party had been formed in 1940, shortly before the MNR itself, and it had played an important role in radicalizing the mine labor movement, but now it was competing directly with the more centrist MNR. En Marcha published an article, "Communism and tin," denouncing the manipulation of the workers. [37]

When Paz Estenssoro was prevented from showing up on April 5, the MNR militancy staged a demonstration anyway as great numbers of people flocked to the airport and then poured through the streets from El Alto to the Plaza Venezuela. Describing the occasion in its fifth issue, En Marcha declared that the manifestation revealed the "immense popularity" of the MNR, even though it leader was not there to greet the multitudes. The newspaper printed five photographs of the huge crowds and noted that they were disciplined, mature crowds, who did not think of "sterile vengeance... but rather of the construction of a better Country." There was not a single hostile cry to the opposition, En Marcha reported, referring to the crowd as "the army of the National Revolution..." These great numbers of people, the newspaper continued, were made

145

up of "the exploited middle class, workers and campesinos...
the national majorities" which had fixed definitively upon the
MNR as "their instrument of liberation." In a time when many
demonstrations were staged, En Marcha pointed out that this
had been based on sincere enthusiasm and spontaneous attendance, since the party could not commandeer government workers and force them into the streets, as the ruling regime did.
The banner headline at the top of the front page heralded a
quotation from Paz Estenssoro, I WILL FULFILL MY DUTIES AT
YOUR SIDES. In the middle of the page another striking
typographical display, including the V-signal, read, THE PEO-
PLE HAVE SPOKEN: WE WILL OVERCOME. Another banner at
the bottom of the page proclaimed, THESE ARE THE PEOPLE
WHO FIGHT FOR THEIR LIBERTY. [38] These headlines--and
others like them--were important propaganda devices in a
country with a great amount of illiteracy and marginal literacy.
Some persons might grasp the headlines and the pictures without being able to read the articles. The sheer sensational
character of the headlines also must be taken into account; this
was a journalistic technique new to Bolivian journalism in the
size of the type-face involved with En Marcha's headlines.
People had the impression that something important was happening, and many of them wanted to be a part of it.

The size of the MNR demonstration on April 5 alarmed the
authorities, however, and the inevitable crackdown came in
outlying parts of the country. La Paz was too visible, with
foreign journalists arriving in town to cover the elections, but
elsewhere repression became the order of the day. Police in
Oruro confined MNR candidates Manuel Barrau and Carlos
Montellano, En Marcha reported in an issue that came out only a
week before the elections. Police in Santa Cruz attacked MNR
demonstrations, and other clashes occurred in Sucre, Tarija,
Trinidad and Cobija. Meanwhile, at La Paz, the center of
political power, the MNR newspaper proclaimed in a two-line
banner at the top of the front page, THE ONLY OPPOSITION
SLATE IS DRS. PAZ ESTENSSORO AND SILES ZUAZO. Prominent pictures of the two candidates and a message from Siles
Zuazo also were featured. [39]

When the ninth issue of En Marcha came out only two days
before the elections, an editorial headlined THE PEOPLE OPPO-
SITE THEIR DESTINY came down hard on continued government
harassment of the opposition in the campaign. When President
Urriolagoitia declared the elections, En Marcha recalled, he had
said that all contenders would have maximum guaranties. But
the newspaper charged that the mining electoral district of La
Chojlla, strong for the MNR, had been annulled or gerryman-
dered; there also were duplicate and fraudulent inscriptions by
the Partido de la Unión Republicana Socialista (PURS, United

Víctor Paz Estenssoro, major architect of the MNR and three-time revolutionary president, is featured on April 5, 1951 in En Marcha, launched by the MNR to support his first bid for the presidency.

Republican Socialist Party), a coalition of factions from the Republican party which supported the status quo governments between 1947-1951. Opposition voters had been struck off the rolls, En Marcha continued, and MNR candidates had been jailed less than fifteen days before the election, along with detentions and persecutions throughout the republic. The government had impeded the return of Paz Estenssoro from exile, countenanced "massacres' in the streets of La Paz, Trinidad and other cities, closed the MNR offices and ransacked those of En Marcha, the newspaper charged. Actually, it continued, the declarations of Urriolagoitia about fair elections where for export only "in the mad desire to prolong a regime of infamy, systematic robberies and massacres that have no parallel in the history of Bolivia." Urriolagoitia and his officials had made a mockery of the Constitution and the UN Charter of Human Rights, En Marcha declared; the penal code and the law of responsibilities had sanctions applicable to any wrong-doers in the electoral process, but they had not been invoked. En Marcha commented, in one of the many strong statements made before the elections which reveals why the government tried to silence the opposition newspaper, "We declare that the present electoral process is fundamentally vitiated by the Government in favor of the official candidates." En Marcha added that police reports of MNR violence were false, and at any rate the United Nations also recognized the right of resistance. The major headline in this last issue before the elections was THE PEOPLE WILL TRIUMPH WITH PAZ ESTENSSORO AND SILES ZUAZO. The MNR leader had sent in an article on how Gosálvez, the official candidate, had served all of the oligarchical governments. [40]

The next issue of En Marcha appeared on May 12, six days after the elections when the vote count was fairly complete, and startled men in the street with its blazing headline, THE MNR CANDIDATES OBTAIN ABSOLUTE MAJORITY. In this regard, the MNR newspaper was optimistic but understandably so since a mere plurality--which the party seemed to have won--would have thrown the elections into the Chamber of Deputies where the old guard political parties held sway. Since 112,298 voters turned out, (44.7 percent of the electorate), according to La Razón, it was necessary for Paz Estenssoro to get at least 61,150 votes to obtain an absolute majority--half of the voters plus one. Thus, En Marcha claimed that the MNR nominee had obtained 68,457 votes to 37,934 votes for Gosálvez; also, Siles Zuazo got 67,984 votes to 36,238 for PURS vice-presidential candidate Roberto Arce. La Razón on May 15, however, reported that Paz Estenssoro had received only 54,129 votes to 40,381 for Gosálvez, and Siles Zuazo 52,602 to 30,202 for Arce. Undoubtedly one set of figures was inflated while the other was whittled down, with various districts still not reporting, but the MNR realized it was in trouble. A headline at the bottom of the front page of En Marcha on May 12 carried a threatening note: THE PEOPLE WILL DEFEND THEIR ELECTORAL VICTORY. Nevertheless, the votes tallied by either count were impressive because never before in a Bolivian election had the opposition come out ahead. The tally would have been even greater, En Marcha asserted, if there had not been so many irregularities and outbursts of official violence on election day. Local MNR leader Ovidio Barbery was machine-gunned down in the streets during the elections in Santa Cruz; another MNR official was shot to death in Sorata. There was violence in Mizque, Challapata, Sacaba and other towns, En Marcha reported. The newspaper also charged that tens of thousands of "paper citizens," with false names inscribed on electoral rolls, had cast their votes for the official candidates. In all the departments of Tarija, including the hometown of Paz Estenssoro, not a single MNR party member had been allowed to vote, En Marcha maintained.

This was the single most stridently militant issue the MNR newspaper had issued to date; the editors feared that the election would be stolen from them, and they were determined to prevent this. An article was entitled, "Neither the persecutions nor the massacres have been able to destroy the revolutionary conscience of the Bolivian people." A banner headline on an inside page trumpeted, THE PEOPLE HAVE TRIUMPHED! While "Officialism won in some provinces by bullet and club," another story declared, "the people in the democratic fight for their liberation have conquered with order and discipline." Trying to overcome its reputation for violence and even thuggery, the MNR presented itself in the pages of En Marcha as a peace-loving and law-abiding political movement. An editorial headlined, "Peace for Bolivia," stated that the elections, despite official pressure and machinations, demonstrated that the people had given "their repudiation to the methods of force, to the arbitrary and anti-constitutional measures that have been the norm of the present Government." The MNR, the editorial continued, had no hatred, vengeance or desire for reprisals, but it would fight "to the single man" to defend its "unassailable" electoral victory. To mend its fences with the ultimate arbitrating force in Bolivian society, the MNR addressed one of its "Letters to the People" to the military, appealing to their civic spirit, nationalist sentiment, and guardianship of the Constitution. In other words, the MNR did not want the army to step in to resolve the electoral crisis since those in control of the armed forces were conservative in character, for whom the MNR was anathema. The open letter in En Marcha stated that enemies had tried "to create abysses [between the army and the MNR] that do not exist..." On the contrary, the letter continued, the MNR "has no differences, no antagonisms with the army nor with any member of the army." It concluded its direct personal appeal to the ranking military men, "You are in the same trench with the Nationalist Revolutionary Movement."

Surprisingly, the traditional newspapers of La Paz came to the aid of the MNR as the political future of Bolivia seemed clouded by the inconclusive elections. Discussing "The triumph of the MNR and the national press," En Marcha predicted that Urriolagoitia would not honor the electoral results and commended its journalistic opponents who maintained that he should. La Razón was quoted from an editorial headlined, "Legality," that "Today... [the MNR] had received from the citizenry, thanks to the democratic system, an evident proof of confidence." El Diario declared that Congress should act only on the basis of "legality and impartiality," not partisan interests, and Ultima Hora pointed out, "It is very serious to play with the faith of the people." [41]

The words of La Razón were particularly magnanimous since the Aramayo newspaper had lashed out at the MNR at every stage of the 1951 electoral campaign because of the nationalist group's unceasing propaganda attacks against "the mining super-state" which the MNR claimed conducted all of Bolivia's affairs. La Razón vehemently denied this allegation. The newspaper, owned and directed by the Aramayo tin-mining family, incredibly replied that "the Bolivian mining industry does not exercise, not try to exert, any political power." [42] After the elections, La Razón was appalled at the strong showing of the MNR, which the newspaper had been doing its utmost to discredit since 1946. The stand-off should have been resolved by congressional decision among the three top candidates, as the Constitution of 1947 provided, but La Razón opposed any situation in which the MNR could possibly win:

> Through the ruinous splintering of the other political parties, the national majority--relative or absolute--has expressed its confidence in the same party [the MNR] that only five years ago was dramatically expelled from power, that agitated, before and afterwards, for the open resistance of great sectors of opinion, and that merited the severe and unanimous criticism of the national press. [43]

Under such pressure from all sides, Mamerto Urriolagoitia on May 16, 1951 handed the Bolivian government over to a ten-man military junta led by General Hugo Ballivián Rojas and fled to Chile. This defection created a new word in the Bolivian vocabulary--a mamertazo which brought even greater repression to the country as the military resorted to every tactic to keep the lid on as social pressures continued to mount in Bolivia.

Strikes and public demonstrations were prohibited, and the junta imposed censorship immediately upon taking command. Los Tiempos, the regional newspaper of Cochabamba, the second largest city in Bolivia, reported that it was actually censored only on the night of May 17, 1951. Looking back, Los Tiempos found Urriolagoitia respectful of press freedom, although there were occasional irregularities--mainly against En Marcha--by his police general Isaac Vencenti. Meanwhile, a communique by the MNR charged that under the Ballivián junta, there was "tacit muzzling of the press" in La Paz. [44]

With the denial of constitutional forms in Bolivia, En Marcha entered its most difficult period in a physical sense--as it faced more police brutality than ever before--but it also held a propaganda ace since the newspaper could capitalize on the unjust and illegal treatment the MNR received at the hands of the authorities. It is easier to convey the plight of the underdog to a sympathetic audience than to attempt to explain away the privileges of the rich and powerful. Under the harshest of conditions, En Marcha managed to get out five more issues before the successful rebellion of April 9, 1952. At least two of these were no more than mimeographed sheets, but they continued the struggle.

The first issue after the takeover by the military was one of these mimeographed efforts, which consisted only of five pages and bore no date or number, but proudly listed the names of the editors above the masthead. A front-page editorial, "Dictatorship," argued that the military junta "in no way expresses the sentiment of the National Army..." The newspaper was referring to the support which lower echelons of the armed forces had given to the Toro, Busch and Villarroel experiments in national socialism. But of greatest concern to En Marcha in this contraband issue--since the newspaper had not bowed to censorship--was the continuing abuses against the press, despite the protestations to the contrary of the minister of government destined for foreign consumption. The fact was, En Marcha said, that editors and newsmen were jailed throughout the country. The directors of En Marcha had escaped imprisonment, but for the sixth time "police hordes" had invaded the newspaper's office, ransacked it, and padlocked the door. Thus, the editors resorted to the lowly mimeograph machine to still get their message onto the streets. The contents did not suffer from the less sophisticated technology, however. In this issue En Marcha reprinted the statement of Paz Estenssoro made in La Razón of Buenos Aires on May 22, 1951. [45] It was undoubtedly a welcome voice for the party faithful in the deepening dark that was enveloping Bolivia.

"The press under the dictatorship" continued to be the

theme of the twelfth issue of En Marcha, also mimeographed and consisting of four pages smaller than sheets of typing paper. The MNR newspaper denounced once again the total censorship under the junta, and it came to the aid of Renato Tapia Caballero, copy editor of El Diario, who was being pursued by the police. En Marcha said it wished to denounce equally "the continuous attacks that our newspaper has received, which though not closed, has not been able to publish its editions normally, because of the persecution which the editorial and print-shop personnel suffer and the continuous assaults and confiscations of which it has been the object." For the militancy of the MNR came word that Juan Lechín, the popular labor leader who had cast in the lot of his mine workers with that of the MNR, was confined in Santo Corazón in the tropical eastern department of Santa Cruz. All MNR prisoners from the Panóptico Nacional (national penitentiary) in La Paz also had been removed there, En Marcha reported, making a mockery of the amnesty granted after the junta took over, a move denounced as designed merely to assuage international opinion.

This diminuitive En Marcha asked for donations of newsprint, stencils, ink and so forth to continue the propaganda effort. Along that line, it was announced that the new periodical for MNR youth, Resistencia, had appeared. And a watchword or countersign for the MNR was included in a small box on the front page: "To the party members: DISCIPLINE, PROPAGANDA, ORGANIZATION." [46]

The role of the military in national life preoccupied En Marcha from this point until the successful overthrow of armed rule after April 9, 1952. An editorial in January 1952 headlined, "The MNR opposite the Military Junta," attacked the golpe of May 16, 1951, when Urriolagoitia voluntarily relinquished power to the Bolivian military to prevent the MNR from taking office. Later the ex-president claimed he had discovered a secret pact between the MNR and the Bolivian Communists, but most observers felt this was simply one more machination-- similar to the "Nazi putsch" charge of 1941--to keep the MNR out of power at any cost. En Marcha editorialized in January 1952, "What has happened since May 16 demonstrates the harsh reality of events that ever deepens the chasm between the privileged few of the Rosca who have everything in excess and the people are deprived even of their daily bread." Among the national goals of the MNR, the editorial listed "the dominion of the Bolivian economy over the well-being of the productive classes of Bolivia, incorporation of the campesino into national life, intensification and diversification of production, identification of the armed institutions with the people and the full exercise of liberty and democracy..." With those goals in mind, En Marcha called upon the Military Junta to honor its

pledge of returning the country to constitutional rule by holding elections in the first months of 1952. The MNR newspaper
stressed "the basic principle that the armed forces should
separate themselves from political tasks, in conformance with
what the Constitution dictates." En Marcha added that the MNR
would be "loyal to its pledge to the Army Command in the sense
of cooperating patriotically toward a peaceful solution of the
political problem..." [47] Here the editorial writer was speaking with his fingers crossed behind his back because the MNR--
as Paz Estenssoro would admit later to the sixth party conven-
tion--did not want a pacific solution of the political frustrations
which had arisen out of the mamertazo. The MNR, which had
thrived on controversy since its inception, actively sought more
persecution and abuses so that public opinion would support the
revolutionary party when its seized power by force. This was
the same tactic which Francisco I. Madero, the political figure-
head of the Mexican Revolution, had used there in the elections
of 1910. In a recently discovered letter to United States
publisher William Randolph Hearst, Madero said his only purpose
in running against aging dictator Porfirio Díaz--in impossibly
rigged elections--was to soften up popular opinion for the
coming revolution led by one unjustly denied election. [48] In
Bolivia, forty years later, En Marcha continued attacking the
opposition by printing pictures of two corpses with the caption,
"This is the work of the Urriolagoitia Government." This is the
inheritance that the Junta received." Paz Estenssoro was still
in exile in Argentina, but Siles Zuazo, described as the
"champion [paladín] of the resistance," was busily at work in
the underground in La Paz preparing the approaching
revolution. [49]

En Marcha was not the only newspaper which opposed
military rule in Bolivia. Although more conciliatory, El Diario
came out with an editorial entitled, "People and army united in
a common desire," which was reprinted in Los Tiempos of
Cochabamba with the latter newspaper's comment that it reflected "with some spontaneity and sensibility the currents of opinion..." The El Diario editorial urged the general staff to go
ahead with its position of holding elections, noting:

> The 21st of July of 1946 marked a hard experience
> that should not be forgotten. The violence and
> blunders of some military chiefs in the government
> placed the people opposite the Army, with the bloody
> consequences that all remember and condemn. Five
> years of separation from the government and from the
> partisan fights have permitted it [the army] to enter
> into a stage of reorganization. The initiative of the
> Chief of General Staff is looking for a way so that
> work is not wasted and history does not repeat itself,

while it is still time to save the honor of the Army, separating it from power, by virtue of the legal fulfillment of its word pledged before the country. [50]

Because of this editorial, the editor of El Diario was called to the office of the minister of government, a military officer, and roundly rebuked. Thus, all newspapers in Bolivia experienced not only official censorship under the Military Junta but also unofficial intimidation, which had a chilling effect upon what the more traditional newspapers would print. In the tense atmosphere, some newspapers closed down completely for brief periods of time. Los Tiempos of Cochabamba, for example, announced at the close of February 1952 that it would not appear for the first three days of the following week, explaining, "The special situation that arises these days seems to forbode new threatening clouds of anxiety and anguish. One hopes that the political parties and the authorities will maintain the serenity and concord necessary for the good of the community." [51]

If the newspapers on the right were having difficulties, En Marcha was more sorely pressed. The fourteenth issue of the journal, which reached the streets on January 19, 1952, was confiscated by the police in great quantities. In its next edition, En Marcha expressed its indignation and sympathy for "the canillitas [newsboys], who were attacked with billy-clubs [laques], detained in police cells, and beaten barbarously in the streets, while the numbers of 'En Marcha' that they had for sale were confiscated, causing them through this extreme and unlawful measure the loss of their miserable livelihoods." Meanwhile, the MNR newspaper complained, the prensa rosquera (oligarchical press) said nothing. [52] The government charged that an MNR revolution had been set to explode on February 9, 1952, and rounded up thirty-one party members, including En Marcha editor Raúl Murillo y Aliaga, confining all of them on the Isla de Coati in Lake Titicaca. [53]

Even in the outlying districts of Bolivia, police repression was stepped up. In Cochabamba a university student, Carlos Sagarnaga, was arrested for distributing copies of a flyer from the local feminine cell of the MNR, which in the words of Los Tiempos "grows stronger every time with the moral penicillin that the government injects daily." Strong-arm methods were bound to strengthen the isolated cells of the MNR, winning adherents through sympathy to an increasingly popular cause. The flyer for which this student was arrested analyzed the press of La Paz, classifying as rosquero newspapers: La Razón, El Diario, Ultima Hora, Antorcha (publication of the Falange Socialista Boliviana), La Tribuna and Momento. Papers considered to be on the side of the people were En Marcha, El Guerrillero, El Campesino and others, organs of different cells of the MNR. [54]

Meanwhile, party officials in La Paz were trying other ways to whip up popular resentment against the Military Junta, hoping for a cascading effect of wrath and indignation. On February 9, 1952, the MNR called for a cabildo abierto (open town-meeting) at the University of San Andrés at 5 p.m. En Marcha hit the streets that morning with the banner headline, ALL THE PEOPLE TO THE UNIVERSITY. The accompanying story explained that the object was "to ask in CABILDO ABIERTO greater attention from the public powers for the people." A photograph of Paz Estenssoro was captioned, "President elect of Bolivia and chief of the National Revolution." A story on the front page was headlined NEITHER HATRED NOR VIOLENCE, but the tone of the En Marcha was clearly becoming more assertive. The opening paragraph under that headline, for example, declared, "No one can deny that the MNR with its enormous majority force, with its vigor as a young party, with its five recent years of struggle and intense experience, is the only defined and solid force in the present hour."

To allay fears among the middle class that the MNR was Marxist and dedicated to a radical levelling of Bolivian society, En Marcha printed an editorial on "Capitalism and nationalism" in which it said the two forces "are not opposing principles; both can develop in harmony when unfolding capital increases the economic forces of the Nation." The tragedy of Bolivia's experience in the past, the editorial continued, was that antinational capital had despoiled the country of its resources without returning anything. Moreover, some of that capital was foreign: The Patiño interests were partly financed with United States capital, Aramayo by Swiss and Hochschild by Argentine. [55] Occasional editorials such as the above have led some observers to conclude that En Marcha was a rightist publication. [56] It was not. Within the contest of the existing Bolivian press, it was far to the left and interpreted MNR directives faithfully. What both the party and the newspaper were trying to was to assuage the fears of all sectors of society. They were not asking for a consensus but they were trying to forge a working alliance; if this pragmatic approach meant watering down the party's intentions on some occasions, it was considered a necessary expedient.

When the Military Junta announced a date for new elections, the hand of the MNR was forced. Decisive action had to be taken before another parody at the polls would divert public opinion. In the confusion, it was rumored that the MNR would make various alliances to push itself over the top in the next go-round. But Germán Vera Tapia, who led the MNR revolt in Cochabamba in 1949, was quoted by Los Tiempos as saying, "The MNR will not make a pact with communism nor with the nationalist parties who have delivered themselves to the Rosca..." Los Tiempos, owned and edited by Demetrio Canelas, was in many respects the most acute political observer on the Bolivian scene. Initially friendly to the MNR but later attacking the successful revolutionary party with fury (see Chapter 7), the newspaper had the second largest circulation in Bolivia after Aramayo's La Razón. Located at some distance from La Paz, Los Tiempos had breathing space in which to ponder political events at the capital. By March 1952 the newspaper realized that the MNR was plotting revolution, with Hernán Siles Zuazo in the La Paz underground making overtures to the military and the Carabineros, but it did not say so directly. Canelas through his editorials deplored any extra-legal assumption of power and denounced any revolution as a viable means of solving Bolivia's problems. Not realizing that a new kind of social revolution was in the wings, Canelas demanded to know what the countless revolutions in Bolivia's past had accomplished. Meanwhile, Los Tiempos noted in passing that En Marcha, the regional publication of the MNR in Cochabamba, would reappear on March 23, 1952 [57] Two weeks later the country would be plunged into a bloody internal confrontation with social and economic overtones new to the history of Bolivia.

When fighting broke out in La Paz on April 9, 1952, during Holy Week, it was impossible for the newspapers in the capital to publish. These were the main sources of news for the handful of journals in the rest of the country, so they also faced a void of information as to what was happening in the city. Radio Illimani, the state transmitter established in 1937, had been captured by the MNR rebels and was the only radio station broadcasting from La Paz on April 9 and 10. From its bulletins and propaganda messages, Los Tiempos of Cochabamba was able to piece together the only journalistic account of the fighting, extremely valuable because the radio broadcasts otherwise would have been lost. [58] This, then, is how one conservative but reasonably objective newspaper viewed the opening wedge in the social transformation of Bolivia.

When the edition of Los Tiempos for April 10 came out, it bore the banner headline on the front page: AFTER TEN MONTHS AND THIRTEEN DAYS THE MILITARY JUNTA OF GOVERNMENT CONFRONTS A SUBVERSIVE MOVEMENT. The lengthy subhead, which imparted the details, described the coalition between the MNR and General Antonio Seleme, minister of government and head of the independent Carabinero forces, as "surprising." This revolutionary grouping seemed to be dominating, Los Tiempos reported, "but the situation is still indefinite." Meanwhile, the subhead announced that within the columns of the newspaper would be found the pronouncements of the revolutionaries, who had promised to convoke new elections soon.

These were the news stories which followed: Radio Illimani went on the air at 7 a.m. on April 9, announcing that General Seleme was military chief of the revolution and Siles Zuazo, the MNR second-in-command, civil chief in the absence of Paz Estenssoro. It was also announced that General Humberto Torres Ortiz, chief of the army general staff, "is in plain agreement with the revolution." (This was intended as a propaganda device to weaken the solidarity of the army ranks and win over the younger officers to the MNR cause.) The main purpose of the Radio Illimani broadcasts was to spread propaganda, not to impart information. Thus, alternating announcements with Bolivian folkloric music, men and women announcers said repeatedly:

- "The revolution is underway!"

- "The revolution is consolidated!"

- "57 districts throughout the republic back the revolution, together with the mining and railroad unions!"

- "Potosí, Oruro, Sucre and Cochabamba have seconded the revolution!"

- "In Sucre the people and the Carabineros have united jubilantly to celebrate the victory!"

- "The Army, the People and the Carabineros are united to consolidate the revolution."

The campaign and psychological warfare continued throughout the day. Announcements indicated that constitutional guarantees would be restored for all citizens, without distinction. The broadcasters also charged the Military Junta with deceiving people with talk of forthcoming elections. The MNR position itself, however, was unclear: at first, it was announced that new elections would be held; later, it was asserted that the results of the May 6, 1951 elections would be honored. Meanwhile, the MNR propagandists declared that Bolivia would be liberated from the power of la Rosca and the oligarchy it represented.

As for the military action, Radio Illimani gave highly favorable reports of the day's fighting and issued directives to the people from time to time. It reported that the Lanza Regiment was opposing the revolution in the suburb of Miraflores, so there was a necessity of building barricades there. People sympathetic to the revolution were called to the plaza in front of the ancient cathedral of San Francisco to receive arms; this call later was cancelled, when it was announced that thousands of arms already had been distributed. Seeking always to minimize casualties, Radio Illimani declared, with a wanton disregard for the truth, "The revolution has imposed its authority without shedding a single drop of blood." Repeatedly it was said on the first day that no one was injured or killed. "The shots that you hear in various sectors of the city have been authorized as simple demonstrations of jubilation and should not cause alarm," Radio Illimani announced as it sought to soothe concerned residents of the city.

At 10 a.m. the total triumph of the revolution was announced, adding that General Torres Ortiz, head of the army, had joined the rebels and General Crespo had ordered all troops to return to their quarters. This was premature as the fighting lasted for three bloody days, with the edge seeming to go toward the rebels on the first day, against them on the second, and bringing them victory on the third. When the 10 a.m. announcement was made, however, it was necessary to offer a political plan for the claimed triumph. General Seleme, head of the Carabineros, broadcast a communique in which he affirmed that constitutional guarantees would be upheld, urged everyone to cooperate in the maintenance of order, declared that the vanguard of the MNR, the Chaco veterans and the young military, "had retaken once and for all the road of the law," and announced that the air force had come over to the revolution. To underscore the significance of Seleme's statement, Radio Illimani announced, "The commands of the corps of Carabineros throughout the nation are with the revolution."

At the same time, Hernán Siles Zuazo, the civil head of the revolt in the absence of Paz Estenssoro, went on the air to calm the populace whose feelings of anger were boiling to the surface. Siles enjoined them: "The people have broken their chains, without fear or hatred, and we call upon all the citizens to back this movement that has no intention of vengeance. We will demonstrate that we know how to forgive and to build. No one should fear reprisals. The army and the people are identified [with each other]. This revolution was not born of hatred, but of the desire to assure for Bolivia, for us and ours, a better future. All violence will be condemned by the political committee of the MNR." Later, as looting broke out in some sections of the city, Radio Illimani broadcast the slogan, "People of La Paz, avoid the attacks [on shops] which some rogues are trying to carry out.'

As 30,000 demonstrators flocked to the Plaza Murillo, the radio station began transmitting items for foreign as well as domestic consumption. It asserted, "The government of the MNR will maintain cordial relations with all the democratic countries; it will respect treaties in force and it will re-establish constitutional guaranties." At the same time, to obtain a good international image--something which the MNR had never enjoyed--the party's propagandists declared, "The revolutionary movement that has just arisen will respect all political tendencies so that united all the Bolivians can contribute to the greatness of the country."

Comments on the manifestation in the Plaza Murillo also were flashed from time to time. Radio Illimani reported, "A great popular demonstration, headed by the women of the feminine section of the MNR, is traversing the central streets of the city." Again, the radio station observed, "Finally, after six years, all Bolivians are gathering to reconstruct what others have destroyed."

Demetrio Canelas, owner and editor of Los Tiempos, was not content to let his reporting of the insurrection rest solely on what he and his staff could glean from the MNR reports over Radio Illimani. Another source of information was the Argentine station, Radio Belgrano, which reported at midnight on the first day of fighting that the Carabineros had surrendered. Relying on wire-service reports from the beleaguered Bolivian capital, Radio Belgrano said the Carabineros had capitulated under an attack by the Bolívar Regiment which descended upon La Paz from the airport of El Alto. Nevertheless, Radio Belgrano also announced that people in the streets of La Paz were crying vivas for the MNR and Villarroel and repeatedly, "Power awaits Paz Estenssoro." Seleme was quoted as saying, "This is a revolution of the people. The Government Junta will be mixed." He added that Paz Estenssoro would return to La Paz immediately from his exile in Buenos Aires. Radio Belgrano also reported that a cabinet crisis in the Military Junta on the night of April 8, when some members resigned, triggered the decision by the MNR to act quickly.

Los Tiempos also printed a United Press dispatch from La Paz by Luis Zavala, but this was buried on the fifth page of the newspaper, revealing the lack of confidence which Bolivian editors had in the international news services. Dated April 9, the dispatch gave a quite different view of what was happening in the capital city. It prematurely stated that the MNR had defeated the Military Junta "after a brief revolution..." The United Press said the shooting began at 6 a.m. with pistol and machine gun firing in the streets of La Paz. An hour later there was firing of about five minutes duration. The dispatch said, "It is still not known if there were casualties in the skirmishes of short duration in the streets of this capital." At 7:15 a.m. the MNR reportedly announced over Radio Illimani that the revolution had triumphed, even though the artillery regiment Bolívar, loyal to the junta, was still fighting in the Villa Victoria section. Trucks with armed civilians raced through the streets bearing signs, VIVA ESTENSSORO!

Meanwhile, Radio Illimani kept up its propaganda barrage. Appeals were made to various sectors of Bolivian society. Juan Lechín, head of the powerful FSTMB or miners' union, spoke over Radio Illimani at 10:55 a.m. pledging the adherence of his organization to the revolution. He called the MNR uprising "an eminently popular revolution, whose advent brings the destruction of the mining rosca. The mines will return to their rightful owner, which is the people itself..." One citizen gave a short, impassioned speech in Aymará to the campesinos around La Paz. The Federación Sindical de Empleados de Bancos y Ramas Anexas (Bank Employees Federation) announced its support for the revolution, asking that all union organizations be restored. And the chief of the student organization Federación Universitaria, Mario Guzmán Galarza, also spoke on Radio Illimani, declaring among other things, "This is the day of glory for the triumph of the MNR revolution." These personal testimonials were intended to give the impression that a fierce groundswell of public support had come to the aid of the MNR and their Carabinero allies. It was carefully orchestrated and exceedingly well done.

As the day of April 9 progressed, Radio Illimani made it clear that a body of basic points had been agreed to by the MNR: international treaties would be respected; relations would be maintained with all democratic countries; the Constitution would be restored; the MNR revolution would remain faithful to democratic principles; radio and telegraph communications had been restored throughout the country; and there had been no bloodshed. While it is true that the fighting was more severe on the second and third days, it was transparently untrue that there were no casualties on the first day. The MNR undoubtedly wanted to maintain public calm, not discourage possible recruits from joining the fight, and to overcome its image as a party of violence.

In the remaining phases of the struggle, loyal army units fought their way uptown from the military barracks in San Jorge. The garrison of Viacha was advancing on La Paz to lend its support to the Military Junta. Artillery, mortars and planes strafed and bombed the MNR street fighters; the picture seemed so dark that General Seleme sought refuge in the Chilean embassy on the second night of fighting. But the MNR fought on, conquered arsenals along with their badly needed supplies of ammunition, and finally overpowered the dispirited military on the third day.

Fighting broke out elsewhere only in the mining center of Oruro. Los Tiempos described the situation in Cochabamba, which probably was typical of the rest of the country. In the early morning, the prefect of Cochabamba, a creature of the central government, said the Military Junta still ruled in La Paz, but no one of the prefecture answered the phone after noon. The Región Militar posted troops at the four corners of the plaza and assigned pickets to patrol the city, but the MNR had control of the casa municipal, the mayor's offices, where MNR partisans were proclaiming the revolution from the balconies. Trucks filled with men shouting revolutionary slogans made a few desultory turns around the plaza, the only other visible sign of the supposedly triumphant revolution. The reporter, who described the city as being under "an apprehensive atmosphere," was told by a bystander, "Right now no one rules in Cochabamba." The Los Tiempos writer described it as much like August 29, 1949, when Germán Vera led the MNR outbreak that mushroomed into war. [59]

En Marcha did not appear again until April 28, almost three weeks after the successful MNR rebellion and the first issue of the newspaper since February 9. A two-line banner headline read MILITARY AND CIVILIANS RESPONSIBLE FOR MASSACRES AND SCANDALS TO THE PENITENTIARY. In an editorial, En Marcha compared what happened after the triumph of April 9 with the aftermath of July 21, 1946, when Villarroel and his aides were shot down and hanged from lampposts in the Plaza Murillo where other officers were dragged from the prison and lynched as late as October. After the MNR victory, by way of contrast, there was no vae victus as the Rosca had predicted--nothing more than contempt for the conquered. On July 21, the people witnessed "the crime organized by anti-national interests which launched to the most savage and unheard of excesses gangs [who were] drunk and paid to execute in the name of the people..." En Marcha maintained. April 9, on the other hand, the newspaper continued, was "the civic explosion of the people [who] pursued no other thing than the re-conquest of their usurped rights, their liberty trampled under foot and their sovereignty outraged... April 9 is, then, the reply of right to crime." [60]

The self-righteousness of En Marcha could not hide the fact, however, that the MNR in power--after suffering persecutions for six years--had as little tolerance for the opposition as its hard-nosed predecessors. This was especially true in the area of press freedom where the MNR moved swiftly to silence opposition in La Paz. On April 30, 1952, the Asociación Departmental de Periodistas (State Association of Journalists) of Cochabamba issued a resolution urging the MNR government to protect La Razón, the Aramayo newspaper which was being harassed by mobs, so that it could publish again (see Chapter 6); release the jailed editor of La Tribuna, and also free the editor of El Diario, Hugo Gonzáles Rioja. Juan del Valle, pseudonym for a writer for Los Tiempos, commenting on freedom of the press in his column, "Someone Has to Say It," reminded the MNR that it had sworn upon taking office that the Bolivian press "will develop without obstacles of any kind." Juan del Valle recognized there was a period of "collective psychosis" following every revolution, but the time had come to return to legal norms. In this regard, the MNR also had promised to issue a supreme decree to repeal that dictated in September 1951 by the Military Junta annulling the Press Jury, constituted of experts to hear libel cases. [61] Yet nothing had been done, and there were important cases pending. The Falange Socialista Boliviana, the rightwing party modeled on the Spanish Falange, for example, announced that it would sue En Marcha for libel in articles about its role in the April revolution. Named in the suit was Raúl Murillo y Aliaga, the editor of En Marcha who once had been an FSB member, and who had criticized the political party severely in the columns of his newspaper. [62]

Whether with official sanction or not, there were other abuses against the opposition press that were as brutal an any registered during the course of the sexenio. Los Tiempos reported that a band of about twenty MNR partisans with faces blackened as a disguise invaded on April 23 the only newspaper published in the remote northern town of Trinidad, Eco del Beni, which opposed the new government. They allegedly threatened the ancient editor, Sergio Becerra, who was the only editorial worker in the shop, scattered the type and made off with some equipment. [63] In other instances, official acts closed down means of public communication. By fiscal order, for example, Carabineros and agents of the police closed Radio Cochabamba on June 12, 1953, accusing it of complicity in the operation of the clandestine FSB station Antorcha, which had been captured on June 8. [64]

To justify these measures and defend its other public acts, the MNR recognized immediately after taking power that it needed an official spokesman. La Calle had been the unofficial voice of the party for five years after the MNR was founded in 1941, and En Marcha had been established specifically to serve as propaganda arm of the movement for the elections of 1951. But after April 1952, what kind of newspaper would best serve the MNR cause? Paz Estenssoro vetoed the resurrection of La

162

Calle, for it had been an organ of the opposition; it was bred and born to oppose, and the party needed positive support now. [65]

Clearly, a new newspaper was needed for a fresh image for the MNR, but that would take time. Meanwhile, En Marcha, which began appearing daily in early May 1952, would be the ORGAN OF THE NATIONAL REVOLUTIONARY MOVEMENT as its masthead proclaimed, as a stop-gap measure. The newspaper was printed on the press that formerly served La Noche. Two newspapers were printed on the same press; although they were very opposed in political philosophy, En Marcha came out in the mornings and La Tribuna, owned by Mario Flores, in the after-noons. La Tribuna ceased publication when the MNR bought its press in 1952 to put out La Nación, the official newspaper the party had been planning. It first hit the streets on Octo-ber 12, 1952, Columbus Day or día de la raza (Day of the Race) as it is known in Latin America. Since La Nación was a morning newspaper, there had been some thought of continuing to issue En Marcha in the afternoons, but the press facilities were no longer adequate to put out two newspapers, especially in view of the wider circulation planned for La Nación. After the revolt of April 9-11, the circulation of En Marcha itself had risen to 15,000-18,000 daily--a respectable figure for the journalistic market of La Paz--and for the first time a newspaper supported itself by advertisements as well as street sales. [66]

Thus, with La Nación waiting in the wings, En Marcha bowed out of the picture on October 1, 1952, having printed 142 editions in its hectic career. On the occasion of what was believed to be its demise--but which turned out to be pre-mature--Murillo discussed "Our contribution to the triumph of the National Revolution," including many facts in the history of En Marcha already presented here. He commented, "to that glorious uprising [April 9], our daily contributed powerfully in the second stage of its life." The first stage had been the efforts to win the elections of 1951; the second stage came to put the MNR in power. Whether by elections or by force, the party was in power; therefore, Murillo concluded, "We have fulfilled our duty and we will not say goodbye, but so long." [67]

It was wise for Murillo to keep his foot in the door, for the reports of the death of En Marcha, as Mark Twain noted about himself, were greatly exaggerated. The newspaper would come back on three separate occasions as the personal political expression of Murillo and the unofficial voice of the rightist, pro-Siles and anti-Lechín sector of the MNR. In retrospect, it was also wise for the party to dump En Marcha for its editor became increasingly conservative and engaged in wild personality brawls that were disruptive within the shaky coalition of the MNR. Briefly, the newspaper first reappeared between April 14 and August 5, 1953, when most MNR officials overlooked the growing petulance of Murillo because of the editor's staunch support of the party in the past. The second and third reappearances were more ideologically oriented. Opposed to the skyrocketing demands of organized labor and especially to the mine workers' flambuoyant chief Juan Lechín, Murillo revived En Marcha between February 9 and December 19, 1957, to support President Siles Zuazo and the monetary stabilization plan which labor so vehemently opposed. Finally, En Marcha was resuscitated in 1959, when Murillo was a deputy, to oppose the presidential aspirations of Lechín in the upcoming 1960 elections. [68]

When Murillo cranked up En Marcha as a weekly tabloid in 1957 to go after his arch-enemy Lechín, the editor noted that his newspaper had no official support or connection whatever. Therefore, he reasoned, it was "a movimientista voice in the deepest and most authentic sense of the word," against extremes of both right and left. "Since the hard years of the sexenio," Murillo reminded his readers, "'En Marcha' has been the banner of rebellion for the people of Bolivia and of its majority party, the National Revolutionary Party..." Fate, however, had intervened. "Factors apart from the will of its editors compelled that during the last few years this authentically nationalist and popular voice cease to circulate with its sound preachments and its compact columns carrying their message to the people of Bolivia." [69]

It soon became all too clear, however, that this En Marcha would serve as nothing more than a vehicle of rabid personal attacks against Juan Lechín. For example, an editorial cartoon depicted the labor leader as a monk surrounded with voluptuous women--a slur against his alleged profligate life and hypocrisy. The feud with Lechín became obsessive as Murillo denounced the labor leader in issue after issue of his revived newspaper. Lechín introduced foreigners into national politics. Lechín cooperated with the Military Junta of General Ballivián. [70] Most heinous, however, was the labor leader's opposition to the stabilization plan recommended by United States expert George Jackson Eder, designed to halt Bolivia's runaway inflation through an austerity program that would have reduced drastically the real wages of the miners. Another editorial cartoon showed Lechín saying, "I'll prosper with inflation without going down in the mine. Don't talk to me of stabilization. I am not Lechín, I am Lechón [sucking pig.]" [71]

Despite its inglorious end, however, En Marcha deserves a

special place in the history of MNR propaganda efforts. Established as the first official party organ to garner support for the 1951 elections, the newspaper did so spectacularly against great adversity. Its editor Raúl Murillo y Aliaga was not a brilliant journalist, but he was tenacious--and that was the quality which the MNR needed at the time. Whether the party failed to get the required absolute majority of votes in 1951, or whether the fruits of victory were snatched from its grasp did not really matter. Public opinion had been set up for the revolutionary blow planned all along; the MNR had won the image of a combative party led by idealistic young men who had been persecuted throughout the sexenio, a persecution capped by denying the party peaceful access to power in the elections of 1951.

That contest was a turning point in the development of the MNR; with the aid of En Marcha for the first time the movement offered a presidential candidate. Even during the Villarroel regime the MNR had only the shadowy representation of three ministers in a predominantly military cabinet. The Catavi interpellation of 1943 had won them that representation, but it was to require the elections of 1951 to establish the MNR firmly on the national stage. In that sense, En Marcha was the single most significant propaganda organ of the MNR during its existence. It was a tremendous feat for a small newspaper to win the most votes for its candidate since the opposition had never come out ahead in a Bolivian election. And this was achieved against police repression and the absence of Paz Estenssoro to prosecute his own campaign.

The fact that the MNR won its biggest margins in the cities indicates that En Marcha, distributed almost exclusively in those centers, pinpointed its target of the middle class and workers successfully. The MNR revolution which began on April 9, 1952, would not have been possible without the middle class. Through ten long years La Calle had instilled a sense of social conscience in that class; in a few short months En Marcha was to channel that craving for social justice and self-improvement into victory at the polls and--when that was denied--victory in the streets. The revolution had begun and newspapers would continue to be the medium of communication through which discussion of the great public questions of the day--or opposition to them--would be carried out. La Nación, the new official MNR newspaper, following in the footsteps of La Calle and En Marcha, did not operate in a vacuum, however. It faced the threat of powerful opposition from La Razón, organ of the tin-mining giant Carlos Víctor Aramayo, in La Paz and Los Tiempos, the conservative vehicle of Demetrio Canelas, in Cochabamba. Before examining how the official MNR press dealt with the major revolutionary issues, it is necessary to consider this press of the Bolivian right. These newspapers did not nip at the heels of the MNR press through the years: they went for the jugular, and leading the pack was La Razón which had dominated Bolivian journalism for decades.

Chapter 6

THE DEATH OF LA RAZON

> I am not going to shoot the people of
> Bolivia to protect Señor Aramayo. [The
> case of La Razón] concerns the liberation of
> the Bolivian people from Señor Aramayo.
>
> --Víctor Paz Estenssoro,
> quoted in Los Tiempos,
> June 10, 1952.

> Political passions should not stain the good
> name of any government regime in Bolivia,
> with the obliteration of that accredited
> national newspaper [La Razón].
>
> --Los Tiempos,
> Oct. 19, 1952.

While the attitude of the established revolutionary press toward the great tin miners, the Indians and the military would reveal much of the thrust the Revolution was taking (see Chapters 8-10), the press of the right was also important in determining that direction. As Augusto Céspedes has stated emphatically, "The process of the press of the right crushed the revolutionary processes." [1] The kingpin of that opposition press--one which did not survive the Revolution of 1952--was unquestionably La Razón, the powerful spokesman of the Aramayo tin-mining family. By examining the attitudes of La Razón on key events of this period, one can determine why it was not allowed to continue publication once the MNR had gained power.

Founded in 1917 by the physician José María Escalier to boost his presidential aspirations, La Razón was soon acquired by the Aramayos. The head of the family, Carlos Víctor Aramayo, had an annual income of more than $1,500,000, but he was doing more than merely dabbling in La Paz journalism. He consciously set out to make La Razón the organ of his personal interests, which meant that he would brook no opposition from labor unions or countenance any attempts at social reform in

Bolivia. La Razón soon captured the widest circulation in Bolivia and gained an international reputation as an extremely well-edited newspaper, even though it was the most reactionary of the capital dailies. [2]

La Paz in 1917 was not a propitious place in which to launch a newspaper. The overwhelming majority of Bolivians could not read, and the man in the street seldom had money, even half a peso, to squander on a newspaper: for that amount he could take food home to his hungry family. Yet until universal suffrage was granted by the MNR in 1952, the Bolivian literate elite was an audience worth cultivating. This was the class that held the reins of political, social and economic power. Although La Razón's circulation was always small in terms of journalism in industrial societies--never more than 50,000--the newspaper's impact was great and at times decisive.

The early days of La Razón, as with many a newspaper, spawned a number of traditions and legends. Under the first editor, Alfredo Infante, staff members worked without pay, getting only free bus fare and movie passes. The newspaper was hand set entirely long after the Linotype machine had effected a journalistic revolution elsewhere. One typesetter was especially valued, for he was the only staff member who could decipher the difficult handwriting of President Bautista Saavedra (1921-1925), a fact which revealed how closely the newspaper was linked with the governing oligarchy. Adherence to the government line was fraught with its own dangers, however, as when "incendiary bands of vandals" destroyed the La Razón plant in 1920. [3] At first, La Razón was printed on an ancient flatbed press hand fed by an Indian. In the early years, before the newspaper acquired major wire services, its only foreign coverage was supplied by one correspondent in Buenos Aires. [4]

La Razón reacted immediately to the Catavi mine massacre of 1942--that angry confrontation which shaped opposition to the oligarchy more than any other single event. Without exception, the newspaper could see no possible good coming from the labor movement and saw behind the desire of the Catavi miners to raise their daily wages from about 75 cents to $1.50 a day "the avid tentacles of communism." [5] An examination of La Razón's editorial reactions to other major events of this period will provide clues as to why the newspaper fell victim to the MNR once the latter gained power in 1952. These events are the death of Germán Busch in 1939, the Indian problem, the closing of La Calle in 1943, the regime of Villarroel ending in 1946 and the crucial elections of 1951. These events formed the calendar of the formation of the MNR itself, and it will be instructive to note the kind of opposition which the party had to brook.   This is important because La Razón spoke not only for itself and the Aramayo interests; it set the tone and style of the other rightwing newspapers of La Paz--Patiño's El Diario and Hochschild's Ultima Hora--as well as being an international spokesman for Bolivia.   Of what was the newspaper guilty that its very life was not restored after 1952?

As cited above, La Razón was not immune from violence because it sided with rightist governments throughout its long and eventful career.   The newspaper plant of La Razón was assaulted by leftwing mobs when Colonel David Toro came to power in 1936.   La Calle recalled later that the intervention against La Razón came from the Federation of Labor Workers, the Revolutionary Socialist Committee and the local union of the Workers' Federation.   They did not occupy the physical site of La Razón, however, as happened to La Razón in 1920 and to El Norte in 1930.   Two days after the Toro coup d'etat, La Razón reappeared. [6]

The administration of Germán Busch (1937-1939) was more radical and posed greater problems for La Razón.   Busch was a curious and painful figure in Bolivian history.   He inherited the backlash of the Chaco War which propelled him into the pres- idency after the coup d'etat which ousted General David Toro on July 13, 1937.   The younger and more idealistic army offi- cers had triumphed. [7]

La Rosca, the Bolivian elite, reacted swiftly to the danger which Busch presented to them.   Carlos Víctor Aramayo, owner of La Razón, was charged with financing an abortive rebellion at Palmar on March 26, 1938, led by the ousted President Toro. But Busch would not be intimidated.   His far-reaching reform decree of June 7, 1939 (a symbolic date used by the MNR to announce its program in 1942) struck at the heart of the mining interests by requiring that all expatriate profits be deposited first in the Banco Central de Bolivia to be returned to the owners at the government's discount. [8]   With that decree, although never enforced, Busch signed his own death warrant. He died August 23, 1939, and the pressure exerted upon him by the tin companies and their hangers-on was blamed for his death, an apparent suicide.

Conditions surrounding Busch's death were so tense that newspapers were forbidden to publish--after La Razón already had rushed an extra edition to the streets--and government troops were stationed in all of the printing plants. August 24-26 were declared days of national mourning, with all public and private work stopped.   When public calm was restored, La Razón breathed a sigh of relief: "Although men pass, institutions remain."   With Busch gone, La Razón urged a return "to the tutelary institutions that our forefathers forged"--in short, no more attempts at reform. The newspaper concluded, "Let the tragedy place a parenthesis around all comment...it is enough to know that the dictator rendered justice to himself, leaving to the country a [painful] experience." La Razón noted only two major aspects of Busch's presidency: the "questionable" elections of March 1938 and the implantation of a dictatorship in April 1939. [9]

Circumstances surrounding Busch's death gave rise to immediate rumors that he had been murdered rather than having committed suicide. According to La Razón, the shooting took place at Busch's residence in the suburb of Miraflores when a group was celebrating the birthday of his aide and brother-in-law, Colonel Eliodoro Carmona. After a political conversation at 5 a.m. Busch was visibly disturbed. He declared that he could no longer endure life, took a revolver out of his pocket, and shot himself in the right temple--in the presence of his brother-in-law and a Major Toytia. Military and political leaders met at once in the salón rojo of the Palacio de Gobierno with Vice-President Enrique Baldivieso present. They issued a communique which established a provisional government under General Carlos Quintanilla.

There was, however, a second version of Busch's death: that Colonel Carmona, the brother-in-law of Busch, and others at the party saw Busch and his wife go upstairs to their apartment (both families lived in the same house). Busch was putting his Colt .38 in a desk drawer when there was an accidental discharge. Most persons, however, seemed to accept the suicide explanation, for they knew how temperamental and at times deeply despondent their former leader had been. [10]

Two separate official investigations spanning a period of thirteen years agreed that Busch died a suicide. A proceso (investigation) in 1939 ruled that it was a suicide, with the first bullet from the Colt .38 hitting a desk and the second entering Busch's right temple. Col. Angel Telleria, an expert named to represent the family, was present during the course of the proceso and agreed with its findings. [11] Again, in February 1952 the magistrates of the criminal division of the Superior Court ruled officially that the death of Germán Busch was a suicide and Colonel Eliodoro Carmona was innocent of involvement. [12] So ended, with a bullet in the right temple, Bolivia's first reform movement. There were no observances of the anniversaries of Busch's death for three years, as la Rosca entrenched itself once again under the repressive military regimes of General Carlos Quintanilla (1939-1940) and General Enrique Peñaranda (1940-1943).

If La Razón took a dim view of worker demands at Catavi in 1942, it dealt even more harshly with the campesinos, the Indian masses who made up the great bulk of Bolivia's population. In 1943, for example, the newspaper attacked a proposal for extending liberal education to the Indians: "It is thought that the Indian Should be educated by a humanistic and not a technical criterion, and from this absolute blindness that afflicts those charged with solving this problem can come serious damage to the country." [13] Again, when the first Indian congress was held in La Paz in August 1943, La Razón denounced the event:

[In] this type of gathering demagogic elements always predominate, anxious to obtain political notice by any means. They bring together however many Indians perfectly ignorant of the meaning and scope of these meetings, and they induce them to sow complaints of all kinds and to formulate votes of protest against this or that, without logical foundation and without serious reasons... [We have always repudiated] the political agitators who want to make of every Indian a doctor [of law] who will claim and demand the redemption of his brothers. [14]

Such congresses, the newspaper continued, were planned and carried out by individuals who were not Indians and "are not interested in any way in helping the Indians, but only and exclusively for gaining a political platform which their scarce personal merits could never give them." [15] In short, the government should discourage such gatherings and jail agitators who already had caused huelgas de brazos caídos (passive resistance strikes) on some haciendas. Thus, as with the tin miners, La Razón found absolutely no common ground with the Bolivian Indian--in the world's most Amerindian nation. On the contrary, the Indian was to be kept submerged forever in the most discredited of colonial traditions.

The newspaper was opposed to the legitimate demands not only of the tin miners and Indians, but also to other segments of Bolivia's incipient labor class. In 1944, for example, La Razón reported that an accident on the Uyuni-Atocha railroad which caused the death of the engineer Celestino Luján was caused by his own drunkenness. The Sindicato Ferroviario (Railroad Union) of Uyuni denounced La Razón as "the scourge of the national labor movement." [16] It should not be surprising that such men, peasants, miners and other workers, terrorized La Razón after the MNR Revolution of 1952 and kept the newspaper from reopening.

While La Razón upheld the status quo in Bolivia, the

Peñaranda government took action to silence the opposition press by issuing on December 13, 1943, a decree which outlawed "extremist propaganda" against public order and the institutions of the state, or which fomented labor unrest. [17] La Calle, the MNR spokesman, clearly the target of the decree, was shut down four days later. The Patiño newspaper El Diario did not comment on the shutdown of La Calle, but the Hochschild organ, Ultima Hora, the most responsible of the oligarchical capital dailies, declared:

> There are those who believe that journalistic solidarity is an elastic concept that should be used with friends and repudiated with adversaries. It is, on the contrary--or should be--an absolute concept, lying beyond personal differences. In the name of that solidarity, we express our objection against the suspension of an organ of information [La Calle], because that wounds the very institution of the press. Whatever its ideology may be, every information organ translates the sentiment and thought of one sector of public opinion. The newspaper may be silenced, but that opinion will not disappear. [18]

La Razón, on the other hand, stressed the need for control of the press in wartime. Was the government to allow its dispensations to be the object of mockery? "The clash has been inevitable," the newspaper observed. "Thus, it has come about that the Cabinet has taken harsh measures. It is lamentable that [La Calle] has knowingly given occasion for this." [19] Hence, only one of the three major dailies of La Paz opposed the governmental seizure of La Calle. La Razón, which was to champion freedom of the press so ardently when it was not allowed to publish after 1952, did not extend that freedom to others in 1943. Conversely, the MNR--which knew from direct experience what suppression was like--also suppressed the press during the first few years of its own rule. Moreover, such repression seldom achieves its goal unless it is total, as in Cuba after 1961. In Bolivia on December 20, 1943, only three days after La Calle was shut down, the Peñaranda government was overthrown by a combined MNR and liberal military revolt. It was a miniature dress rehearsal of what was to happen in April 1952 except there was little street fighting. In 1944, La Calle recalled that at that time, a year earlier, La Razón did not have the confidence of the people, who gathered in the morning of December 20, 1943, when the revolt had been successful, and wanted to demolish the building in La Razón and destroy the installations of the newspaper "which today believes itself qualified to direct the same people." [20]

The "Revolution of the Majors" of 1943 saw the installation

of a reform military junta led by Major Gualberto Villarroel (1943-1946). In his first message after being sworn in at 3 p.m. on December 20, 1943, Villarroel said to a representative of the United Press, "As far as what refers to the goals of the new government, we will return to the people the free exercise of their rights. In the international aspect the position of Bolivia will not vary. Order exists throughout the country and in this moment I have received adhesions of all the garrisons." [21] In his Christmas message of December 24, Villarroel added, "Our objective resides in opening up the road to a new life in which, once restored the rights and guarantees the Constitution consecrates, and dignifying the level of material and cultural prosperity of the people, all of the Bolivians can enjoy, far from necessity and fear, the benefits of a free life in a free Country." [22]

La Razón, which did not publish between December 20-26 and then reappeared as a tabloid because of the shortage of newsprint, dutifully printed the president's statements. In its editorial on December 31, the Aramayo newspaper urged "Return to normalcy," stating, "The operation of the Constitution, proclaimed a few days ago for all of the country, returns to public opinion the most important factor of its life. Logically, the restrictions of its application should be eliminated in the most rapid and most complete form that can be possible." Elections should have been held in May 1940 but were postponed due to "exceptional factors." La Razón called for elections at the regularly scheduled time, May 1944. [23]

While such statements may have sounded conciliatory, La Razón was soon opposing tooth and nail the proposed social reforms urged by Villarroel, who stated:

> We are seeking, above all, that the material and human resources of the Country serve to obtain economic and social betterment of the men who humbly work here. We do not recognize artificial privileges, nor of race; human value can only be measured by work; it is therefore that the honorable and working men have nothing to fear in the change which has been produced.

The riches of Bolivia should build schools and roads, necessary for development, Villarroel said, adding these natural resources should also give a just return to capital "and at the same time favor the workers whose sacrifice is undeniable." The former "false democracy" would be replaced by a "regime of mutual and equitable cooperation that portions out to each social sector the elements that it needs for its development." [24]

La Razón ignored these concessions to "a just return to capital" and countered with an editorial on "The impelling capital," which noted that "since some time in these parts [Bolivia] whatever capital achieves is no longer going to reinforce foreign industry, but on the contrary, seeks in Bolivia itself the means of remaining in the country, as the strong investments destined to the land and cattle industry prove..." [25] Again, the newspaper stated editorially, "The life of all of the country is no more than an uninterrupted succession of steps at the margin of the most sacred national interests... What is to be desired, what every citizen who loves his country covets, is that we make the facts match the words..." [26]

La Razón, with its smooth, reasoned words could not obscure the fact that it faced a challenge to the hegemony of the great mining enterprises in Bolivian life even more dangerous than the tentative thrusts of Busch. When Villarroel called upon "the young military forces" to join in his movement for national renovation, La Razón declared such an alliance unconstitutional, similar to the union of soldiers and peasants in Russia in 1917. Forgetting its previous support of Peñaranda and other army heads of state, La Razón argued that the military should be strictly non-political. [27] On only one point could the Aramayo newspaper agree with Villarroel during the early months of his rule. It quoted him out of context as saying that Bolivia should not "disperse its activity in reform experiments." Villarroel was actually calling for substantial, not token, reforms but La Razón mistakenly agreed that "attempts at reform... have thus far been a genuine scourge for the whole country." [28]

Luis V. Zavala, editor of La Razón, also took up the cudgels on the issue of recognition of the Villarroel government by foreign states. At first, Argentina was the only foreign power to recognize the new regime--on January 3, 1944. Shortly thereafter, Zavala wrote that the Junta de Gobierno was composed of three groups: first, the military men; second, chiefs of the MNR, and third, dissident political elements of the parties which had collaborated with the deposed government. Yet, noted La Razón, in spite of the heterogeneous composition of Villarroel's cabinet, "a certain intellectual and moral unity is present in the Junta." La Razón was disturbed by the lack of United States recognition, however, and noted that a confidential agent in Washington, D.C. said the only way Bolivia could get United States recognition was "the necessity of participation by the PIR in the conduct of the national events..." The inclusion of the Marxist party, founded in 1940, in the Bolivian government horrified La Razón, even though the Soviet Union was an ally in World War II. The inclusion of the PIR, wrote La Razón in early 1944, could not help or please Bolivia, the

United States or the PIR itself. [29] Yet only two years later the newspaper would be welcoming the alliance of José Antonio Arze's extremist party to bring the MNR and the reform military to their knees.

Along the same lines, in January 1944 Villarroel wrote, "The reorganization of the political parties is, in effect, one of the most troublesome [issues] within the civic readjustment that all of the Bolivians want." La Razón replied in an editorial, "Premature reorganization," that "the present moment has ceased to be [one of] disturbance; nevertheless, it is still [one of] social and political commotion." Therefore, La Razón concluded, the reorganization of political parties, which would strip perhaps the oligarchy of its ancient accoutrements, was a luxury that the country could not afford. [30]

Yet La Razón was forced to stand by while the Villarroel government made its first tentative efforts toward reform. On January 20, 1944, one month after the coup d'etat which toppled Peñaranda, Villarroel stood on the balcony of the national palace facing the Plaza Murillo and declared, "We must obtain all of the social and economic recoveries for the campesinos, workers and employees. We must obtain recovery [of the rights] of the State itself." In a mass ceremony, the military, workers and members of the MNR pledged to aid the Junta de Gobierno, which took advantage of the occasion to announce the abolition of the reduction of tariffs on foreign goods established by a decree of December 1942. [31] Harking back to the colonial period and the ley residencia, another statute of the Junta ordered that all officials must submit to an inspection of their political and administrative acts when they left office. [32] In early February 1944 a projected civil code was released, and the Villarroel regime granted complete freedom of the press to discuss political issues. In line with this change of policy, the Junta invited the press to tour the Panóptico Nacional or national penitentiary to scotch rumors that political prisoners were being held there. Even La Razón found excellent conditions and reported that the prisoners said their conditions were better than before the coup d'etat. [33]

The patriotic sentiments of La Razón could easily be aroused, however, if foreign statements concerning the country were deemed to be false. Thus, in February 1944 the New York Times reported that the Spanish embassy in La Paz, representing a country which had not broken relations with the Axis, channeled money from the Axis countries into Bolivia to help finance the revolution of December 20, 1943, which overthrew Peñaranda. La Razón, which was soon to have a new editor in the person of Nicolás Ortiz Pacheco, denied this completely in an editorial entitled, "Human fallibility." [34]

On every other occasion, however, La Razón did its very best to apply the brakes to the mild social revolution which the Villarroel forces had unleased. The newspaper compared the Villarroel movement to the first days of the French Revolution and noted: "As a characteristic of the periods immediately following every revolution, one can point out the aggressiveness of that part of the triumphant citizens who feel themselves to be the masters of the new political order without being so." The Aramayo newspaper called upon the Junta to allow opposition political parties for the elections coming up in May 1944. [35]

On one occasion during the Villarroel government, La Razón felt constrained to explain the origin of the term, la Rosca, in an attempt to defuse attention directed at itself. Since the origin of the term has always been in doubt, it is interesting to note La Razón's explanation. At first the term was applied to "a close circle of individuals who, thanks to unbecoming machinations, had succeeded in monopolizing the means of enrichment, at the margin of the law and of rectitude of conscience." Later, La Razón reported, the name was applied to a lodge which collected commercial information. During the Chaco War, it was applied to civilians who made fortunes in the cities and to the military who became millionaires overnight. Now, the newspaper asserted, the term applied to "all the men of fortune, rightly or wrongly achieved... the legion of the privileged." La Razón concluded that the term was misused, showing "an absolute lack of discernment" of those who abused it. [36] In another editorial, "The envious and those envied," the newspaper noted there were various grades of la Rosca today, like the emboscados, a term used by front-line soldiers in the Chaco War to denigrate those in the rear. Moreover, La Razón found a conflict between the old Rosca and the new Rosca which centered on the Villarroel regime. [37]

La Razón came to accept the change in government, although it vehemently disapproved of it. In February 1944 it wrote, "The revolution is a fait acompli and has triumphed. Nothing nor anyone can suppress these two truths. But what next? Evolution toward legality or another revolution?" La Razón came down on the side of the former although it deplored the pulverization of parties which had occurred since the revolt. [38] La Razón, which so vehemently decried fascist influence in the new government at every possibility, wanted a corporate system of representation in the new Convention which the Villarroel forces were establishing. In short, the newspaper wanted the Convention to be made up of "a formation of numerous and representative entities...grouped together by community or by similarity of ideals around persons of prestige..." [39]

La Calle saw a new tactic in the opposition press after David Alvéstegui was named new editor of La Razón in October 1945. The MNR newspaper claimed, "The rosquera tactic is now to ask for marvels for the people, so that they can encounter an echo in the sympathy of the masses." For example, La Razón, in attempting to arouse expectations which could not be satisfied and therefore lead to an overthrow of the Villarroel regime, had asked for "open-air theaters, milk bars [and] vacation housing developments." [40]

The opposition mining press continued to flay the social program of Villarroel, who declared in 1945, "I am more the friend of the poor than enemy of the rich." Attacks became so severe that the ineffective reform government finally seized both La Razón and Ultima Hora after the two newspapers had stirred up the abortive coup d'etat of June 13, 1946. The change in La Razón's editorial policy after its confiscation was startling. For example, the newspaper urged great increases in workers' wages so that more money from the mining industry would remain in the country to build a national market. Confiscated or not, it seemed strange to hear La Razón saying, "Since the colonial epoch, a river of silver has flowed from our mines to Europe, while in this country there remained only holes in the mountains and holes in the lungs of the miners." [41]

This kind of rhetoric was particularly galling to La Razón which had always pictured itself as the champion of the voice of reason in Bolivian affairs. It is not surprising that the overthrow of Villarroel came soon afterward; confiscation of the major mining newspapers was not to be tolerated. Nevertheless, La Razón was far from certain that the new order was firmly on its feet after the collapse of the Villarroel regime. An editorial, "People [be] vigilant!" published on the same day as the revolt, July 21, 1946, declared:

The people should not neglect vigilance. They should remain firm in the post of duty in order to avoid any bloody surprise whatever. With serenity and calm, without excesses nor violent acts that could stain this glorious liberating revolution, we should be on a war footing until the last source of resistance is snuffed out. The MNR has stored arms in different places and in any moment can surprise the people. There is no reason to give credence to rumors. La Razón will provide the people with [information about] everything that happens but it asks the collaboration of all, in order to be alert and avoid acts that are not in agreement with the nobility [of the people] of La Paz. [42]

In another editorial, "The mission of the army," La Razón sought to cajole dissident elements of the military back into the ranks of those faithful to oligarchical interests. The editorial noted, "Forgetting that only a fraction of the armed institution placed itself against the Bolivian people, some want to cast shadows on all of the institution." [43]

On the day after the successful counter-revolt, La Paz paid its traditional obeisance to the memory of the dead. A total of 20,000 persons, according to La Razón, formed a procession twenty-five blocks long beginning at the University of San Andrés, led by the new Junta de Gobierno. The coffins were carried on the shoulders of marching men, and the army band was dressed in civilian clothes. Speeches at the General Cemetery lauded the heroism of the students, workers and Bolivian women. [44]

A few days after the overthrow of Villarroel when his corpse was hanged from a lamppost in the Plaza Murillo, La Razón revealed its real interest in the affair by publishing within an editorial the comment, "There exists the security most complete from which [the country] enters a new period in which there will be no more threats, neither for persons nor for capital." [45] In another editorial, in July 25, La Razón maintained, "Our daily, sequestered and silenced momentarily, returns to occupy the post which duty points out to it, interpreting the feelings of the Bolivian people, translating their patriotic desires and trying to raise on high the cultural index of the country, since that is the mission of a free journalism conscious of the responsibilities which such a noble heritage places upon it." [46]

As La Calle had attempted to discredit the overthrown regime of Peñaranda, La Razón also worked overtime to tarnish the image of Villarroel and his retinue. Fabián Vaca Chávez, writing in the columns of the Aramayo newspaper, called the Villarroel government "A nightmare of thirty-one months" and added: "The 'National Revolution' served [only] to fill the pockets of its disciples. Not a few of them, [in fact] the most, arrived at the government in a state of indigence and left millionaires... The revolution was made by them and for them, and against the country." [47]

In the same vein, an article by Manuel Carrasco discussed "The truth about the events in Bolivia and those responsible." According to the writer, using La Razón as a forum, the most recent revolt overthrew "a regime composed of men intoxicated

LOS UNIVERSITARIOS, UNA VEZ MAS RECONQUISTARON PARA EL PUEBLO BOLIVIANO LA MAS AMPLIA LIBERTAD

EXTRA LA RAZON GRATIS!

LA TIRANIA QUE MASACRO A MUJERES Y NIÑOS COBARDEMENTE HA SIDO APLASTADA POR EL HEROICO PUEBLO EN SU TOTALIDAD

TORRENTES DE SANGRE FUERON DERRAMADOS POR EL REGIMEN EN SU AFAN DE SEGUIR DOMINANDO

El Pueblo Paceño Recuperó con Máximo Heroísmo su Libertad

LA PRIMERA VICTIMA DE LA MASACRE CONTRA ESTUDIANTES

PUEBLO ALERTA!

NO PRETENDEMOS SACAR PROVECHO DEL GESTO HEROICO DEL PUEBLO"

LA JUNTA DE GOBIERNO ESTARA PRESIDIDA POR EL DOCTOR MONJE GUTIERREZ

EL ATAQUE A PALACIO

LA MANIFESTACION ESTUDIANTIL

INTERVENCION DE LA POLICIA

Mañana Daremos Una Edición al Medio Día

EN CAJONES DE MUNICION FUERON HALLADOS RESTOS HUMANOS

EL EJERCITO NO DEBE DISPARAR CONTRA EL PUE[BLO]

La Razón, owned by tin-mining magnate Carlos Víctor Aramayo, distributed this extra edition free on July 21, 1946, after the overthrow and murder of Gualberto Villarroel whom the MNR had supported.

179

by the philosophy built up as a system of domination by the hierarchies of national socialism." Twelve years ago, Carrasco continued, the secret military societies of the young Chaco War veterans were formed. These young men were sent to Europe where they imbibed fascist ideas. They gained power in 1943 with "a group of politicians of terror" whose theme was "blood erases the wrongs." When a revolt in Oruro failed on November 20, 1944, killed in cold blood were Senator Luis Calvo; Carlos Salinas Aramayo, ex-chancellor and professor; Rubén Terrazas, ex-minister of education and professor; Félix Capriles, senator and chief of the Socialists in Cochabamba, General Demetrio Ramos, ex-minister of defense, and five other distinguished citizens. The bodies of Calvo and Capriles were found two months later "in a ravine in the Yungas, devoured by the buzzards, the cranium of Calvo split by a blow from an axe and both men had their hands tied behind their backs. The bodies were found at Chuspipata on January 1, 1945, but the government--according to Carrasco--refused to investigate this crime, "and as a supreme insult [the government] sheltered [those responsible] through an illegal amnesty dictated for their own benefit." [48] The rumored complicity of Villarroel and the MNR in the murder of these men was so persistent that Armando Arce felt the necessity to answer these allegations with a book on the subject immediately after the MNR gained power in 1952.

The other side of the overthrow of Villarroel and the immediate succeeding incidents was published on the tenth anniversary of the leader's death, when La Nación began the serialization of Carlos Montenegro's "The counter-revolution of July 21," which was begun in Argentine exile in 1947 but never completed. In the chapter published, VII, Montenegro blamed the assassination of Villarroel to "a conspiracy of teachers and students." The particularly bizarre death of Villarroel was deliberate "in order to obtain sacrificial blood that would hide the true interests of the counter-revolution before the eyes of the people." Even before that event, the reaction adopted "a new and ferocious watchword--We need them to kill students." Surprise attacks had failed, such as that on June 13, because they encountered no popular echo. Therefore, the teachers' strike was fomented, demanding a 50 percent raise. Elsewhere in the country, striking teachers had accepted a 20 percent raise and gone back to work. Thus, the strike was localized in La Paz in the union of secondary teachers, "most of whom were affiliated with the PIR." After the assassination of Villarroel, the La Paz teachers accepted the same raise. The only participation by the MNR (Paz Estenssoro was the minister of finance) was asking Villarroel to "grant the demands of the teachers without haggling." When the secondary teachers of La Paz refused the government's offer of a 20 percent raise, proposed by the minister of education, the rector of the University, Héctor Ormachea Zalles, was named mediator. Montenegro described him as "one of the most efficacious agents of the circle of the great businessmen, in his condition of millionaire, large landowner, powerful commercial man, Grand Master of Masonry, and through his known efforts on behalf of the Liberal Party, supporter of the finances of Patiño, the railroad monopoly and private banks." Even the foremost newspaper of the mining magnates, La Razón, noted this in its edition of August 21, 1946. Montenegro called the rector an "agente provacateur" since settlement of the strike was in his hands. But, playing a double role, he delayed and the secondary teachers and supporting university students went on strike. La Razón quoted Ormachea Zalles, the rector of UMSA, as saying to the students, "In no moment [would] the university pretend to direct situations once the popular movement consolidates itself, since all, the Rector and the university students in general, otherwise would be shot." Thus did Ormachea Zalles incite the students to armed struggle. The same issue of La Razón reported that on July 14 the university resolved "to adopt a vertical system of organization through cells and factions of combat." On July 15 some thirty-seven revolutionary groups were organized for combat. According to La Razón, "All of these determinations were communicated to the Rector. Thus, he realized 'subversive provocation' in the people but did nothing about it." On July 16 the mimeograph machine was taken from UMSA to "continue the work of the revolutionary propaganda," in the words of La Razón. A public manifestation took place on July 16 even though the Federación Universitaria Local (FUL) did not approve. Students went to the streets unarmed, wanting only an injunction for the teachers. The government thought it was dealing with a simple demonstration. Police placed themselves in a line of combat in the Plaza Murillo and fired in the air; the students retreated, reorganized and continued the manifestation. According to La Razón, it was at that point that police were ordered to fire against the students, who fled in disorder. The police advanced and kept firing. "The firing was long drawn out, said La Razón. Such a confrontation, noted Montenegro, would have been enough to produce a "frightful slaughter" if the government had not shown restraint. Actually, only one student was killed--Camberos. Police recovered the body but not before the students had removed his jacket drenched in blood with which to arouse the multitude. La Razón stated, quite frankly, "the blood of students inflames the people. It is useless, then, [to try to] contain their indignation." With children and women marching at the front, the mob approached the plaza for the second time. If soldiers were firing into the group, reasoned Montenegro, why did the people hurry to the spots where they heard firing? Obviously they were aroused by the jacket, in La Razón's words, "in order to have a bloody banner with which to direct the multitude." Montenegro concluded, "More than aiding the victim, what mattered to them was not the body but its blood." [49]

More violence erupted after the successful coup d'etat when on September 27, 1946, three officers charged with the murders at Chupisata on November 20, 1944, were dragged from their cells in the Panóptico Nacional or national penitentiary and hanged in the Plaza Murillo. La Nación on the thirteenth anniversary of the event recalled what happened on that day: "From the preparations minutely elaborated with a methodical propaganda," the drama unfolded to its grisly end. Lt. Luis Oblitas Bustamante, whose body was hanged from a lamppost in the Plaza Murillo, became a victim because he made a simple protest because he was kept waiting for long periods of time in the Palacio de Gobierno without being received. When he vented his anger, he was charged with an attempt on the life of President Monje Gutiérrez. La Nación stated that the door of the balconies of the presidential palace were thrown open and passersby heard shouts of an "attempt" on the government. Radio Illimani began immediately broadcasting appeals to the people of La Paz to defend the Monje Gutiérrez government against an attempted coup by the MNR. Mobs dragged Oblitas from the police station to which he had been taken, kicking and beating him through the streets until he was shot in the Calle Ayacucho by Meyer Aragón--tried for treason in the Chaco War--and then the corpse of Oblitas was hanged from a lamppost in the Plaza Murillo--a grim reprise of the events of July 21, 1946.

Meanwhile, Majors José Escobar and Jorge Eguino were also wrenched from their cells at the Panóptico Nacional. Escobar was half-dead when he was taken to the Plaza Murillo in a wheelbarrow--also to be hanged. Eguino was taken on foot fourteen blocks. He was hanged also, but when the rope broke, he was shot. The oligarchical press covered these proceedings as if they were normal events in the national life of Bolivia. Even stenographers accompanied the dying men through the streets avid to record their final words. Commented La Nación: "All of the press of La Paz, without exceptions, justified and covered up all three monstrous events." [50]

The overthrow of Villarroel did not bring an end to labor agitation, as another "massacre" occurred at Catavi in May 1949. As the storm clouds were gathering, La Razón stated editorially:

The permanent state of agitation in the principal

mining zone of the country is causing the most grave damages to the Bolivian economy.... It is time that the workers, those who have not yet been subjugated by the forces of demagoguery, comprehend that they are only being used as a pretext and that none of them are qualified, by themselves, as interpreters of the proletarian will, [and therefore] should realize the true situation of the worker. What they are doing is a continuous work of destruction and a planting of hatred that will give the most bitter hours to Bolivia if there is not any reaction in time and they stop giving attention to such senseless preachments. [51]

Once again, as in 1942, La Razón did not exhibit the slightest sympathy for the striking Catavi workers. Once again the stage was set for tragedy when the leading newspaper of Bolivia proclaimed:

Unfortunately the right of strike... has been converted into a political weapon, employed in the majority of cases by demagogues, extremists and in general by enemies of order and legality. Mesmerized, they pretend, at any cost, to provoke anarchy and create a climate favorable to their aspirations at hand and to obtain in this manner privileges and personal benefits. The union dictatorship has come to intolerable extremes.... The workers will not recognize that capital is one of the important factors for the development of collective life, as important as organized labor. [52]

When President Mamerto Urriolagoitia delivered a radio speech on May 28, 1949, he declared that tolerance on the part of the government had been interpreted as weakness. "Democracy is the defense of institutions with a firm hand, if it is necessary..." he added. He charged that the elements displaced by July 21, 1946, were once again trying to give out weapons or fractricidal arms which could lead to civil war. The government, he said, had documents proving a general strike leading to a civil war was planned, "a suicidal and criminal attitude against the entire Republic." Some agitators, he concluded, had been expelled from Bolivia. "whose contact with the totalitarian parties is evident..." [53]

The strike reached an impasse, however, and erupted into violence on Sunday, May 29, when the combined military and Carabineros launched a concerted attack at noon upon the local sindicato building at Catavi. According to La Razón, which chose to overlook this aggression against organized labor, the

183

soldiers once inside the union building found "acts of tremendous cruelty and sadistic refinements." Six captives, held until their leader Juan Lechín--arrested on May 27 and deported--should be allowed to return to Bolivia, were rescued alive; three bodies were found dead, and others had disappeared. One body was said to have been found on the conference table of the sindicato with its brains beaten out.

Five hundred workers were captured, who said in preliminary hearings they had been instructed by Guillermo Lora, the POR leader, and Augusto Céspedes of the MNR. It was claimed that the workers used dynamite in bottles for terrorist effects, grenades made from empty condensed milk cans and dynamite wrapped with wire to hold together grapeshot. At 2:45 p.m. on Sunday, May 29, a strong group of miners gained possession of the hill of San Pedro near the mine of Uncía and attacked the barracks of Miraflores, where the First Infantry of the Colorados Regiment was stationed. On Sunday, all employees--nationals and foreigners--who wanted to be evacuated were taken from the nearby Siglo XX mine to Oruro in army airplanes. At the conclusion of this news column, La Razón stated, "The events of yesterday and today at Siglo XX and Uncía are deplorable and have moved the entire country because of the cruelty and rage with which the great labor leaders proceeded against their own work companions." [54]

The capital press was not hesitant in the slightest to give the most gory details of the fighting. When a Carabinero, for example, approached the door to the union headquarters at Catavi, he fired his weapon to break the lock, and exploding dynamite hidden inside beheaded him. A total of 550 armed miners were captured, however, and near Huanuni troops captured six workers--four of them union leaders--disguised as women. [55]

President Mamerto Urriolagoitia decreed a state of siege throughout Bolivia, but the worker unrest spread. At Siglo XX both military and worker dead totalled thirty-one, and at Huanuni, there were two dead and six wounded. Again editorializing in its news columns, La Razón denounced this "inconceivable criminal violence, especially at Huanuni, where workers on May 30 attacked the local police station, killed two and wounded one. When the Camacho Regiment took over, the workers fled to the hills above the town from which they continued to throw dynamite on the settlement below." [56]

The mining district represented a patchwork quilt of varying opinions or positions on the strike. There were no military forces in any of the Hochschild mines, where pay seems to have been better. The Uyuni and Pulacayo miners demanded return of the imprisoned or exiled labor leaders before they would return to work. Workers at the Aramayo mines declared a strike until the labor leaders were returned, and Oploca also declared suspension of work. [57]

The ministry of government, in announcing the state of siege, said it was necessary "because of finding the country in a state of civil war provoked by the MNR and the POR..." On May 30, 1949, the workers at Colquiri went on strike and also took hostages. Miners at Tazna in the south also walked out, in what La Razón declared was carrying out a plan, unmasked some time before, by the MNR to overcome and disarm troops and police at the mining centers and to use those arms in advancing on the rest of the country. The Aramayo newspaper denounced these "irresponsible and fanatic hordes directed and armed by the MNR and the POR."

No labor dispute for La Razón could simply be a conflict on its own merits: there was a sinister apparatus behind every move for labor to better its condition. The government on this occasion, La Razón warned, had information that the exiled labor leaders used the consulate of a friendly nation to meet and discuss the coming revolution. [58] Meanwhile, the violence escalated. Some eighty persons, all foreigners, were evacuated from Llallagua and Siglo XX. When the widow of the American engineer O'Connor went to look for his body, La Razón reported, she found his eyeballs gouged out and his fingers pulled off. Hugo Portocarrero, the inspector general of labor, sent telegrams to all mining centers warning the workers that strikes for political reasons "or in the aid or solidarity of other institutions" were forbidden by the Ley General del Trabajo (General Labor Law) enacted during the presidency of Germán Busch. At the same time, La Razón editorialized, "It is necessary to demonstrate that without a democratic regime the workers would be submitted to slavery. Without the regime of order, they could not organize themselves in unions. Without the regime of liberty, the agitators at the service of subaltern interests would not have been able to mobilize themselves, as they have done, in an attempt to deal a blow to the death of democracy." [59]

Under the state of siege, Urriolagoita ordered the mobilization of all men between the ages of nineteen and fifty for possible military service. The president was hard pressed. The Union of National Factory Workers went on strike June 1, and the National Confederation of Railway Workers decreed a general strike that would close all of the lines in the Republic. La Razón was livid, attacking the railroad workers for going on a sympathy strike. The newspaper declared, "The national destiny hangs in the balance" and spoke of "this demonstration

185

of suspicious solidarity" which was "the solidarity of crime, backing up the forces of anarchy disposed to destroy the base of our institutions." [60]

In the mining district of Catavi, complete order reigned after the events of May 28-29. Colonel Roberto Ramallo, chief of the garrison at Catavi, said the reason the army did not attack the local union headquarters on Saturday, May 28, was the fear of reprisals against hostages. When they heard on Sunday that two were already dead, they attacked. Later, hostages at Huanuni were rescued, and La Razón published what purported to be a photocopy of the revolt planned by the MNR. [61]

In the wake of these events, which plunged Bolivia into brief civil war two months later, there were desperate efforts by the ruling middle group of politicians to heal the wounds. Urriolagoitia said, for example, "The government never thought for one moment to develop an anti-union political policy." But in an editorial, the Aramayo newspaper also said, concerning some military units who sided with the strikers, "...the errors of some elements do not comprise the entire army, in the same way that bad priests are not the Church." [62] La Razón was not so conciliatory in other ways, however. An editorial of June 5 described how "Impunity encourages crime," attacking the parliamentary impunity of labor leader Juan Lechín and others. The newspaper did nothing to try to heal the wounds of the bloody conflict at Catavi. It quoted Urriolagoita as saying, "No means are excessive when the peace of the nation is threatened." The newspaper ran a long personal account of Elena de O'Connor, the widow whose American husband had been mutilated in the confrontation. [63] Still, the minister of labor, Germán Zegarra Caero, said an agreement was being reached on the mine strikers, and at noon on June 8 all miners were requested to renew their labors. On June 11, it was announced that probably within a week all mine work would be normalized and foreign technicians also would return to their jobs. [64]

After the failure of the Catavi-Siglo XX mine strikes and the short-lived civil war they were intended to set off, described elsewhere, the MNR girded its loins for the elections of 1951, by far the most crucial in the history of Bolivia. The campaign was not without violence. When there was a demonstration for the candidates Gabriel Gosálvez and José Antonio Arze in the Plaza Pérez Velasco upon their return from campaigning in the interior, La Razón alleged that elements of the MNR attacked the manifestation and left two dead and twenty-two wounded. [65] Mainly, however, the Aramayo newspaper fought the MNR candidates on philosophical grounds. On

May 3, 1951, for example, a few days before the scheduled elections, La Razón printed an editorial, "On the road to state slavery," which attacked the opposition for once again raising the specter of a "mining superstate" in its quest for the economic recovery of Bolivia. The only way to do that, reasoned La Razón, was through increased, not curtailed, mineral production. Then the newspaper of Carlos Víctor Aramayo, the newspaper which had helped to make and unmake presidents, made the astonishing statement, "The Bolivian mining industry does not exercise, nor does not try to exercise, any political power whatever." Pressing its own argument, La Razón noted, "It has been known for a long time that without economic liberty there can be no political liberty." Yet for fifteen years Bolivia had been following the line of "socialism" leading to an "omnipotent State." The newspaper declared, "This is the future of progressive servitude which official socialism offers the republic." The end result would be "the spectacle of an army of robots under the discretional arbitration of a state bureaucracy." [66]

Thus, it was not only Paz Estenssoro and the MNR who were attacked by La Razón in the campaign of 1951, but the entire state socialism program launched by David Toro in 1936 and including even those rightwing presidents after the overthrow of Villarroel in 1946. In 1951 the Aramayo newspaper noted that the government of the past four years had led to extreme inflation; there were only 1,582 million bolivianos in circulation in 1948, but 3,431 million in 1951. [67]

There were also 188 candidates for deputies, and the army announced it was ready to suppress any acts of violence on the eve of the election, May 5. La Razón editorialized, however, that the elections would not be fair in view of the police repression, packed electoral boards, falsified civic registers, and the general corruption "which have characterized our political history." The newspaper warned against violence and even more against abstention from the polls, which it pointed out would only passively aid the existing government. Most significantly, this editorial of May 5, only one day before the elections, urged, "The opposition parties ought--and here we make special allusion to that which seems to have adopted violence as a norm of conduct [the MNR]--to avoid incidents that the national conscience repudiates and that serve only to justify official pressure." [68]

The day after the elections, La Razón editorialized under the heading, "At the end of a democratic march," that the elections had been carried out "with an atmosphere of general tranquility and laudable reciprocal respect." There had been deplorable incidents in some districts of the interior, but these were isolated, the newspaper reported. It scored most severely the "deplorable effect" of traditional party divisions. Paz Estenssoro had tried twice to return to Bolivia by plane before the elections, but was thwarted each time. [69] Nevertheless, to the astonishment of many observers, the MNR won a clear plurality in the political field divided six ways but not-- according to the incumbent government--the necessary absolute majority.

An editorial in La Razón on May 8 addressed itself to this point, attributing the strong showing of the MNR to absten- tions--which the Aramayo newspaper had warned against-- especially in the city of La Paz itself. "The atomization of parties served only to disorient the electorate...and the politi- cal mechanism," La Razón observed. Nevertheless, the vote reflected a censure of the present government which had seen productivity diminish seriously and had favored "the most radical currents of opposition." President Urriolagoitia said he would "respect the popular verdict pronounced in the electoral contests." [70]

Surprisingly--to some--La Razón came to the defense of the MNR in the political tug-of-war after the elections, noting that although the constitution required an absolute majority, "...it is also undeniable that the electorate has given its ver- dict and that verdict points out--within democratic norms--the road to follow." At the same time, however, the Aramayo newspaper argued against a congressional decision that would have enabled the MNR to gain power peacefully. La Razón proclaimed, "Through the ruinous splintering of the other political parties, a national majority--relative or absolute--has expressed its confidence in the same party [the MNR] that only five years ago was dramatically expelled from power, that agitated, before and afterwards, for the open resistance of great sectors of opinion, and that merited the severe and unanimous criticism of the national press." The newspaper added, in an aside which underscored the gulf that existed between the established press and the MNR, "It is a historical fact that the general reaction [against the MNR], widely justifi- able, originated in the acts of the same MNR or of the military elements with which they shared the exercise of power." [71]

Bringing up the murders of 1944 and the civil war of 1949, La Razón declared, "If the MNR on its part does honor to legality and submits itself to the norms of respect for human dignity, La Razón will be the first in recognizing it. If this does not occur, La Razón will also be the first in returning, without vacillation, to the same principles that in strict con- science it invokes." [72] At nearly the same time, La Razón also printed what purported to be a photostatic copy of a pact between the MNR and the Communist Party of Bolivia, from which Juan Lechín withdrew as a candidate to throw his weight to the Paz Estenssoro-Siles Zuazo ticket, allegedly agreed upon on the eve of the elections of 1951. The newspaper also printed what was alleged to be the instructions from Paz Estenssoro, still in exile in Argentina, to his second-in-command and vice-presidential running mate, Siles Zuazo, in La Paz. [73] Despite these questionable journalistic tactics, since the documents in question were never verified, La Razón was sanctimonious enough to observe on May 15, 1951, one day before the takeover by the military junta, a usurpation of power to which the newspaper itself had contributed:

> The press constitutes in the modern world the major element of diffusion and perhaps the most powerful instrument to express and shape the thought of the people.... Its role is more transcendental and deli-cate, even, in societies of less stability and culture as our own. [74]

Largely due to the pressure exerted by La Razón to keep the MNR out of the government, despite some protestations to the contrary, President Mamerto Urriolagoitia resigned on May 16, 1951, handing the Bolivian government over to the ten-man military junta led by General Hugo Ballivián Rojas and fled to Chile. This defection, subtly encouraged by La Razón, created a new word in the Bolivian vocabulary--a mamertazo which would provoke the ultimate armed rebellion of April 1952 at a cost of more than 600 lives. It should be emphasized that the elections of 1951 were held with an effective electorate of only 150,000 persons in a country of four million population because voting was limited only to literate, adult, property-owning males. [75] In such a setting the role of the news-papers of the opposition was crucial: La Razón itself reached one-third of the voting public with a circulation of 50,000, not counting secondary circulation, figures which the clandestine En Marcha for the MNR could not begin to reach (see Chapter 5). Thus, the failure of the electoral process in Bolivia in 1951 was also a failure of its journalism, a failure which was to plunge the country into a brief but bloody civil war.

In the year between the abortive elections of May 16, 1951, and the MNR Revolution of April 9-11, 1952, La Razón fought with all the power at its command for a middle-of-the-road approach to Bolivian politics. The newspaper was unsuc-cessful, but an examination of its final issues reveals why it went under. On January 13, 1952, La Razón editorialized that a lack of strong political parties and the emphasis on personal-ismo had been the cause of frequent interventions by the military in the Bolivian government. An accompanying news story stressed the lack of national parties, although the newspaper overlooked the firm national base that the MNR was building as a result of having been denied victory at the polls in May 1951. [76] The newspaper plugged "The function of foreign capital" as a necessity demonstrated by history at a time when many Bolivians wanted control of their own affairs-- economic and political. [77] Three things Bolivia needed to overcome her backwardness, La Razón editorialized on another occasion were capital, immigration and technical experience. [78] The newspaper also still came down hard against labor; when the Supreme Court ruled that judiciary employees could not unionize, La Razón saw this as an "institutional precedent" for all workers in public administration. [79] Again, when public voices were raised in favor of an increase in salaries, La Razón cited the danger of inflation, which the newspaper said it had been emphasizing for seventeen years. [80]

Politically, La Razón dragged its feet on the question of new elections. When the minister of government in early February 1952 said the country would return to its "constitutional course" through elections, La Razón thought this was premature. The newspaper recalled the words of the Junta Militar de Gobierno when it took power on May 16, 1951: "Our activity arises from the firm decision of maintaining public peace and re-establishing the harmonious living together of the Bolivian family. We do not aspire to any other thing than to tranquilize the country and create a propitious atmosphere for the institutional future of the Nation, absent from hatreds, fears and prejudices." These conditions had not been met, La Razón maintained: "the danger of violence and the seed of anarchy have not been extirpated." "Subversion" still existed. Would the elections be honest? The MNR had trucked citizens in the 1951 elections from one district to another to vote fraudulently, La Razón charged, which was the reason for the MNR's large vote. Parties must be reorganized, the Aramayo newspaper declared, thinking probably of a unified party of the right. The climate of extremist agitation must be removed, such as the class struggle through the alliance of the MNR and the Communist Party of Bolivia, reasoned La Razón, adding that the army could not return to its barracks until it could assure the Bolivian people of "a constitutional government inspired by democratic principles." The contrary, editorialized La Razón, "would be to return to the tragic and shameful years in which the MNR made a clean slate of all the rights and guarantees that the law recognizes." Elections in 1952? No, said La Razón, thereby opening the door to violent revolution, because "democratic competence, as with the competence of sports, needs common rules. In such a case, could the MNR, identified with communism, aspire to be considered a democratic party?" [81] It would be a long time before true elections could be held, La Razón maintained, and thereby sealed its own fate. Although the most powerful leader of public opinion in Bolivia, the newspaper did not understand that opinion. It did not understand the appeal of En Marcha, the occasional MNR propaganda sheet, and it sought unsuccessfully to stem the tide of change.

Like a lightning flash which cleared the turbulent Bolivian political skies, the revolt came on April 9, 1952, with severe fighting in the streets of La Paz and the mining city of Oruro. MNR forces were bolstered with the aid of the Carabineros, headed by General Antonio Seleme, but on the evening of the first day of fighting, when it appeared that the MNR forces were losing, General Seleme took refuge in a foreign embassy, giving up any effective claim to command. The tide turned on the second day, and on the third day the MNR forces were in command of the situation. Paz Estenssoro returned from Argentina and was installed as president, honoring his victory in the 1951 elections. Paz Estenssoro refused to give La Razón any protection after the April 9-11, 1952, revolution, when it was menaced by angry mobs. Guillermo Céspedes, the newspaper's editor, repeatedly asked Minister of Government César Aliaga for police protection and was repeatedly refused. Hugo Roberts Barragán, chief of the newly created ministry of propaganda, angrily informed foreign newsmen that "memories of the dead and wounded are too fresh" for the MNR regime to protect La Razón against popular outbursts. The government unpadlocked the newspaper's plant, but when La Razón attempted to publish on April 17, mob pressure and terrorism were renewed. Three station wagons cruised around the newspaper's editorial offices after midnight, full of men shouting, "La Razón will die! The revolution will live!" [82]

Paz Estenssoro was quoted by the New York Times as saying on April 19 that the Bolivian government would not assist La Razón to reopen because it was "an enemy of the Bolivian people." The president asserted there was nothing to prevent the newspaper from publishing, but doing so would be like "waving a red banner before a revolutionary populace which was thus far shown great restraint by refraining from pillage and unnecessary violence." Paz Estenssoro announced that he and other MNR leaders planned to sue La Razón for libel and calumny. [83] Finally, in the middle of June 1952, La Razón dismissed its 300 employees, who had been idle but on the payroll for two and a half months, and closed down completely. [84]

On the other hand, treatment of the other major voice of opposition in Bolivia, Los Tiempos of Cochabamba, was more temperate--for the time being, at least. On November 9, 1953, allegedly government-inspired mobs attacked and sacked the printing plant of Los Tiempos. But the newspaper did survive the Revolution for nineteen months (see Chapter 7) despite stringent attacks upon the MNR and its programs. In April 1952, however, things were quite different. Commenting upon the case of La Razón, the newspaper of Demetrio Canelas editorialized, "The triumph of the nationalist revolution has been characterized by forgetting the offenses of the past and this time we have not seen unfold the persecutions against the conquered, nor have we received in our own printing plant the visit of military nor civil agents, charged with censoring the material of this newspaper, as has occurred in all of the previous revolutions." [85]

Carlos Victor Aramayo, tin magnate and owner of La Razón, fled Bolivia immediately after the revolution of April 9, 1952, telling his managers to suspend editions indefinitely and perhaps for good. From Europe he wrote:

> Passionate elements of the party which has today in its hands the destinies of the country, consider my newspaper [La Razón] as its capital enemy, responsible for the hostilities which they have suffered in the past six years. The [printing] building is constantly patrolled by these citizens and it is probable that any attempt whatsoever to re-establish the editions would provoke resistance of excited groups, which, as is known, are armed. The ministry of propaganda, which has just been created by the new government, has the goal of founding 'a great daily,' as it announced a few days ago. This proposition could only be made effective by the government acquiring the shops of 'La Razón' which are the only ones with the capacity [for such a project]. [86]

La Razón found a powerful international champion in the Inter American Press Association (IAPA), which when it met in Mexico City October 7-11, 1953, declared that freedom of the press did not exist in Bolivia. [87] The IAPA, founded in 1926 and reorganized in 1950, had established a committee on freedom of the press in 1946, a group which was appointed each year by the incoming president. [88] Committee chairman Jules Dubois of the Chicago Tribune, who had made an inspection trip to Bolivia soon after the April 1952 revolution, sent a letter to Paz Estenssoro in 1953 asking guarantees for newsmen and freedom for newspapers in Bolivia to import newsprint. José Fellmann Velarde of the ministry of press, information and culture replied that exiled Bolivian newsmen had participated in conspiracies against the government. He also pointed that IAPA had never intervened against oligarchnical regimes when newspapers were closed and newsmen "killed, imprisoned, tortured and exiled." Moreover, Fellmann Velarde argued, the newsprint restrictions--as well as those on food and other goods--were necessary to protect Bolivia's rapidly dwindling balance of payments. [89] (It is true that the government spokesman La Nación itself suffered from lack of newsprint and was forced to go to tabloid size for a time). Nevertheless, the IAPA compared the plight of La Razón to that of La Presna of Buenos Aires, which was confiscated in 1951 by Juan Domingo Perón, and accused the MNR government of "an act of aggression against the free and independent press." [90]

Thereupon began a vendetta between the Bolivian revolutionary government and the IAPA, made up mainly of newspaper publishers throughout the hemisphere, that was to last two decades. The international association refused to concede that freedom of the press existed in Bolivia as long as La Razón could not publish and Los Tiempos, partially destroyed by mobs on November 9, 1953, was not indemnified. The Bolivian authorities, on the other hand, disputed the right of the IAPA to sit in judgment, since it was composed of entrepreneurs and not workers of the press. Judgments of the IAPA committee on freedom of the press, the MNR maintained, were made only upon hearsay from other newspaper owners and not by proper investigations on the scene. Moreover, in the case of Los Tiempos, publisher Demetrio Canelas himself was a member of the IAPA committee, therefore being both judge and party to the cause. Concerning La Razón, the Bolivian revolutionary government steadfastly refused to admit that the Aramayo newspaper plant in downtown La Paz had been nationalized, although the building did become the headquarters of the ministry of mines and petroleum.

The plight of La Razón's former workers became the concern of the first National Congress of Workers called in 1955 by the Central Obrera Boliviana (COB), the fledgling national labor organization. The congress proposed to the MNR government that La Razón be expropriated since its "voluntary closure" had left 300 workers jobless. But the MNR refused, according to its official newspaper La Nación, precisely because it [the government] knew that proceeding to such an expropriation, even though all of the legal requisites were fulfilled, would be exploited as a sign of repression of liberty of the press." [91]

When the IAPA placed Bolivia on the condemned list year after year, La Nación warned:

Our readers should remember that the Sociedad Interamericana de Prensa [IAPA] is an entity which

193

groups together the proprietors of newspapers of almost all the countries of this hemisphere, which is the same as saying the capitalists who manage the editorial industry...from a point of view purely utilitarian. The conclusions or pronouncements of the committee on freedom of the press of IAPA have to be, inevitably, the result of reports of their own members--also owners--and...many of those informants are at the same time active politicians who are not able to escape from the passion, hatred or prejudice with which they see affairs from their respective viewpoints. [92]

In 1958 when the IAPA at its meeting in Buenos Aires declared that freedom of the press still did not exist in Bolivia, La Nación commented: "Its curious. It is now happening, as rarely came about in the history of this country, that the great majority of the spokesmen for journalism are independent or averse to the politics of the Government and who say what they desire on the spur of the moment, without strictions of any kind," Indignant, the official newspaper continued, "[our critics] are passionate in their language, [inflicting] injury and calumny against the regime, which tolerates them patiently. What greater liberty can one ask?" La Nación described the IAPA as a "capitalist consortium" which did not "defend an idea [freedom of the press] but rather an economic position." [93]

The Bolivian revolutionary government steadfastly defended its position against the repeated strictures of the IAPA. On another occasion, La Nación observed: "The IAPA does not know, or pretends not to know, that after April 9, 1952, the daily La Razón stopped appearing only through the will of its proprietor, fearing certain reactions of the people, to be sure.... But at no time was the plant of La Razón threatened, let alone confiscated, by the Government, making it impossible 'to make restitution' of that which [already] is in the hands of its owner." The MNR newspaper pointed out that in the previous six years, Carlos Víctor Aramayo had made no gesture to reopen his newspaper, nor did he need to obtain governmental approval to do so. "Nevertheless," La Nación concluded, "nothing of this sort has occurred because the oligarchy obtains greater advantages from the silence of La Razón, which permits it to agitate against the Government" in the court of international public opinion. [94]

Actually, Aramayo tried to reopen La Razón on two occasions but was prevented both times from doing so by "spontaneous popular demonstrations in the streets." The Bolivian people had been outraged by La Razón's justifications of the massacres at Catavi in 1942 and at Uncía, Villa Victoria and again Catavi in 1949. The Aramayo newspaper aided the mamertazo of 1951, La Nación charged, publishing falsified documents of an alleged pact connecting the MNR and the Bolivian Workers Federation with the Communist Party, which triggered the military takeover. After the revolution of 1952, Aramayo offered to let Paz Estenssoro name a new director for La Razón, suggesting Walter Montenegro, but the MNR refused, saying there were no obstacles to resumed publication and declining to intervene in the internal affairs of the newspaper. La Nación drily recalled that La Razón had applauded the closing of La Calle, spokesman for the MNR, in 1943 and the closing of an independent daily of the left, La Noche, property of Gustavo Chacón, in 1949. [95]

In 1959 La Nación noted with dismay that Bolivia was once again blacklisted, yet the IAPA declared that there was freedom of the press under the regime of Anastasio Somoza in Nicaragua. On that occasion, La Nación welcomed the creation of the Agencia de Prensa Latinoamericana (Latin American Press Agency, more commonly known as Prensa Latina) which was to start functioning under Cuban auspices within several weeks, even though the newspaper had been lukewarm to the Cuban revolution. [96]

Augusto Céspedes, as editor of La Nación (1956-1959), delighted in taking swipes at Jules Dubois, chairman of the IAPA committee on freedom of the press, when La Razón and Los Tiempos first went under. Céspedes wrote in 1959, "When the Cuban Revolution... did not threaten to be more than one of the inoffensive exultations of the Caribbean, Jules Dubois found in Castro--who is now an enemy of 'liberty'--a savior, a great democrat and the expulsor of a tyrant." [97] Another victim of Céspedes' trenchant pen was Argentine publisher Alberto Gainza Paz of La Prensa, large-scale cattle rancher and subsequent president of the IAPA. Céspedes referred to the IAPA as "constituted by retired colonels [Dubois] and bovine oligarchies that mix news the same way they breed cattle." [98]

Time and again the MNR government urged representatives of the IAPA to visit Bolivia to see for themselves whether or not freedom of the press existed there. In 1959 Carlos Morales Guillén, minister of government, invited William H. Cowles, then president of the IAPA, to make such an inspection tour. But Céspedes noted sardonically, "If Cowles comes--a very unlikely thing--this has to be his verdict: Bolivia is a dictatorship and señor [Jorge] Carrasco [publisher of El Diario] lives with a militia bayonet pointed against his chest, although those inconveniences do not stop him from preparing editorial coups as interesting as that of April 19." (This referred to the most serious attempted counter-revolt against the MNR, organized by the extreme rightwing Falange Socialista Boliviana, FSB, Bolivian Socialist Falange.) No, editor Céspedes saw quite another outcome: "On the contrary, Cowles will repeat his nefarious report, Colonel Dubois will continue writing cretin chronicles for the Chicago Tribune, Gainza Paz will continue selling cows and newspapers, the great defenders of freedom of the press will keep on getting fatter and, once again, President Eisenhower will appear perplexed by the inexplicable Latin American bad will against his country..." [99]

Significantly, when the Interamerican Congress of Working Journalists met in Lima August 18-22, 1960--a meeting not covered by the American wire services--this group of newsmen pronounced against infringements on freedom of expression in Cuba, Haiti, the Dominican Republic and Paraguay but--unlike the IAPA--did not find cause for alarm in Bolivia. [100] When the Interamerican Federation of Professional Journalists was formed at that meeting, La Nación applauded the action. The newspaper noted that the IAPA did not concern itself with "the economic anguishes and social disadvantages that grieve the workers of the press [in Latin America]." [101] Again, when Pope John XXIII criticized the capitalist press for biased coverage of underdeveloped countries, La Nación took advantage of the occasion to lash the IAPA once more for having the audacity to set up "a kind of permanent Inquisition" that takes upon itself the task of judging Latin American people without "any investigation whatever." [102]

The official press of the Bolivian National Revolution did not attempt to paint an unblemished picture of the relationship between government and opposition newspapers there. In 1960, when the IAPA meeting in Buenos Aires declared that freedom of the press existed in Argentina but not in Bolivia, La Nación quoted two Cochabamba newspapers by way or refutation. The independent El Mundo dismissed as pure fantasy the IAPA report that "the [Bolivian] government controls the newspapers and the opposition lacks means of expression." The Cochabamba newspaper admitted that the MNR government owned such newspapers as La Nación and La Tarde of La Paz and El Pueblo of Cochabamba, but the majority of newspapers were either independent or in the opposition. El Mundo agreed, however, that freedom of the press did not exist in Bolivia during the first few years of the revolution, as when El Diario of La Paz appeared with blank columns to dramatize MNR censorship, but "it is false to say that all of the dailies that now circulate in our country belong to the Government of the MNR." El Pueblo, the MNR newspaper of Cochabamba, noted the irony in the IAPA's deciding that freedom of the press did exist in Argentina, pointing out that on the very day that the organization was assembling there, the government of Arturo Frondizi closed down La Razón of Buenos Aires and imprisoned its editor. Moreover, El Pueblo maintained, 90 percent of the radio outlets in Argentina were controlled by the government and four million peronistas not only did not have a single newspaper spokesman but also could not even vote. [103]

La Nación summed up the attitude of the MNR toward the IAPA over the case of La Razón in 1958, six years after the newspaper had failed to reappear:

As for 'La Razón,' an error is committed in the flagrant falsity of affirming that [the newspaper] is currently in the hands of the Government which impedes its publication. All of Bolivian public opinion knows this is not so. The shops of the said press continue belonging to the Aramayo Mines enterprise and the newspaper can publish when and how their proprietors decide. But it is necessary to note that in this case, as in all, la Rosca operated agilely. It knows that it is doing more damage to the Government maintaining those shops closed than by publishing the daily. This circumstance favors its tendentious propaganda abroad, where the details of our internal political life are not known. [La Rosca] takes advantage of every opportunity to speak of the 'muzzling' of 'La Razón"...but foolish speech has its limit: the truth perfectly comprehended by the public conscience. [104]

The case of La Razón of La Paz was never settled to the owner's or IAPA's satisfaction, but the conflict did reveal much of the sharp duality of Bolivian life. [105] Pitted against the modern city of La Paz and its Western-style journalism were the vast majority of the people of the countryside, eking out a bare living through primitive subsistence farming. There are vast differences between Bolivian culture and our own. As one small indication of this, there are no words in the Quechua language, spoken by the large bulk of Bolivian Indians, for "newspaper" or "to read," since their Incan forebears had no written means of expression. What then does an abstract concept such as "freedom of the press" mean to such people? They are interested in more adequate food for their families, better shelter and clothing, schools and medical care. "Freedom of the press" as practiced in La Paz by Aramayo and others did not free these campesinos from their rural and psychological isolation, but on the contrary fought consistently to keep them a submerged class. [106]

La Razón was an inappropriate newspaper for an emerging nation; it was, as Augusto Céspedes has said, un periódico millonario o de lujo ("a millionaire or luxury newspaper"). The people were ignored almost altogether and they resented it. It has been asserted that the Indians could not have known what was being said in the pages of La Razón because the vast majority of them could not read. Nevertheless, newspapers were posted on the walls of buildings in downtown La Paz where literate men would read them to their less fortunate fellows, and the news traveled by word of mouth. The extremely conservative editorial views of La Razón rankled deeply among the workers and campesinos of Bolivia, and when social revolution came in 1952, it seemed only natural that La Razón should be part of the old order to be swept away. No newspaper can continue to exist, for better or worse, by flying directly in the overwhelming face of public opinion, and when workers and campesinos harassed La Razón in April 1952 and prevented it from reopening, it was as if an entire people were cancelling their subscription to a newspaper that had attempted to hold them in bondage. The same handwriting also appeared on the wall for Los Tiempos of Cochabamba, a satellite newspaper for the Aramayo interests, but that journal also refused to heed the message.

Chapter 7

THE TIMES AND LOS TIEMPOS

In confused times of great calamities, the
paths of good and evil seem to join.

--Demetrio Canelas,
Jan. 10, 1938.

...we cannot free ourselves from the
oppressive conditions that confront the
world and the country in which we live.
Everywhere reigns uncertainty, oppression,
injustice. To the present evils must be
added the obscure predestinations of the
immediate future. No one is sure of tomor-
row.

--Christmas editorial note,
Los Tiempos,
Dec. 25, 1952.

The fate of Los Tiempos of Cochabamba, owned and edited
by Demetrio Canelas, was intimately bound up with what the
Bolivian National Revolution was trying to accomplish. As La
Razón was the bellwether of the opposition press in the capital,
Los Tiempos led the opposition in the hinterlands. Perhaps
precisely because the Aramayo newspaper was located at the
seat of power in La Paz, it was silenced when the revolution
first broke out, whereas Los Tiempos was allowed to survive
the April 9 revolt for nineteen months before it went under on
November 9, 1953, in circumstances that still comprise the
biggest riddle of the Revolution. We will see (Chapter 9) how
Los Tiempos adamantly fought the agrarian revolution sweeping
the Cochabamba valley, which was certainly the immediate
provocation for the newspaper's demise, but its total philosophical outlook--which militated against every aspect of the MNR
revolution--brought harassment from the central authorities
ranging from heavy-handed police action to the cutting off of
supplies of newsprint, a tactic which Juan Perón of Argentina
had found effective against La Prensa not long before. Canelas, a systematic political thinker in his own right, survived all

199

of these threats to the existence of Los Tiempos. Thereupon, it seems that the MNR government decided to use force to close the newspaper although its version of the final incident is quite different from that of Canelas. At any rate, it was José Fellmann Velarde, one of the high MNR officials in La Paz, who allegedly led the attack upon the printing plant of Los Tiempos on November 9, 1953, which closed the newspaper until 1967, three years after the MNR itself had been overthrown.

Why couldn't the MNR tolerate the continued existence of this newspaper? First of all, it was not simply a regional newspaper, the only one in Cochabamba. It had the second largest circulation in Bolivia, second only to Aramayo's La Razón, and that circulation was national in scope. Los Tiempos had two correspondents in La Paz, two in Oruro and one each in Potosí, Tarija, Santa Cruz and Sucre, with numerous stringers in the provinces. [1] The newspaper even had a correspondent in Europe, Juan Pereira Fiorilo, who covered the 1952 disarmament talks in Paris. [2] On the home front, Demetrio Canelas was the most astute political analyst writing in the Bolivian press, whether one agrees or disagrees with his conservative political stance. This chapter will detail how that stance led to the destruction of his newspaper and his own exile. It is in many respects a sad story because Canelas fought for the wrong causes; he was out of touch with the society in which he lived, and no newspaper can fight indefinitely the overwhelming weight of adverse popular opinion. The times were out of joint for Los Tiempos.

The newspaper was founded on September 20, 1943, shortly before Major Gualberto Villarroel came to power. Thus, from Villarroel to Paz Estenssoro, Los Tiempos spanned ten of the most tempestuous years in Bolivian life, from the dress rehearsal of a social revolution to the revolution itself. The origins of the newspaper are shrouded in secrecy, however. Although Demetrio Canelas, born in 1879, had owned and edited La Patria of Oruro beginning in 1923, he did not immediately take charge of the new newspaper in his hometown of Cochabamba. Director for the first year was his brother, Julio César Canelas, later imprisoned at the concentration camp of Corocoro by the MNR. [3] Significantly, the printing equipment for Los Tiempos was sold to the Canelas family for a pittance by Carlos Víctor Aramayo, who perhaps wanted to extend the influence of La Razón into the second largest city in Bolivia.

Nevertheless, it was Demetrio Canelas who was the guiding light of the newspaper from its inception. Having played an important part on the national stage, he was not unknown to Bolivian readers. Delegate to the League of Nations, he was also deputy in several congresses and president of the Chamber of Deputies. Most importantly, he was minister of war under President Daniel Salamanca during the Chaco War. As head of the Genuine Republican Party, he accompanied Salamanca to the front in 1934 and was imprisoned there with him at Villa Montes. [4] Obsessed with Salamanca all his life, Canelas regularly printed a column in Los Tiempos on "The Thoughts of Salamanca" almost two decades after the former president's death in 1935. [5]

Personally, Canelas was somewhat stuffy and the butt of many jokes in the opposition press. El Universal in 1933 ridiculed his epicurean tastes and modish dressing style acquired during his education in Geneva. The newspaper, in its satirical column, "Men of the Day," noted: "Canelas speaks quietly, very low, carefully, as if he were dictating an editorial.... One must come into his presence submissive, obedient, not interrupting his conversation so as not to deprive history." [6] El Universal also attacked the political leader for his "feminine delicacy in the face of popular mockery..." [7] La Calle later had a field day when Canelas allegedly took records from the Chamber of Deputies to change versions of speeches he had made during the Chaco War. [8]

Soon after its founding, Los Tiempos was faced with the first wrenching change in Bolivian life as Major Gualberto Villarroel was swept to power in the revolt of December 20, 1943, almost exactly one year after the massacre at Catavi. When Villarroel's vague reforms ended on July 21, 1946, with the body of the unfortunate president dangling from a lamppost on the Plaza Murillo, the newspaper of Canelas could not contain itself, addressing the fallen chieftain directly:

> You have died to serve as a lesson. This form of death, which Providence has afforded, causes us to shudder to the depth of our bowels, but this is the way the hydra of seven heads of the military dictatorship that is destroying Bolivia throughout all of its life should die once and for all.... Upon this death the Bolivians can erect a new life, without more revolutions, without more military caudillos, without more tyrants. May this example be fecund, now and forever. And may God receive you in his infinite Mercy because he has chosen you to serve, from the lamppost on which you were hung, as a sign of repentance and reconciliation. Amen. [9]

From this moment on, the MNR--which had supported and participated in the government of Villarroel--knew that it had an implacable enemy in Demetrio Canelas and his newspaper, Los Tiempos. Representing the aristocracy in Bolivian life and tied to the Catholic Church--as the above quotation demonstrates all too clearly--the newspaper had little or no sympathy for the underdogs in Bolivian society. Just as it later championed the great landowners in the agrarian struggle, Los Tiempos saw in the Villarroel interlude a threat to almost every facet of a complex, interlocking, dominant social structure. On the day of the overthrow of Villarroel, Major René Guiroza Paz Soldán showed up at the Los Tiempos offices to censor the newspaper, something never attempted during the rule of Villarroel himself. [10] Nevertheless, three days later, Canelas was still extolling this most brutal overthrow in Bolivian history:

> The triumph of the popular revolution is an event of exceptional dimensions in the political history of Bolivia. This revolution has not been the end of a political party, nor of a caudillo, nor of a confabulation of military men in command of troops, as have been the thousand and one revolutions that fill Bolivian annals. It has been a gesture of collective heroism in which have participated men, women and children, guided by an uncontainable rage, in the face of a regime stained with blood, blood shed not in legitimate actions of attack and defense, but in forms of the most refined and abject criminality. [11]

Nevertheless, Los Tiempos was not hostile to the MNR itself in the wake of the Villarroel episode. Dispersed and repressed after 1946, the MNR sought to regroup but the nascent political party, charged by military partisans of having abandoned their leader in his final hours, was harassed and persecuted across the land. Canelas, a firm believer in constitutional procedures, wrote at the time, "That system [of persecution] has ended by converting into true reality that which at the beginning was mere fantasy." In other words, repression was strengthening the MNR. Canelas sustained a strong fight against the persecution, especially after the beginning of 1948, the year before the outbreak of civil war in Bolivia. Gabriel Arze Quiroga, writing several years later in La Nación, noted that Canelas thus "demonstrated his consummate knowledge of human psychology and sociology." This persecution provided the precipitating factor of the attempted golpe of August 1949. Elected MNR deputies, denied the right to fight in the parliament, chose to carry their fight to the streets, with the outbreak of hostilities on May 1 and 2, 1949, in La Paz and later, May 27 and 28, at the mining centers of Siglo XX, Llallagua and Huanuni. [12] The MNR had planned to seize power by capitalizing on scattered labor strikes, but the effort failed and party leaders were driven into exile--many, along with Paz Estenssoro, into neighboring Argentina.

The early favorable or at least neutral attitude toward the MNR by Los Tiempos reveals the bankruptcy of the older parties and the desperate need for men like Canelas--on the brink of disaster--to grasp at any available straw. As early as 1944, just a year after the founding of the newspaper and during the rule of Villarroel himself, Los Tiempos editorialized that Villarroel would not have the same freedom to act as his intellectual precursor Germán Busch had with the Convention of 1938. Busch's only political support was the amorphous, symbolical Legión de Excombatientes (Legion of War Veterans) which he could make appear and disappear at will. On the other hand, Villarroel must contend with the MNR and the Stalinist PIR (Partido de Izquierda Revolucionario, Party of the Revolutionary Left), "two adult entities with strong characteristics, especially the MNR." The newspaper added, "The MNR, through its numerical force and also through its spiritual inclination, is called to weigh in the balance, to an extent that one cannot yet predict and that depends on the greater or lesser capacity it shows to play its role in the drama that will unfold next August [when elections were scheduled]." [13]

After the MNR gained power by force on April 11, 1952, Los Tiempos adopted an ambivalent position. In the first place, the newspaper called for "Constitutional government" in an editorial, declaring that the MNR government would not be constitutional until Congress began functioning again. Moreover, the newspaper declared, this matter was delaying recognition of the new government. "Meanwhile," it continued, "declarations issued by some ministers on revolutionary plans, makes one suppose that it is in their minds to proceed not as a constitutional government, but as a revolutionary committee." [14] At the same time, Los Tiempos deplored on April 25 popular disturbances in Oruro, the first since the MNR took power, in which a mob seized property imported by W.R. Grace Co. and sold by Said-Yarur, monopoly concessionaire in the production and distribution of shirts and sheetings in Bolivia. The Los Tiempos editorial compared this action to the mob seizures of Major Escobar and Eguino from the national penitentiary after the upheaval of July 21, 1946, and hanging them in the Plaza Murillo--the first damaging act committed during the interim government headed by Tomás Monje Gutiérrez. In conclusion, the newspaper moralized, "popular currents should be heard by the governors. But at no time should the rabble take justice into their own hands." [15]

On the other hand, by contrast, Los Tiempos pointed out that the MNR had the most solid base of any party in Bolivian history and had obtained the greatest victory in the May 1951 elections. Therefore, the new political grouping need not fear the traditional parties, which were moribund before April 9. At the floodtide of the MNR honeymoon in power, the Cochabamba newspaper declared, "The MNR, among the different political parties of the country, is the one which [can give] Bolivia a relatively long era of political peace and fruitful labor. But that depends on the condition of not renewing the obsessive and destructive politics of its predecessors." [16]

On another occasion, Los Tiempos applauded the literacy campaign undertaken throughout the country by the MNR, using the party's pyramidal structure for instruction. In the MNR departmental command in Cochabamba, for example, a certain number of illiterates would be assigned to each cell to be taught to read and write. "In this manner," the newspaper noted, "the MNR--apart from its recruiting action--has taken itself to fulfill a cultural campaign of positive benefit." [17]

The roots of cooperation between Los Tiempos and the MNR go even deeper than this. In 1951, when the party desperately needed publicity for the May elections--its first chance to return to power since the overthrow of Villarroel and the aborted civil war of 1949--Los Tiempos devoted a page periodically to the doings of the MNR. Edited by Wálter Guevara Arze, this public surfacing of a party that had been persecuted and harassed by the military government appeared prominently on the second page. First appearing on April 8, 1951, the series ran for nine installments before the May 6 elections, always accompanied by the MNR V-signal made by the index and second finger and signifying "Venceremos" (We Shall Conquer.) [18] One wonders if Demetrio Canelas would have been so generous, if he could have looked into the future and witnessed the destruction of his own newspaper allegedly by the party he helped in 1951.

Los Tiempos always believed that the MNR won the elections of May 1951 fairly and honestly. At the beginning of 1952, the newspaper asserted, "The MNR as a party whose weight has been evidenced in the elections of May, by virtue of [considerable] numbers, does not in reality need any pact [with other parties] in order to triumph in just and free elections. The Party maintains itself organized and disciplined and only waits for the Government to convoke the announced [run-off] elections." [19]

When those elections were not forthcoming, talk began to circulate that the MNR would take by force what had been denied it at the polls. This was the point at which Los Tiempos parted company with the National Revolutionary Movement, declaring in early February 1952: "...what is certain is that the Bolivian community in its entirety is far from participating in revolutionary dispositions, whether they be red

[Trotskyite POR or Stalinist PIR] or brown [MNR]. The people one bumps into daily in the streets speak badly of the government but reject every new revolution. The only revolution that everyone desires is that which will put an end to all revolutions." [20]   A few days later, Los Tiempos attacked the MNR for its strong nationalism:

> It is difficult to fix the ideological position of the nationalist Revolutionary Movement, if we take into account that the nationalisms never have signified a philosophical or political position, [but rather] they have always obeyed reasons of sentimental character. Contemporary history has demonstrated that rabid nationalisms have fatal consequences for many peoples.   In Europe, Italy and Germany suffered the consequences of Nazism and fascism.   Many place the MNR in the same line followed by the FSB [Falange Socialista Boliviana, a rightwing party formed in 1937], tinted from time to time with known Marxist phraseology.   Both parties have an inclination for totalitarian principles.   Their leaders are the standardbearers of nationalism, although each one marches by a distinct path. [21]

As the showdown between the MNR and the forces of the status quo neared, Los Tiempos stepped up its attacks on revolution as a viable means to solve national problems.   The newspaper vigorously defended capitalism against the strictures of "revolutionary propagandists," noting that all the advances and amenities of modern life were due to capital, not labor.   Bolivia lived in misery despite her enormous natural resources precisely because she did not have the capital to exploit them. On the other hand, "The revolutionary parties speculate with the present miseries and want not only to maintain them but to sharpen them, to achieve through hunger their plans to demolish the social order.   It is for this reason that they intensify their preachings against capital and capitalism and 'imperialism.'" [22]

Ever putting more distance between itself and the MNR, Los Tiempos was virulently attacking the party by February 1952.   In a passage revealing his strict legalistic orientation, Canelas wrote, "The transformation of the political parties into subversive bands, guided by necessity and vengeance, is one of the dangers that confronts Bolivia under the permanent system of exercising implacable persecutions against political adversaries."   Although Los Tiempos had spoken frequently of the persecution of the MNR by the Ballivián junta after the elections of 1951, this system was not the creation of the PURS (Partido de la Unión Republicana Socialista).   It was practiced by the MNR during the Villarroel period, and by all the governments that preceded the MNR. All questions of principle or doctrine, the newspaper lamented, were subordinated to personal rivalries. [23] In this sense, Los Tiempos was correct in recognizing Paz Estenssoro as another caudillo and seeing beneath the surface the opportunism inherent in the MNR.

Only eight days before the MNR revolt of April 9, Los Tiempos launched its most virulent attack on the party that seemed to be giving up its victory at the polls for hand grenades in the streets. "Paz Estenssoro represents more than the electoral majority [in the elections of May 6, 1951, in which he opposed five other candidates]. He represents the reprisals, the hatreds, the grudges, the compressed violence against the vital interests that sustain the fragile armor of the national Bolivian aggregate. These interests have opposed themselves, oppose now and will oppose tooth and nail the entrance of this vengeful force into the government." [24]

Always a stickler for constitutional norms, Los Tiempos was horrified at the rapidity and sweep of the social changes unfurled in La Paz after April 1952. These provoked an attempted counter-revolt in early January 1953, which prompted the newspaper to state: "The revolutionary process...has gained...its own velocity, independent of the action of the Government. The Government still has sufficient power to stimulate that velocity, but it now seems impotent to bridle it, much less to stop it. The Government, therefore, has no other alternative than to let itself be carried by the current." [25]
This referred more than anything else to the agrarian depredations launched against landowners in the Cochabamba valley, but it also accurately marked the momentum of the Revolution in other areas such as the universal vote and nationalization of the tin mines. Steadily the newspaper of Demetrio Canelas and the MNR grew further and further apart, with little common ground left between them. Curiously, Los Tiempos still used the columns of La Nación, the official MNR newspaper, for its source of information about happenings in La Paz. The Cochabamba newspaper had a column with the standing headline, THE EVENTS OF LA PAZ ACCORDING TO THE OFFICIAL DAILY. This was sub-headed, "the most complete account." [26] It seems that Canelas the journalistic entrepreneur took precedence over Canelas the disgruntled politician. Or, on the other hand, maybe this was simply a way of placating the central authorities while Los Tiempos girded itself for the fight of its life.

The opening salvo in the harassment of the Cochabamba newspaper came with the imposition of labor fines on Los Tiempos in 1952. On October 29 a man claiming to be a labor judge came to the newspaper's offices on payday and demanded to see if increased backpay ordered by the government was included in the workers' checks. Clerks explained that a lawyer was arranging this. Angry and offensive, the judge, Samiramis Jaldin, fined Los Tiempos 120,000 bolivianos on the spot; this amount was increased to 500,000 bolivianos on November 4. Canelas wrote in the pages of his newspaper, "...since it has existed, Los Tiempos never deviated from its line of conduct, neither before the threat of death, nor of fines, and we hope that, God willing, it will maintain its tradition to the end of its days." [27] It seems that the fines were not justified because they were later dropped by the MNR government, but at the time they were intended to exert some muscle against a recalcitrant opposition newspaper.

Los Tiempos again found itself in trouble concerning some false details it had published on the attempted counter-revolt of early January 1953. Always having to walk a tightrope in the revolutionary situation, the newspaper apologized in an editorial headed, "Road of thorns for 'Los Tiempos.'" The editors admitted they were wrong in having published a false broadcast by Radio Belgrano in Argentina that university leader Guzmán Galarza had captured the chancellery during the fighting in La Paz. Actually Los Tiempos had made a contrite apology the previous day under the title, "Flying saucers in Cochabamba," but MNR attacks upon the newspaper led to this second explanation. Los Tiempos maintained that the error did not mean, as the government press had charged, that the Cochabamba newspaper was trying to divide the government or represented the Rosca, imperialism or Patiñismo. [28]

Nevertheless, the continued strictures of Los Tiempos against every aspect of the revolutionary program brought a groundswell of public protest. By early 1953 workers' groups-- probably including the same men who had forced the closure of La Razón--were demanding that Los Tiempos be confiscated. Coming to the defense of the Cochabamba newspapers were such groups as the Society of Writers and Artists of Bolivia, which resolved:

That the daily Los Tiempos is a news-dispensing institution morally tied to the general interests of the Bolivian people; that it is the permanent defender of civil liberties and free thought, being therefore unjust and unlawful the campaign of some nuclei of anarchic agitation, bent on annihilating in Cochabamba said organ of civic expression which honors national journalism. [29]

The Inter American Press Association got wind of the

matter and sent a telegram to Paz Estenssoro in early February 1953 urging him not to honor the petition to expropriate Los Tiempos and establish censorship in Cochabamba. The Bolivian ambassador to the United States, Eduardo Arze Quiroga, denied that the MNR had any intention of doing either. Meanwhile, the Bolivian president's secretary, Roberto Méndez Tejada, replied to the IAPA telegram, emphasizing that the government had no intention of acceding to the request for the expropriation of Los Tiempos formulated by labor organizations, "notwithstanding this daily's having published tendentious and false information." The MNR official added that there was no censorship in Bolivia of the press or radio or any other organ of diffusion "because the Government finds itself firmly backed by the great national majorities." [30]

This did not bring an end to the agitation, however. On April 16, 1953, Los Tiempos noted that labor leaders were continuing to threaten the newspaper. In self-defense, Canelas wrote that in the rapid succession of revolts and changing governments, both military and civil, since 1943 when Los Tiempos was founded, "The press has not escaped this period of confusion." Nevertheless, Los Tiempos claimed it was the only newspaper to protest vigorously the attempts against the press under Mamerto Urriolagoita (1949-1951) and General Hugo Ballivián (1951-1952). Los Tiempos declared in 1953, "[We were] the only tribune of defense for those persecuted and we noted at various opportunities that persecution, confinement and exile would [only] bring a great wave of vengeances." [31]

Repression became more direct when the chief editor of Los Tiempos, Oscar Dorado Vásquez, was arrested by police on the night of May 13, 1953. Dorado, who had been a journalist for twelve years and was president of the Association of Journalists of Cochabamba, was working late in the Los Tiempos offices with his colleague, Samuel Mendoza. A flurry of activity at the city hall prompted them to go to inquire of Mayor Rafael Saavedra if this meant a crisis in the departmental MNR. The mayor denied anything unusual was going on, but Dorado was arrested upon returning to the newspaper. He was in exile in Chile forty-eight hours later, where he wrote a series of eight articles on his experiences that were published in Los Tiempos. The first one concluded, "I have fear for the Bolivian people; always so suffering, always deceived, and never satisfied.... [but] ideas do not die with arrests or exiles." [32]

On May 15, two days after Dorado's arrest, Los Tiempos blasted the action in an editorial headlined "'Los Tiempos' under police hostility." Earlier the newspaper had criticized the police for the detention of a campesino official on May 12. In the editorial, Canelas declared, "Regardless to what party are affiliated those who suffer injustices, they have always had in Los Tiempos a podium to defend their rights." Now that one of its own editors had been arrested and spirited away in the night, the newspaper harkened back to its historical origins: "Our daily began its existence in September 1943, entering the journalistic world not as an instrument of combat, as has been and still continues being the usage of Bolivian journalism, born under the favor of some form of protection, now of the government, then of its adversaries, and of determined interests, having as their mission the defense or attack upon them." On the contrary, Los Tiempos declared that it had established a reputation for impartial commentary, "until having constituted itself as the first informative instrument for the popular conscience, not only of our own district, but in all of the Republic." [33]

Whether as a result of pressure or not, editorials disappeared from Los Tiempos except for the one noted above during this period immediately following the arrest of Dorado. Some innocuous editorials appeared, such as "Results of the Italian elections" on June 10, but the first local editorial, concerning a labor demonstration in Cochabamba, did not appear until June 13, a month after the arrest of Dorado. Radio Cochabamba supported Los Tiempos after the arrest of Dorado, [34] but other groups were also harassed by the police. Four cadets were arrested by police chief Major Emilio Arze Zapata for distributing La Voz del Cadete (Voice of the Cadet). The charge was "clandestine distribution of pamphlets without imprints." In other words, only officially recognized publications could be issued. Arze Zapata told Los Tiempos this was necessary because of terrorist plans afoot in Cochabamba. [35]

But the weapon used by the MNR government most effectively against Los Tiempos was neither punitive taxation nor direct police harassment. It was a weapon perfected by Juan Domingo Perón of Argentina against La Prensa before its ultimate confiscation in 1951--the curtailment or severe rationing of newsprint to opposition journals, forcing them to reduce the size of their editions, limit circulations or go out of business altogether. Paz Estenssoro had spent the exile years of the sexenio (1946-1952) in exile in Buenos Aires where he had witnessed the muzzling of la Prensa, and MNR journalists and intellectuals such as Augusto Céspedes had worked on the nationalized newspaper. Defending the abolition of a free press, Céspedes said later, "Carrying out a social revolution is like marrying a woman: you cannot marry only part of her." [36] Critics of this kind of ruthlessness, such as Los Tiempos, quoted the Conference of Chapultepec and Article 19 of the United Nations Declaration of the Rights of Man, which was paraphrased in part as saying, "the most odious system [to silence opposing voices] recently put into practice, is that of establishing the rationing of newsprint." [37] The system had the advantage to the MNR government of its being able to maintain that diminished supplies of newsprint to Los Tiempos resulted from a genuine shortage and lack of foreign exchange to buy more. In part, this was true because La Nación, the government's own organ, was forced at times to reduce its size or print on available colored paper.

The agency which channeled the flow of newsprint to the handful of newspapers in Bolivia was the Subsecretaría de Prensa, Informaciones y Cultura (SPIC). In July 1953 it advised Canelas, who had sought foreign exchange for paper already at the port of Arica in nearby Chile, that SPIC "has the monopoly of importation of paper and it is not possible to attend this class of isolated orders since they nourish the black market." On July 8 Canelas replied that his supply of paper on the docks at Arica had been there since February 1953, before SPIC ordered the monopoly control of paper, but the agency still would not release it. Always the jurist, Canelas pointed out that regulations could not be retroactive. Bowing before central authority, Canelas wired that if SPIC would not release all of the paper, at least 50 tons were desperately needed if Los Tiempos--the only newspaper in Cochabamba-- were to continued publishing. [38] Meanwhile, the shortage of paper caused gaps in Los Tiempos' printing schedule. During this period the people of Cochabamba were lucky to have a newspaper one day out of three. [39]

A meeting of the departmental COB (Central Obrera Boliviana, Bolivian Worker Central) on July 14 discussed the possibility that Los Tiempos would close down if it did not receive newsprint. According to a report of the meeting in Los Tiempos, some were in favor of this, calling the newspaper "a reactionary daily, imperialist and oligarchial (rosquista)." Although some complained that Los Tiempos did not publish all of the union communiques, others thought that Cochabamba should not be without a newspaper. One speaker urged that Los Tiempos pass under the control of COB, but the Los Tiempos writer reminded his readers that the Sindicato de Fabriles (Manufacturer's Union) had issued a resolution to that effect months ago, without any effect whatever. [40]

When SPIC finally made its decision on the quota of newsprint for Los Tiempos, the newspaper was aghast to find that it had received only ten rolls a month, whereas it used two rolls a day and had 185 rolls waiting in the fifty tons at Arica. The newspaper was insisting on forty tons a month, hoping to go to ten or twelve pages because of increased news and other material. Los Tiempos called the SPIC decision "a mockery." The newspaper announced it would suspend publication on July 6, explaining that it had been able to hang on this long by going to six pages and reducing circulation from 10,000 to 5,000. [41]

Declaring that the government was engaged in a "conspiracy" or "machination" against it, Los Tiempos editorialized that the MNR was determined to close the newspaper during the month of July for two reasons--to clear the way for an official newspaper to start up in August, using the machinery of El País of Oruro, and to prevent Los Tiempos from publishing reactions to the agrarian reform slated to be decreed on August 2. Giving further details of its experience with the La Paz bureaucracy, the newspaper charged that SPIC had ordered the Banco Central not to grant Los Tiempos any foreign exchange, although the bank itself had authorized the importation of newsprint in October 1952. Other newspapers were in a similar position, Los Tiempos pointed out, having ordered their paper before the imposition of monopoly control by SPIC, but they had received their newsprint. [42]

Meanwhile, the plight of Los Tiempos was polarizing the Cochabamba community. On the night of July 28 students paraded before the newspaper's building shouting "Confiscate Los Tiempos" and "Los Tiempos belongs to the Yankees." [43] On the other hand, the Cámara Departmental de Industria (State Chamber of Commerce) sent telegrams on July 20 to Paz Estenssoro and Carlos Wálter Urquidi, minister of information, supporting Los Tiempos' claim to newsprint. [44]

Finally, it was El Diario of La Paz which came to the regional newspaper's rescue. Los Tiempos would have had to cease publishing altogether if the capital newspaper had not loaned it six tons or twenty rolls of newsprint in late July. Days earlier Canelas had sent a telegram to SPIC pointing out the mechanical difficulty of printing a six-page edition and the speculation arising from the lowered circulation of Los Tiempos. His request for the immediate delivery of twenty rolls of newsprint was surprisingly granted, but with this notation, "What seems strange is that in spite of our good will 'Los Tiempos' is publishing versions that are not true [respecting our assurances that you would have adequate paper]." [45] The heavy-handed hint for Los Tiempos to draw back from its criticism of SPIC, coupled with the carrot of a small amount of newsprint, was obvious.

More trouble from the student sector came on July 28 when youths gathered at the Facultad de Medicina (Medical School) approved a four-point program which included the immediate confiscation of Los Tiempos. Other points:

• Everyone who did not agree with the students were traitors to the people and San Simón University.

• All private colegios (high schools) in Cochabamba should also be confiscated immediately.

• A general mobilization of the University was decreed for as long as necessary.

This issue is important because students were instrumental in the initial assault on Los Tiempos on November 9, 1953, but the newspaper in July treated their meeting with scorn and derision. An editorial headlined, "Work of a few fanatics," compared this kind of rally to a Jacobin Club, or better, Committee of Public Safety of the French Revolution. The students complained that Los Tiempos did not publish their communications, but Canelas replied only that the Penal Code, adopted in 1834, prohibited the confiscation of private property for political reasons. So too did the Constitution which stated, "Confiscation will never be applied as a political punishment." Los Tiempos noted that the building of La Razón in La Paz had been confiscated as part of the property of Compañía Aramayo de Minas during the tin expropriation, "But the shops of this newspaper have been respected until now." [46] On the following day, Los Tiempos protested that the gathering in the hall of the Facultad de Medicina included many non-students. There was no discussion and no votes taken, claimed the newspaper, which also found the student communique false and misleading. Canelas called for a plebiscite which would reveal the strength of leftists in the University, but this was never carried out. The suggestion did serve, however, to widen the gulf between the newspaper publisher and his young opponents. [47]

Meanwhile, the battle of the newsprint continued. Canelas experienced the classic runaround so well known to all but Bolivians of the higher classes. On July 29, 1953, he sent a telegram to his agent in La Paz advising him to pay the importing firm La Papelera for the twenty rolls of paper approved by SPIC. But the agency reneged on its promise: The agent replied that La Papelera maintained it had not received an order, and SPIC had not received a request. The agent said Canelas should send his request to SPIC. Firing off a letter to the agency on the same day, the publisher pleaded that his paper supply would last only until August 2. In another telegram sent at the same time he urgently requested ten tons of newsprint to avoid paralyzation of his editions. [48]

Once again the editorial guns of Los Tiempos were trained on the problem. Canelas printed copies of the exchange of correspondence between him and his agent in La Paz, La

Papelera and SPIC. In an editorial of August 1 he denounced the "machination of the office of assistant secretary of press [SPIC] to deprive this daily newspaper of paper." Canelas warned the ministers of labor and economy that his workers would be out of work after Sunday, August 2, including the canillitas (news vendors) who made their sole living that way. The editorial concluded that SPIC "is guided by the deliberate intent to cause an independent newspaper to disappear, which is at this time the only one published in Cochabamba." [49]

At the same time, Canelas received a telegram of July 30 from SPIC authorizing five tons of newsprint. Replying, Canelas added in a postscript, "We must reiterate our surprise at this system of [small] doses [of newsprint] which does not permit us to be sure of the continuation of our editions except for a week ahead." Los Tiempos advised the authorities in La Paz that it needed to plan at least a month ahead, and it claimed the rights of any licit business established in conformance with the laws of the country. In a boxed note in the same edition, the newspaper explained that the special agrarian reform issue planned for the day of the signing of the decree, August 2, had to be cancelled for lack of paper. The editors noted that Los Tiempos would not reappear until the five tons of newsprint reached Cochabamba, possibly on the national airline, Lloyd Aéreo Boliviano. [50]

The worst fears of Canelas were realized. Between August 2 and 22, Los Tiempos was able to publish only two editions--on August 5 and 9. Five rolls of newsprint arrived by air on August 5, sufficient only for these two editions. On August 8 Canelas wrote to the chief of labor in Cochabamba urging him to put pressure on SPIC for more paper. What would be the obligation of Los Tiempos to its workers if they must be fired? the publisher asked. He also sent a telegram to Paz Estenssoro, asking now for only twenty tons a month for strictly local circulation and another telegram to SPIC begging for a few more rolls by air. [51] Again, the request of twenty tons monthly was repeated. On August 14 SPIC authorized ten rolls, enough for only five restricted local editions. The newspaper was also having mechanical difficulties and was unable to obtain the parts to repair its presses.

Nevertheless, Los Tiempos was garnering some popular support in its native city. Eleven civic organizations sent a joint protest on August 10 to President Paz Estenssoro and Vice-President Siles Zuazo. [52] The effect of such remonstrances can be doubted, but they helped to adorn the columns of Los Tiempos and make the plight of the newspaper an international issue. At the darkest period of the struggle for newsprint, Canelas left Cochabamba to attend the ninth general assembly of the Inter American Press Association, which then represented more than 300 member newspapers, beginning September 8 in Mexico City, where he continued to plead the case of his newspaper. [53]

The slow strangulation of newsprint for Los Tiempos weakened the newspaper but did not kill it. Dismayed by its continued sporadic editions, MNR strategists in La Paz may have decided to try another tactic--that of force, as applied on November 9, 1953 when students and campesinos, allegedly led by MNR members such as José Fellmann Velarde, dismantled and sacked the newspaper plant. If this is true, the question remains why the MNR allowed Los Tiempos to continue publishing for nineteen months after the outbreak of the revolution, whereas La Razón in the capital was not permitted to survive the MNR insurrection by one edition. Nevertheless, there was a concerted effort to silence Los Tiempos after the newspaper appeared so adamant on the agrarian reform issue (Chapter 9). A brief look at other issues will illustrate why the MNR could no longer tolerate the existence of Los Tiempos by November 1953 when the Revolution was struggling desperately to consolidate itself.

The tragedy of Los Tiempos was that it could see the problems of Bolivia but could not face up to their solutions. Canelas was not a monster. A humane and enlightened man with the norms of Western democracy instilled by his Swiss education, he refused to consider social revolution as the only means capable of re-distributing power and wealth in Bolivia. A systematic political thinker and staunch supporter of the capitalist status quo, he viewed everything in the bleak light of a legalism which had never served Bolivia. Canelas deplored "revolutions" as means to solve the problems of the country, but he confused the many coup d'etats of Bolivian history with the genuine and far-reaching social and economic changes attempted by the MNR after 1952. Just five days before the outbreak of fighting in La Paz on April 9, 1952, Canelas in a long editorial reviewing the country's history came to the conclusion that political parties as such had become obsolete after the Chaco War with national and international political questions replaced by social and labor problems and the emergence of the class struggle. Noting that 85 to 90 percent of the Bolivian people worked, Canelas declared, "All of this population is inflammable, at the service of revolutionary parties. The multiplicity of these revolutionary parties is proof without doubt of the volcanic condition in which the country lives, because of bad governments and inflation." [54]

When fighting broke out in La Paz on April 9, Canelas sat glued to his radio, listening to the blow-by-blow descriptions of the struggle after the MNR had seized Radio Illimani in La Paz and Radios Popular and Rural in Cochabamba. Then the 73-year-old journalist entitled his front-page editorial, GOD PROTECT BOLIVIA. He informed his readers, "The revolution, in synthesis, has begun with little ambience and, up till now, its victories have been only verbal." [55]

Because the MNR had departed from constitutional norms to become outright revolutionary--even though it claimed to have won a majority of the votes in the May 1951 elections--Los Tiempos turned against the party. Earlier the newspaper had respected the social goals and viability of the new political grouping, but immediately after the April 9 revolt it criticized the MNR for setting itself up as a revolutionary committee rather than duly constituted government. Why were run-off elections not held? Why were large numbers of persons held as political prisoners? On May 24, 1952, Los Tiempos reprinted an editorial from Rebeldías of Postosí which was intended to hold the party to its promises. The editorial noted that the MNR V-sign for Venceremos ("We shall conquer") now stood to the opposition for Vigilancia ("Vigilance") and Veremos ("We shall see"). Specifically, opponents vowed to watch out to see if the MNR nationalized the mines, realized the agrarian reform, lowered the cost of living, nationalized the railroads, improved working conditions, respected freedom of press, respected labor's right to organize and strike, and made effective the "anti-feudal and anti-imperialist" struggle. Would the party implant in Bolivia a "fecund era of social and economic transformation"? Would at last justice, right, liberty, order and peace reign in Bolivia? Would the MNR moralize the public administration? "In conclusion," the editorial stated, "[We want to see] if the present government fulfills all the postulates and all the promises scattered by its President, apart from demagoguery, opportunism and the base personal appetites which have never been lacking in the national political gloominess." [56]

It is ironic that Los Tiempos should be encouraging a far-left view of the MNR Revolution by reprinting the above editorial, but the newspaper was intent upon embarrassing the party whenever possible, disseminating dissent from any quarter. It must be stressed again, however, that Los Tiempos approved in principle many of the MNR reforms but differed only in how they should be carried out. The extent of the social changes was also in dispute; if Canelas could have had his way, the agrarian reform program would have been emasculated.

On the first major reform launched by the MNR--the universal vote decreed on July 21, 1952, on the sixth anniversary of the murder of Villarroel--the newspaper vacillated. As early as the elections on May 6, 1951, Los Tiempos had demonstrated vividly that Bolivia could not in any sense call herself a democracy, with suffrage limited to adult, literate, property-owning males. The newspaper pointed out that of a population of about 3,900,000 at that time, only 205,000 were literate, but past experience showed that only about 140,000 actually went to the polls. In other words, only 5 percent of the Bolivian people could vote but those who actually exercised this right were only 3 percent. To win, a presidential candidate needed half of those 140,000 votes, or 70,001. Thus, Canelas pointed out with cool logic, Bolivian governments could be based on the will of only 1.75 percent of the population. [57]

In early 1952, before the April 9 showdown, Los Tiempos continued discussing the issue of restricted suffrage:

> There is no legal possibility of maintaining public order because they always try to give stability to minority governments, as if a pyramid could rest upon its apex instead of its base. The institutional life of Bolivia lacks a mechanical foundation. The governments are formed by minority interests, who sustain their trenches with open force against the majority currents, so that these always have to resort to armed force [to overthrow them].

This, according to Canelas, was one of the profound constitutional contradictions of Bolivian "democracy." There could not be majority government because the majority of the Bolivian population was outside political life, and secondly because within the minority nucleus that had a political conscience, most were in violent divergence with the interests that had in their hands the vital resources of the nation, creating conflict without resolution. Prophetically, the newspaper publisher concluded, "The day when the true Bolivian majority enters the government, blood will flow and the historical, social and economic architecture [of Bolivia] will collapse." [58]

This apocalyptic vision of the national future led Canelas to support initially the universal suffrage decree of July 21, 1952. He decided that ballots would be preferable to bullets. Praising the measure which gave votes to Indians for the first time, proposed by Villarroel in 1945, the editorial was headlined "Perhaps they will do it better." One could not argue with the logic of the decree, the publisher wrote, since the basic democratic principle was rule by the popular majorities. He added, "Since it is undeniable that 70 percent of the Bolivian population is constituted by these native materials [Indians], the government in good law should be exercised by them, and not by the white or mixed [morena] minority." [59]

Canelas had second thoughts, however, about his first magnanimous reaction. Two days after the above editorial, he vigorously attacked the universal vote in an editorial headed "Political sovereignty and native masses:"

> The application of the universal vote in a racial conglomerate, constituted in its majority by illiterates, runs the risk of being translated into a grotesque electoral farce, discrediting the democratic principle in its very source.... Such amplification of the vote will serve, for the time being, only to place an invincible electoral capital in the hands of the Government. Native masses of both sexes, lacking in general in political and institutional concepts, will be mobilized as stupid ingredients to weigh in the electoral balance. With these artificial citizens lacking in civic convictions and free will, their votes will be manipulated. This, in the final analysis, will contribute to make more muddy and perhaps more laughable Bolivian democracy. [60]

This complete turnabout reveals that Canelas, upon thinking things over, was willing to see his professed democratic and legal ideals evaporate like the morning mist if their implementation should threaten the economic and social privileges of his class. He saw--probably correctly--that the universal vote was a calculated attempt by the MNR to consolidate its regime by anchoring itself in the countryside. History was to prove otherwise, as the campesinos turned out to be essentially conservative, but the prospect was frightening to men like Canelas in 1952.

On economic matters, the newspaper publisher was equally severe. To give only one example, he attacked in October 1952 a measure to make all wage increases retroactive to April 9. Calling this "The second pillar of the National Revolution," Los Tiempos cited as reasons for the decree that it would put buying power in workingmen's pockets, decrease the profits of firms, and gain political adhesion of the working masses. Canelas found all three motives reprehensible. The first would lead to inflation and people working less since they tended only to fulfill their immediate needs. As for the second, businesses had always been the best lookers-after of their own working people, as the Constitution recognized. And the third was but another way for the MNR in a pragmatic or opportunistic way to embed itself more deeply in power, as with the universal vote and agrarian reform. [61]

The third great postulate of the Revolution, nationalization of the three major tin mines, met with similar resistance from

Los Tiempos. The newspaper mounted a campaign to stop the nationalization of October 31, 1952, defending the sanctity of private capital. In carrying out the action, the MNR was fulfilling a campaign promise that was more than rhetorical in nature; the international firms of Patiño, Hochschild and Aramayo each had annual earnings greater than the Bolivian national budget. As such they were a symbolic and real threat to national sovereignty, but this did not prevent Canelas from defending them as "captains of industry" rather than "robber barons." After nationalization, Los Tiempos did everything in its power to discredit government operation of the mines, not taking into account that plant installations had become antiquated, foreign technicians had fled, and veins of tin were playing out. In August 1953, for example, the newspaper proclaimed that nationalization of the tin mines had not been successful, even taking into account the lower world tin prices after the close of the Korean war. What went wrong? "It is conceded true everywhere and at all times that [government] administration is disadvantageous, irresponsible and causes rapid demoralization when it invades the field of commercial and industrial exploitation." Canelas saw an even greater danger in the device, for "The politics of linking the public and private economy to the destiny of every political party that rises to power is very dangerous for the future of Bolivia." [62]

Thus, Los Tiempos opposed every major reform pushed through by the MNR. The newspaper was on a collision course with impatient officials in the capital, and that crash exploded on November 9, 1953. Three months after the signing of the agrarian reform decree, campesinos and others attacked and destroyed the Los Tiempos plant. The violence of the confrontation produced in the exterior one of the greatest controversies of the Bolivian National Revolution. Along with La Razón, the case of Los Tiempos became a cause celebre among the proprietors of the hemisphere's press. What happened? Lee Hills, former president of the IAPA, gave this version in 1969: "The late Demetrio Canelas, of Los Tiempos, Cochabamba, Bolivia, saw his newspaper destroyed by government-inspired mobs, and then he was thrown in prison and threatened with execution as a traitor for not bowing editorially to the government. IAPA protests saved him." [63]

But the MNR spokesman La Nación gave quite a different account in 1959, relying on a dispatch from Cochabamba by its correspondent Julián Cayo. This newsman, sifting the evidence six years after the event, reported that Los Tiempos had not been "destroyed" at all. Two line-casting machines were not injured while a third and the press itself were damaged only slightly and were functional again after light repairs. In fact, Canelas' "destroyed" press was first sold to Critica of

218

Cochabamba, then to Crónica of the same city, and finally to Progreso of Santa Cruz, where it continued in service.

Cayo reconstructed the events of November 9, 1953. That morning, he said, the people of Cochabamba were told by radio that a counter-revolution led by the FSB had broken out in their city. The rebels used the Los Tiempos building as their citadel. After the noon hour, the plant of Los Tiempos was taken by MNR-controlled students against machine-gun fire from the building. The students were about to print the first issue of El Proletario when mobs of campesinos invaded and occupied the building. On November 10 the student group, Avanzada Universitaria, again gained control of the building for four hours. It was they who reported that the equipment had been damaged only lightly. Some fifty workers lost their lives putting down the attempted counter-revolt.

The MNR correspondent found it ironic that Canelas had used illiterate peons to carry his editorials from his nearby estate of Pucara to Cochabamba. They were "innocent porters of editorials which argued that it was necessary to perpetuate the order of a powerful bossism," Cayo wrote. He also charged that Canelas had conspired openly with the Rural Federation of Landowners to bring about the attempted counter-revolt of November 9, 1953, maintaining that the publisher had no social conscience whatsoever. He had used pongos (serfs) both in his country house and in the plant of Los Tiempos itself, where they could be seen "running like souls in pain to fulfill the domestic commands of the patrón." The MNR writer concluded, "The campesinos, dressed in coarse flannel and wearing sandals, watched terrified the operation of the Linotypes and the press which was publishing the newspaper that was inciting repression of the agrarian revolution underway." [64]

A politically combative and articulate man, Canelas was not to let these charges go unanswered. He presented his version of these events in a book published in Cochabamba in 1960, after he had returned from exile, entitled Los Tiempos, Independent Newspaper, History of Ten Years of Journalism. For the first time, his petitions to the government were presented to public view because Los Tiempos itself did not resume publication until 1967. The aging publisher reminded his readers that when the MNR was defeated in 1946, "the only newspaper that tried to put a stop to the policy of [police] vengeance [against the MNR] was Los Tiempos and the only one also that sheltered in its columns the publications of that party in defense of its rights." Canelas maintained that because of that policy Los Tiempos came to be the most sought after newspaper in Bolivia. [65]

In this statement of January 10, 1954, Canelas described as "false and absurd" the MNR charges that the Los Tiempos plant had served as a bastion for the counter-revolutionary FSB forces on November 9, 1953. On the contrary, the FSB uprising served only as a pretext for José Fellmann Velarde to rush to Cochabamba and oversee the destruction of the newspaper. Canelas himself was in his apartment on the second floor of the building when fighting broke out on the morning of November 9. Anticipating trouble, he sent his employees home and locked the building before fleeing to the home of his sister where he followed the day's events on the radio. Later he pieced together this narrative. Mario Buzmán Galarza, a student leader, took charge of reorganizing the newspaper after the building was seized. Fellmann Velarde, director of SPIC throughout Paz Estenssoro's first term, showed up and declared that such use of Canelas' property "would solve nothing" since in a few days it would have to be returned to its owner. According to Canelas, it was Fellmann Velarde who personally ordered the destruction of the shops and offices of Los Tiempos, including the sacking of his own living quarters. For this purpose, a brigade of armed Indians was brought to Cochabamba from Ucureña, and Fellmann Velarde personally directed the assault. The attackers were aided by "street thieves," all of whom gutted the building. A large crowd gathered outside to watch the vandals, who also stole or destroyed Canelas' private library--the largest such collection in Cochabamba--and made off with 500,000 bolivianos in cash. Throughout the day the beleaguered publisher called the prefecture, even before the beginning of the sacking, seeking protection for his property, but nothing was done. As Canelas exclaimed later, in recounting the incident, "Never had such a spectacle been seen in Cochabamba, and its memory will last for generations." [66]

José Fellmann Velarde gave quite a different account in an interview with the author in 1973. A historian and novelist of considerable attainment who served the MNR faithfully, Fellmann Velarde maintained that even if Los Tiempos were not openly involved in the attempted FSB coup of November 9, 1953, the newspaper was morally culpable for making the "psychological preparations" for the revolt in its columns. Moreover, it was a serious attempt to overthrow the MNR government, with fighting breaking out in La Paz as well. The FSB captured two barrios there, the wealthy neighborhoods of Calacoto and Obrajes, before the insurrection collapsed. Fellmann Velarde heard that angry campesinos were converging on Cochabamba and he flew immediately to the stricken city. His only mission, he insisted twenty years later, was to persuade the campesinos to restrain themselves to manifestations or parades. For this peace-keeping purpose, he took along Ñuflo Chávez, the Indian minister of campesino affairs. They were not successful, however, insofar as the sacking of the Los Tiempos building was concerned. [67]

The personal fate of Canelas was precarious. As he picked up the narrative again, a delegation of MNR officials appeared at his sister's house that evening to arrest him. José Canedo López, one of the directors of the MNR, blamed Los Tiempos for the bloody events of the day and declared it was "a newspaper which should exist no longer." He added, "Once and for all this taboo should disappear." All of the male members of the Canelas family, including the three brothers of Demetrio Canelas, were imprisoned or persecuted. The newspaper publisher himself was taken to La Paz where he remained confined for forty days. Although the newspapers and press associations at the time reported that he was held for "treason and attempted assassination," there were no charges filed against him. Finally, he was freed on December 22 with the stipulation that he could not leave the finca (large estate) of Angostura in the district of Cochabamba. This order of confinement was lifted after an interview with the minister of government on January 5, 1954. Meanwhile, the government decreed the embargo of all of Canelas' remaining goods to pay benefits to his former employees. Bitter and bewildered, the publisher complained, "There are no longer any authorities to safeguard life and property [in Bolivia]. I myself cannot define my position as a resident under these new circumstances." [68]

But the troubles of Demetrio Canelas were only beginning. Technically free, he could not get his passport stamped to leave the country. He then obtained diplomatic asylum from the papal nuncio, Sergo Pignedolli, from which refuge he finally obtained a safe-conduct pass to go into exile in Chile. Writing to Wálter Guevara Arze, minister of foreign relations, Canelas had the temerity to maintain, "I do not participate in political activities, as is publicly notorious..." Becoming ever more querulous, he issued a parting shot: "The only thing certain [in Bolivia today] is that no one is sure of his freedom when he is not a friend of the Government." [69]

After an amnesty was granted by the new MNR President, Hernán Siles Zuazo, Canelas returned to Bolivia in September 1956, where he immediately set about obtaining government indemnization for the damage done to his printing plant. In a petition to the minister of government and justice on September 10, 1956, the publisher called the assault on his newspaper "the most sensational act of vandalism within memory in that city [Cochabamba]." Canelas also declared that "Freedom of the Press... has suffered in this case the most flagrant injury of our history." He pointed out that the prefecture of Cochabamba had issued a resolution in 1955 providing that the Los

Tiempos building be returned to its owners. Referring again to the charges that he had fomented the 1953 uprising, Canelas maintained that he read these allegations in the newspapers from his prison cell in La Paz. He had written to the minister of government, Federico Fortún, asking that a judicial process be instituted against him so the truth might be established. The letter was returned with the notice that Canelas was incommunicado. [70]

Actually, the Los Tiempos owner did receive support from the prefecture of Cochabamba. On February 27, 1957, it offered written testimony of the disputed events. The statement noted that the FSB captured the plaza of Cochabamba on the morning of November 9, 1953, and the public buildings surrounding it, but not the building of Los Tiempos. After MNR partisans, leading a counter-attack, secured the public buildings again, armed groups thought that some falangistas might have taken refuge in the plant of Los Tiempos. The windows and doors were shuttered and locked as Canelas had left them, but the mob broke in anyway. They proceeded to dismantle the installations and to ransack the living quarters of Canelas, hoping to find subversive propaganda. They found none, but by then the mob was intent on looting. After it was all over, the ministry of government instructed the fiscal officer of the district and the chief of police to make an inventory of the remaining goods belonging to Los Tiempos. [71]

Canelas' efforts to obtain redress from the MNR government led only to his second exile from the country. Two days after his petition to the minister of government and justice on September 19, 1956, armed forces (probably militiamen) entered his house in La Paz. Fearing imprisonment again, Canelas sought diplomatic intervention and obtained a safe-conduct to flee to exile in Buenos Aires. [72] The matter was now out of his hands, but the question of indemnification for the alleged loss of the Los Tiempos printing equipment was to keep the Inter American Press Association, the hemispheric organization of newspaper publishers, stirred up for almost two decades.

The IAPA accepted completely Canelas' version of these events, which silenced Los Tiempos until the newspaper reopened under Carlos Canelas in 1967--three years after the overthrow of the MNR government. Throughout the twelve years that the MNR held power (1952-1964) the IAPA year after year declared that freedom of the press did not exist in Bolivia. The organization's price tag for lifting this onus was for the government to allow La Razón to reopen and to indemnify the Canelas family for damages done to Los Tiempos. Actually, the IAPA heard only one side of the story. In 1962, for example, Samuel Mendoza, last editor of the newspaper before it went under in 1953, told the IAPA meeting in Santiago de Chile that Los Tiempos had been assaulted by the MNR because the newspaper had denounced Communist infiltration in the government. It was also revealed at the 1962 meeting that the IAPA had been studying the possibility of guaranteeing a loan for the acquisition of new equipment for Los Tiempos, a project which was later abandoned. [73] Finally, at the 1969 meeting of the IAPA in Washington, D.C., it was announced that the civilian government of Luis Adolfo Siles Salinas in Bolivia had appointed a commission to ascertain the amount of damage suffered by Los Tiempos, [74] but the Canelas family never received payment of damages. Earlier, Canelas had tried to hold a public sale of the machines left over from the sacking of his newspaper plant, but he had to let them go in a private sale for only $15,000. In a public statement, he advised that "the reappearance of the daily Los Tiempos is considered for the time being impossible." [75]

During these years the MNR official newspaper, La Nación, kept up a running battle with the IAPA, ridiculing its pretensions as watchdog of freedom of the press in the hemisphere. When some Bolivian exiles in Chile in 1958 appealed to the reports of the IAPA as authoritative sources of what was happening in Bolivia, the newspaper stated:

...as if we did not know that in what pertains to Bolivia those reports are inspired by the tales of Señor Demetrio Canelas, member of that organization of merchants of printed paper and proprietor of the newspaper Los Tiempos which served as a material barricade for the falangistas of Cochabamba when in 1953 they tried to alter the public order. The people took that barricade, destroying part of the installations, and Señor Canelas, instigator of the revolt, still has the nerve to ask for an indemnization. [76]

On another occasion, La Nación proclaimed in a headline, THE LITTLE VOTES OF IAPA MEAN NOTHING TO BOLIVIA. The "Blackmail" of Demetrio Canelas had grown old, the newspaper declared. It added, "The IAPA has touched the depths of loss of reputation as a society of merchants of journalism, many of them as illiterate as Gainza Paz, exploiters of journalists who know how to write." [77] Again, the MNR spokesman noted that in its latest release from New York, the IAPA had included colonies in its annual report with equal status as the independent Latin American nations. Thus, Belize (British Honduras) counted the same as Guatemala, and the Dutch Antilles or Dutch Guiana as Mexico or Venezuela. La Nación commented, "The IAPA has arrived, then, at the extreme of forming the coarsest, most stupid, most impudently childish concept about 'freedom' [of expression] upon trying to place together on the same level the rights of colonies with those of republics. This constitutes an insult to public opinion throughout the continent, including the United States." [78]

When Canelas returned to Bolivia in 1958 from his second exile, he continued to play a role in the political arena even though he no longer had his newspaper to back him. When a "Society of the Free Press" was proposed in Bolivia, a letter writer declared in the columns of La Nación, "nothing can convince me that the idea does not belong to don Demetrio [Canelas], who has wanted to create in Bolivia a miniature replica of the IAPA." [79] In February 1960 the journalistic entrepreneur called for "the greatest cabildo abierto [town meeting] of our history." Those who would be invited to this select gathering would be, in Canelas' words, "those who represent Bolivia." The publisher said he wanted to do this in November 1958 but the MNR was too unified then. The purpose of the cabildo was to obviate the universal vote, whether through "functional senates" or through this type of cabildo for "national salvation." [80] Nor did the other MNR reforms set any better with Canelas with the passage of time. In 1960 La Nación headlined an article by Guillermo Alborta Velasco that agrarian reform for Canelas was "The zero hour of calamities." [81] When two representatives of the IAPA arrived in La Paz in 1961, Demetrio Canelas was at the airport to meet them. La Nación seized upon the occasion to point out once again that the publisher's "destroyed" presses had been sold and he had opened a new printing shop in Cochabamba with the proceeds. [82]

These were among the last public activities of Canelas, who died in 1964--having lived to see the forces of General René Barrientos overthrow the MNR soon after Paz Estenssoro entered his third term as president. As Demetrio Canelas recedes into history, how does one evaluate him? First, it is necessary to consider his age, which probably influenced his political and social outlook. He was 73 years old when the MNR Revolution began in 1952 and 85 years old at the time of his death. His ties to the landowning class of Cochabamba also influenced the course of Los Tiempos which finally proved suicidal in 1953. Even his opponents had grudging respect for him, however. La Nación, responding to an interview with Canelas in El Mercurio of Santiago de Chile in 1955, conceded:

He is intelligent, without doubt; but a long past of frustrations has caused that intelligence to be locked up within himself, to create a fantastic universe from which he refuses to leave. For that reason it is sadder still that that universe is not a Bolivian

224

universe, wide and clear, but a universe of the Rosca. [83]

Later, in 1959, Canelas assumed the presidency of the Committee of National Unity and wrote a letter from Santa Cruz, published in El Diario, decrying the "fearful hunting of human beings" that MNR militiamen were carrying out against the dissidents of that city. He also accused the government of "the extermination of hordes of juveniles." Since Canelas had been chancellor during the Chaco War, La Nación headlined its reply, SENILE NOSTALGIA FOR KILLINGS. The newspaper commented, "Canelas represents, in effect, one of the last surviving signs of that Bolivian generation that is sealing its demise with decades of humiliating intellectual pongueaje [servitude] to the oligarchy." [84]

These criticisms, while harsh, are essentially accurate, but one other jibe at the publisher was not. When Canelas published a letter in Presencia attacking the MNR Revolution, La Nación published a cartoon showing Canelas with a halo above his head and a copy of Los Tiempos sticking out of his back pocket, standing behind Germán Busch. The young reform president was seated at his desk, with Canelas guiding Busch's right hand, holding a revolver, to his head. This was manifestly unfair since Los Tiempos was not even publishing in 1939 when Busch committed suicide. The newspaper did not appear on the journalistic scene until 1943, but the jingle which accompanied the cartoon revealed the distaste with which the MNR establishment--and many Bolivians--viewed the Cochabamba newspaper:

Los Tiempos is gone forever
already it is forgotten
more than forgotten--disbelieved
by the sins into which it has fallen. [85]

One of the final and most telling attacks upon Canelas appeared in the MNR afternoon newspaper La Tarde in early 1960. Written by Luis Alberto Viscarra, the article was headlined, "Canelas, the sorcerer who survives." Everyone had expressed amazement that the publisher had surfaced again with a series of articles attacking the Revolution in "a local morning newspaper." As chancellor during the Chaco War, Canelas was charged with hiding a peace offer from Paraguay and with purchasing the island of Coati as a concentration camp for critics of the Salamanca regime. Viscarra, author of the article, ascribed Canelas' long life to the possibility that hell refused to receive him! Despite such excesses, the article struck a note of truth when it concluded, "The world of Demetrio Canelas has died, in part destroyed by him himself.

225

Within that tribal world, reduced to 200 families that tyrannized the country, Canelas was the grand wizard." [86]

In conclusion, the somewhat arrogant personality of Canelas was intimately tied up with the operation of his newspaper because personalism was still the dominant factor in Bolivian journalism. All the wizardry of that personality could not keep Los Tiempos afloat, however, as accelerating social changes wracked the Cochabamba valley. Some may say that Canelas was courageous in his role as the only real opposition voice in Bolivia during the first nineteen months of the MNR Revolution. Others might describe him as foolhardy. In a sense, Los Tiempos became the successor by default to the defunct La Razón of La Paz as spokesman for the conservative interests of Bolivia. Canelas owed Carlos Víctor Aramayo, tin magnate owner of La Razón, something for having set him up in business in Cochabamba in 1943.

Nevertheless, Los Tiempos bore the indelible imprint of Demetrio Canelas, who survived the era in which he was more comfortable. His Nineteenth Century liberal ideas were no longer suitable for a country in social convulsion, and he would not change or bend those rigid principles in which he believed: freedom of the press, parliamentary government, unrestricted private enterprise. He flirted briefly with the universal vote as a concept but backed away when that concept became reality. Also, he opposed nationalization of the tin mines and other MNR reforms, making a clash between Los Tiempos and the central government inevitable, a clash more serious than the withholding of newsprint or police harassment.

The issue which tipped the balance was Los Tiempos' stand on agrarian reform (see Chapter 9). The newspaper resorted to scare tactics to block land redistribution, but all of those scare tactics could not deter the agrarian revolution underway in the Cochabamba valley and elsewhere. Although students and MNR members took part in the events of November 9, 1953, it was mainly Indians who led the assault on the Los Tiempos plant and destroyed much of its interior. The depth of their bitterness was evidenced by the fury of the assault as the second major opposition voice in Bolivia was silenced. Against the journalistic manipulations of La Razón and Los Tiempos, it was necessary to juxtapose official versions--overcoming almost half a century of retrograde Bolivian social thought--by La Nación and later La Tarde, both MNR newspapers, on the burning issues of the day--nationalization of the tin mines, the agrarian question and the role of the military. These had been questions to which the tin-mining press had seldom addressed itself, although they touched the lives of all Bolivians. Although Los Tiempos was to reappear in 1967, at the time the

Canelas newspaper joined <u>La Razón</u> in silent ignominy, victims of those who had never received nor understood these newspapers.

Chapter 8

THE 'TIN BARONS' AND NATIONALIZATION OF THE MINES

> The MNR has made its state of war against the mining interest the major warhorse to gain adherents. Its present underground campaign of propaganda continues playing that record ever more loudly.
>
> --Los Tiempos,
> Jan. 11, 1952

> Nationalization of the tin mines was not a simple demagoguic act with ruinous consequences [as the reactionary sectors charge] but rather the most important of the measures initially adopted by the first revolutionary Government...
>
> --La Tarde,
> Jan. 25, 1961

Since its discovery at Llallagua near the turn of the century, tin has been a raw nerve running through the body politic of Bolivia. Replacing the silver mania of the colonial period, tin came to be the new monocultural export product that accounted for 76 percent of the country's foreign exchange earnings. It in effect caused the removal of the capital from the tropical lowlands of Sucre to the tin-dominated altiplano of La Paz. Three men and their international cartels controlled this overwhelming influence on Bolivian life, which made and unmade presidents and monopolized the press of La Paz. These men--Simón I. Patiño, Mauricio Hochschild and Carlos Victor Aramayo--were such visible targets for the ills of Bolivia that they were the first, and always the most acute, propaganda focus for the MNR.

The influence of these Big Three tin producers on the national life of Bolivia cannot be exaggerated. For example, the defeat of President Hernando Siles in 1930 by Republican landowners and the Patiñista Liberals placed in power a Junta Militar presided over by a Patiño manager. [1] Exactly how

229

much production did they control? In 1945, when Bolivia achieved her greatest production to that time of refined tin ore--43,147 metric tons--the Big Three accounted for these shares of that production: Patiño, 45 percent; Hochschild, 28 percent, and Aramayo, 7 percent. Thus, collectively the Big Three accounted for 80 percent of Bolivia's tin production, while the small producers contributed only 11 percent and the Banco Minero, 9 percent. [2] This kind of economic preponderance, coupled with collusion with the state, produced such sad chapters in the history of Bolivia as the Catavi mine massacre of 1942 and many other labor clashes that saw government troops and national police pitted against striking miners. As the Commission on the Nationalization of the Mines concluded in 1952, "The life of an entire Nation cannot depend upon the caprice of three persons however powerful they may be.... The mining workers have the right to be free of the permanent threat of new massacres." [3]

Fissures between the Bolivian government and the major tin producers first began to appear in the administration of Germán Busch (1937-1939), although as early as 1918 Gustavo Navarro had pleaded for "Mines to the state, lands to the Indians" in his polemical work, Renacimiento del Alto Perú (Rebirth of Bolivia). It took more than twenty years, however, for the first assertion of the autonomy of the government over the mining interests. On June 1, 1939--a symbolic date used by the MNR to announce its program in 1942--the young and impetuous Busch struck at the heart of the mining companies by requiring that all foreign earnings must first be deposited in the Banco Central de Bolivia to be returned to the owners at the government's exchange rate. [4] This in effect was the Bolivian government's first attempt to tax the mining interests, although the decree was never enforced. Nevertheless, the government's foot was in the door, and with the Gualberto Villarroel reform regime, a decree of April 3, 1945 re-established the obligation of sale to the government of 100 percent of the value of tin exports, making the earlier Busch decree enforceable. [5]

Neither of these actions would have been possible without the work of early propagandists urging public opinion to fight for a more responsible relationship between the tin companies and the government. La República, for example, which was one of the first voices for social justice in Bolivia, was declaring in headlines as early as 1932, HOW THE GREAT FORTUNES ARE MADE.--Today as yesterday they flee [the country] without leaving more than perversion of public officials and professional servility.--They had not only positive guarantees but also the docility of the Government, the parliament and justice." [6] El Universal added its voice to the rising chorus of denunciation, declaring in 1935, THE DOG IN THE MANGER IS THE MINING INDUSTRY."--There are mine owners who have high tax rates and do not pay them even with outside aid..." [7]

Leading the attack, however, was La Calle which pulled no punches in its frontal assault on the "mining super-state." in 1936, the same year that it was founded, La Calle ran an article headlined, "Bolivia today is as colonial as Alto Perú two centuries ago..." The article pointed out that the treasurer of silver-rich Potosí sent a balance statement to the king of Spain on June 16, 1784, which showed that between the discovery of silver there in 1545 and 1783, production had amounted to $920,513,893--a greater quantity than that produced by all of the nations of Europe put together. And the same thing had happened with tin during the past thirty years, the article continued: "The tin riches drawn out from the bowels of the earth with superhuman sacrifices...[once] converted into gold, flow into the coffers of the potentates who form the superstate. Our country lies under their dominion without restrictions and our people are dying of misery." [8]

One of the difficulties in getting sentiments such as these across, however, was that the Big Three monopolized the La Paz press. As El Universal pointed out in 1935, Patiño was the major share holder of El Diario and Aramayo owned La Razón outright. Together, these two powerful newspapers had manipulated public opinion for twenty years. [9] Hochschild also had entered the journalistic arena with Ultima Hora, and all three newspapers gathered in the lion's share of circulation in La Paz. Theirs were the voices with which the middle and upper classes reckoned. As President Víctor Paz Estenssoro recalled in 1956:

> All of the life of this country was submitted to that domination [of the large mine owners]. The press: Some dailies were the property of the mining Enterprises and others were controlled by the mining companies. There was no public opinion which the press translated in this country; it was the opinion of the mining companies. The intellectuals had no future whatever if they were not paid by the Rosca and naturally they had to write in favor of it. [10]

This exclusion from the larger circulation of the Bolivian press perhaps made more shrill the voice of La Calle in its earnest desire to be heard, but the newspaper did not resort only to blatant rhetoric. It also examined the tin companies as economic institutions that were not fulfilling their obligations within the context of Bolivian life. The major companies were actually a drag on the economy, the newspaper declared in early 1937. It noted that Bolivia was not even meeting the tin quota assigned to it by the International Committee in London, despite the government's lowering of the amounts to be turned over to the state for discount, bettering of the exchange rate for these divisas, and "the elimination of all motives that could make exploitation difficult." Yet only one major tin company had taken advantage of these incentives. The alternative La Calle found in the title of its editorial, "Toward intervention in the mines." [11]

Luis Peñaloza, later to be the first historian of the MNR, raised similar questions in an article of 1945 entitled, "Mining and neo-mercantilism." He blamed the governments of the past for not applying heavier taxes during the boom wartime years of 1914-1919 and 1940-1943. Except for reduction on additional tax on wolfram of July 7, 1944, taxes on the mining industry had not changed since 1940--even though the producers were making a windfall with World War II profits. The current tax of 15 to 20 percent should be raised, Peñaloza concluded, since the mining sector contributed only 283 million bolivianos to the general budget of 1,200 million bolivianos. [12]

The lack of social sensitivity of the large-scale tin producers came into sharp focus in 1937 when the minister of education and Indian affairs asked them to contribute toward a goal of 10 million bolivianos for establishing Indian schools in the countryside. The Association of Industrial Miners declined the request flatly, stating vehemently, "This Association has no other character then that of an entity representative of the firms associated in it to assume the defense of the mining interest of the country before the Public Powers or other institutions." [13] This provided considerable grist for the propaganda mills of La Calle, augmented when Carlos Víctor Aramayo personally turned down the request the following month. Aramayo maintained that his company had not declared a dividend from 1930 to the end of 1936 because of "the extremely high percentage of giving over foreign exchange which is imposed on us, as well as the exchange rate that we receive for said foreign currency..." Aramayo did not let it rest there, however, adding pointedly, "I allow myself to be of the opinion, moreover, that public education should be under the charge of the State and should be financed by means of the taxes that the Treasury collects." Aramayo concluded that the situation "does not permit us to divert funds for social problems such as you bring up." [14]

La Calle had a field day when it reported that Mauricio Hochschild had contributed 100,000 bolivianos toward the Indian schools under the headline, NOTWITHSTANDING HIS STATUS AS FOREIGNER. In a comment preceding the minister of education's reply to Aramayo, the newspaper referred to the mine owner as "the proud, stingy and insensitive capitalist," recalling that Aramayo had been minister of the treasury during the administration of José Luis Tejada Sorzano (1935-1936) when nothing was done by the state to further Indian education. Aramayo, the newspaper charged, earned more than 1 million bolivianos a year between 1933 and 1935, before the government of Colonel David Toro. [15]   Showing the lack of social conscience by Aramayo, La Calle front-paged a story a month later that José María Gamarra, the king of coca, would make a solid contribution to the Indian school fund from the fortune which he had made in the drug traffic from the Yungas.   The implication was clear that even those who were on the questionable side of the social register in Bolivia were more sympathetic to the needs of the people than the Oxford-educated Aramayo. [16]

And so the debate raged back and forth.   While poverty and misery reigned in Bolivia, it was charged that Patiño had a fortune of 600 million dollars, making him the fifth or sixth most wealthy man in the world. [17]   La Calle never ceased to underline, usually with great irony or sarcasm, the disparities in Bolivian life when one could be so opulent while his workers were paid fifteen to seventeen cents a day.   When Dr. Pedro Escudero, director of the National Institute of Nutrition of Argentina, reported that the vast majority of the Bolivian people lived at starvation level, La Calle followed up with an editorial declaring "The Rosca is the culprit for the malnutrition of the people," reminding its readers that Aramayo had always insisted that "Bolivia should only be a mining country."   The statement, which had created a scandal among the Bolivian intellectuals who were to form the MNR, implied that Bolivia could produce tin best and need not concern herself with foodstuffs. [18]

La Calle also claimed during the Villarroel administration that the great mining corporations during the interim presidencies of Carlos Quintanilla and Enrique Peñaranda (1939-1943), the time when the MNR was being formed, had received 2,500 million bolivianos. [19]   Also, less than two months before the overthrow and murder of Villarroel, the Oruro Company announced that it planned to close its mines at San José and Machacamarca, firing 1,600 workers.   La Calle, now the unofficial spokesman for the MNR, reported that the state would intervene, using the mines as a yardstick for the labor-cost claims of the great mining enterprises. [20]

The MNR stepped up its personal attacks upon the so-called "tin barons" during the six-year interlude between the toppling of Villarroel in 1946 and the successful MNR revolution of 1952. The Big Three tin potentates were high-profile targets, almost symbolic representations of the vast inequities in Bolivian life, and as such they were ideal for the propagandists. They were singled out as a "devil theory" of what ailed Bolivia, just as the American propagandists who drafted the Declaration of Independence personified all of their hatred in the figure of George III. Curiously, it was not the richest tin magnate, Simón I. Patiño, who drew the most fire. Nor, was it the second most wealthy, Mauricio Hochschild, but rather the third, Carlos Victor Aramayo. This was because Aramayo was most powerful in the journalistic arena in La Paz, owning La Razón which had the largest circulation of any newspaper in the country. Let us consider these men in order.

Simón I. Patiño, discoverer of tin at Llallagua, was a mestizo who denied his racial heritage; he seemed to despise his Indian roots as well as other Bolivian realities, living most of his life abroad. He never identified with the national purpose of Bolivia, which gave him his staggering wealth reputed to be 600 million dollars. When Bolivia was reeling under the inflation and high cost of prosecuting the Chaco War, Patiño "generously," as La Nación later recalled bitterly, loaned only a few thousand dollars to buy some transport airplanes for the Army in the Chaco campaign. The niggardliness of the tin king was a bitter pill for the Bolivian people to swallow for they were suffering from rampant inflation after inconvertible paper money had been introduced in 1931. The Chaco War itself cost more than 400 million bolivianos, adding to the "Emergency Loan of 1933" which placed the same amount at the disposition of the government, while the Big Three tin companies continued to drain the country of about the only resource which could be used to pay off these sums, astronomical for a poverty-stricken country. [21]

Fiscal irresponsibility bordering on arrogance was the charge most often made by the MNR press against Patiño. In 1936, for example, La Calle charged that Patiño had robbed the state of more than 50 million bolivianos by refusing to pay legal taxes. The exchange rate was set at fifty bolivianos to the dollar, the newspaper charged, only as an advantage for the great mine-owners since this reduced the amount of taxes paid on foreign exchange, while for the common man the cost of living had increased 120 percent. [22] Shortly thereafter, La Calle noted that the country had decreed the death penalty for illegal exportation of national gold, but the inhabitants and residents could have objects of art. The newspaper commented, with the irony which made it famous, "Don Simón I. Patiño, for example, can order a statue to be set up with a net weight of a thousand kilos of pure gold in the stables of the Palacio Portales or in the pigpen of Pairumani--if by chance the irony occurs to him to leave something in Bolivia..." [23]

Humorous paragraphs of the column, "The Lamp of Diógenes" written by George Bernard Chopp, also lambasted Patiño. On one occasion, for example, it was noted that the La Paz dailies had carried on their front pages the preceding day a United Press dispatch from Paris that Simón I. Patiño's ten gardeners had gone on strike. Commented Chopp, "This story deals with a true and of course sensational innovation, which has merited the honors of the first page and the biggest head-lines." [24] This topic was milked for all the humor possible in succeeding issues of La Calle. On the next day, Chopp reported in his column that "Alcides Argüedas has declined to be rector of the Central University in view of the low budget. With that criterion, neither would he accept the job of gardener for Patiño in Paris." Finally, there was this parting shot: "The light and electric power firm of Cochabamba declines to pay bonuses to its employees, adducing that its major share-holder, the poor Don Simón I. Patiño, does not even have the money to pay his gardeners in Paris." [25]

Day by day La Calle hammered away at the overwhelming power and influences of the Patiño corporation. In 1936 the government printed a document supposedly proving that the government of Daniel Salamanca (1931-1934) had let Patiño off from paying his taxes for a bribe of one million bolivianos. [26] During the period of Villarroel (1943-1946), an administration in which the fledgling MNR shared power, the attacks on Patiño enterprises were stepped up. In 1944, La Calle noted that an Associated Press dispatch--not printed by the mining press-- stated that Patiño Mines cleared $2,271,414 in the first six months of 1944, compared with $2,076,528 in a similar period for 1943. This represented, the AP reported, a profit of 16.45 percent on a capital of $13,803,160 or more than 40 percent a year. [27]

The flow of such profits could not go untapped by the state for long. A law of December 29, 1944, required the tin companies to pay taxes on dividends; thus, in early 1945 La Calle reported that Patiño Mines and Enterprises and associated members of the Patiño group paid 19,613,541 bolivianos as taxes on dividends for 1944. The money, the newspaper announced, would go for public works in Potosí on the eve of its fourth centenary. [28] Wage disputes also were settled in favor of the workers during the Villarroel period. For example, it was ruled that Patiño Mines must pay workers 12 million bolivianos in increased back pay from January 1 to June 15, 1945, after strenuous efforts in this direction by the labor leader Juan Lechín, the Federación Sindical de Trabajadores Mineros de Bolivia (FSTMB, Federation of Bolivian Mining Workers) and mediation by the government. [29]

The facts were powerful enough in themselves, but a concerted editorial crusade against Patiño Mines required greater initiative. In early 1946, La Calle asked educator Alfredo Guillén Pinto to write an article about the educational services provided by the mining company. The result, published prominently in La Calle, showed that Patiño miners did not get the efficient education to which they had a right, including adult schools, scholarships for children and technical education. [30] At the same time, the specter of corruption also was exploited to its fullest. Thus, La Calle reported in May 1946 that Patiño had been charged with defrauding the state of 200 million bolivianos in seventeen years through not paying the taxes to which everyone in Bolivia was subject. The MMR newspaper noted that El Diario, "that sturdy pillar of fiscal integrity," had not said a word about the matter. [31]

Corruption struck closer to home when Lloyd Duame, general manager of La Unificada mine for Patiño, went to Juan Lechín's home in La Paz on June 13, 1945, and offered the labor leader 50,000 bolivianos if he would see that negotiations for salary increases then underway would result in what management wanted. Lechín, son of an Arab father and Indian mother and a former soccer hero, went directly to the ministry of labor, La Calle announced, and reported the attempted coima or bribe. Two meetings were then held between Lechín and Daume in the Hotel Sucre; when money finally changed hands, the mine manager was arrested. [32] The incident not only provided excellent propaganda material for the opposition press, but it also launched Lechín upon a long and stormy career as head of the mine workers.

Because of these stinging attacks and also perhaps because it felt vulnerable, the Patiño corporation acquired El Diario in 1948 to fight back. Villarroel had been overthrown and dead for two years, but the uneasy truce of the sexenio threatened the grip which the great mining companies still held on popular sympathies. Seeing the writing on the wall, Patiño Mines formed the firm Hemisphere Promotion which included El Diario under its corporate umbrella. [33] Although Patiño held an interest in the newspaper before, the new arrangement guaranteed complete control and polarized the press of La Paz even further as the showdown between the MNR and the tin interests loomed nearer.

Even after the death at the age of eighty-four of Simón I. Patiño on April 20, 1947, the reform-minded press of La Paz did not cease to attack the Patiño family. His son Antenor Patiño, reputed to be one of the twenty richest men in the world, was a favorite target because of his romantic imbroglios, which were widely reprinted in the Bolivian press even after the MNR Revolution got underway. It may have been an attempt to draw attention from the fact that the nationalized tin mines were not doing so well, but at any rate the Patiño name was seldom absent from the official MNR press. Thus, La Nación followed the tin heir's matrimonial difficulties with great interest. In 1959 the newspaper announced that the Superior Court of Paris had granted a divorce between Antenor Patiño, whose fortune was estimated at $100 million, and María Cristins de Borbón, specifying that she receive half of his income since 1931. La Nación alleged that Patiño had obtained a Bolivian diplomatic passport and scored "his always unmerciful attitude against the interests of our people, which he never tires of extorting, whether it be only to pay the consequences of an exotic marriage that, from beginning to end, represents a history of sweat and tears for Bolivia." Indemnification for the Patiño tin holdings in Bolivia nationalized in 1952 really amounted to "a simple gift, obtained [through United States policy]...on the basis of pressures and blackmail." Most galling was that the money had gone to settle the divorce of Patiño from the French aristocrat. The newspaper fumed:

> The heir of the fortunate miner Simón I. Patiño has demonstrated himself in effect as the painstaking swindler of the Bolivian people, doing honor to the tradition of his progenitor. And he has done it not for the adoration of the fortune itself, ambition in which the miner had no equal, but rather to satisfy his luxurious lovesong, first, and then to finance one of the most expensive divorces which one can remember in the world. [34]

The story did not end there. Blocked in the French courts, Patiño turned elsewhere. In early 1960 La Nación began reprinting a series of articles about the "King of Tin" from Novedades of Mexico City. Thus it became known in Bolivia that Patiño had finally received a divorce from María Cristina de Borbón without having to pay any alimony. The MNR newspaper commented in an editorial note, "The 'King of Tin,' notwithstanding flaunting that title throughout the world, thanks to the fortune extracted from the mines of Bolivia and continuing to receive plentiful indemnization from this country, has abandoned his ex-wife, not even recognizing that she might have him ennobled eventually." [35] In the second installment, Patiño was reputed to be one of the twenty richest men in the world. His ex-wife reportedly asked for a settlement of $250 million, estimated at half his fortune, but the Mexican court granted the divorce with no alimony. All Patiño lost was a fee of $300,000 for his lawyer, and he reportedly had asked for

Mexican citizenship. [36] In the third installment, it was reported that the Supreme Court of Mexico had ruled that Antenor Patiño Rodríguez could remarry at once, but his ex-wife could not remarry for two years. It was deemed doubtful that Mexico, if it granted citizenship, would also give Patiño a diplomatic passport such as the one which he obtained upon leaving Bolivia. [37]

During the divorce proceedings, Armando Arce--former editor of La Calle--arrived in Mexico as the Bolivian ambassador and offered these tidbits about Patiño's background which also were printed in Novedades and reprinted in La Paz. By 1920, Arce recounted, the hold of the Big Three on the tin-mining industry of Bolivia was consolidated. The first denunciation of Patiño and his fellow mining magnates was made a year earlier, in 1919, by the minister of the treasury, José Luis Tejada Sorzano. Speaking before the interpelation of the cabinet in December 1919, he declared:

> The development of fortunes in our country has no parallel with the development of public finances; a single citizen [Patiño] possesses by himself alone greater resources than those of the nation, with preponderant action upon the energies of the whole country. Our tributary system, based on taxes on consumer goods, weighs on the popular classes and leaves the capitalists almost free from any fiscal imposition. These great industrialists, favored with benefits so immense, ought to share at least a part of their earnings with the general prosperity. Until today all of the attempts at bettering the country have failed because of the harsh resistance of these misers.

Later, when the delegation from Santa Cruz asked Patiño to finance a railroad from Cochabamba to their city isolated in the southeast, Arce said the mining magnate answered from his residence abroad, "I have no interest in making investments in that country." Again in 1932 after fighting had begun with Paraguay, President Salamanca asked for a loan from Patiño, who was then the Bolivian ambassador to France. The terms were so severe, however, that the Bolivian president sent another cable to Patiño: "Go to Geneva to sign a little loan which they offer us in conditions more favorable than yours." Patiño was said to be at that time a member of the Schneider-Crusot consortium which was selling arms to Paraguay. Meanwhile, the miners of Patiño Enterprises, Inc., were paid fifteen cents a day, Arce maintained. [38]

After his divorce, Patiño took up residence in England

238

where, like his father, he denied in a magazine article that he was mestizo. How could he do otherwise, demanded La Nación, since the tin heir was now in the "very center of the Aryan race." The newspaper continued, "Culturally, mestizaje is the nationalization of the invader, his adhesion to the land." This kind of status Patiño could never accept, La Nación declared, and in its last comment on the expatriate multi-millionaire added, "Patiño no longer exists for Bolivia." [39]

In retrospect, however, it was not the newspapers which wounded the mining interests most deeply, but rather the book Metal del diablo (The Devil's Metal) published by Augusto Céspedes in 1946 with the subtitle, "The Life of a King of Tin." In this book Céspedes, who had won literary fame throughout the continent ten years earlier with Sangre de mestizos (Blood of Half-Breeds), electrified the literary world with what could be called a forerunner of the New Journalism—that written with fictional techniques but based solidly on fact. Although another name was used, Céspedes' work of biting social realism referred in detail to the life of Simón I. Patiño. The book excoriated his cruelty and indifference, but it was not without the saving grace of Céspedes' sardonic humor. In discussing the massacre at Catavi--with which the book ends--a reporter asks, "Is it true that there were 300 dead?" And a spokesman for Omonte, the fictional counterpart of Patiño, says, "Oh, no.. One must always divide by ten. You know, the exaggerations..." [40]

Céspedes has since revealed that the Patiño interests tried to suppress this novel. Before the book was published, according to Céspedes, the Patiño manager, José Santos Quiroga, visited the writer in his Buenos Aires hotel room and tried to bribe him with $20,000 not to publish Metal del Diablo. Céspedes said he replied, "I write my novels to publish them, not to sell the original manuscripts." Again, when Hollywood was talking about filming the book, the Patiño family allegedly exerted pressure and the project was dropped. A friend of Céspedes who lived in the United States, Carlos Salamanca, told the Bolivian writer that he had made a mistake in not using Patiño's real name in Metal del diablo to create a scandal, possibly bring on a libel suit, and achieve notoriety for the work. As it was, however, Céspedes was content with its propaganda effect at home, and it certainly gave a dramatic boost for nationalization of the tin mines once the MNR gained power. [41]

The staying power of Metal del diablo was evidenced when as late as 1960 Lima police confiscated copies of the book carried by Bolivian journalists on their way to Europe. Likewise, according to the publication Bohemia, police in Buenos

Aires were also continuing an intensive campaign against book-stores selling works of "propaganda," including the confiscation not only of Metal del diablo but also the Diary of Anne Frank, Juan José Arévalo's, The Shark and the Sardines, and an edition of the speeches of Fidel Castro. [42] There were also repercussions of "the fact is stranger than fiction" variety. After Augusto Céspedes returned from a trip to Europe in 1960, he commented upon the version of a lunch offered by the Patiño family in Paris--a lunch attended by a Chilean who described it in a letter to a friend on the staff of La Nación. The lunch was presided over by Graciela, the only daughter of Simón I. Patiño, and the Chilean was impressed that one 84-year-old woman sported five strands of pearls and a diamond ring "as big as a paving stone," and that he was returned to his apartment in a Rolls-Royce. Commented Céspedes: "The foregoing mixture of invited quests seems to be a repetition [of the theme] that reality outdoes fiction in 'Metal del Diablo' where a zoological garden also figures in the house of Omonte. And neither does there lack the invited poor person [who is] dazzled by 'the royal treatment' because they dispatch him to his boarding-house in a Rolls-Royce." [43]

Another prime target of the MNR press was Mauricio Hochschild, a German Jew naturalized in Argentina, who had pulled himself up by the bootstraps to become the second most wealthy and powerful tin miner in Bolivia. La Calle always maintained that Hochschild circumvented the laws of the state. In 1943 the MNR spokesman ran a series of articles on "How Busch proceeded against the abusive millionaire" in 1939 when Hochschild was arrested and almost put to death. [44] Busch wanted the death penalty for Hochschild in a cabinet meeting of July 5, 1939, for sabotaging the decree of June 7, 1939, which required all of the mining companies to channel their foreign exchange through the national bank for discount. Hochschild had said the miners should ignore the decree. Five ministers agreed with Busch, according to La Calle, that Hochschild indeed should be shot. Therefore, Busch ordered the police chief to shoot the mining tycoon at 6 a.m. the next day, but the cabinet members backtracked and talked Busch out of it. The next day Hochschild was called to the palace where he excused his conduct before Busch and left hurriedly. The Bolivian president, watching the retreating figure of Hochschild, turned to one of his ministers and said, "Look, what a good-looking corpse for a dead man!" [45]

Actually, Hochschild was the only one of the Big Three who bothered to live in Bolivia and seemed to have paid his ordinary taxes. [46] Nevertheless, this did not blunt the drive of La Calle to get him, alleging that the tin miner had been in collusion with the government on numerous occasions. In 1942, for example, La Calle alleged that Hochschild for ten years had charged the ministry of national defense "millions of bolivianos and thousands of pounds sterling" for hauling non-existent freight on his Atocha-Villazón railroad. [47] Concerning the same affair, the title of an article proclaimed, "Hochschild defrauded the state of more than one million bolivianos in the Chaco War." [48] La Calle drummed away on this single theme from March through November, 1942. Finally, the quarry was flushed out: Hochschild sent a letter to Demetrio Canelas, president of the Chamber of Deputies, which was printed in full, occupying two newspaper pages in La Calle on November 10, 1942, under the banner headline, HOCHSCHILD, MASTER OF BOLIVIA, PONTIFICATES... On the next day, the newspaper asked under another heading, "To whom do we owe that Bolivia should be the most wretched country in the world? This letter from Hochschild to Canelas does not say." [49]

Undoubtedly some of the hatred for Hochschild stemmed from his Jewish background at a time when La Calle was attacking the Jews viciously. But more than that was his alleged meddling in domestic political affairs. His status as a foreigner irked many Bolivians because he was absorbing wealth that could have gone to nationals, and he was interfering in domestic politics. At least, that was the picture which La Calle tried to paint. In 1942 the newspaper reported that Hochschild was running his main lawyer, Torrico Lemoine, for deputy; now, decried La Calle, a mere phone call could get all the laws that Hochschild wanted! [50] Also, Hochschild was on the scene and he was therefore vulnerable to charges of manipulation of the domestic political process. On another occasion, for example, La Calle charged that all of the "Independents" were actually in Hochschild's pocket. [51]

This theme was played time after time. The tin magnate was accused of exerting influence in other agencies of government as well. In late 1942, La Calle asked, in the heading of an article, "Is the exchange rate of minerals in the hands of Mauricio Hochschild once again? Explosive coup at the Banco Minero." [52] In another article's title the newspaper proclaimed, "Now Hochschild is the seller of quinine for the government.--The state works for Hochschild." [53] Direct political action seemed to be feared most, however, as in 1943 when La Calle headed a third article, "Hochschild will decide the election of the presiding officer of Congress.--No national representatives [but] preferably a lawyer of the big enterprises to preside over Congress." [54] And it was charged that "Standard Oil, Hochschild and the PIR [will predominate] in the governing bodies of the [two] chambers." [55]

Hochschild came into direct confrontation with the law

again during the Villarroel administration in 1944. The government claimed that a complot had been discovered on April 28: Hochschild and others were arrested, and a state of siege was declared throughout Bolivia. The government charged on April 30 that Hochschild and others had sought to bribe General César Menacho, some colonels and troops with 10 million bolivianos. La Calle described the general's "gloomy action in the Chaco War where all of his heroism consisted in breaking the record as a shooter of poor Indian soldiers." As for the colonels, the newspaper added, "In the same war they distinguished themselves as weighers of potatoes in the rearguard..." The linkage of Hochschild to this attempted coup was significant, whether justified or not, because he personified the resentments which many Bolivians had been feeling since the Chaco War. The MNR launched a 20,000-man street demonstration which filed through La Paz shouting "Down with the Rosca!" [56] On May 24 Hochschild asked for his liberty "in order not to damage the war effort of the United Nations." Villarroel replied that Hochschild would be tried by the judicial system, although he finally was placed in liberty on June 16, with the provision that he not leave the country. [57]

As evidence that the editorial crusades of La Calle did not simply evaporate into thin air, the Atocha-Villazón railroad scandal aired by the newspaper brought results. In December 1944 the Permanent Fiscal Commission ordered Hochschild to repay 6,358,033 bolivianos to the state for fraudulent billings of hauling troops and material during the Chaco War. [58] La Calle was exuberant, proclaiming in a headline, HOW M. HOCHSCHILD DEFRAUDED THE STATE OF SEVERAL MILLIONS. [59] The funds of the South American Mining Company, Hochschild's firm, were frozen to be audited on December 9, 1944; the freeze on funds was lifted on December 12 but the audit continued. Nevertheless, during this process the Commisión Fiscal Permanente allowed Hochschild to appeal to the ministry of the treasury before paying restitution. [60]

The alleged machinations of Hochschild were revealed in a dramatic highlight of the debate on establishing an investigative commission on freedom of the press in September 1945 in the national Convention. Armando Arce, speaking against the project, read a document which purportedly revealed that Hochschild in the United States had approached Bolivian military officials and offered to stop paying salaries of newsmen defaming Bolivia--in the pages of Ultima Hora and elsewhere--if the Bolivian government would stop obliging the mining companies to give 100 percent of foreign exchange for discount after the exportation of minerals. Arce indicated that Major José Escobar in Washington, D.C., kicked Hochschild out of his office after hearing the proposal. [61]

In the closing months of Villarroel's regime, more government attacks were launched against the Hochschild holdings. In March 1946 the government charged that Hochschild had not done the necessary work to legitimize his concession of waters on the Río San Cristobal in the province of Larecaja granted in 1929. La Calle trumpeted in the heading of an article, "Hochschild continues extracting great utilities from the state at the margin of the law." The newspaper also printed a private accusation that Hochschild had ignored the foreign exchange decree of July 7, 1939--designed partly to protect small producers--and continued to gobble up such producers. [62]

The most sustained and vicious of the attacks upon the Big Three, however, was aimed not at Patiño or Hochschild, the two bigger producers, but at Carlos Víctor Aramayo, who claimed a weak third of the country's tin production. Aramayo, born in Paris in 1898, was detested for his Western pretensions, and more importantly because he owned La Razón, the most powerful journalistic voice in Bolivia. Aramayo's whole life was a negation of his Bolivian origins; Costa du Rels in his biography of Aramayo's father, Félix Avelino Aramayo, recounted that after graduating from Oxford, Carlos Víctor Aramayo tried to enlist first in the English and then in the French army but succeeded in neither as World War I broke out in 1914. [63]

Ridiculed as a dandy who sported fancy Piccadilly clothes and feigned an English accent, Aramayo spent little time in Bolivia and scoffed at the country's laws, the opposition press maintained. When his father died, La República charged that millions of the Aramayo fortune passed from Félix Avelino Aramayo to Carlos Víctor without the state getting one cent in inheritance taxes. [64] During the Chaco War, El Universal featured Aramayo in one of its profiles in the column, "Men of the Day," and found him to be: "Man of the world, neither politician nor literary person, neither republican nor socialist, neither liberal nor nationalist...To don Carlos only money is necessary.... It would occur to no one to pursue don Carlos Víctor Aramayo the day after a revolution." The column also noted that Aramayo had been the Bolivian ambassador to the Court of St. James for several years without making much of an impact on Bolivian-English relations. [65] Did the young tin tycoon have wider political aspirations? El Universal reported in 1934 that Aramayo was planning to return to La Paz from Europe, noting that since Franz Tamayo had declined the presidential candidacy for the Genuinos, it was rumored Aramayo would accept. [66]

That never materialized but Aramayo did pull strings from behind the scenes. In 1936, soon after La Calle started publishing, the newspaper singled out the political dilettante for a major attack, proclaiming in a heading, "The Aramayo firm is the strongest exploiter of rosquero capitalism. Its decision to intervene in politics is clearly demonstrated." The article stated:

One sees his agents, well known because the stinginess of the famous London millionaire [does not allow him] ever to change his subalterns, [who] move with unaccustomed activity fishing unwary ones and with the manifest desire of suggesting to indifferent ones that Aramayo is an angel descended from the sky and that his mere presence can make the price of tin and the value of the pound go up.

La Calle charged that Aramayo once had suspended the exportation of tin rather than pay the amount of divisas (foreign earnings) his firm should have turned over to the state. Moreover, Aramayo was said to have imposed "the famous decree" upon Tejada Sorzano (1935-1936) which reduced the quantity of divisas that the mineowners had to sell for government discount; thereby, the price of tin rose 120 percent a pound. La Calle called this "the most criminal negotiation in favor of the mining interests and against the State. The capitalist press praised the decree--it was their duty--and the people were deceived one more time." [67]

Political inclinations did crop up when Aramayo decided to be a candidate for senator from Potosí in 1942. La Calle noted at the time that he had been "the silent deputy" at the side of Daniel Salamanca in 1916 as a Genuino, but the newspaper charged that the Genuinos were only interested in the money the young man had inherited from Avelino Aramayo "to check the Liberals who were aided by Patiño." [68] During the course of the campaign, La Calle flagellated the younger Aramayo, calling him an "enemy of national industry." [69] The attacks continued on into 1943. On the occasion of his birthday in that year, La Calle declared in a headline, WE SALUTE ARAMAYO! adding in a subhead, "We invite him to show a single work of his that benefited the country." Again, in another heading the newspaper asserted, "The patriotism of Aramayo is only measured in vile metal.--They did not accept him in the Foreign Legion but he was a minister of state in Bolivia." [70]

The lack of social consciousness or involvement by Aramayo was continually presented to the readers of La Paz. La Calle devoted much space to an incident of 1943, for example, when the matrons of La Paz asked Aramayo and others for donations for a chapel of Señor del Gran Poder (Lord of Great Power). Aramayo did not answer the letter personally, and his

244

administrator refused a donation. La Calle called this "an inadmissible discourtesy not only in a type educated in England, but even in the primary school of Tupiza..." The newspaper recalled that Aramayo had given nothing for Indian schools two years earlier and declared that the tin magnate treated all needs of society with disdain. When he once returned from London, La Calle asserted, Aramayo refused to pay 5,000 bolivianos on liquor he was importing, alleging a diplomatic status which he then did not have. Daniel Salamanca wrote out a check, paying the customs out of his own pocket, La Calle maintained, regaling the public with this bit of gossip about the inaccessible Carlos Víctor Aramayo. [71]

More serious charges were leveled against the tin king third in wealth but perhaps foremost in political involvement. In 1944 La Calle declared in an article's title, "Aramayo was the biggest beneficiary of the socialist revolution of [May 17] 1936," which brought Lt. Col. David Toro to power. By June 6, the newspaper charged, Aramayo through a beneficial contract had cornered all of the gold in the four provinces of the department of La Paz. [72] By 1945 Aramayo was fighting cancellation of the gold contract awarded by Toro. La Calle editorialized on "The fight against the Toro-Aramayo contract," and criticized Aramayo for having said, "Bolivia should only be a mining country. Other countries produced better and more cheaply everything that is needed [here] for provisions." [73] But Aramayo's gold interests continued to plague him; in later 1945, La Calle declared in a story's heading, "The democrat of gold [Aramayo] attacks the Convention." Further, when Aramayo assailed the law of voluntary retirement for workers on jurisprudential grounds, La Calle countered with an editorial, "Social politics and 'jurisprudence.'" [74] The sister of Aramayo, Gladis Luisa, denounced him for not paying inheritance taxes according to the law of December 29, 1944, after their father, Félix Avelino Aramayo, had died in France. [75] But the crowning blow came when an article in La Calle charged that Aramayo had paid David Alvéstegui, editor of La Razón, to erode the prestige of the Villarroel government because of the cancelled gold contract. [76]

The perceived hypocrisy of Carlos Víctor Aramayo also came under attack by La Calle, quoting an editorial from La Razón which commented on a Panamerican Union call for an inter-American conference on conservation. Heading its own response, "Accusations against the big mining interests," La Calle noted that no one had ravaged the countryside more than the Big Three, and yet the Aramayo newspaper had had the gall to state:

...that in Bolivia not only are cultivated lands

abandoned...; the national forests are destroyed by irresponsible persons; valuable species of our flora and fauna are on the point of disappearing, and finally no organisms exist to watch over the development of the industries that make use of the resources that the earth offers, in order to establish the appropriate bases of their labor and to contribute to their protection. [77]

Shortly thereafter, when Aramayo returned to Europe after one of his brief visits to Bolivia, La Calle had a field day, declaring "His Majesty don Carlos V" had left. "And what does it matter to him?" the MNR asked, continuing with heavy irony:

He did not spend his money... subventioning mercenary pens, mixing a hot bath of the refined and infamous in political polemics, and providing his emissaries with banknotes, machine-guns and bullets? "Well," the powerful señor of money said to himself without doubt, "my engagement has terminated. I gave my silver and they were not able to do anything..." But nevertheless, what a tortuous drama our simple people have lived, our simple Bolivian people always tormented, always by the lustful and macabre imagination of the playwrights of gold and tin. The final act has ended. There remain here the dead. The millionaire has gone... [78]

After the Revolution of 1952, Aramayo continued to be the prime target of the MNR press. Simón I. Patiño had died in 1947, and Mauricio Hochschild had bowed quietly out of the picture. Again, it was Aramayo's ownership of La Razón which continued the vendetta. When the newspaper could not resume publication after April 9, 1952, because of hostile mob action and a lack of protection by the state, it became a cause celebre for the Inter American Press Association (see Chapter 6). This exacerbated a highly volatile situation in Bolivia; for the new revolutionary government to get on its feet, it needed a breathing space of calm and quiet. This it did not receive. Numerous attempted coups were launched against the MNR, the most serious one being on April 19, 1959, which La Calle charged was financed by none other than Carlos Victor Aramayo. La Nación, the official MNR newspaper, bannered a headline the day after the attempted golpe which declared, ARAMAYO RECOVERED IN BLOOD THE DOLLARS THAT HE INVESTED IN CONSPIRACY. An editorial maintained that it was Aramayo's money which had financed the attempted golpe through the Falange Socialista Boliviana (FSB). The uprising, which was put down by miners' militias in La Paz with campesino militiamen on the alert in Cochabamba, cost more than 100 lives. [79]

Mine-owner Carlos Víctor Aramayo is depicted in a comic-book biography of Víctor Paz Estenssoro as an evil man whose newspaper La Razón scourges the workers. A fictitious headline states, "The best Indian is a dead Indian."

The editorial of April 21, 1959 in La Nación was entitled, "Now Carlos Víctor Aramayo can be content." The government newspaper saw Aramayo money still at work in the opposition press in La Paz playing down the magnitude of the event. Thus, on April 22, 1959, La Nación observed:

> The inexplicable continues. Two days ago more then a hundred persons were shot to death as a result of a bloody putsch. The partisan promoters of the killing seem to act, nevertheless, with all the impunity necessary, utilizing its press in order to continue its propaganda after the turmoil suffered, disregarding the sanction which the Law places in the hands of the Government for the defense of a Revolution harassed relentlessly, in a continuous and bloody way by the enemies of the historic pledges of our people.

La Nación on the same occasion published an editorial warning that "The people honest and loyal to the truth should put themselves on guard against the sinister propaganda of the Rosca." The newspaper also criticized the small headlines of the opposition press which recounted the events of April 19, 1959, "as if they were dealing with news about Sunday picnics or sporting events..." [80]

Aramayo as the sole remaining activist of the Big Three might well have had a part in this attempted coup of April 19, 1959, as well as those of May 14 and October 21 of the preceding year. Whether he actually did or not, however, is almost beside the point because the MNR press created the impression that he was squarely in the middle of the conspiracies. As such, these attempts to overthrow the MNR government actually strengthened it, providing considerable raw material to be refined as propaganda for the masses. The same morality play was enacted in March 1960 when the minister of government, Carlos Morales Guillén, released a letter from the PURS chief Enrique Hertzog from exile in Buenos Aires, dated January 23, 1960, purportedly to Carlos Víctor Aramayo. The tin magnate was not named, but the letter closed with a salutation to his wife, María René. In the letter, Hertzog allegedly asked for money to finance invasions of Bolivia from Argentina, Brazil and Peru before the June elections, claiming he had military support in those countries. Initially, he proposed an alliance with the FSB, but this was withdrawn later; the letter occupied almost an entire page of La Nación and created a sensation.

An editorial declared that the principal agents of the plan--Hertzog and Aramayo--"are the most discredited elements in the last thirty years of national politics." The editorial, "Rebels at the doors," continued:

The very mention of the identity [of the principal agents of the plot] reveals the low ends of a conspiracy nourished by traffickers and exploiters who try, with the same money exploited from the people of Bolivia, to impose their domination once again. At the head of these are found the ataxic and stuttering millionaire Carlos V. Aramayo, genuine representative of the decadence of the mining Rosca, financial promoter of the conspiracy, and a comic figure of Bolivia: the insane physician Enrique Hertzog, mental patient once confined in Chulumani, forced to resign by his own partisans convinced of his ineptitude and foolishness.

Details of the letter revealed that Hertzog thought the conspirators would need ten or twelve thousand dollars for the FSB in La Paz, $200,000 in Peru, two million Argentine pesos for an operation from Pilcomayo, and one million for the town of Roboré on the Brazilian border. "At any rate," Hertzog allegedly wrote, "it will be a cheap operation. Fidel Castro raised $1.5 million in Venezuela alone for his cause and the Paraguayan liberals and febreristas have just received, also from Venezuela, $500,000 to begin [their operations]."

In short, La Nación concluded, the entire scheme was the product of "minds unsettled by impotence," who revealed their very weakness in saying that this would be "our last chance." In the pages of El Diario, Hertzog denied having written the letter, and this denial also was printed in Ultima Hora. La Nación quoted the minister of government as saying it had been expected that it would only be a matter of time before the former head of state would deny the sensational letter. [81]

In later years, Aramayo continued to surface in the Bolivian press. In 1960, for example, it was widely reported in the MNR newspapers that he had initiated court action in Paris against the French journalist Lucien Dequenne for having published in Combat three articles in which he wrote that Aramayo had paid his mine workers before World War II "the incredible sum" of fifteen cents a day for eight or nine hours of work. [82] Thus, in view of the MNR press, Carlos Víctor Aramayo faded from the Bolivian stage much as he had entered it--in scandal and disgrace.

Given this framework of personal attacks upon the Big Three tin mine owners, how did the Bolivian press react when nationalization of their holdings actually began in late 1952? The view of an opposition newspaper may be helpful to determine by indirection the thrust of the official press. Los Tiempos of Cochabamba, owned and edited by Demetrio Canelas, editorialized frequently on the nationalization of the mines in the first few weeks and months after the successful MNR insurrection of April 9-11, 1952. Exactly one month after that outbreak, Los Tiempos noted that the Partido de la Izquierda Revolucionaria (PIR, Party of the Revolutionary Left) a Marxist party formed in 1940, claimed to have been the first party to urge nationalization of the tin mines. Their production then would have been used to vitalize other economic sectors, especially agriculture. The Falange Socialista Boliviana (FSB, Bolivian Socialist Falange), an extreme rightist party patterned after the Spanish Falange, also had urged "progressive nationalization" in an eight-point program. The MNR position, as explained by Wálter Guevara Arze, was that the mines were a national asset and should be administered by the nation, not just by the miners. Los Tiempos pointed out that this was in direct contradition to the famous Thesis of Pulacayo drafted by the Partido Obrero Revolucionario (POR, Workers Revolutionary Party), a Trotskyite party affiliated with the Fourth International, which said that the workers should take direct control of the mines. Throwing up its hands in horror, the Canelas newspaper quoted Carlos Víctor Aramayo from an earlier work:

> ...it is well known that all of the states are axiomatically incompetent to manage industries and businesses, which they have demonstrated to satiety as many times as they have tried it. Our state has gone even further and proved its incapacity to perform services relatively simple, which are within the normal attributions of every state more or less organized, and which in other countries are satisfactorily fulfilled such as the mails, telegraph service, custom duties, taxes... If our fiscal authorities have failed invariably, from the beginnings of the republic until today, in the performance of these elemental functions, what probabilities are there that they can achieve success in the administration of a business infinitely [more] difficult, complicated and fortuitous as the mining business? [83]

After the Commission on Nationalization of the Mines was established on May 29, 1952, Juan Lechín Oquendo, leader of the mine workers and minister of mines and petroleum, expressed the government's point of view at the opening of the commission's deliberations:

> ...the insurrection of April is the bloody creation of our future, gestated painfully in the bowels of economic colonialism and the decision of the Government of the National Revolution to nationalize our principal mining wealth. [This] cannot be considered as a

250

simply progressive means in our slow economic evolution, but as the beginning of a radical and profound transformation of the social-economic structure of the country. [84]

In the midst of the Cold War, Los Tiempos did not hesitate to raise the specter of international communism in the government's drive to nationalize the tin mines. Raúl Vargas Guzmán wrote that the MNR needed three victories for attainment of its goals. The first two had been achieved: triumph in the May 1951 elections and the April 9 revolution; but the third must be triumph over international communism. However, Los Tiempos headed an article, "The nationalization of mines is of Bolivian and not Russian nature, and it has been decided to involve Bolivia in the southern block, a high official of the MNR tells us." [85]

Meanwhile, the new MNR government took over a monopoly of mineral exports on June 2, 1952, less than two months after taking power, as a means to gauge the actual production of the Big Three companies. It was determined that between January and May of 1952, Patiño produced 6,989 tons of fine ore, averaging 1,398 tons monthly and earning United States $17,652,129 or more than 3.5 million dollars a month. Hochschild produced 2,698 tons of fine ore or a monthly average of 521 to earn a total of $6,573,267 or about 1.3 million dollars monthly, and Aramayo produced 989 tons of fine ore, earning $2,493,882 or about half a million dollars monthly. [86]

Thus painting the Big Three as sturdy pillars supporting the economy of the state, Los Tiempos also expressed alarm against the rising clamor for nationalization of the mines. It noted in September 1952 that the commission appointed by Paz Estenssoro in mid-April, headed by Wálter Barrau, had 120 days to present its findings on nationalization of the mines. Barrau had said this would be carried out on "judicial bases," but time was running out. Students, unions, Communist parties had all urged seizure of the mines without indemnification, Los Tiempos reported, rather than legally expropriating them under the clause of public utility. The Cochabamba newspaper also noted with dismay that the MNR continually whipped up and kept alive hatred of the big mineowners, most recently charging them with buying arms for subversive plots. This might mean, Los Tiempos surmised, that the MNR had already decided on attachment of the mines without compensation. [87]

In fact, the Central Obrera Boliviana (COB), the central labor organization after 1952, voted for the mines to be nationalized without indemnification and to be put under control of

251

the workers. [88]   As the time neared for decision by the commission, Los Tiempos stepped up its campaign against nationalization.   In a title for an article by Juan Pereira Fiorilo, writing from London, for example, the newspaper declared, "Nationalization of the mines is the work of demagoguery and intemperance." [89]   When the nationalization was carried out on October 31, 1952--the second major decree by the MNR after granting the universal vote on July 21, 1952--ceremonies were held at the Campo María Barzola, the field near the Siglo XX mine were striking miners were shot down in 1942 during the Catavi massacre, with María Barzola apparently the first victim. Los Tiempos printed the decree nationalizing the mines and devoted another page to the speeches, [90] but the newspaper of Demetrio Canelas was not about to give up the fight.   Early in November 1952 it entitled a report of a talk by the PIR leader, Ricardo Anaya, at a university round-table, "The decree of nationalization of the mines is not a reality, scarcely a promise." [91]   And Los Tiempos also sought to put the brakes on the revolutionary process with the signing of the nationalization decree.   Under a heading, "Political outgrowths of the nationalization of mines," the newspaper declared that after the signing of the decree Bolivia could enjoy "a period of institutional stability and tranquility in all spheres of activity." [92]   The newspaper seemed to be whistling in the dark against the specter of agrarian reform (see Chapter 9) which hung especially heavy over the agriculturally rich Cochabamba valley.

Immediately after the ceremonies solemnizing nationalization of the tin mines at Siglo XX, Los Tiempos printed an editorial favoring private initiative over bureaucratic action in the mines. The newspaper asked if production would be the same under government management and commented:

It is usual nowadays to execrate the mine owners and to present them as social vampires that feed on human blood.   These notions form part of the catechism idola fori of our peculiar historic moment, charged with explosive materials.

But where, the editorial asked, would the Bolivian economy be without the intrepid risks of the early mining magnates? [93]

At the time of nationalization of the major mines, the newspaper also expressed its dismay at the one-sided nature of the public debate, noting in an editorial that the commission, which had not yet made its report, had been releasing accusatory charges against the mining interests to the public.   Los Tiempos hoped that portions dealing with the legal, economic and social aspects of nationalization also would be made public. It objected that nationalization was vindictive and punitive.

The mine interests were on trial but had not yet been given the opportunity to be heard. They should have the chance to answer the major complaints against the Big Three, Los Tiempos argued, including the flight of profits to the exterior, evasion of taxes and exploiting workers to the point of massacre. [94]

Yet when nationalization came on October 31, 1952, Los Tiempos found the Bolivian public ready for it. A few days before the signing of the decree, the newspaper pointed out that the Patiño interests owed 168 million dollars to the government; Hochschild, 171 million and Aramayo, 54 million. This was a debt to the state of more than 393 million dollars; moreover, the companies also owed a total of 14 million dollars in other settlements. Therefore, popular opinion was deemed ready to accept nationalization of the major tin mines. Los Tiempos editorialized, "Few times has there been observed in the country a coincidence of sentiments more vehement than which concerns nationalization of the three mining firms. This should not be attributed solely to the efficacy of the tenacious propaganda carried out by the MNR... propaganda participated in by other political parties. The mining enterprises are, perhaps, in the most part responsible for the state of hostile opinion created against them for not having followed a political policy of radication in the riches of the subsoil." [95]

The price of tin, rapidly spiraling downward, was to plague the MNR in the early years of nationalization. Shortly before the signing of the decree, Los Tiempos noted that the two pillars of the National Revolution were nationalization of the tin mines and increasing salaries in all branches of work; the third would be agrarian reform. Concerning the first, Los Tiempos noted that Bolivia had told Stuart Symington, head of the Reconstruction Finance Corporation in the United States, that it could not produce tin for less than $1.50 a pound, but she was getting a price of only $1.17 1/2. Therefore if production continued under nationalized mines as before, it would cost Bolivia $132 million to produce tin sold for $102 million, based on the amount of tin sold in the last year under private ownership. In fact, Los Tiempos argued, the most Bolivia could hope for would be a price of $1.25. "Therefore," the newspaper concluded, "the first column of the National Revolution is not constructed as would be the desire of everyone, with horns of plenty capable of satiating our necessities with a stream of dollars." [96]

A year later the situation had deteriorated even further. In October 1953, Juan Lechín, minister of mines and petroleum and mine union leader, said that the cost of producing nationalized tin was $1.03 for a pound of fine ore, but the price had gone to below 80 cents for this amount. The slack was taken up by issuing more paper money, which had resulted in galloping inflation. At a production of 30,000 tons annually or sixty million pounds of fine tin ore, Bolivia was losing $7,800,000; at the official exchange rate of 190 bolivianos to the dollar, this would be 1.5 billion bolivianos; at the actual exchange rate of 750 bolivianos, it would be 5.9 billion bolivianos. The possible long-range solutions which Los Tiempos saw were modernizing work techniques; exploiting only the richest deposits and laying off workers, and building a smelter at Oruro. Also, Bolivia should ask the International Bank for Reconstruction and Development for loans for industrial diversification and the building of hydroelectric plants and highways. [97]

At the time of nationalization of the major tin mines in 1952, Los Tiempos was a reluctant handmaiden at the wedding. The newspaper published, for example, "Illusions of Nationalization," written in 1949 by Alfred Edwards, a member of the British Labor Party. [98] Los Tiempos pointed out that José Manuel de Ugarte had introduced a bill to nationalize the mines in the Chamber of Deputies in 1933, to no avail, and the newspaper also ran excerpts from the pessimistic view presented by Robert Arce in "Nationalization of the Mines," reprinted from the Revista Económica of Oruro. [99] Meanwhile, the diplomatic staff of Bolivians abroad was drumming up support for the imminent nationalization. Hernán Siles Zuazo, vice-president and the Bolivian delegate to the United Nations, spoke in early December 1952 before the Economic and Financial Committee of the UN, endorsing the right of nations to nationalize their riches. Bolivia was joined by Uruguay and supported by Yugoslavia, Chile, Ecuador and Iraq. [100]

The act of nationalizing the Big Three tin companies, although viewed as a political necessity by almost everyone, did not end immediately the influence of the huge corporations on Bolivian life. Propaganda was still the order of the day. José Fellmann Velarde, for example, speaking in the campaign of 1956, declared: "Now in Bolivia there are two and a half million beings who eat bread, meat and sugar; and this hurts the oligarchical reaction since there will not be imported for them anymore English shoes and French perfumes [bought] with the effort of the workers of the mines." [101]

When a former member of the oligarchy, Alberto Ostria Gutiérrez, published from his Chilean exile a frontal assault on the MNR in 1954, Un pueblo en la cruz, El drama de Bolivia (A People Crucified, The Drama of Bolivia), La Nación maintained that the book was paid for and distributed free by the "tin barons." The book was translated into English and published in 1958 as The Tragedy of Bolivia. During the early years of the Bolivian National Revolution it was one of the few works in

English on Bolivia available on United States library shelves, where it undoubtedly twisted perceptions with its extremely biased view of the Bolivian situation. For one thing, it linked the MNR in its early stages of development to the Nazi movement in Germany (see Chapter 4). The book must have been subsidized by someone, and it is likely that it was Carlos Víctor Aramayo, although La Nación did not mention him specifically, referring instead to "the 'gentlemen' of the mining diplomacy" and "the mining-feudal oligarchy." [102]

A lingering refrain from the propaganda war over the nationalization of the major tin producers was whether or not they should be compensated for their seized property. At first, the government took the position that the mining companies owed them rather than the other way around because of not paying back taxes. This was not a new charge brought against the tin producers; as early as 1944 the Permanent Fiscal Commission under its president Walker Crespo said that the Patiño group owed Bolivia some 24 million bolivianos; Hochschild, 20 million, and Aramayo, 18 million "through bad application of the laws that govern mining taxes.." [103] After a running debate following nationalization of the major tin mines, the Supreme Court decided in 1955 not to pay the amount of 340 million dollars that Patiño Mines Enterprises Consolidated had demanded for its nationalized property. The reason: The court decided that Patiño Mines owed more than that in back pay and social benefits to its mine workers. [104]

Finally, the Bolivian government agreed to allow a portion of the tin sold abroad to go to the Big Three for compensation of their holdings. This was fraught with controversy in itself, however, as the views of what was justly owed to the major tin producers varied widely. In 1958, for example, the Corporación Minera de Bolivia (COMIBOL, Bolivian Mining Corporation), the state mining agency founded after the nationalization of 1952, in a report to the government maintained that Patiño Mines owed the government of Bolivia $2,778,410 "owing to the fact that the representatives of this firm in the exterior are continuing to deduct the corresponding quotas for indemnification notwithstanding that the payment [already] has surpassed the noted quantities." The amounts owed to the Big Three were taken directly from their own books of accounting, La Nación explained, in which Patiño acknowledged a net worth of $3,559,696 while the smaller producers of Hochschild came in at $8,786,338 and Aramayo, $7,253,409. Why the discrepancy between them and the man who controlled almost half of Bolivian tin production? Obviously, La Nación observed, Simón I. Patiño had undervalued his property grotesquely to defraud the nation of taxes, declaring less value for his belongings than the much smaller mines of Hochschild and Aramayo. [105]

While this controversy raged back and forth, the official MNR press acknowledged in the pages of La Tarde in 1960 that the experiment in the nationalization of the mines had been in several respects a failure. In an editorial on the eighth anniversary of the event, the MNR afternoon daily which supported Lechín's aspirations to the presidency, declared, "The visible objectives of nationalization of the mines have been three: political, social and economic, of which we can say that the first has been the only one satisfactorily fulfilled up to the present." [106]

The question of indemnification of the Big Three were partly political backlash from the harsh reality that the tin mines were playing out, installations and plans had been sabotaged by fleeing foreign personnel in 1952, and the miners themselves had become an inflated bureaucracy with two workers above ground for every one below. Social costs of the mining establishment also ran inordinately high, as heavily subsidized pulperías or company stores sold goods and necessities to the miners at far below cost. The miners had reluctantly bitten the bullet during the currency stabilization of Hernán Siles, accompanied by his hunger strike in 1957, but they were prepared to go no further. Thus, the question of compensation for those men who had stripped Bolivia of her natural riches was highly volatile. In November 1960, La Tarde announced that conversations had reopened between the ministry of mines and representatives of Patiño for a definitive settlement of compensation to all of the Big Three. Yet the newspaper noticed the unfairness of this procedure, pointing out that the international price of wolfram had been $20 a unit while the Big Three had waited and sold for $53, but the Bolivian government had not received any taxes or divisas on the difference. [107]

In the early 1960s another element entered the picture as Bolivia sought to resuscitate its ailing mining industry with international aid in the famous Operación Triangular (Triangular Plan). Under this arrangement, a bitter pill for Bolivian labor to swallow, the United States, West Germany and the Inter-American Development Bank would provide the capital and the technical know-how to reorganize the tin industry in Bolivia. No sooner had the plan been announced, however, than Ñuflo Chávez Ortiz, minister of mines and petroleum, in 1961 called Carlos Víctor Aramayo, the only member of the Big three still hovering on the horizon, a "blackmailer" intent upon destroying the Triangular Plan by persuading the German minister Salzgitter not to cooperate unless Aramayo were indemnified more than the total for both Hochschild and Patiño. An article in La Tarde called Aramayo's attitude "untimely and anti-juridical." [108] But an editorial on "Mining indemnifications" noted in

256

August 1962 that the Bolivian government wanted to make a total settlement with all of the Big Three. [109]

In May 1960, shortly before Paz Estenssoro was to begin his second term in the presidency, Oscar Gómez wrote an article on "The nationalized mines" which began the series, "Present and Future of the national Revolution" in La Tarde, which was established by Paz Estenssoro in 1959 to advance the presidential aspirations of Juan Lechín in 1960 because Hernán Siles controlled La Nación, which was plugging the presidential bid of Wálter Guevara Arze. The article stated: "To give the exploitation of the large mines to private capital [once again] is something that one cannot even imagine; it would be to decapitate the National Revolution." Gómez admitted that the state mining sector "confronts serious difficulties and has come to be an economic problem for all of the country..." It was no secret, he added, that the mines were operating at a loss. The Central Obrera Boliviana (COB, Bolivian Labor Central) and Federación Sindical de Trabajadores Mineros de Bolivia (FSTMB, Bolivian Mine Workers Federation), Bolivia's first miners' federation formed in 1944 and the backbone of COB, must increase production, stop excessive demands and end the frequent strikes. A miner in South Africa received $19 (225,000 bolivianos) a month, Gómez reported, which was the same as in Bolivia, but whose miners also received fringe benefits of family subsidy, medical and pharmaceutical attention, foodstuffs and other benefits. The miners must sacrifice, Gómez demanded, so that the state could earn dollars to industrialize the country--providing jobs for superfluous miners and other workers. "Anarcho-syndicalism is creating the most serious problems for the National Revolution," the article declared and noted that reactionary spokesmen decried "the farce of the nationalization of the mines," "the bankruptcy of the nationalized industries," and "the farce of economic liberation." These critics charged that the miners had only changed their old masters for the labor bureaucrats. The article concluded, "The proletariat should be the advanced directors of the National Revolution," but this could only be done if they acted with responsibility. [110] At the same time, La Tarde was stressing "The importance of the private mining sector," although by this it meant only the small producers. [111]

In retrospect, the "tin barons" were the most natural propaganda target for those who were to form the MNR and later the party itself. They were highly visible objectives and they were vulnerable. With the exception of Hochschild, they did not bother to pay their taxes or to work for national betterment, as their notorious refusal to aid in financing schools for Indian children testified. Moreover, the luxurious and ostentatious life of Patiño and Aramayo abroad was used to

257

underscore the sacrifices which the mine workers at home had to make to support such lifestyles.

Augusto Céspedes' Metal del diablo, published one year--in 1946--before the death of the tin king, capped much of the propaganda that La Calle had been churning up for ten years. Perhaps this book was to change the course of Bolivian history even more than Carlos Montenegro's Nacionalismo y coloniaje. The latter appealed to Bolivian intellectuals; the former to the broadest spectrum of Bolivian life. Céspedes' work was a classic anti-capitalist statement; it did not lure adherents--it shamed those who would not go along with its basic thesis. This was that single individuals such as Patiño should not have such overwhelming industrial and political power in Bolivia. It was the capstone to the argument for nationalization of the Big Three tin holdings, and as such it was a masterful piece of propaganda with few equals in the Western world. In the English-speaking world, John Steinbeck's Grapes of Wrath or Erskine Caldwell's Tobacco Road come to mind as extremely pungent works of social realism aimed at improving the society with which they dealt. Céspedes revealed in an interview in 1973 that he believed the United States produced the best novelists in the world in the 1930s, citing as the most influential for him Steinbeck, Caldwell, John Dos Passos, Theodore Dreiser, Ernest Hemingway and--most of all--William Faulkner. [112]

Metal del diablo was not an end in itself, however; the book also spurred more reporting and increased propagandizing of the "tin barons" in the popular media--especially the newspapers--as well. This came to be so intense and repetitive that El Nacional of Caracas exclaimed in a headline in 1955, ENOUGH OF THE PATIÑOS! The accompanying story asserted that "...the Patiño family has come to be much better known than the curves of Marilyn Monroe or the amorous adventures of Errol Flynn." [113] The Venezuelan newspaper failed to realize however, that the movie stars alluded to were the opiate of the masses, while jibes and stabs and sniping at the "first family" of Bolivia were designed to awaken the people from their indifference or lethargy.

At any rate, the propaganda campaign was successful. From the very beginning the MNR had advertised nationalization of the major tin mines as its foremost goal. It rode this horse to power and after successfully seizing the government in April 1952, it had no choice but to carry out the ritual upon which it had embarked for power: nationalization of the major tin mines. There was not nearly as much opposition to this plank in the MNR platform as, later, to agrarian reform (see Chapter 9) because the major latifundistas lived in Bolivia and were a more vocal opposition than the expatriate tin miners. Nevertheless, Patiño Mines acquired El Diario totally in 1948 to increase the impact of its voice in the Bolivian body politic. The effort did not succeed because most of the Bolivian people were fed up with the posturings and social irresponsibility of the Big Three tin magnates--again with the possible exception of Hochschild-- and welcomed any "news" which reinforced their preconceived views of the lives and work of the "tin barons."

Exploiting this aspect of Bolivian life, which was the easiest road for the MNR propagandists to take, was to prove to be a doubled-edged sword, however. By denigrating the Big Three tin producers, the MNR was implying that it could run the mines much better once nationalization had taken place. This was not the case. The MNR inherited rapidly depleting mines, a flight of departing technicians, and an unruly labor force which under the demagoguery of Juan Lechín seemed to think that the mines were theirs as spoils of war. Therefore, dealing with the extremely delicate problem of indemnification--apparently forced upon the MNR as a prerequisite for continued United States aid--kept the party propagandists busy. Likewise, it was difficult to sell monetary stabilization in 1957 or the Triangular Plan in 1960, but the MNR press continued as straight-faced as it could.

Nevertheless, it must be remembered that it was tin miners who fought in the streets of La Paz on April 9-11, 1952, even before the Carabineros joined them. It was tin miners who left their work when the national Revolution was threatened on any number of occasions after that, roaring down into La Paz in their trucks and brandishing sticks of dynamite and rifles. Up until 1964 the miners really believed that is was their revolution and they fought to defend it. This was a master-stroke of the MNR propagandists: Bolivia was tin; if something was wrong with Bolivia, something was wrong with the tin industry. Change one and you change the other. Although the economic reality of the tin-mining industry remained much the same, the propaganda had worked. The Bolivian people were stimulated by the psychological and political effects of nationalization, regarded as an assertion of nationhood. Meanwhile, other thorny problems such as agrarian reform were waiting in the revolutionary wings, soon to crowd their way onto center stage.

Chapter 9

THE INDIAN PROBLEM AND AGRARIAN REFORM

> Everything the Bolivian peasant has today as material and spiritual riches is purely Spanish... It should be clearly established that "the Indian" only exists and should only exist as the past and as history, and in no way should serve as a dynamic element in the social, economic, racial and artistic conformation of Bolivia.
>
> --Jorge Pinto de la Torre,
> testifying before the
> Agrarian Reform Commission
> in La Paz, quoted in
> Los Tiempos, July 31, 1953.

No problem of Bolivian life permeated the country more deeply before 1952 than that of the campesinos--the Indians of the countryside--but none was discussed less. To a large extent, theirs was the forgotten plight of forgotten men. The lot of the mining workers involved only about 35,000 of the country's laborers, but theirs was a vocal minority increasingly heard. On the other hand, the Indian subsistence farmers comprised almost two-thirds of the nation's population, but they had few spokesmen. The La Paz press reflected this silence, with the exception of La Calle which ceased to publish after 1946. Thus, the redemption of the Indians was not high on the list of priorities of the MNR. In fact, agrarian reform was forced on the party--although it had paid lip service to the issue before--once the violence and terrorism of the Cochabamba valley had begun. As a result, the opposition press used the confrontation to attempt to discredit the MNR, although La Nación after October 12, 1952, said little about the problem. To understand the dilemma, therefore, it is necessary to turn away from the city-oriented newspapers of La Paz and to consult instead the pages of Los Tiempos, the conservative newspaper published by Demetrio Canelas in Cochabamba, the hub of the richest agricultural region in Bolivia and the scene of the densest Indian population.

One man who spoke out in favor of the Indians was

261

Gustavo A. Navarro, the Bolivian writer whose commitment to social justice led him to adopt the Bulgarian pen-name Tristán Marof in honor of the Soviet Revolution. He was the first to bring the problem of the Indian to the attention of his fellow countrymen. As early as 1918, with his Renacimiento del Alto Perú (Rebirth of Bolivia), Marof was thinking the unthinkable among the Bolivian elite from whose ranks he had come: that the Indian was a human being and should be treated as such. In 1934, Marof wrote, "No people have been so subjected, in such absolute form, as the Indian people. Even the Jews under the rule of the Pharaohs still had their leaders, their religion and their prophets. But the Indian has been stripped of everything, from his land to his way of thinking." [1]

Thus, the campesinos were at the margin of national life and suffered accordingly--until they took matters into their own hands in the Cochabamba valley after the successful MNR revolt of April 1952. There, with increasing acceleration, they forced their grievances directly upon the national authorities and public opinion. The leading bellwether of the latter was the only newspaper of the area, the daily Los Tiempos of Cochabamba, founded in 1943 by Demetrio Canelas with printing machinery sold to him at a pittance by Carlos Víctor Aramayo, Big Three mining magnate and owner of La Razón of La Paz. Apparently Aramayo wanted to consolidate his sway over Bolivian public opinion by subsidizing Los Tiempos, which was to have the second largest circulation in the country.

It is not surprising that Canelas would view the gathering storm of bloodshed and agrarian seizures in 1952 and 1953 with fear and resistance because he himself was a terrateniente or large landowner who personally had much to lose. From his nearby estate of Pucara, Canelas saw much of the ancien regime washed away in 1952 as terror and depredations swept the Cochabamba valley. The view from Pucara encompassed more than the rolling acres of the finca, however: it was a view conditioned since colonial times which considered property and power and social dominance as a matter of course in the scheme of things. This attitude was the view of most of the Bolivian elite. Since it was sharpened in the intensive agricultural district of the Cochabamba valley, it is this local perspective--viewed through the pages of Los Tiempos--with which this chapter concerns itself.

Cochabamba is the hub of the world's most Amerindian nation, which has the greatest concentration of Quechua and Aymará-speaking peoples. [2] The census of 1950 classified 63 percent of the population as Indian, although the aboriginal tribes of the eastern rainforests were not included. In the next census of 1970 between 55 and 60 percent of the 4,658,000 people were found to speak Quechua and Aymará, and 40 to 45 percent, Spanish. Thus, as blacks are being "bleached" in Brazil, Indians in Bolivia are slowly entering the minority but dominant culture, although the word cholo is preferred to mestizo to denote one of mixed blood or customs. [3]

Indians in Bolivia were systematically excluded from participation in national life until the Bolivian National Revolution began in 1952. Until then, the culture of most of the bolivian people remained embedded in the Sixteenth Century, perpetuated by an illiteracy rate of more than 60 percent. [4] Indians were so despised by the Bolivian elite before the MNR revolution that the worst epithet one could hurl at another was indio! (Indian!) Since 1952, the word indio has been expunged from the official vocabulary in favor of campesino: literally, "country dweller." [5]

Before the agrarian reform of 1953, which eventually redistributed more than one-third of all of Bolivia's agricultural lands to Indian peasants, men were bound to the soil as pongos (serfs). They were also called pegujaleros or compañeros. In exchange for working for the estate owner three to five days a week and rendering occasional personal service, the pongo was allowed to work a small subsistence plot of land. Before 1952, advertisements in La Paz newspapers noted how many men were to be transferred with the land being sold, and it was customary for Indians entering the presence of their patrones to kneel until receiving permission to rise. As anthropologist Paul Radin has noted, "Of few mature and complex civilizations has time, corruption and exploitation taken so devastating a toll as of that of the [Bolivian] Aymará and Quechua." [6]

Estates or fincas in the Cochabamba valley were not as extensive as those elsewhere in Bolivia because of the richness of the agricultural land, but smaller holdings and overcrowding only made the regimen upon the Indians more severe. According to Rafael Reyeros, the department of Cochabamba with 59,657 square kilometers had only 71,907 property owners among 627,600 inhabitants. In other words, about 13 percent of the people owned all of the land, and many of these were the small holdings. [7]

Nevertheless, on the eve of the agrarian revolution, Los Tiempos denied vehemently that feudal regimen of landholding dominated the Cochabamba valley. The newspaper noted in 1952 that three types of property-holding had predominated historically in Bolivia: (1) the state-owned land of the Inca period, (2) division of land and labor under the Spanish encomienda system; and (3) progressive fractionalization of fundos or large estates as colonos or tenant farmers bought their pegujales or usufruct plots. Some of the latter, according to Canelas, were extensive enough to support cattle. Therefore, the condition of the Indians had been steadily improving, Canelas maintained. After buying his pegujal, the Indian usually stayed on to work for his ex-patrón as a compañero or arrimante. In 1952, on giving this distorted historical sketch, Canelas repeated that the agrarian problem was not one of dividing the land, but rather improving the conditions of life and the social-educational outlooks of the Indians. [8]

On another occasion, in early 1953, Los Tiempos declared that if the original property system in the Spanish new world was feudal, it no longer was. Some encomiendas had been expropriated by the national governments for charity or educational purposes. Others entered the market or were inherited; in either case, they were likely to be fractionated. As for the pegujaleros, they too were regulated by normal civil law. The newspaper maintained, "They are free men. They are not bound to the soil except through their will and convenience. When they wish, they can leave their fields, as they do constantly, looking for other activities, better conditions of life." Sometime, in fact, Los Tiempos stated, they bought land of their own: "There are hundreds of them in our valleys which have made themselves small and medium and even larger landowners." Thus, the newspaper concluded, to speak of feudal landholding in 1953 was sentimental; some obligations of feudalism, such as pongueaje (including compulsory domestic service) had survived to the present time, but this was common to many countries of the world, including Russia after the Revolution of 1917. [9]

Los Tiempos always looked at the world around itself through rose-colored glasses tinted to the specifications and needs of its proprietor Demetrio Canelas. At times this distortion exceeded the bounds of credibility. In the same article cited above, for example, Canelas maintained that the Indians themselves looked at the many institutions and customs which oppressed them with equanimity. Thus, he pointed out that decrees in Bolivia in 1945 had liberated campesinos from gratuitous services. Yet where pongueaje persisted, wrote Canelas, it was "by voluntary accord and with adequate remuneration." In the type of convoluted and wishful thinking that marked his class, the newspaper editor added, "Many Indians like to lend this service [pongueaje] which places them in contact with civilized customs." [10]

In short, most of the Bolivian elite saw in the Indian masses of Bolivia only what they wanted to recognize. yet in reality three centuries of Spanish rule had destroyed the complex social organization of the Indian people. Regarded mainly as a labor force to be exploited or heathen souls to be saved, Indians were parceled out as forced laborers in the mines (under the mita system) or as wards to be Christianized and protected while working for the great landowners (under the encomienda system). After 1650, land titles were distributed openly by the Crown apart from encomiendas. As the encomienda declined and ultimately disappeared in the Eighteenth Century, haciendas proliferated. After Bolivia obtained independence from Spain in 1825, the Indian communities lost even the slight protection they had received from the Crown, and the great estates steadily encroached upon their lands. Thus, by 1952, only 3,783 free Indian communities were left in the entire country, which is as large as Spain and France combined. [11]

This economic subjugation was accompanied by psychological degradation. Writers of the Nineteenth Century, according to Harold Osborne, "decried [the Indian] unmet as one brutish and bestial, sub-human of intellect, impervious to education, resistant to progress, an economic liability, a drag on development and a disgrace..." [12] Many intellectuals led in the onslaught against Indian culture. The novelist Nataniel Agüirre, for example, spoke in Juan de la Rosa of Quechua as "that most ugly jargon used by the brutalized children of the sun." [13] And while the elite may have read and praised the great indianista novels coming out of Ecuador and Peru in the 1930s and 1940s, they still regarded the Indians of their own country as "men impermeable to progress." [14]

Then came the disastrous Chaco War with Paraguay (1932-1935), which cost Bolivia 60,000 dead, 70,000 square kilometers of land and 50 million dollars. Indians ignorant of Spanish or even the meaning of the word "Bolivia" were hauled to the faraway front in the desolate southeastern Chaco to fight for an imcomprehensible cause. The effect of the Chaco War on the Indians, however, has been keenly debated. United States scholars tend to think the war had little impact upon the Indians. Herbert S. Klein has written, "Cut off from the other classes, speaking their own tongues and dying together for a useless and inexplicable cause, they [the Bolivian Indians] had no chance to enlarge their horizons or challenge their old assumptions." [15] James M. Malloy believes "[Indian] veterans returning from the front brought with them at least an awareness of a larger world...[but] there is as yet little evidence of a direct impact of the war on the Indian mass." [16] Some Bolivian scholars take exception to this, however. Abelardo Villalpando, for example, believes the Chaco War was the cause of a great indigenous awakening, since the obvious inequities of that conflict revealed to the Indian his treatment as an inferior. [17]

265

If this was the case, such a change in social outlook of the Bolivian Indian surfaced very rarely in the Bolivian press. Illiteracy and lack of access to the dominant mining press muzzled the Indian masses, although El Universal and La Calle began to speak for them. But Bolivian historian José Fellmann Velarde believes this concern for the Indian was "more a sentiment, a vague compulsion to improve somehow the situation of the campesino, rather than a concrete program with social content." [18]

An article by Nazario Pardo Valle in El Universal in 1933 represents the fanciful view of the Bolivian Indian taken by the La Paz press. Discussing the attitudes of indigenous elements to the Chaco War, Pardo wrote that the Indians of Paraguay had to be lassoed or subdued by deceit to get them to the fighting front, whereas Bolivian Indians were clogging the recruiting stations. (If so, it is probably because they had heard they could get better food there.) Pardo wrote with respect of the Bolivian Indians' religious faith, noting that they always prayed before going into battle. These quaint people, he added, had great admiration for airplanes, always piling out of their huts to wave their arms and throw their hats into the air when one passed over. Even when one visited the isolated Bolivian Indian villages, Pardo concluded, one would be besieged with, "Tell us about the war, tell us about our fatherland!" whereas the Paraguayan Indians had a high desertion rate. [19]

Actually, this was inflated war propaganda by the respected La Paz newspaper El Universal which later opposed the war with courage and distinction. Despite these trumpetings of the newspaper in 1913, the fact remained that the Indians of Paraguay were better incorporated into national life and therefore they fought better. El Universal itself noted later that Paraguay had a newspaper published in the Guarani language, El Enanito, established in the town of Ayala as early as 1935. [20] Bolivia, on the other hand, had no Quechua newspaper until 1971 when a few issues were published by the brief government of General Juan José Torres.

La Calle (1936-1946), edited throughout its tempestuous existence by Armando Arce, was the first newspaper in Bolivia to open its columns to Indian writers, which infuriated upper-class persons. One M. Teresa Solari Ormaches, who identified herself as a "white lady," protested in a letter to the editor of La Calle that an earlier article appearing under the name of Chipana Ramos, an Indian woman, was "a fraud" because she could not have written it. Señora Solari, the letter writer, charged that this "deceit" was indicative of the "indigenous entity that loans itself as an unconscious mass to such dissimulations and hoaxes." [21] The letter was answered in an article by a man who signed himself, "Tomás Mamani (Indian)." He wrote, "The responsibility of the 'cultured' press is revealed by the fact that there are persons satisfied to assure us, over their signature, that the Indians are an unconscious mass. So it is. The 'conscious' persons have taken advantage of this unconsciousness to regard us as beasts and to attribute to us defects and bad inclinations such as deceit..." [22]

This kind of open discussion was indicative that the plight of the Indian--the overwhelming national majority--had at last surfaced in the Bolivian press. Those who first discussed the problem were likely to take harshly stringent views of its solution. In a banner headline of 1934, for example, El Universal signaled its intent to discuss THE GREATEST PROBLEM OF BOLIVIA: THE INDIAN under the subhead, "How to resolve it in logical and permanent form." The article was generally sympathetic, noting that the occasional uprisings on the altiplano could be attributed to "alcohol, vagrancy, shyster lawyers and economic slavery." Nevertheless, the cure proposed was harsh indeed--especially for the newspaper which was the first to discuss the serious social problems of Bolivia. The Indian should be submitted to military discipline, the article declared, being organized into agricultural battalions of men between the ages of seventeen and sixty. They would be directed by a committee composed of agronomists or "practical farmers," proprietors, and one representative of the government in each military zone. Each zone would have a vocational agricultural school with compulsory attendance required for those between seven and sixteen. The Indians would receive daily wages for their battalion work and plots of land for their subsistence. Thus, the plan would have substituted merely a military regimen for the previous civilian autocratic one, but the writer did cite the need for a comprehensive agrarian law. [23]

The continuation of this article was even more unsympathetic, declaring that one of the major reasons for the uprisings on the altiplano was the "subversive propaganda" of the pettifogging lawyers who stirred up the Indians. The "shyster lawyers" were designated "the worst social plague that exists in Bolivia." Nevertheless, the writer warned that force would intensify the problem. He added: "The only way of pacifying radically the Indian race is to take away their alcohol and incorporate them into civilization, not an artificial civilization, but rather an effective civilization, instructing them in rational form." In short the Indian would still be bound to the land, but he would receive just pay for his work, relative comfort in his home, food and clothing for his children, hygiene and order. [24] Despite such restrictive projects as these, there existed early yearnings toward genuine and far-reaching agrarian reform. Some North American scholars have denied this, maintaining that the MNR embraced agrarian reform only when it was forced upon the party by the seizures of land in the Cochabamba valley and elsewhere. This is not entirely true. While the 1941 MNR platform was vague on the point, there were later--more concrete--statements on the matter by the highest party leaders and others. In one of the weekly press conferences he instituted, Villarroel declared in 1945 that "the Indian problem is not so much one of lands but rather of management, because we have more than enough lands and what we lack is organizing an economic and social system for the Indian, to which it is necessary to give the sufficient capacity to develop himself as an active element in the national economy." The military president, with whom the MNR shared power, added that since the Indian had no concept of private property, cooperatives would be the best solution. [25]

In the same vein, party intellectual Carlos Montenegro declared in an interview in 1945 with Alberto Morales Jiménez that he was preparing a short, concise, clear exposition of the Bolivian agrarian problem for distribution in Mexico. Montenegro, Bolivian ambassador to Mexico under the Villarroel government, had captured the MNR revolutionary zeal with his analysis of national reality, Nacionalismo y coloniaje, published in 1943. He was also the most outspoken of all the MNR propagandists or theorists on the agrarian reform question. He was not willing to settle for cooperatives--as did Villarroel--simply because the Indians had never been individual proprietors. On the contrary, Montenegro declared in an interview with the Mexican paper, El Nacional, "Agrarian reform is an urgent-- perhaps desperate--necessity for Bolivia, which should redeem approximately two millions of Indians that live in my country dispossessed of land." [26]

Nevertheless, agrarian reform was not a major propaganda thrust for the MNR. Such reform threatened more people than did nationalization of the major tin mines, and the propaganda seldom reached the Indians of the countryside. On the other hand, there is some evidence that these scattered ideas on agrarian reform did filter down among the Indian masses of Bolivia. This was clear when Los Tiempos of Cochabamba reprinted in January 1952--on the very eve of the National Revolution--the program for an Indian congress that was to meet in the province of Pacajes in the department of La Paz. The document, signed by "Condor Kunka," was first published in the newspaper La Patria of Oruro, and the eleven points revealed the degree to which politicization of the Indians had gone. They demanded:

• Full citizenship with all the privileges and rights which the other inhabitants of Bolivia enjoyed.

• The opportunity to contribute to the National Treasury the same as anyone else, so they would therefore have the right to obtain aid and assistance.

• New division of the communal lands which had not been done for more than half a century, desperately needed because of the increase in population.

• Readjustment of the land tax in accordance with inflation and loss of real income.

• Organization of agricultural cooperatives to increase production.

• General compliance without exceptions for military service, "which is for our youth a school that stimulates the patriotic sentiment transforming them into men convinced of their obligations and rights both for their country and their people..."

• A strong tax on alcohol to combat alcoholism.

• Expansion and betterment of the educational system for their children.

• Adult education stressing vocational agriculture.

• Creation of mobile sanitation units.

• Elimination of the 100 bolivianos head tax for women and reduction of that for men from 200 to 100. Working men could pay fifty and contribute two days of work.

Significantly, in the one point referring to agrarian reform no expropriation of privately owned land was countenanced; these Indians simply wanted the law carried out in reviewing the tenure patterns of the communal lands of the indigenous communities to distribute more land among the inhabitants. The increase in population had brought about "abnormal situations" which forced the comunarios who had no land to rent it or flee to the cities and mining centers, swelling the proletariat there and producing the phenomenon known as "abandonment of the countryside" (abandono del agro). [27]

This problem of over-crowding and subsequent fractionalization of Indian lands was most severe in the intensive agricultural district of the Cochabamba valley, where the conservative daily Los Tiempos held sway. Publisher and editor Demetrio Canelas realized the explosive nature of the Indian problem facing him and other great landowners. On March 15, 1952, only three weeks before the outbreak of revolution, Canelas wrote in an editorial:

> The revolutions which occur in Bolivia, for one triumphant party to replace another conquered one in the exercise of power, have occurred an infinite number of times. We are all tired of these revolutions, which convert from one day to the next the persecuted of yesterday into the persecutors of tomorrow, in nefarious succession. Bolivia, as a nation, is on the point of liquidating itself... In the final analysis, no revolutionary cause ever triumphs, but rather some revolutions collapse after others in apocalyptical succession.

Canelas went on to note that less than 10 percent of the Bolivian people ever wanted revolution. The Indians, constituting 60 percent of the population, "are indifferent because they belong to the native races, for whom everything is the same." [28]

This insensitive and traditional view of the Bolivian Indians was deceptive, however. To the surprise of Canelas and other observers, changes in the attitude and behavior of the Bolivian Indian came rapidly after the MNR revolution of 1952. The supposedly "unconscious mass" of Indians throughout the countryside knew what was happening in La Paz and responded accordingly. The Indians would wait no longer for agrarian reform: they seized lands and terrorized their former patrones, especially in the Cochabamba valley where the peasant uprisings of 1952-1953 were so bloody that some landowners actually appealed for United States intervention. [29]

Los Tiempos, which had the second largest circulation in Bolivia next to La Razón, survived the MNR revolution for nineteen months before resuming publication in 1967. Under its reactionary publisher Demetrio Canelas, who had edited the daily since founding it in 1943, Los Tiempos fought the MNR reforms every inch of the way. The issue of agrarian reform was especially sensitive to Canelas, himself a large landowner. Expropriation of land--even with compensation to the owners-- and its redistribution to peasants was not simply an economic threat. As James Malloy has pointed out, "to threaten the agrarian structure was to threaten a complex system of values and a way of life traceable to colonial times." [30] Moreover, the Indian was particularly despised in the Cochabamba valley because of his sheer numbers. As United Nations aid official

Carter Goodrich, who witnessed the 1952 revolution, observed later, "a municipal official in Cochabamba... told me that the only solution for the problems of the country was to exterminate the Indians and replace them with European immigrants." [31]

Because of difficulties in publishing, news of the April 9-11 street fighting in La Paz and Oruro which inaugurated the Bolivian National Revolution did not appear in Los Tiempos until April 19, 1952. An account of the fighting issued by the ministry of propaganda filled two and a half columns on an inside page, and also prominently displayed was an article, "Vanguard of the MNR of Santa Cruz suggests agrarian revolution." Oscar Barbery Justiniano, chief of the Santa Cruz MNR vanguard, urged immediate nationalization of the mines, but added as the second point of the Vanguard's platform: "The agrarian problem is another that weighs heavily on the economic and social life of the Bolivian people." Barbery urged land for all who wanted it, through immediate liquidation of the institution of latifundium, a large tract of land of which much remained idle. The regional MNR leader noted that regulations would have to guide the process of devolution of land to assure production levels that would meet national self-sufficiency. As for the Indians themselves, he pointed out that theirs was not a racial but rather an economic problem which could be resolved by elevating their standard of living and helping them to reach economic independence, "all through the tutelary action of the new revolutionary government." [32] This pronouncement coming from the hinterlands scarcely a few days after the outbreak of the 1952 revolution reveals that the problem of the Siamese twins of agrarian reform and redemption of the Indians was more in the forefront of the consciousness of MNR planners than has previously been suspected. It was, indeed, to become a major propaganda motif through direct agitation in the countryside that would bring the lifestyle of Canelas and others crashing down around them as the revolution progressed.

Nevertheless, Canelas and his newspaper Los Tiempos were not drastically opposed to the MNR revolution from the very beginning. On April 20, 1952, for example, the main story on the front page, from the United Press, was headlined, THE NEW GOVERNMENT OF BOLIVIA IS CONSIDERED AS ONE OF THE MOST GENUINELY DEMOCRATIC OF THE CONTINENT. There was an editorial on recognition of the MNR government by Spain--one of the first countries to do so--and comments by Chancellor Wálter Guervara Arze, visiting Cochabamba, on the need for agrarian reform and reorganization of the military. Guevara Arze also noted the need for a communications revolution in his country, pointing out that there were only 300,000 radios in Bolivia, or enough for only 10 percent of the population. [33]

271

Again, Los Tiempos was not hostile to the National Revolution until it became clear that agrarian reform would be a real goal of the new administration. On April 26, 1952, the newspaper printed in an editorial the five aims which Paz Estenssoro had listed for the MNR revolution: (1) to assure food supply for a hungry people; (2) to nationalize the Big Three tin mines; (3) to divide the land among the campesinos; (4) to punish those responsible for the massacres of the Holy Week uprising; and (5) to put an end to pilfering from public administration. [34]

Within three days of the above announcement, Los Tiempos was training its editorial guns on the proposed agrarian reform--a theme it was to sound frequently and with vehemence in the months ahead. On this particular occasion, the newspaper printed an article by Damián Z. Rojas, who noted that land reform had been tried in Bolivia ever since the days of Bolívar and Santa Cruz, but it had always been ineffective and counter-productive. Rojas pointed out that the latifundistas used extensive methods of agriculture, letting the land rest eight to ten years after a crop was harvested to restore the soil. Moreover, they had the capital to buy machinery--and a foreign-made plow cost 20,000 bolivianos--better seeds, fertilizer, and irrigation. On the other hand, if the land were parceled, the latifundista would no longer have a labor source: production would be only for the subsistence of farm families. To illustrate the tragic outcome of one such agrarian reform scheme, Rojas recalled that at one time Indians were given three fanegas of land (about 4.77 acres) called sayanas. Reviewing boards or mesas revisitadoras were established to distribute the land among the Indians. The last revistado was Delfin Arce, who was killed and eaten by the natives while fulfilling his function in one of the provinces of the Department of Oruro. "Since then," Rajos remarked drily, "they suspended the functions of the reviewing boards." Rojas concluded that "expropriation will produce disorder and chaos without attaining the desired illusion." [35]

On May 1 Los Tiempos stepped up its attacks on revolutionary reforms under its own editorial signature, after labor unions and university committees came out for nationalization of the tin mines and agrarian reform. Canelas noted that within the diversity of Bolivia there was not one agrarian problem, but many. In a statement revealing his inmost prejudice, the editor added, "the Indian himself is a problem upon which have accumulated so many negative sediments that his 'humanization,' in the sense of his incorporation into civilized life has become an impossible [inabordable] task." Canelas spoke out passionately for the benefits of private initiative, private enterprise and private capital. He declared that the government, rather

272

than nationalize capital, should give it "a friendly and hospitable treatment. One cannot prevent capital from fleeing through police methods, nor much less, anti-capitalist preachments time after time. Capital is a fleeting guest par excellence. In order to retain it one must give it a propitious climate." [36]

The first straw in the wind appeared in the columns of Los Tiempos on May 21, 1952, when it was reported that government officials in La Paz had sent a telegram to the nuns of Santa Clara informing them that their finca, one of the richest in the Cochabamba Valley--which had been temporarily sold to Indian syndicates in 1938--would be taken over by the MNR government and administered by Andrés Román. Bristling with indignation, Los Tiempos pointed out in a boxed story that the monastery, as an individual, had personal rights which could not be violated without due process. In its standing column, "Political Notes," the newspaper also discussed "Recrudescence of the anti-religious fight" and "The Catholic church and capitalism." [37]

The cloud on the horizon grew darker when reports began filtering into Cochabamba of outbreaks of fighting between Indians and their proprietors in the hinterlands. Los Tiempos noted with alarm the reports which "speak of a general movement of racial agitation, which already has had partial outbursts in some remote fincas." The newspaper also reported with dismay gatherings of campesinos in various provinces of Cochabamba, and a meeting on the very outskirts of the city itself. On the previous Sunday more than 300 men and women in the zone of Tamborada had met on land belonging to the University; the police of Cochabamba dispatched a picket of Carabineros, but they arrived an hour after the meeting had dispersed. It was reported that no mass meetings would be held in the future--that only delegates selected by the people would confer. Nevertheless, Los Tiempos cited informants who believed "the directors of the racial agitation will be announcing the establishment of a new government in a short time, which will immediately decree the division of lands among the Indians, with the extermination of all the patrones. 'There will not remain one owner alive,' declared the informant." [38] These fears were partially realized when the landowners of the province of Tapacari on June 18 asked guarantees from the prefecture, the local arm of government. Los Tiempos printed their letter, which began, "The agitation of indigenous campesinos has extended throughout all of the country and it is obtaining dangerous characteristics." [39]

In an editorial headlined "Race struggle versus agrarian reform," Los Tiempos declared, "The native masses, themselves decadent, are facing now an adversary [the patrones] in

273

greater decadence." The newspaper made it clear which side it was on in this internecine struggle, however. It added:

> The Indians announce now that they, on their own account, will carry out the agrarian revolution. This is a warning alarming in the highest degree. The forces that move the Indian, after so many centuries of oppression, are forces of revenge, which are not channeled toward an organic evolution, but toward bloody anarchy, that can translate itself into the saddest events. [40]

In a subsequent editorial, Canelas identified as the two biggest problems of the National Revolution those of nationalization of the tin mines and the agrarian problem, which he considered more serious. Strikes of passive resistance and agitations in rural areas were critical because they had diminished the percentage of land planted. Seeking to identify outside interference to explain what was dismaying him, the editor continued, "There are reasons to suppose that we are in the beginnings of racial uprisings and that these movements count on the approval of the constitutional authorities..." He concluded that the agitations "constitute a mechanical fermentation, which in the given moment will carry out plans forged by those who operate behind the scenes." [41] Time and time again Canelas also stressed that Bolivia would have no true economic independence unless she became self-sufficient in food production, which could not be achieved by returning to the subsistence farming of the past. [42]

The situation was so confused that Rafael Gumucio, head of the Rural Federation, an organization of the big landowners, denied in the columns of Los Tiempos a police chief report that landowners were responsible for Indian agitation, which he said would be suicidal. [43] Gumucio was probably sincere, but his disclaimer reflected the narrow vision of the landowning class, which could not see that their policies contained the seeds of the destruction of their entire class. Los Tiempos took up this line of argument by lashing out at police authorities who attributed Indian agitation to the fact that some patrones had not honored judicial decisions. One landowner in Cochabamba was sent to jail for this, Los Tiempos noted, but the general turmoil could not be explained by these particular cases. The newspaper added:

> This movement is the work of systematic instigation, through careless statements [by agitators] in the indigenous centers, making the Indians suppose that the lands will be divided up among them; that in the future they will have no obligation whatever toward

the patrones; that the government will enforce all their rights, etc. [44]

Most dismaying to Los Tiempos and its proprietor was the belief that the central authorities of La Paz had favored these reunions of Indians. The newspaper reported that MNR officials of Sucre had led an Indian parade in that city; the minister of Indian affairs had attended a rally at the Malico hacienda in Cochabamba; the prefect and other local authorities had appeared at a rally in Ucureña, which was to become the cradle of the agrarian revolt. Moreover, MNR support went beyond symbolic appearances at popular rallies: directors of Indians in the zone of Tamborada were employees of the University, and an official commission was said to be making the round in the region of Tupiza to organize syndicates or rural unions. Even the president of the republic, Víctor Paz Estenssoro, was going to the Indian districts. The results of all this, Los Tiempos predicted, would be both lowering of food production and "fervor of the native masses in which are resurging ancestral rancors and desires for historical redress..." The writer did not understand why the central government was pursuing such a course. It would only make food prices go up and "it raises on the horizon the sinister cloud of a racial civil war." Los Tiempos concluded:

We are all conscious of the fact that the past, present and future of Bolivia carry upon their shoulders the accusatory charge of having maintained the majority of the national population in abjection and vassalage. No one would oppose or rather all would salute, like a dawn which illumines the horizon after a night of four centuries, the social and agrarian reform which will make it possible for the Indians to leave their present condition. [45]

Nevertheless, the newspaper of Demetrio Canelas--while applauding the principle of agrarian reform--would not go along with the violent way it was unfolding in the Cochabamba Valley and elsewhere. The same editorial warned in its conclusion, "Social and agrarian reform can only come about as the fruit of patient study in the cabinet, never as the fruit of demagogic agitations." [46] Canelas probably hoped that such projects would be shelved if left to governmental discretion--as they always had been in the past--and such statements as this would toll the note of opposition that Los Tiempos was to sound over and over again as the civil unrest spread.

The newspaper also attacked the Indians as a race, mixing invective with condescension. Discussing the "Problem of the Indian" on August 2, 1952, the Day of the Indian created by

Germán Busch in 1937, Los Tiempos conceded that there had been brilliant Indians, such as the writer Pazos Kanki, but these had been rare exceptions. What were the reasons for the backwardness of the Indians? "Among them in first place is the rearguard nature of these races, upon which weigh centuries of vassalage, which have deteriorated their moral and physical values," Los Tiempos declared. Getting in its usual pitch, the newspaper concluded, "It is wrong to believe that the problem of the Indian is a problem of civil law, which [for solution] only needs modification of the regimen of property." [47]

Events threatened to move too quickly even for the central government as the unrest mounted. When Ñuflo Chávez, the Indian minister of Indian affairs, spoke before the Rural Federation of Cochabamba on September 22, 1952, he assured the big landowners "that the ministry of Indian affairs has nothing to do with constituted enterprises." [48] Shortly thereafter, violence in full force erupted in the Cochabamba Valley. In early November, 4,000 Indians destroyed the corregimiento of Colomi, burned hacienda houses in the area and terrorized the patrones. [49] The central government tried to deprecate this incident. Roberto Méndez Tejada, Paz Estenssoro's secretary, told El Diario that the reports from Colomi were completely false. Travelers, he maintained, mistook the fiesta of Candelaria for an uprising, although some Indians did get drunk and threw some rocks at windows of one of the houses. In an editorial, Los Tiempos vigorously deplored "this official adulteration of the reality of the facts" and noted moreover that Indians demonstrating in Ylury on the previous day had carried red flags. Los Tiempos sent along its editor when a commission of the Rural Federation and a fiscal went to Colomi to investigate the situation themselves, and the newspaper reported that the disorders had been verified. [50]

Canelas took advantage of the Colomi incident to do some agitation of his own. In a strong editorial, he declared, "It is impossible that those events could have occurred if their authors were not sure of impunity." Observing that rural agitation was "the most tremendous social tragedy of all time," he again implied that the MNR and its minions had instigated the affair. "The devastating band seems to have been formed by wandering persons," Los Tiempos stated. Afterwards Canelas reported solemnly, loyal Indians met their patrones in their ruined houses with tears in the Indians' eyes. As is frequently the case when the essence of an institution is threatened, outside agitators were blamed for the disruptions in the Cochabamba valley. Canelas also seized the occasion to extol the virtues of his own threatened class: "In all of the civilized countries, the agriculturist is considered as the essence of the nationality, the depositary class of tradition, forger of the concept of the country, working the land to feed the peoples." [51] At about the same time, a call was issued for the convening of a cabildo abierto or open town meeting to study the growing agrarian unrest, with invitations going to the prefecture of the department, the mayor, rector of the university, the Rural Federation, chambers of industry and commerce, and the Pro-Cochabamba committee, formed as a defensive maneuver to include the key upper-class elements of the community. [52]

Despite the propaganda thrust of his own comments in the pages of Los Tiempos, Canelas did not close the columns of his newspaper to spokesmen of the Indian community. On November 15, 1952, for example, he printed a three-point communication from the Federación Sindical de Trabajadores Campesinos (Union Federation of Farm Workers) of Cochabamba, charging that the "alarmist" news of Colomi published by the: "prensa rosquera" (plutocratic press), calling the incident there an uprising or insurrection, was part of a counter-revolutionary plan to denigrate the campesinos. This attitude constituted "a true incitation to massacre," the document declared. The events of Colomi, it continued, were spontaneous and restricted, not the work of "demagoguic...agitators," a convenient invention of the landowners. No, the document insisted, the violence was due to "the tremendous conditions of misery and exploitation [of the Indian], and to the inhuman abuses committed by the feudalism surviving in the countryside." Contributing to the unrest had been exactions and maltreatments by the corregidor, patronal threats to kill syndical leaders, and heightened rumors that the oligarchy was preparing a punitive expedition against the Indians. Army machine-guns and rifles--with munitions--had been found in the houses of finca owners. Col. Armando Pinto Tellería, who had opposed the Revolution of April 9, had been seen in the region, and workers of Cliza said proprietor Ramón Ledezma had 100,000 bolivianos in his house, provided by the Rural Federation and parties opposing the MNR, to buy arms for the "capitalist counter-revolution." [53]

Although he printed such a damaging document, Canelas did so partly to refute it and partly to exploit its belligerent nature. He commented that failure to incorporate the Indians into national life had been due to two major factors. The first was political instability, which had not allowed any program the continuity needed for effectiveness, and the second was "the deep backwardness of the native races [as a result of] centuries of servitude." Obviously frightened at the prospect, Canelas declared, "This creates a situation of national emergency, which shakes to its roots the social and political structure of Bolivia." For the first time, Canelas came out openly for land reform which would allow Indians to become small proprietors, but only after careful study and through legal channels. He also advocated--as did the cientíﬁcos before the Mexican Revolution of 1910--the importation of European colonists, "who would introduce their modern techniques and their customs, contributing to civilize our Indians by proximity." [54]

Time and time again Canelas hammered away at the theme that the Indian problem was more complex than it appeared. In December 1952 he declared, "It is an error to suppose that the physical and spiritual misery of our Indians is the consequence of the sordid exploitation by which they are victims of the patrones." Perhaps exploitation was true in exceptional cases, Canelas maintained, but the fact was that Indians had more capital at their disposal with which they could save to buy land--an action advanced as the solution of the agrarian problem--than 80 percent of the middle class. In fact, Canelas believed, in a gross distortion of the situation, that Indian savings were actually causing a currency shortage. At any rate, he insisted that the agrarian problem was extremely complex--a multiple problem--and each region must have its own peculiar solution. Yet Canelas himself advanced simplistic solutions to the Indian problem; in a six-point program for education for the Indians he included "uniformity of dress in men and women throughout the entire country, so that primitive vestments will not establish a complex of racial differences." This uniformity, which would have deprived Bolivia of her rich diversity, was urged to begin in the schools and ultimately would have erased Bolivia's most priceless heritage. [55]

While the war of words progressed, practical action also was initiated by the Rural Federation, with the publicity support of Los Tiempos. In December of 1952 a delegation of four men, including Carlos Canelas, brother of the publisher, went to La Paz to interview the revolutionary president, Víctor Paz Estenssoro. They reportedly got him to agree to these four points: (1) a competent commission would be constituted to study agrarian reform, with the concurrence of the Sociedad Rural Boliviana; (2) while this commission deliberated, the status quo would remain in effect; (3) national decrees would be issued ordering Indians back to work under existing laws, avoiding capricious local interpretation of such laws; and (4) a thorough investigation of the agitators among the Indians, analyzing their sources of funds and what they were preaching. [56]

This attitude, if presented accurately, revealed an essentially conservative position toward the question of agrarian reform on the part of the MNR. Actually, the party based in

La Paz was not alone in seeking to enlist the Indians in its ranks. The Partido Obrero Revolucionario (POR, Workers Revolutionary Party) sought to extend its base of power from the mines to the countryside and combed the latter seeking support. Víctor Villegas, director of the POR spokesman, Lucha Obrera, on a swing through the interior told Los Tiempos that the COB, national labor union, wanted to create a Confederación Nacional de Trabajadores Particulares (National Confederation of Private Workers) before the National Congress of Workers would be held in La Paz in January 1953. COB also first urged the arming of campesino militias:

> We will not permit the reorganization of the army in its traditional form. The army ought to fulfill technical work in the industrialization of the country and the development of agriculture. The [Indian] unions will be converted into armed militias in order to serve and defend their own revolution. [57]

The radical position of COB pushed Los Tiempos closer to the MNR position. In an editorial the newspaper declared that the MNR seemed to want de jure agrarian reform, that is, reform carried out though constituted legal channels, while COB, if it did not get the above, would press for de facto agrarian reform, that is, seizure of the land in an agrarian revolution. COB was quoted as saying, "Agrarian reform is an imperative that has the characteristics of an historical sine qua non. It is now impossible to continue...this chronic secular crisis. The dilemma is stated." [58] The Indians reflected a will of their own, however, as they rejected both COB and the MNR organization behind it. In February 1953 Abraham Lazarte Lizarazu, founder and leader of the Sindicato Agrario de Tiquipaya and secretary of educational questions of the Central Campesina de Quillacolla, said that the campesinos would not be organized within COB, but rather would form their own Central Campesina de Bolivia with its seat in Cochabamba. This was never effected with any great strength, but it did reveal the independence of the Indian movement. [59]

Meanwhile, the Indian problem pressed closer and closer upon Cochabamba, hub of the most densely populated Indian area of Bolivia. A reunion of 10,000 Indians representing 114 sindicatos of the Federación de Trabajadores Campesinos, held in the Cochabamba stadium in late December 1952, prompted Canelas to headline an editorial, "Agrarian Reform should be taken seriously." It was Canelas who interviewed some of the campesinos on the road and found they did not know the motive of the gathering. Others said they were called "to take part in the division of lands." After giving a colorful description of the concentration of Indians at the Cochabamba stadium,

Canelas noted that they were peaceful but, on the other hand, one could not tell how the Indian really feels, unless he was drunk. One indiecito ("little Indian") had come all the way from Potosi, but the writer wondered why they presented such a miserable appearance when they earned between 80 and 100 bolivianos a day as farm workers. Revealing a sad lack of communication and understanding, but also a surprising honesty, Los Tiempos declared, "As for the political ends of this mobilization, we must say again that we cannot comprehend them." But such reunions would not solve the agrarian problem. Government ministers, the newspaper continued, were wasting their time attending and speaking at such gatherings; they should be working out a viable agrarian plan. Moreover, sindicato organizers were exploiting the Indians, obtaining money for their own travels, sending commissions to La Paz, buying vehicles, obtaining land titles, and so forth. Agrarian reform, Los Tiempos concluded, should not be an act of historical vengeance: "Now it seems necessary to put an end to street theatricalities and to dedicate ourselves to work seriously, the Indians in cultivating their fields and the governors in giving to their plan of reform an operative and fertile conformation." [60]

Again, assessing the status of Bolivia at the end of 1952, Los Tiempos found agrarian reform to be hung up on "an intense labor of racial exacerbation among the native masses, with the danger of creating grave conflicts in the future." For the first time, the newspaper charged that Communist agents had infiltrated the sindicatos or rural unions. [61]

As 1953 opened, Los Tiempos reported official action to stop the agitation in the countryside, which was seemingly a change in government policy. Reflecting a basically paternalistic view toward the Indians, an editorial stated, "If these assaults have still not been executed in global scale, affecting all the rural properties of the valleys, it is because the campesinos, in general, are peaceable people, who oppose passive resistance to criminal plans." Then adopting a more threatening tone, the editorial continued, "There is, however, within all the possibilities, that, once the conflagration is set off for the extermination of the patrones, 'in a single night,' as have some of these agitators been preaching, the Indians, without exception will be hunted down in all of the fields and places." [62]

In a more positive vein, Los Tiempos began devoting an occasional page to "Rural Notes," which was described as the official publication of the Rural Federation of Cochabamba. The pages, of which at least nine appeared before the newspaper folded on November 9, 1953, dealt with technological matters related to farming but was obviously a propaganda attempt to stem or at least control the direction of agrarian reform. An editorial note, "Our aims," pointed out that the viewpoint of the page would be "at the margin of every simplistic or demagogic purpose." [63] Nevertheless, the page was openly partisan in favor of the large landowners. As a propaganda device, however, it was too little and too late to contain the rushing tide of upheaval in the Cochabamba valley.

Such devices came in for criticism by the opposition. After insistent rumors that campesinos of Torrecillas, Matarani and Cayarani had risen up, Víctor Zannier, coordinator of Indian affairs in Cochabamba, said that "the most drastic sanctions [will be applied] against all the patrones who are accomplices in the rosquera counter-revolution and propagate false and tendentious news that provokes a state of anxiety and intranquility in the population." [64]

The momentum was clearly turning toward the side of the campesinos as disturbances proliferated in the countryside by April 1953. Los Tiempos noted with dismay that the police were showing an attitude of tolerance toward the agitators and demanded to know if this were a deliberate and predetermined government policy. Or, the newspaper postulated, perhaps the government was simply afraid to alienate the powerful potential political support of the campesinos. The universal vote of August 12, 1952, had altered for all time the balance of political power in Bolivia. Nevertheless, the newspaper wanted to know if fincas where violence broke out were those of men who opposed agrarian reform. Landowners were telling Canelas, he wrote, that they would rather have the report at once from the Agrarian Reform Commission, set up earlier and deliberating in La Paz, in order to avoid more drastic direct action. Perhaps the government could no longer rein in the movement, as Canelas feared, for "we are at the mercy of a general enveloping operation..."[65]

Only a few days later Canelas published an editorial headlined, "Social justice through hatred" which deplored the deteriorating situation in the Cochabamba valley. The editorial referred to "the process of social and economic disintegration of Cochabamba's agriculture, on the eve of the promulgation of new laws that will give a new face to the countryside." The editorial called the wave of violence "the logical ferment of the irresponsible preaching of a group of Communist syndical directors." [66]

Los Tiempos took advantage of such charges to publish interviews with campesinos--probably faked--in the pages of the newspaper that was the most vehement opponent of agrarian reform in Bolivia. Thus, Indians were quoted on one occasion as saying, "We want to get our lands with the sweat of our brows and we repudiate the Communist campesinos." These were the words of syndicate directors from Ana Rancho and Víctor Paz Estenssoro, who added, "We do not wish to assault outside estates, and we await the agrarian reform to buy lands with our own moneys. We are not rosqueros but we are Catholics and movimientistas." [67]

By April 25, 1953, slightly more than a year after the Bolivian National Revolution broke out, Los Tiempos reported that 85 to 90 percent of the rural landowners had fled to the cities, fearing a St. Bartholomew's massacre of land propri-etors. The newspaper noted that terror, whipped up by out-side agitators who had nothing to do with agriculture, was the tactic of the Indians, and the malefactors had impunity. Los Tiempos decried an Informative Bulletin of April 20 published by the sub-secretary of press, information and culture and headlined, THE SUPREME GOVERNMENT IS IN FAVOR OF THE CAMPESINOS. The publication stated that the minister of government, Federico Fortún, had given orders that police were not to interfere in Indian-landlord disputes. In the longest editorial Canelas had ever written occupying more than one column of wide type, the journalist asserted that no politician or political party had ever failed to support agrarian reform, but the MNR rejected the proffered cooperation of the rural associations, seeming intent "to exterminate a social class, or at least to leave it in ruins." Once again the newspaper sought to explain away all the troubles which afflicted the Cochabamba valley by blaming everything on outside agitators:

The campesinos are instruments, innocent for the most part, in the hands of these instigators of crimes. Most of the natives take part in the mob actions against their will, under threat of reprisals, fines and corporal punishment. They declare, when they are outside the hypnotic control of the instiga-tors, that they are against all forms of violence and that they do not desire to be owners of lands robbed from their patrones. [68]

Los Tiempos abhorred the defiance of the Indians when it was learned they were harvesting crops directly in the absence of the terrified landowners. A news item reprinted from La Nación, the official MNR newspaper in La Paz, pointed out that campesinos of ten haciendas and eight communities were har-vesting the crops directly to prevent their loss, and these would be placed in special places for sale to provision the people directly. An hacendado of the region of Pojo reported that the campesinos had harvested all of the maize and potatoes because he could not go to his own finca because of threats against his life. Therefore, having no rent whatsoever, he had decided to sell his cattle and sent slaughter men to the hacienda but the Indians would not allow them near the corrals, declaring that "the patrón cannot sell anything." [69]

As events slid toward chaos in the Cochabamba Valley-- threatening to strangle the supply of foodstuffs for the cities--the MNR government took action on April 30, 1953, by issuing a decree that Los Tiempos hailed as one that would save "days of bloodshed for Bolivia." Paz Estenssoro ordered all campesinos back to the supervised harvest; all disputes, pending establishment of the agrarian reform law, would be mediated by a Junta de Conciliación established by the inspectors of farm work. Meanwhile, all attempts on property or lives would be punished to the full extent of the law. Los Tiempos maintained there were "super-abundant" lands in the public domain which could be used for agrarian reform; for the first time, the newspaper also conceded that unused parts of the present privately owned haciendas could be used to establish places for small Indian proprietors or European immigrants "to reactivate and modernize exploitation [of the land]." Despite such minimal conciliatory gestures, however, Canelas remained adamant in his main opposition to economic and social readjustment in the countryside:

> The idea of making agrarian reform blaze like a banner of bloody struggles, inciting one class to destroy another, is one of the most unhappy ideas that we have seen appear in the course of our already abundantly unhappy history.

On May 3, 1953, Canelas also reported that the hacendados were arming themselves for self-protection, and he substantiated his view that the difficulties were whipped up by "outside agitators" by revealing that the Indians called such persons Los mineros or the miners, who probably came from the MNR and POR-dominated mining districts. [70] To add to the fears of the upper class came news in early May that Indian militias were being formed. Los Tiempos reported that a battalion of 2,000 campesinos had been formed in Arani but they had only four rifles with which to train, and their leaders had gone to La Paz to seek more arms. It was not certain, the newspaper noted, whether the arms of other Indians groups had come from raided haciendas or directly from the government. Víctor Zannier, coordinator of campesino affairs in Cochabamba, declared he had 600 armed men at his call, but Los Tiempos discounted this. Nevertheless, the newspaper admitted that the Indians had not only rifles but also machine-guns, which they were being taught to use by ex-army men. However, most of the Indians at the gatherings, which were being held with increasing frequency, had only their traditional macañas or wooden swords edged with sharp flint and some type of old shotguns. Angrily, Los Tiempos pointed out that Article 171 of the Constitution stipulated that all of the armed forces owed obedience to the state, did not interfere in civilian affairs and were subject in all things to military regulations. [71]

Fear and rumors were so palpitant in Cochabamba that Canelas referred to them in an editorial as a "popular psychosis." Rumors flew, for example, that Eduardo Ferrufino, a collaborator on Los Tiempos and friend of Canelas, had been quartered by the Indians and eaten "piece by piece." There were also rumors of uprisings at Tarata, Cliza, Totora, Vila Vila, Independencia, Colomi, Pojo and elsewhere. Yet travelers said the countryside was calm. As Canelas declared: "The rumors are uncontrollable. No one is able to bridle the gossip of the streets and markets. This empty talk enters into homes and offices and centers of entertainment as freely as the air which one breathes." [72]

As the Agrarian Reform Commission, headed by MNR second-in-command Hernán Siles, continued its deliberations in La Paz, Los Tiempos again denied that the Bolivian landholding system was feudal. The newspaper maintained that there were no more than half a dozen hacendados of today who could be traced to colonial encomenderos—in Cochabamba, not a single one. Revealing how far out of touch it was with the actual situation, Los Tiempos declared that the problem in Bolivia was to find farm labor, not farm land. The government should encourage colonization; yet several hundred colonizers at Chapare were unable to sell their farm products because there was no road for 200 kilometers between Cochabamba and Todos Santos. The newspaper declared:

Judging by the official and officious literature in circulation, the agrarian reform is being planned in the sense of an economic and historic reprisal of one class (perhaps more exactly, of one race) against another and not, as it should be, pursuing the general reactivation of the agricultural industries and the renewed impulse of the principle of private property as the base of national development. [73]

In early July 1953 the Agrarian Reform Commission visited Cochabamba to study the situation firsthand, and Los Tiempos greeted them with an editorial headlined, "Institutional order endangered by campesino agitations." Turmoil whipped up by the Indian syndicates "is gaining systematic and intensified violence, the newspaper claimed, while police action against the

Falange Socialista Boliviana and other "subversives" was stepped up. Los Tiempos saw a concerted drive in this contradictory effort and declared that Bolivia was no longer a country of law. [74]

The rift between Los Tiempos and the MNR was widening all the time, mainly because of the continued agrarian unrest. In an editorial of July 5 headlined, "Grave dangers now confront the nation," the newspaper noted with dismay successful armed attacks against the towns of Tarata, Cliza, Tiraque, Punata, Villa Mendoza, Vila Vila and smaller places. Where did the Indians get the arms? One observer, Serafín Iriarte, reported that "millions of bullets have been fired against the city of Tarata." The newspaper stated that even the vast uprising headed by Tupac Amaru in 1780 did not demonstrate such rapid operations, with Indian fighters deployed so extensively. Los Tiempos concluded:

> What is certain is that all of the frail institutional, economic and political architecture of Bolivia is threatened with imminent collapse if this racial war breaks out on a national scale, as may happen in the course of a few weeks, in the event that a well-studied plan is not adopted to ward off these dangers.

The newspaper also warned that the entire MNR program itself could collapse in the vortex of the agrarian reform issue which the party had unleashed, "with the country falling into an orgy of unchecked extremisms." To lend substance to its prophecy, Los Tiempos reported with horror that in the uprisings, churches were being profaned, and white women were forced to kiss the feet of Indians, pleading for their lives and those of their families. [75]

On the issue of campesino violence, Los Tiempos was riding a raging tiger: at first the newspaper exploited the fears of those who lived within the relative protection of the cities, but as the unrest spread this tactic was abandoned for what seemed to be a genuine and frightened plea for federal intervention. On July 9, 1953, Los Tiempos declared that the agrarian revolt had reached national scope with its center at Ucureña. From La Paz came word that the recent uprisings were political in nature since the Indians believed that the MNR government was about to be attacked by the right. The Cochabamba newspaper said this may have been true at the beginning of the campesinos' marches upon the towns concerned, but any political character gave way to a racial character once the attacks were underway. Los Tiempos feared that the spread of violence could become "a second racial movement, comparable to

285

the revolution of Tupac Amaru in 1780" except that then whites had the arms to fight Indians; now the MNR government supported the campesinos, and the MNR controlled the nation's arms. [76]

Part of the impetus of the stepped-up attacks by the Indians was that they believed actual land division would be held on August 2, 1953, the day of the promulgation of the agrarian reform decree, and the campesinos wished to demonstrate their strength. There were reports of outbreaks throughout the country, although outside the Cochabamba valley they were directed at private holdings rather than towns. In the raids, the Indians were obtaining arms and ammunition, and Los Tiempos expressed the opinion that the ultimate aim of the movement was "the extermination of everything that remains of the white race." [77]

Los Tiempos was not the only newspaper outside La Paz which deplored the ominous agrarian situation. Although it had the second largest circulation in the country, the Cochabamba newspaper was seconded by La Patria in the mining center of Oruro. Los Tiempos reprinted an editorial from La Patria which maintained that the state had the organisms and legal faculties to control the disorders but would not do it. The newspaper, which represented the same class views as Los Tiempos, concluded:

> All of the violations that are not punished, all of the attempts that go directly to undermine the stability of the Republic, in order to create anarchy, not only represent the most serious danger for the peaceful citizen of the street, but the most immediate threat that obstructs the very Government of the Nation, whose powers are usurped without any other argument than caprice and brute force. Only the judging and punishing of the guilty rebels can return tranquility to the Bolivian people. [78]

A few days later, Los Tiempos agreed that order should be re-established in the countryside as a base for agrarian reform. The newspaper noted that the first governmental argument for arming the Indians was that they would be needed to defend the agrarian reform, but "never has it been insinuated, in any part of Bolivia, the intention of resisting the agrarian reform on the part of the proprietors." Secondly, it had been argued that the campesino militias were necessary to defend the MNR government. But, objected Los Tiempos, "The Government, whatever it be, cannot rely as a point of support of its stability on the campesino masses, lacking in discipline and organic conceptions." [79]

On the eve of the promulgation of the agrarian reform decree, Los Tiempos saw, in a shake-up of personnel in the Comando Departmental of the MNR and the mayor's office, steps to prevent the outright outbreak of fighting if the agrarian reform, when announced, would not be acceptable to some elements. The writer believed that the MNR had become more polarized between right and left elements, but the latter had been stirring up the countryside, and they were more expert propagandists, using slogans of the Soviet Union. [80]

The denouement of the agrarian reform struggle also frightened Canelas and his large landowning friends. At first, it was believed that the sixty-page decree would be signed in Cochabamba, with 40,000 Indians converging upon the city for the ceremony. The Comité Pro-Cochabamba formed a five-man committee which met with the prefect, Gabriel Arze Quiroga, to protest the gathering of so many natives in Cochabamba, but on the next day, July 25, 1953, it was announced that the agrarian reform decree would be signed in nearby Ucureña. [81] At the same time, Paz Estenssoro met for more than four hours with delegates from campesino syndicates from all over the country in the Red Salon of the Palace of Government on July 23. The president explained that the August 2 signing of the agrarian reform would be the supreme decree only, which must be followed later by enabling decrees. In the summary of La Nación, Paz Estenssoro said "the Government of the National Revolution has the firm goal of liquidating the unproductive latifundium." Hernán Siles, the vice-president who had headed the Agrarian Reform Commission, declared that the agrarian reform decree was designed so that "all the workers of the countryside will find in this means [re-distribution of land] a true salvation of a new social order since the campesinos during many, many years have been totally neglected in Bolivia." Both Paz Estenssoro and Siles impressed on the campesino leaders the need for "perfect order" throughout the republic if the agrarian reform were to work, and the latter listed four principal complementary parts of the program: (1) agricultural credit; (2) mechanized service, or providing tractors and plows; (3) education in the countryside, especially to combat illiteracy; and (4) hygienic services. [82]

Canelas sought to block or blunt the agrarian reform to the bitter end. When the contents of the agrarian reform decree were released, however, the newspaper owner thought it would not be a problem for either campesinos or proprietors. The law stated that young men over eighteen years of age, or fourteen if married, and widows with children would be the owners of the parcels of land which they previously had worked. The Indians themselves would pay off the cost of the land with 25-year bonds drawing 2 percent interest. The decree would affect all properties except those of the state, universities and other autonomous institutions, not including municipalities or religious units. [83] Canelas was especially pleased that the Indians getting titles to their pegujales would pay for them over the years according to their means. Canelas claimed that the Indians he had talked with in the office of Los Tiempos had reiterated over and over that they wanted to buy their land, not rob it from former owners. As a case in point, Indians of Angostura had refused parcels of land taken from a private finca--parcels they did not consider theirs and therefore vulnerable to future court action. Heaving a sigh of relief, Los Tiempos editorialized, "The inciting efferescence of mortal antagonisms in the breast of the national community ought to pass [now] like a grim nightmare." [84]

The nightmare was not quite over, however, for the privileged few of the Cochabamba valley who witnessed the signing of the agrarian reform decree on August 2, 1953, did so with trepidation. Campesinos began arriving in Cochabamba by train on the evening of July 30 when about 2,000 came in eight cars of the Bolivian Railway from La Cumbre and Suticollo. The chief of police in Cochabamba, Capt. Juan Pepla Gonzáles, issued a communique at 11:30 p.m. telling the people of the city not to be alarmed and that "the Police Authority is alert to whatever act of sabotage that goes against the Supreme Decree of the Agrarian Reform [and will] restrain with energy any elements that try to disturb the order of the town." [85]

The full scope of the agrarian reform decree was still not known, however. The Commission on Agrarian Reform had rendered a four-volume report after four months of labor, but Los Tiempos had to headline its article on July 30, "Depth of the agrarian reform not revealed." The newspaper quoted Hernán Siles who cited the noble example of Lanza, a guerrillero of the independence movement who, upon freeing the slaves, freed his own. Siles was quoted as saying that "there are members in the Agrarian Reform Commission and in the government of the National Revolution who upon formulating the project of agrarian reform that we place in your hands, have collaborated in it with the clear knowledge that they were sacrificing their own interests in the properties which they inherited from their ancestors or which they acquired with honest work." [86] A later account by La Nación revealed that Paz Estenssoro himself lost 2,500 hectares he had inherited in the province of Entre Ríos in Tarija, and five other cabinet members or officials also lost land, especially the Indian head of the ministry of campesino affairs, Ñuflo Chávez, who lost an "enormous" property in Chávez province. [87]

As the day of August 2, 1953, dawned bright and clear in

the Cochabamba valley, Canelas greeted it with an editorial which called agrarian reform "the event of highest consequence for the existence of Bolivia..." Nevertheless, the newspaper editor found "justified inquietude" reigning in the country, since the agrarian reform was going to be implanted as "a movement of racial and historical revenge, rather than being placed on the plane of a pacific evolution, made auspicious by the cooperation of all the classes that make up the fragile and sickly Bolivian population." Los Tiempos reported rumors that leftist extremists were urging the Indians to disregard the agrarian reform decree and seize the land themselves immediately.

Preparations for the signing of the decree had been elaborate and thorough. Armando Montenegro, mayor of Cochabamba, named a new park Plaza de la Reforma Agraria in honor of the occasion. Flags were flown from all private and public buildings. The cinematographic department of the Universidad Mayor de San Simón in Cochabamba filmed all of the ceremonies at Ucureña, and Radio Popular of Cochabamba, owned by Víctor Veltze, broadcast all of the ceremonies at Ucureña, hooked into a national network. Radio Illimani did the same on short wave tied into an international network. Paz Estenssoro was scheduled to arrive at the Cochabamba airport at 8 a.m. via Lloyd Aéreo Boliviano for the ceremony set for 10 a.m. along with all members of his cabinet; also invited were United States and other foreign diplomats. Some 200,000 Indians were expected to be present. [88]

Paz Estenssoro rode in an open car into the center of Ucureña, through many pine arches erected in his honor along the way. A multitude of Indians awaited the president, hailing him as if he were a Roman conqueror. Many carried banners, standards and signs praising Paz Estenssoro, the national Revolution and agrarian reform; some Indians climbed trees around the plaza to watch better. The agrarian reform decree was read in Spanish, Quechua and Aymará, and the immense crowd was delighted when Wálter Guevara Arze, minister of foreign relations, spoke to them in their native Quechua. Paz Estenssoro, after reading the decree, said, "From this moment you are owners of the lands where you work," touching off a tremendous ovation. The president added, "Just as the government has complied with its promise, it is necessary that you fulfill yours, working more to produce more."

The day went off without a hitch, although Los Tiempos reported several possible incidents. There were rumors that a Molotov cocktail had been discovered on a man in the crowd, but the Los Tiempos writer saw the bottle was empty, with a dynamite cap that never would have exploded. Later, it was rumored that a hand grenade had been placed under Paz Estenssoro's car, but neither was this proved. A man with dynamite was found near the radio broadcasting equipment, but the chief of police said most rumors probably dealt with the simple explosives the Indians had brought with them to express their jubilation, but police investigated the rumors nevertheless. Miners from San José guarded the speaker's platform during the ceremonies. [89]

Fausto Reinaga, a champion of the Indian cause in the popular press but regarded as something of a crank in La Paz, also witnessed the signing of the agrarian reform decree and described his emotions in the prologue to his fifth book, Belzú: "With a fistful of land in their hands and the radiant light of liberty on their faces, my brother Indians continued dancing as I left Ucureña..." [90] Also present was Edward J. Sparks, who was to serve as United States ambassador to Bolivia from June 1954 to November 1956, and who recalled the signing of the agrarian reform decree later:

I remember vividly an enormous crowd of Indians silently listening to the proclamation in Spanish of the Agrarian Reform decree. Then the Foreign Minister, Wálter Guevara Arze, stood up and extemporaneously summarized the decree in Quechua. What a sensation to see that silent mass come to life! [91]

Perhaps all of the fanfare impressed Canelas himself because Los Tiempos was muted in its attacks on the agrarian reform for the next several weeks. The new wave was presaged by a column by "Chacarero" on August 5 which applauded the agrarian reform decree and told Paz Estenssoro, "You will be the Messiah of three million comrades." The writer proclaimed that the decree of August 2 would rank in historical significance with the battle of Ayacucho, whereby Peru obtained her independence from Spain. Praising the president for fulfilling his word to the Bolivian people, the column concluded, "Paz Estenssoro has played his most recent card on August 2, demonstrating to the people that brought him to power that he is not a Communist, nor is he in agreement with the anarchist doctrine of the Soviet cells. He is a nationalist because his labor proves it. We the workers of the land salute you with admiration and respect." [92]

The honeymoon did not last long, however. On the same day that Canelas allowed the above column to be printed in his newspaper, he again criticized the agrarian reform, declaring it would cause a general decline in food production. Because of the catastrophic low price of tin Bolivia did not have the foreign exchange to buy needed imports of essential meat, sugar, flour and oils. Therefore, what the agrarian reform needed were (1) stockpiles of food to carry over the period of adjustment; (2) technical assistance; (3) sanitary posts or mobile hygienic service; (4) campesino housing appropriate to each region; and (5) an educational campaign stressing an intensive literacy drive. Without these complementary services, Canelas declared that the agrarian reform "is destined to remain only an aspiration placed on paper, without modifying the condition of the campesinos." [93]

As early as August 22, 1953, Los Tiempos proclaimed that the expected results of the agrarian reform plan had not materialized. The pegujales plan of Canelas had not worked out because the colonos or share-croppers believed that they held the plots in usufruct as their exclusive possession and did not need to pay for them. Moreover, all feudal work obligations had been removed and farm workers must now be paid a minimum of 200 bolivianos a day. One proprietor in Totora, a physician, told Los Tiempos that he had fifty colonos which he needed to work 100 days a year; wages alone, therefore, would cost him 1 million bolivianos and he had never received more than 500,000 bolivianos in proceeds from the finca in any one year. Therefore, he was abandoning his finca and practicing his profession in Cochabamba.

To make the picture more dismal for landowners of the region, the Indians were again attacking fincas and towns. When Canelas asked one Indian why he was armed, the campesino replied, "They say that there has to be war." The newspaper proprietor feared that a movement was underway to seize all the land in a revolution of rising expectations, but he took some solace in the establishment by the MNR of the Servicio Nacional de Reforma Agraria, which Los Tiempos hoped would pacify the country again and intensify agricultural production. [94]

Agrarian violence did in fact become a reality of Bolivian life once again. Los Tiempos reported bloody conflict among campesinos themselves over parcelization of the land, and conflicts between and among various campesino syndicates. Moreover, the Indians were choking the cities, where they got involved with conflicts with urban residents and each other. [95] On another occasion the newspaper declared that unrest in the countryside was not the result of opposition of landlords to the agrarian reform, but of fighting among the Indians themselves. They had shown themselves to be incompetent in managing their own agricultural affairs, Los Tiempos editorialized, adding: "Among the masses of workers in the country, the campesino worker not only has shown himself the one most inclined to accept the demagogic preachments, but what is worse, he has abandoned his labors." The newspaper declared that the government should subsidize landowners to pay the minimum rural wage of 200 bolivianos a day and offer credit and technical assistance for them. [96]

The agrarian reform also sparked factional disputes within the MNR. Los Tiempos severely criticized Ñuflo Chávez for resigning as minister of campesino affairs in late August at the very moment when the agrarian reform was underway. The newspaper speculated that Chávez may have been kicked out because he had used force in dealing with some Indian uprisings on the altiplano and at Ayopaya. [97] On the local scene, the controversy over patronage for regional functionaries revealed a struggle for control between the syndicate of Cochabamba and that of Cliza. The former was under the control of José Rojas; the latter, Agapito Vallejos. This, in miniature, Los Tiempos pointed out, marked the division that had always existed within the MNR itself. There were three ministers who inclined toward an extreme or Marxist position, the newspaper maintained, who denounced other ministers as "small bourgeois reformers and not revolutionaries." Paz Estenssoro was playing one group off against the other; who, Los Tiempos wondered, would he support in the Cochabamba valley campesino dispute? [98] When the infighting between the campesino syndicates broke down into violence and recriminations, Los Tiempos headed an editorial, "Agents of chaos in agrarian unions," and declared: "This invasion by the syndicates into the political field is the most disquieting and perturbing phenomenon for the existence of the institutional regimen of the Nation." [99]

The above statement appeared less than six weeks before campesino and MNR mobs destroyed the printing plant of Los Tiempos. It was exactly in such dogmatic certitudes as blasting the political activity of the campesino unions that lay the seeds of the newspaper's destruction. Despite a brief truce at the time of the signing of the agrarian reform decree, Los Tiempos was intransigent on that topic, which Paz Estenssoro believes was the major achievement of the MNR. [100] Los Tiempos was not a community newspaper but a spokesman for the privileges of a special class. It concerned itself with the agrarian reform question more than any other opposition newspaper in post-revolutionary Bolivia, more than either El Diario or Ultima Hora. This may be regarded as only natural since Cochabamba was located in the heart of Bolivia's richest agricultural district, but Los Tiempos also was a national paper--with the second largest circulation in the country--which sold copies on the streets of La Paz and other cities. So it was that the newspaper proclaimed with indignity in September 1953 that the Cochabamba area was experiencing the brunt of the agrarian reform. Of the forty-nine major haciendas that had been expropriated by that time, thirty-five were in Cochabamba and only fourteen in other districts. Los Tiempos declared this was reminiscent of the aftermath of the 1946 revolution when Villarroel's hometown of Cochabamba suffered the brunt of reprisals. Moreover, the engineer Ceballos Tovar had warned beforehand that redistribution of the land would cause the collapse of the Cochabamba economy, and the land was being given to miners, not campesinos. [101]

True to its character to the very end, Los Tiempos printed this editorial on the eve of the newspaper's own demise. In a sense, Los Tiempos fell victim to its own propaganda because the constant ranting against violence or political involvement by the Indians produced exactly that result. Deploring violence, the newspaper tried to keep the lid on a burgeoning social movement which could no longer be contained, and this in turn produced more violence. All of the considerable weight of Los Tiempos could not deter the agrarian revolution underway in the Cochabamba valley and elsewhere. If anything, the newspaper probably hastened the final settlement as it painted a picture of things darker than they actually were--a picture which prompted officials in La Paz to appoint the Agrarian Reform Commission and hurry it through its four-month labors.

Secondly, Los Tiempos never had any sympathy for the plight of the campesinos, who formed a majority of the community which the newspaper ostensibly served. Los Tiempos fought agrarian reform every inch of the way--even after it became a fait acompli--with all the resources at its considerable command, but to no avail. The case of Los Tiempos and the terror of the agrarian revolt in the Cochabamba valley in late 1952 and early 1953 demonstrates that no newspaper can go against the overwhelming tide of public opinion. Most Indians could not read the pages of Los Tiempos, but were aware of what the organ of Canelas--with his close ties to the Rural Federation--was saying, and they resented it deeply. Attacks upon Canelas and Los Tiempos were made at campesino gatherings and word passed from mouth to mouth. Finally, about three months after the agrarian reform decree was signed, campesinos and others attacked and destroyed the Los Tiempos plant on November 9, 1953. The newspaper had survived the 1952 revolution for nineteen months, but it signed its own death warrant in opposing agrarian reform so vehemently. Meanwhile, once the great landowners had been brought to heel, the official MNR press stepped up its attacks on the traditional military, hoping to domesticate the last remaining power bastion in Bolivia.

Chapter 10

IMAGE AND ROLE OF THE MILITARY

Our nationality has never had any meaning
other than armed struggle.

--Carlos Montenegro,
quoted in La Nación,
August 8, 1958

Thus the Army [before 1952]...had become
an insatiable parasite in whose bosom ges-
tated all of the torments that bloodied this
country.

--La Nación, April 30, 1955

As intensive as was the drive to justify nationalization of
the tin mines and the uncertainty surrounding agrarian reform,
another problem brooding over the Bolivian National Revolution
came to be regarded as more menacing. It was the role of the
military in the new order, for MNR planners knew from the
many interventions by the army in internal political matters
throughout Bolivian history that their social and economic
reforms were not safe until the military were brought to heel.
Thus, one of the major propaganda thrusts of the MNR in
power was to discredit the old, predatory army and to build up
the image of the new military dedicated to the service of the
people.

Paz Estenssoro did not abolish the pre-1952 Army once he
gained power, as is commonly thought, but he did cashier and
exile some 300 officers known to have served the oligarchy
faithfully in the past and to be adamantly opposed to the social
and political philosophy of the MNR. As President Paz Estenssoro said in a New Year's message at the close of 1952, "The
government oligarchy until April made of the National Army an
instrument of force designed to maintain itself in power. We
have returned to the Armed Forces their dignity and their true
function, eliminating all those from their files who turned their
arms against the people." [1] Then in an effort to build a new

295

military more representative of the Bolivian people, quota systems were inaugurated in the officer-training schools so that for the first time cadets would come from the ranks of the workers, campesinos and MNR members. These young men learned technocratic skills and also studied the historical and sociological realities of Bolivia. Not only did they constitute a déclassé army acquiring a social conscience, but also they were put to work as worker battalions fanned out over Bolivia engaged in road building, school construction, irrigation projects and colonization in the eastern tropical lowlands. This not only was an economic benefit for impoverished Bolivia but also got the army recruits to identify more with the common people of the nation, and to cause these same people to fear the military less. It was not always so. Before the elections of 1951, as the MNR spokesman La Nación pointed out, "democracy" meant only fifty years of the three P's--plata, pisco, y palo ("money, brandy and the club.") [2]

It was as wielder of the club that the Army darkened the pages of the Bolivian history. Corrupt senior officers viewed the military as simply a stepping stone to high political office, especially the presidency, and in return they were all too willing to place their troops at the disposal of the oligarchy. Brutal confrontations between the army and miners or other workers punctuated Bolivian history in the Twentieth Century, and outrage over these clashes fed the desire to transform radically the social structure of the country. Thus, the propaganda attack launched by the MNR on militarism focused first on the abuses of the old army, including the "massacres" that dot the Bolivian historical landscape and which were recited over and over in the official press with all the hypnotic effect of a litany.

The evolution of the Bolivian military presented a dismal picture in other ways to the MNR propagandists. First of all, the army was never large; the officer corps was a self-contained caste which intrigued constantly after José Antonio de Sucre established it in 1826. Sixty years of political infighting and jockeying for power kept the institution divided and weak. Large numbers of troops, which Bolivia could ill afford in any event, were not necessary for military chieftains intent only on capturing the presidency. Meanwhile, preparations for the defense of Bolivia went begging. Thus, when the War of the Pacific broke out with Chile in 1879, Bolivia had only 2,165 men under arms, and again only 6,418 on the eve of the Chaco War with Paraguay. [3] The ratio of officers to these troops, which had numbered five or six thousand at the time of the wars of independence, was inordinately high, and they came almost exclusively from the ranks of the upper classes. At the time of separation from Spain, these officers learned that force was a difficult thing to argue with, and <u>pronunciamientos</u> against the government became commonplace.

A propaganda booklet put out by the <u>Subsecretaría de Prensa, Información y Cultura</u> (SPIC) after <u>the MNR gained power charged that these officers</u> were allied with the great landowners--who also commanded Indian labor--or were themselves <u>terratenientes</u>. Thus, the semi-feudal colonial tradition was <u>continued with an</u> interlocking tripartite alliance of church, military and landowners dominating the social structure. SPIC noted that the landowners lacked the "ideological unity and internal consistency" to maintain power and therefore they turned to the military. After the War of the Pacific political parties developed which brought to a temporary end the <u>caudillos</u> parading through the presidential office, but the <u>parties</u> reflected class alignments rather than mass interests. Thus, the Liberal party was founded in 1885 by General Eliodoro Camacho, but after the Federal Revolution of 1899 it wrenched power from the landowners and allied military and placed it in the hands of the new tin magnates. An army was reorganized, SPIC continued, "that would respond to the ideological interests of the nascent bourgeoisie and to the new conditions of imperialist exploitation of the country." [4]

Professionalization of the army began after 1905 with the suppression of the <u>fuero militar</u> (legal privileges), and the introduction of methodical and modern organization, instruction and training. The Liberals brought in alien military training missions [5] and obligatory military service became law. For a time the army became apolitical but, after 1918 moral decay set in; the first <u>camarilla</u> (secret lodge), the Twentieth Century's answer to the <u>intrigues</u> of an earlier time, was formed in that year. The Liberals still respected the economic power of the landowners, however, which encouraged them to reorganize in the <u>Partido Republicano</u> during the economic crisis of 1920. Later, despite the efforts of Busch and Villarroel, the army continued to be "an instrument of unconditional oppression of the oligarchy." [6]

Against such harsh judgments were posited the effusive statements of career military men steeped in the romanticism of their craft. A brief dip into the literature will convey the flavor of the idealism upon which the Bolivian military fed so long that they themselves came to believe the rhetoric. Consider, for example, what Nicanor Aranaves had to say in discussing in 1918 the revolutionary changes of government in Bolivia:

Revolutions are saintly and necessary when they have
as their object to cast from the land an unbearable

tyranny, an absolutism cloaked with the mantle of law, a despotism oppressive of citizens' guarantees, of all the rights stated in the Constitution. Then all peoples have the right to reconquer their lost rights. [7]

And General Carlos Blanco Galindo, surveying the military history of Bolivia in 1922, did not concern himself with the civil struggles in which so many army factions had taken part, noting only in passing that Bolivia had gone through "a long period of civil wars, whose study under the military aspect will not interest anyone other than Bolivia herself." [8]

The inflated view of the army's role as the "tutelary" institution in guiding the country's destiny did not, of course, disappear with the Revolution of 1952. Colonel M. Fernando Wilde C., writing a military textbook in 1963, one year before the MNR was overthrown by combined forces of the army and air force, said that any modern army needs "a disciplined and conscious element...that which is constituted like a large family and serves as the national equilibrium between law and obligations, guarantees liberty and creates sovereignty, secures order and impedes anarchy." [9]

The MNR, on the other hand, took a more realistic view of the role of the military in the modern state. Wálter Guevara Arze put it best in 1954:

For a long time we had to accept the fact that the army was, for all practical purposes, an armed political party, maintained with the money of the people. Its organization, which proved not to be good enough to win the international wars in which we were involved, was nevertheless better than that of any other party in an incipient democracy. Under such conditions, its political preponderance was little short of being absolute and invincible. [10]

This autopsy of the baleful effects of militarism on Bolivian national life continued throughout the twelve-year span of La Nación, the official MNR spokesman, or as long as the party it represented continued in power. The propaganda campaign, which filled more space in the official newspapers than any other issue, was double-edged: first, it was necessary to expose the old army and then to build a positive image of the new déclassé army which studied sociology and history as well as artillery and engaged in public works projects throughout the country. The former task was easier; the mass of the Bolivian people felt no affection for their armed forces and were prepared to believe the worst because they had witnessed it unfold. The first line of attack against the old army was scoring its frequent interventions in civil life.

The most tragic aspect of this intervention--a charade carried out time after time--was that despite the frequent changes in rulers in the presidential palace, nothing really changed in Bolivian life. As La Nación once counted with dismay, the country had experienced more than 200 palace uprisings, barracks revolts and coups d'etat in less years than that of national life. "It was sufficient," the newspaper noted, "for a colonel or sergeant to post his troops in the four corners of the main plaza to consummate a 'revolution,' and another military figure, obscure and ambitious, would put on the Medallion of the Liberator, symbol of presidential command." [11]

This deeply engrained habit of Bolivian politics--of gaining power by force--certainly did not end with the triumphant MNR insurrection of April 1952. When another in a series of seemingly endless complots against the MNR government was put down in July 1956, La Nación again pointed out, "The barracks revolts which were habitual for conspirators of the past were simply changes of the guard.... Scarcely no more than a change of persons was realized, as in comedies when in order not to tire the public, characters enter and leave [the stage] but the heart of the drama remains the same." [12]

Recounting the dismal record of military intervention in Bolivian governments, La Nación once pointed out that there had been two classes of generals catapulted to power by the "mining super-state:" the commanders who gained power directly, as General Blanco Galindo in 1930, General Carlos Quintanilla in 1939, and General Hugo Ballivián in 1951--"all without the slightest right to do so and only as a result of an agreement with la Rosca in order to figure as 'President of the Junta' or as 'Provisional President.'" The second type, La Nación continued, was exemplified by General Enrique Peñaranda who maintained the fiction of democratic government by getting together "rummage sales" of civil parties in order to be designated the only candidate for the presidency. [13]

Since the time of David Toro and Germán Busch there had been reform-minded elements within the military, but they did not come to the forefront until Peñaranda was overthrown on December 20, 1943. This successful "Revolt of the Majors" stemmed from the foundation of a war school composed of select military youth and headed by Major Gualberto Villarroel. La Nación credited this institution with inculcating in addition to the usual military studies "a stage of political and administrative preparation...[which] provoked the revolution of December 20, 1943." During the sexenio which followed the overthrow and murder of Villarroel in 1946, more than a hundred army officers suffered exile or persecution. Others sacrificed their careers by siding with the MNR in the civil war of 1949. [14]

MNR officials sought to stem the overweening personal ambition on the part of some officers at every occasion, whether in speeches or in articles for the press. For example, when Vice-President Siles Zuazo gave a bust of post-independence hero Andrés de Santa Cruz to a military school in Cochabamba in 1955, he drew a moral lesson that may not have squared with history, but which got across a point that the MNR believed more important. Siles said, "And the fact is that he [Santa Cruz] was a military man of civil vocation tempered by the fire of culture; a magistrate in uniform who understood that the Army was a simple instrument to assure the well-being and happiness of his fellow citizens and not a pedestal from which to attain doubtful laurels of personal eminence." [15]

Even when the army did not intervene directly in civil affairs, the propaganda theme continued, it was corrupt and easily manipulated by the ruling oligarchy. This in itself contributed to civil unrest, as after the MNR was denied election in 1951, or perpetuated an unjust economic system. As La Nación put it, "The Army, in Bolivia, under the domination of the oligarchy, constituted a serious problem for constitutional stability, because it was the political instrument of the feudal-mining [clique], and served their interests on the exploitation by this legendary 'mining camp.'" [16]

Still, it was the army's direct intervention in the nation's past that drew the sharpest fire from the MNR press--perhaps because it was highly visible and subject to ridicule. On one occasion, for example, La Nación chided an opposition news-paper, which wanted the "old army" back, by reminding its adversary of the political anecdote, "l don't change. What changes are the governments." The official MNR newspaper continued, "To defend the massacring army [which] degenerated to the category of praetorian guard, as the rosquera press is doing today, is to show one's claws too soon." [17]

Intervention by the military in civilian matters of state was usually bloodless, however, and in the ritualistic propaganda of violence common to so many Latin American countries, blood is an essential ingredient. Thus, after the MNR gained power in 1952 one of the most successful of its propaganda techniques was to rehash time and again the "massacres" which the former military had perpetrated on Bolivian labor and campesinos. Most of these clashes in the Twentieth Century had been real enough, [18] but at times the extent of casualties was blown out of all proportion. La Nación, offering its readers a synopsis of Bolivian history in the Twentieth Century, placed seven massacres among the fifteen most important events in the nation's life: that at Uncia in 1924; the Catavi massacre of December 1942; campesino massacres at Ayopaya and Caquiaviri; the massacre of Potosí when "creole Communists" Villalpando and Pedrazas machine-gunned down more than twenty workers; the masacre blanca (bloodless massacre) of Catavi, when thousands of miners were fired en masse; the second Catavi massacre of May 1949 after the worker deputies of the MNR had been expelled from Bolivia, and the massacre in the working section of La Paz at Villa Victoria. [19] Shortly afterward, La Nación added the elections of May 1949 as another bloody chapter in Bolivia's tragic past when a peaceful reunion of the MNR was machine-gunned in the Plaza Murillo under orders of the government of President Hertzog. [20]

It was important to focus the propaganda sights on the most recent period of Bolivian history because that would justify the armed intervention by the MNR itself on April 9, 1952. Thus, when El Diario published an open letter to Paz Estenssoro from two members of Acción Democrática Latino-americana in 1956, criticizing the MNR president for what they deemed to be violations of human rights in Bolivia, La Nación replied: "...there has not been repeated nor will there be repeated in Bolivia the case of collective killings of workers so common in other epochs of Hertzog and Urriolagoitia: there you have Catavi [1942], Villa Victoria, Potosí, La Paz, Huanuni, like accusing names of the most grave political crimes whose responsible [agents], now contrite, act as defenders of the rights which they brutally violated." [21]

Having staked out the Bolivian historical landscape with these somber landmarks, the MNR propagandists then sought to flesh out these outlines with greater detail, taking up each "massacre" in turn.

After the carnage at Catavi in 1942, the most serious clash between workers and troops took place at Potosí on January 28, 1947. Violence erupted when miners sought the release of leaders imprisoned after July 21, 1946. They sought an interview with Abelardo Villalpando, the prefect of Potosí, and Gualberto Pedrazas, chief of policy--both prominent members of the PIR. But rather than release the jailed union leaders, the officials ordered police to fire on the protesters with carbines and machine-guns. The delegation retreated to the mines carrying their wounded comrades. The workers then returned to the city en masse where they were met by the army and police with automatic arms and mortars. In 1956 La Nación claimed that 370 miners had been killed, carrying no other weapons other than their traditional sticks of dynamite. The

MNR newspaper blamed the PIR for purposely staging the confrontation to discredit the MNR, with whom they were vying for political leadership in the mines. Actually, this propaganda ploy was to answer charges made by Wálter Guevara Arze at the seventh MNR convention that Juan Lechín had deliberately whipped up the Catavi massacre of 1949 for propaganda purposes. [22]

As the civil war of 1949 broke out, the MNR charged further depredations against organized labor. Another clash at Potosí resulted in twenty-seven persons killed. La Nación maintained in 1956 that if Monsignor Cleto Loayza, bishop of Potosí, had not intervened on that occasion the dead would have been more than 200. At the same time, the newspaper charged, Hertzog ordered the killing of workers and citizens in La Paz on May 1 and 2, 1949. Shortly afterward, he entered a mental sanitarium in Chulumani, and his successor Urriolagoitia declared Llallagua to be a military district and surrounded it with five regiments. Juan Lechín, leader of the FSTMB and senator, was arrested in La Paz and exiled to Chile, and MNR members elected in the congressional elections of 1949 were not allowed to take office. [23]

This civic violence in La Paz triggered the second Catavi massacre on May 19, 1949, when in addition to the ground assault, two planes bombed the mining camp. The number of dead was not known, but La Nación in 1956 published the names of ten army officers, headed by Ovidio Quiroga, commander in chief of the army, and two Carabinero officials as responsible for the confrontation. Significantly, La Nación charged that the "intellectual author" of the second Catavi massacre was La Razón, owned by the tin mining magnate Carlos Víctor Aramayo. A third clash at Catavi on August 28, 1949, brought military occupation of the mining zone by Colonel Rubén Rioja Aponte, commander of the Regimiento Andino. A famous photograph, published again by the MNR newspaper, showed Urriolagoitia shaking the hand of the military commander while the manager of the Patiño mines stood by, smiling. [24]

La Nación reprinted selections from La Razón at the time of the 1949 Catavi massacre, when the Aramayo newspaper stated, "The attack upon the residences of Siglo XX came about through the procrastination of Colonel Ocampo." La Nación commented, with deep sarcasm, "The military officers of the Rosca always delayed, as at Nanawa, Boquerón and a thousand other sites of the Chaco. They only arrived in time for the cocktails." La Razón went on to say that the number of miner casualties was not known, although it was affirmed there were more than a hundred. The newspaper listed no wounded or killed among the army or Carabinero troops, leading La Nación to comment, "In such actions, it is customary that not a single military man falls. They must have invented radar several years before the Europeans. All of the casualties were miners." [25]

More grist for the MNR propaganda mill was provided by the massacre of Villa Victoria, said to have begun in a working-class section of La Paz on May 18, 1950. On April 11 of that year the government of Urriolagoitia declared illegal a strike by bank employees, joined by other unions through the Comité de Emergencia. The government warned that if the strikers did not return to work, they would lose their jobs, all social benefits, and also be subject to penal laws for disrupting public order. La Nación in 1956 again blamed La Razón for the "inciting action" that led to bloodshed when regiments of infantry, cavalry, artillery, police forces and planes were all used against the striking workers. There was "systematic and indiscriminate" firing of machine guns into the crowd, La Nación recalled: when the workers resisted, the machine guns and carbines were augmented with mortars, artillery and air bombing. La Nación said the number of victims was "incalculable," although the newspaper had earlier given the grossly inflated figure of 2,000 dead, [26] hauled away in garbage trucks and buried in a common grave. Editorialized La Nación: "This event and those which preceded it, explain with clarity why the people cannot show esteem for the armed forces, which intermittently had been the instrument of repression for any demand and for every aspiration. This explains and justifies the present divorce between the Army of that time, at the service of the feudal mining interests, and the Bolivian people." [27]

When Ovidio Quiroga Ochoa from exile in Chile protested this steady stream of denunciations of the old army, La Nación recalled that the former commander-in-chief had also been responsible, along with David Toro, for the massacre at the Cine París in La Paz on June 28, 1930, when thirty-five were killed and hundreds wounded. That slaughter had prompted a letter from "Bolivian Mothers" saying, "The people are beginning to look upon the uniform with horror." Nevertheless, the MNR newspaper did print Quiroga's manifesto, "In defense of the Armed Forces of Bolivia." The exiled officer admitted his participation in the events at Catavi and Villa Victoria, but he protested the use of the word, "massacre." This, he explained, was a Gallicism that in Spanish meant the same as "to assassinate," which in turn meant to kill treacherously, with premeditation. "The professional military of the Armed Forces of Bolivia have never killed with treachery and premeditation," Quiroga objected. "To impute this crime to them is to calumniate them with baseness and villany. All this about the 'massacres' of Catavi and Villa Victoria is one of the many infamies with which the MNR has poisoned popular sentiment, trying to make the people an adversary of the Army..." On the contrary, Quiroga maintained that the army had been called into Catavi in 1949 after several engineers had been slain, and the soldiers recovered more than two thousand Molotov cocktails.

Quiroga also claimed that the civil war of 1949 had been aided by Juan Domingo Perón from neighboring Argentina. The miners of Catavi again rose in arms and attempted to take contiguous towns, committing various atrocities. As for Villa Victoria, "it was a theater of a bloody episode prepared exclusively by the MNR." After distributing arms and ammunition, including light machine guns they had allegedly obtained from Perón, the MNR launched a strike with the aid of students which immediately became open rebellion. The insurgents gained control of the University of San Andrés and other strategic sites from which they exasperated the army command. Ably commanded, they took positions in the groves of Villa Victoria. When the police could not re-establish order, the army was called in, and the ensuing battle lasted for two days and one night. Four officers and twenty-three Carabineros were wounded, along with various conscripts, and among the dead were Carabinero Captain Javier Ceballos and six soldiers.

Moreover, Quiroga concluded, it little behooved the MNR to point an accusing finger at needless violence when they themselves had assassinated twelve prominent political figures, including four officers and one union leader, on November 20, 1944. [28] Since regaining power, the MNR was charged by Quiroga with ordering the police of Potosí to fire with machine guns to put down a campesino uprising on Las Cañanas, hacienda of Gustova Dazi. He also accused the MNR regime of using slow torture on political prisoners and maintaining concentration camps set up by its Coordinación Política. [29]

While the attack upon the old army continued, despite such protestations as those by former commander Quiroga, the propaganda campaign to sell the new army to the people of Bolivia was stepped up. This was more difficult than the opening phase of merely discrediting the army of the ancién regime because it was relatively easy to heap hatred and abuse upon an institution which large numbers of Bolivians despised anyway. It took greater persuasion to convince the people that the new army really was reconstituted and that it would play a beneficial role in the new state. An army was needed in post-revolutionary Bolivia because of the many attempts by the extreme right to unseat the MNR and also to keep recalcitrant labor and campesinos in line. The militias these latter two groups formed, which shall be discussed later, were for the most part green and unreliable; they could not be counted upon to defend the central government in a showdown, although they could be used as a counter-balance to the regularly established military. La Nación might say, "Counter-revolution [will not succeed because] one reality is evident: The Bolivian people are terrified by the past," [30] but the MNR was vulnerable to overthrow because of its swift and far-reaching social and economic changes which alienated successive segments of its original coalition. Therefore, an army was necessary and it became the job of the MNR propagandists to sugar-coat the pill in presenting a revamped "new" army to the people. The major themes, while always contrasting the new army to the old, were that the new officer corps was drawn from broader social classes, along with conscription itself, and both were working in the celebrated "civic action" programs to build desperately needed public works for Bolivians rather than to mow them down in the indiscriminate slaughter of the periodic "massacres" of the past.

The idea was to create a "new soldier" much as Ernesto "Che" Guevara had wanted to create a "new man." This soldier would be identified with the Bolivian National Revolution: he would defend it and he would help to carry out its programs. José Fellmann Velarde, one of the propaganda kingpins of the new regime, expressed this best in a column for La Nación in 1955, "Military men with revolutionary consciences," in which he said: "An army with a political conscience did not suit the oligarchy's interest in any way whatsoever because the military man, having a political conscience, would no longer place his sword for sale. And what the Rosca and their agents wanted, more than any other thing, were military men with their swords for sale. There you have our agitated history, cut to pieces by the blows of the military swords." [31] Another voice pointing out the necessity for a new army was that of Captain Oscar Daza Barrenechea, who quoted "a distinguished revolutionary military man" in La Nación as saying, "You know, Captain, that the Spanish Republic failed because it did not have the sufficient capacity to organize its own Army; rather, it counted for security on the old Monarchical Army which, as we well know, was trampled upon and later destroyed." [32]

The fact was, however, that much of the officer corps had been left intact--through necessity--and it would take time for the younger déclassé officers to reach command positions. It was a race against time and a calculated gamble--one which the MNR eventually lost in 1964 when it was overthrown by the combined army and air force--but it was a concerted and sustained propaganda drive throughout the 1950s and early 1960s. There were many pockets of resistance against a new image for the military, including the old romanticism which seemed to permeate the officer ranks. The rhetoric might be recast in revolutionary terms, but such effusive statements as the following revealed that the higher officers were still living in the never-never land of military glory and personal honor. Such sentiments could easily be swayed to the service of another cause. Colonel Gualberto Almos A., minister of national defense, on the Day of the Armed Forces in 1955 referred to the National Revolution as the "second independence" of Bolivia and identified Busch and Villarroel as the "two great soldiers of the Chaco." Colonel Almos went on to describe the symbolism of the Bolivian flag: the red represented the sacrifice or martyrdom of Busch and Villarroel; the yellow signified the riches of the nationalized mines, and the green, the hopes of the valleys and tropics through the "evangelical" agrarian reform. [33]

Other officers, whose speeches, letters and articles were faithfully printed in La Nación, sought a more realistic view of the armed forces. Almost as if to convince themselves, they repeated time and again that the Bolivian military had been transformed into an apolitical force identified with the people and with the goals of National Revolution. There was almost a magical quality in this incantation, as if saying it would make it so, but beneath the soothsayer's charms lurked the original beast. Thus, Colonel René González Torres, chief of the general staff, said in eulogy to Villarroel on the ninth anniversary of his death in 1955: "The political conscience is such in the Armed Forces that we have overcome the epochs of the cuartelazo [barracks revolt], we have thrown out the military caudillos for good, to convert ourselves into the firm depositaries of the popular will and sovereignty." [34] La Nación agreed, noting in an editorial on the civic action programs that the famous slogan from Bolivia's past, "the Army does not deliberate," no longer applied. [35]

To identify the new army with the people of Bolivia was a major element of MNR military policy and the propaganda campaign which accompanied it. As an editorial in La Nación entitled "Troops as people" expressed it, "The army is the people, the army exists through the people and in their function, in order to fulfill the will of all and not that of the minority integration of a caste." [36] Later, when the army was being rebuilt during the administration of Hernán Siles (1956-1960), La Nación printed an editorial on the "Obligatory popularity of the army" which declared: "The Revolution convinces, speaking clearly about the place that the Army occupies within the revolutionary status. Its end is not the restricted defense of the Supreme Government but the armed safeguard of all that which signifies the nationality.... An army that is not popular loses its vital reason to exist because it is anti-national." [37]

This process received its first impetus from Paz Estenssoro who as revolutionary president after 1952 was torn between the desire to abolish the army or recast it along more modern lines. In his second yearly address of August 6, 1953, the MNR president declared:

> The Army, in all of the epochs of history and in all the countries on earth, has constituted the mechanism of coercion of the State, placed at the service of those who have political power in their hands. Bolivia has not been an exception. During its long period of hegemony, the feudal and mining oligarchy, who were the owners of power, created an Army structured and educated in order to serve them and whose bodies of Chiefs and Officers were chosen, principally, from among the sons of the dominant classes. [38]

Thus, to destroy this caste structure--which in the past had colored the view of the armed forces on all political, social and economic issues--Paz Estenssoro established quotas for all cadets entering officer training. Thirty percent would be sons of the working class, 20 percent from the campesino sector, and a whopping 50 percent must be siphoned from the sons of MNR members. [39] It was a daring experiment in social egalitarianism within the military, the first such scheme in Latin America which sought to ameliorate if not destroy the class-consciousness of the former military elite who identified strongly with the wealth and privilege from which they had sprung.

Defense of the new system, which ruffled the feathers of many old-guard officers and their families, became a top priority for MNR propagandists. A publication of SPIC, for example, titled Philosophy of the National Revolution, stressed the "social sensibility" of the new technical army. Class constitution in the past had prevented the old army from serving as "defender of the anguished aspirations of the multitudes," the pamphlet stated. Harking back to its first attack upon the political voraciousness of the old army, the tract added that "its directors saw in the army only a springboard of force to arrive at commanding situations within the country." [40] But under the new system, as La Nación commented later, things were changing radically. The new déclassé army was "an army [that] carries the germs of victory or defeat which have been transmitted to it by the men organized socially and who form a nation. An army is what the society is from whose womb it has been born." [41]

Changing the socioeconomic composition of the incoming classes of cadets was not enough to break down class and racial barriers, however, if the methods of instruction in the military schools were to remain the same. Thus, as La Nación pointed out, the revolutionary government closed its Colegio Militar (Military School) "where cadets were formed in the molds of the oligarchy." Immediately, the new Colegio Militar Coronel Gualberto Villarroel was created on July 23, 1953, "where the new officers are formed with revolutionary mentality" and where greater attention was given to aviation and modern engineering techniques to be used by a self-supporting army. The MNR newspaper added:

> The Army, as an apparatus of coercion that the classes or groups who are in power dispose to keep them there or for using it in certain opportunities against the other classes, in Bolivia constituted the docile instrument of the feudal mining oligarchy. It was an army of caste which the privileged joined, with a training that isolated it from the people and where was imparted a strictly military instruction, leaving aside Bolivian reality... [42]

On the second anniversary of the Colegio Militar Coronel Gualberto Villarroel, it was revealed that the new officer training institute had thirteen civilian instructors compared to nineteen military. In addition to the physical sciences-- algebra, geometry, physics and the like--the young men were trained in the geography and history of Bolivia, literature, political education, psychology, natural sciences and Quechua, Aymará and English. Captain Wálter Rodríguez Michel, speaking at the anniversary celebration, said the School was now open to the sons of workers, campesinos and the middle class, and he referred to the Army as "uniformed workers." [43] This type of training in the liberal arts, as well as the technical instruction needed to carry out the civic action programs, was carried over to the Carabineros as well. After 1958, everyone graduating from the Academia Nacional de Carabineros received the title of Bachelor in Humanities, reflecting the broader scope of their preparation. [44] This kind of humane training for the military, previously unheard of in Bolivia, was designed to humanize what had been an aggressive and insensitive institution.

Did this amount to indoctrination, as some critics of the MNR charged? The decree which reorganized the armed forces stated that the military institutions would thereafter be constituted "by elements of the middle class, workers and campesinos, which, in addition to the technical training corresponding to the military art, should be educated to respect and protect the national sovereignty and the popular aspirations, and to defend the riches of the country in the face of the ambitions of the oligarchy..." [45] President Siles Zuazo, outlining the four essential functions of the armed forces in his message to Congress in 1958, said these were to preserve internal order; cooperate in production for self-sufficiency, eliminating an expensive bureaucracy; participate in the construction of public works vital to the nation; and "operate as a school of cultural transformation for the contingents of conscripts." [46] Thus, indoctrination was unabashedly embraced, as when Colonel Inocencio Valencia Valle, commandant of the Colegio Militar Coronel Gualberto Villarroel requested that the National Youth Command of the MNR send a group of young intellectuals to his institution to give conferences to the cadets on the National Revolution. Four were chosen to do so. [47] In an editorial, La Nación explained this process:

> In what refers to the study of the social conditions of the country and to the knowledge of the postulates of the National Revolution, the programs are ample and the reasons that originated the 9th of April are taught to the future conductors of the National Army in such a manner that when they have the armed forces under their command they will direct them toward the defense of the People that suffered and endured during a century, until finding their redemption with the National Revolutionary Movement. Now it will no longer be possible for the officers graduated from the Military School, transformed materially and spiritually by the Revolution, to create--as before--a privileged caste formed to oppress the people and serve the omnipotent capitalists... [48]

Nevertheless, there were those who felt that all the work done to renovate the military structure by the MNR had merely replaced one hierarchy with another: the MNR had substituted its own young men for those who had previously come from the oligarchy, and there was little difference in the outlook or practices of the "new" military. Thus, a radio station in La Paz attacked the government in 1958 for sending a group of cadets from the Colegio Militar to Buenos Aires for the inauguration of newly elected President Arturo Frondizi. The radio station, unnamed in the reply by La Nación, charged that the cadets were nothing more than "sons of the hierarchies of the regime" looking for "vacations paid by the people." Indignant, La Nación responded, "The cadets of the Colegio Militar Gualberto Villarroel are not exactly the 'darlings' of the massacrers who educated the oligarchy to defend the interests of the tin rosca. They are youths of the people educated to respect the will of the people and those whom the oligarchy cannot count upon any longer as cannon fodder for their protection." [49]

The fear that the MNR was entrenching itself in power through a brainwashed military establishment proved to be unfounded with the passage of time, and in fact the failure of the propaganda effort was becoming apparent quite early. It was not until 1959, for example, seven years after the start of the Revolution, that a successful national Célula Militar (military cell) was established by MNR members within the military. There had been other cells attempted before, Captain Oscar Daza Berrenechea wrote in discussing "The soldier in politics" for La Nación, but they had all failed because of poor leadership. The average officer, Daza found, preferred to keep his politics in the private aspect of his life, although there was a transformation among the troops because the universal vote had made citizens of the common soldiers, too. [50]

Seeking further to reinforce a technocratic officer corps which would be loyal to the goals of the Revolution, Paz Estenssoro created the School of Higher Military Studies in early 1961. General Eliodoro Murillo, speaking at its dedication, explained the objectives of the new institution. There would in fact be a fusion of military and liberal arts concepts. Thus, national defense and military organization would be stressed, but in a unique manner, in "military art and science, comprising systematic analysis and interpretation of diverse factors: political, economic, social, etc." [51]

A broadly educated officer corps loyal to the National Revolution would have been useless, however, without adequately trained troops to place at their disposal. In this regard, a conscious effort was made to improve the living conditions of common soldiers so that more would be attracted to the service. This was more than just an improvement in their physical surroundings, with better food, uniforms and barracks facilities. There was a startling change in psychological attitude toward the recruits: no longer would they be treated as dumb brutes or herded around and exploited. La Nación discussed "The new conscripts" in a column printed in 1955, noting that if "Blue blood is no longer requisite to enter into the Colegio Militar," the changes in the enlisted ranks were equally dramatic:

Today the conscripts have a decent life. They are offered humane treatment. Far off in the distance of time and space lies the tyranny of the Lieutenant to the enlisted officer. The bullying of the Corporal upon the ignorant. Belonging to the past [is] that abuse of: 'Soldier, take this bill. Buy bread, cheese, sweets, cigarets and bring me change of 50 cents.' The epoch will pass also, I imagine, of the assistant who has to wash the diapers of the

Captain's babies. And who was obliged to cook. To wash the floors. And go to the market. In sum, to do everything in the house of the officer, except be instructed in how to serve his Country. There is no doubt. The New Army is part of the liberation of all citizens, promoted and made reality by the Government of the People. [52]

The facts seemed to bear out this lyrical description of life in the new army. In the first two days of the annual conscription in 1955, for example, long lines formed to enter military service. Perhaps better food was the main attraction, but so many campesinos and others showed up in La Paz that only 4,000 out of 7,000 could be processed. Of these, 76.6 percent were found to be fit for service and 8.9 percent unfit. The remaining men went into two types of auxiliary service. (In 1957 a bill was introduced into the Senate for obligatory civil service in public works and communications or education for those young men ineligible for military service.) [53] At the time of the swollen conscription lines in 1955, La Nación declared that "no longer are we dealing with an army in which reigned only a discipline of iron developed in exercises of trememdous inutility, in long guard watches, in empty marching repeated a thousand times and in ornamental parades. Thus, the army was only a plaything..." [54] Colonel Cupertino Ríos, commander of the military region of La Paz, also noted in 1956 the "extraordinary enthusiasm" of the conscripts, "above all those of the campesino class who have come voluntarily from distant provincial cantons, with no necessity, as has been done before, of sending them transportation to bring them to this city." [55]

The better educated officer class and the better treated conscripts found their confluence in the civic action program, a process of beating swords into plowshares that was widely publicized in the press. There were three main goals of the civic action plan: to use the army as a source of labor to build an infrastructure--roads, schools, potable water supplies and the like--to further the economy of the nation; to colonize the lowlying eastern lands to relieve population pressure from the crowded altiplano; and through both of these projects to make the army self-sufficient and no longer a burden on the treasury. The "parasitical army" of the past, La Nación repeatedly pointed out, used to consume a third of the national budget. [56] As Colonel Gualberto Olmos, minister of national defense, told La Nación in 1955, the greatest need of the armed forces was to become self-supporting so they could be freed once and for all from the national budget. This also would invigorate the national economy, he said, adding:

I want to note this point...that the previous governments as much as the officers of the Old School were
rooted and molded in archaic concepts in what
referred to the country's economy; therefore, as a
result of this there was neither comprehension nor
harmony between the Government and the Army, and
the old generals did nothing more than make unlimited
demands on the State. The Army's budget thus came
to be an excessive charge for the taxpayer since
considerable sums already were destined to the bud-
gets of the other Portfolios. [57]

The agricultural production of the army in the colonization
projects steadily whittled down the amount of money which the
MNR had to funnel directly into the armed forces. Paz Estenssoro, addressing the seventh convention of the MNR in 1956,
announced proudly that production profits by the army had
been 91 million **bolivianos**, even after a subsidy to raise the
salaries of officers. The excess was used to buy tractors,
tools, other agricultural implements and supplies. The MNR
president drew applause when he declared, "They did not
pocket the money, as did the old colonels." [58] Paz Estenssoro summed up the transformation of the armed forces:

In the Army has operated not only a change in spirit,
but also the Army has been converted into a collaborator with the force that the people of Bolivia are
carrying out to develop the economy.... The new
Army, the Army of the national Revolution, is no
longer an instrument of oppression as was that of the
oligarchy. It is the Army composed of the people, an
Army at the service of the people, an Army that is
collaborating with the constructive force of Bolivia.
[59]

The building of infrastructure projects in the settled areas
of Bolivia was not as spectacular as the colonization program,
perhaps because the soldiers had a personal incentive in the
latter. The projects in which the labor of soldiers was used to
build and maintain public works should not be overlooked,
however. The press at all times kept the public amply informed
of these projects, and speeches by governmental officials--
viewed as an educational or propaganda effort in themselves--
referred to them constantly. The army cooperated with the
Corporación Boliviana de Fomento and other central agencies to
finance its projects, [60] which came to be so universally
accepted that it was maintained the mission of the armed force
had come to be "comprehensive works of development." [61]
The major contribution of the air force was through the newly
created Fuerza Aérea de Producción, composed mainly of the

former Transportes Aéreas Militares and integrating a network of commercial routes throughout a country that desperately needed transportation to outlying areas. [62] These military activities were so successful that they spilled over into other national departments. In 1958, for example, the minister of campesino affairs, Vicente Alvarez Plata, asked the minister of national defense to divert the excess of conscripts in 1958 to the ministries of agriculture and campesino affairs so they could be used to build small irrigation dams in various parts of the country. [63]

Finally, after careful study the Consejo Nacional de Desarollo (National Council of Development) approved a five-year plan for the armed forces in early 1962. It stressed the opening of roads in important but previously inaccessible regions, the building of airports which serve for the movement of garrison troops as much as to facilitate commerce and industry, and the composition of an accurate national map. Production and colonization projects would continue, for the Council found that the soldiers knew that their personal or professional conditions could not be improved unless Bolivia won the struggle for a "Free Economy." Editorial comment in La Nación noted, "It is worth saying that when an Army does not have arms in its hands, but rather the instruments of work, the fact is that the Army is more than the people doing militia service." [64]

The conjunction of military reorganization and agrarian reform--which Paz Estenssoro has called the single greatest achievement of the Bolivian National Revolution--occurred in the colonization program. Regiments of conscript farmers spear-headed the way for the greatest internal migration in Bolivian history; by 1973, Paz Estenssoro estimated that at least 200,000 persons--and probably more than 300,000 or 400,000--had been relocated in agricultural projects in the tierras bajas (lowlands) of the east and north. Paz Estenssoro believed it to be an "absurd myth" that the campesinos of the altiplano did not want to leave their traditional homes for the colonization areas; actually, they flocked to such areas, sometimes pushing ahead of the bulldozers carving out access roads. [65]

But it was the military who first showed the possibilities of farming in these tropical regions. In 1954, for example, a corporation was formed by supreme decree between the ministry of national defense, which provided 100 conscripts, and the military pension fund, which contributed 25 million bolivianos to develop 600,000 hectares in the zone of Alto Madidi. In four years the project had built a landing strip, a breeding station, a nursery garden, and the men had planted 70,000 coffee trees, along with helping various groups of forester colonizers. [66]

On another occasion, La Nación lauded the work of colonizers in an editorial, "New concept of military service." It noted in 1955 that 650 men nineteen years old had been sent on a colonization mission to the Oriente. These men would get their own choice of plots in Montero and Ichilo after their term of military service was up, thus effecting a redistribution of population. [67] Each conscript worked twenty hectares of land; at the conclusion of his service, he could either elect to keep them for the rest of his life or return to his place of origin. José Fellmann Velarde, writing in La Nación, noted, "It is to be hoped that, having become fond of the land which has given its first fruits, the soldiers converted into citizens and proprietors, will prefer to put down roots where they have a security and a future." [68]

This procedure was modified somewhat in later 1955. Mayor Roberto Lemaitre, speaking on "The new productive army," detailed plans for colonization in the Oriente. Since there was a two-year conscription, families of the colonizing soldiers would arrive in the second year, which would be characterized "by the gradual diminution of the military aspect to the simple operation of control and statistics." At the end of the second year, provisional titles of four years would be given to those who desired them, marking a testing period during which the settlers would repay the state "a part of the expenses effected in their installation but remaining free to dispose of the product of their plantings as they please." [69] Actually, perhaps the provision of family life was unnecessary, for as Paz Estenssoro told the seventh convention of the MNR in 1956, of the 1,300 men in the Regimiento Colonial who had left La Paz for colonization in Santa Cruz in April 1955, only eighteen had deserted, fewer by proportion than those of the Regimiento de Viacha stationed on the altiplano. [70]

What the press strived to put across most forcefully, however, was that these were pay-as-you-go operations; they were organized as if private capital were financing them, and they were expected to be self-sustaining and eventually profitable. In 1956, for example, the Corporación Boliviana de Fomento organized a division in Cochabamba for colonization in the Oriente. They were distributed in four regiments of 500 each at Mineros, Chane, Surutú and San Miguel where they cultivated maize, rice, yucca, vegetables and other products appropriate for those regions. [71]

The civic action program, supported by a favorable press, was thus relatively popular, but in other areas the MNR military policy met stiff opposition. The greatest hostility from the oligarchical newspapers was not against the organization of a new army along technical and déclassé lines, but the contin-

314

uance of armed militias--both miners and campesinos. The miners had fought in the streets of La Paz and Oruro during the successful revolt of April 9-11, 1952, and the campesinos had seized arms during the agrarian upheavals in the Cochabamba valley. Exactly how many of these armed civilians roamed the towns and countryside cannot be known, but to the former oligarchy they seemed omnipresent. This dispersal of power was ominous to the ex-ruling class because it threatened the monopolistic structure of the army which had supported them in the past. One of their favorite lines of argument was that the indiscriminate possession of firearms threatened the public safety. Próspero Morales Pradilla, writing for La Nación, dispelled this fear when he noted in 1955 that 100,000 campesinos were armed, along with 50,000 to 80,000 miners and other organized workers. Nevertheless, in La Paz where there were 8,000 or 10,000 rifles and about 500 machine guns, there were only eleven violent deaths in one year, Morales Pradilla reported, whereas there were eleven homicides every week in Bogotá, the "Athens of the Americas." [72]

Nevertheless, to former landowners who had sought refuge in La Paz from the terror in the countryside, it was frightening to watch thousands of armed campesinos participate in the holiday marches down the Prado. The protocol for such demonstrations was interesting since it revealed the relative importance the MNR leaders attached to the various sections of the military and paramilitary. On the fourth anniversary of the 1952 overthrow, for example, the parade lasted seven hours. The troops of the army led off, followed by the chief of the general staff and the chiefs of staff of the army and air force. Next came the corps of Carabineros and finally the seemingly endless stream of militias, all giving the V-signal when they passed the reviewing dignitaries looking down from the balcony of the palace of government. [73]

The MNR was proud of its armed citizenry and praised it at every opportunity. This was not merely a gesture of good will, but an indication of dependency: it was hoped the militias--like the Carabineros--would serve as a counter-balance to the regular army, which by no means had been dismantled, if it should return to its old predatory ways. As Paz Estenssoro phrased this in a state visit to Peru in 1955, "Since the Revolution started, our Army has ceased to be the springboard for the oligarchy. We put at the head of it officers who proved their honor and patriotism in the Chaco. Before, the mine owners could buy two or three regiments; now they would have to buy all the campesino and working masses." [74] Abroad it was widely misunderstood that the standing army had been completely abolished and replaced with the worker and Indian militias. Ex-President Enrique Hertzog made such a charge in an article published in La Razón of Buenos Aires, but Colonel Pablo Acebey B., military attaché of Bolivia to Argentina, denied publicly that "the Army has been dissolved and the arms given to union leaders." [75]

In a sense, the MNR followed a schizophrenic military policy and this made propaganda justification difficult. The regular army was suspect; yet it was retained. On the other hand, the militias were praised profusely, but they were not maintained and in fact pleas to beef them up went unheeded. This, in 1953, for example, the Confederación Universitaria Boliviana (CUB) petitioned the MNR government for more arms for the working class and an intensification of the organization of armed units of workers, campesinos and students. [76] Their call went unanswered, however, even though La Nación could later declare, "The revolutionary military regime, defending all the national rights of sovereignty, can sustain itself only in the military effectiveness of its human masses. In other words: a revolution such as this cannot know it is secure without sustaining itself in a people of warriors." [77]

As the elections of 1956 approached, which would mark the first transfer of MNR power, the young revolutionary regime was skittish about possible repercussions. La Nación repeated the words that Siles Zuazo uttered immediately after the 1952 rebellion that "These rifles are our best guarantee." [78] Shortly before the elections, Paz Estenssoro granted an interview to Edward Morrow of the New York Times which was revealing. At the time, units of the MNR were patrolling the streets of La Paz twenty-four hours a day. Paz Estenssoro noted that he had asked for 500 men in the Villa Victoria section but 1,500 militiamen showed up with their arms. As special groups on six-hour shifts patrolled every block of the capital, Paz noted, "We can win any battle in the field" with the militias. This should not be interpreted, however, he added, that the armed forces themselves were not available for defense. Paz explained that the danger would last until August 6 when his successor would be installed, which would be the first time in thirty years that the President of Bolivia would give command to an elected successor--since Hernán Siles' father received a peaceful transfer of political power from Bautista Saavedra in 1926. [79]

The spectacle of armed militias especially awed foreign correspondents. David Brinkley, in his half-hour documentary program for NBC, devoted a segment to armed miners rushing into La Paz in their trucks brandishing rifles and sticks of dynamite to defend the Revolution whenever the alarm sounded. Examples of this Bolivian version of Minutemen rushing to the defense of the Revolution were frequent during the early years of the MNR in power, but gradually declined as the Revolution continued to stabilize itself. Thereby the militias were allowed to atrophy; they were not needed so much, or so it was thought, as on the morning of October 21, 1958, when some 300 armed miners from Milluni swept into La Paz in trucks to put down another Falangist attempted coup d'etat. [80] Donald Loomis, correspondent for McGraw Hill, noted that "we are not accustomed to see a people armed; since World War II, I have not seen a parade which suggested so much to me." In an editorial commenting upon Loomis' statement, La Nación declared that if the National Revolution meant anything at all, it was this: "that in Bolivia democracy is armed and that, therefore, it rules with its superior human and political orientation the life of a people that never knew anything but the 'benefits' of armed regimes without law and without patriotism." [81]

To those who protested the extra-legal character of the militias, La Nación responded that there had always been secret armies in Bolivia's past. The newspaper recalled the famous Sección Segunda (Second Section) during the time of Hertzog, Urriolagoitia and Ballivián. This infamous unit was "composed of a body of detectives and a numerous network of agents especially charged to watch, arrest, confine, exile and torture the political adversaries of those regimes of the oligarchy. Far off and unhealthful places such as Santo Corazón, Chapare, Caranavi, Coati, Ichilo and so many others were concentration camps" where for months and years citizens of the opposition were detained, especially militants of the MNR. But at that time, La Nación demanded, who objected to the Sección Segunda? [82]

In 1958 the MNR newspaper devoted a front-page editorial to "The armed militias" to answer a campaign of recent months in the opposition press to dissolve them. In that campaign the conservative press was charged with using every means to discredit the militias, calling the campesinos of Ucureña "bands of habitual criminals" and the workers' militias "a grave threat to the public peace." To "prove" their charges, the opposition newspapers had magnified incidents or invented them, La Nación charged.

Once again, the best defense for the MNR newspaper was a vigorous offense, repeating the theme of past clandestine groups armed by the oligarchy. The Liberal party had its Guardia Blanca (White Guard) that had taken the lives of numerous citizens; the Republicano had, in their time, the famous Guardia Republicana whose dreaded agents were called "sheep" for their blind obedience. The Genuine Republicans, in their turn, possessed Father Ibar and his "Janizaries." The newspaper noted, "From that time dates the practice of forcing

317

political prisoners to drink motor oil, a usage revived during the sexenio and now barred from the political struggle." La Nación charged that the FSB had its Camisas Blancas (White Shirts) which periodically murdered MNR workers, and after the overthrow of Villarroel in 1946, presidents of the sexenio had their sadly celebrated "Revolutionary" legions. [83]

"The oligarchy also occupied itself in organizing armed civil militias" La Nación headlined an article in late 1958. According to La Razón of October 10, 1946, the governing Junta after the murder of Villarroel authorized the first steps toward organizing civil forces in zones commanded by Chaco War veterans. Groups such as 21 de Julio, Lopera, Acción Civil Revolucionaria and others were active in realizing this objective. The question arose, however, as to what to call the new armed civilians who took part in the events of July 21, 1946. Names suggested where Guardia Republicana, Milicia Civil de Seguridad and Guardia Civil. [84]

"On the other hand," La Nación editorialized, "the armed [MNR] militias are not mercenary bands nor groups of rich brats [señoritos] at the age of proving their valor. Every rifle which the [MNR] militia possesses has been wrenched from an enemy in plain fight, risking their lives. And if they save those rifles, it is because with them they are defending more than the government itself--[they are defending] their own convictions and class interests. They are partisan organizations united in the fight against the reaction..." [85]

La Nación did not always have the time to take such a reflective view of the situation. Day-to-day events called for immediate response, as when El Diario broke the story in May 1958--despite the censorship imposed by a state of siege--of a counter-revolutionary golpe in Santa Cruz, the eastern region long known for its separatist tendencies. The opposition newspaper was especially alarmed that campesino militiamen from Ucureña had been used to put down FSB uprisings in Santa Cruz, Camiri and Choreti on May 14, 1958. FSB leader Mario Gutiérrez and the members of his Comité Revolucionario had urged the uprising from Radio Grigota. El Diario described the outbreak "as part of a national plan" and published on its editorial page on FSB document two months old which alluded to "a tremendous and dangerous situation of civil authority [policiaria]" in the region caused by the presence of troops from Ucureña. La Nación countered by quoting an announcement from the Dirección de Informaciones that these Indian militia were under responsible command of officials of the army. Moreover, they were brought to Santa Cruz in trucks on May 16 and returned to Ucureña on May 19. A statement by the supreme government declared, "This kind of information [that published by El Diario] far from truthfully orienting public opinion tries to deceive it, inciting it to deeds of uncontrolled violence such as those which the same newspaper promoted by means of a systematic campaign of adulteration of the truth that lasted six months culminating with the situation of July 1946." [86]

Following this line of attack, La Nación asked in September 1958 what would happen in the case of a successful counter-revolution. "[The country] would enter into chaos, undoubtedly, because the regime that followed would have to improvise an army and a police force faithful to it, as it faced an army and a police with revolutionary sensibilities. And if this could happen, consider the armed resistance of miners, factory workers, artisans and employees, and then with strictly tactical criteria, one would arrive at the conclusion that the counter-revolution would machinate not the death of the MNR, but the death of Bolivia." [87]

The militia was also regarded as a counter-balance to recalcitrant labor, as the hardships of the revolution increased. In 1958 La Nación described the militias as "partisan organizations united in the fight against the reaction and union organizations, nourished from their fight for better living conditions, [which] have not always demonstrated themselves as unconditional supporters of the government." [88] A ten-day strike by bank employees was ended in 1959 when miner militias and crowds presented a show of strength on January 22. As it turned out it was the Carabineros who peacefully removed the strikers from their union headquarters. [89]

The MNR press also viewed the militias almost as an extension of the universal vote granted in 1952. In 1959 La Nación defended universal suffrage against the continued armed attacks on the MNR government: "The parties opposed to the Revolution continually opt for methods of force for the conquest of a power which is denied them by the universal vote. In such circumstances it is natural that the classes which represent the human basis of the Revolution, safeguard the maintenance of the new order in all terrains. The militias are not private organizations: they are and they act within the Revolutionary State." [90]

As the elections of 1960 approached, the greatest attack of the opposition press was against the universal vote, viewed cynically as an artificial means to broaden the base of MNR support. La Nación noted the place of the militias in this new political process of Bolivia: "The social power of the universal vote came to be backed in the Revolution by the possession of arms and the organization of the worker and campesino militias." [91]

Of peculiar sensitivity to the MNR government was the continued existence of the campesino militias, a factor not envisioned in the MNR master plan. In 1955, three years after the revolution began, the Chilean journalist Raúl Aldunate Phillips interviewed Paz Estenssoro on this matter and included the conversation in his book, Trás la cortina de estaña (Behind the Tin Curtain). Paz insisted that the Bolivian army had never been abolished but simply changed to a technocratic status. And the popular militias? asked Aldunate. "They exist and they are indispensable," Paz replied. He noted with satisfaction that seven regiments of the Rosca had been defeated in La Paz and Oruro in the April 1952 insurrection by the combined miners and Carabineros. Paz told the Chilean journalist, "You would have found it interesting to have seen six regiments of campesinos with arms, perfectly disciplined, parade on April 9, 1955." The reporter replied, "How can one reconcile that, Mr. President, with the existence of the army? An army jealous of its honor cannot accept the existence of such organizations." Paz replied that these were problems that would have to be solved in the future. He explained that 300 regular Army officers had been cashiered after the 1952 revolt, and there remained about the same number on the rosters. Some were even generals, he noted, such as Calleja and Tavera. "Little by little, we are forming new squadrons until we obtain the restoration of a new army," he concluded.

The Chilean journalist's eye caught the details of Paz Estenssoro's office. There was a Mauser carbine on his desk, along with two large fingers cast in tin giving the "V" signal of Churchill, which Paz explained in Bolivia meant not only "Victory" but "Venceremos" ("We shall overcome"). On the walls, a much larger portrait of Villarroel dominated others of Bolívar and Sucre, and over the doorway was a Sacred Heart of Jesus. [92]

At times, the official MNR press made exaggerated claims about the strength of the armed forces backing the Revolution. The MNR journalist Julián Cayo, for example, wrote in 1959 that the forces of the National Revolution constituted 95 percent of the Bolivian people, made up of workers, campesinos and middle class--all oriented by the doctrine of the MNR. Cayo described the miners' militias as the most revolutionary and most mobile, since they could be put into action in any part of the country. Also, he noted, they had combat experience that would enable them to fight under any conditions.

Next in terms of effectiveness came the revolutionary classes of the cities, which had four components: the zonal commands of the MNR, the armed militias, the workers' unions and special forces of control. These were the forces that made possible the successful insurrection of April 1952. They specialized their activities later as an armed vanguard of the classes they represented, and they could be used to back up the armed forces. They could act rapidly, and their principal strategy was the revolutionary offensive, which had routed the frequent attempts at counter-revolution.

Third came the campesinos, said to represent 80 percent of the Bolivian population. Their focal point was Ucureña, cradle of the agrarian union movement in the Cochabamba valley, and the campesino "regiments" distributed throughout the country. The campesinos from Ucureña formed a mobile force of national action while the other campesino "regiments" carried out local missions. Noting the chilling effect of the campesino militias, Cayo wrote, "Their importance is so great that it is almost not necessary for them to realize operations on a grand scale." The "army" of Ucureña, the organized forces of the cities, and the proletarian miner forces acted separately, Cayo pointed out, but if necessary they could act in coordination. "Nevertheless," Cayo concluded, "it seems that it is not necessary to display so much force against subversive enemies, whose qualitative force is deficient and whose quantitative power is insignificant." When would Bolivia cease to be an armed camp? "Only the disappearance of the enemy forces can determine the disappearance of the combative organization of the vanguard of the National Revolution." [93]

Within the regularly constituted armed forces, the MNR thought it could count on the allegiance of the Carabineros, a national police force similar to those created in other Latin American countries—especially Chile—as a counter-balance to the army. Moreover, when the Bolivian Carabineros under General Antonio Seleme went over to the MNR insurgents in April 1952, the fate of the oligarchy was sealed. [94]

La Nación in 1960 included in its series of "Government Programs of the MNR" an installment which gave the history of the Carabineros. Beginning as a municipal body under Sucre, they were placed under departmental prefects after the first half of the Nineteenth Century and finally became a national organization in 1910 under the direction of the president and the minister of government. They were known as Security Police until after the Chaco War, when they were reorganized under an Italian training mission into the national Corps of Police and Carabineros. A National Academy of Carabineros was founded for their training, and in 1960 Paz Estenssoro proposed creating a Higher School of Carabineros to provide technical and sociological training similar to that provided for the new army. [95]

   In Bolivia the formation of the Carabineros did not serve
as a counter-balance to the regular military, however. Until
1952 they had always acted in concert with the army, as at the
Catavi mine massacre in 1942. The Carabineros, as a national
police force, also were implacable enemies of the campesinos.
La Nación recalled in 1955 how the old Carabineros had been in
the service of the oligarchy, and as defenders of the status
quo it was part of their job to impede the entrance of campesinos into the cities; frequently the country people were arrested and made to perform "the most vile tasks" in a cruel effort
to stem the migration from countryside to city. [96] An editorial in La Nación in 1955, upon the graduation of forty new
officers, declared that the Bolivian Carabinero "is now no
longer the servile uniformed man, now no longer the execut-
ioner of his own brothers." [97] Again, on the Day of the
Police and Carabineros the same year, the newspaper stated:
"We reiterate the concept that the Carabineros have ceased to
be the repressive elements of the ideals of the people. In their
[future] evolution, the Carabineros will be a solid pillar in the
structuring of a new Bolivia, serving with efficient protection
all the social strata of the people, helping the child, the needy,
the defenseless woman, the old and the weak. The profound
revolutionary sentiment of the Carabineros of Bolivia is the
magnificent foundation upon which will be built all these advantages for the Bolivian people." The newspaper also noted that
two fundos (haciendas) had been given to the Carabineros to
provide both for their self-sufficiency and for the building of a
School of Carabineros. [98]

   The creation of a new image for the Carabineros was not
an easy task for the MNR press because it meant constantly
repeating the same theme--as for the reconstituted army
itself--that the national police force was no longer a predatory
unit used to put down labor strikes and civil protest. The
Carabineros themselves realized the need for reorganization,
however, so the official press could also report the speeches of
its commanders. Lt. Col. Víctor Ramírez Bedregal, for example, proved to be a good propagandist himself when he declared
in 1955: "The olive green uniform will no longer be stained
with the blood of the people, because we the Carabineros are
the people armed, disposed to defend the Revolution to the
ultimate sacrifice and to the last breath." Programs of civic
action would be part of the regimen of the national police
force, as well as that of the army, he continued: "The Corps
of Carabineros will be an institution of peace, but always
disposed to maintain the internal peace of the Republic. For
this [purpose] its greatest present preoccupation is that of
giving technical training to its squadrons and amplifying the

professional knowledge of its members to convert itself into an organism capable of cooperating with greater effect in the plans of industrial diversification begun by the Government of the MNR." [99]

General Cuadros Quiroga spoke in a similar vein upon the graduation of a new group of Carabinero officers in 1957: "...the National Corps of Carabineros and Police, free from all the obstacles which impeded its resurgence, has entered a stage of total transformation, leaving behind the antiquated mold which characterized it, in order to convert itself into an institution of true social protection, such as that pointed out in the Organic Law of Police." [100]

The rhetoric of Carabinero officials speaking at official functions and the propaganda of La Nación seemed to nourish and fortify each other. In 1956 the official MNR newspaper commented editorially on the anniversary of the National Corps of Carabineros, recalling a machine gun attack upon unarmed Carabineros in Cochabamba on November 9, 1954. After 1952, La Nación asserted, "the defenders of order and public security have seen to it that the country ceases to fear them and identifies them with the function for which they are destined: the defense of social peace." [101] "Social peace," of course, was peace against the almost continuous attempts made upon the MNR by the FSB; in the days of the oligarchy, the phrase would have meant peace from labor strikes.

One of the ways in which the MNR oriented itself in regard to its new military policy was to compare events in Bolivia to those elsewhere in the hemisphere. When Juan Domingo Perón fell on September 19, 1955, La Nación did not comment editorially until September 24, when its tone was unusually hostile toward Argentina where MNR leaders had obtained exile during the sexenio until they were temporarily expelled after the unsuccessful attack upon Villazón from Argentine soil in 1949. Paz Estenssoro had been an ardent admirer of peronismo, and he subsequently had to deny that Perón helped to finance the MNR revolt of 1952. Upon the fall of the flambuoyant Argentine leader, however, La Nación declared that the coalition of labor--the Confederación General de Trabajadores of Argentina--with the military had contained the seeds of its own destruction. In another commentary of September 28, "Lessons of reality," the MNR newspaper emphasized that the Bolivian National Revolution came to power in April 1952 against the army, not with its support--as did Perón with the Grupo de Oficiales Unidos in Argentina. "The Army which Bolivia is building today," La Nación continued, "is the Army of work and workers; the regrettable distinctions of caste have been stripped from validity in its files." In other words, the newspaper continued, "if the Army brought Perón to power, the Army, with the same logic, has shown him the way to exile. [Such are] military logic and tactics." [102]

Comparison with another neighbor to the South was made in 1958 when Germán Quiroga Galdo, speaking in the Chamber of Deputies, asked why there had been no militarism in Chile before that time. The tensions of civil and military conflict there had been resolved early, he noted, between Bernardo O'Higgins--representing the military tradition--and Diego Portales, representing aristocratic civilismo. "Thus, in Chile there appeared first the rivalry between civilismo and militarismo, that which subsequently became general in all of the Continent as a result of the wars for independence, an event which left without stable occupation an increased number of audacious military chiefs." Quiroga believed that continued intervention by the military in civil affairs had been spared Chile partly because of the racial and lingual unity there. At the time of independence, he pointed out, there were less than 10 percent of Araucanian Indians in a population of one million. "On the other hand," he continued, "in the other countries--principally in Bolivia and Peru--the process of biological democratization operated with the tonic of a strong wind from the sea.... [In Bolivia] contrary to what happened in Chile, the military man neglected his profession and was converted into a politician." Since then the destinies of the two countries were intertwined until the culmination of the War of the Pacific. "While in the neighboring country, civil spirit gained dominance over political power, in Bolivia the influence of the military and demagogues was accentuated to the point that, however inorganic and incipient [they were]., nothing or very little could be done to preserve the vital interests of the country," he concluded. [103]

Closer in time to the Bolivian experience was the Cuban Revolution, which aroused cautious enthusiasm in the MNR press. On one point, however, writers noted that the two revolutions crossed paths by defeating the old military. As Jean Tropsius wrote in La Nación in 1959, the greatest triumph of the Cuban Revolution was the success of a people in arms against the regular army. "Unfortunately," he continued, "the countries of America have not achieved the grade of moral stature that permits the existence of regular [armed] forces without these constituting a threat for civil liberties.... In America presidents are manufactured in the barracks, and it was the generals who were called to the first magistrature, almost as a consequence of the exercise of arms." In the fighting of April 1952, he added, the Bolivian people won "not so much by the vote of arms, but because the arms that the regular Army carried were turned away before the horror that

324

implied using them against men, women and children who possessed the right... The armed people surrendered before the people in arms." The army should aid the people, Tropsius stressed, "at least through its neutrality." He proclaimed, "There is not a beast that does not tremble upon killing his brother or father. And that is what happens when line troops face a mass of citizens [with the resulting] massacre." He concluded that guerrilla tactics, "the oldest form of war strategies known to man," had been used with telling effect in Cuba where "the Government of Batista, with all its power, never was able to contain the skirmishes..." [104]

The Bolivian view of the Cuban Revolution again presented itself when foreign journalists came to observe the 1960 elections. Several interviewed Augusto Céspedes on the radio, including Domingo Aroza and Hipólito Molinari of Radio Rivadavia of Buenos Aires and an unidentified reporter for Verde Olivo of Havana, the official organ of the Cuban revolutionary army. One of the prominent questions asked was whether the worker and campesino militias were still the "vigilant symbol" protecting the Bolivian National Revolution. Céspedes responded: "The people armed is the sign of every great revolution. Upon destroying the oppressor's [military] apparatus, one must necessarily arm the people to defend their conquests. This system, imposed by events, does not impede the education of a regular Army to identify itself totally with the Revolution, which is also the Nation." [105]

The reconstruction of the traditional army fell to the lot of Hernán Siles Zuazo (1956-1960), with massive infusions of United States military aid, considering the small size of the Bolivian military. [106] Ironically, Siles derided the old army in the first speech of his candidacy in 1956, declaring "the Byzantine discussions of doctors, periodical massacres in the mines and cities, and campaigns of extermination of the Indians in the countryside [to perpetuate] the most unmerciful exploitation of the Bolivian people, were the typical form of the pretentious semicolonial culture." [107] But when the transfer of presidential power took place on August 7, 1956, Paz Estenssoro in his message to Congress did not mention the armed forces. Siles, on the other hand, as his speech was summarized in La Nación, stated that "it is imperative to watch over [the army's] respectability so that it may fulfill its specific function in defense of the national sovereignty, always with performance of its productive activities." [108]

Siles was a more conservative member of the MNR coalition in economic matters, pushing through the stabilization plan of 1957 at a cost of great erosion of his personal popularity, but he had fought in the streets of La Paz against the old army in

April 1952. Why then did he consent to rebuilding this powerful and unpredictable force? His defenders say the process was underway before he became president. They point out that expenditures for the armed forces climbed to second place in the national budget for 1956, with only education receiving more, and this was carried out during the seven final months of Paz Estenssoro's presidency. [109] The recovery of the armed forces' position was real in the psychological sense, as well. Chief of Staff Armando Fortún Sanjinés stated in a Christmas message to the people and the army at the close of 1956, "We are able to say at the end of this year that we have gotten back our fueros [rights], regaining government and popular confidence, once again assuming our place as tutelary Institution of the Country and its interests." [110] Finally, on September 26, 1957, President Siles and his cabinet reorganized the armed forces on expanded lines with greater control of the institution's fate in the hands of the high-ranking military officers. [111]

Again, why did Siles reactivate the Frankenstein's monster of the Bolivian National Revolution? Paz Estenssoro, looking back from the vantage point of 1973, regarded the reconstruction of the regular army as the greatest error of the Revolution. It was begun by Siles because of his confrontation with Juan Lechín, the popular labor leader, during the stabilization crisis of 1957 and later as Lechín's ambitions grew to include the presidency in 1960. Lechín had most of the sindicatos behind him; Siles had only a very small minority of the labor movement under the leadership of Juan Sanjinés Ovando, so the MNR president increased the army. Ironically, the "new" army thus became the personalist instrument in the hands of the MNR president just as it had been manipulated by the oligarchical presidents before 1952. When Paz Estenssoro returned to the presidency in 1960, with Lechín as his vice-president, he found a "completely new" situation compared to 1956. Two powerful officers, Alfredo Ovando Candia and René Barrientos Ortuño headed the army and air force, respectively. These were the men who were to lead the golpe against Paz Estenssoro soon after he began his third term in 1964. To complicate matters further, there were increased Falange uprisings against the MNR government after 1960--in Santa Cruz and later Camiri--and a strengthened army was necessary to defend the government. But as Paz Estenssoro recalled in 1973, he did not know if there was a genuine identification of the armed forces with the revolutionary movement, and the error made by the MNR lay in not defining the depths of this commitment. [112]

This error was really a failure in propaganda because the best type of shaping public opinion is that which allows one to

BOLIVIA RATIFICO A VICTOR PAZ

Esta madrugada: 608.206 votos el MNR

LA NACION

DIARIO DE LA MAÑANA

EL PUEBLO SE HA PRONUNCIADO POR EL RESPETO A LA CONSTITUCION

René Barrientos Ortuño votó en Colegio Nacional Ayacucho

La Nación, official spokesman for the MNR during its twelve years in power, proclaims on June 1, 1964 the election of Víctor Paz Estenssoro to his third term in the presidency. Five months later he was overthrown by his vice-president, Air Force General René Barrientos Ortuño (lower right).

fathom what the opposition is thinking. The MNR official press was more concerned about feedback from another source, however--the opposition press in La Paz. This was readily available and had to be refuted, if possible, because it nurtured the seeds of rebellion in the armed forces, but La Nación did not ascertain what those military feelings and aspirations were. The exchange with the opposition press on the military question was almost a continuous process during the twelve years the MNR was in power. [113] One has only to read the record of this exchange to know that freedom of the press, despite the protestations of the Inter-American press Association, did exist in Bolivia during these years--and dangerously so. As La Nación commented in 1958, the reorganization of the army and police had been discussed in the opposition press so frequently that golpistas believed they did not have to worry about the efficacy of the traditional military. [114] This constant harping on the theme by the reactionary press that Bolivia's "cherished" institution of a strong military was being destroyed was summed up in 1960 when La Nación charged that the remnants of the Rosca were hoping--and had always done so--that the army could be used to exploit the divisions within the MNR. The party's official newspaper commented in exasperation, "The question of the army is agitated by the tendentious and felonious rosquera press on as many occasions as is possible." [115] On another occasion, La Nación printed an article under the headline, "The rosquera press continues intriguing in the command of the armed forces." More significantly, the subhead read, "Only revolutionaries have the right to talk of the Armed Forces." [116]

The role of the armed forces in the new revolutionary state was the focal point of the propaganda battle during the twelve years that the MNR held power. Nationalization of the tin mines was an emotional propaganda issue that could be readily exploited; it had been in the national consciousness ever since the 1920s, and the MNR after the party's formation in 1941 used its patriotic appeal to ride to power. Once the mines were nationalized, however, the usefulness of the issue had expired; the official press after 1952 made little effort to explain why the nationalization had not brought the promises envisioned. Agrarian reform was quite different; it was a fait accompli that kept outstripping the efforts of MNR planners to keep up with it. It needed little justification because it was innately just and overdue; most of the large landowners had left the country, and city dwellers had other interests. The Indians, most of whom could not read anyway, did not need to be told that the agrarian reform was in their best interests.

But the issue of military reform sliced across all of the other issues and became the rock upon which the MNR ship of state foundered. It was a difficult issue and one which received more attention than any other. Nevertheless, it was not handled well, failing to convince even the MNR leaders of the danger of a revived military establishment. However, no amount of propaganda probably could have overcome the prerogatives of a military caste developed over one hundred years unless the armed forces were abolished altogether, and this was impossible. By about 1960, the militias--which had once been touted as the answer to Bolivia's endemic militarism--had become hardly more than a footnote to the history of the Bolivian National Revolution. The workers' militias were defending only their own interests, and the campesino militias, according to La Nación, had degenerated into caciquismo, the ancient manipulation of men by an Indian chief, perverting in the case of the militias a social phenomenon into mere personal utilization. [117]

Most ironically, the Bolivian military during the MNR years became a pawn in the hands of the MNR leaders as surely as it had served the oligarchical presidents before 1952. On the left of the party spectrum, Lechín and his labor followers wanted a weak military so there would never again be massacres of workers in Bolivia, and their economic gains would not be taken from them. Siles and the right wing of the MNR wanted to rebuild the armed forces along modern lines to control labor and the campesinos. From time to time, La Nación reported and attempted to deny renewed clashes between the army and the campesinos, as in 1960. [118] There were also periodic attempted coups de'etat by the FSB, so frequent that they had all the novelty of the common cold. Paz Estenssoro, whose terms in office bridged the weakening of the army first and then its continued reconstruction with United States aid and training missions, was caught in the middle and wavered on the issue, which kept the newspapers and the government stirred up. The military itself, however, listened to the rhythm of a deeper propaganda than the daily newspaper page. Although some wrote brief pieces for the La Paz press, and their speeches were extensively reported, they soon lapsed back into the rhetoric and beliefs that had been instilled in them long before 1952. The MNR drove the military back to the barracks for twelve years, a remarkable achievement in itself, but unfortunately officers like Barrientos and Ovando simply watched and waited. Meanwhile, the MNR press sought justification elsewhere, attempting to orient the Revolution in the broader currents of world history.

Chapter 11

SHOCK OF RECOGNITION:

THE BOLIVIAN PRESS VIEWS

THE MEXICAN AND CUBAN REVOLUTIONS

The case of Mexico is an example for all of America.

--La Calle, Dec. 18, 1936

The example of Bolivia has reverberated in the Antilles with the accent of Cuba's own and definitive affirmation.

--La Nación, Jan. 4, 1959

These quotations from the Bolivian newspapers, La Calle, an opposition newspaper which served as spearhead of the Movimimento Nacionalista Revolucionario before the party was formally organized in 1941, and La Nación, the official spokesman for the MNR during the twelve years the party held power (1952-1964), reveal that the Bolivian National Revolution did not occur in a vacuum. On the contrary, the torch was passed from Mexico, whose social and economic revolution got underway in 1910, to Bolivia who in turn passed it on to revolutionary Cuba in 1959. This is not to say that any kind of "domino" effect was in play during these first three great socioeconomic revolutions in Latin American history, but rather that there were intellectual spillovers, especially in the popular press. Nations know themselves better by feedback from world opinion, and by measuring their accomplishments against those of other countries. Bolivia sought her own revolutionary moorings by examining and commenting upon the social changes which became profound in Mexico after 1934 and launched in Cuba after 1959--and those thwarted in Guatemala in 1954. [1]

Time and distance muted the impact of the Mexican Revolution upon Bolivia, but the press played an important role in each movement and there were occasional contacts between the two nations before 1952. [2] Next to Europe, Mexico was the most fashionable place for Bolivian exiles to seek refuge, and several shared in print their observations of the Mexican Revolution with their fellow countrymen. The changes being wrought in the Mexico of Lázaro Cárdenas (1934-1940) made an especially heady brew for Bolivian writers still chafing from the bitter experience of the Chaco War (1932-1935). Also as Bolivians coming from the most Amerindian country in the world, they felt a racial affinity with the mestizo and Indian republic of the north. Independent socialist Tristán Marof published México de frente y perfil (Mexico in Front and Profile) in 1934, but the Bolivian writer who brought the Mexican revolutionary experience home most poignantly was Roberto Hinojosa, the unpredictable MNR journalist later murdered in the overthrow of the reform Bolivian regime of Major Gualberto Villarroel (1943-1946).

Denied exile in Peru after the abortive uprising which he led at the town of Villazón on the Argentine border in 1930, Hinojosa went on to Mexico where he published at least seven books and pamphlets dealing with the Mexican Revolution. In El Tabasco que yo he visto (The Tabasco Which I Have Seen) published in 1935, he declared, "Mexico... is for us, the South Americans, the intellectual and social meridian that orients our anxieties and nourishes our sacrifices." [3] Hinojosa admired the generosity of the Mexican Revolution in allowing its detractors full freedom of the press, a freedom which he considered was converted into counter-revolutionary license. [4] In the same work cited above, issued by the Mexican Office of Publications and Propaganda, the Bolivian writer summed up his creed:

What did I pursue with the revolution of Villazón...? The same things that the revolutionaries of Mexico pursue: to divide the land and give it totally to those who work it; to eliminate the caverns of fanaticism which are called churches; to socialize education; to unionize the intellectual and manual workers; to close the prostitute presses and send to jail the journalists who serve Capitalism and the Vatican. [5]

Soon after this work appeared, however, the extreme socialist government of Tomás Garrido Canabál in the state of Tabasco was intervened by the federal government, which marked the beginning of Hinojosa's disillusionment with the Mexican Revolution. After the Second Congress of Socialist Students of Mexico met in Uruapán in 1935, Hinojosa published Justicia social en México (Social Justice in Mexico) in which for the first time he criticized the Revolution. He called it an intuitive revolution which lacked the discipline of scientific socialism; in fact, it had a "reformist character" because the country had no great masses of industrial workers to fit the Marxist pattern of class struggle, and from this stemmed "the vacillating and hybrid ideology of the Constitution of 1917." [6] Finally, in his La saeta rota (The Broken Arrow) of 1940, Hinojosa rejected completely the Mexican Revolution, finding it neither "integral nor permanent, neither in time nor space" because it was not part of the "Universal revolutionary movement." [7]

Hinojosa's ideas, however unformed or chaotic, filtered down to some Bolivian readers, but it was the newspaper La Calle which presented day to day the most complete and detailed picture of the Mexican Revolution available to Bolivians. [8] Newspapers have the advantage of frequent publication and relatively wide circulation: La Calle reached many more readers than the limited-circulation pamphlets and books of Hinojosa. Thus, the La Paz newspaper found much to admire in revolutionary Mexico--although similar reforms seemed far on the horizon for backward Bolivia--especially in the agrarian reform program of Cárdenas, who redistributed more land than all of the preceding revolutionary Mexican presidents combined. Under the leadership of Cárdenas, relations between the two countries improved. Bolivia raised its diplomatic mission in Mexico to the level of an embassy in January 1939, and in April of that year Mexico sent two commissions of experts on irrigation to Bolivia. [9]

Every year on September 16, the anniversary of Mexican national independence, La Calle commented editorially on the grand experiment to the north. In 1938, for example, in an editorial headlined, "México, country of the effective revolution," La Calle proclaimed: "Because the Mexicans have proceeded with sincerity and valor, without negating their principles and without being intimidated by the threats of capital, Mexico now presents itself as the most authentic American nationality." [10] Again, in 1940, La Calle commented, "Mexico is for Bolivians a magnificent historical and ethnic paradigm in which Bolivian problems seem identical, although on an enlarged scale." [11] At the same time, the newspaper INTI, edited by Hernán Siles, who later was to become MNR president (1956-1960), editorialized that the Mexican Revolution constituted--while World War II raged in Europe--a "history lesson for the Indo-Mestizo people of this continent" in contrast to the "advance of the decadent and convulsive Western Culture." [12]

After the reform-minded Villarroel regime gained power in Bolivia in 1943, friendly overtures to Mexico became more pronounced. In 1944, for example, the great cholo educator Franz Tamayo as president of the Bolivian Convention rendered homage to Mexico on September 16. On the same occasion, MNR deputy Hernán Siles declared, "The Mexican revolution preceded the Russian revolution, and had to suffer also, as we did, the Calvary of non-recognition by the [obstruction and] incomprehension of the Mexican rosca." The Bolivian minister of foreign relations added, "Today... we initiate our revolution in equal or similar circumstances of collective social desire. Mexico is a symbol, as many other countries [such] as Russia and France which sacrificed a portion of their lives to see resolved their economic, political and social problems." [13]

In the spring of 1945, when the world was preparing for peace, Chancellor Gustavo Chacón and Víctor Paz Estenssoro returned elated to Bolivia from the hemispheric conference at Chapultepec in Mexico City. The latter declared, "The Bolivian revolution [of Villarroel] can count on continental comprehension." He added, "Mexico knows now that Bolivia also finds itself engaged in the fight for its economic liberation and the well-being of its peoples." Paz Estenssoro added:

Mexico is a nation that stimulates whoever visits her. For us she is, moreover, a living experience that will save us from many errors. I am very glad to have had the opportunity of visiting that country that is gathering the fruits of its own great national revolution and that is generously interested in the future of the other American nations. [14]

Bolivian identity with the Mexican revolutionary experience did not lessen as the days of the Villarroel reform interlude dwindled. On September 16, 1945, La Calle editorialized, "We salute Mexico, the great republic of indomitable courage that made possible the first triumph of the people against misery and pain." [15] Two days later, Alberto Mendoza López as president of the Convention rendered this homage: "Mexico is a revolutionary example for all of the Latin American peoples, a mestizo people who rise in insurgence on the continent." [16]

Bolivia also had its effect upon its neighbor to the north. At the International Conference of Labor held in Mexico City in May 1946, Bolivian delegate César Toranzos pushed through adoption of the fuero sindical or labor rights as codified in the Bolivian Constitution of 1945. The motion was unanimously approved by the labor delegates of twenty-one nations after the employers had rejected it in commission session. The renowned Mexican labor leader Vicente Lombardo Toledano spoke in favor of the motion, and another Mexican delegate declared, "The Bolivian Revolution is at the vanguard of Latin American democracy." [17]

By mid-century the Mexican Revolution had congealed,

however, swerving sharply to the industrial right with the administration of Avila Camacho beginning in 1940. Nevertheless, the mystique of the Mexican Revolution continued to exert its power as the second social and economic revolution in Latin American history got underway in Bolivia in 1952. Vicente Lombardo Toledano was dispatched as the official Mexican representative to the ceremony nationalizing the major tin mines at Catavi in 1952, and Mexican land redistribution expert Edmundo Flores helped in the Bolivian agrarian reform program.

There were also a few other cultural contacts. Revolutionary Bolivia did not experience the renaissance in art which exploded in Mexico after 1910, but the Mexican School of Modern Painting in 1958 did exhibit the work of Miguel Alandia Pantoja, whose revolutionary mural covered one side of the former La Razón building, later converted into the ministry of mines and petroleum. Once a miner who had fought in the Chaco, Alandia Pantoja was forty-three years old at the time of the Mexican exhibit of his work. In the forefront of the Bolivian labor movement, he had founded the first Central Obrera Boliviana union in the tin mines. Art critic Miguel Duhal Krauss, writing for Mañana of Mexico City, compared his work favorably to that of the great Mexican muralist, José Clemente Orozco. [18]

When La Nación took over the Bolivian propaganda effort after 1952, eulogies for the Mexican Revolution increased in tempo. Typical was an editorial of September 16, 1958, which stressed--not altogether accurately--the similar Indian racial compositions of both countries. Referring to "the great Aztec nation" which was the scene of the first Latin American social revolution, the editorial glowed in its praise of the Mexican Revolution:

> [Mexico is] the paradigmatic case of what our peoples are capable of making in all of the fields of life when they believe in their destiny and when they base their history on their own people. Mexico is, in effect, what can be called a typical mixture of the American. A mestizo country watered with the belligerent and insurgent blood of the revolutionaries destined to expel...the economy of the foreigner, Mexico is the closest case to Bolivia in the battle without quarter which we are fighting. [19]

The editorial emphasized that Mexicans had achieved an indigenous expression of revolutionary change "which gave back to the country its own characteristics and its own voice, rather than introducing unsuitable foreign ideologies." The editorial cited the resurgence of Mexican painting and the literary work of Mariano Azuela and Martín Luis Guzmán, "but the true actor and hero of the American feat which is bearing fruit in Aztec soil is the people of Mexico, whose resolution, whose definitive sense of the American constitute an unconfused bulwark of the American culture, in the lively reply of native forces to the reiterated economic and cultural incursion of the foreigner." The editorial conceded that Mexico is "a difficult land, as our own..." but added, "Perhaps for this in itself, more than any other reason whatsoever, it behooves us to remember this date [September 16] as if it were our own." [20]

Bolivia also derived sustenance from the very age of the Mexican Revolution--the fact that it had survived for almost half a century. Fearful of losing their precarious grip on power, MNR leaders pushed through far-reaching changes in Bolivia swiftly. Whereas Mexico did not dare to nationalize United States oil holdings until 1938--more than a quarter of a century after the Mexican Revolution had begun--Bolivia moved within months to nationalize the internationally owned Big Three tin interests. Whereas Mexico did not achieve massive land reform until the administration of Lázaro Cárdenas (1934-1940), Bolivia redistributed one-third of her agricultural lands to peasants within twelve years. Despite such bone-wrenching changes in Bolivian society, however, critics of the MNR left-- dominated by Juan Lechín and his tin miners--complained that the Revolution was moving too slowly. La Nación replied in 1959:

> If all this process [of the Bolivian Revolution] has still not culminated in the institutional stage, the fact is that one cannot demand more from time than it permits. The clearest example we have before us is Mexico, where the Revolution has become institution- alized only after decades. [21]

Bolivia, through its official voice of La Nación, did not hesitate to side with Mexico in any criticism of the United States. After the visit of Mexican President Adolfo López Mateos (1958-1964) to Washington, D.C., in 1959, the Bolivian newspaper quoted him as saying, "For Mexico and for all of Latin America the major problem is that of relations with the United States, but for Mexico that problem is less each time." La Nación added that the problem was cultural as well as eco- nomic, stating, "Culturally, contrary to what the formal propa- ganda of Pan-Americanism tries to impose, it is certain that there is not one America but two and that this division should not result in an opposition, as has happened in most events, but in a friendship which respects the fact of the difference." [22]

López Mateos was especially regarded by Bolivia for his efforts to create a bloc of Latin American nations of producers of raw materials. When he announced in early 1960 that he would visit Bolivia--along with Argentina, Brazil, Chile, Peru and Venezuela--the MNR and its organ La Nación rejoiced. An article by Juan José Río was headlined, "Adolfo López Mateos will bring the voice and experience of the Mexican Revolution," and once again the newspaper began printing articles on Mexican agrarian reform. [23] Bolivia--desiring to create some distance between herself and the United States, to overcome the massive infusion of American aid--lauded the Mexican president's efforts to create a common market of raw material producers. And once again La Nación denounced the inter-American system dominated by the United States: "Pan-Americanism, or what has been understood by it, refers above all to a kind of inclusion of the Latin American destiny and conduct in those of the United States, an imperial power, distant and distinct from us although coinciding in certain world democratic constants." [24]

Preparations for the arrival of López Mateos caused great excitement in Bolivia. Armando Arce, former editor of La Calle and ambassador to Mexico, was called back to brief his superiors before the arrival of the Mexican presidential party. Arce came to La Paz on January 22, 1960, and continued on to Santiago de Chile to join the entourage of López Mateos before it arrived in Bolivia. Arce, a warm admirer of Mexico, had called the country "a model for the peoples of the world, and especially for us the Latins" soon after arriving there as ambassador in 1959. [25] On the occasion of the visit of López Mateos, the Mexican ambassador to Bolivia, Jesús Reyes Silva, gave La Nación a collection of clippings from the Mexican press which had resulted from Arce's diffusion of Bolivian revolutionary thought and actions there. [26] The MNR newspaper stated in an editorial:

> Mexico and Bolivia have two great [common] points of identity in the Revolution and in the Race.... In this secular struggle, the Mexicans are in the forefront. In no other part [of the world] has been achieved such a systematic maturity of rediscovery of the native which is at the same time construction of the American culture. This robustness... [which] now moves Mexico is the result of the Revolution which--if it cost work and tears--was also necessary for the conquest of a future that, if there is no treason or surrender, will also be that of Latin America. [27]

La Tarde, the MNR afternoon paper, also waxed enthusiastic over the state visit of López Mateos. On January 30 the newspaper put out a special issue dedicated to Mexico, with a banner headline at the bottom of the front page in bold red ink proclaiming, TWO INDIAN PEOPLES WITH A COMMON DESTINY. An editorial entitled, The symbolism of Mexico for America," cited Mexico as "the first people of Brown America [America Morena] which has managed to consummate with success its national revolution.'" The editorial continued:

> Mexico now is a great nation that not only has prestige among the nations of this continent, but also among those of the whole world. Mexico is a nation admired and respected, precisely because of its revolution.... Now Villa, Zapata and Madero are no longer the "bandits" that the reactionary press of the continent called them in the early revolutionary period. [28]

On January 31, 1960, the day before López Mateos was to arrive in La Paz, President Siles held an hour news conference with the Mexican journalists who preceded him. The Bolivian president, who had greatly decreased political oppression of the opposition during his term (1956-1960), declared, "We are a government that has nothing to hide," and he referred to the Mexican Revolution as the "older sister of our Revolution." [29]

Unforeseen events doomed the López Mateos' visit to failure, however, as the weather made it impossible for his plane to land in La Paz on February 1. To help blunt disappointment caused by the cancellation of his visit, the Mexican president broadcast a message to the Bolivian people from the Chilean coastal city of Arica. Among other things, he declared, "In Mexico and Bolivia social evolution is giving its just content to the dignity of life and to overcoming [the miseries of] human life." López Mateos spoke of the similar peoples of Mexico and Bolivia, their common fight against privilege, and their parallel revolutions, ending with his plea for a Latin American common market. [30]

La Nación also took advantage of the planned visit by the Mexican president to score once again what it considered the inequities of the Pan American system. An editorial entitled "Revolution and continental unity" noted that any Latin American union was still an incipient ideal--"with appearances of myth and with poor and limited objective criteria"--despite its early expression by Simón Bolívar. But the very fact that the ideal survived attested to its popularity, La Nación stated, concluding, "Among the revolutionary movements of the continent exists a clear agreement that...Revolution is the only road for Latin American unity." [31]

This editorial was prepared in advance, but the cancellation of López Mateos' visit aroused deep resentment in Bolivia. The official press considered the incident to be an unforgivable diplomatic slight. On February 2, La Nación stated in an editorial that the previous morning--when López Mateos was to have arrived in La Paz--began cloudy but soon cleared up. Information from Panagra Airlines showed "with certain bitter evidence" that the weather was nothing but a pretext "for an inexplicable disposition not to come." The editorial continued, "At eleven, a splendid sun dried up the humidity of the previous days. But the spirit of the people who had awaited the President of Mexico was not so clear nor so smiling...." La Nación, despite its superlatives for Mexico in previous issues, now declared that the friendly feelings of Bolivia for Mexico at such a distance were more historical than commercial, and the flight cancellation had revealed "that the Mexican government was not as close to Bolivia as had been thought." Armando Arce was ordered to report to La Paz at once, and Juan Luis Gutiérrez Granier, the Bolivian ambassador in Lima--next stop on López Mateos' trip--proclaimed sudden illness and attended none of the programs there in homage to the Mexican president. [32] La Tarde, the MNR afternoon paper, also protested the incident in an editorial headlined "Unjustified rebuff." La Tarde stressed that the juridical equality of all states--whatever their size--referred to dignity, too, and López Mateos had offended the dignity and sovereignty of Bolivia by not coming beyond Arica. [33] Then the matter was dropped in the official Bolivian press until February 13 when La Nación charged--with a degree of paranoia--that the whole affair had been a conspiracy engineered by la Rosca in connivance with Panagra. [34]

The momentary disappointment over the cancellation of López Mateos' trip did not permanently injure relations between Bolivia and Mexico, however. The MNR press continued to uphold the Mexican Revolution as a shining example of profound social change, hoping thereby to stimulate enthusiasm for the flagging Bolivian National Revolution. [35] Mexico responded in September 1960 by sending a good-will mission of technical assistance from Petróleos Mexicanos (PEMEX) to aid the similar Bolivian state petroleum corporation, Yacimientos Petrolíferos Fiscales Bolivianos (YPFB). The gesture was greeted with editorial applause in La Nación, which used the rare device of repeating the same editorial the following day. [36] Mexican journalist Antonio Vargas MacDonald accompanied the group of PEMEX experts, and his series of articles written for Novedades was reprinted in seven installments in La Nación under the heading, "Parallelism between sister nations." [37] Finally, when the new Mexican ambassador Jesús Reyes Ruiz arrived on November 15, 1960, he offered the Bolivian people "the fruits of the experience which the Mexican people won with their revolution, provided that the government of Bolivia esteems it pertinent, in accordance with its own high national interests." He proposed to López Mateos a plan of technical cooperation between Mexico and Bolivia. [38]

If Bolivia expressed admiration for the Mexican experiment, it also voiced concern for the social revolution of Jacobo Arbenz in Guatemala, overthrown with United States aid in 1954--only two years after the Bolivian Nation Revolution had begun. The interest of Bolivia in the Guatemala debacle was far from academic, for the Andean nation feared that similar tactics might be used against her if the National Revolution went too far to the left. In 1959 La Nación reprinted an editorial comment from the New York Daily News aimed directly at Bolivia: "It seems to us that it is time for Secretary of State Christian A. Herter to have his boys set themselves to studying carefully the methods that Dulles used to save Guatemala." [39]

The tragedy of Guatemala found continuing echoes in the Bolivian official press. United States intervention through the Central Intelligence Agency in a small and underdeveloped country evoked protests motivated by self-defense. Firsthand knowledge of Guatemala was scarce in Bolivia, but La Nación reprinted an article by Juan José Arévalo, reform president of Guatemala (1945-1950), that originally appeared in the review Entre Columnas under the title, "The Caribbean, the world and nonsense." Arévalo, who preceded Arbenz in the presidency of Guatemala and who was more committed to democratic social change, traced United States intervention in his country back to Franklin Delano Roosevelt who tended to think in forces of good (Churchill, Stalin and De Gaulle) and forces of evil (Hitler, Mussolini and Franco). This was admissible in time of war, in Arévalo's view, but since then in peacetime the United States news agencies continued to take the line of the State Department which divided the world between the good West and the bad East. The news agencies "still offer this stupid division of the world, and classify ideologies with a cartographic criterion," Avévalo wrote. "A meridian that passes through Hamburg or its immediate vicinity served approximately to fix the ideological borders," he added. Arévalo rejected "the stupid pretension of resolving the afflictions of mankind by pigeon-holing the plurity of [the world's] problems into two insurmountably divided camps."

Arévalo, who had given conferences on the defense of Guatemala in Chile, Bolivia, Ecuador and Uruguay, declared that Latin America deserved a better fate than "the resignation of being miniscule nations submitted to the master of the 'Occident' which is the United States" simply because of the geographic fate of being on the same side of the Hamburg meridian. The result of Roosevelt's simplistic thinking was that the two super powers in their desire to divide up the world were trying to force all of the world into the situation of colonies, the former Guatemalan president continued.

The tragedy of the Caribbean, Arévalo maintained, was that commerce and governing had always been confused:

This is the sea and this is the country where Jacobo Arbenz dared to plan and construct a pier as property of the State where ships other than those of the United Fruit Company could arrive. This is the sea and this is the country where Jacobo Arbenz, president of the Guatemalans by the will of the Guatemalans, planned and carried out the most just and patriotic distribution of idle lands, in order to multiply the national riches, to free the enslaved peasant, to make less expensive and brighten the life of the humble people. But, ah!... Among the owners of the monstruous latifundios, occupying the better lands of the Republic, was the United Fruit Company, the only owner of docks and transport, that was not accustomed to being treated in a form so disrespectful. And Jacobo Arbenz had to pay, according to them, for the crime of having tried to make his country into a nation. [40]

The fate of Guatemala was always an ominous cloud on the horizon for Bolivia--as well as for other small or weak Latin American countries. Despite the sympathetic attitude of Dr. Milton Eisenhower and the informed diplomacy of career ambassadors in La Paz which had brought about massive United States aid to Bolivia, there were occasional outcries in Congress that the United States was supporting a Communist revolution there. One such statement by Senator L.F. Sikes in 1960 concluded that Guatemala should be "an example for the other countries of Latin America" since it had attained a "notable consolidation of anti-Communist forces" after the overthrow of Arbenz. La Nación was quick to reply forcefully to the words of Sikes:

In reality, this deals with a live and lacerating problem for the Latin Americans who saw repeated in Guatemala the calamities of simulated or armed [United States] intervention [of an earlier era], giving the lie to the official norms [the juridical equality of nations and non-intervention as reaffirmed in the Treaty of Río de Janeiro] to which the Department of State claims to be adhering.

On the contrary, La Nación continued, to act as the United States had acted in Guatemala was self-defeating for it would prepare, with certainty, "the easy broth for the demagogic prosperity of communism, for the chauvinist way, although such contradictory labor is carried out in nothing less than the name of anti-communism--fear, banner and dogma of the North Americans [who are] more preoccupied with their phobias than with the interior problems of Latin America--which is organizing popular movements thinking only in themselves and neither in communism nor in anti-communism." [41]

La Tarde also recalled the sad lesson of Guatemala where constant internecine warfare had followed the stemming of a genuine social revolution. Fedor Yunque in his column, "Our Vision of the World," noted in 1962 that free elections had been held in Guatemala in 1944 and 1950. But the Guatemalan president, Manuel Ydígoras Fuentes (1958-1963), installed in office with no election, was arguing "that he is defending the nation against 'communism,' while in reality, he is against the people against whom the counter-revolution is clearly working." [42]

Both Mexico and Guatemala offered clear-cut historical examples for the MNR press of social revolutions which either succeeded or failed, but the case of Cuba after 1959 was more confusing and tested the mettle of MNR writers who tried to keep up with the rapidly unfolding events in the Caribbean. The first reaction in La Nación to the Cuban guerrilla campaign of Fidel Castro, which got underway in December 1956, came in July 1958 after the Brazilian review Maquis had printed an article saying that Oscar Unzaga de la Vega, leader of the Falange Socialista Boliviana (FSB), and other rightwing FSB conspirators were threatening to turn Bolivia into another wartorn Cuba. Commented La Nación:

> The political position of Fidel Castro does not interest us, whatever it may be. But it is worthwhile to point out his irreducible tenacity, his personal fearlessness. He has prepared a trench for himself and from it he fights for his ideas, giving an example of manhood and courage. Unzaga, on the other hand, is a creature of propaganda. Never has he even been seen leading a street demonstration. He incites his 'white shirts;' he urges them to defy danger, but he himself, with all his beard, astutely looks after his own skin in the shadow of his mysterious hiding places. [43]

Later, Bolivia claimed to have influenced the course of the Cuban Revolution in its early days. After the July 26 Movement emerged triumphant in Havana on January 1, 1959, La

342

Nación recounted how a group of Cuban exiles in New York had turned for advice in the early 1950s to Hernán Siles, then vice-president and chief of the Bolivian delegation to the United Nations. Siles talked with the group for more than three hours, according to La Nación, which observed, "Above all, it intrigues them to know how a people without arms [the Bolivians in 1952] had managed to conquer a regular army endowed with all the means of combat." Later, these and other Cuban exiles maintained "close contact" with various directors of the MNR, La Nación asserted, who acted "apart, of course, from the function of Government, but [were] sympathizers of the popular movement in Cuba." [44]

This assertion was never confirmed nor denied by Siles or any other high-ranking MNR official, but after Siles became president in 1956, he authorized Chancellor Víctor Andrade while on a visit to the United States in late 1958 to suggest the mediation of three countries--Bolivia, Ecuador and Uruguay--to stop the civil war in Cuba and try to convince Fulgencio Batista to stop the bombardment of villages. These three small countries, Siles reasoned, could not be accused of intervention, but the rapid course of events in Cuba annulled this aspect of Andrade's mission. [45]

In the heady early days of Castro's triumph, the MNR press joined in the general rejoicing that another Latin American dictatorship had been felled. HONOR TO THE CUBAN PEOPLE! proclaimed a headline in La Nación when the news was first announced to the Bolivian people on January 4, 1959. The newspaper asserted that Batista's army "rather than being defeated by the adversary, was defeated by itself" since his 50,000 well-armed soldiers had little to fight for in a land marked by tyranny. The fall of Batista, as with so many other Latin American dictators, La Nación declared, "resulted as much as anything else from popular sentiment which one day says 'Enough,' and nothing can contain its sweeping force, which is that of reason." La Nación noted "almost an exact parallel" in Bolivia when the dictatorial military junta took over after the contested elections of 1951. This "Praetorian guard" was overthrown after only three days of fighting in April 1952 because "despite the human and material means [the oligarchical army officers had] at their command in order to resist, they were already defeated by themselves, for they were defending an unjust cause." A boxed insert announced that Bolivia would be one of the first nations to recognize the new government of the Republic of Cuba. [46]

The editorial page of this issue of La Nación of January 4, 1959, carried no fewer than ten articles on the Cuban Revolution--a mixture of analysis, advice for Castro, and pride that

Cuba had followed in Bolivia's revolutionary footsteps. At one point the newspaper made the exaggerated claim that "In America, the honor of being the pioneer of a nationalist revolution with profound popular content has fallen to the Bolivian people," an assertion which ignored the Mexican Revolution of 1910 altogether. Another commentary in the same issue corrected this, however, noting that Bolivia had experienced "the first contemporary nationalist revolution in the Continent." [47]

On this occasion of the advent of the Cuban Revolution, La Nación examined the trajectory of Bolivia's own revolution after almost seven years in power and drew cautionary lessons for Cuba derived from other Latin American social movements. Acción Democrática during its first period of government in Venezuela between 1945 and 1948, and the Alianza Popular Revolucionaria Americana when it shared power in Peru during the same period both failed because they had not destroyed the feudal structures of their countries left over from the colonial inheritance, according to La Nación. "Power," the newspaper continued, "is purely formal and precarious without this objective, and the oligarchy, conserving its economic power, can oust them [reform or revolutionary movements]," which is what happened in both Venezuela and Peru. "The example of Bolivia can serve once again," commented La Nación, referring to the overthrow of the coalition MNR-Villarroel government in 1946, since "Our experience is instructive in that the oligarchy is like an octopus with a thousand heads that lives latently in permanent conspiracy." [48]

Drawing a more recent lesson from Bolivian history, the decision to maintain the armed miner and campesino militias to offset the power of the reduced army after the victory of 1952, La Nación warned:

The civil guerrilla fighters of Fidel Castro, conquerors of a powerful reactionary army, will have to be maintained for a long time if Castro does not want to frustrate his movement. They are the only forces in which he can have confidence, while he consolidates the structure of a true revolutionary army.... A revolution takes time to consolidate itself... [and until then] the militias are by themselves an institution imposed by the necessities of the Revolution.

The newspaper also recalled that the government of Rómulo Gallegos was overthrown in Venezuela in 1948 "as a consequence of not having changed the army of [Juan Vicente] Gómez [who held power from 1908 to 1935] for a popular armed force." [49]

There were, of course, comparisons that could not be made

344

between insular Cuba at the crossroads of the Caribbean and inland Bolivia isolated in the Andean knot of the South American heartland. Moreover, each country had a different racial composition: Cuba enjoyed a more homogeneous population, white with a considerable admixture of Negro and slight Indian elements, while Bolivia was a society sharply demarcated between its minority white and majority Indian population, with the aspiring mixed class in between. La Nación pointed out another major contrast: "Naturally, the economy of Cuba cannot be compared to that of Bolivia. That country [Cuba] of eight million inhabitants has revenues that double, for example, those of Argentina. Its sugar provides for more than 50 percent of the free world's consumption. [In Cuba] there are resources with which to construct progress." [50] In making this last comment, La Nación was answering the famous complaint voiced by the Bolivian middle class that all their revolution had accomplished was to socialize poverty, since Bolivia before the revolution was poorer than any other Latin American country except Haiti. [51]

The decade of the 1950s would be known as that as "cudgelling the dictators," La Nación exulted, as a common desire for national liberation swept Latin America. Bolivia led in the assault on authoritarian rule with its successful revolution of 1952, followed by the overthrows of Gustavo Rojas Pinilla of Colombia in 1957, Marcos Pérez Jiménez of Venezuela in 1958, and then Fulgencio Batista of Cuba in 1959. La Nación could not have foreseen the resurgence of militarism throughout the hemisphere in the 1960s nor the course of the Cuban Revolution itself, but in early January 1959 it had nothing but words of praise for the young leader of the Cuban Revolution: "Fidel Castro is a symbol of admirable struggle, resistance and tenacity because he knew how to interpret the aspirations and desires of his people. Bolivia...from its own position of struggle, salutes the dawn of freedom in Cuba and renders homage to its famous fighter." [52]

As in large segments of the world press, however, La Nación's honeymoon with Fidel Castro came to an abrupt end when the Cuban leader consented to summary executions of Batista officials after kangaroo trials in the Havana stadium. By the end of March 1959, firing squads had shot down 483 persons--by official count. On January 16, 1959, La Nación printed an article by Luis Ayala Claure eulogizing Castro's successful revolt, "The liberation of a great people," but an editor's note preceding the article stated that it had been written before the beginning of the executions "which are tarnishing the brilliance of the revolutionary victory." The MNR newspaper emphasized, "It is the desire of all America, sympathetic to the Cuban movement, that the wave of terror stop." [53] A column on January 17, "Shadows on a glorious victory," followed by several others, in similar vein, contrasted the persecutions suffered by the Cubans under Batista to those endured by the MNR during its six years out of power between 1946 and 1952. Yet, La Nación recalled, the theme of the MNR had been "Volveremos y perdonaremos" ("We shall return and we will forgive"), a motto "carried out to the letter" after 1952. The columnist conveniently forgot the political prisoners and concentration camps of the first Paz Estenssoro administration, but it was true that revenge in Bolivia did not reach the point of killing, as in Cuba. "If there are or were crimes [in Cuba]," continued the MNR writer, "let justice punish them. But let the moral hierarchy of the movement remain on high, for its stability, for its security and for the peace of our brothers, the noble people of Cuba." [54]

The campaign by La Nación against the Cuban executions was reconsidered after Castro spoke to 350 foreign journalists on January 21 and accused them of distorting the news from Cuba. In an editorial entitled, "Cuba before international opinion," La Nación stated:

> ...Fidel Castro made a grave charge to the foreign news agencies, whom he accused of spreading biased propaganda against his movement, adulterating the truth of what is now happening in Cuba. He attributed to that campaign the formation in the last few days of an international opinion suspicious and distrustful of the revolution led by him, and he asked that those agencies act with greater honesty and responsibility in the face of events unfolding there.

La Nación did not find such charges far-fetched "because in the case of Bolivia more than one time certain foreign correspondents sent dispatches embellished to the taste of the displaced [oligarchical] interests." The newspaper continued:

> The Cuban revolution [has] concluded one state of its struggle, but now begins the most difficult, in which [Cuba] will have to face the secret resistance of her adversaries, which there as here are a force to be reckoned with because they retain economic power and are not accustomed to fight on open ground. Fidel Castro asks for peace to work for the progress of his country. We hope he gets it. After six years and nine months, we ourselves still have not obtained it. His fight from the position of power will certainly be harder than from the Sierra Maestra. [55]

After La Nación sent René Zavaleta Mercado as its own

correspondent to Havana in later January 1959, a more balanced picture of the Cuban Revolution began to appear. He wrote that the Cuban government faced the hard choice of either shooting guilty Batista officials or granting them systematic impunity, thereby risking their comeback, and in the early days of the Cuban Revolution he had the insight to write that it might become "progressive imperialism" to haunt the hemisphere. [56] La Tarde, the MNR afternoon daily, also sent a correspondent to Cuba in May 1960. Under the heading, "Reporting Cuba--panorama of a revolution," Carlos Montaña Daza, assistant editor of the newspaper, filed five dispatches, preceding them with this caveat: "...the Cuban Revolution cannot be considered [only] as a political event... It has projections in the scope of the moral, because it tends to dignify the human being and to return to him the spiritual health weakened by the predominance of a minority social class that despised the human condition." [57]

On the issue of the rapid trials and executions in Havana, La Nación objected to Herbert Matthews' interpretation in the New York Times that this violence meant a real social revolution was underway in Cuba, not simply another coup d'etat with nothing more than a change of rulers at the top. It was impossible, maintained La Nación, to measure the magnitude of any social revolution merely by the degree of its violence: the Bolivian National Revolution got underway in 1952 with only about 600 casualties whereas hundreds of thousands of deaths in la violencia of Colombia after 1948 had not insured social change there. On the contrary, maintained La Nación, a social revolution could be determined only by advances in all of a country's aspects of development--political, social and economic--and therefore "we cannot assert with any certainty at this time that the Cuban revolution can be considered as such." [58]

Jorge Coimbra, comparing the immediate aftermaths of the Cuban and Bolivian revolutions, repeated the theme of the MNR's forgiveness of its former adversaries and Castro's vengeance. "[But] perhaps Castro...wants to do justice in a heated climate [of opinion] before the natural propensity of the men, who had the courage to fight against a powerful apparatus of dictatorial repression, to take pity on their own [former] executioners [which] would prevent merited punishment for the despots." Still, the writer for La Nación believed that Bolivia had chosen the right path, and he concluded, "Happily there is still time [in Cuba] to open the law books and apply their inescapable mandates." The "International Commentary" column in the same issue of La Nación, signed with the pen-name "Gryb," reminded Bolivian readers that Batista had been responsible for perhaps as many as 20,000 deaths, although the

347

writer conceded that innocent Cubans could be punished as well as the guilty by the manner in which the trials were being held. [59]

As time softened the impact of the trials, however, and as a few Bolivians traveled to Cuba bringing back firsthand impressions of a society undergoing changes for the better, the image of the Cuban Revolution improved in the official Bolivian press. For example, an interview with Adalid Balderrama, Bolivian delegate to a forum on Agrarian reform held in Havana in August 1959, was headlined in La Nación, THE CUBAN REVOLUTION IS PROFOUND AND COUNTS ON THE ADHESION OF ITS PEOPLE. Accompanying the interview was a photograph showing a vast multitude of Cubans celebrating the first July 26th of Castro in power, which La Nación claimed refuted a picture released by an unnamed Western news service that depicted only hundreds of persons at the rally. [60]

One of the devices used by the MNR press to bring a wider understanding of the Cuban Revolution to Bolivian readers was to reprint articles from prestigious publications throughout the hemisphere. Of natural interest to Bolivia was the Cuban agrarian reform, and a series on this topic was reprinted in La Nación from Bohemia of Havana in late 1959. [61] Another series on "Cuba and us," dealing with the significance of the Cuban Revolution for Uruguay--a country which had undergone evolutionary change--was reprinted in La Tarde from Marcha of Montevideo in early 1960. [62] La Nación also reprinted from Marcha a favorable article "Ideology and revolution" by Jean Paul Sartre, written after the French philosopher had visited Cuba. [63] Also of interest was a long summary of C. Wright Mills' Listen, Yankee! reviewed by K.S. Karol and reprinted from L'Express of Paris. La Nación noted that the Columbia University sociologist had been giving a series of lectures in Mexico when he decided to go to Cuba, where Castro appeared at his hotel room with a copy of The Power Elite under his arm, saying, "This was our principal guidebook in the Sierra Maestra..." [64]

In general, the MNR press tended to treat the Cuban Revolution in its early days with caution. Thus, by early 1960 such articles were beginning to appear in La Nación as that by the Bolivian writer Mario Diez de Medina, "Fidel Castro, enigma of the Caribbean: Redeemer or phony?" [65] The Bolivian press also became involved at an early stage in the debate over alleged Communist infiltration of the July 26 Movement. Immediately after José Antonio Tabares, revolutionary Cuba's first ambassador to Bolivia, had arrived in La Paz and presented his credentials in early January 1960, he held a news conference that lasted for three and a half hours and which stressed that the Cuban leaders were "thousands and thousands of kilometers away from communism." The MNR, which itself had fought off labels of being either fascist or Communist in its early years, could identify easily with the Cuban ambassador's next words, probably well-chosen for the effect: "I am sure that if our Revolution had come about in 1940, they would have called us fascists." [66] Tabares expressed his firm attachment to the revolutionary cause of the Bolivian people, which caused El Diario to declare him persona non grata for meddling in Bolivia's internal affairs. La Nación responded to El Diario's editorial with a long polemic by Federico Joffre Chávez boldly headlined, CUBA SUPPORTS THE BOLIVIAN REVOLUTION. [67] When Tabares gave a banner commemorating the July 26 Movement to the MNR youth organization of La Paz, La Nación gave extensive coverage to his speech and later reported that MNR youth delegates had been invited to attend the First Congress of Latin American Youths to be held in Havana on July 15-30, 1960. [68]

Nevertheless, there were ominous straws in the wind. In an editorial column of 1960, prophetic in view of Che Guevara's ill-advised Bolivian adventure of 1967, La Tarde called for "Revolutions without exportation." The writer of this regular column, "Our View of the World," Fedor Yunke, admonished, "...Latin American revolutions cannot be material for export, contrary to what President [Osvaldo] Dorticós [of Cuba] has clearly said. The situation of each country is such that, although revolution on the continent is a general necessity, this nevertheless must come about by its own and individual paths." [69]

As early as July 1960, La Nación expressed alarm over the apparent drift of Cuba toward Marxist-Leninist ideology. In an editorial, "Grave dilemma of the Cuban case," the newspaper warned her sister republic:

It is absolutely inadvisable to begin to mold a national insurgency in connivance with theories or forces foreign to western political characteristics. Because in such an enterprise not only does one run the risk of alienating the sympathies of countries that can have the most well-founded affinity with the revolutionary ideal, but also one decrees the suffocation of the social experiment itself.

Foreseeing an eventual confrontation between Cuba and the United States, La Nación noted with pride that Bolivia's own revolution had been national and had stimulated yanqui assistance rather than exacerbated the United States' "natural distrust." Nevertheless, the editorial noted that although the "style of struggle" had been very different in Bolivia than in Cuba, "the human objective was the same." [70] This editorial brought a quick response from José Antonio Tabares, the Cuban ambassador to Bolivia, whose statement was published in La Nación on the following day:

> As to the solidarity of the peoples of America, we want it, we demand it and we have it, but we should not forget that during the Guatemala operation the governments of Latin America, deaf to the clamor of their own peoples, folded their arms. That the voice of Chancellor Toriello found no echo in the Conference of Caracas, but rather in the popular masses. That the governments aligned themselves with [John] Foster Dulles against Guatemala. [71]

After this point, relations between Bolivia and Cuba began to deteriorate. When Castro attacked both the Mexican and Bolivian revolutions in August 1960 "as articles of North American manufacture," La Nación was indignant, stating "the historical truth is that both knew how to master the imperialist impetus" of the United States and that the Bolivian Revolution was neither "Made in U.S.A." nor "Made in U.S.S.R." [72] Additional resentment surfaced when Bolivian Communist members Federico Escóbar, a labor leader at Catavi and Catalina Mendoza, another union leader of La Paz, denounced the Bolivian Revolution while on a trip to Cuba, prompting vigorous rebuttal in the columns of La Nación. [73]

The most serious breach between the two nations occurred in December 1960 when La Nación accused "activists" in the Cuban Embassy of stirring up trouble in the Bolivian countryside. Specifically, the MNR newspaper charged that the Cubans had arranged a campesino meeting at Achacachi where they formed the Partido Agrario Nacionalista (PAN, National Agrarian Party) and published a manifesto signed with the pen-name Julián Apaza Catari, the Indian patriot who besieged La Paz in 1780 and was executed. Subsequently, the party died an embryonic death, but at the time La Nación editorialized, "Unfortunately, Bolivia already has enough native agitators for us to be able to tolerate in addition to foreign agitators." [74]

Such disagreements caused articles favorable to the Cuban Revolution to disappear from the MNR press, and little more was said of that country until the Bay of Pigs invasion of April 17, 1961. On the day of the attack, the afternoon MNR daily La Tarde rushed a unique extra edition to the streets and used the biggest headlines of its existence to herald the news: EXTRA! CUBA BURNS: THE INVASION COMMENCES. [75]

The first editorial comment in La Tarde did not appear until April 19 when a columnist observed that the creation of new resistance within and without Cuba demonstrated "how necessary and indispensable it is for a revolutionary government to return to the institutional regime of democratic elections, with the participation of the entire people through the universal and unrestricted vote, as Bolivia did in 1956." [76] The fate of Brigade 2506, trained in Guatemala and Florida by the CIA, was announced in another immense headline of April 20: K.O.: SMASHING VICTORY FOR FIDEL CASTRO. Despite the fact that Bolivia was under a state of siege, which prohibits the gathering of crowds, a huge meeting in support of Castro turned into a street riot as demonstrators stoned the buildings of El Diario and Presencia, both of which had criticized the Cuban Revolution. La Tarde also reported that the FSTMB, in the name of 58,000 Bolivian miners, sent telegrams to Castro, the United Nations, and the General Confederation of Cuban Workers protesting "the barbarous aggression of yanqui imperialism against the Cuban people." [77]

More forceful editorial comment on the Bay of Pigs appeared in La Nación, revealing once again that the morning MNR paper was more vigorous than La Tarde, its sister afternoon publication. Teddy Cordova Claure, later to be press secretary for General Juan José Torres and to suffer five bullet wounds in the overthrow of that regime in 1971, wrote the invasion commentary for La Nación. A gifted writer of fiction as well as a journalist, [78] Cordova Claure began his commentary, "Soviets supply the armament, North Americans contribute the dollars, and Cubans shed the blood." He added that no one expected the confrontation so soon, but the quick defeat of the landing force and taking 1,179 prisoners obviously indicated that Castro was backed by the popular will of the Cuban people. "At the moment it is apparent that 200,000 militiamen are much more in the right then 5,000 doubtful invaders," the writer commented. He also berated "this almost insane struggle in which the Latin Americans share a good part of the blame," for allowing Cuba to be caught between the world's two power blocs. [79]

Sympathy for the Cuban regime engendered by the abortive Bay of Pigs invasion faded in Bolivia after Castro made his famous speech of December 3, 1961, in which he declared, "I am a Marxist-Leninist, and I will be until the day I die." La Nación expressed dismay, noting that the speech had caused "profound rejoicing in certain circles, stupor and perplexity in others, and in the greater part of our American world [a sense of] deep deception." The newspaper recalled that it had been a hope shared by all to see Castro in power during the dark days of the Batista dictatorship, but "Today...we discover, through the very words of Castro himself, that behind the banners of democracy and liberty blazed, secretly and with dissimulation, the Communist flag." A column by "Tácito" severely criticized the "deaf indifference" and "blind enthusiasm" of those who continued to applaud Castro regardless of his deeds--"the sacrifice of the labor movement, the suppression of free expression, and even the persecution of his own friends, helpers and allies." [80] Finally, Huga González Rioja, editor of La Nación, offered a signed article, "Castro: Invulnerable of conquered?" in which the Bolivian journalist saw a great danger in over-reaction to events in Cuba by the United States, which in the future might view all popular movements--national democratic movements such as that of Bolivia--as potential threats to western democracy. The editor wryly concluded, "Cuba, after all, is not everything." [81]

Shock waves from the Caribbean island continued to shake Bolivian domestic politics, however, After Castro's revelation the MNR press downgraded the Cuban Revolution more sharply, but it still enjoyed wide support among Bolivian workers. When the Central Obrera Boliviana, the national labor organization, staged a massive street manifestation in La Paz in January 1962 to support Cuba, an engineer was shot and killed when an anti-Castro mob attacked the demonstrators. La Nación was aghast, headlining its commentary, "The Cuban contest should not be washed in Bolivian blood." With all the forceful language at its command, La Nación denounced the entangling of Bolivian citizens in Cuban affairs, calling this "a vacuous lack of knowledge of our own problems [and an] almost blind and suicidal desertion." Bolivia had its own peculiar national voice which would be raised at the upcoming second Punta del Este conference, the newspaper commented, adding:

> Meanwhile, to open battle on our soil and water it with blood for something that is not entirely vital for us, is nothing more than a rite of useless fanaticism, an obstinacy without any probability of accomplishing anything, because in the final analysis the Cuban dispute will be settled in its own atmosphere and not by transference. [82]

Partly to placate the pro-Cuban sentiment of her own domestic left, Bolivia attempted to heal hemispheric wounds at the Eighth Meeting of Foreign Ministers at Punta del Este in January 1962. José Fellmann Velarde, representing Bolivia, stressed non-intervention and self-determination, and he opposed punitive measures against Cuba. Nevertheless, as La Nación reported, he also pointed out that only those governments were legitimate which originated from free, mass elections as in revolutionary Bolivia. [83] "Tácito" called the conference premature, maintaining it should not have been held until concrete results had been obtained from the first conference at Punta del Este held in August 1961 at which the Alliance for Progress was approved. [84] Fears were also expressed in the MNR press that reprisals--such as not granting Alliance for Progress aid--might be taken against those nations, including Bolivia, which had not lined up with the United States against Cuba at the second Punta del Este meeting. [85]

On a tour of South America, British historian Arnold J. Toynbee said in Peru that the second Punta del Este conference by expelling Cuba from the Organization of American States had done nothing more than make a hero of Castro. To his great disappointment, Toynbee could not travel to the high altitudes of Bolivia because of a heart condition, but La Nación echoed his words:

> Castro by himself is not a great thing... The only way of curing fidelismo is the Alliance for Progress... If those Latin Americans who have hoarded up riches are ready and disposed to divide their lands and pay their taxes... Castro will have no importance; if they don't do it, Castro is important.

The newspaper considered it unfortunate that Toynbee's judgment could not be applied retroactively to the deliberations of the second Punta del Este conference, where Cuba was ostracized and possibly martyred by a majority of the Latin American republics. Bolivia--along with Argentina, Brazil, Chile, Ecuador and Mexico--refused to vote for the ouster of Cuba. "To safeguard liberty," La Nación stressed, "the condition sine qua non is to base its pedestal on the abolition of [economic] slavery and misery," not to quarantine Cuba in the futile hope its challenges would disappear. [86]

Bolivia continued to fear the backlash of the socialist experiment in the Caribbean, however. The MNR newspaper printed in full, for example, an editorial from El Diario, the Spanish-language daily of New York where Cuban exiles were exerting an influence, that the United States should not only isolate Cuba but also stop "with the uninterrupted backing of millions of dollars a month earmarked for the Communist regime of Bolivia." Castro called the Cuban exiles gusanos (worms), and La Nación, protecting Bolivia's own flanks, called them pirañas, the flesh-devouring fish of the Amazon. [87] La Nación began printing such commentarios as "The freezing of salaries in Cuba, lessons for armchair leftists," [88] but mainly, the MNR newspaper called on its readers to look more toward Bolivia's own internal problems and less toward external affairs:

In fact, Cuba is converted today into a point of friction between the two great ideological blocs that dispute world hegemony. Around [the future] of the Island is developing, in effect, one of the most dramatic, although fortunately still bloodless battles of positions, to such an electrifying point that it is beginning to influence with mutedly violent characteristics the spirit of countries as distant as our own. In groups somewhat deviated from the Party itself [the MNR] there are manifestations of that Cuban hypnotic effect, with dimensions we cannot judge less than alarming.

La Nación urged the superior councils of the MNR, charged with supervising the ideological and political control of all elements of the party, "which is needed so badly in these moments, in one single convergent trend [to deal with] the immediate goals and true urgency of our cause." [89]

The plea to maintain a calm perspective on Castro was useless, however, under the extreme tensions of the Cuban missile crisis of October 1962. Sides were sharply drawn in the confrontation between the United States and the Soviet Union that brought the world to the edge of nuclear warfare, and once again violence erupted in faraway Bolivia. Groups for and against Castro fought furiously in La Paz on October 26, with the cost of several lives and numerous wounded, which prompted La Nación to ridicule those "who pretend to decide the fate of that regime [Cuba] on our soil," in an editorial headlined, "Bloody transplant of an exterior quarrel." [90] On the following day, the newspaper again denounced "a fanaticism bordering on stupidity [which] has sought to determine the Cuban question in the streets of La Paz," producing more casualties than the recent five-day civil war in Argentina. With chagrin La Nación pointed out that in no other part of the world--neither in Havana nor in Moscow or Washington--had the problem of Soviet missiles on Cuban soil provoked violence. Only in Bolivia had actual fighting occurred. "The consequence of this collective misconduct," the newspaper warned, "is that the country gains an aura of bloody barbarity, while the world smiles to itself, including certainly Cuba, where not a single beard has been drenched in blood." [91]

On substantive issues of the United States naval blockade of Cuba and the rattling of nuclear sabers to force removal of the Soviet missiles, a column by "Tácito" approved these decisive measures against "an unquestionable risk for hemispheric security" but noted there were other threats to the Americas equally dangerous--those of disease, illiteracy and poverty. [92] The writer implied that Cuba was dealing effectively with these problems, while the United States was dragging its feet on programs promised by the Alliance for Progress.

Officially, Bolivia took an even tougher line against United States policy in the crisis. Back in the Organization of American States after having left briefly over the Lauca river dispute with Chile, Bolivia was present to abstain with Mexico and Brazil from recommending the use of armed force against Cuba. Bolivia nevertheless recognized her obligations under the Inter-American Treaty of Reciprocal Defense signed at Rio de Janeiro on September 2, 1947, and during the Cuban missile crisis La Nación printed the full text of the Rio Treaty. [93]

The major thrust of editorial comment by the MNR press on the Cuban missile crisis was that Cuba had sold her soul to the Soviet Union. "Tácito" pointed out, in a column headlined "The self-determination of peoples," that Castro had played no part at all in determining the fate of his country--a fate which was decided solely between Kennedy and Khruschev. Actually, it was Mikoyan who went over the Cuban premier's head in arriving at a settlement with the United States, but the writer concluded, "The naked and horrible truth which international politics has revealed in these last hours, should make all of America stop and think, for in the face of this truth [the absorption of Cuba into the Soviet camp], neither the boastings of [Cuba] propaganda nor demagoguery has a validity anymore." [94]

An editorial in La Nación on "The destiny of 'negotiable' peoples," made the same point even more forcefully, but the writer noted that Cuba had perhaps received something in the resolution of the crisis--an alleged pledge by the United States never again to invade the island. In fact, he added, the hypothesis had been raised that the whole Cuban Missile crisis had been engineered for only one reason--to insure the continuance of the Castro regime by establishing bargaining power through the installation of the missiles. [95]

The question of economic or cultural dependence touched a raw nerve in Bolivia, the recipient of much aid and advice from the United States. Some observers claimed that only Mexico was fortunate enough to have begun her social revolution in 1910, seven years before the Bolshevik upheaval in Russia, for the second and third such revolutions in the hemisphere had been split between the two competing world powers dominant in the 1950s--Bolivia going the way of the United States and Cuba veering toward the Soviet Union. The MNR press used the occasion of the revelation of Cuba's subordination to the Soviet Union during the missile crisis to deny that Bolivia had been equally absorbed by the United States. In two major editorials,

La Nación went to great lengths to deny this allegation. On the eve of the missile crisis, the newspaper noted the build-up of economic and military aid by the Soviet Union in Cuba and concluded:

It is... necessary to understand that we Bolivians are not losing our conscientious independence of yanqui capitalism by the simple fact of accepting... a cooperation sine qua non for solving [our] crisis which should be resolved in deeds, and positively. [96]

Again, after the missile crisis, La Nación seemed to be applying a double standard in drawing a cautionary tale from the recent occurrences in the Caribbean:

This series of events goes to prove the ability painfully but effectively demonstrated by the Bolivian Revolution [to prove] her autonomy as a movement of national liberation. Although it is evident that we act within the mechanisms of the West and receive North American cooperation, such circumstances have not cancelled either our independence or sovereignty. [97]

In one of the final comments on the Cuban missile crisis, "Tácito" reiterated the theme of Cuba's having become a pawn in a larger Cold War political chess game over which it no longer had any control:

Cuba presently constitutes a neuralgic and dangerous point [of contention] not only for the western world--in which she plays the role of a spearhead for communism--but also for the Soviet system, for [Cuba] lies at the crossroad where the two postures of Marxist-Leninist thought are debated: war or co-existence as a means to do away with the capitalist system. [98]

In retrospect, the Cuban Revolution was a painful experience for Bolivia long before Che Guevara brought the lesson home. On one hand, it felt a filial benevolence toward social change elsewhere in the hemisphere--much as Bolivia itself delighted in claiming descent from the Mexican Revolution--but on the other hand, it felt threatened by Cuba's forthright embrace of Marxist ideology. For that matter, the Cuban Revolution also became an embarrassment for Mexico when the aging ex-president Lázaro Cárdenas, surrounded by a coterie of young radicals, persisted in lauding Castro, warts and all. As events turned out, both countries, despite their reservations, did not reject the Cuban Revolution--until Bolivia broke diplomatic relations after the right-wing military seized the revolution in 1964. Mexico remained steadfast, insisting on keeping one door in the hemisphere open to Cuba when all others had been slammed shut.

Thus, both the Mexican and Cuban revolutions had more impact upon Bolivia than as mere occasions for propaganda trumpetings. Fore-shadowing the Bolivian National Revolution of 1952, La Calle heard--or thought she heard--an evocative call from the Mexican experience. Bolivia also identified later with revolutionary change in Cuba, but only in ambivalent postures. By 1959, Bolivia's dependence upon aid from the United States was deemed too essential for Bolivia to loudly proclaim direct kinship with Cuba. MNR editorial writers were torn between the desire to accept other social revolutions in the hemisphere and their own need to consolidate revolution at home. To some observers, the shedding of Bolivian blood on Bolivian soil in defense of the Cuban Revolution--in the wake of the Bay of Pigs invasion and later missile confrontation--revealed that Bolivia's own social experiment had not gone far enough or fast enough. Thus, it is not surprising that the official MNR press tried early on to claim the mantle handed down by the Mexican Revolution and later made half-hearted gestures toward passing that mantle on to Cuba.

In a sense, these maneuverings were refreshing because they meant the breakdown of the traditional isolation of Bolivia. These propaganda forays also meant that Bolivia was in the revolution market for earnest, although the divergence between word and deed could not long be concealed. It is perhaps symptomatic that the strongest identification between Bolivia and Cuba came in the early days of Castro's triumph when he did not hesitate to throttle the Cuban press in favor of forced economic and social development. In January 1959, when the fall of Batista brought hopes that freedom of the press would soon be restored in Cuba, La Nación demurred: "But liberty is so relative that, finally, we do not know how Castro can allow freedom of the press, since those faithful to Batista will rise in rebellion and do with him [Castro] what he did with his caudillo [strong man]. Castro cannot grant liberty of action to the censerbearing journalists of Batista without placing in danger the conquest of the July 26 Movement." Inevitably, the writer for La Nación concluded, Castro's partisans would cool off and begin to side with the opposition, an inevitable process "which is--don't forget it--the temperamental range of opinion in Hispanic America." [99] But overriding concern for the control of national press systems was the keen desire of the Bolivian National Revolution to obtain a favorable world press.

Chapter 12

FOREIGN COVERAGE: THE CULTURAL CHASM

Many times, our country has been presented as something deformed.

--La Nación, Oct. 26, 1961

Isolated on the roof of the Americas, Bolivia has never
enjoyed a good world press--"good" not in the sense of flatter-
ing statements but simply in getting accurate statements about
Bolivian affairs out to the broader international community.
This problem was acutely heightened by the fact that the
Bolivian National Revolution began in 1952--only seven years
after the close of World War II and at the height of the Cold
War. Either ignored or misrepresented, Bolivia became the
unknown soldier of the Cold War as the winds of doctrine
shifted. At first it was a beneficiary of the Cold War and then
its victim. By the later 1950s, Bolivia was receiving more
United States aid per capita than any other country in the
world, [1] but at the same time the Bolivian military establishment, which had been partially dismantled in 1952 in favor of
popular militias, was slowly rebuilt under the fiction that a few
thousand Indian and cholo [mixed] troops were important for
hemispheric defense in the age of inter-continental ballistic
missiles. Thus, in its ambivalent policy, the United States put
the kiss of death on social change in Bolivia. Thereafter, the
outside world witnessed the overkill in wiping out Che Guevara
and his misguided band in 1967 and the attempt to recapture
reform made by General Juan José Torres in 1970-1971, but in
all other ways Bolivia was consigned to oblivion. [2] It remains
today--like Guatemala--another skeleton of the Cold War strewn
along the way to détente or Armageddon. Bolivia under
General Hugo Banzer Suárez proscribed all political parties and
labor unions. The country became simply one more armed
enclave among the military regimes of Latin America which
oppress their own peoples until the fragile return to democracy
under Walter Guevara Arze and Bolivia's first woman president,
Lydia Gueiler Tejada.

The world press heightened the suspicions of the Cold War

359

itself. [3] Since an informed diplomacy rests ultimately on an informed public opinion, it is important to try to determine what United States and European wire services have reported about Bolivia since 1952. How did she become the "unknown soldier"--in both the literal and ironic sense--of the Cold War?

Whenever news from Bolivia hits the copy desks of United States newspapers or magazines, editors seem to reach for their strongest action verbs and most dramatic nouns or adjectives to headline the articles--many of which are written in similar vein. Thus a change of rulers at the Palacio Quemado is not simply a coup d'etat: it is another "Blowup in Bolivia." Political difficulties are described as "Chaos in the Clouds," and labor disputes become "Tin-Plated Trouble." This "Tormented, Grim Land," [4] is wracked with perpetual "revolutions" as writers once confused either palace or barracks revolts, usually bloodless, with genuine and far-reaching social change. Even such a distinguished correspondent as John Gunther summarized Bolivia in 1941 as "a primitive mountain state in the high Andes, predominantly Indian. Important as a source of tin." [5]

In this way, stereotypes were fastened on the public consciousness to such an extent that readers were almost totally unprepared to grasp what occurred in Bolivia after 1952. With no knowledge aforethought, much of the United States press, feeding on its own engrained concepts, did not comprehend what was unfolding in Bolivia. Life, for instance, tagged the revolution which began in 1952 "Bolivia's Annual Revolt," [6] even though the MNR was to bring the country unprecedented stability for twelve years despite the wrenching social readjustments. [7] It is not the purpose of this chapter, however, to criticize adversely United States coverage of Latin American affairs. That has been done elsewhere. [8] Rather, we shall examine from the historical perspective how Bolivia herself viewed foreign coverage of its own social revolution--and the problems and anxieties which the world press caused it.

With world attention riveted on the Italian invasion of Abyssinia in the 1930s, the isolated Chaco struggle received little notice outside the Americas, but it did reveal to Bolivian middle-class intellectuals the desperate plight of their country. Bolivia faced problems more severe than any other country in the hemisphere except Haiti: extreme poverty, class and caste discrimination, political corruption and cynicism, and an economic monoculture. Tin production, the country's major export earner, was dominated by some of the world's richest men-- Simón I. Patiño, Mauricio Hochschild and Carlos Víctor Aramayo--who ignored the welfare of their 35,000 mine workers much as the great landowners mistreated their pongos (serfs).

The Big Three mine owners returned very little in taxes to help to develop Bolivia's infrastructure or to diversify her economy. As one writer put it, when the MNR shared power with Major Gualberto Villarroel (1943-1946), the tin tycoons left behind "only holes in the mountains and holes in the lungs of the miners." [9]

After gaining power on their own hook in 1952, the MNR leaders knew from their own journalistic experience the advantage of a favorable press. They remembered vividly that recognition of the Villarroel government by the United States had been delayed six months in 1943-1944 because of the "fascist" label slapped on the MNR by diplomats and newsmen whose judgment was colored by what was happening in wartorn Europe. The importance which MNR officials attached to a responsible world press was voiced many times, as during the eight-day visit to Bolivia by President-elect José Figueres of Costa Rica in September 1953. On that occasion, President Paz Estenssoro declared:

> ...international understanding is fundamentally important for a revolutionary State such as ours. When a revolutionary Government appears in the aggregate of the nations of the continent, it awakens misgivings in non-revolutionary governments; the true orientation of this revolutionary Government is disfigured abroad. Control by the news agencies of the means of public information, which the great economic interests generally have at their service, gives versions of what happens in the country governed by a revolutionary party completely distinct from reality, showing it in the most unfavorable aspect. [10]

This was by no means the first time that the MNR deplored what it considered the ineptitude or deliberate distortions of the foreign wire services. In 1946, for example, La Calle, which was then the MNR spokesman, reprinted a statement by the Peruvian Aprista leaders Luis Alberto Sánchez and Manuel Seoane from El Diario Ilustrado of Santiago de Chile. One of the men, who had held a news conference, declared, "Information from the news agencies cannot be taken very seriously." To back up their point, they cited the case of El Comercio of Lima, which had supported all oligarchical regimes in Peru. The editor of El Comercio was also the head of the Associated Press (AP) bureau in Lima; his brother headed the United Press bureau, and the editor of the afternoon edition of El Comercio was also responsible for the Reuters agency. La Calle, decrying this ingrown and monopolistic situation, asserted that the same situation applied in Bolivia. [11]

As the news agencies used more and more nationals or persons married to nationals of Latin American countries as stringers, partly to improve their coverage, this practice also came under criticism. In 1959, for example, La Nación, official spokesman for the MNR during its twelve years in power, demanded the firing of a woman named Betsy Zavala Pabón who reported for the United Press from La Paz. Her offense was the lead paragraph in a story--which La Nación printed in photostat from La Prensa of Buenos Aires--originating from La Paz on April 18, 1959: "The official organ 'La Nación' reappeared yesterday, directed by the deputy of the extreme left, Augusto Céspedes." La Nación objected strongly to this label of "extreme left" applied to its editor, noting that the United States news agencies frequently used the terms, "left," "leftist" or "leftwing," but very seldomly "right," "rightist" or "rightwing." The MNR newspaper charged that this overworked and inaccurate usage, in the specific case of Céspedes, stemmed from the maliciousness of correspondents who had personal grudges to settle. Moreover, La Nación maintained, these stringers had no experience in journalism but merely aped the worst of foreign practices. La Nación recalled that in the days of La Razón, pay on that newspaper owned by Carlos Víctor Aramayo was so low that workers moonlighted for the United Press--carrying over to their foreign news assignments the prejudices and practices of the powerful Aramayo tin-mining family. On other occasions, La Nación called for Bolivians to report Bolivian news to the world via the international news agencies, but in this instance the MNR newspaper headlined its commentary, "It would help good relations with the United States if the news agencies had foreign correspondents." [12]

One of the most serious events in which the MNR press claimed that the country was being treated unjustly by the wire services centered on the death of Oscar Unzaga de la Vega, head of the Falange Socialista Boliviana (FSB), founded in 1937 and modeled upon the Spanish Falange, during its attempted coup of April 19, 1959. This was the strongest attempt to unseat the MNR during its twelve years in power. After the course of the day's fierce fighting, Unzaga was found shot to death in the bathroom of a house in a residential area of La Paz. The MNR claimed that Unzaga had committed suicide, along with a trusted aide, but loyal party followers maintained that both had been murdered. First to feel La Nación's wrath was Martín Leguizamón, United Press International (UPI) correspondent in Santiago de Chile. He reported that MNR militiamen had surprised Unzaga and other FSB members while they were attending a mass in a cathedral in downtown La Paz. He wrote that Unzaga was shot down with "a burst of machine-gun fire that practically cut his body into two sections at the waist, and he later received two shots in the head from different weapons as a coup de grace." [13]   The story was based on the reports of FSB exiles reaching Santiago, but it was completely false.

The UPI again was called to task two days later after a story was filed from Lima reporting that a man named Eleodoro Ventocilla had a manuscript supposedly written by Unzaga in 1954 entitled, "Yo seré asesinado ("I will be assassinated"), which Time-Life was expressing an interest in buying. Ventocilla claimed that Unzaga had given him the manuscript in Caracas in 1954 when he was seeking aid from the rightwing military dictator, General Marcos Pérez Jiménez.   Even supposing the document were genuine, La Nación demanded to know, who would give credence to a prophecy written five years before the alleged assassination?   La Nación concluded, "Now the news from United Press International comes not a posteriori, as generally happens, but rather a priori..." [14]

As the days passed, versions of Unzaga's death proliferated as the UPI filed contradictory accounts based on interviews with FSB exiles in different capitals.   Why the news agency did not try to verify and reconcile these stories perplexed La Nación, which also saw an inclination by the UPI to regard as objective news reporting the practice of simply attributing such statements without investigating their truth.   As United States editors sadly learned during the heyday of Senator Joseph McCarthy, objectivity cannot be obtained simply by putting quotation marks around direct statements.   In the case of Unzaga's death, La Nación charged, "the UPI lies simultaneously in Río de Janeiro and Buenos Aires, but in different ways. Thus we have Unzaga dead in diverse times, places and attitudes, without the least care for the scandal of these contradictions." [15]

On the other hand, when the grandaughter of the Bolivian ambassador to Paraguay disappeared in Asunción, the UPI reported, "It is said in diplomatic circles that the Ambassador, [Luis] Arduz Daza is an elderly career diplomat who has passed the greater part of his life outside his country, and he had never mixed in politics. FOR THIS REASON... [the theory] is discarded that... [the disappearance of the girl] may deal with the vengeance of some political [FSB] exile."   On the contrary, La Nación quickly pointed out, Arduz Daza was not a career diplomat, he had always lived in Bolivia and he was one of "the most active, oldest and decided [members] of the MNR." [16]

This   boiling   controversy   over   the   circumstances   of Unzaga's death stirred up by the press became so intense that the MNR government invited a commission of experts designated by the Organization of American States to make an independent,

363

on-the-spot investigation. President Hernán Siles hoped thereby to put an end to the rumors and speculation that Unzaga had been killed in cold blood. The commission ultimately agreed with the government's explanation of suicide, but in the course of the long investigation the four major news services implied that it was nothing but a white-wash. La Nación attacked UPI, AP, Reuters and Agence France Press for their coverage of the investigation, accusing them in a headline of attempting to "sabotage" the National Revolution. [17] The French news agency added insult to injury, in La Nación's view, by attributing a denigrating statement about Bolivia to Daniel Schweitzer, a member of the OAS mission, who supposedly remarked to the Chilean minister of foreign relations that "lesser officials at the Chilean Embassy in La Paz want to change stations or better yet return to Chile because of the continuous unrest on the altiplano." [18]

The major target of MNR complaints about foreign handling of Bolivian news was the UPI, perhaps simply because this agency turned out more copy on Latin America than any of its competitors. [19] A case in point was a paragraph from a United Press dispatch covering the speech of Fidel Castro in the United Nations on April 21, 1959: "The delegates of Nicaragua and Bolivia joined in the applause, NOTWITHSTANDING that Castro had referred to the democratic representative governments 'that include the majority of those here represented.'" La Nación headlined commentary on this error, "The U.P. tries to catalogue [President] Siles among the dictators of America," whereas actually he had been freely elected in 1956 by the largest turnout in Bolivian history. [20]

Part of the difficulty in covering Latin American news is the propensity of wire service reporters to cull some of their material from the national newspapers where they are stationed--thereby rehashing an essentially conservative version of contemporary history written to please the oligarchical owners of most of the hemisphere's press. [21] In July 1959, for instance, the UPI picked up the accusations of Jorge Vaca Díez and other FSB exiles printed in the conservative Chilean press that MNR miner and campesino militias had slaughtered many people in an attempted FSB coup in Santa Cruz, the eastern tropical boom town long known for its separatist tendencies. El Diario Ilustrado of Santiago had first printed the assertions of Vaca Díez and his companions under such headlines as "They denounce monstrous genocide against the people of Santa Cruz" and "Bolivian falangists affirm that more than a thousand cruceños fight on in the forests." La Nación questioned the shaky source of the UPI story under its own headline which probably erred in the opposite direction, "It's a strange genocide without a single victim." [22]

The MNR newspaper even accused the UPI after 1958 of faking pictures in its coverage of Latin America. According to a spectator, La Nación reported, UPI photographer Andy López in Havana tried to get a campesino to raise his left clenched fist in the Communist salute, as Cubans gathered to celebrate the July 26th anniversary in 1959--long before Cuba became overtly a Marxist state. The incident reminded La Nación of a similar one which happened in Bolivia during the government of Villarroel:

> ...a foreign review, specialized in investigating fascism in South America, published the cliché of a gymnastic gathering in Bolivia, in which the children made the athletic salute, raising the outstretched right hand: proof that the Government was educating its youth in fascist ways. [23]

On another occasion, La Nación noted with obvious satisfaction how a sister publication had met the problem of foreigners "photographing slander." After Life en Español published a series of stark photographs of the favelas or slums of Río de Janeiro, the Brazilian review O Cruzeiro countered by publishing pictures of New York slums, one of which showed an abandoned child covered with cockroaches. [24]

Another clash with UPI came in January 1960 when the news agency issued a dispatch from La Paz quoting the Cuban ambassador to Bolivia, José Antonio Tabares, as saying that Che Guevara was a Communist and the Cuban people were not ready for elections. PRELA (Prensa Latina) of Havana denounced the inaccuracy of the UPI story, as did all of the Bolivian reporters who had attended the press conference with Tabares on January 19. What the Cuban ambassador actually said, according to La Nación, was that Guevara was a Marxist and elections would have to be organized before they could be held in Cuba. A second PRELA dispatch from Havana reported that the UPI correspondent in La Paz, Betsy Zavala Pabón, herself denied the accuracy of the quotations. The changes then, reasoned La Nación, were made by UPI editors in New York--whether through simple ignorance or willful misrepresentation. [25]

When the UPI covered the 1960 presidential elections in Bolivia, La Nación had the opportunity to weigh the merits of reporting by traveling versus permanent resident correspondents. UPI newsman James Whelan was dispatched to back up resident correspondent Betsy Zavala Pabón. The former offended MNR authorities by reporting the Falangist version of their abstention from the polls on Sunday, June 5, "under the threat of genocide" in Santa Cruz. In reality, reported La

Nación, the FSB had won more than 2,000 votes there. Whelan also reported seeing five young men at one gathering with rifles, despite the fact that the government had prohibited arms since the previous Friday.

La Nación criticized the reporting of Ms. Zavala more severely. She counted five armed militiamen at the airport, five more at an intersection, and seventy soldiers at the Casa Municipal, where the votes were to be counted. The lead paragraph of her story of June 5 was, "Numerous electoral irregularities were observed by the UPI in a rapid swing through La Paz following the tracks of presidential candidate Paz Estenssoro." La Nación, conceding that Ms. Zavala could certainly count well, replied with heavy irony, "The foreign reader will think, naturally, that the armed formation [at the Casa Municipal] was there to massacre the Electoral Court in broad daylight, and not to guard the ballot boxes nor to guarantee the election returns." Ms. Zavala saw "government" trucks hauling voters to the polls, reported that only MNR ballots were available in the Indian village of Tachachirá, and found armed soldiers also in "the traditionally turbulent Plaza Murillo." She reported the Communists in La Paz had obtained the unbelievably low figure of 115 votes, and charged that even those ballots were thrown in with the MNR returns. La Nación pointed out this was impossible since colored ballots were used in largely illiterate Bolivia. Actually, according to the unofficial count, the Trotskyite Partido Obrero Revolucionario won 449 votes in La Paz, and the Partido Comunista de Bolivia got 1,505. [26]

La Nación was at a loss to explain the discrepancies between Ms. Zavala's reporting and the facts, but one study has revealed that national reporters for the Associated Press learn quite early what kinds of stories will please their superiors, the editors or "gatekeepers" in New York, and thus send exactly what gets the best play, thereby perpetuating stereotypes of Latin America in the United States press. [27]

One of the things which irritated La Nación most about coverage of national events by the foreign news agencies was that seldom did they ever issue corrections or retractions. UPI ignored the newspaper's challenges to the facts of its coverage of the 1960 elections, and again turned a deaf ear when La Nación claimed it was simply untrue the six students were killed in the disturbances of October 23, 1961, as UPI had reported. On the latter occasion, the newspaper declared editorially:

> The lamentable thing, in this and other cases, is that the great international news agencies such as UPI, trusting in the impartiality and truthfulness of their

correspondents, broadcast to the four winds whatever news they send because of its sensational character. Later, if they [the news agencies] should receive some correction or contradiction, they do not publish it because they give it no importance. [28]

On the other hand, La Nación noted on another occasion, at times the distortion of the news became so grotesque that the bias could no longer be denied. Such was the case when the Brazilian state elections of 1962 gave support to Joao Goulart, whom the news agencies had dismissed as a nationalistic leftist with no future whatever. La Nación commented:

Really, whatever news of transcendent importance is transmitted by the news agencies [is done so] at their pleasure and taste. Moreover, beforehand the public is prepared to receive that previously seasoned news. Nevertheless, when the crudity of the events becomes patent, the artificially inflated globe bursts and the reality remains nakedly exposed...The press should fulfill a function of faithful service to the people, based on veracity in the news and honesty in commentary. The journalistic organs that do not respond to this demand, do nothing more than convert themselves into a kind of soporific sedative that maintains the people...in a comfortable drowsiness that does not succeed in transforming the reality to which they will have to awaken later, and certainly not very pleasantly. [29]

Another major criticism of the wire services voiced in La Nación was that they were geared to crisis reporting, as correspondents hop-scotched from one capital to another whenever turbulence boiled to the surface, with very little follow-up or attempt to report causative factors. La Nación also detected what it considered selective dismissal of major stories, as in the case of Guatemala after 1954:

No sooner had [Colonel Carlos] Castillo Armas arrived at power in Guatemala than the same news agencies which had launched a huge press campaign against the 'filocomunista' regime of [Jacobo] Arbenz rapidly forgot the Guatemala affair and condemned it to the destiny of the archives...Silence. That was the countermand of the high commands of propaganda. All the world forgot the matter, although it was too transparent not to comprehend the sad role which Democracy played there. [30]

At times sheer speculation--and the inadequate preparation

of their correspondents--brought the major United States news agencies into direct contradiction with each other. This happened when Paz Estenssoro before his second inauguration in 1960 visited President Arturo Frondizi in neighboring Argentina. Although the heads of state conferred behind closed doors, James Whelan of UPI reported that the meeting augured "a swing to the right" in Paz Estenssoro's second term in office, while the AP correspondent, not named, found that the encounter indicated Paz would take "a more leftist line than supposed..." [31] On another occasion, Francis McCarthy of UPI, who accompanied Adlai Stevenson on his South American trip in 1961, reported that Bolivia was engaged in "a fight to the finish against attempted Red coups d'etat," when actually it was the rightwing FSB that was most to be feared. [32]

At other times, it was the deprecating tone of news agency dispatches that rankled Bolivian readers. This was the reaction to an article sent by the AP correspondent in La Paz--a Bolivian--and published in El Mercurio of Santiago de Chile under the headline, "Three of every five registered for the Bolivian presidential elections are illiterate." The headline was accurate enough, but the body of the story expressed disapproval of the universal vote granted in Bolivia in 1952, considering it to be a Machiavellian maneuver by the MNR to insure its continuance in power; by coupling land reform with universal suffrage, the MNR created a power base among the majority of illiterate campesinos that was well nigh unassailable. The AP correspondent found this to be "dirty politics but this underdeveloped Mediterranean country of South America is notable for its political violence." [33]

When some observers expressed the belief that MNR officials were too thin-skinned about such statements, La Nación noted that the shoe could be placed on the other foot. A sharp-eyed editor for the newspaper noticed that Selecciones, the Spanish edition of Reader's Digest, censored its own material bound for Latin America to eliminate anything that might tarnish the image of the United States. Was there a double standard on sensitivity? As a case in point, La Nación translated and printed two paragraphs describing anti-Yankee sentiment in Japan which had been deleted from the article, "Turbulent Tokyo," in June 1960. The editorial writer for La Nación considered this "self-censorship" to be most curious:

> Propaganda in the great Democracy of the North... believes surely that there are things which should not be put within the reach of minors, which in this case are we the Latin Americans. That is why facts and observations published in the English edition of Reader's Digest are not reproduced in the Spanish

version for use by the underdeveloped peoples of these latitudes. [34]

With their overwhelming clout, the international news agencies--and especially those based in the United States--were active partners in this cultural penetration or imperialism. With no other wire service available to them for many years, Latin Americans were forced to view the world--and even their own region or country--through the eyes of foreign reporters or editors who belonged to a different world. As Juan José Arévalo, former president of Guatemala, expressed it in 1959, "The Spanish and the English in America are two categories that cannot intermix. Moreover, they are antagonistic... We the Latin Americans do not want to be put in the same pocket with the North Americans, because their life-style has nothing in similar with ours." [35]

In short, wire-service reporters had been culturally conditioned by the needs of the highly industrialized societies of the United States and Western Europe, steeped in the concepts of representative democracy and freedom of the press, and committed to an international laissez-faire economic system. Moreover, they frequently applied these alien yardsticks with rigor and at times with arrogance. With traditional up-the-ladder training, they tended to regard the world as a gigantic police court with good guys and bad guys--depending on whether or not Latin American leaders lined up with the United States in the atmosphere of the Cold War which the press itself did much to foment. Thus, UPI was advertising its services with a large poster of Fidel Castro with these words in big, boldface type underneath: HELP PUT CASTRO IN HIS PLACE. TAKE UPI. [36]

Latin American publishers and others early recognized the great need for better news coverage of their region. In 1926, those gathered at the First Pan-American Congress of Journalists, a precursor of the Inter American Press Association, found the news flow between Latin America and the industrialized world to be imbalanced, and they called for the establishment of a regional news agency. [37] This objective became lost, however, as the IAPA gained in strength and reflected essentially the wishes of the predominant United States publishers who perhaps did not want to encourage competition against the AP or UPI.

Significantly, the plea for a Latin American news agency was voiced loudest in those countries in the throes of social revolution--Bolivia after 1952 and Cuba after 1959--because of their bitter experiences with the well-established news agencies. Thus, when the Cuban Revolution was only a month old, La

Nación correspodent René Zavaleta Mercado quoted Castro as saying in a press conference held in Havana on February 1, 1959: "We no longer take the international news services, but for you--the Latin American journalists--there is no other remedy except to accept whatever the cables tell you, and they are not Latin American." [38] La Nación itself echoed Castro's words about three months later:

> The insularity of the Latin American nations is not unknown nor a secret to anyone. Not only do we not know each other but we do not have the instruments to do so.... The Latin Americans do not know the news of Latin America except through agencies [which are] not Latin American, lacking therefore the sub-stances, imponderable and incomprehensible in their inmost recesses to the foreigner. For the opinion of sister nations, our [current] history is too scattered in information at times false, but always incomplete. Whether imperialism exerts pressure for this to hap-pen is another problem, but for these reasons and for those that the entire Indo-American world knows, it is an inevitable imperative that the revolutionary and democratic movements that form part of continental nationalism lend their aid to the creation of a Latin American press agency already proposed publicly by such men of great American renown as [Rómulo] Betancourt and Castro. Our information must be in our hands. [39]

Help in this matter came from Pope John XXIII, who declared late in 1959 that the capitalist news agencies--through their built-in and unconscious biases--could not report ade-quately the news of the developing world. The needs and aspirations of the exploding Third World either went unnoticed or were reported in terms of what events there meant to the northern hemisphere's industrial community, the Pope main-tained. Applauding his words, La Nación commented, "How could the Pope ignore the propagation of historical fiction [by the major news agencies] that has nothing to do with enlighten-ment or honest information?" The Pope noted that the shib-boleth of the Western world was freedom of the press, whereas what the Third World needed was freedom of information. Concerning the latter, La Nación observed that the emerging peoples of the world knew they were the object of lies and distortions, for the most part, in Western wire services, but they could no longer be hoodwinked by the "cult of objectivity" in the news reporting which had little to do with their own reality. La Nación stressed the moral aspect paramount in the Pope's message:

Through the enormous apparatus of the colonialist incursion, the weak peoples, who are the recipients of that propagandistic bombardment, are taught that they are useless, impotent and inferior and that, therefore, since all of their attempted revolts are fruitless from the beginning, what they should do is to submit to the useful, the powerful and the superior [peoples]. The Christian doctrine that plants the idea of substantial equality among men cannot do less than reject these anti-human methods. [40]

Thus, when the first Third World news agency, Agencia de Prensa Latinoamericana (PRELA), began functioning with Cuban capital in June 1959, La Nación greeted its appearance on the international scene with jubilation. The newspaper exclaimed, "Castro is, for [those of us who fight] imperialism and its press, an unexpected and lucky conjunction [of events]." [41] Prensa Latina, as it was usually identified in datelines, was a direct result of the Cuban Revolution and inextricably tied to its fate. For some observers, it was too nationalistic, reporting the hemisphere's news only from the viewpoint of national liberation, with Cuba held up as the prime example. In some respects, it was the underground news agency for the Americas, just as the Liberation News Service was to supply underground newspapers in the United States with news and features. Some called it the TASS of the hemisphere, while others argued that its distortions to the left were no more pronounced than the biases to the right of AP and UPI.

As time passed, other alternatives were considered to the problem of Latin American nations informing themselves about each other. One of the recommendations of the second World Encounter of Journalists held in Baden, Austria, October 18-22, 1960, was for the under-developed countries to form news gathering and reporting cooperatives, including radio and television. [42] This suggestion, which had been spectacularly successful for Excélsior of Mexico City since 1932, was perhaps too optimistic for countries with scant resources. Nevertheless, General Juan Velasco Alvarado sanctioned the device for El Comercio in Lima after 1968, and General Juan José Torres was on the point of sanctioning it for El Diario of La Paz when he was overthrown in August 1971.

Another response to the formation of the Cuban news agency occurred in 1961 when UNESCO journalism experts meeting in Paris called for the "creation of a cooperative Latin American news agency, operated by information enterprises of the region." [43] This did not come about, however, until January 13, 1970, when thirteen leading Latin American newspapers formed LATIN, a Latin American regional news agency. Privately owned by daily newspapers of seven Latin American nations, it was not strictly a cooperative, however, since it was not owned and conducted by its workers. Designed to correct deficiencies of the large foreign news agencies already operating in Latin America, it was unfortunately soon competing with them in stereotyped coverage of regional events. Thus, in the first three years of its existence, sports coverage and political news increased dramatically, while news of foreign relations, economics and culture all declined by wide margins. [44]

Although discomfort with the established wire services was endemic in Bolivia, it was the news magazine Time which caused the greatest furor in the twelve years that the MNR held power. The imbroglio began when Time quoted an unidentified United States official at the Embassy in La Paz as saying, in the Latin American edition of March 2, 1959: "The only solution to Bolivia's problems is to abolish Bolivia. Let her neighbors divide up the country and the problems." There is no evidence that any official anywhere said such a thing, but the quotation was a stab to the heart of Bolivian national sensibilities. When the 670 copies of this edition of Time arrived in La Paz, President Siles ordered them confiscated. But on March 2, 1959, the Time article was printed in all of the newspapers of the capital. Rioting students seized and burned the copies of Time. Two days of disorder, which on the third day spilled over into the cities of Oruro and Cochabamba, threatened to make La Paz the scene of another bogotazo. Some 900 United States residents in the capital were placed under protective guard in one of the suburbs, while planes stood by to evacuate them, if necessary. The United States Embassy, attacked twice during the melee, denied that any of its personnel had made such a statement, which was probably the invention of one of the Time re-write men in New York. The final toll of Time's sensational brand of journalism: two dead, thirty-eight policemen injured, and $50,000 property damage in La Paz and $20,000 in Cochabamba. [45] Also wrecked, along with United States Information Service libraries in La Paz and Cochabamba, were the aspirations of Clare Booth Luce, former ambassador to Italy, who wanted to become the United States ambassador to Brazil. She withdrew her nomination, then awaiting confirmation by the Senate, convinced that the Time debacle in Bolivia would make her persona non grata in neighboring Brazil. [46]

Typical of Bolivian reaction to the insulting Time quotation was a front-page article in La Nación by René Zavaleta Mercado, who declared:

It is for the Bolivians and not the North Americans to decide upon the future of this country. Once again it is imperialism, pretentious successor to the colonialism of the Spaniards, which wants to dissolve our country, because it knows that the [Bolivian National] Revolution has been made against it.... A nationality is not 'business.' One cannot say [even] sportingly: to divide [Bolivia] is the easiest and most economical way. [47]

Reaction to the Time incident varied widely in the United States. Senators Hubert Humphrey of Minnesota and Wayne Morse of Oregon came down on the side of Bolivian sensibilities, while Styles Bridges of New Hampshire said, "The action of the rabble was not justified; it was not avoided, and it demonstrates a lack of esteem [for the United States]." Bridges wanted to suspend all economic aid to Bolivia, and he also urged that United States troops be sent into the troubled country. [48]

On the other hand, La Nación reaped a windfall by reprinting in full sixteen articles and editorials throughout the month of March 1959 from other segments of the Latin American press which expressed solidarity with Bolivia. [49] The incident also stimulated editor Augusto Céspedes to write a long historical article which traced the roots of entreguismo, or giving up national territory, fifty years back to the Liberal Party. His article concluded, "The Liberal Party can therefore add to its tradition that of being a precursor of Time.... To hell with the decadent democrats!" [50]

In retrospect, no other single incident furnished as much propaganda mileage to La Nación as did the Time article. Although news of the original story broke in the Bolivian press on March 2, 1959, La Nación was still commenting bitterly upon the episode as late as May 18. During this time, La Nación charged that Carlos Víctor Aramayo, the former tin magnate, had planted the quotation in the Latin American edition of Time as the first step toward a rightwing golpe in Bolivia. The MNR newspaper quoted Aramayo as saying before the article appeared, "This week Time is going to give a sensational blow against the government of Siles." The name of Aramayo seldom appeared in La Nación without a jibe at his Oxford education and his pretentious English accent. On this occasion, La Nación quipped, "What a shame that the English pronunciation of Carlos Víctor does not harmonize with the journalistic cockney of Time." [51]

There is some evidence that the attempted FSB coup d'etat of April 19, 1959--the most serious challenge to MNR hegemony in its twelve years in power--was triggered by the disorders following the Time story of March 2, 1959. This was the opinion of the Mexican philosopher Leopoldo Zea, who noted in an article published in Novedades of Mexico City near the end of April 1959, "This [Time] article also served to stimulate those opposing the Bolivian government to attempt a coup that was frustrated by the immediate intervention of the people...[which] made it unnecessary for the army to subdue the revolt." [52]

The Time incident and Bolivia's experience with the foreign wire services should not be taken to mean that the Bolivian National Revolution received only unfair treatment in the United States press. There were many favorable comments as well. The New York Times, for example, was generally sympathetic to the social changes being wrought in Bolivia. This attitude stemmed mainly from the informed editorials of Herbert L. Matthews, who had been reporting and commenting on Latin American affairs since 1949. Another warm friend of Bolivia was the columnist and radio commentator, Drew Pearson. Perhaps more than anyone else, he painted a sympathetic picture of the history unfolding in Bolivia. [53]

In addition to improving foreign news coverage of Latin America, the problem remains of how the region is best to inform itself. Clearly, the United States and European wire services have failed at this task, and cultural penetration--in the sense of viewing the world through eyes of others--has spilled over into the electronic media as Walter Cronkite of CBS News was once dubbed into Spanish and syndicated in Mexico. Moreover, LATIN has failed to fulfill this need in its brief existence, competing now with the traditional news agencies, and Prensa Latina of Cuba is too biased in the opposite direction. As Pope John XXIII suggested, perhaps the answer lies in worker cooperatives such as Excélsior of Mexico City. Labor is more closely tied to the realities of developing Latin America than are the oligarchical elites. But traditional views of Western industrialized societies regarding the sanctity of freedom of the press and private property will have to be modified substantially to give such agencies a chance to function and to prove themselves. Perhaps in the future there can be a genuine regional news organization that neither imitates the older news agencies--as LATIN does--nor descends to polemics with datelines--as Prensa Latina does.

In the context of the Cold War, however, the news received from Latin America by the industrialized northern hemisphere is a much more critical factor. On balance, foreign coverage of Bolivia since 1952 has been sketchy and misleading. Probably no other area of the world received less coverage in the United States press than Latin America except Africa, and that imbalance has been reversed in recent years. In one sense, the scanty coverage of the Bolivian National Revolution in the United States media was an advantage, since it allowed United States career diplomats to carry out their economic aid programs without interference from Congressmen incited by an irresponsible press--the same press which bungled the nearby Cuban story so badly.

But far outweighing that advantage, if it can be called one, was the disadvantage caused by the lack of public understanding of what was happening in Bolivia and elsewhere. This vacuum of reliable information gave the Pentagon free rein to influence State Department policy and to make much of Latin America an armed camp. As the memory of the democratic reforms effected by the MNR in Bolivia faded into the recent past, the proto-fascist state headed in turn by Generals René Barrientos, Alfredo Ovando Candia, Hugo Banzer and others remained the legacy of uninformed diplomacy and public opinion. As Víctor Andrade, Bolivian foreign minister, commented acidly during the Time affair, "I think the whole trouble is the United States was forced to take a leading role in the world before it was really ready. Your people need some preventive education before going abroad." [54]

Conclusion

JOURNALISM AT THE BARRICADES

While much of the international press painted a distorted or insensitive picture of events in Bolivia, the official press of that country faced its own imminent extinction. Forces were at work which would spell the end of the twelve-year-old Bolivian National Revolution. Even though manipulation of the Bolivian press had been successful in popularizing the MNR reforms among civilians, no amount of propaganda could blunt the drive by the military to regain its traditional status.

In this regard, the MNR collaborated in engineering its own destruction. After 1952 civilian militias composed of miners and campesinos had been formed as a counter-balance to the reduced military establishment, and déclassé recruiting of cadets had been instituted, but the militias withered away and the new technocratic training for officers did not have enough time to prove itself. Thus, Hernán Siles Zuazo (1956-1960) started to rebuild the traditional military with United States aid and training missions.

Paz Estenssoro, who did not reverse this trend in his second period in the presidency (1960-1964), has since called this the greatest single mistake of the Revolution. [1] In 1964, when Paz Estenssoro decided that the Revolution could not continue without his guidance and opted for a third term, he was forced to accept popular Air Force General René Barrientos Ortuño as his vice-presidential running mate. Within four months of the third inauguration of Paz Estenssoro, he was overthrown by the rebuilt military machine headed by Barrientos, marking the beginning of eighteen years of military rule. This period was lightened only by occasional flickerings of return to democracy with the elections by congress of interim presidents Wálter Guevara Arze in 1979 and Lydia Gueiler Tejada later that year. Finally, in October 1982 former MNR president Hernán Siles Zuazo (1956-1960) and his Popular Democratic Union were inaugurated as an elected government, followed by that of major architect of the MNR and three-time revolutionary president Victor Paz Estenssoro (1952-1956 and 1960-1964) in August 1985.

The overthrow of the MNR by the military on November 4,

1964, did not mean that the reforms of the Revolution partly
brought about by the press had come to an end, however.
Forces were in motion which could be halted but not reversed.
The propaganda had taken root. Even though military factions
sparred for control of political power after 1964, they did not
attempt to dismantle the Revolution. Nationalization of the tin
mines, agrarian reform and universal suffrage all remained,
although the latter was observed more in the breach than in
practice. Thus, in this military interregnum--with some populist overtones--revolutionary reforms may have been halted for
the time being, but they were not expunged from the books or
popular consciousness.

Thus, after more than three decades since the beginning
of the Bolivian National Revolution, what can be said in summary of the role of the press in that socioeconomic movement
that promised to transform Bolivia? Crane Brinton has
observed that social revolutions occur only when there are
improvements, touching off a spiral of rising expectations. But
Bolivia between 1932 and 1952 was economically a stagnant
society as far as the middle and working classes were concerned, and Indians lived beyond the margins of national life.
It required a vigorous press to break this centuries-old mold
and to arouse a people from stagnation and despair to launch a
revolution.

The Chaco War (1932-1935) itself was a watershed in
Bolivian history since the humiliating defeat by Paraguay
aroused national inquiry and soul-searching. The few voices
which surfaced would have gone unheard, however, without a
popular medium of diffusion. This meant newspapers. Books
and pamphlets were more expensive and largely available only to
the thin middle class. Magazines were also a luxury and never
prospered in Bolivia. Radio was controlled by the government
or vested interests, and television had not yet appeared on the
horizon.

Thus, it was newspapers which had to serve as the vehicle
for social change in Bolivia, and that quest produced some
distinguished and courageous journals. El Universal, presaged
by La República, gained the highest circulation in La Paz by
opposing the Chaco War and thus becoming the first mass-based
newspaper in Bolivian history. Divorced from political control
by this wider base of support, El Universal, the training
ground for a generation of Bolivian writers, started discussing
social reforms for the first time in Bolivian history. It defied
the entrenched conservative newspapers of the Big Three tin
consortiums in La Paz, called collectively "the tin curtain" by
opponents which was quickly drawn closed whenever vested
interests were threatened.

El Universal did not hesitate to lift that curtain to reveal what happened behind it, and as a pioneer it inspired other small opposition newspapers such as INTI on which editor Hernán Siles Zuazo, who was to serve his country twice in the presidency, made his public debut. But the newspaper which most stimulated the Bolivian National Revolution was La Calle, which in an aggressive manner voiced the concerns of previously inchoate masses. For the most crucial decade of the MNR's development, from the newspaper's founding in 1936 to its demise in 1946, La Calle set the national agenda for opponents of the oligarchial rule. It witnessed the birth of the MNR in 1941 and the brutal overthrow in 1946 of Gualberto Villarroel in whose government the MNR had participated. La Calle championed the cause of the MNR even though the party disclaimed any connection with the newspaper, not wishing it to be discredited as simply another political sheet.

La Calle achieved its leadership role by practicing what was later called in the United States in the 1960s "advocacy journalism." The press was put at the barricades in a society so stratified there was little or no chance of self-adjustment. The newspaper of the MNR advocated, in ostensible news columns laced with editorial comment, issues both good and bad. It championed the cause of miners and their families slain at Catavi in 1942, which first launched the MNR to national prominence, but it also exploited the anti-Semitism latent in Bolivian life in an effort to arouse class-consciousness.

Perhaps the experience of La Calle best illustrated that it is easier to oppose social injustice rather than to sustain social reform. When a newspaper spokesman was needed for the elections of 1951, the MNR did not revive La Calle but rather used a new voice, En Marcha, to help obtain a plurality--if not an absolute majority--for the MNR. Paz Estenssoro has indicated that he never expected to win what he considered the rigged elections of 1951 but that he participated to justify the armed rebellion to follow, and for this a newspaper voice was necessary. Again, when the MNR did gain power by force on April 9-11, 1952 the party did not resurrect La Calle as its spokesman, launching first La Nación (1952-1964) and later La Tarde (1959-1962).

While some might contend that official newspapers have little credibility, this was not the case in Bolivia. These major newspapers and their satellites helped to define the issues and offer solutions to the complicated questions of granting universal vote, pushing through nationalization of the major tin mines and legitimizing the agrarian reform. Their efforts to redefine the role of the military were less successful, but they did bring public attention to bear on this problem as well. One advantage of an official press--when opposition newspapers such as El Diario, Ultima Hora and Presencia are allowed to function--is that it provides greater freedom of the press when the government has its own spokesman in the journalistic arena to outshout opponents rather than silence them.

There was censorship during the first two years of MNR rule when the government feared counter-revolution by the Falange Socialistia Boliviana and others. But La Razón, owned by the powerful Aramayo tin-mining family, was prevented from reopening in 1952 not by government action but rather popular wrath. The MNR refused to protect the newspaper, declaring that it would not shoot Bolivians to protect the property of Aramayo. Circumstances surrounding the assault on Los Tiempos of Cochabamba on November 9, 1953, are more confused. It is not clear whether owner and editor Demetrio Canelas participated in a counter-revolt against the MNR on that day, provoking the attack on his newspaper. Nor is it clear whether the MNR government sought to control the angry crowds or incite them. Los Tiempos, unlike La Razón which never reappeared, started up again in 1967, but a careful study of the files of both newspapers reveals why they fell victim to a social revolution which neither understood.

Some observers think that concepts of press freedom in Western industrial democracies, with three or four centuries of give-and-take between government and press, are not appropriate for emerging Third World countries. [2] In the latter, participants believe the question which should be asked is not freedom from what--censorship or other restraints--but rather freedom for what? Freedom to carry out social reforms or freedom to obstruct them? To MNR revolutionaries the Bolivian press was free only if it was responsive to the needs of society--hence the decision not to aid in the continued publication of La Razón and Los Tiempos. Nevertheless, there was complete freedom of the press in revolutionary Bolivia after the first two years in power by the MNR.

It has been suggested that the Alliance for Progress did not succeed in the 1960s partly because it failed to develop a mystique to convince the oligarchies to give up at least part of their power in return for a more equitable society. The MNR, on the other hand, evolved its own social mystique after thirty years of opposition to the status quo. Disillusioned by the Chaco War, young men wanted to communicate their feeling about the misconduct of national affairs. But where would they do this? The press of La Paz was owned or controlled by the Big Three mining interests, and El Universal had been closed. And so some of those who were to form the MNR decided to start their own newspaper, La Calle, which perhaps shaped the party after its birth in 1941 as much as the party shaped the newspaper. Guillermo Lora, leader of the Trotyskite POR, correctly described the early MNR as a propaganda group which became a party of the masses. [3]

The crucial question, however, was to whom did La Calle direct its message? Judging from the contents of the news-paper, it was aimed at the emerging middle class, always one cut above poverty themselves--those who could read and found little of interest in the mining press. They aspired to a better social status for themselves and other less fortunate Bolivians. The MNR sought to tap the political support of the middle and lower classes through La Calle and other publications. News-papers and literature indicted Bolivian society for wrongs dating back centuries, touching off the second social and economic revolution in Latin America. The press was enlisted to serve at the barricades in this transformation, and it did so creditably. The Bolivian National Revolution could not have readjusted society to the extent it did without the support of the middle class, and the MNR cultivated that support assidu-ously. Perhaps the MNR press was more effective in the long struggle to power than in effecting the reforms themselves, but it did pre-condition the majority to accept those changes and to support the Revolution in its early years. Moreover, after the initial revolt of April 9-11, 1952, MNR leaders clearly believed that a flow of words could continue to be as effective as a fusillade of bullets.

FOOTNOTES

Introduction

1. Carlos Montenegro, Nacionalismo y coloniaje, su expresión histórica en la prensa de Bolivia (La Paz, 1953), p. 203.

2. Interview with Víctor Paz Estenssoro, La Paz, Bolivia, August 11, 1973.

3. La Nación, February 6, 1960.

4. Herbert S. Klein, Parties and Political Change in Bolivia, 1880-1952 (Cambridge, 1969), p. 424.

5. Remarks by Víctor Paz Estenssoro, President of Bolivia, before the National Press Club (Washington, D.C., 1963), p. 2.

Chapter 1

1. The circulation of El Universal was placed at 34,000 in its edition of April 10, 1933.

2. Herbert S. Klein, Orígenes de la Revolución Nacional Boliviana, La crisis de la generación del Chaco (La Paz, 1968), 205. Also closed were Acción of Sucre and La Crónica of Cochabamba.

3. Tristán Marof, La tragedia del altiplano (Buenos Aires, [1934]), 142-143.

4. This synopsis of the war is drawn from Robert Barton, A Short History of the Republic of Bolivia (La Paz, 1968), 229-240. For an excellent brief analysis of the historical significance of the conflict, see the foreward by Charles W. Arnade to David H. Zook, Jr., The Conduct of the Chaco War (New Haven, Conn., 1960). The latter is the most impartial account of military, diplomatic and political aspects of the war.

5. La Nación, March 17, 1956.

6. This historical sketch of La República can be found in the article, "Twelve years," July 12, 1932.

7. Ibid., July 21, 1932. For examples of Saavedra's contributions, see Aug. 5 and 6, 1932, and especially "A port upon the Paraguay [river]," Aug. 12, 1932.

8. Ibid., Feb. 6, 1932.

9. Ibid., March 29, 1932.

10. Ibid., April 1, 1932.

11. Ibid., April 5, 1932.

12. Ibid., May 4, 1932.

13. Ibid., Feb. 23, 1932. The article was signed with the pen-name, Fray Paliza.

14. Ibid., July 8, 1932. Emphasis of capital letters in original.

15. Ibid., "Our diplomatic failure," Aug. 10, 1932, and see also July 27, 1932.

16. Ibid., July 20, 1932.

17. Ibid., July 22 and 24, 1932.

18. Ibid., Aug. 26, 1932. The article was signed only by J.T.

19. Porfirio Díaz Machicao, Historia de Bolivia, Salamanca, La guerra del Chaco, Tejada Sorzano, 1931-1936 (La Paz, 1955), 149 and 154.

20. Both excerpts are quoted in ibid., 149.

21. Ibid., 191-192.

22. The attack by Ultima Hora is mentioned in Céspedes' dispatch in El Universal, March 27, 1933. The later comment is from Augusto Céspedes, Crónicas heroicas de una guerra estúpida (La Paz, 1975), comprising all his war disptaches, collected by Jerry Knudson, footnote 2, p. 180. A list of the correspondents who went to the front is given in footnote 1, [p. 9].

23. An example of Bolivian censorship during the Chaco War is recounted in Céspedes' dispatch of July 6, 1933 on soldiers who had tunneled under a mountain for the defense of Nanawa.

24. Céspedes, Crónicas heroicas, footnote 1, p. 162. The quotation was originally from Salamanca o el metafísico del fracaso (La Paz, 1973) and refers to a flight which Céspedes made over the Chaco in 1963.

25. Céspedes, Crónicas heroicas, 162. The article, entitled "The malign spirit of the Chaco," appeared in La Nación of Santiago de Chile in June 1935.

26. El Universal, March 18, 1933. The dispatch was filed from Villa Montes on Feb. 18, 1933, which illustrates the difficulties of communication with the Chaco front.

27. Ibid., March 17, 1933. The dispatch was dated Feb. 12, 1933.

28. Céspedes, Crónicas heroicas, 164. This article appeared in La Nación of Santiago de Chile in June 1935.

29. El Universal, March 20, 1933. The dispatch was dated Feb. 25, 1933.

30. Ibid., March 21, 1933. The dispatch from Fort Ballivián was dated Feb. 25, 1933. Also, March 23, 1933, dispatch from Fort Ballivián of Feb. 26, 1933.

31. Ibid., March 22, 1933. Dispatch from Fort Ballivián, Feb. 25, 1933.

32. Ibid., March 25, 1933. The dispatch from Muñoz was dated March 2, 1933.

33. La Nación, Santiago de Chile, June 21, 1935. The article is included in Céspedes, Crónicas heroicas, 157-161.

34. Ibid., 161.

35. Ibid., 157. The article, "The pila and the boli, Two soldiers of America," appeared in La Nación of Santiago de Chile, June 21, 1935. Ellipses in the original.

36. The Chaco War dispatches of Carlos Montenegro, never collected before, are available on microfilm from the author. They appeared in El Universal on the following dates in 1934: Jan. 20, 22, 23, 24, 25, 26, 27, 29, 30, 31; Feb. 1, 2, 3, 7, 8, 9, 10, 17, 19, 20; March 10, 12, 14, 15, 16, 17, 20, 22, 27; April 24; May 2, 4, 5, 11, and Dec. 3.

37. El Universal, March 14, 1934.

38. Ibid., Feb. 10, 1934. Young literary figures mentioned in the dispatch are Guzmán de Rojas, Jorge de la Reza, Alberto de Villegas and Salamanca Figueroa. Best analyses of literature and the Chaco War are Jorge Siles Salinas, La literatura boliviana de la Guerra del Chaco (La Paz, 1969) and Murdo J. Macleod, "The Bolivian Novel, the Chaco War, and the Revolution," in James M. Malloy and Richard S. Thorn, eds., Beyond the Revolution, Bolivia Since 1952 (Pittsburgh, 1971), 341-365.

39. El Universal, Feb. 16, 1933.

40. Ibid., March 17, 1934.

41. Ibid., Oct. 29, 1934.

42. Interview with José Fellmann Velarde, La Paz, June 19, 1973. The ministry of propaganda during Busch's presidency was under the direction of the late Mario Flores, who later had great success in Argentina as a writer of sainetes or one-act farces.

43. El Diario, Jan. 24, 1935.

44. El Universal, Dec. 24, 1934.

45. Interview with Augusto Céspedes, La Paz, Aug. 9, 1973.

46. El Diario, Jan. 10, 1935.

47. The only file for El Universal which the author could find is in the Biblioteca del Congreso in La Paz. There one can consult copies from Jan. 2, 1933 (1st year, No. 31) through Aug. 23, 1935 (3rd year, No. 596).

48. El Universal, Jan 2, 1933.

49. Ibid., March 31 and April 29, 1933.

50. Gutiérrez also published under the pen-name, Juan de la Vía. Carlos Montenegro and Armando Arce paid him homage in El Universal, May 23, 1934.

51. Ibid., Nov. 23, 1934.

52. Ibid., Feb. 21, 1934.

53. Ibid., May 25, 1934

54. Ibid., Jan. 12, 1935.

55. Ibid., Jan. 27, 1934.

56. Ibid., Jan. 25, 1934. See also Feb. 19, 1934.

57. Ibid., Dec. 4, 1934.

58. Ibid., Jan 3, 1935

59. The column first appeared in El Universal on June 14, 1933.

60. El Universal, May 24, 1933. Kundt believed the reason for the declaration of war was to blockade Bolivia--gaining thus what could not be won on the battlefield. For editorials on the early stages of the war, see

"Toward the end," May 20, 1933, and "Absurd Paraguay," June 9, 1933.

61. See Carlos Montenegro, "The Indian, A great soldier," ibid., May 4, 1934.

62. Ibid., June 12, 1933.

63. Ibid., July 30, 1934.

64. Ibid., Dec. 27, 1933. El Universal learned about this not from the Argentine newspaper itself but from someone who had read it in Arequipa and sent a telegram.

65. Ibid., april 13, 1935.

66. Ibid., June 7, 1934.

67. La Calle, July 12, 1936. The editorial was headlined, "Deserters with a program."

68. El Universal, Jan 5, 1934.

69. Ibid., Nov. 28, 1934.

70. Ibid.

71. Ibid., Jan, 15, 1935.

72. Ibid., July 24 and 27, 1935.

73. Ibid., Nov. 30, 1934.

74. Ibid., Dec. 4, 1934.

75. Ibid., Dec. 15, 1934.

76. Ibid., Dec. 5, 1934.

77. Ibid., Dec. 14 and 17, 1934. See also "The last visions of the past regime...", Dec. 20, 1934.

78. Ibid., Dec. 5 and 11, 1934.

79. Ibid., Feb. 15, 1935.

80. Ibid., March 20, 1935.

81. Ibid., May 7, 1935.

82. See, for example, the accounts by Aníbal Alaiza, ibid., May 29 and 30, 1935, and Lorenzo Ramos Tincupa, June 4 and 5, 1935.

83. Ibid., May 27; June 11, 12, 14 and 27, 1935. An account of the last days of fighting is given on July 6, 1935.

84. Ibid., July 27, 1935.

85. Ibid., July 20 and Aug. 12, 1935.

86. Ibid., Aug. 14 and 16, 1935.

87. Ibid., June 26, 1935.

88. Ibid., Aug. 16, 1935.

89. Ibid., July 29, 1935.

90. Ibid., July 4, 1935.

91. Ibid., Aug. 23, 1935. It is difficult to ascertain the exact closing date of El Universal because newspaper files in Bolivia are notoriously incomplete. Aug. 23, 1935, is the last issue in the file of El Universal at the Biblioteca del Congreso in La Paz, apparently the only public collection of the newspaper.

92. La Nación, Sept. 6, 1960.

93. Ibid., Feb. 6, 1960.

94. Rodolfo Salamanca Lafuente, "Periodismo," Presencia, Aug. 6, 1975.

95. Issues of INTI available at the Biblioteca del Congreso, La Paz, are 1st year, No. 41 (Aug. 13, 1940) to 2nd year, No. 302 (July 16, 1941).

96. The editorial appeared in INTI on Dec. 28, 1940. Martha Mendoza's article appeared on Feb. 20 and March 1, 1941.

97. See "José Antonio Arze speaks," ibid., April 4, 1941.

98. Ibid., Oct. 29, 1940 and May 24, 1941.

99. Ibid., May 15, 1941.

100. Ibid., Sept. 10, 1940.

101. Ibid., April 5, 1941.

102. Ibid., April 6, 1941.

103. Ibid., April 16, 1941.

104. Ibid., May 21, 1941.

105. Ibid., June 24, 1941.

106. Ibid., May 8, 1941.

107. Ibid., July 11, 1941.

108. Ibid., July 12, 1941.

109. Ibid., July 16, 1941. Ellipses are in the original.

110. Interview with Victor Paz Estenssoro, La Paz, Aug. 11, 1973.

Chapter 2

1. For analysis of these two regimes, see Herbert S. Klein, "David Toro and the Establishment of 'Military Socialism' in Bolivia," The Hispanic American Historical Review, Vol. 45 (February 1965), 25-52, and "Germán Busch and the Era of 'Military Socialism' in Bolivia," ibid., Vol. 47 (May 1967), 166-184.

2. Listed in the bibliography of Herbert S. Klein, Parties and Political Change in Bolivia, 1880-1952 (Cambridge, 1969), 424.

3. La Calle, June 27, 1937.

4. Ibid., June 23, 1936.

5. Ibid., July 4, 1936.

6. Ibid., Feb. 19, 1937.

7. Ibid., June 24, 1936.

8. Ibid., Feb. 16, 1937.

9. Ibid., July 1, 1936.

10. Ibid., July 23, 1936.

11. Ibid., Nov. 12, 1936.

12. Ibid., June 26, 1936.

13. Ibid., June 23, 1937.

14. Ibid., July 1 and 9, and June 13, 1937.

15. Ibid., Jan. 19 and 22, and March 6, 1937.

16. Ibid., Feb. 25 and March 4, 1937.

17. Ibid., Feb. 26, 1937.

18. Ibid., April 17, 1937, and Nov. 28, 1936.

19. See "Urban evolution of La Paz;" Augusto Céspedes, "Restoration of paceñismo," and an editorial, "The progress of La Paz" in La Calle on the city's independence day of July 16, 1936, and an article by Luis Iturralde Chinel, "A brief history of the city of La Paz," ibid., July 17, 1936.

20. Ibid., April 27, 1937.

21. Ibid., July 2 and 4, 1936.

22. Ibid., July 9, 1936, "Something about the proletarian schools;" René Chávez Muñoz, "Justice for the Teacher," July 7, 1936, and Faustino Suáres Arnex, "Toward integral reform of education," July 12, 1936.

23. Ibid., Jan. 21, 1937, and May 1 and 3, 1946.

24. Ibid., Oct. 30, 1945.

25. Ibid., June 28, 1936.

26. Ibid., April 25, 1946.

27. Ibid., June 26, 1942.

28. Ibid., July 14, 1936.

29. Ibid., Nov. 12, 1936. The newspaper claimed the next day that those responsible were José Daniel Antelo, Carlos Ardiles Arce and an American named Mogg.

30. Ibid., March 27, 1946.

31. Ibid., March 28, 1946.

32. Ibid., April 16, 1946. The reply was probably written by Augusto Céspedes.

33. Fairly complete files of La Calle may be found in the Biblioteca Municipal and the Biblioteca del Congreso, both in La Paz.

34. La Calle, Sept. 23, 1944.

35. Ibid., June 23, 1936.

36. Ibid.

37. Ibid.

38. Ibid.

39. Ibid., June 24, 1936.

40. Ibid., July 3, 1936.

41. Ibid., July 7, 1936.

42. Ibid., July 12, 1936.

43. Ibid., July 15, 1936.

44. Ibid., Sept. 27, 1936.

45. Ibid., Oct. 21, 1936.

46. Ibid., Oct. 23, 1936.

47. Ibid., June 24, 1936.

48. Ibid., June 28, 1936.

49. Ibid., Nov. 25, 1936.

50. Interview with Augusto Céspedes, La Paz, Aug. 9, 1973.

51. La Calle, June 25, 1936.

52. Ibid., June 24, 1936.

53. Ibid., July 14, 1936.

54. Ibid., July 24, 1936.

55. Ibid., July 26, 1936.

56. Ibid., July 30, 1936.

57. Ibid., Aug. 29, 1936.

58. Ibid., Aug. 30, 1936.

59. Ibid., Dec. 5, 1936.

60. Ibid., Jan. 11, 1946.

61. Ibid., June 25, 1937.

62. Ibid., July 1, 1937.

63. Ibid., June 27, 1937.

64. Ibid., July 3, 1936.

65. Ibid., June 29, 1937.

66. Ibid., Feb. 26 and 27, 1946.

67. Ibid., Feb. 27, 1944.

68. Ibid., July 4, 1939.

69. Ibid., April 6, 1944.

70. Ibid., Aug. 15, 1944.

71. Ibid., Feb. 17, 1946.

72. Ibid., March 18, 1937.

73. Ibid., May 13, 1937.

74. Ibid., June 24, 1936. The initial series was continued on June 24, 26, 27 and 28, 1936.

75. Ibid., June 30, 1936.

76. Ibid., July 1 and 2, 1936.

77. Ibid., July 5, 1936. See also July 7, 1936.

78. Ibid., July 11, 1936.

79. Ibid., July 5, 1936.

80. Ibid.

81. Those attacked in the La Calle series, all in 1936, were Siemons & Rapp Inc., June 28; Martin Wargas "Ilimited," June 30; Arthur Ayza, adviser to Rapin, July 1; Charles Calvino, Standard Oil, July 2; Joseph Estaño Riverside, July 3; Joe Mary Coca, July 4; Raft Ugarte, July 5; M. Miki Midinittique, July 7; Monsieur Ernest de Saint Mines, July 8; Signore Domenico Soligno, July 9; Nicholas Tocuyarur Pacha, July 10; and August Tin Mines Fajador, July 12.

82. See Carlos Montenegro, Frente al derecho del estado el oro de la Standard Oil (el petróleo, sangre de Bolivia) (La Paz, 1938).

83. La Calle, March 16, 1937.

84. Ibid., March 18, 1937. See also the editorial of March 19, 1937, "Toward intervention in the mines."

85. "The people and Standard Oil," La Calle, April 3, 1937, and "Foreign opinion supports us," April 13, 1937.

86. Ibid., April 23, 1937. See also the editorial, "The politics of Standard Oil," May 6, 1937.

87. Ibid., June 20, 1937.

88. Ibid., July 20 and 21, 1938.

89. Ibid., "The decision of the Supreme [Court] in the demands of Standard Oil," Sept. 18, 1938; "Diplomatic sophistries of Standard Oil," Feb. 14, 1939, and "Suspicious delay," Feb. 19, 1939.

90. Ibid., March 9, 1939. See also the editorial of March 10, 1939, "The morality of the country offended," and March 14, 1939, "Standard Oil fakes discontent."

91. Ibid., Feb. 12, 1942.

92. Ibid., Feb. 27, 1942.

93. See also the editorial of March 8, 1942, ibid., "The 'arrangement' between P[eñaranda] and Standard Oil is a contract of sale or indemnization?"

94. Ibid., April 1, 1942.

95. Ibid., Nov. 11, 1942.

96. Ibid., Sept. 2, 4, 5, 6, 8, 9, 10, 11, 12, 13, 15, 16, 17, 18, 19 and 27, 1936.

97. Ibid., Sept. 3, 10 and 17, 1936.

98. Ibid., Sept. 18, 1936. Walter E. Montenegro replied to this on Sept. 24, 1936. Other writers who expressed their views, all in 1936, were Augusto Guzmán, Sept. 26; Juan Cabrera Carcia, Oct. 2; Félix Eguiño Zaballa, Oct. 3; Leland Stowe, Oct. 12; Luis Iturralde Chinel, Oct. 15,; and one who preferred to remain anonymous, Oct. 18.

99. Ibid., Sept. 27, 1936.

100. Ibid., Sept. 29, 1945.

101. Ibid., March 30, 1939.

102. Ibid., July 14, 1937.

103. Ibid., July 15, 1937.

104. Ibid., July 20, 1937.

105. Ibid., July 29, 1937.

106. Ibid., Nov. 5, 1938. See also further editorial comment and the text of the Socialist Manifesto itself in the issue of Nov. 6, 1938.

107. INTI, Dec. 10, 1940.

108. La Calle, May 12, 1943.

109. Interview with Rodolfo Salamanca de Lafuente, La Paz, July 27, 1973.

110. La Calle, May 12, 1943.

111. Ibid., May 13, 1943.

112. Ibid., June 19, 1942.

113. Ibid., June 22, 1943.

114. See especially El Jefe (comedia política) (La Paz, 1965) and Breve biografía de Víctor Paz Estenssoro, vida y trasfondo de la política boliviana (La Paz, 1965).

115. Alfredo Ayala Z., Historia de Bolivia, Vol. VI, Bolivia en el siglo XX, del liberalismo a la segunda república (La Paz, 1968), 220.

116. Porfirio Díaz Machicao, Historia de Bolivia: Toro, Busch, Quintinilla, 1936-1940 (La Paz, 1957), 101-104.

117. La Calle, Aug. 24, 1939. Again on Oct. 4, 1939, La Calle proclaimed in a banner headline on an inside page, "There is no doubt that general Busch committed suicide and that he was not assassinated." The subhead pointed out that this was the opinion of Dr. Benigno Palacios, the fiscal ordered to investigate the case.

118. Ibid., Sept. 2, 1939.

119. Ibid., May 17, 1942.

Chapter 3

1. La Nación, Feb. 6, 1960.

2. Interview with Víctor Paz Estenssoro, La Paz, Aug. 11, 1973.

3. The La Noche review was reprinted in La Calle, April 12, 1946.

4. La Nación, May 31, 1961.

5. Ibid., Oct. 24, 1955.

6. See, for example, El Diario of Aug. 6, 1937, when Argüedas was trying to discredit the "military socialist" rule of Toro, president of the military junta of government. Argüedas charged that funds of 2,000 pounds sterling or 320,000 pesos had been diverted to send two generals to Europe. Subsequently, Argüedas and El Diario denied that the names of Generals Sanjinés and Cortadellas had been mentioned in the article's draft. La Calle, Aug. 12, 1937, retorted, "Here practically no one [is willing to admit he] writes anything."

7. La Calle, April 22, 1944. Author of the reply was "Heródoto Mamani."

8. Ibid., June 3, 1944. The counter-attack against Argüedas continued in the issue of July 15, 1944, with an article, "Finally, how should history be written?" by "Huijlla Doctora." Both articles, by their style, seem to be the work of Céspedes.

9. Ibid., July 22, 1938. Despite the virulence of its attacks on Argüedas, La Calle itself asked on Nov. 25, 1938, "Is Bolivia a [viable national] state?"

10. Interview with Víctor Santa Cruz in La Paz, June 27, 1073. Born in 1902, Santa Cruz has been active in Bolivian journalism for more than half a century.

11. Carlos Montenegro, Nacionalismo y coloniaje, Su expresión histórica en la prensa de Bolivia (La Paz, 1953), 203.

401

12. A review of Nacionalismo y coloniaje that appeared in La Calle on June 4, 1944, considered Carlos Montenegro superior to Gabriel René-Moreno, the great Bolivian historian who died in 1908 and had worked mainly in the colonial period. Therefore, the review stated, he was unable "to obtain the formation of a total interpretation of our history."

13. In addition to articles cited elsewhere, the only pieces signed by Montenegro that I could find in La Calle were a tribute to the Bolivian poet Jaime Mendoza on Jan. 31, 1943; two significant articles on the Magruder Mission on Feb. 5 and 6, 1943; a homage to the journalist J. Cirilo Barragán on May 11, 1944; a historical account of the impact of the Argentine press in Bolivian history, May 28, 1944; and a critique of the paintings of Reque Meruvia on Aug. 18, 1944.

14. Ibid., Oct. 14, 1936.

15. Ibid., June 15, 1937. In the introduction to his reportage of the conference, Montenegro was identified as "one of the founders of this newspaper." Céspedes maintains that only Armando Arce and himself started the daily.

16. Written during the Buenos Aires peace conference, the book was published in La Paz in 1938 by the publishing firm "Trabajo" which promised a series of works "that will analyze Bolivian problems in the light of a modern, anti-imperialist criterion." The Attila quotation is the title of Chapter 3, pp. 51-70.

17. Carlos Montenegro, Documentos (La Paz, 1954), 10 and 76. According to La Calle, Feb. 28, 1942, the central committee of the MNR voted to supply the services of lawyers Hernán Siles Zuazo and Alberto Mendoza López to prosecute a criminal suit against unidentified alleged authors of libel against Semanario Busch. Apparently, this was not carried out and Montenegro left soon thereafter for Cochabamba to run as an MNR candidate in the upcoming elections.

18. Montenegro, Documentos, 114-115.

19. A fragment of this work, begun about 1940, "Kocha Pampa, myth, history and destiny," was published in La Nación on Sept. 14, 1959.

20. Watch for the forthcoming Ph.D. dissertation on Montenegro by James Doyle, graduate student in history at

402

Temple University.

21. La Nación, March 12, 1960. The advice was apparently heeded when Paz Estenssoro selected Juan Lechín as his running mate in 1960, but it was forgotten by 1964 when Paz ostracized organized labor and opted for a third term supported only by a few campesino unions and a military vice-president, General René Barrientos, soon to turn against him. The deathbed quotation of Montenegro was printed in La Nación on Dec. 27, 1960, reported by Federico Fortún, secretary of the National Political Control of the MNR.

22. La Calle, June 4, 1944.

23. La Nación, Oct. 29, 1955.

24. René Zavaleta Mercado, El asalto porista (La Paz, 1960); Estado nacional o pueblo de pastores (El imperialismo y el desarrollo fisiocrático) (La Paz, 1963), and La revolución boliviana y la cuestión del poder (La Paz, 1964).

25. Ricardo Anaya, Nacionalización de las minas de Bolivia (Aspecto económico, social y cultural de la historia y la revolución) (Cochabamba, 1953). The full citation for Fernando Díez de Medina's work is Literatura boliviana, Introducción al estudio de las letras nacionales del tiempo mítico a la producción contemporanea (Madrid, 1959).

26. Tamayo's central work was Creación de la pedagogia nacional (La Paz, 1910), which advocated education for Bolivia's Indian masses, but he opposed agrarian reform in a parliamentary debate with Paz Estenssoro during the Villarroel period. Interview with Paz Estenssoro, La Paz, Aug. 11, 1973. Fausto Reinaga, who scathingly attacked Paz Estenssoro in print in 1949, tried in a haphazard and romantic fashion to link Tamayo directly to the MNR to ingratiate himself with the party once it had gained power by publishing Franz Tamayo y la Revolución Boliviana (La Paz, 1956). He failed to do so. He also attempted to start an Indian Party of Bolivia in 1970, but neither that effort nor his several works on indianista and indigenista literature were taken seriously in Bolivia.

27. La Nación, March 12, 1960.

28. Ibid., Dec. 27, 1960.

29. Interview with Augusto Céspedes, La Paz, Aug. 9, 1973.

30. Ibid.

31. Jerry W. Knudson compiled the articles, for which he is given credit on page 7, Crónicas heroicas de una guerra estúpida (La Paz, 1975).

32. La Calle, Aug. 25, 1936. The review originally appeared in the Chilean review, Acción Social.

33. Ibid., Aug. 15, 1936.

34. Ibid., April 9, 1937.

35. Ibid., March 3, 1944.

36. Ibid., Oct. 27, 1939.

37. Ibid., Dec. 16 and 10, 1939.

38. Ibid., March 9, 1940.

39. Ibid., June 16 and July 7, 1944.

40. Ibid., Jan. 20, 1944.

41. Ibid., March 3, 1944.

42. Ibid., April 5, 1945.

43. INTI, Jan. 3, 1941, and La Calle, June 22, 1946.

44. La Calle, April 9, 1942.

45. Ibid.

46. Ibid., April 10, 1942. El Diario's summary appeared on April 9, 1942.

47. Ibid., May 6, 1942.

48. Ibid., Nov. 20, 1942.

49. Ibid., Jan. 31; Feb. 2, 5 and 7; March 3, and June 19, 1943. See also Feb. 23, 1943, which concerns several topics but has no interview or photograph.

50. Ibid., March 2, 1943.

51. Ibid., July 2, 1943. See also, "With Paz Campero they have saved the United Nations," June 17, 1943, and

"What is nationalism in Bolivia and what is Nazism in Europe," June 18, 1943.

52. Ibid., June 26, 1943. See also, "The Unified Socialists will abolish private property and put the rich to the sword?" June 29, 1943.

53. Ibid., Sept. 2, 1943.

54. Ibid., Dec. 12, 1943.

55. Ibid., Dec. 14 and 15, 1943.

56. Interview with Augusto Céspedes, La Paz, Aug. 9, 1973.

57. La Nación, April 17, 1959.

58. A complete text of the speech may be found in La Nación, Nov. 23, 1957. An interesting interview with Céspedes was printed in Vanguardia, July 29, 1971.

59. This biographical information on Arce is taken from an interview with Enrique Fairlie Fuentes in Intermedio of Bogotá on March 1, 1957, when Arce was ambassador to Colombia, and reprinted in La Nación, March 25, 1957. See also an article on Arce taken from La Gaceta de la Prensa of Madrid and reprinted in La Nación, Aug. 14, 1959. Arce read the latter and noted there were no mistakes. Ibid., Aug. 20, 1959.

60. La Calle, May 23, 1943.

61. Ibid., July 1, 1944.

62. Ibid., July 2, 1944.

63. Ibid., July 4, 1944.

64. Ibid., Feb. 7, 1946. The speech was broadcast on Feb. 6, 1946.

65. The article originally appeared in El Siglo on Feb. 14, 1946, and was reprinted in El Diario on Feb. 22, 1946. La Calle, March 8, 1946.

66. Ibid., May 8, 1946.

67. La Nación, Sept. 6, 1960.

68. Ibid., Aug. 21, 1958.

69. Ibid., Sept. 27, 1958.

70. This is the interpretation of Christopher Mitchell, Department of Politics, New York University.

71. La Calle, April 15, 1943.

72. Ibid., Dec. 16, 1943. See also comments by Augusto Céspedes, Dec. 12, 14 and 15, 1943.

73. Ibid., Jan 1, 1944.

74. Ibid., Dec. 21, 1943.

75. Ibid., Dec. 22, 1943.

76. Ibid., Dec. 26, 1943.

77. Ibid., Dec. 30, 1943.

78. Ibid., Feb. 9, 1944.

79. Ibid., March 1, 1944.

80. Ibid., March 9, 1944.

81. Ibid., March 22, 1944.

82. Ibid., May 17, 1944.

83. Ibid., May 25, 1944. The four candidates listed were David Guerrero, province of Ituralde; Raúl Ramos, Poopó; Gustavo Adolfo Otero, Larecaja, and Gustavo Navarro, Potosí.

84. Ibid., Sept. 21, 1941.

85. Ibid., Oct. 3, 1944.

86. Ibid., April 14, 1944.

87. Ibid., April 18, 1944.

88. Ibid., March 5, 1944.

89. Ibid., March 23, 1944.

90. Ibid., March 3, 1946. For more on the Blue Book, see Chapter 5. Peñaranda from Arica had continued to criticize the new government. See ibid., Jan. 4 and 5,

406

1944.

91. Ibid., Jan. 6, 1944, and Feb. 3, 1945.

92. Ibid., June 9, 1946, and Feb. 12, 1944.

93. Ibid., April 4, 1945.

94. Ibid., July 14, 1945. The final vote in the convention was 42-30 in favor.

95. Ibid., June 10, 1944.

96. Ibid., May 11 and 26, 1945.

97. Ibid., May 30, 1945.

98. Ibid., Feb. 12, 1944. Céspedes rejoined the La Calle staff as assistant editor, and Montenegro went to work with the MNR.

99. Ibid., May 16, 1944.

100. Ibid., July 26, 1944, and Oct. 12, 1945.

101. Ibid., Oct. 6, 1945.

102. Ibid., Jan. 11, 1944.

103. Ibid., Jan. 25, 1944.

104. Ibid., July 9, 1944.

105. Ibid., Nov. 25, 1944.

106. Ibid., June 8 and 29, 1945.

107. Ibid., Aug. 29, 1945.

108. Ibid., Dec. 19, 1945. The editorial was entitled, "La Rosca with an anti fascist mask." See also the editorial, "Anti-fascist jingles," Dec. 27, 1945.

109. Ibid., Feb. 10, 1946.

110. Ibid., Feb. 19, 1946.

111. Ibid., May 8, 1946.

112. Ibid., Feb. 12, 1946.

113. Ibid., June 15, 1946.

114. Ibid., June 13, 1946.

115. Ibid., June 14, 1946.

116. Ibid.

117. Ibid., June 18, 1946.

118. Julio Díaz Argüedas, El derumbe de una tiranía (La revolución de julio de 1946) (La Paz, 1947), 101-103.

119. La Calle, July 6, 1946.

120. Ibid., July 9, 1946.

121. Ibid., July 12, 1946.

122. Ibid., July 14, 1946.

123. Ibid.

124. Ibid., July 18, 1946.

125. Ibid., July 11, 1946.

126. Ibid., July 18, 1946.

127. Interview with Augusto Céspedes, La Paz, Aug. 9, 1973.

128. Interview with Tristán Marof, La Paz, July 6, 1973.

129. Interview with Jacobo Libermann, La Paz, Aug. 8, 1973.

Chapter 4

1. Tristán Marof, El peligro Nazi en Bolivia, Discursos
    pronunciados en las sesiones de la H. Cámara de Dipu-
    tados el 27 y el 30 de agosto de 1941 por el doctor
    Gustavo A. Navarro, representante por Sucre (La Paz?
    1941?), 5 and 24.

2. The three dismissed MNR ministers were Víctor Paz
    Estenssoro, Rafael Otazo and Wálter Guevara Arze. Two
    other MNR cabinet members, Augusto Céspedes and Carlos
    Montenegro, had been dropped earlier.

3. Jerry W. Knudson, "Antisemitism in Latin America:
    Barometer of Social Change," Patterns of Prejudice
    (September-October 1972), 5-9.

4. La Calle, May 10, 1939. An editorial comment on June 6,
    1940, denied that a "fifth column" was operating in
    Bolivia.

5. Ibid., June 8, 1940.

6. Roberto Hinojosa, Al pueblo boliviano (Mexico, D.F.,
    1936), 6 and 11.

7. Roberto Hinojosa, Justicia social en México (Mexico, D.F.,
    1935), 70.

8. Roberto Hinojosa, Vórtice (Política internacional) (Mexico,
    D.F., 1936), 87-94, 15, 16 and 7. Hinojosa also blamed
    "the homosexual leaders of Bolivia" for the country's
    plight after the Chaco War. Al pueblo boliviano, 5.

9. Roberto Hinojosa, El mito del Rhin (Vida, pasión y gloria
    de Adolfo Hitler) (Monterrey, Mexico, n.d.) and Ecce
    Homo (Vida, pasión y milagros de Adolfo Hitler). No
    bibliographical information on the latter is given in Arturo
    Costa de la Torre, Catálogo de la bibliografía boliviana,
    Libros y folletos, 1900-1963 (La Paz, 1966).

10. Interview with Augusto Céspedes, La Paz, Aug. 9, 1973.

11. Interview with Tristán Marof, La Paz, July 6, 1973.

12. Interview with Victor Paz Estenssoro, La Paz, Aug. 11, 1973.

13. El Diario, Jan. 5, 1935.

14. La Nación, July 21, 1955.

15. El Diario, Jan. 20, 1935.

16. El Universal, March 28, 1933.

17. Ibid., April 11 and May 31, 1933. See also an article by Edmundo Guibourg, "Hunting Jews in Germany," April 11, 1933.

18. La Calle, July 2, 1936.

19. Ibid., June 8, 1838. See also editorial, "Selection of immigrants," Nov. 13, 1938.

20. Ibid., Nov. 17, 1938.

21. Ibid., May 28, 1939. See also editorial notes of July 9 and 13, 1939.

22. Ibid., Feb. 27 and March 19, 1940.

23. Ibid., Aug. 11, 1940.

24. Ibid., Sept. 4, 1940.

25. Ibid., Sept. 12, 1940. Demetrio Canelas, later to found the opposition newspaper Los Tiempos in Cochabamba in 1943, spoke in favor of this project.

26. Ibid., Oct. 25, 1940.

27. Other aspects of the Jewish affaire are discussed in Herbert S. Klein, Parties and Political Change in Bolivia, 1880-1952 (Cambridge, 1969), 307-308.

28. INTI, Dec. 5 and 6, 1940. See also the editorial, "The accusation," in the latter issue, and La Calle, Dec. 5, 6 and 12, 1940.

29. Mark Wischnitzer, To Dwell in Safety, The Story of Jewish Migration Since 1800 (Philadelphia, 1948), 198-199.

30. Interview with Tristán Marof in La Paz, July 6, 1973. Víctor Paz Estenssoro in an interview of Aug. 11, 1973,

in La Paz conceded that Marof's early socialsit thought had helped to shape the MNR, "but one cannot copyright ideas."

31. Tristán Marof denuncia a los viles calumniadores del Nazismo criollo (Broadside, n.p., n.d.) See also his 26-page pamphlet, El peligro Nazi en Bolivia (La Paz, 1941?)

32. Cole Blasier, "The United States, Germany, and the Bolivian Revolutionaries (1941-1946)," The Hispanic American Historical Review, Vol. 52 (February 1972), 26-54.

33. Céspedes first analyzed the "putsch" in La Calle on July 19, 1942. He next examined it and the Blue Book in an article which covered four pages of La Calle on May 25, 1946. It also occupied Chapter IV of El presidente colgado (Buenos Aires, 1966), 59-77, and was ultimately disposed of in "A falsified letter in search of an author," Presencia, Jan. 3, 1972. Also, the matter was discussed in an interview with Céspedes in La Paz, Aug. 9, 1973.

34. La Nación, June 7, 1959.

35. INTI, May 24, 1941.

36. Céspedes, El presidente colgado, 60-62. Emphasis in the original.

37. Ibid., 57.

38. Ibid., 65.

39. An architect, N. Ondarza and a man named Schrott, manager of Lloyd Aéreo Boliviano, also were arrested and confined briefly. Céspedes called this feeble round-up "a feat for which Peñaranda received hundreds of cablegrams of congratulation." Ibid., 65 and 76. Also, La Calle, July 19, 1942.

40. Ibid.

41. Céspedes, El presidente colgado, 70.

42. Quoted in La Calle, July 19, 1942.

43. Ibid.

44. Ibid.

45. Céspedes, El presidente colgado, 69.

46. La Calle, July 19, 1942.

47. Those whose names were printed on the broadside were José Cuadros Quiroga, Wálter Guevara Arze, Jorge Lavandenz, Alberto Mendoza López, Rafael Otayo, Hernán Siles Zuazo, Arturo Pacheco and Raúl Molina Gutiérrez. Céspedes in El presidente colgado, 66, fails to mention Pacheco, but his name was included in the newspaper accounts in La Calle, July 19, 1942 and May 25, 1946.

48. Quoted in ibid., July 19, 1942.

49. Ibid. On July 24, 1942, Céspedes, Montenegro, Cuadros Quirago, Guevara Arze, Molina, Otaco, Pacheco and Siles were sent to confinement at San Ignacio and Santa Ana de Velasco. Armando Arce was imprisoned at Sorata and Lavandenz at Chapare. Paz Estenssoro during all this was in his hometown of Tarija.

50. La Calle, May 25, 1946.

51. Ibid. Also, Céspedes, El presidente colgado, 72.

52. Carlos Montenegro, Documentos (La Paz, 1954), 10.

53. Céspedes, El presidente colgado, 77.

54. Alberto Ostría Gutiérrez, Una revolución trás los Andes (Santiago de Chile, 1944) and The Tragedy of Bolivia; A People Crucified (New York, 1958).

55. See Jerry W. Knudson, "The Bolivian Immigration Bill of 1942: A Case Study in Latin American Anti-Semitism," American Jewish Archives, Vol. XXII, No. 2 (November 1970), 138-158.

56. La Calle, Sept. 16, 1942.

57. Ibid., Sept. 26, 1942.

58. Ibid., Sept. 16, 1942.

59. Ibid., Sept. 20, 1942.

60. This is the conclusion of James Doyle, a Ph.D. candidate in history at Temple University working on Carlos Montenegro. Doyle interviewed Cuadros Quiroga in La Paz in 1975--shortly before his death.

61. La Razón printed no editorial comment on the immigration bill, perhaps not to offend Hochschild. El Diario on Sept. 19, 1942, argued for a "good" immigration bill that would exclude "parasitical groups." For reports of the debate on the excluding immigration bill, see El Diario for Sept. 18-20 and 22, 1942. See also the article, "The Jew and the future of Latin America," by Waldo Frank, Sept. 27, 1942. Frank made a special point to visit Bolivia while the immigration bill was being debated.

62. Ultima Hora, Sept. 22, 1942.

63. Ibid., Sept. 23, 1942. For other attacks in the column, "Nightcap," on opponents of Jewish immigration, see Ultima Hora for Sept. 22-25 and 30, and Oct. 1-3, 5 and 16, 1942. For other editorial comment in Ultima Hora on the immigration bill, see Sept. 24 and 26, and Oct. 1, 2 and 7, 1942. See also the article by Lucio Lanza Solares, "The immigration question in the Chamber of Deputies," Sept. 23, 1942.

64. Ibid., Sept. 21, 1942.

65. Ibid., Sept. 26, 1942.

66. Ibid., Oct. 2, 1942.

67. La Calle, April 29, 1942, listed the names of all those who voted against the exclusion of Jews in 1941. Those who voted for it were called "Defenders of the Bolivian people." PIR members Alfredo Arratia, Abelardo Villal-pando and Fernando Sinani all voted "in favor of the Jews (who would believe it!) and against the workers and exploited classes of Bolivia." For other slashing anti-Semitic attacks in La Calle, triggered by debate on the 1942 immigration bill, see the issues of Sept. 16, 23-26 and 29; Oct. 2-4, 6-8, 15-17; Nov. 11, and Dec. 5, 1942. Of particular interest is the article by Carlos Salázar, "Materialist foundation of anti-Semitism, The necessity of settling the problem with apolitical criterion," Sept. 24, 1942.

68. Interview with Víctor Paz Estenssoro in Lima, Aug. 16, 1968.

69. La Calle, May 25, 1946.

70. Interview with Augusto Céspedes, La Paz, Aug. 9, 1973.

71. INTI, June 29, 1941.

72. La Calle, Jan. 4, 1942.

73. Ibid., Feb. 8, 1942.

74. Ibid., Feb. 24, 1942.

75. Ibid., Feb. 28 and April 29, 1942.

76. Ibid., Feb. 13, 1942.

77. Ibid., May 14 and 15, 1942.

78. Ibid., Aug. 15, 1942.

79. Ibid., Sept. 13, 1942.

80. Ibid., Oct. 7, 1942.

81. Ibid., Jan. 13, 1944.

82. Ibid., Nov. 6, 1945. See also, "Once again the pass-ports," May 30, 1943.

83. Ibid., April 5, 1946.

84. Ibid., June 15, 1943.

85. Ibid., Aug. 30, 1944, "Eliminating the corruptors from the judiciary." See also, "The Supreme Court, instrument of antinational reaction," Aug. 22, 1944; "How is the Supreme Court formed?" Aug. 24, 1944; "The Supreme Court and Masonry," Aug. 25, 1944, and "The country against Masonry," Aug. 31, 1944.

86. Ibid., Sept. 1, 1944. See also, "The 'scientific' Masons," Sept. 2, 1944.

87. Ibid., Sept. 6, 1944.

88. Ibid., June 30, 1940.

89. INTI, Jan. 31, 1941.

90. Ibid., Feb. 15, 1941.

91. Ibid., June 18, 1941.

92. Ibid., June 21, 1941.

93. See, for example, ibid., July 10, 1941.

94. La Calle, July 16, 1942.

95. Ibid., June 10, 1943.

96. Ibid., June 8, 1943.

97. Tristán Marof denuncia...

98. La Calle, May 1, 1943.

99. Ibid., May 8, 1943.

100. Ibid., Jan. 16, 1944. The Tiempo cover story appeared on Dec. 31, 1943.

101. La Calle, Jan. 22, 1944.

102. Ibid., July 22, 1943.

103. Ibid., May 28, 1944.

104. Ibid., Sept. 30, 1944. See also the editorial, "Antifascist varieties," Jan. 13, 1946, and "The Nazi-fascists of today are the same as fifty years ago," Jan. 25, 1946.

105. Ibid., Nov. 18, 1942. See also comments in the column, "Politics of the Day," Dec. 10, 1942.

106. Ibid., Jan. 28, 1944. Ellipses in the original.

107. Ibid., Feb. 1, 1944.

108. Ibid., June 11, 1944. Ellipses in the original.

109. Ibid., Oct. 25, 1944.

110. Ibid., Feb. 26, 1946.

111. Ibid., April 14, 1946.

112. Ibid., June 20, 1946.

113. Interview with Jacobo Libermann, La Paz, Aug. 8, 1973.

114. La Calle, June 27, 1943. See also, "What is nationalism in Bolivia and what is Nazism in Europe?" June 18, 1943.

115. Ibid., Nov. 8, 1945.

116. Ibid., Feb. 19, 1946.

117. Ibid., April 26, 1946. Ellipses and capital letters in the original.

118. Augusto Céspedes, "Recuerdos peronistas," Visión Boliviana (April-May, 1973), 16.

119. Ibid., 16-18.

120. La Calle, Feb. 25, 1944.

121. Ibid., Sept. 20 and 21, 1944.

122. Ibid., Feb. 22, 1945.

123. Ibid., Feb. 23, 1945.

124. Ibid., March 28, 1945.

125. Ibid., March 31, 1946.

126. Ibid., June 5, 1946.

127. Interview with Augusto Céspedes, La Paz, Aug. 20, 1976.

128. La Calle, Jan. 16, 1944.

129. Víctor Paz Estenssoro, Discursos parlamentarios (La Paz, 1955), 221-222. Views on the early anti-Semitism of the MNR also were expressed by Paz Estenssoro in interviews in Lima, Aug. 17, 1968, and La Paz, Aug. 11, 1973.

Chapter 5

1. Interview with Víctor Paz Estenssoro, La Paz, Aug. 11, 1973.

2. Juan J. Vidaurre, "Brief history of the MNR press. The present press: Decalogue," La Tarde, July 29, 1960.

3. La Razón, Aug. 23, 1946.

4. Ultima Hora, Aug. 10, 1946.

5. La Razón, Jan. 1, 1947. See also Guillermo Bedregal, La revolución boliviana, Sus realidades y perspectivas dentro del ciclo de liberación de los pueblos latino-americanos (La Paz, 1962), 23-24.

6. Carlos Montenegro, Culpables (La Paz, 1955), 36.

7. La Razón, July 21, 1946.

8. Ibid., July 24 and 25, 1946.

9. Alfonso Finot, "Así cayó Villarroel" y defensa de mi relato, "Así cayó Villarroel" (La Paz, 1966), 68-69. The original account was published in Los Tiempos of Cochabamba in May 1948 and also in Presencia of La Paz in June 1965. It was first published as a pamphlet, Así cayó Villarroel, Dos palabras por Alfonso Finot (Buenos Aires, January 1948).

10. Ibid., 28.

11. Alberto Ostria Gutiérrez, The Tragedy of Bolivia, A People Crucified (New York, 1958). The allusion to the Finot story is in Un pueblo en la cruz, El drama de Bolivia, 2nd ed. (Santiago de Chile, 1956), 106-107.

12. This letter by Paz Estenssoro, dated March 31, 1951, was published in Ultima Hora, April 4, 1951. Paz attempted to rectify other statements made by Finot in his original account of January 1948. Finot's reply to Paz appeared in El Diario, April 22, 1951. The original declarations of General Damaso Arenas were published in El Diario, Aug.

10, 1946. The documents by Colonels Pinto and Ponte were printed in the La Paz press on March 1, 1951, and April 28, 1951, respectively. All of these citations are from Ostria Gutiérrez, Un pueblo en la cruz, 107, footnote 88.

13. Finot, Así cayó Villarroel, 94. The story by Matte Alessandri appeared in Las Noticias de Ultima Hora of Santiago de Chile, April 17, 1960.

14. Interview with Víctor Paz Estenssoro, La Paz, Aug. 11, 1973.

15. Alfredo Ayala Z., Historia de Bolivia, Vol. VI, Bolivia en el siglo XX, Del liberalismo a la segunda república (La Paz, 1968), 287-291. Urriolagoitia had been acting president since May 7, 1949, while Hertzog was in a hospital in Chulumani.

16. Víctor Paz Estenssoro, Mensaje a la VI convención del MNR (La Paz, 1953), 10.

17. Interview with Víctor Paz Estenssoro, La Paz, Aug. 11, 1973.

18. Interview with Raúl Murillo y Aliaga, La Paz, June 20, 1973.

19. En Marcha, March 31, 1951.

20. Interview with Raúl Murillo y Aliaga, La Paz, June 20, 1973.

21. Interview with José Fellmann Velarde, La Paz, June 19, 1973.

22. Interview with Raúl Murillo y Aliaga, La Paz, June 20, 1973.

23. En Marcha, March 13 and 31; April 5, 1951, and Jan. 19, 1952.

24. En Marcha, March 22, 1951.

25. Ibid., March 13, April 5 and May 12, 1951.

26. Ibid., March 13, 22 and 31, 1952. The huayño presented in the latter was "Always."

27. Ibid., March 22, 1951. The editorial cartoon is also from

this issue.

28. Ibid., March 31, 1951.

29. Ibid., March 22, 1951.

30. Ibid.

31. Ibid., March 31, 1951.

32. The six sets of presidential and vice-presidential candidates were Guevara Arze and Abelardo Villalpando, Party of the Revolutionary Left; Bernardino Bilbao Rioja and Alfredo Flores, Party of the Bolivian Socialist Falange; Tomás Manuel Elio and Bailón Mercado, Liberal Party; Gosálvez and Roberto Arce, Party of the Social Democratic Alliance; Guillermo Gutiérrez Vea Murguía and Julio Salmón, Bolivian Civic Action, and Paz Estenssoro and Siles Zuazo, MNR. Ayala, Historia de Bolivia, 301-302.

33. Ibid., 301 and 303.

34. En Marcha, March 31, 1951.

35. Ibid. This issue of En Marcha also printed an article, "I am a Movimientista, says Juan Lechín," and carried an account of the "massacre" at Villa Victoria, a working-class neighborhood of La Paz, in 1949.

36. Ibid., April 5, 1951.

37. Ibid. The informe of Froilán Calderón was dated Feb. 2, 1951.

38. Ibid., April 10, 1951. Other articles in this fifth issue were "Chaco veterans and the May elections;" "Our right to a port on the Pacific;" "Dr. Hernán Siles Zuazo, candidate of the people;" "The MNR defends labor;" "Miners under the terror," and a letter from Paz Estenssoro to Celestino Pinto.

39. Ibid., April 29, 1951. Other propaganda pieces were "The people and the 'saviors of the country'" and "Heroism has conquered the tyranny."

40. Ibid., May 4, 1951. Another article was headlined, "The people mocked the official binomial."

41. Ibid., May 12, 1951.

419

42. La Razón, May 3, 1951.

43. Ibid., May 10, 1951.

44. Los Tiempos, May 17, 1951.

45. En Marcha, n.d. Mimeographed.

46. En Marcha, n.d. Mimeographed.

47. Ibid., Jan. 19, 1952.

48. Jerry W. Knudson, "When Did Francisco I. Madero Decide on Revolution?" The Americas, A Quarterly Review of Inter-American Cultural History, Vol. 30, No. 4 (April 1974), 529-534.

49. En Marcha, Jan. 19, 1952. At this point, only Raúl Murillo y Aliaga was listed as editor.

50. Los Tiempos, Jan. 13, 1952.

51. Ibid., Feb. 24, 1952.

52. En Marcha, Feb. 9, 1952.

53. Los Tiempos, Feb. 24, 1952.

54. Ibid., Feb. 29, 1952. Another youth arrested, Angel Peña, was said by his parents and friends to be completely apolitical.

55. En Marcha, Feb. 9, 1952.

56. James M. Malloy, Bolivia: The Uncompleted Revolution (Pittsburgh, 1970), 230.

57. Los Tiempos, March 19, 1952.

58. The only nearly complete file of Los Tiempos anywhere is in the Library of Congress, Washington, D.C. At the time, La Paz libraries were not collecting provincial journals, and the files of the newspaper itself in Cochabamba were destroyed when a mob sacked and burned the building on Nov. 9, 1953.

59. Los Tiempos, April 10, 1952.

60. En Marcha, April 29, 1952. Articles in this issue included, "The formidable push by the MNR and

Carabineros obtained the triumph of the REVOLUTION;" "The popular strategy defeats the uniformed mercenaries," and "The rosquero diplomats betray us with [Spruille] Braden."

61. Los Tiempos, May 1, 1952.

62. Ibid., May 25, 1952.

63. Ibid., April 26, 1952.

64. Ibid., June 14, 1953. Owners of Radio Cochabamba were Hugo Maldonado, Oscar Salinas and Daniel Landaeta.

65. Interview with Víctor Paz Estenssoro, La Paz, Aug. 11, 1973.

66. Interview with Raúl Murillo y Aliaga, La Paz, June 20, 1973.

67. En Marcha, Oct. 1, 1952. After April 9, 1952, the slogan, "Year of the National Revolution," appeared above the newspaper's masthead.

68. La Nación, Jan. 30, 1959.

69. En Marcha, Feb. 9, 1957.

70. Ibid., Nov. 21, 1957. See also, Sept. 12 and 19; Oct. 3, and Dec. 28, 1957. It was charged on July 11, 1957, that because of these unrestrained personal attacks, there was a move underway to censor En Marcha.

71. Ibid., June 20, 1957. En Marcha supported stabilization in an editorial of March 7, 1957, and on other frequent occasions.

Chapter 6

1. Interview with Augusto Céspedes, La Paz, Aug. 9, 1973.

2. Tristán Marof, La tragedia del altiplano (Buenos Aires [1934]), 138-141.

3. La Nación, March 19, 1959.

4. La Razón, Jan. 1, 1943.

5. Ibid., Aug. 13, 1943.

6. La Calle, June 18, 1938.

7. See Herbert S. Klein, "David Toro and the Establishment of 'Military Socialism' in Bolivia," The Hispanic American Historical Review, Vol. 45 (February 1965), 25-52, and "Germán Busch and the Era of 'Military Socialism' in Bolivia," ibid., Vol. 47 (May 1967), 166-84.

8. Porfirio Díaz Machicao, Historia de Bolivia: Toro, Busch, Quintanilla, 1936-1940 (La Paz, 1957), 101-104.

9. La Razón, Aug. 24, 1939.

10. Ibid.

11. El Diario, Sept. 21, 1939.

12. La Razón, Feb. 16, 1952.

13. Ibid., Jan. 30, 1943.

14. Ibid., Aug. 12, 1943.

15. Ibid.

16. La Calle, June 14, 1944.

17. La Razón, Dec. 14, 1943.

18. Ultima Hora, Dec. 18, 1943.

19. La Razón, Dec. 18, 1943.

20. La Calle, Feb. 26, 1944.

21. La Razón, Dec. 27, 1943.

22. Ibid.

23. Ibid., Dec. 31, 1943.

24. Ibid., Jan. 3, 1944.

25. Ibid., Jan. 18, 1944.

26. Ibid., Jan 20, 1944.

27. Ibid., Jan. 22, 1944.

28. Ibid., Jan. 24, 1944.

29. Ibid., Jan. 14, 1944.

30. Ibid., Jan. 21, 1944.

31. Ibid.

32. Ibid., Jan. 30, 1944.

33. For the civil code, see ibid., Feb. 10 and 17, 1944. On freedom of the press, see Feb. 16 and 20, 1944. See also the editorial, "Projections of freedom of the press," Feb. 27, 1944.

34. Ibid., Feb. 2, 1944.

35. Ibid., Feb. 6, 1944. The editorial was entitled, "Dangerous partisans."

36. Ibid., Feb. 9, 1944.

37. Ibid., Feb. 10, 1944.

38. Ibid., Feb. 18, 1944.

39. Ibid., March 25, 1944.

40. La Calle, Oct. 27, 1045.

41. La Razón, July 2, 1946.

42. Ibid., July 21, 1946.

43. Ibid., July 23, 1946.

44. Ibid.

45. Ibid., July 24, 1946.

46. Ibid., July 25, 1946.

47. Ibid., July 28, 1946.

48. Ibid., July 30, 1946. See also the article, "How the bodies of Calvo, Salinas, Terrazas, Ramos and Soto were found," July 31, 1946.

49. La Nación, July 21, 1956.

50. Ibid., Sept. 27, 1958 and Sept. 27, 1959. In the latter issue there is an article by Jacinto Oblitas Benavente, the father of Oblitas.

51. La Razón, May 25, 1949.

52. Ibid., May 29, 1949.

53. Ibid.

54. Ibid., May 30, 1949. For editorial comment, see "The events of Catavi," same issue.

55. Ibid.

56. Ibid., May 31, 1949.

57. Ibid.

58. Ibid.

59. Ibid.

60. Ibid., June 1, 1949.

61. Ibid.

62. Ibid., June 2, 1949.

63. Ibid., June 5, 1949. See also the editorial, "The people defend their liberty," June 6, 1949.

64. Ibid., June 7, 1949.

65. ibid., May 1, 1951. the editorial was entitled "Independent and responsible unionism."

66. Ibid., May 3, 1951.

67. Ibid., May 4, 1951.

68. Ibid., May 5, 1951.

69. Ibid., May 7, 1951.

70. Ibid., May 8, 1951.

71. Ibid., May 10, 1951.

72. Ibid.

73. The alleged MNR-Communist Party pact is found in ibid., May 16, 1951, and Paz Estenssoro's instructions to Siles Zuazo, May 17, 1951.

74. Ibid., May 15, 1951.

75. Ibid., May 6, 1951.

76. Ibid., Jan. 13, 1951.

77. Ibid., Jan. 26, 1952.

78. Ibid., Feb. 20, 1952.

79. Ibid., March 1, 1952.

80. Ibid., March 30, 1952.

81. Ibid., Feb. 9, 1952.

82. New York Times, April 19, 1952.

83. Ibid., April 20, 1952.

84. Newsweek, June 23, 1952.

85. Los Tiempos, April 19, 1952. The editorial was entitled, "The case of La Razón."

86. Ibid., May 7, 1952. For other comments on the La Razón case in Los Tiempos, see June 10, July 11, and Oct. 19,

1952.

87. New York Times, Oct. 6, 1953.

88. Mary A. Gardner, The Inter American Press Association: Its Fight for Freedom of the Press, 1926-1960 (Austin, 1967), 159.

89. New York Times, Oct. 6, 1953.

90. Newsweek, June 2, 1952.

91. La Nación, Oct. 23, 1955.

92. Ibid., March 24, 1958.

93. Ibid., Oct. 11 and 12, 1958.

94. Ibid., Oct. 16, 1958.

95. Ibid., March 11, 1959.

96. Ibid., June 3, 1959.

97. Ibid., Oct. 3, 1959.

98. Ibid., July 19, 1959.

99. Ibid., Dec. 4, 1959.

100. Ibid., Aug. 10 and 24, 1960.

101. Ibid., Aug. 25, 1960.

102. Ibid., Dec. 14, 1959. See also Dec. 18, 1959.

103. Ibid., Oct. 31, 1960. For other criticism of the IAPA, see also May 23 and 31, and Nov. 16, 1958; Oct. 6, 7, 10 and 30, and Dec. 4 and 9, 1959; Feb. 25, and Aug. 23 and 28, 1960; and Oct. 23, 24 and 28, 1962.

104. Ibid., May 28, 1958.

105. See Jerry W. Knudson, "The Inter American Press Association as Champion of Press Freedom: Reality or Rhetoric? The Bolivian Experience, 1952-1973," paper presented to the Association for Education in Journalism, Fort Collins, Colo., August 1973. Available through ERIC.

106. See Jerry W. Knudson, "The Peruvian Press Law of 1974: The Other Side of the Coin," <u>Mass Comm Review</u>, Vol. 5, No. 2 (Spring 1978), 7-13.

Chapter 7

1. Los Tiempos, Sept. 20, 1953.

2. Ibid., Jan. 16, 1952.

3. Ibid., Sept. 20, 1953.

4. El Universal, Nov. 30, 1934.

5. See, for example, Los Tiempos, Feb. 4, 1953.

6. El Universal, Feb. 21, 1933.

7. Ibid., July 30, 1935.

8. La Calle, July 8 and 10, 1936.

9. Los Tiempos, July 24, 1946.

10. Ibid., July 21, 1946.

11. Ibid., July 24, 1946. The editorial was headlined, "21 of July! Popular revolution that marks the beginning of a new era."

12. La Nación, Aug. 27-30, 1957. Letter from Gabriel Arze Quiroga to Federico Gutiérrez Granier, Cochabamba, Sept. 14, 1949.

13. La Calle, July 13, 1944. This editorial was reprinted from Los Tiempos of July 9, 1944.

14. Los Tiempos, April 24, 1952.

15. Ibid., April 25, 1952.

16. Ibid., April 27, 1952.

17. Ibid., April 6, 1952.

18. The "Page of the MNR" appeared on April 8, 12, 19, 22, 27 and 29; and May 4, 5 and 27, 1951.

429

19. <u>Los Tiempos</u>, Jan. 12, 1952.

20. Ibid., Feb. 13, 1952.

21. Ibid., Feb. 17, 1952.

22. Ibid., Feb. 22, 1952.

23. Ibid., Feb. 29, 1952.

24. Ibid., April 1, 1952.

25. Ibid., Jan. 7, 1953.

26. See, for example, <u>Los Tiempos</u>, Jan. 8, 1953.

27. Ibid., Oct 30 and Nov. 4, 1952. A letter from R. Cabero, administrator of the newspaper, to the <u>Jefe del Trabajo</u> was also printed, Oct. 30, 1952.

28. Ibid., Jan. 16, 1953.

29. Ibid., Feb. 1, 1953. The resolution was dated Jan. 31, 1953, in Cochabamba and was signed by Javier del Granado, president, and Jaime Canelas López, secretary.

30. Ibid., Feb. 22, 1953. See also Feb. 6 and 7, 1953.

31. Ibid., April 16, 1953.

32. Ibid., May 29, 1953. This article from Antofagasta was dated only May 1953. Other installments appeared in <u>Los Tiempos</u> on June 3, 6, 7, 11, 23 and 27; and July <u>9, 1953.</u> Dorado's pseudonyms on <u>Los Tiempos</u> were Juan del Valle, Ocky (sports) and Repo<u>rtero X.</u>

33. Ibid., May 15, 1953.

34. Ibid., May 16, 1953.

35. Ibid., May 21, 1953.

36. Interview with Augusto Céspedes, La Paz, Aug. 9, 1973.

37. <u>Los Tiempos</u>, May 10, 1953.

38. Ibid., July 11, 1953.

39. Ibid., July 15, 1953.

40. Ibid., July 17, 1953.

41. Ibid., July 19, 1953.

42. Ibid., July 21, 1953.

43. Ibid., July 29, 1953.

44. Ibid., July 21, 1953.

45. Ibid., July 29, 1953.

46. Ibid., July 30, 1953.

47. Ibid., July 31, 1953.

48. Ibid. Canelas reprinted the complete texts of all these telegrams in his newspaper.

49. Ibid., Aug. 1, 1953. The editorial was headlined, "The problem of provision of paper for 'Los Tiempos.'"

50. Ibid., Aug. 2, 1953.

51. Ibid., Aug. 9, 1953. The article was entitled, "The assistant secretary fulfills his plans of interrupting the editions of 'Los Tiempos.'"

52. Ibid., Aug. 22, 1953.

53. Ibid., Aug. 25, 1953.

54. Ibid., April 4, 1952.

55. Ibid., April 10, 1952. The banner headline on the front page read, AFTER TEN MONTHS AND THIRTEEN DAYS THE MILITARY JUNTA GOVERNMENT CONFRONTS A SUBVERSIVE MOVEMENT.

56. Ibid., May 24, 1952.

57. Ibid., May 1, 1951. This item in "National Happenings" was subtitled, "Incurable sorrows of Bolivian democracy."

58. Ibid., Jan. 5, 1952. The editorial was headlined, "An aspect of the Bolivian crisis."

59. Ibid., July 23, 1952.

60. Ibid., July 25, 1952. The Liberal Party deplored the

431

universal suffrage in a resolution of Aug. 23, 1952. On Sept. 19, 1952, Los Tiempos also printed an interview with René Canelas, professor of constitutional law at San Simón University in Cochabamba, on the universal vote.

61. Ibid., Oct. 29, 1952.

62. Ibid., Aug. 28, 1953. The editorial was entitled, "The Revolution and private initiative."

63. Lee Hills, "The Story of the IAPA," Nieman Reports, Vol. 23, No. 1 (March 1969), 6.

64. La Nación, Oct. 16 and 20, 1959. For other comments on the case of Los Tiempos, see also March 24 and 25, 1955; Aug. 27-31, 1957; May 28, Oct. 11, and Dec. 25, 1958; Aug. 17 and 24, Sept. 1, and Oct. 9, 1959; Feb. 13, March 10, May 12 and 22, and Oct. 19, 1960; and Feb. 24 and Oct. 21, 1961.

65. [Demetrio Canelas], Los Tiempos, Historia de diez años de periodismo (Cochabamba, 1960), 221.

66. Ibid., 221-224.

67. Interview with José Fellmann Velarde, La Paz, June 19, 1973. Fellmann Velarde held four positions in the MNR government: minister of state, executive secretary of the MNR political committee, private secretary to the president, and sub-secretary of press, culture and propaganda.

68. Canelas, Los Tiempos, 224-226.

69. Ibid., 226-227. The letter was dated Jan. 20, 1954.

70. Ibid., 229-231.

71. Ibid., 228-229.

72. Ibid., 232-233.

73. [IAPA], XVIII Annual Meeting, October, 1962 (Mexico City, 1963), 160-169.

74. [IAPA], XXV Annual Meeting, October, 1969 (Mexico City, 1970), 161-162. Also, letter to the author from James B. Canel, general manager, IAPA, June 27, 1972.

75. Canelas, Los Tiempos, 233.

76. La Nación, May 28, 1958.

77. Ibid., Oct. 19, 1960.

78. Ibid., Oct. 19, 1961.

79. Ibid., Dec. 25, 1958.

80. Ibid., Feb. 13, 1960. La Nación published letters from other newspapers attacking the universal vote. See, for example, March 10, 1960.

81. Ibid., May 22, 1960.

82. Ibid., Feb. 24, 1961. See also the editorial by Hubo Vial, "Freedom of press in Bolivia," Oct. 21, 1961.

83. Ibid., March 25, 1955.

84. Ibid., Aug. 17, 1959. Canelas was attacked again on Aug. 24, 1959, with the statement, "There are appearing machinators of intrigues that still survive, such as Canelas."

85. Ibid., Sept. 1, 1959.

86. La Tarde, Feb. 13, 1960.

Chapter 8

1. La Nación, Sept. 18, 1958.

2. La Calle, Feb. 2, 1946.

3. Comisión de nacionalización de minas. La nacionalización de las minas, Decretos (La Paz, 1952), 11.

4. Porfirio Díaz Machicao, Historia de Bolivia: Toro, Busch, Quintanilla, 1936-1940 (La Paz, 1957), 101-104.

5. Comisión de nacionalización, 9.

6. La República, July 9, 1932.

7. El Universal, March 29, 1935.

8. La Calle, June 25, 1936.

9. El Universal, Feb. 6, 1935.

10. Víctor Paz Estenssoro, Mensaje del 9 de abril (La Paz? 1956), 3.

11. La Calle, March 19, 1937.

12. Ibid., Jan. 25, 1945. See also "Economic reality of the Banco Minero de Bolivia," March 16, 1945, and "The whys of previous permissions for importation," Aug. 21, 1945.

13. Ibid., Feb. 20, 1937.

14. Ibid., March 21, 1937.

15. Ibid., March 3, 1937. See also the editorial comment, "Inexplicable representation," March 24, 1937.

16. Ibid., April 20, 1937.

17. Paz Estenssoro, Mensaje del 9 de abril, 3.

18. La Calle, May 16 and 22, 1946. See also editorial, "Evasions of the miners," May 9, 1946.

435

19. Ibid., May 14, 1946.

20. Ibid., May 19, 1946.

21. La Nación, June 5, 1956.

22. La Calle, June 26, 1936.

23. Ibid., July 1, 1936.

24. Ibid., July 8, 1936.

25. Ibid., July 9, 1936.

26. Ibid., July 10, 1936.

27. Ibid., Oct. 17, 1944.

28. Ibid., Jan. 6, 1945.

29. Ibid., June 15, 1945.

30. Ibid., Jan. 20, 1946.

31. Ibid., May 24, 1946.

32. Ibid., July 24, 1945.

33. La Nación, June 17, 1958. Author of the article was José Fellmann Velarde.

34. Ibid., July 3, 1959.

35. Ibid., Jan. 8, 1960. Author of these articles, which appeared in Novedades in December 1959, was Agustín Barrios Gómez.

36. La Nación, Jan. 9, 1960.

37. Ibid., Jan. 10, 1960.

38. Ibid., Jan 13, 1960. Author of the Novedades article, "'The Devil's Metal' and Bolivia," was Graciela Mendoza, who also quoted the book by Ernesto Galarza, El caso Bolivia.

39. La Nación, May 20, 1960.

40. Augusto Céspedes, Metal del diablo (Buenos Aires, 1960), 266.

41. Interview with Augusto Céspedes, La Paz, Aug. 9, 1973.

42. La Nación, Nov. 15, 1960.

43. Ibid., Nov. 29, 1960.

44. An account of the incident favorable to the mining magnate is Luis Adrián R., Secuestro Hochschild (Buenos Aires, 1951).

45. La Calle, Oct. 12 and 14-16, 1943. See also "Luis Herrero, Busch's minister, speaks about the shooting of Hochschild..." Nov. 5-7, 1943.

46. La Calle, Nov. 10, 1942.

47. Ibid., March 5-7, 1942. See also "Hochschild tries to stop Parliament from examining the subsidy of the Atocha-Villazón railroad," July 24, 1942.

48. Ibid., March 12, 1942. Coverage of the railroad scandal continued on Sept. 12 and 15, and Nov. 7, 1942.

49. Ibid., Nov. 10 and 11, 1942.

50. Ibid., March 24, 1942.

51. Ibid., July 30, 1942.

52. Ibid., Nov. 21, 1942.

53. Ibid., Sept. 26, 1943.

54. Ibid., Aug. 6, 1943.

55. Ibid., Aug. 10, 1943.

56. Ibid., April 29 and 30, 1944.

57. Ibid., May 24 and June 16, 1944.

58. Ibid., Dec. 3, 1944.

59. Ibid., Dec. 8, 1944.

60. Ibid., Dec. 9 and 12, 1944, and June 20 22, 1945.

61. Ibid., Sept. 23, 1945.

62. Ibid., March 10 and 14, 1946.

63. Ibid., Oct. 9, 1943.

64. La República, Jan. 24, 1932.

65. El Universal, Feb. 23, 1933.

66. Ibid., Sept. 14, 1934.

67. La Calle, June 24, 1936.

68. Ibid., Feb. 22, 1942.

69. Ibid., July 9, 1942.

70. Ibid., Oct. 8 and 9, 1943.

71. Ibid., Dec. 9, 1943.

72. Ibid., Oct. 27, 1944.

73. Ibid., Oct. 26 and 27, 1944, and Nov. 24, 1945.

74. Ibid., Dec. 1 and 2, 1945, and Jan. 3 and 5, 1946. See
    also the editorial, "Another fraud of Aramayo," Jan. 9,
    1946.

75. Ibid., Jan. 9, 1946.

76. Ibid., April 9, 1946.

77. Ibid., June 9, 1946.

78. Ibid., June 19, 1946. Ellipses in the original.

79. La Nación, April 20, 1959.

80. Ibid., April 22, 1959.

81. Ibid., March 9 and 11, 1960. See also, "Hertzog demon-
    strates in his letter hatred for [everything] national and
    various [other] degenerations," March 9, 1960. Gerardo
    Schamis, Argentine ambassador in La Paz, said his
    country would guard her borders with Bolivia carefully.
    Ibid., March 11, 1960. See also commentary on different
    reactions, ibid., March 12, 1960: "Distortion of the news
    in Venezuela;" "Indignation against the Bolivian
    government," by Peruvian Chancellor Alvaro Garrido;
    "Cooperation from the Argentine government," and "No
    response by Brazil."

82. La Nación, Sept. 13, 1960.

83. Los Tiempos, May 9, 1952.

84. Comisión de nacionalización, 18.

85. Los Tiempos, May 13 and 14, 1952. See also, "Special commission will study nationalization of the mines," May 15, 1952.

86. Ibid., Aug. 5, 1952.

87. Ibid., Sept. 3, 1952.

88. ibid., Oct. 17 and 18, 1952. Biographical data on members of the commission to study nationalization of the mines was given on Oct. 31, 1952.

89. Ibid., Oct. 11, 1952.

90. Ibid., Nov. 4, 1952.

91. Ibid., Nov. 5, 1952.

92. Ibid., Nov. 6, 1952.

93. Ibid., Oct. 24, 1952.

94. Ibid., Oct. 23, 1952.

95. Ibid., Oct. 26, 1952.

96. Ibid., Oct. 28, 1952.

97. Ibid., Oct. 2, 1953.

98. Ibid., Nov. 11-13, 1952.

99. Ibid., Nov. 25, 1952, and Feb. 6, 1953.

100. Ibid., Dec. 11, 1952.

101. La Nación, May 26, 1956.

102. Ibid., April 13 and June 18, 1958.

103. La Calle, Dec. 15, 1944.

104. La Nación, Aug. 2, 1955.

105. Ibid., Aug. 10, 1958. See also, "COMIBOL report," Feb. 17, 1960, and "Indemnification to the Patiño group," Feb. 18, 1960.

106. La Tarde, Oct. 31, 1960.

107. Ibid., Nov. 23, 1960.

108. Ibid., April 25 and 26, 1961. See also, "Triangular Plan or the liquidation of COMIBOL," Aug. 11, 1961; "Víctor Paz: The Triangular Plan will benefit the workers," Aug. 29, 1961; "Triangular Plan: There is no opposition. The mining workers reveal their maturity and their responsibility," Aug. 30, 1961, and "Personages voice their opinions concerning the 'Triangular Plan,'" Aug. 31, 1961.

109. Ibid., Aug. 19, 1962.

110. Ibid., May 28, 1960.

111. Ibid., Sept. 14, 1960. See also, "Defense of the little mining interests," June 3, 1961; "The new mining code," Oct. 9, 1961, and "National foundries for tin," Nov. 17, 1961.

112. Interview with Augusto Céspedes, La Paz, Aug. 9, 1973.

113. Reprinted in La Nación, Jan. 17, 1955.

Chapter 9

1. Tristán Marof, La tragedia del altiplano (Buenos Aires, [1941]), 42. Marof published some 25 books and pamphlets. Also important in discussing the Indian problem was his La justicia del Inca (Brussels, 1926).

2. Ruth Stephan, ed., The Singing Mountaineers, Songs and Tales of the Quechua People (Austin, 1957), 5, has noted that "the Quechua language, which derives from the court language of the Incas, is spoken more extensively now than at the end of the Inca reign in the sixteenth century." Quechua is the major Amerindian language; perhaps as many as 18 million people in South America speak it, while about one million speak Aymara. J.E. Monast, Los indios aimares (Buenos Aires, 1972), 9.

3. Richard W. Patch, "Population Review 1970: Bolivia," American Universities Field Staff Reports, West Coast Latin America Series, Vol. XVIII, No. 1 (December 1970), 2-4 and 6-7. See also his "The La Paz Census of 1970, With Comments on Other Problems of Counting People in a Developing Country," ibid., Vol. XVII, No. 12 (June 1970). Demographically, Bolivia is not typical of Latin America: population growth is less, the country is not over-populated (although the population is maldistributed), and countryside to city migration is slight.

4. Patch, "Population Review 1970," 5-6. The figure of 60 percent illiteracy counts only those over 15 years of age and probably does not include many functional illiterates.

5. Harold Osborne, Indians of the Andes, Aymaras and Quechuas (London, 1952), xi, noted: "The very name 'Indians' had no other justification than the famous blunder of Columbus. Its continued use had a twofold disadvantage. It encouraged the tendency to lump all the people of the New World together as 'backward' races... And it has encouraged the quite false supposition that all the peoples of the Americas are united by links of conscious kinship."

6. Paul Radin, Indians of South America (New York, 1942), 277.

441

7. Quoted in Los Tiempos, Nov. 14, 1952. The full citation for Reyeros' work is Historia social del indio boliviano, "El ponqueaje" (La Paz, 2nd ed., 1963).

8. Ibid., Dec. 9, 1952.

9. Ibid., Feb. 12, 1953.

10. Ibid.

11. Hans C. Buechler and Judith-Maria Buechler, The Bolivian Aymará (New York, 1971), 3.

12. Osborne, Indians of the Andes, 201.

13. Quoted in ibid., 201.

14. La Nación, Nov. 30, 1962.

15. Herbert S. Klein, Parties and Political Change in Bolivia, 1880-1952 (Cambridge, 1969), 189.

16. James M. Malloy, Bolivia: The Uncompleted Revolution (Pittsburgh, 1970), 75. The U.S. anthropoligist Richard W. Patch does believe that the Chaco War stimulated Indian aspirations.

17. Abelardo Villalpando R., El problema del indio y la reforma agraria (Potosí, 1960), 4-5. La Tarde, MNR newspaper, noted on April 4, 1960, that the Indian had been taken to the Chaco "like the lamb to the sacrificial pyre..."

18. José Fellmann Velarde, Historia de Bolivia (La Paz, 3 vols., 1968-1970), III, 138.

19. Nazario Pardo Valle, "The Indians and the war," El Universal, March 24, 1933.

20. Ibid., March 19, 1935.

21. La Calle, April 10, 1946.

22. Ibid.

23. El Universal, Jan. 13, 1934.

24. Ibid., Jan. 15, 1934.

25. La Calle, July 27, 1945.

26. Ibid., March 14, 1945.

27. Los Tiempos, Jan. 19, 1952.

28. Ibid., March 15, 1952. Canelas noted that of the other 40 percent of the population, some 20 percent formed part of the bureaucracy--fiscal and municipal administration, army, judiciary and the like--and thus supported the incumbent government.

29. Interview with Douglas Henderson, United States ambassador to Bolivia, La Paz, June 28, 1968.

30. James M. Malloy, "Revolutionary Politics" in Malloy and Richard S. Thorn, eds., Beyond the Revolution, Bolivia Since 1952 (Pittsburgh, 1971), 124.

31. Carter Goodrich, "Bolivia in Time of Revolution," ibid., 18.

32. Los Tiempos, April 19, 1952.

33. Ibid., April 20, 1952. An expanded version of Arze's comments filled two-and-a-half columns in the issue of April 22, 1952.

34. Ibid., April 26, 1952.

35. Ibid., April 29, 1952. The article was headlined, "The latifundio and [methods of] farming."

36. Ibid., May 1, 1952. The editorial was entitled, "Concerning revolutionary reforms."

37. Ibid., May 21, 1952.

38. Ibid., June 17, 1952. The editorial was headlined, "Vast campesino agitation."

39. Ibid., June 18, 1952.

40. Ibid., June 21, 1952.

41. Ibid.

42. Ibid., June 24, 1952. The editorial was entitled, "Economic independence."

43. Ibid., July 3, 1952.

44. Ibid., July 18, 1952, The editorial was headlined, "Privileged juncture is in risk of being lost."

45. Ibid.

46. Ibid.

47. Ibid., Aug. 2, 1952. The newspaper added, "Neither the Indians nor the whites [chapetones] of 1952 are worth what they were worth in 1780 [the time of the revolt of Tupac Amaru]."

48. Ibid., Sept. 23, 1952. On the following day in Cochabamba, Los Tiempos interviewed Guillermo Alborta, minister of agriculture.

49. Ibid., Nov. 7, 1952. See also the column on Sept. 24, 1952, by "Labrador" on "Disorder in the countryside."

50. Ibid., Nov. 9 and 11, 1952.

51. Ibid., Nov. 12, 1952. Significantly, the editorial was entitled, "Problem of the Indian converted into the problem of the patrón."

52. Ibid., Nov. 9, 1952.

53. Ibid., Nov. 15, 1952. The document was dated Nov. 11, 1952, and was signed by Sinforoso Rivas, secretary general, and Agapito Vallejos, secretary of [public] relations.

54. Ibid.

55. Ibid., Dec. 6, 1952.

56. Ibid., Dec. 16, 1952.

57. Ibid., Dec. 2, 1952.

58. Ibid., Dec. 20, 1952.

59. Ibid., Feb. 22, 1953.

60. Ibid., Dec. 23, 1952. The speech at the reunion by Ñuflo Chávez, minister of Indian affairs, was printed Dec. 25 and 28, 1952.

61. Ibid., Dec. 28, 1952.

62. Ibid., Jan. 25, 1953.

63. The first installment appeared in Los Tiempos on Feb. 10, 1953, followed by others on March 3, 10, 18 and 25; April 1, 14 and 23, and May 7, 1953.

64. Ibid., April 8, 1953.

65. Ibid., April 17, 1953.

66. Ibid., April 19, 1953.

67. Ibid., April 23, 1953.

68. Ibid., April 25, 1953.

69. Ibid., May 1, 1953.

70. Ibid., May 3, 1953. It was also reported on May 5, 1953, that the decree of April 30 and the absence of Víctor Zannier, coordinator of the campesinos, had brought tranquility back to the countryside. Nevertheless, hacendados were said to be arming themselves at Totora, Pojo, Tacopaya and elsewhere.

71. Ibid., May 9, 1953.

72. Ibid., May 13, 1953.

73. Ibid., June 25, 1953.

74. Ibid., July 1, 1953. See also the article of July 4, 1953, "Preoccupation in the agrarian reform commission for events in the valley."

75. Ibid., July 5, 1953. On July 8, 1953, the newspaper reported that Víctor Zannier, head of the office of Indian affairs in Cochabamba, had attributed the "bloody events" to the villagers of Tarata and Vila Vila.

76. Ibid., July 9, 1953. The editorial was headlined, "Projections of the indigenous movement."

77. Ibid., July 11, 1953. In the attack upon Tarata, for example, Indians reportedly seized 70 rifles and two cases of bullets.

78. Ibid. The editorial, "Sanction against the rebels," appeared in La Patria, July 7, 1953.

79. Los Tiempos, July 15, 1953.

80. Ibid., July 19, 1953.

81. Ibid., July 23-25, 1953.

82. Ibid., July 25, 1953. It was pointed out that the directory of fundamental education of the ministry of campesino affairs would work for basic education in the countryside.

83. The text of the agrarian reform decree may be found in La Revolución Nacional a través de sus decretos más importantes (La Paz, 1955), 41-80.

84. Los Tiempos, July 28, 1953. The editorial was entitled, "Campaign of racial revenges [is] contrary to the public good."

85. Ibid., July 30, 1953.

86. Ibid., July 30, 1953.

87. La Nación, Jan. 24, 1960.

88. Los Tiempos, Aug. 2, 1953.

89. Ibid., Aug. 5, 1953.

90. Ibid., Sept. 19, 1953. Another extract from this book, headlined, "Without the Indian there would be no Bolivia," was printed on Oct. 1, 1953.

91. Letter from Edward J. Sparks to the author, June 30, 1974.

92. Los Tiempos Aug. 5, 1953.

93. Ibid.

94. Ibid., Aug. 22, 1953.

95. Ibid., Aug. 23, 1953.

96. Ibid., Aug. 27, 1953.

97. Ibid., Aug. 28, 1953.

98. Ibid., Sept. 22, 1953.

99. Ibid., Sept. 29, 1953.

100. Interview with Víctor Paz Estenssoro, La Paz, Aug. 11, 1973.

101. Los Tiempos, Sept. 4, 1953.

Chapter 10

1. Interview with Víctor Paz Estenssoro, Lima, Aug. 16, 1968, and Víctor Paz Estenssoro, Mensaje de año nuevo (La Paz, 1952), 9.

2. La Nación, May 16, 1956.

3. Julio Díaz Argüedas, Historia del ejército de Bolivia, 1825-1932 (La Paz, 1940), 20 and 33.

4. Sub-Secretary of Press, Information and Culture, Filosofía de la Revolución Nacional (La Paz, n.d.), 76-79.

5. In the first three decades of this century, these training missions came from Germany, under the leadership of Major (later General) Hans Kundt on four assignments between 1911 and 1933--the last directing Bolivian troops in the Chaco. Díaz Argüedas, Historia del ejército, 758-776.

6. Sub-Secretary of Press, Information and Culture, Filosofía, 76-79, and Julio Díaz Argüedas, El derrumbe de una tiranía (La revolución de julio de 1946) (La Paz, 1947), 11-12.

7. Nicanor Aranzaes, Las revoluciones de Bolivia (La Paz, 1918), i.

8. C[arlos] Blanco G[alindo], Resumen de la historia militar de Bolivia (Guerras de la independencia e internacionales) (La Paz, 1922), 98.

9. M. Fernando Wilde C. Historia militar de Bolivia (La Paz, 1963), 21.

10. Wálter Guevara Arze, Planteamientos de la Revolución Nacional en la décima conferencia interamericana (La Paz, 1954), 27. English translation in the original.

11. La Nación, June 16, 1956.

12. Ibid., July 2, 1956.

13. Ibid., Sept. 6, 1959.

14. Ibid., Dec. 3, 1962. See also Jaime Ayala Mercado, "New conscience of the army and the air force," Dec. 7, 1962.

15. bid., Aug. 27, 1955.

16. Ibid., Oct. 7, 1955.

17. Ibid., Oct. 9, 1957. The debate over the role of the military in the revolutionary government also brought heated exchanges in the letters-to-the-editor columns of the La Paz press. See the statement by General Julio Prado Montaño, minister of defense, and all other command officers in La Nación, Oct. 9, 1957, backing Siles but objecting to the term "institutional" army used by El Diario which, they believed, tended to restore the stigma of "the massacring army at the service of the oligarchy." See also the letter from Montaño to José Carrasco Jiménez, editor of El Diario, on Oct. 12, 1957, reprinted in La Nación, Oct. 14, 1957. Montaño, speaking only for himself, called it a "criminal intention" to suggest doing away with the Bolivian army, one which would lead to "inevitable chaos."

18. There has been no systematic study of clashes between the military and campesinos, but for labor see Agustín Barcelli S., Medio siglo de luchas sindicales revolucionarias en Bolivia (La Paz, 1956).

19. La Nación, Sept. 18, 1958.

20. Ibid., Sept. 28, 1958.

21. Ibid., Feb. 25, 1956. The two Latin American Democratic Action (ADL) members were Nicolás Besio Moreno and Estala Acosta Lecube. The president and secretary of the Tupaj Katari center for social studies, González Sánchez de Loria and Ernesto Landivar, sent a letter denying charges that human rights had been violated in Bolivia. See also the letter from Manuel Frontaura Argandoña, secretary to the president, to Besio Moreno of the ADL, Feb. 28, 1956.

22. Ibid., Jan. 28, 1956.

23. Ibid., May 1, 1956.

24. Ibid. Held responsible for the second Catavi massacre were Mamerto Urriolagoitia, Alfredo Mollinedo, Ovidio

Quiroga, Isaac Vicenti, Ernesto Monasterio, Gastón Arduz Eguía; Cols. Roberto Ramallo, Armando Ichazo, Rubén Rioja and Enrique Vacaflor; Col. of Carabineros Váldez Anibarro and Lt. of Carabineros, Luis Elío Alborta. Those who piloted the bombing planes were Capts. Fernando Etchenique and Hernán Justiniano Melgar.

25. Ibid., May 29, 1956.

26. Ibid., May 1, 1956.

27. Ibid., May 18, 1956.

28. See Pedro Zilveti Arze, Bajo el signo de la barbarie (Matanzas de noviembre) (Santiago de Chile, [1946]).

29. La Nación, Oct. 25, 1957. Quiroga said he had the "diligent advice" of Pedro Zilveti Arze in drafting his manifesto, "In defense of the armed forces of Bolivia."

30. Ibid., April 19, 1955.

31. Ibid., April 20, 1955.

32. Ibid., May 5, 1955. The column was headlined, "The army of the National Revolution."

33. Ibid., Aug. 9, 1955.

34. Ibid., July 22, 1955.

35. Ibid., Aug. 25, 1955. The editorial was entitled, "The army's labor." See also, "The army in the Revolution," March 16, 1956.

36. Ibid., Aug. 8, 1958.

37. Ibid., Nov. 28, 1859.

38. Mensaje del presidente constitucional de la república de Bolivia, Dr. Victor Paz Estenssoro a su pueblo (La Paz? Aug. 6, 1953), 20.

39. See Robert J. Alexander, The Bolivian National Revolution (New Brunswick, N.J., 1958).

40. Sub-Secretary of Press, Information and Culture, Filosofía, 75.

41. La Nación, Oct. 19, 1961. The newspaper was reporting

a conference given by Alfredo Franco Guachalla, minister of work and social security, in the Institute of Higher Military Studies. His remarks were continued in the issues of Oct. 20 and 21, 1961.

42. Ibid., Feb. 3, 1956. The occasion of this commentary was the graduation of the first class of pilots from the Colegio Militar de Irpavi.

43. Ibid., Aug. 17, 1955. There were also five civilian administrators at the Colegio and thirteen military command staff. Main speaker for the day was Col. Inocencio Valendia Valle, commander of the Colegio.

44. Ibid., Sept. 28, 1958. This information was from the address of President Hernán Siles Zuazo to Congress.

45. Quoted in ibid., May 21, 1955.

46. Ibid., Sept. 28, 1958.

47. Ibid., Feb. 12, 1956.

48. Ibid., Feb. 9, 1955.

49. Ibid., April 19, 1958.

50. Ibid., Sept. 28, 1959.

51. Ibid., Feb. 28, 1961. See also the editorial, "Late PURS alarm for a political army," Jan. 4, 1961.

52. Ibid., July 5, 1955.

53. Ibid., Feb. 19, 1957.

54. Ibid., April 30, 1955.

55. Ibid., April 3, 1956.

56. Ibid., Feb. 3, 1956.

57. Ibid., March 18, 1955.

58. Ibid., Jan. 8, 1956.

59. Víctor Paz Estenssoro, Informe a la VII convención nacional del Movimiento Nacionalista Revolucionario (La Paz, 1956), [28].

60. See the article by Lt. Col. Hugo Antezana C. about the road to Ichilo, a joint project between the army and the Corporacion Boliviana de Fomento, La Nación, Nov. 30, 1961.

61. Ibid., Oct. 22, 1961. See also the editorial, "The army in action," Nov. 16, 1961, which applauded the 12-year civic action plan.

62. Ibid., May 8, 1955.

63. Ibid., Jan. 30, 1958.

64. Ibid., Jan. 11, 1962. See also Jan. 26, 1962, for a speech by Juan Luis Gutiérrez Granier, minister of national defense, "The armed forces in the plan of economic-social development," and editorial comment, "The new military mentality."

65. Interview with Víctor Paz Estenssoro, La Paz, Aug. 11, 1973.

66. La Nación, April 26, 1958.

67. Ibid., May 8, 1955.

68. Ibid., May 10, 1955.

69. Ibid., May 19, 1955.

70. Ibid., Jan. 8, 1956.

71. Ibid., May 7, 1956.

72. Ibid., May 2, 1955. El País of Montevideo reported on Oct. 23, 1958, reprinted in La Nación on Nov. 4, 1958, that the MNR had about 80,000 armed men in both the miners' and campesinos' militias, probably a more accurate estimate.

73. Ibid., April 11, 1956.

74. Ibid., Aug. 1, 1955, reprinted from La Prensa of Lima, July 31, 1955. Paz Estenssoro, on a state visit to General Manuel A. Odría of Peru, added that soon the Bolivian army would no longer be a charge of the state. Its double function was to defend the terrirotial integrity and to work through its squadrons of engineers and electrical technicians to open roads, study hydroelectric possibilities and to place in cultivation previously unused

lands.

75. Ibid., Jan. 7, 1956.

76. Sub-Secretary of Press, Information and Culture. El M.N.R. Gobierno de obreros[,] campesinos y gente de la clase media. Mensajes y manifiestos del 1 de mayo [1953], 43.

77. Ibid., May 29, 1958. The author was "Uyustus," writing in the column, "Theory and Action."

78. Ibid., Aug. 15, 1955. Siles was quoted in an editorial, "On the next elections."

79. Ibid., March 21, 1956.

80. Ibid., Oct. 22, 1958. See also Oct. 21, 1958, when La Nación replied to an El Diario editorial of Sept. 17, 1958, under the heading, "The militias and the army."

81. La Nación, April 13, 1956. The editorial was entitled, "Armed democracy."

82. Ibid., Sept. 24, 1958. Title of the editorial was "Rule of security and public order."

83. Ibid., Sept. 16, 1958.

84. Ibid., Dec. 25, 1958.

85. Ibid., Sept. 16, 1958.

86. Ibid., May 28, 1958. The headline referred to "subversive affirmations" by El Diario.

87. Ibid., Sept. 19, 1958.

88. Ibid., Sept. 16, 1958.

89. Ibid., Jan. 23, 1959.

90. Ibid., Feb. 18, 1959.

91. Ibid., Sept. 28, 1959.

92. Ibid., Dec. 11, 1955. Other installments of the interview were printed on Dec. 7-10 and 13, 1955.

93. Ibid., Feb. 28, 1959. J. Cayo, "Evaluation of the

revolutionary forces."

94. See Antonio Seleme Vargas, <u>Mi actuación en la Junta Militar de Gobierno con el pronunciamento revolucionario del 9 de abril de 1952</u> (La Paz, 1969).

95. La Nación, Oct. 8, 1960.

96. Ibid., April 23, 1955. The editorial was headlined, "Armed forces and production."

97. Ibid., Feb. 14, 1955.

98. Ibid., June 24, 1955.

99. Ibid., June 25, 1955.

100. Ibid., Dec. 29, 1957. See also the issue of Dec. 30, 1957, which reported the speech of Lt. Col. Carlos Godoy Godoy at the graduation of officers from the National Policy Academy.

101. Ibid., June 24, 1956.

102. Ibid., Sept. 24 and 28, 1955.

103. Ibid., Sept. 19, 1958.

104. Ibid., Jan. 7, 1959. The commentary was entitled, "Army, people in arms."

105. Ibid., June 8, 1960.

106. For information and comment on the U.S. military aid, including the Bolivian congressional interpelation of late 1962, see ibid., Feb. 3 and May 30, 1956; April 30, 1957, and Dec. 9, 1962.

107. Ibid., Feb. 4, 1956.

108. Ibid., Aug. 7, 1956.

109. Ibid,, Dec. 28, 1956. The ministry of national defense received 3,569,006,186 bolivianos, compared to 4,250,063, 063 for education and fine arts.

110. Ibid., Dec. 25, 1956.

111. Text of the reorganizaiton decree is given in ibid., Oct. 6, 1957. For other commentary on the relationship

between Siles and the military, see June 17 and Oct. 4, 1957, and march 6, 1958. See also Hernán Siles Zuazo, Cuatro años de gobierno revolucionario, 1956-1960 (La Paz? 1960?), [13] and [60-64].

112. Interview with Víctor Paz Estenssoro, La Paz, Aug. 11, 1973. Another factor which strengthened the army's hand was the Río Lauca dispute with Chile. See La Nación, Dec. 12, 1961, and the editorial, "Bitter aftertaste of Praetorianism," Sept. 8, 1962.

113. See, for example, "Generals of the Revolution," ibid., Dec. 24, 1955; "The army and the press," Oct. 17, 1957; response to an El Diario editorial of Oct. 18, 1957, in La Nación, Oct. 19, 1957; "An army for liberty," Oct. 29, 1957; "Correction and tolerance," Oct. 20, 1957; "The national army, the reactionary press and the campesinos" and "The horde of 'El Diario'" by Amado Canelas, June 27, 1958; Presencia, Aug. 23, 1959; El Diario, Aug. 24, 1959; Ultima Hora, Aug. 25 and 26, 1959; La Nación, Aug. 26, 1959; "The army" in El Diario, Nov. 30, 1959, commented upon in La Nación, Dec. 1, 1959, in the article, "Nostalgic reminiscences of the Liberal Patiñista dean on the Praetorian army of tin;" "The new Bolivian army," Feb. 20, 1960; "Another oligarchical record: 16 dead and 106 wounded," March 20, 21 and 26, 1960; speech of General Luis Rodríguez Bigegain, army commander-in-chief, July 22, 1960; report of General René González Torres in Presencia, commented upon by La Nación, Oct. 29, 1960, and General Humberto Moreno Palacios, "Revolutionary politicization of the army," Dec. 12, 1962.

114. Ibid., Nov. 18, 1958.

115. Editorial, "Nationalism of the army," ibid., Jan. 11, 1960.

116. Ibid., May 13, 1960.

117. Editorial, "Deflection of the militias," ibid., June 18, 1960.

118. Ibid., June 19, 1960. Campesinos in one valley designated a military zone petitioned COB to mediate the immediate withdrawal of army troops, charging they had killed 25 campesinos on one occasion.

Chapter 11

1. See Jerry W. Knudson, "The Press and the Bolivian National Revolution," Journalism Monographs, No. 31 (November 1973) and other articles by the same author, not cited previously, "U.S. Coverage since 1952 of Bolivia: The Unknown Soldier of the Cold War," Gazette, No. 3 (1977), 185-197; "Bolivia's Popular Assembly of 1971 and the Overthrow of General Juan José Torres," Special Studies No. 52, Council on International Studies, State University of New York at Buffalo (April 1974); "Bolivia--Where Critics Need Courage," International Press Institute Report (January 1974), 1 and 18, and "Press Women of Bolivia," Matrix, Women in Communications (Winter 1973-74), 8-9 and 21.

2. See Jerry W. Knudson, "The Press and the Mexican Revolution of 1910," Journalism Quarterly (Winter 1969), 760-766.

3. Roberto Hinojosa, El Tabasco que yo he visto (2nd ed., Mexico, 1935), 98 and 101.

4. Ibid., 103.

5. Ibid., 106. Hinojosa lost a diplomatic appointment when he applauded Mexico's defense of Nicaragua. Later, he spoke against the Mexican church in universities in Buenos Aires, Río de Janeiro, Asunción and La Paz.

6. Roberto Hinojosa, Justicia social en México (Mexico, 1935), 7-9 and footnote 2, pp. 7-8.

7. Roberto Hinojosa, La saeta rota (Mexico, 1940), [11].

8. See, for example, La Calle, "Agrarian cooperatives in Mexico," Oct. 17, 1936, and "Socialist activities of Mexico," Nov. 17, 1936. La Calle interviewed the Mexican ambassador to Bolivia on Dec. 17, 1936, and editorialized on the Cristo rebellion in "The shadow of Christ in Mexico," Dec. 25, 1936. Carlos Medinaceli wrote on "The literary production of the Aztecs" on Dec. 31, 1936. See also Maurice Halperin, "Mexico reborn," April 29 and 30, 1937.

9. Ibid., Jan. 11 and April 5, 1939.

10. Ibid., Sept. 16, 1938.

11. Ibid., Sept. 15, 1940.

12. INTI, Sept., 15, 1940.

13. La Calle, Sept. 17, 1944.

14. Ibid., March 16, 1945.

15. Ibid., Sept. 16, 1945.

16. Ibid., Sept. 18, 1945.

17. Ibid., May 5, 1946.

18. La Nación, Sept. 7, 1958.

19. Ibid., Sept. 16, 1958.

20. Ibid., The same issue of La Nación reprinted an article by the famed Mexican sociologist and historian, Jesús Silva Hertzog, "The Mexican and his sojourn," concluded on Sept. 17, 1958.

21. Ibid., Jan. 4, 1959. On Sept. 16, 1959, La Nación reprinted an article by Adolfo López Mateos, "The agrarian reform has elevated popular dignity." On Jan. 25 and 26, 1961, the newspaper also reprinted an article from Life by Columbia University historian Frank Tannenbaum on the 50th anniversary of the Mexican Revolution, "The triumphal march of an insurgent people."

22. La Nación, Oct. 14, 1959.

23. The Río article is from ibid., Jan. 6, 1960. For agrarian reform, see a story reprinted from Novedades of Mexico City, "After 45 years the adjudication of lands continues in the agrarian reform of Mexico," La Nación, Jan. 20, 1960.

24. Ibid., Jan 21, 1960. The same issue indicated that El Universal of Mexico City had reported unofficially that during his trip Adolfo López Mateos would invite five presidents to pay a return visit to Mexico--Hernán Siles of Bolivia, Arturo Frondizi of Argentina, Juscelino Kubitschek of Brazil, Jorge Alessandri of Chile and Rómulo Betancourt of Venezuela.

25. The statement was made in an interview with Armando Arce by Graciela Mendoza, entitled, "Bolivia, or the awakening of a people," published in the Mexican review Hoy and reprinted in La Nación, Jan. 24, 1960.

26. Ibid., Jan. 23, 1960. A biographical synthesis of Adolfo López Mateos' life was published in La Nación on Jan. 25, 1960.

27. Ibid., Jan. 30, 1960. An article by Huáscar Montenegro in the same issue was entitled, "Mexico and the resurrection of America."

28. La Tarde, Jan. 30, 1960. See also a series of articles by Lucio Mendieta y Núñez, "An objective balance of the Mexican Revolution," which appeared in La Tarde on June 29 and 30, and July 1 and 4, 1960. An article from Visión, "Thus the Mexican Revolution evolved," appeared in La Tarde on Sept. 10 and 12, 1960.

29. La Nación, Jan. 31, 1960. In the same issue was a long article on "Historic Mexico."

30. Ibid., Feb. 1, 1960.

31. Ibid.

32. Ibid., Feb. 2, 1960. The editorial was headlined, "Mexico: Between the Revolution and protocol, History of a cloudy day."

33. La Tarde, Feb. 1, 1960.

34. La Nación, Feb. 13, 1960.

35. See, for example, all from ibid., Ramón Fernández Fernández, "The present Mexican agrarian problem (Ejidal politics)," June 27, 1960; Raúl Alfonso García, "Fifty years of the Mexican Revolution," Nov. 20, 1960, and Alberto Morales Jiménez, "The Mexican Revolution," Nov. 23, 1960.

36. Ibid., Sept. 7 and 8, 1960.

37. Ibid., Oct. 22-28, 1960.

38. Ibid., Nov. 15, 1960.

39. Ibid., July 29, 1959.

40. Ibid., Sept. 5, 1959.

41. Ibid., Feb. 27, 1960.

42. La Tarde, March 19, 1962.

43. La Nación, July 15, 1958.

44. Ibid., Jan. 4, 1959.

45. Ibid.

46. Ibid.

47. Ibid. Italics added.

48. Ibid.

49. Ibid.

50. Ibid.

51. James M. Malloy, Bolivia: The Uncompleted Revolution (Pittsburgh, 1970), 340. Stanislav Andreski in Parasitism and Subversion: The Case of Latin America (London, 1966), 232, commented that Bolivia had experienced a "revolution at starvation level."

52. La Nación, Jan. 4, 1959.

53. Ibid., Jan. 16, 1959.

54. Ibid., Jan. 17, 1959. See also the columns by Juan José Capriles M., "Don't stain the glory of the brave," and Gryb, "The executions in Cuba," Jan. 18, 1959.

55. Zavaleta Mercado's dispatches from Cuba began with "The antecedents of fidelismo" in ibid., Jan. 30, 1959, and continued through "Ambivalence of the middle class," Aug. 1, 1959. Book-length treatments of the Cuban Revolution by Bolivian writers were rare, among them Amado Canelas O., Cuba, Socialismo en español (La Paz, 1964).

56. La Nación, Jan. 25, 1959.

57. La Tarde, May 6, 1960. In succeeding installments, Montaño Daza declared in the issue of May 7, 1960, that whoever held the Columbia military base outside Havana would rule Cuba, interviewed President Osvaldo Dorticós

on May 10, and discussed Cuban agrarian reform on May 11 and Cuban-U.S. relations on May 12, 1960.

58. La Nación, Feb. 3, 1959.

59. Ibid., Gryb's column was headlined, "Revolutionary indecisions." See also, "Crime does not correct crime," Feb. 8, 1959.

60. Ibid., Aug. 10, 1959.

61. The series was reprinted in ibid., in 1959 under the general heading, "Agrarian reform in Cuba," with these installments: "A poor people in a rich land," Sept. 23; "Mortal blow to the heart of the latifundio," Sept. 24; "The arguments of the old latifundismo," Sept. 29; "Agrarian reform in Cuba, Sugar in the opposition," Sept. 30, and "Everyone a proprietor, Catholic opinion," Oct. 3.

62. La Tarde reprinted the series under the general heading, "Problems of America," in its issues of Jan. 17-19 and 21, 1960. See also Luis Alberto Viscaria, "Cuba: Revolution and diplomacy," Jan. 23, 1960.

63. La Nación, May 4, 1960.

64. Ibid., Jan. 19, 1961.

65. Ibid., Jan. 18, 1960.

66. Ibid., Jan. 19, 1960.

67. El Diario, Jan. 18, 1960, and La Nación, Jan. 22, 1960.

68. La Tarde, Feb. 15, 1960, and La Nación, March 25, 1960. The conference was reportedly called by youth organizations in Cuba, Chile and Venezuela. See also, "Letter to the students of Chile," by Osvaldo Dorticós, president of Cuba, printed in La Nación on May 20 and 21, 1960.

69. La Tarde, June 9, 1960.

70. La Nación, July 11, 1060.

71. Ibid., July 12, 1960.

72. Ibid., Aug. 14, 1960. The editorial was entitled, "National filiation of our revolution."

73. Ibid., Aug. 20, 1960.

74. Ibid., Dec. 16 and 17, 1960. See also the editorial of Dec. 18, 1960.

75. Huge headlines also appeared in La Tarde on April 18, 1961: FIDEL SPEAKS! RUSSIA: WILL AID THE CUBAN REGIME. REBELS: BOMBARDED BY MIG PLANES.

76. Ibid., April 19, 1961.

77. Ibid., April 20 and 21, 1961.

78. Ted Cordova Claure's most successful novel was Cita en Tierra - Coraje (La Paz, 1970).

79. La Nación, April 21, 1961. See also the article in the same issue by Luis Antezana E., "The sardine eats the shark." "Tácito" on April 29, 1961, discussed the conflict between the secret invasion and the press in a free society, "Kennedy and the Fourth Estate."

80. Ibid., Dec. 5, 1961.

81. Ibid., Dec. 6, 1961.

82. Ibid., Jan. 24, 1962.

83. These views were expressed in the column, "Another view," by Hugo Vial, ibid., Jan. 28, 1962.

84. Ibid., Jan. 30, 1962.

85. Ibid., Feb. 1, 1962.

86. Ibid., Feb. 7, 1962. "Tácito" commented upon "Toynbee and the agrarian reform" in the issue of Feb. 10, 1962, which also included a commentary, "Democracy should listen to Toynbee." La Nación also applauded Mexico's open-door policy toward Cuba in an editorial on Sept. 23, 1962.

87. Ibid., Feb. 10, 1962.

88. Ibid., Sept. 2, 1962.

89. Ibid., Sept. 4, 1962

90. Ibid., Oct. 27, 1962.

91. Ibid., Oct. 28, 1962. The editorial was headlined, "Sequels and lessons of a bloody episode." A column by "Tácito" in the same issue, "Blood again," closed with the statement that it was time for Bolivians to observe hombría (manhood) rather than machismo (demonstrative maleness).

92. Ibid., Oct. 25, 1962.

93. Ibid., Oct. 27, 1962.

94. Ibid., Oct. 30, 1962.

95. Ibid., Nov. 13, 1962. Another column by "Tácito"--the last to discuss the Cuban missile crisis--appeared on Nov. 22, 1962, and was entitled, "Tension diminishes in the Caribbean."

96. Ibid., Sept. 23, 1962.

97. Ibid., Oct. 31, 1962.

98. Ibid., Nov. 13, 1962.

99. Ibid., Jan. 16, 1959.

Chapter 12

1. James W. Wilkie, The Bolivian Revolution and U.S. Aid since 1952, Financial Background and Context of political Decisions (Los Angeles, 1969), 13. A total of 275.9 million dollars was disbursed by the U.S. through 1964.

2. See Jerry W. Knudson, "Bolivia's Popular Assembly of 1971 and the Overthrow of General Juan José Torres," Special Studies No. 52, Council on International Studies, State University of New York at Buffalo (April 1974).

3. James Aronson, The Press and the Cold War (Boston, 1970), 153-179, discusses the effect of the Cold War on Cuba. See also, Bernard C. Cohen, The Press and Foreign Policy (Princeton, 1963) and Herbert I. Schiller, Mass Communications and American Empire (New York, 1970).

4. Titles, in order, are from U.S. News & World Report (Nov. 9, 1964), 6; Time (March 2, 1959), 25; Newsweek (Aug. 19, 1963), 48, and Life (June 30, 1961), 66-74.

5. John Gunther, Inside Latin America (New York, 1941), frontispiece.

6. Life (April 28, 1952), 34.

7. Major syntheses of the Bolivian National Revolution are Robert J. Alexander, The Bolivian National Revolution (New Brunswick, N.J., 1958); James M. Malloy, Bolivia, The Uncompleted Revolution (Pittsburgh, 1970), and Malloy and Richard S. Thorn, eds., Beyond the Revolution, Bolivia Since 1952 (Pittsburgh, 1971).

8. Jerry W. Knudson, "Whatever Became of 'The Pursuit of Happiness'?" The U.S. Press and Social Revolution in Latin America," Gazette, International Journal for Mass Communication Studies, Vol. XX, No. 4 (1974), 201-214.

9. La Razón (after it was confiscated by the Villarroel regime), July 2, 1946.

10. Estamos en la época del gobierno del pueblo (La Paz,

1953), 13-14.

11. La Calle, Feb. 22, 1946.

12. La Nación, April 30, 1959. On this occasion, the newspaper also denied an AP report that the MNR was taking
part in preparations for a Communist youth festival.

13. Ibid., May 5, 1959. In the same issue, La Nación
charged that La Prensa of Buenos Aires had also invented
its story that falangistas, surprised by the government
attack, had sought refuge in the building of Radio
Illimani to escape being stoned. On the contrary, the
MNR newspaper maintained, they did so to seize the station to broadcast the insurgents' manifesto. See also La
Nación, May 9, 1959, when the newspaper asked if former
Aramayo employees had written the radio script.

14. La Nación, May 7, 1959.

15. Ibid., May 27, 1959.

16. Ibid. Capital letters in the original.

17. Ibid., May 16, 1959. The entire heading was, "The
correspondents of foreign news agencies do not desist in
sabotaging the National Revolution."

18. Ibid., July 26, 1959. Consoling words for the MNR from
other segments of the Latin American press were
reprinted in La Nación. See, for example, Maguel Loria,
"Two suicides in twenty years: Despised Bolivia and her
Revolution" from El Universal of Mexico City (no date
given), reprinted in La Nación, May 22, 1959.

19. The United Press and International News Service were
combined as the UPI in 1958.

20. Ibid., May 5, 1959. Emphasis in the original.

21. Marvin Alisky, for example, found U.S. coverage of
Batista's Cuba to be dependent on the unreliable Havana
press for story leads. See "The Cuba Nobody Knew,"
Nieman Reports (April 1959), 2 and 29.

22. La Nación, July 15, 1959.

23. Ibid., July 25, 1959. The commentary was headed,
"Record of UPI in Cuba: Photographing slander."

24. Ibid., Sept. 10, 1962.

25. Ibid., Jan. 22, 1960.

26. Ibid., June 7 and 9, 1960.

27. Al Hester, "The News from Latin America via a World News Agency," paper presented to the Association for Education in Journalism meeting at Fort Collins, Colo., in August 1973.

28. La Nación, Oct. 26, 1961. On this occasion, the newspaper agreed with FSB deputy Mario Gutiérrez Gutiérrez, who said at a press conference in Buenos Aires several weeks earlier that foreign representatives of the news services should be replaced by Bolivian journalists.

29. Ibid., Oct. 11, 1962. These thoughts were expressed by "Tácito" in a column, "Distortion of the news and the elections in Brazil."

30. Ibid., Sept. 27, 1959.

31. Ibid., July 21, 1960.

32. La Tarde, July 3, 1961. La Tarde was published between 1959 and 1962 as an official afternoon daily of the MNR government.

33. La Nación, April 5, 1960.

34. Ibid., June 15, 1960. Even the title of the article was changed--from "Turbulent Tokyo" to "Tokyo, the Largest City in the World."

35. Ibid., April 28, 1958.

36. The author saw this poster in the UPI offices in New York in the spring of 1971.

37. Mary A. Gardner, The Inter American Press Association: Its Fight for Freedom of the Press, 1926-1960 (Austin, 1967), 3-13.

38. La Nación, Feb. 1, 1959.

39. Ibid., April 28, 1959. In the same issue, it was noted that national correspondents for the foreign news agencies were "without exception" former employees of Aramayo and therefore biased. La Nación urged that they be

replaced "with foreign elements that constitute a guarantee of impartiality in the task of giving the world news of what is happening in Bolivia." See also, "The news agencies should designate foreign correspondents in Bolivia," April 29, 1959.

40. Ibid., Dec. 14, 1959. See also Creyente Seglar, "A warning from the Pope to the hypocritical and pharisaical press," Dec. 18, 1959.

41. Ibid., June 3, 1959.

42. Amont the delegates from 62 countries, Luis E. Heredia represented Bolivia. Author of Prensa y nacionalismo (Potosí, 1955), Heredia was the most embittered critic of the oligarchical Bolivian press before 1952, the "great press of Wall Street," and the international news agencies. After the meeting in Baden, he journeyed on to Moscow and also spent fifteen days in Peking, where he interviewed Mao Tse-Tung. La Nación, Dec. 25, 1960, and Jan. 8, 1961.

43. Meeting of Experts on Development of Information Media in Latin America. Report of the Meeting - Santiago, Chile, 1-13 February 1961 (Paris, 1961), 10.

44. John Spicer Nichols, "LATIN--Latin American Regional News Agency," paper presented to the Association for Education in Journalism meeting at San Diego, Calif., in August 1974, Table B. The founding newspapers were O Estado and Diario Popular of Sao Paulo, and Jornal do Brasil and O Globo of Rio de Janeiro, Brazil; El Mercurio and La Tercera de la Hora of Santiago, Chile; El Tiempo of Bogotá, Columbia; El Comercio of Quito, Ecuador; Excélsior of Mexico City; El Comercio and Expreso of Lima, Peru; and El Nacional and La Verdad of Caracas, Venezuela. By 1972, LATIN dispatches represented a minimum of 26 percent of the total wire service copy in all the member newspapers. Nichols, "LATIN," 12.

45. Time, March 16, 1959.

46. La Nación, March 5, 1959. See also March 7 and 10, 1959.

47. Ibid., March 1, 1959.

48. Ibid., March 5, 1959.

49. Reprinted (all dated are 1959) were articles or editorials

from Ultima Hora of Santiago de Chile (March 3), La Nación, March 9; El Debate of Santiago (March 3), March 12; El País of Montevideo (no date given), March 14; El Espectador of Botatá (no date given), March 15; the Houston Chronicle (March 5), March 16; El Mercurio of Santiago (no date given), March 17; La Nación of Santiago (March 4), March 18; La Prensa-Gráfica of San Salvador (March 2), March 20; El Pueblo of Madrid (March 11), March 21; La Crónica of Lima (March 16,), March 23; Topaze of Santiago (no date given), March 25; La República of San José, Costa Rica (March 7), March 26; Hoy of Mexico City (March 14), March 21 and April 1, and La Esfera of Caracas (no date given), April 3, among others.

50. La Nación, March 7, 1959.

51. Ibid.

52. Ibid., May 18, 1959. The original date of publication in Novedades was not given. The article was reprinted in La Nación under the heading, "The peoples take the initiative." For other comments on the Time episode, see La Nación for March 7-9 and 31; April 27, and June 2, 1959.

53. See, for example, Pearson's broadcast of Aug. 29, 1955, printed in La Nación on Sept. 23, 1955, and his column of March 7, 1959--commenting on the Time incident--which was reprinted in La Nación on April 17, 1959. Pearson was one of the few U.S. observers who saw the need and value of the armed militias. Another was David Brinkley of NBC News. Others were appalled by the spectacle of a people armed.

54. Time, March 2, 1959.

Conclusion

1. Interview with Víctor Paz Estenssoro, La Paz, Bolivia, August 11, 1973.

2. See, for example, Jerry W. Knudson, "Freedom of the Press in Latin America: Another View," Studies in Latin American Popular Culture, Vol. 2 (1983), pp. 239-243, and John Spicer Nichols, "Freedom of the Press in Latin America: A Questionable Concept," paper presented to Illinois Association for Latin American Studies and St. Louis Latinamericanists, November 30, 1979.

3. Herbert S. Klein, Parties and Political Change in Bolivia, 1880-1952 (Cambridge, 1969), p. 424.

and the Soviet Union,
355-356
United States naval
blockade, 354-355, 356

Dawson, Allan, 115-116
Day, Benjamin, 41
Daza Barrenechea, Captain
Oscar, 305
Daza, Hilarión, 25
Dazi, Gustavo, 304
de Borbón, Maria Cristina,
237
de Machaca, Jesús, 92
de Mora, Juan Miguel, 126
de Santa Cruz, Andrés, 300
de Sucre, José Antonio, 296
de Villegas, Alberto, 16
Delgado, Oscar, 29
Democracy is Enough, 115
Democratic Union, 129
Dequenne, Lucien, 249
Devil's Metal, The, 68,
77-78, 239, 258
Diario, El
and the Chaco war, 13
on freedom of the press,
196
and Los Tiempos, 211
on military rule, 153-154,
318-319
and the 1951 elections,
150
on propaganda, 18-19
owner, 3
Diario Illustrado, El, 361,
364
Diary of Anne Frank, The,
240
Díaz Argüedas, Julio, 96
Díaz, Porfirio, 39
Dictator Self-Destroyed,
The, 83
Diez de Medina, Eduardo,
106
Diez de Medina, Mario, 348
Dorado Vásquez, Oscar, 208
Dorticós, President
Osvaldo, 349
Dos Passos, John, 258

Dreiser, Theodore, 258
Du Rels, Costa, 243
Duame, Lloyd, 236
Dubois, Jules, 192, 195

Eco de Beni, 162
Edwards, Alfred, 254
Eguino, Jorge, 182, 203
Eisenhower, Dr. Milton, 341
Enanito, El, 22
En Marcha
association with the MNR,
138-139
circulation, 139-140
cost of, 139
final days of, 162-166
founding, 138
influence of, 140-141
police assaults against,
140, 142, 154
resurrection of, 163-164
Escalier, José Mariá, 167
Escóbar, Major José, 182,
203, 242
Escudero, Pedro, 233
Espada, Joaquin, 31, 111
Estigarribia, Lt. Col. José
Félix, 27-28
Excélsior, 371, 374
Executions of November 20,
1944, and the National
Revolutionary Movement,
The, 86

Fabulosa Mines Consolid-
ated, 56
Falange Socialista Boliviana,
138, 162, 196, 246, 285,
362
fascism, 93-94, 125-126,
131-132
Faulkner, William, 258
Federación de
Ex-Combatientes, 143
Federación Obrero Sindical,
98
Federación Sindical de
Empleados de Bancos y
Ramas Anexas, 160
Federación Sindical de

477

Saavedra, President Bautista, 9, 168
Saeta Rota, La, 333
Sagarnaga, Carlos, 154-155
Salamanca, Carlos, 239
Salamanca, Daniel, 19, 24, 40, 55
  closing El Universal, 7
  and La República, 10-13
  resignation, 24
Salamanca Lafuente, Rodolfo, 31
Salamanca or the Metaphysics of Failure, 83
Salamanca, Rafael, 25
Salinas Aramayo, Carlos, 32, 62, 64, 180
Salmón, Julio, 104
Salzgitter, 256
Sánchez, Luis Alberto, 125, 361
Sangre de Mestizos, 13, 74, 239
Sanjinés Uriarte, Mario, 138-139
Saravia, José Luis, 74
Sartre, Jean Paul, 348
Selecciones, 368
Seleme, General Antonio, 156-157, 321
Semana Gráfica, 13
Semanario Busch, 67, 72, 107
Seoane, Manuel, 125, 361
Servicio Intercontinental de Periodistas, 72
Shark and the Sardines, The, 240
Sick People, 69
Siglo, El, 85
Sikes, Senator L. F., 341
Siles Zuazo, Hernán
  and agrarian reform, 284-285, 287
  education budget, 98
  elected president 1982, 377
  election of 1951, 189
  journalism career, 29, 30
  and López Mateos, 338

and the military, 325-326, 377
on the Mexican Revolution, 334
Sindicato de Fabriles, 210-211
Sindicato Ferroviario, 171
Síntesis Económica Americana, 72
Social Democratic Alliance Party, 143
Social Justice in Mexico, 332
Sociedad Rural Boliviana, 278
Society of Writers and Artists of Bolivia, 207
Solari Ormanchea, Teresa, 266
Sombras de Mujeres, 16
Sorzano, Tejada, 26, 50, 244
Soviet Revolution, 106
Spanish Civil War, 60
Sparks, Edward J., 290
Stalin, Josef, 115, 127
Standard Oil, 8, 57-59, 71, 108, 241
State Association of Journalists, 162
Steinbeck, John, 258
Stevenson, Adlai, 368

Tabares, José Antonio, 350
Tabasco Which I Have Seen, The, 332
Taborga, Major Alberto, 92
Tamayo, Franz, 73, 76, 143
Tamayo, José, 124
Tamborini, José P., 129
Tapia Caballero, Renato, 152
Tapia, Luis A., 21
Tapia, Vera, 156
Tarde, La, 9, 133, 196, 226, 256, 257, 348, 351
taxation, 21
Tejada Sorzano, José Luis, 19, 24, 40, 55-57, 233, 238
Telleria, Colonel Angel, 170

circulation, 7
closed by Salamanca, 7,
  21, 22, 24
final issue of, 28
founding of, 20-21
headlines in, 20
humor in, 20, 23
and the propaganda
  campaign, 18-19, 23-28
and Salamanca, 7, 21, 22,
  24-25
sensationalism in, 21-22
and tin mining, 230-231
Unzaga de la Vega, Oscar,
  362-364
Uruguay, 8
Urquidi, Carlos Wálter, 211
Urriolagoitia, Vice President
  Mamerto, 137, 148, 150-
  152, 183, 189, 208, 302
USSR, 74, 126-127

Vaca Chávez, Fabián, 127,
  178
Vaca Diez, Jorge, 364
Valverde Figueroa, Juan, 63
Vargas MacDonald, Antonio,
  339
Velasco Alvarado, General
  Juan, 68, 371
Velasco, Gastón, 63
Vencenti, Isaac, 151
Ventocilla, Eledoro, 363
Verde Olivo, 325
Villa Montes, 14
Villa Victoria Massacre, 301,
  303, 304
Villalpando, Abelardo, 265,
  301
Villarejos, Francisco, 13
Villarroel, Major Gualberto
  and La Calle, 91-97
  fascism and, 93-94
  murders of November
    1944, 85-87
  Nazism and, 126
  overthrow of, 68, 81, 82,
    98-99, 133-134, 135-137,
    178-182
  publication of

Montenegro's Nationalism
  and Colonialism, 16, 40
and La Razón, 134,
  172-178
revolt against, 94-95
sharing power with MNR,
  37, 40
social reforms, 91-92,
  172-175
teacher's strike, 97-98
Villazón, 103
Virriera Pacieri, Carlos, 106
voting rights reform, 4, 92,
  215-217, 319-320

War of the Pacific, 8
War of the Triple Alliance,
  8
Well, The, 13
Welles, Sumner, 92, 115
Wendler, Ernst, 107
Whelan, James, 365
White Guard, 317
Wilde, C., Colonel M.
  Fernando, 298
Wilkie, Wendell, 81
wire services, 361-375
Women's Shadows, 16
Worker Union Federation, 98
Workers Revolutionary
  Party, 40, 143, 205, 250,
  279
World War II, 33, 101-132

Ydígoras Fuentes, Manuel,
  342
Yunke, Fedor, 349

Zannier, Víctor, 281
Zarate M., Gover, 32
Zavala, Lois V., 174
Zavala Pabón, Betsy, 362,
  365-366
Zavaleta Mercado, René, 73,
  346-347, 372
Zea, Leopoldo, 374
Zegarra Caero, Germán, 186
Zilveti Arce, Pedro, 86
Zuazo Cuenca, Julio, 26
Zweig, Stefan, 118

ABOUT THE AUTHOR

Jerry W. Knudson is professor of communications at Temple University. A former newsman, he has taught both journalism and Latin American history after earning his B.S. at the University of Kansas, M.A. at the University of Minnesota, and Ph.D. at the University of Virginia.

He has traveled and done research in eleven Latin American republics, but the major focus of his work has been Bolivia which he has visited periodically since 1968.

He has lectured on journalism throughout Bolivia for the United States Information Service, and he also served as consultant for American University's second edition of Area Handbook on Bolivia.

He was also one of the first members of the Press Committee established by the Latin American Studies Association in 1974 to evaluate and make recommendations for improvement of United States news coverage of Latin America.